The Mildly Handicapped Student

The Mildly Handicapped Student

Edited by

Ted L. Miller, Ph.D.
Associate Professor
Department of Special Education and Counseling
The University of Tennessee
Chattanooga, Tennessee

Earl E. Davis, Ed.D.
Professor of Education
Department of Special Education and Counseling
The University of Tennessee
Chattanooga, Tennessee

Grune & Stratton
A Subsidiary of Harcourt Brace Jovanovich, Publishers
New York   London
Paris   San Diego   San Francisco   São Paulo
Sydney   Tokyo   Toronto

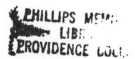

Library of Congress Cataloging in Publication Data
Main entry under title:

The mildly handicapped student.

   Includes bibliographies and index.
   1. Mentally handicapped children — Education —
Addresses, essays, lectures. I. Miller, Ted L., 1947 –
II. Davis, Earl E. (Earl Edwin), 1935 –
LC4601.M53   371.92′82   81-7107
ISBN 0-8089-1441-3   AACR2

Grune & Stratton, Inc.
111 Fifth Avenue
New York, New York 10003

Distributed in the United Kingdom by
Academic Press Inc. (London) Ltd.
24/28 Oval Road, London NW1

Library of Congress Catalog Number 81-7107
International Standard Book Number 0-8089-1441-3

Printed in the United States of America

Contents

Part V   The Mildly Handicapped: A Future Service Distinction?

Acknowledgments

Written efforts rarely reach completion without a fair number of trials and tribulations. This book certainly was not the exception. As usual, specific individuals emerged who helped complete this book. Without these people's assistance and encouragement, it would be doubtful if the project could have reached fruition. The editors are particularly grateful for the careful and meticulous efforts demonstrated by each contributor. We are in debt to these busy and talented people who were able to find the time to produce chapters that seldom required corrections. We are additionally grateful to the production staff at Grune & Stratton who exhibited copious quantities of patience, diligence, and tremendous competence. Their encouragement was always stimulating if, at times, a bit guilt-producing. Finally, we would like to thank Ms. Nan Holt, our uncommonly noble departmental secretary, for typing all the correspondence and corrections associated with each manuscript. To these fine people, and doubtless to others who played lesser roles, we are sincerely grateful.

Preface

Introductory textbooks in special education constitute the medium by which most professionals initially view the field. Such texts usually present a survey, or a general overview, of the field with individual chapters covering each of the recognized exceptionalities. Subsequent textbooks, those usually used in a second course in special-education training, often build upon this basis by providing an in-depth view of a particular exceptionality. Although this training practice may have been adaptive in the past, special education is presently embarked in a state of rapid change. Not all of these sources of change are readily identifiable, but it may be suspected that the pressures for accountability and the concommitant re-emphasized need for instructional pragmatism have encouraged a large number of training programs to rethink the use of this "classical" sequence of instruction. The question that provided the impetus for this book was, What functional differences must the teacher be prepared for as he or she considers the three traditional handicapped groups: learning disabled, mildly (educably) mentally retarded, and mildly behaviorally disordered?

On one side of this argument there is considerable evidence suggesting that the individuals may be distinguished conceptually—at least some of the time—on a number of dimensions. An equally compelling argument, however, dictates that this is possible only when groups, not individuals, are considered. These dimensions are the result of research scientists' efforts, which have been far more viable for heuristic purposes rather than for actual use in contemporary educational practice. Which of these views is more accurate is a matter of conjecture and personal perspective on the nature of special education.

There is evidence, however, that more than a few factors are coalescing to produce a reorganization of some of these categories into a more educationally oriented structure, namely the "mildly handicapped," a term conceived for this text. The remarkable success of behavioral techniques is seemingly not dependent upon the nuances associated with categorical labels. Since the individual educational plan is student-specific, little can be gained from labeling. The curriculum and diagnostic techniques used in schools overlap across all categories (particularly the mildly handicapped group) to a tremendous extent. There is, to our knowledge, no aptitude-by-treatment interaction that can be based upon the diagnosis of handicapping conditions. Another sign, that is less student-centered, includes the fact that a substantial proportion of states have undertaken noncategorical teacher certification or they have established procedures that foster training in ways that de-emphasize institutions categories. A large number of teacher training institutions have begun to follow this certification lead. In short, a proliferation of evidence has emerged that indicates some sentiment and acceptance of a mildly handicapping concept, at least within the service delivery system.

Should the concept of mildly handicapped be considered a trend or, as has happened in special education with other practices, should it be considered a passing whim? Although this question is examined in this book, it is clearly far too great to be attacked on all facets in one textbook. The authors were asked to express their views within defined, germane aspects of the specific issue. No attempt has been made to form a conclusion, since any conclusion would be premature. The reader may indeed feel that the authors share diverse opinions on the concepts and that the issues will not be resolved quickly nor easily. The authors point out that differences do exist but that these differences are, at least in part, only pertinent to some aspects of special education. Instruction, as it is currently conveyed, may not be one of the pertinent aspects. To use a metaphor, we have been using a brush that is too broad to paint a very delicate instructional portrait.

Whatever the ultimate evidence for the mildly handicapped concept— whether it be in favor of, or detrimental to it—what we hope to have constructed here is a provocative examination that may be useful for the fields' practitioners and for those who train practitioners. Regardless of the answers to the issues raised in this book, a discourse should be established on this topic. It is our hope that this book represents an initial review of what we believe to be a most important and fundamental concept for the education of the majority of handicapped students.

Ted L. Miller
Earl E. Davis

Contributors

Randy Elliot Bennett, Ed.D.
Director, Special Education
Division of Educational Services
Educational Testing Service
Princeton, New Jersey

Douglas Cullinan, Ed.D.
Associate Professor
Department of Learning,
  Development, and Special
  Education
School of Education
Northern Illinois University
DeKalb, Illinois

Earl E. Davis, Ed.D.
Professor of Education
Department of Special Education
  and Counseling
The University of Tennessee
Chattanooga, Tennessee

Michael H. Epstein, Ed.D.
Associate Professor
Department of Learning,
  Development, and Special
  Education
School of Education
Northern Illinois University
DeKalb, Illinois

George W. Fair, Ph.D.
Associate Professor
Special Education Program
The University of Texas at Dallas
Richardson, Texas

Patricia Gillespie-Silver, Ed.D.
Associate Professor
Early Childhood/Special Needs
University of Massachusetts
Amherst, Massachusetts

Libby Goodman, Ed.D.
Director, Special Education for
  Administrative Services
Philadelphia Public Schools
Philadelphia, Pennsylvania

Jay Gottlieb, Ph.D.
Associate Professor
Department of Educational
  Psychology
New York University
New York, New York

Edward Earl Gotts, Ph.D.
Director, Childhood and Parenting
  Division
Appalachia Educational Laboratory
Charleston, West Virginia

Jerry C. Gross, Ph.D.
Director, Office of Special Education
Long Beach Unified School District
Long Beach, California

George B. Helton, Ph.D.
Associate Professor of Psychology
The University of Tennessee
Chattanooga, Tennessee

Lester Mann, Ph.D.
Professor, Continuing Education in
  Communication Disorders
The Pennsylvania State University
Radnor, Pennsylvania

James K. McAfee, Ph.D.
College of Education—Special
  Education Teacher Certification
  Program
Continuing Education
The Pennsylvania State University
Radnor, Pennsylvania

Ted L. Miller, Ph.D.
Associate Professor
Department of Special Education
  and Counseling
The University of Tennessee
Chattanooga, Tennessee

Joyce Ness, M.Ed.
Supervisor of Learning Disabilities
  Program
Montgomery County Intermediate
  Unit
Norristown, Pennsylvania

Melinda Parrill-Burnstein, Ph.D.
Director, Institute for Child and
  Family Development and
  Research, and
Department of Psychiatry
Emory University School of
  Medicine
Atlanta, Georgia

Marianne Price, Ed.D.
Director of Learning Disabilities
  Program
Montgomery County Intermediate
  Unit
Norristown, Pennsylvania

Henry Reinert, Ed.D.
Professor, School of Special
  Education and Vocational
  Rehabilitation
Department of Special Learning
  Problems
School of Education
University of Northern Colorado
Greeley, Colorado

Ann C. Sabatino, M.S.
Doctoral Student
Department of Special Education
Southern Illinois University
Carbondale, Illinois

David A. Sabatino, Ph.D.
Professor of Special Education
Department of Special Education
Southern Illinois University
Carbondale, Illinois

John Salvia, Ed.D.
Professor, Division of Special
  Education and Communication
  Disorders
The Pennsylvania State University
University Park, Pennsylvania

Denise Sedlak
Graduate Assistant
Department of Special Education
Southern Illinois University
Carbondale, Illinois

Robert A. Sedlak, Ph.D.
Associate Professor
Department of Special Education
Southern Illinois University
Carbondale, Illinois

Paul T. Sindelar, Ph.D.
Assistant Professor
Division of Special Education and
    Communication Disorders
The Pennsylvania State University
University Park, Pennsylvania

Cecelia Steppe-Jones, Ph.D.
Associate Professor
Department of Special Education
North Carolina State University
Durham, North Carolina

Les Sternberg, Ph.D.
Associate Professor
Exceptional Student Education
Florida Atlantic University
Boca Raton, Florida

Mollie Stitt, M.Ed.
Learning Disabilities Coordinator
Prince William County Schools
Manassas, Virginia

Stephen S. Strichart, Ph.D.
Professor, Division of Psycho-
    Educational Services
School of Education
Florida International University
Miami, Florida

Sara G. Tarver, Ph.D.
Assistant Professor
Department of Studies in Behavioral
    Disabilities
University of Wisconsin
Madison, Wisconsin

Carol Lynn Waryas, Ph.D.
Executive Director
Avondale House
Houston, Texas

Edward A. Workman, Ed.D.
Assistant Professor
Department of Psychology
The University of Tennessee
Chattanooga, Tennessee

The Mildly
Handicapped
Student

PART I

Three Categories of Exceptionality

Ted L. Miller
Earl E. Davis

1

The Mildly Handicapped: A Rationale

Special education provides appropriate instruction to students who, in some way, are not "normal." To accomplish this, special education is unique in four areas: methodology; diagnosis and evaluation; programming and services; and research (Kneedler & Tarver, 1977). It is also special because of the extraordinary legal and legislative actions of the past decade and the resulting precedents, guidelines, and incentives that are now associated with it.

Interestingly, changes in any of the unique features of special education usually create alterations in the others. Changes in special education programming may thus alter requirements in diagnosis, the outcome of special education research may affect programming, and so on. Logically, then, the rather dramatic changes in special education of the past decade or so also have had a "ripple effect" into other areas of the profession. One of the more important of these areas concerns the definition of that population of students who are to be served by special education. From existing evidence, it is clear that there has been a marked alteration in the age of handicapped public school populations, which now ranges from 3 to 21. But additional changes may also be underway, including a restructuring of the categories under which students now enter special education.

Conceivably, an alteration of the categorical arrangements that now exist could occur in several ways: (1) attempts at redefining existing categories could occur; this is, indeed, a seemingly perennial process for some categories; (2) a completely novel structure might be created within which existing categories would be broadly expanded or limited; or (3) a category-free approach might emerge. Although it is impossible to predict which approach will become dominant, it is possible to consider the classification structure for a particular group of students. In the main, this group of students is the least different from "normal," generally requires the least extensive services, and comprises the largest proportion of the handicapped population now served by special education. Members of this group are sometimes arbitrarily termed the mildly handicapped and include the educably mentally retarded (EMR), the learning disabled (LD), and the mildly behaviorally disordered (BD). While other groups might be included (e.g., the so-called slow learners), in this chapter "mildly handicapped" refers to the LD, EMR, and BD only.

3

THE CATEGORICAL LINK IN SPECIAL EDUCATION

In examining the feasibility of alterations in categorization, it is clear that special education instruction is unique because it proceeds from the assumptions that the students' needs and characteristics and/or tasks are atypical. It is on the basis of these fundamental assumptions that instruction must be developed and provided in a modified format. In considering any categorical approach to special education, it must be established whether the utility or benefits of the concept of any special classification are superior to the utility or benefits derived from a particular *process* of classification. A move toward complete noncategorization might be seen as a rejection of the belief that *any* classification system is useful or desirable. Such an approach has been both criticized (e.g., Hobbs, 1975) and supported (Forness, 1974), but, as Hallahan and Kauffman (1978) pointed out, advocates of noncategorical special education often limit the extent of the approach:

> . . . there are a few special educators who believe that children from all of the areas of exceptionality, except the gifted, have so much in common regarding educational needs that there should be separate classes for each of these areas. . . . Many people, however, advocate noncategorical special education only for the learning disabled, the mildly disturbed and the mildly retarded. (p. 45)[1]

An examination of Hallahan and Kauffman's (1978) position does not suggest that categorical systems be eliminated; it suggests that some modifications of the current process be adopted. Certainly, the proper use of categories must be carefully undertaken for ". . . the manner in which differences among children are conceptualized ultimately dictates the practices used to identify and serve exceptional children" (Wyne & O'Connor, 1979, p. v).[2]

If the concept of categorization is accepted in principle, even to a limited degree, then the task of defining appropriate and acceptable limits to the classification process must be faced. Clearly, developing an acceptable process has long been a goal of special education; since the beginning of the century, the study of characteristics of learners who might need specialized educational services has been refined. This refinement still continues and is evident in the existence of some exceptionalities that were virtually unrecognized or were contained within larger categories less than three decades ago. There are numerous reasons for the investment of energy and time that continues to be put into classification strategies. However, two factors seem especially prominent as critical impetuses of a categorical approach to special education. The first of these is the need for discovery of patterns of individual differences and the subsequent analysis of these differences for heuristic research purposes. This is in response to the demand of educational research that carefully defined categories must be specified and ma-

---

[1]Reprinted with permission from Hallahan, D. P., & Kauffman, J. N. *Exceptional Children: Introduction to special education.* Englewood Cliffs: Prentice Hall, 1978.

[2]In this vein, Simches (1970) noted that "We cannot continue to use taxonomy of labels that have a tendency to homogenize children into meaningless diagnostic label categories based primarily on psychometrics, medical findings or psychiatric examinations" (p. 10).

nipulated and, ultimately, that outcomes must be recorded in a manner that allows replication, hence "proof," of the event (Kerlinger, 1979).[3] Support of categorization also evolves from the long-term influence of the erroneously termed (Kauffman & Hallahan, 1974) medical model. A principle element of this model is the nosological approach to treatment, an approach that places extensive emphasis upon the categorical viewpoint. Briefly, the nosological concept may be expressed in the following way: if the characteristics of one group of students can be identified and discoveries are made concerning the treatment strategies most effective for the group, then a particular student as a member of some group can be most appropriately served through the strategies found effective for the specific group. Treatment strategies, then, are closely bound to specific categories.

The influence of science and the medical model in service strategies has helped to entrench the categorical approach in special education. Also, the discoveries of science led to changing implementation practice, which, in turn, determined new avenues of (categorically dictated) research. It is obvious that contemporary literature is, usually as a starting premise, structured about categories.

Categorization has led special education into several practices, including individualized instruction through diagnostic-prescriptive teaching, placement strategy, ability training, the use of profiles of abilities to establish educational programs, and various research emphases, e.g., categorical comparisons. Not all of these practices have been successful, but the categorical orientation has served special education well; despite its shortcomings, it has been a large contributor to the general development of the field. Hobbs (1978) noted that without the identification and recognition afforded by labels, the essential funding for the field could not have occurred—an argument echoed by Lieberman (1980) and reviewed by Lilly (1979) and many others. Perhaps it is necessary to accept some negative results of categorization while refining the instructional utility that can be gained from the approach.

SOME ISSUES RELATED TO THE CONCEPT OF THE MILDLY HANDICAPPED

Doubtless, many issues influence the development—or lack of development—of the concept of the "mildly handicapped." Concerns might include traditional factors such as research or programming, or they might include specific subsets of any or all of these factors. Three particularly important subsets require attention if a high-incidence group called "the mildly handicapped" is to emerge in a useful fashion: (1) prevalence; (2) behavioral characteristics; and (3) training procedures and certification policies.

---

[3]It is probably erroneous to believe that the categories now in existence are necessary to scientific investigation in special education. In fact, some authors (e.g., Cohen, 1976) have argued that the categories now used are so sloppily defined that the progress of science in special education has been impeded. Despite this observation, it seems clear that the current categories have, by some alchemy, become incorporated into our research. As a result, much, if not most, of the contemporary study of exceptional individuals is category specific.

Prevalence of the Mildly Handicapped

As any reader of a classical "introductory" textbook is surely aware, the number of persons afflicted by particular handicapping conditions can only be approximated. There are several reasons for this, including (1) the vagueness of current definitions of handicapping conditions; (2) the confusion between the concepts of incidence and prevalence; and (3) a shift in identification of students as a result of the social acceptance of specific categories.

The vagueness of current definitions is probably the best known and most frequently discussed source of difficulty in establishing incidence or prevalence. For instance, the categorical definition of learning disabilities has been shown to be vague, to vary from state to state, and, therefore, to promote quite different programs and estimates of the number of students involved (Gillespie, Miller, & Fielder, 1975; Lloyd, Sabatino, Miller, & Miller, 1977; Mercer, Forgnone, & Wolking, 1976). Definitions of behavioral disorders have also been shown to vary significantly across certifying agencies (Epstein, Cullinan, & Sabatino, 1977; Kauffman, 1977), while shifts in criteria for establishing mental retardation have not only greatly "reduced" the number of persons termed retarded but have also greatly reduced the numbers of students considered educable mentally retarded. It may easily be recognized that such shifts, however warranted, sharply limit the precision by which individuals can be identified as members of a subgroup. The problem is further confounded by the need to establish *which* handicap is most appropriate. For example, in some summaries (e.g., Hallahan & Kauffman, 1976) it is concluded that a sizeable proportion of learning disabled students possess IQs considerably below "normal" intelligence; simultaneously, a large number of learning disabled students also appear to possess characteristics more commonly associated with behavior disorders. It would appear then that definitions now in use are imprecise and allow considerable overlap between the handicapped and non-handicapped and within the various handicapping conditions.

The second major problem concerning mildly handicapped pupils is an apparent confusion within the literature concerning the concepts of prevalence and incidence. Marozas, May, and Lehman (1980) recently pointed out confusion between the terms by demonstrating that common introductory texts define the terms differently, exchange definitions, and even use the terms interchangeably. Marozas et al. suggested that incidence be used to represent new cases over a given period of time while prevalence be used to indicate the number of persons who have some particular condition at any given point in time (following Morton & Hebel, 1978). However, the current confusion makes the study of actuarial figures a difficult and somewhat suspect undertaking. This analysis suggests that current estimates may be inaccurate.

Finally, there is the least often discussed aspect of estimating numbers of mildly handicapped students: categorical shift. Categorical shift refers to a major change in the occurrence of some handicaps that is not based on etiological or treatment concerns. Such concerns could perhaps be socially motivated, economically motivated, or the result of a paucity (or surfeit) of categorically trained teachers. Tucker (1980) recently demonstrated one case that illustrates this concept. In his study, Tucker described the growth of the special education population from less than 1 percent of the school population in 1973 to just over 5 percent in 1977. Substantial as this growth may be, the development of one category has been phenomenal: in 1972, LD represented about 10 percent of all special education classifications; by 1977, LD represented 43.9 percent of all special education classifications. This growth in the acceptance of LD has resulted in a decline in other categories, particularly EMR. Additionally, Tucker's data suggest that one problem of categorical arrangements—ethnic imbalance—has not gone away over the years but has simply reasserted itself through the medium of the LD category. Tucker suggested that LD provides "alternate placement for children not succeeding in general education" (p. 104) and may represent nothing more than a catchall for poorly succeeding students. Whether this is true or not, it seems that either (1) a categorical shift developed from the effects of the learning disability label or (2) behaviorally, the categories of LD and EMR are difficult to distinguish. Either way it appears that many children who would have been described as EMR in 1970 are now described as LD. Therefore, if these trends are accurate and externally valid beyond Tucker's Texas sample, it is quite possible that an enormous categorical shift is occurring along with the expansion of students involved in special education.

Because of such factors (and many others may exist), the task of determining the prevalence of any of the three categories discussed here is difficult. Beyond this, the task of estimating the prevalence of a mildly handicapped population is fraught with additional problems since the category "mildly handicapped" does not officially exist. Nevertheless the following information is pertinent in the estimation of membership in this category.

The learning disabled population has been reckoned to range from 1 to 30 percent (Kirk, 1976), although the National Advisory Committee on Handicapped Children (1968) suggested a more conservative prevalence of 1–3 percent. The prevalence of retardation is perhaps 1–3 percent, with the majority (about 2.3 percent) considered mildly retarded (Payne & Mercer, 1975). According to Kauffman's review (1977), behavior disorders may range from a low of 2 percent to a high of 10 percent, with, again, the majority considered mild behavior disorders.

A summation of these percentages may well not be an accurate reflection of the prevalence of mildly handicapped students. Nevertheless, simple addition of the lower estimates (learning disabled, 1 percent; mildly mentally retarded, 1 percent; and mildly behaviorally disordered, 2 percent) reveals minimal prevalence of mildly handicapped students at 4 percent of the school-aged population. Use of the upper boundaries might include 15 percent or more of the student population. While it is probable that the "true" prevalence lies somewhere between these figures, it is clear that a significant number of students could be considered mildly handicapped if the LD, BD and EMR categories are included. Should the category become officially accepted, it is obvious that the majority of special education students would be described as mildly handicapped.

Behavioral Characteristics

The most significant reason for considering the mildly handicapped as a group lies in the potential similarity of behavioral characteristics. While the students may maintain some categorical uniqueness, it is doubtful that this uniqueness is as prevalent as was once thought. There are several lines of contention to support this position. For example, Lilly (1979) argued that for the schools, at least, "emerging special education programs place primary *functional* emphasis on the *functional* problems of education setting . . . " (p. 2). He also pointed out that students "differ on a continuum of functional ability levels, and students in EMR, BD, and LD classes are more *like* than *different* from their peers in regular classes" (p. 46). Thus, in Lilly's view (1979), the categories of children defined here as mildly handicapped are perhaps very similar to nonhandicapped peers in a total sense; variation appears in the functional (presumably learning) problems of the mildly handicapped. It is important to note the use of the term functional, for this implies that the salient differences of mildly handicapped pupils are not necessarily pervasive. They are, rather, classroom-specific learning behaviors.

Hallahan and Kauffman (1976, 1977) are among the more prominent chroniclers of the similarities of BD, LD, and EMR classifications. Paralleling Lilly's (1979) contention that there are more similarities than differences between nonhandicapped and mildly handicapped peers, Hallahan and Kauffman (1977) asserted that "there is no rational basis, in terms of instructional efficacy, for grouping children in accordance with some of the categorical labels now in use" (p. 139). Within a behavioral framework and with primary consideration for instruction, they found that problems in definitions are but one reason for examining the existing categories of special education. There are several others, including the fact that historical examination of the three categories reveals a considerable number of factors in common. There often is difficulty in differentiating emotional disturbances and mental retardation (Balthazar & Stevens, 1975), and many of the major constructs of learning disabilities were derived from the study of mental retardation (Hallahan & Cruickshank, 1973). Beyond this, the existing data provide evidence of behavioral overlap among the three categories. Indeed, the major variable in terms of behavioral characteristics appears to be the *frequency* of particular behaviors; the same behavioral characteristics overlap in all of the categories. It may be expected then that any given behavior may occur in all categories, for it is primarily the frequency of a specific behavior per category that separates the groups (Hallahan & Kauffman, 1976).

Anna Gajar (1979, 1980) examined the similarities of the various categories that operationally define the mildly handicapped. In one paper (Gajar, 1979), similarities and differences among the educable mentally retarded, the learning disabled, and the emotionally disturbed (ED) were explored. The cognitive, affective and demographic patterns, three key characteristics, were examined in 378 children (86 girls, 292 boys; 122 ED, 135 LD, 121 EMR). Significant differences were found among the groups in intelligence, with EMR children scoring below both ED and LD children. Differences were noted in the degree of underachievement across categories but members of all three groups were underachievers. In the analysis of affective behavior, BD/ED children were significantly different from LD and EMR children on conduct disorders and personality and were different from EMR students in immaturity and inadequacy. All groups were lower on conduct disorders and personality problems than on inadequacy and immaturity. Demographically, a high proportion of students were of minority background (33 percent); there were more boys than girls (a ratio of 3:1); 84 percent of the students were from relatively low social positions; and there was a tendency for black students to be disproportionally labeled as EMR. As Gajar (1979) noted, both similarities and differences were detected, and, while the study cannot be broadly generalized to other systems, there appears to be evidence of failure in current identification procedures.

In a second paper, Gajar (1980) again analyzed cognitive, affective, and demographic procedures across EMR, LD, and BD/ED categories. In this study, however, the background variables were used to predict the value of background characteristics in discriminating among the three categorical groupings. Data were collected for each of the three domains of interest and were submitted to a discriminant analysis. Results indicated that 81.8 percent of the cases were correctly classified, with 91 percent of the EMR cases correct, 81 percent of the LD cases correct, and 73 percent of the BD/ED cases correct. In short, the data collected adequately classified a substantial proportion of the students involved in the study. However, as Gajar noted, there remains a question of instructional relevance in the categorical distinction. The similarities are so striking that the differences may be eliminated for the purposes of instructional practice. Therefore, there is less than complete agreement that the differences that existed in the study are directly applicable to instructional planning.

How do the functional differences of students vary? Of what importance are these differences? As Hallahan and Kauffman (1977) and other authors (Bateman, 1967; Hewitt, 1968; Reynolds & Balow, 1972) suggested, categorical criteria that are noneducational are not of significance to educators. Therefore, two questions arise. Might some current conceptualizations represent differences, but differences not essential to programming? Might individual differences other than those now commonly measured better serve functional distinctions? Although neither question is fully answerable, two papers assess these issues.

Neisworth and Greer (1975) considered a distinction between the genotype and phenotype of behavior after the designation offered by Stuart (1970). The genotypic designation refers to the putative causes of behavior, explains what the student "is," and relates predispositions toward specific behaviors; behaviors are seen as phenotypical expressions of the genotypes. In contrast, the phenotype represents a focus upon the surface behaviors, that is, what a person observably does. Little if any reference is given to causes or etiologies.

From this structure, Neisworth and Greer established and considered the premise (abbreviated for our purposes here) that mild mental retardation and learning disabilities may constitute independent genotypes, even though this is probably *not* the case (see Hallahan & Cruickshank, 1973). Following this, the authors found reason to accept significant phenotypic similarities as a point that led them to conclude that "divergent causes or conditions can produce the same or similar problems in functioning" (Neisworth & Greer, 1975, p. 18). In short, Neisworth and Greer illustrated that even with assumed independent genotypes, phenotypes may be quite similar. Therefore, current categories of mild disabilities are conceptualized on presumably different genotypes—a point of understandable research interest. But, this seems to be an instructionally less valid concept since (1) genotypes are not now readily malleable; (2) genotypes have always been identified through the mask of phenotypes, i.e., behaviors; and (3) it is phenotypes that are of concern to educators. In sum, then, current categorical differences among mildly handicapped children are based upon analysis of unproven genotypes. Considering that relatively similar behaviors are measured to provide evidence of genotypic difference, it is no wonder that confusion often reigns in deciding what genotype, i.e., classification of handicap, best describes a particular student. The futility of programming from our existing knowledge of genotypes is painfully obvious.

Assuming that current, predominantly genotypic classifications are possible, are they desirable? That is, wouldn't other classification systems, perhaps ones built upon phenotypes, be more appropriate for educators? In an important paper, Becker (1978) noted that considerable debate has taken place concerning the merit of mixing the categories of emotionally disturbed and brain-damaged children (Bower, 1965; Mesinger, 1965) (the latter categorically now served through Public Law 94-142 presumably as learning disabilities). The argument has had some unsurprising results. For example, California now serves learning disabled, emotionally disturbed, and educable mentally retarded students under the generic label "learning handicapped." According to Becker, two closely related assumptions arise concerning the advocacy of generic categories. The first is that there is an overlap of child characteristics. The second is that because of the overlap, the students should be similar to teach and, therefore, the labels are of no instructional value.

Becker sought to investigate differences between California's educationally handicapped and educable mentally retarded children. Forty educationally handicapped and 20 educable mentally retarded children with a mean age of about 10 years served as subjects. The educationally handicapped group was divided into a group with 20 learning disabled students and a group with 20 emotional-behavioral problems; thus, in effect, the study is a comparison of EMR, LD, and BD/ED students. Five tasks were given the children: Digit Span, Raven Progressive Matrices, Matching Familiar Figures Test, a puzzle task, and a rod and frame test (a measure of field dependence/independence). All except the Matching Familiar Figures Test yielded significant differences. Accordingly, Becker drew the following implications. First, there may not be homgeneity among the various groups of mildly handicapped students, and this is particularly true of mental age; i.e., students placed together by chronological age might have quite different mental ages. Second, perhaps the nature of educational programs should be quite different, concentrating, for example, on the reduction of behavior on the one hand and the development of language skills on the other. Third, the assumption that teacher training can proceed on a high incidence basis is closely linked to the homogeneity of students. Because of differences among the groups, Becker suggested that teacher competencies are not overlapping and that teachers therefore require a broader preservice base and special modifications in inservice training. Finally, Becker pointed out some potential problems created by the approach. IQs, for example, might vary within a group as much as from 48 to 125. As Becker wrote, "How will the bright educationally handicapped child feel about being with a child who has a IQ that is 77 points lower?" (p. 510).

In sum Becker projected a cautious attitude toward the mixing of the learning disabled, the emotionally disturbed, and the mildly retarded. He also pointed out that students, teachers, and state certifiers all have a sizable stake in the issue. Considering Hallahan and Kauffman's (1977) earlier remarks, Becker argued that homogeneity emerges only when students are described on mental age not chronological age—though chronological age is used in contemporary practice. Thus, according to Becker, more research is needed, since the arguments begun years ago (Bower, 1965; Mesinger, 1965) remain unresolved. But it should be pointed out that the factors discussed by Becker may or may not separate functional differences, for the strength of the educational argument for categories rests upon the degree to which the test score differences necessitate particular instructional strategies. An analysis of the test data demonstrated differences among students; whether these differences can be applied to instructional practice remains in doubt. In truth, there is little evidence that suggests even a group-related functional relationship, and, in fact, categorical overlap might be expected in practice. That these differences are obstacles in a practice that emphasizes individualized instruction remains unproven.

Teacher Preparation and Certification

Two potential obstacles to the development of a "mildly handicapped" classification are teacher preparation and teacher certification. Generally, teacher preparation refers to the specific course content that leads to professional certification within a given state. Certification represents official sanction to instruct within carefully defined dimensions. Teacher preparation models vary considerably, and certification practices may be widely different; for example, some states do not have distinct standards for special education certification.

Teacher preparation in special education has a long history. However, by far the most dramatic increase in training was initiated by the Federal government in 1958 through PL 85-926, and expanded in 1963 through PL 88-164.[4] By 1978, approximately 45 million dollars had been provided to all agencies involved with training. It is a matter of record that the initial support for training was strongly categorical in nature. It was not until the early 1970s that the Bureau for the Education of the Handicapped (BEH) began procedures to promote a movement away from categorically based teaching training. Interrelated teacher-training programs and the move toward competency-based training were among the more prominent factors stressed by BEH but other ideas were also considered. As a result, according to Lilly (1979): (1) noncategorical teacher-training programs are now commonplace; (2) teachers are prepared to deal with both academic and social problems; and (3) competency-based programs (i.e., specific skills) are now stressed in training. These changes have had overwhelming impact upon the concept of noncategorical special education, particularly in the recognition of the mildly handicapped (Lilly, 1979).

> As colleges and universities began to develop "interrelated" special education training programs, it became clear that the overlap between various categorical training proposals was phenomenal. As one teacher was heard to remark, "When you examine methods courses in EMR, LD, and BD, you're always meeting yourself coming around the corner." (p. 413)[5]

---

[4]PL 85-296 was enacted by the Federal Government to provide support for the preparation of leadership personnel and teachers working with mentally retarded students. PL 88-164 expanded this original law to all areas of special education.

[5]From *Children with exceptional needs: A survey of special education* by Stephen Lilly, editor. Copyright © 1979 by Holt, Rhinehart and Winston. Reprinted by permission of Holt, Rhinehart and Winston.

Since teaching is the end result of training and certification, it seems that the similarities of instructional needs of the three groups are in fact a guideline for future direction. As was pointed out earlier, this has not had so great of an impact upon research or evaluation, though ultimately it probably will. The point, however, is that service delivery may be more and more directed toward the noncategorical approach.

Weintraub, Abeson, and Braddock (1975) described the need for certification (and training) to reflect the actual needs of special education students:

> . . . each state must carefully reexamine its present system of defining and classifying children to ascertain if the system is stigmatizing children beyond that which is necessary and whether the system is related to the educational needs of the child. (p. 25–26)

In this light, Connor (1976) noted a number of trends that seem to suggest a movement away from strict categorical arrangements. First, teacher education programs are preparing future teachers to operate in a variety of ways. Second, there are major attempts to provide retraining of other teachers with an eye toward individualizing instruction. Third, a "trend toward cross categorical teacher education continues as recognition of the folly of clear-cut single disability emphasis spreads" (p. 375). Finally, there is a movement toward competency-based teacher education, a move that shows the specific skills that teachers should possess. It may be seen that by 1975 both teacher certification and teacher training were moving away from a strict categorical view of exceptionality. Recent information has documented a sustained change in both teacher training and teacher certification regarding the concept of noncategorical, or generic, approaches. Two examples, one concerning certification practice, and one concerning training patterns, may be illustrative.

Belch (1979) examined the current status of noncategorical teacher certification across the United States. Supporting Connor's position in his initial review (1976), Belch noted that noncategorical teacher certification is not new and may be traced through the writings of Laycock (1934), Lord (1956), and Reynolds and Balow (1972). Citing Smith and Neisworth (1975), Belch discussed the often-stated difficulty of attempting to teach categorically unique instructional procedures in view of the fact that such specifics are seldom shown to be effective. Given this training difficulty, the topic of Belch's study emerged: Is there a trend toward comprehensive (noncategorical) certification of special education teachers? Accordingly, Belch submitted a questionnaire to State Directors of Teacher Education and Certification of all states and the District of Columbia. A 100 percent return was received and the following data emerged: 11 states now award comprehensive certification; 12 states are actively moving toward such certification or contemplate it for the near future; and 27 states do not have such certification or contemplate its adoption in the near future. In short, about half of the states now award or are considering the development of such comprehensive certification. Belch concluded that the trend is in line with the move toward competency-based certification and that certification practices may well be aimed toward noncategorical arrangements. In the future, the balance may well shift to the general certification pattern.

Training and certification practices obviously share a reciprocal relationship;

the results of Belch's study (1979) ought to suggest alterations in teacher-training programs. In a study conducted by the Council for Exceptional Children (1978), 550 colleges and universities were asked to supply information concerning the types of certification for which their programs prepared students. About 33 percent of the responding institutions indicated that their programs offered generic programs. While these data are subject to some error (due to unspecified return rates and the fact that commonality of meaning of the term *generic* is not assured), it would appear that a substantial proportion of teacher education programs now offer generic training. Without doubt, the certification pattern is being responded to by supporting training programs. As may be seen from the Belch (1979) and Council for Exceptional Children (1978) data, emphasis seemingly is being placed upon generic training and certification. While a clear trend is not yet in evidence, it is certain that training and certification are no longer categorically dominated.

SUMMARY

This chapter briefly examined a rationale for the mildly handicapped, a group operationally composed of the mildly behaviorally disordered, the learning disabled, and the mildly mentally retarded. Both impetus and cautions for the development of the category were found through current trends and seem, on balance, to suggest that the development of the concept is likely. An initial discussion found that a totally categorical or a categorical-free model of special education is seldom advocated, most authors preferring to focus on the educational, hence functional, relevance of any categories that emerge. Further discussion found considerable overlap in characteristics among the LD, BD, and EMR, and a trend toward less categorically structured teacher preparation programs. Overall, it was surmised that a substantial number of students might be mildly handicapped and that current categorical shifts have changed proportions within recognized categories even while the absolute number of students served continues to grow. In short, several lines of evidence suggest that a valid rationale is evident, and, though the concept is not yet fully developed, it is now implemented in some locations and may soon appear in others.

REFERENCES

Balthazar, E. G., & Stevens, H. A. *The emotionally disturbed, mentally retarded.* Englewood Cliffs: Prentice-Hall, 1975.

Bateman, B. Implications of a learning disability approach for teaching educable retardates. *Mental Retardation*, 1967, *5*, 23–25.

Becker, L. D. Learning characteristics of educationally handicapped and retarded children. *Exceptional Children*, 1978, *44*, 502–511.

Belch, P. J. Toward noncategorical teacher certification in special education—Myth or reality? *Exceptional Children*, 1979, *46*, 129–131.

Bower, E. M. The return of Rumpelstilskin: Reaction to Mesinger's article. *Exceptional Children*, 1965, *32*, 238–239.

Cohen, S. A. The fuzziness and the flab: Some solutions to research problems in learning disabilities. *Journal of Special Education*, 1976, *10*, 129–136.

Conner, F. P. The past is prologue: Teacher preparation in special education. *Exceptional Children*, 1976, *42*, 366–378.

Council for Exceptional Children. Educational Research Information Center (ERIC) Clearinghouse on Handicapped and Gifted Children: Fact Sheet, 1978.

Epstein, M., Cullinan, P., & Sabatino, D. A. State definitions of behavior disorders. *Journal of Special Education*, 1977, *11*, 417–425.

Forness, S. R. Implications of recent trends in educational labeling. *Journal of Learning Disabilities*, 1974, *7*, 57–61.

Gajar, A. H. Educable mentally retarded, learning disabled, emotionally disturbed: Similarities and differences. *Exceptional Children*, 1979, *45*, 470–472.

Gajar, A. H. Characteristics across exceptional categories: EMR, LD, and ED. *Journal of Special Education*, 1980, *14*, 155–164.

Gillespie, P., Miller, T. L., & Fielder, V. D. Legislative definitions of learning disabilities: Roadblocks to effective service. *Journal of Learning Disabilities*, 1975, *8*, 660–666.

Hallahan, D. P., & Cruickshank, W. M. *Psychoeducational foundations of learning disabilities*. Englewood Cliffs: Prentice Hall, 1973.

Hallahan, D. P., & Kauffman, J. M. *Introduction to learning disabilities: A psycho-behavioral approach*. Englewood Cliffs: Prentice Hall, 1976.

Hallahan, D. P., & Kauffman, J. M. Labels, categories, behaviors: ED, LD, and EMR reconsidered. *The Journal of Special Education*, 1977, *11*, 139–149.

Hallahan, D. P., & Kauffman, J. M. *Exceptional children: Introduction to special education*. Englewood Cliffs: Prentice Hall, 1978.

Hewitt, F. M. *The emotionally disturbed child in the classroom*. Boston: Allyn & Bacon, 1968.

Hobbs, N. (Ed.). *Issues in the classification of children* (Vols. 1 & 2). San Francisco: Jossey-Bass, 1975.

Hobbs, N. Classification options: A conversation with Nicholas Hobbs on exceptional child education. *Exceptional Children*, 1978, *44*, 494–497.

Kauffman, J. M. *Characteristics of children's behavior disorders*. Columbus: Merrill, 1977.

Kauffman, J. M., & Hallahan, D. P. The medical model and the science of special education. *Exceptional Children*, 1974, *41*, 97–102.

Kerlinger, F. M. *Behavioral research: A conceptual approach*. New York: Holt, 1979.

Kneedler, R. D., & Tarver, S. G. (Eds.). *Changing perspectives in special education*. Columbus: Merrill, 1977.

Kirk, S. A., Samuel A. Kirk. In J. M. Kauffman &

D. P. Hallahan (Eds.), *Teaching children with learning disabilities: Personal perspectives*. Columbus, Oh.: Charles E. Merrill, 1976.

Laycock, S. R. Every teacher a diagnostician. *Exceptional Child Review*, 1934, *2*, 47.

Lieberman, L. M. Noncategorical special education. *Journal of Learning Disabilities*, 1980, *13*, 65–68.

Lilly, M. S. *Children with exceptional needs: A survey of special education*. New York: Holt, 1979.

Lloyd, J., Sabatino, D. A., Miller, T. L., & Miller, S. R. Proposed federal guidelines: Some open questions. *Journal of Learning Disabilities*, 1977, *10*, 69–71.

Lord, F. E. A realistic look at special classes. *Exceptional Children*, 1956, *22*, 321–325.

Marozas, D. S., May, D. C., & Lehman, L. C. Incidence and prevalence: Confusion in need of clarification. *Mental Retardation*, 1980, *18*, 229–230.

Mercer, C. D., Forgnone, C., & Wolking, W. D. Definitions of learning disabilities used in the United States. *Journal of Learning Disabilities*, 1976, *9*, 376–386.

Mesinger, J. F. Emotionally disturbed and brain damaged children—Should we mix them? *Exceptional Children*, 1965, *32*, 237–238.

Morton, R. F., & Hebel, J. R. *A study guide to epidemiology and biostatistics*. Baltimore: University Park Press, 1978.

National Advisory Committee on Handicapped Children. *Special education for handicapped children*. First annual report. Washington, D.C.: U.S. Department of Health, Education and Welfare, January 31, 1968.

Neisworth, J. T., & Greer, J. G. Functional similarities of learning disabilities and mild retardation. *Exceptional Children*, 1975, *42*, 17–21.

Payne, J. S., & Mercer, C. D. Definition and prevalence. In J. M. Kauffman & J. S. Payne (Eds.), *Mental retardation: Introduction and personal perspectives*. Columbus, Oh.: Charles E. Merrill, 1975.

Reynolds, M. C., & Balow, B. Categories and variables in special education. *Exceptional Children*, 1972, *38*, 357–366.

Simches, R. F. The inside-outsiders. *Exceptional Children*, 1970, *37*, 5–15.

Smith, R. M., & Neisworth, J. T. *The exceptional child—A functional approach*. New York: McGraw-Hill, 1975.

Stuart, R. B. *Trick or treatment: How and when psychotherapy fails*. Champaign, Ill.: Research Press, 1970.

Tucker, J. A. Ethnic proportions in classes for the learning-disabled: Issues in nonbiased assessment. *The Journal of Special Education,* 1980, *14,* 93–106.

Weintraub, F. J., Abeson, A. R., & Braddock, D. L. *State law and education of handicapped children: Issues and recommendations.* Reston, Va.: Council for Exceptional Children, 1975.

Wyne, M. D., & O'Connor, P. D. *Exceptional children: A developmental view.* Lexington, Ma.: Heath, 1979.

Sara G. Tarver

2
Characteristics of Learning Disabilities

Although official recognition of learning disabilities as a category of exceptionality is of relatively recent origin, the historical roots of the field are deep. Current thinking and practice have been traced to theories and concepts of the 19th century (Hallahan & Cruickshank, 1973; Wiederholt, 1974). Wiederholt's two-dimensional framework (1974) illustrates the diversity of this history. A tripartite "type-of-disorder" dimension encompasses spoken language disorders, written language disorders, and perceptual and motor disorders. A developmental-phase dimension divides time into a foundation phase (circa 1800–1930), a transition phase (circa 1930–1960), and an integration phase (circa 1960–1970).

In the foundation phase, theories about the nature and causes of the different types of disorders were formulated. These theories were translated into practice during the translation phase, which produced a wide variety of assessment instruments, teaching methods, and educational/training programs. Recognition of the overlap among the symptoms associated with the three types of disorders, in concert with recognition of the common concerns of parents and professionals across disorders, culminated in the integration phase.

While detailed accounts of this rich history are available (see, for example, Hallahan & Cruickshank, 1973; Wiederholt, 1974), the major purpose of this brief recapitulation is to show how occurrences of one phase gave rise to those of the next, eventually leading to the official "birth of the field" in 1963. Specific events are mentioned only to the extent necessary to illustrate threads of thinking that have shaped the present view of learning disabilities.

SPECIFIC DISORDERS

Spoken Language Disorders

Spoken language theorists of the foundation phase were primarily concerned with the localization of speech functions; they sought to determine which areas of the brain housed the different functions involved in speech. A variety of spoken language disorders, *aphasias,* were observed in patients having suffered brain

17

damage and later, after autopsy, the type of disorder was correlated with the locus of the brain lesion. For example, Wernicke identified four types of aphasia—motor, conduction, sensory, and total—and proposed corresponding brain centers. Sensory aphasia, i.e., inability to understand spoken language, came to be called Wernicke's aphasia because Wernicke was the first to document difficulties in interpreting spoken language. Similarly, a cortical area related to the production of speech came to be called Broca's area because Broca was the first to note the association between damage to this particular area and loss of the ability to speak (T. Bryan & J. H. Bryan, 1978b).

During the foundation phase, disorders of understanding and producing spoken language came to be called *receptive aphasia* and *expressive aphasia*, respectively. Also, reflecting a shift in emphasis from brain structures to brain functions, references to sensory and motor areas gave way first to references to sensory modalities, and later to perceptual modalities (e.g. visual and auditory modalities). Both the receptive/expressive and the visual/auditory distinctions were incorporated into the well-known model of psychoneurological learning disorders developed by Johnson and Myklebust (1967; Myklebust, 1954) and also into the Illinois Test of Psycholinguist Abilities (ITPA) (Kirk, McCarthy, & Kirk, 1961), one of the most popular assessment instruments developed in the transition phase. The ITPA assesses visual-motor and auditory-vocal channels of communication along one dimension and receptive, organizing, and expressive processes along another.

The ITPA was designed to assess intraindividual, as well as interindividual, differences in a variety of psycholinguistic processes in such a way that the resultant assessment information would lend direction to remediation. Corresponding teaching techniques and materials were developed by Bush and Giles (1969) and Minskoff, Wiseman, and Minskoff (1973).

Written Language Disorders

The most extensive written language theory of the foundation phase was that of Samuel Orton (1937). Although Orton did not seek to establish one-to-one correspondences between specific language disorders and loci of brain lesion in the same sense that his spoken language counterparts had, his theory of hemispheric dominance did ascribe language functions to a single hemisphere of the brain and attribute written language disorders to damage or dysfunction of that hemisphere alone. Orton's theory also emphasized the associative areas and functions of the brain; associations among visual, auditory and motor functions were deemed essential to reading, writing, and spelling.

Orton's etiological views also differed from those of the earlier spoken language theorists in that he considered certain disorders to be the result of heredity rather than brain damage. He explained *strephosymbolia* (a condition characterized by letter and word reversals, mirror writing, and reading from right to left rather than left to right) in terms of the genetic transmission of mixed dominance, i.e., right-handedness in combination with left-eyedness or vice versa. This mixed hand–eye dominance was thought to reflect a lack of hemispheric dominance for language functions. It was posited that the subdominant hemisphere housed the mirrored forms of the letters and words contained in the dominant hemisphere; thus, failure to suppress the subdominant hemisphere when engaged in written language activities resulted in the emergence of mirrored images, which, in turn, produced reading and spelling errors such as *was* for *saw* and *b* for *d*.

Although Orton's mixed dominance theory has been refuted, it is of historical significance because it was one of the first to propose etiological factors other than brain damage. In addition to his emphasis on heredity, Orton also discussed developmental aspects of written language disorders and mentioned possible environmental influences. For example, he suggested that our environment, because it is designed for right-handed persons, (e.g., right-handed scissors and desks) makes it difficult for left-handed persons to develop unilaterality. The terminology adopted by Orton's coworkers during the transition phase reflects his influence, including such terms as *developmental dyslexia* (deHirsch, 1963) and *maturational lag* (Bender, 1963).

Orton's emphasis on associative functions is clearly reflected in the visual-auditory-kinesthetic triangle that forms the basis of the popular Orton-Gillingham multisensory method of teaching reading, writing, and spelling (Gillingham & Stillman, 1956). Instruction begins with teaching the sight, sound, and feel of the letters of the alphabet through carefully structured and sequenced lessons involving much repetition and drill.

Perceptual and Motor Disorders

Wiederholt's third historical vein (1974), the perceptual and motor disorders vein, clearly has its roots in the study of mental retardation (Hallahan & Cruickshank, 1973). Goldstein's observations (1939) of the behavior of brain-injured soldiers formed the basis of much of the later research of Strauss and Werner (1942; Werner & Strauss, 1941), which led to characterization of the *exogenous* (presumably "brain-injured") mentally retarded child as one who exhibits: (1) perceptual disorders, including figure-ground perceptual distortion; (2) conceptual disorders, including organization problems and confusion of words symbolizing concepts; and (3) behavioral disorder, including hyperactivity, distractibility, explosiveness, and disinhibition.

Similar characteristics were documented for cerebral-palsied children by Cruickshank and colleagues (Cruickshank, Bice, & Wallen, 1957). More importantly from a learning disabilities perspective, Cruickshank called to the attention of physicians, psychologists, and educators the fact that similar behaviors were exhibited by children who, although they had no known brain damage, were being labeled as having "minimal brain damage," "minimal brain dysfunction," or "central nervous system dysfunction." Distractibility was thought to be the core characteristic of these children, one that could explain other symptoms such as hyperactivity, disinhibition, impulsivity, and perseveration (Cruickshank & Paul, 1971). An emphasis on the perceptual, relative to the motor, aspects of perceptual and motor disorders was clearly evident in Cruickshank's work.

In contrast to the perceptual emphasis of Cruickshank is the motor emphasis of Kephart (1960, 1971). In his early work with Strauss (Strauss & Kephart, 1940), Kephart observed poor motor coordination in mentally retarded children and subsequently developed a perceptual-motor theory in which motor development plays a more basic role than perceptual development per se. According to this theory, motor differentiation and motor integration are prerequisite to the development of a perceptual-motor match. This perceptual-motor match, in turn, is prerequisite to the development of perceptual integration and concept formation.

Attempts to translate the perceptual and motor theories of the foundation phase into practice during the transition phase took two distinctly different directions, paralleling the theoretical distinctions of Cruickshank and Kephart. While Cruickshank and his colleagues (Cruickshank, Bentzen, Ratzeburg, & Tannhauser, 1961) developed a structured classroom approach designed to eliminate distracting stimuli from the school environment, Kephart (1960, 1971) developed a perceptual-motor training program for slow learners.

Cruickshank's structured classroom was an expanded and refined version of the structured teaching environment developed earlier by Strauss and Lehtinen (1947) in an institutional setting. To avoid unnecessary distraction, teachers were instructed to wear plain clothing and no jewelry; colorful bulletin boards and pictures were prohibited; windows were painted; and cubicles were provided for individual study. In addition, motor involvement was recommended as a means of focusing the child's attention on the learning task. Kephart's perceptual-motor program includes a variety of gross and fine motor activities such as walking-board and balance-beam exercises, chalkboard exercises, and games such as making angels in the snow.

The Integration Phase

Although the events of the foundation phase fell primarily within the province of the medical profession, those of the transition phase were shared by a number of professions including medicine, psychology, language therapy, optometry, and education. Education came to play an increasingly greater role during the integration phase.

The professionals concerned with learning disorders during the transition phase differed greatly in terms of theoretical underpinnings, nomenclature, and treatment-training practices. Such diverse backgrounds made intercommunication exceedingly difficult; thus, confusion grew. There is little wonder that the parents of the children with learning disorders became even more confused than the professionals. In the face of much conflicting information about etiology, diagnosis, and treatment, they did not know what caused their child's disorder or what to do about it. Some parents, having had their child's problems diagnosed as "dyslexia" in one setting, "aphasia" in another, and "minimal brain dysfunction" in still another, did not even know what to call their child's disorder. Out of this confusion evolved a recognition of the need for a unified, organized effort on behalf of all children with learning disorders. Parents began to voice their concerns, not only to professionals dealing with learning disorders, but to legislators as well.

On several occasions in the 1960s, professionals convened to attempt to lend direction to this movement on behalf of children with learning disorders (Clements, 1966; Cruickshank, 1966). The most fruitful conference proved to be one initiated by parents: "The Conference on Exploration into Problems of the Perceptually Handicapped Child," in Chicago in 1963 (Kirk, 1976). It was at this conference that Kirk, in his keynote address, mentioned that the term *learning disabilities* had been used to refer to children exhibiting disorders in

. . . development, in language, speech, reading, and associated communication skills needed for social interaction. In this group I do not include children who have sensory handicaps such as blindness or deafness. . . . I also exclude from this group children who have generalized mental retardation. (p. 256)[1]

As an outcome of this conference, the parents organized a national association, the Association for Children with Learning Disabilities (ACLD), which was and is composed of both parents and professionals. It was not until 1968 that a national organization exclusively for professionals was recognized—the Division for Children with Learning Disabilities (DCLD) of the Council for Exceptional Children (CEC). In the interim, ACLD had been lobbying for inclusion of learning disabilities in legislation for the handicapped. Their efforts resulted in passage of the Children with Specific Learning Disabilities Act of 1969.

DEFINITIONS AND IDENTIFYING CRITERIA

Incorporated into the Children with Specific Learning Disabilities Act of 1969 is the following definition of learning disabilities, recommended to Congress by the National Advisory Committee on Handicapped Children (1968):

Children with special learning disabilities exhibit a disorder in one or more of the basic psychological processes involved in understanding or in using spoken or written language. These may be manifested in disorders of listening, thinking, talking, reading, writing, spelling, or arithmetic. They include conditions which have been referred to as perceptual handicaps, brain injury, minimal brain dysfunction, dyslexia, developmental aphasia, etc. They do not include learning problems which are due primarily to visual, hearing, or motor handicaps, to mental retardation, emotional disturbance, or to environmental disadvantage.

Attempts to implement the law in accord with this definition have revealed several shortcomings. Two of the most publicized criticisms of the definition are as follows: (1) It is so vague that it allows for the identification of large numbers of children who were never intended to be designated as learning disabled (Cruickshank, 1976; Kirk, 1976; McIntosh & Dunn, 1973). Widespread overidentification has resulted in a situation referred to as the "learning disabilities bandwagon" (Blatt, 1979); and (2) The exclusion of other mildly handicapped children—educable mentally retarded and mildly emotionally disturbed children—is unwarranted because the three groups are more similar than they are different (Hallahan & Kauffman, 1976, 1977).

In hopes that the 1969 definition might be replaced by a more satisfactory one in the Education for All Handicapped Children Act of 1975 (Public Law 94-142), new definitions were formulated and discussed extensively in the early and mid 1970s. In response to the criticism that the 1969 definition allows for overidentification, some of these definitions stated more explicitly the lines of demarcation of the category of learning disabilities; however, the suggested demarcation criteria differed. The following definition formulated by a learning disabilities committee

---

[1]Kirk, S. A., Samuel A. Kirk. In J. M. Kauffman & D. P. Hallahan (Eds.), *Teaching children with learning disabilities: Personal perspectives*. Columbus, Oh.: Charles E. Merrill, 1976.

of the National Project on the Classification of Exceptional Children (Hobbs, 1975) delimits the population on the basis of a perceptual-neurological locus:

> *Specific learning disability*, as defined here, refers to those children of any age who demonstrate a substantial deficiency in a particular aspect of academic achievement because of perceptual or perceptual-motor handicaps, regardless of the etiology or other contributing factors. The term *perceptual* as used here relates to those mental (neurological) processes through which the child acquires his basic alphabets of sounds and forms. (p. 306)[2]

Kirk (1976) continued to recommend delimiting on the basis of the specificity of the learning disability, stating that

> Mentally retarded children have learning problems, hence the move to label them "general learning disabilities" instead of "mentally retarded." Indeed all exceptional children—the deaf, the blind, and others—have learning problems. But these children are not children with *specific learning disability*, that is, a learning disability in one area when all other functions are intact. (p. 258)[3]

Demarcation on the basis of severity, and the need for special, rather than simply remedial, education was recommended by McIntosh and Dunn (1973):

> Children with major specific learning disabilities (MSLDs) are those 1.0 to 2.0 percent of the school population (1) who display one primary severe or moderately severe discrepancy between capacity and performance in a specific basic learning process involving perception, conception, or expression associated with the areas of oral and written language or mathematics; (2) yet whose MSLDs are neither mental retardation nor any of the other traditional handicapping conditions; (3) but who may have one or more additional, secondary traditional or specific learning disabilities to a milder degree; (4) none of whom have MSLDs that can be adequately treated in the regular school program when only remedial education is provided as an ancillary service; (5) not more than one half of whom have MSLDs that can be adequately treated in the regular school program even when special education consultant-helping teacher services are extensively provided; (6) half or more of whom therefore, will require more intensive special education instruction under such administrative plans as the resource room, the combined resource room and special class, the special class, and the special day and boarding school; and (7) yet any of whom may also require other remedial and special education services to deal with their secondary traditional or specific disabilities. (p. 542)[4]

In contrast to the three definitions above is the definition of Hallahan and Kauffman (1976, 1977, 1978), which broadens former views of learning disabilities. Expressing the hope that a learning disabilities definition that recognizes the heterogeneity of the learning disabilities population would be adopted, Hallahan and Kauffman (1976) suggested that the term *learning disabilities* be used to "re-

---

[2]Reprinted with permission from Wepman, J. M., Cruickshank, W. M., Deutsch, C. P., Morency, A., & Strother, C. R. Learning disabilities. In N. Hobbs (Ed.), *Issues in the classification of children* (Vol. 1). San Francisco: Jossey-Bass, 1975.

[3]Kirk, S. A. Samuel A. Kirk. In J. M. Kauffman, & D. P. Hallahan (Eds.). *Teaching children with learning disabilities: Personal Perspectives*. Columbus, Oh.: Charles E. Merrill, 1976.

[4]Reprinted with permission from McIntosh, O. K., & Dunn, L. M. Children with major specific learning disabilities. In L. M. Dunn (Ed.), *Exceptional children in the schools: Special education in transition* (2nd ed.). New York: Holt, Rhinehart and Winston, 1973.

fer to learning problems found in children who have traditionally been classified as mildly handicapped, whether it be emotionally disturbed, mildly retarded, or learning disabled'' (p. 28). At a later date, Hallahan & Kauffman (1978) described their definition as one that

> . . . posits that a learning-disabled child is simply one who is *not achieving up to his potential*. He may be at any intelligence level. He may have a learning problem for any number of reasons, some perceptual and some not. . . . He also may or may not have emotional problems. (p. 125)[5]

These authors claimed that their definition offers two major advantages: (1) it avoids the problem of looking for hard-to-detect neurological and/or perceptual causes; and (2) it lends recognition to the similarities of children traditionally defined as mildly retarded, mildly disturbed, and learning disabled.

The United States Office of Education (USOE) (1977), after considering these and other contrasting definitions of learning disabilities, concluded that the only generally accepted definitional criterion is that there is a major discrepancy between expected achievement and ability that is not the result of other handicapping conditions. Several procedures and/or formulas for quantifying this discrepancy have been proposed. The one included in the 1976 proposed rules and regulations of PL 94-142 specified that the child's achievement should be "at or below 50 percent of his expected achievement level in order for a severe discrepancy to exist" (p. 52405). During hearings on the proposed rules and regulations, negative reactions to the formula referred to four areas (USOE, 1977): (1) the inappropriateness of attempting to reduce the behavior of children to numbers; (2) the psychometric and statistical inadequacy of the procedure; (3) the fear that use of the formula might easily lend itself to inappropriate use to the detriment of handicapped children; and (4) the inappropriateness of using a single formula for children of all ages, particularly preschool children.

After conducting a study to determine the effectiveness of the formula, USOE decided to delete it from the final rules and regulations. Other approaches considered for determining the existence of a severe discrepancy were (1) the requirement of a major discrepancy between verbal and performance scores on the Wechsler Intelligence Scale for Children (WISC); and (2) the requirement that each area of information processing be subdivided into discrete functions and analyzed in terms of their effects on achievement. Both of these approaches were rejected because it was felt that extensive research would be required before they could be made applicable. Continuing interest in the development of acceptable procedures for quantifying the discrepancy is indicated by recent publications of new approaches (Danielson & Bauer, 1978; Lavine, 1978; McLeod, 1979; Schere, Richardson, & Bialer, 1980).

The 1976 proposed rules and regulations also included a statement, in accord with the definition proposed by McIntosh and Dunn (1973), that no more than 2 percent of the school-age population could be counted as children with specific learning disabilities. However, this proposed 2 percent cap, like the proposed discrepancy formula, was deleted from the final rules and regulations.

---

[5]From Hallahan, D. P., & Kauffman, J. M. *Exceptional children*. Englewood Cliffs: Prentice-Hall, 1978. Reprinted by permission of Prentice-Hall, Inc., Englewood Cliffs, New Jersey.

A number of people objected to that part of the official definition that excludes emotionally disturbed and mentally retarded children from the learning disabilities category. No changes were made, however, in the exclusion clause, and those exclusions are now statutory.

Included in the final rules and regulations were the following criteria for determining the existence of a specific learning disability (USOE, 1977, p. 65083):

(1) The child does not achieve commensurate with his or her age and ability levels in one or more of the areas listed in paragraph (a)(2) of this section, when provided with learning experiences appropriate for the child's age and ability levels; and

(2) The team finds that a child has a severe discrepancy between achievement and intellectual ability in one or more of the following areas:

    (i) Oral expression;

    (ii) Listening comprehension;

    (iii) Written expression;

    (iv) Basic reading skill;

    (v) Reading comprehension;

    (vi) Mathematics calculation; or

    (vii) Mathematics reasoning.

        (b) The team may not identify a child as having a specific learning disability if the severe discrepancy between ability and achievement is primarily the result of:

        (1) A visual, hearing, or motor handicap;

        (2) Mental retardation;

        (3) Emotional disturbance; or

        (4) Environmental, cultural or economic disadvantage.

The learning disabilities definition included in the final rules and regulations is, except for minor changes in wording, the same as the 1969 definition (USOE, 1977):

"Specific learning disability" means a disorder in one or more of the basic psychological processes involved in understanding or in using language, spoken or written, which may manifest itself in an imperfect ability to listen, think, speak, read, write, spell, or to do mathematical calculations. The term includes such conditions as perceptual handicaps, brain injury, minimal brain dysfunction, dyslexia, and developmental aphasia. The term does not include children who have learning problems which are primarily the result of visual, hearing, or motor handicaps, of mental retardation, of emotional disturbance, or of environmental, cultural, or economic disadvantage. (p. 65083)

Publication of the final rules and regulations also included the following statement of the basic concepts from which they were developed (USOE, 1977):

Those with specific learning disabilities may demonstrate their handicap through a variety of symptoms such as hyperactivity, distractibility, attention problems, concept association problems, etc. The end result of the effects of these symptoms is a severe discrepancy between achievement and ability. If there is no severe discrepancy between how much should have been learned and what has been learned, there would not be a disability in learning. However, other handicapping and sociological conditions may result in a discrepancy between ability and achievement. There are those for whom these conditions are the primary factors affecting achievement. In such cases, the severe discrepancy may be primarily the result of these factors and not of a severe learning problem. For the purpose of these regulations, when a severe discrepancy between ability and achievement exists which cannot be explained by the presence of other known factors that lead to such a discrepancy, the cause is believed to be a specific learning disability. (p. 65085)

Different reactions to the final rules and regulations were expressed by Senf (1978), editor of the *Journal of Learning Disabilities* and Larsen (1978), president of the DCLD. Senf pointed out that, although the definition retains the phrase "*disorder* in one or more of the basic psychological processes," the criteria for identifying specific learning disabilities essentially redefine the condition as *underachievement*. Senf contended that the underachievement criteria are inadequate for the identification of learning disabled children at preschool and kindergarten ages, and that the rules, as presently stated, are applicable only to education; other concerned professions are ignored. Larsen (1978) presented the view that learning disabilities are basically educational problems and wrote that the rules place the responsibility for the management of learning disabled children where it should be—on the shoulders of educators.

Incidence Estimates

Estimates of the incidence of learning disabilities have ranged from 1 to 30 percent (Kirk, 1976). The National Advisory Committee on Handicapped Children, which formulated the official 1969 definition, recommended a 1–3 percent figure. The recently proposed 2 percent cap is in accord with this conservative estimate; however, its deletion from the final rules and regulations may be indicative of higher incidence figures to come.

The prediction of higher incidence figures is consistent with a major change in the definition of mental retardation that occurred in the 1970s. The 1961 definition of mental retardation specified an IQ cutoff point of one standard deviation below the mean, whereas the revised 1973 definition specified a cutoff point of at least two standard deviations below the mean (Grossman, 1973). Therefore, many children who would probably have been classified as educable mentally retarded prior to 1973, i.e., children with borderline and dull normal IQs (70–89), and who also exhibit a discrepancy between ability and achievement, are presently eligible for inclusion in the learning disabilities category.

Etiology

A host of organic, biological, and environmental factors have been purported to cause learning disabilities (Hallahan & Kauffman, 1978, pp. 126–129; Tarver & Hallahan, 1976, pp. 8–12). In the foundation phase, and even into the transition phase, learning disorders were assumed to be the result of organic factors such as brain damage, central nervous system dysfunction, or genetic inheritance. While the emphasis has clearly shifted to environmental etiological factors, there is some current evidence to suggest that learning disabilities, or at least some types of learning disabilities, are due to organic factors such as chromosomal irregularities (Waldrop & Halverson, 1971) and heredity (Owen, Adams, Forrest, Stolz, & Fisher, 1971).

Separating environmental-ecological factors from organic-biological ones is exceedingly difficult (Hallahan & Cruickshank, 1973). Organic factors such as brain damage can be the result of conditions associated with poverty and/or environmental disadvantage, e.g., malnutrition and inadequate medical care. Furthermore, some etiological factors that were previously viewed as organic causes are currently viewed as ecological ones. Mayron (1978), for example, contended that anxiety, malnutrition, toxicity, allergy, and electroradiation are five general ecological factors that can cause learning disabilities.

The popular contention that learning disabilities are really teaching disabilities reflects the view that poor teaching causes learning disabilities (Cohen, 1971). This view is consistent with the notion that educators can teach any child anything if they know enough about how to teach it (Engelmann, 1977). This is not to say that educators deny the proposition of multiple causation, but that they consider it to be more efficacious to focus on the deficient academic skills themselves rather than to attempt to discern more basic causes.

LEARNER CHARACTERISTICS

Interest in the language and perceptual-cognitive characteristics of learning disabled children has been apparent throughout the development of the field. Documentation of academic and intellectual characteristics has been required by the discrepancy clause of the USOE definition. An upsurge of interest in social-affective characteristics has become evident during the last decade. More importantly, an emphasis on the interrelatedness of these various aspects of the child's total functioning seems to be emerging at present.

Demographic and Developmental Characteristics

Subsequent to passage of the Children with Specific Learning Disabilities Act of 1969, federal funds were allotted for the establishment of Child Service Demonstration Centers in learning disabilities. Kirk and Elkins (1975) conducted an empirical study of the characteristics of over 3000 children enrolled in these centers in 21 states and summarized their demographic data as follows:

1. Most of the children were in the lower elementary grades.
2. The sex ratio was three boys to one girl.
3. Approximately two-thirds of the children were rated as having reading problems.
4. The median educational retardation was one grade below the mental age reading grade expectancy.
5. The retardation in reading and spelling was one half of a grade more than the retardation in arithmetic.
6. The distribution of IQ contained a larger proportion with below-average ability than is found in the general population of children.

More recently, a series of developmental studies conducted at the Frank Porter Graham Child Development Center in North Carolina (McKinney & Feagans,

1980) produced the following generalizable findings about learning disabled children in the elementary grades:

1. Regarding academic achievement, learning disabilities (at least as manifested in the early elementary school years) seems to be a mildly handicapping condition. However, academic retardation becomes progressively greater over the elementary years and is more generalized than previously thought; learning disabled children are as far behind in math as in reading.
2. Regarding intellectual ability, learning disabled children do not show an atypical pattern of abilities; rather, they perform at a generally lower level that is still within the normal IQ range.
3. Regarding adaptive behaviors in the regular classroom, learning disabled children differ from their normally achieving peers; these differences are associated with academic competencies and not with social-affective competencies.
4. Regarding language development, learning disabled children differ from normally achieving peers in expressive language but not in ability to comprehend abstract conceptual information.
5. Regarding cognitive development, learning disabled children reveal general cognitive immaturity and perceptual processing difficulties; their difficulties do not reflect specific kinds of perceptual errors and do not appear to be due to impulsivity.

Intellectual Characteristics

IQ scores on individually administered, standardized tests of intelligence such as the WISC and revised WISC (WISC-R) have been used almost exclusively as measures of intellectual potential. These tests are divided into performance and verbal scales. Each of these scales is composed of five subtests purported to measure the components of intelligence. Three hypotheses, which have been widely investigated, are (1) high performance–low verbal IQ is characteristic of the learning disabled; (2) greater-than-average subtest scatter (variability) is characteristic of the learning disabled; and (3) a particular subtest profile, other than that indicated by the performance–verbal distinction, is characteristic of the learning disabled.

The first hypothesis has received support from studies by Ackerman, Peters, and Dykman (1971); Anderson, Kaufman, and Kaufman (1976); Smith, Coleman, Dokecki, and Davis (1977a); and Zingale and Smith (1978). However, most of these authors emphasized the fact that this pattern was not found in all learning disabled subjects; high verbal–low performance and no verbal–performance discordance patterns were observed in some cases. A series of studies with children exhibiting the three performance–verbal patterns found the high verbal–low performance pattern to be more highly associated with achievement in reading and reading-related skills than the other two patterns (Rourke, Dietrich, & Young, 1973; Rourke & Finlayson, 1978; Rourke, Young, & Flewelling, 1971), suggesting that the opposite pattern—high performance–low verbal—may be characteristic of that subgroup of learning disabled children whose underachievement is in the area of reading.

Group comparisons of the subtest scatter of learning disabled children with that of other children have shown the scatter of the learning disabled to be (1) greater than that of educably mentally retarded and emotionally disturbed children (Gajar, 1979); (2) similar to that of low-achieving normal children (Ysseldyke, Shinn, McGue, & Epps, 1980); and (3) no different from that of a normal control group (Ackerman et al., 1971). Comparisons with normative data have yielded conflicting findings. Anderson et al. (1976) reported no differences, whereas Tabachnick (1979) reported greater scatter for a learning disabled group. However, Tabachnick (1979) also found that the range of verbal scores was greater for learning disabled children below 11 years of age than it was for those above 11 years of age.

A number of researchers have sought to delineate a subtest profile characteristic of the learning disabled by recategorizing the WISC-R subtests. Bannatyne (1968, 1974), for example, first proposed three categories (*spatial,* composed of the Picture Completion, Block Design, and Object Assembly subtests; *verbal conceptualizing,* composed of the Comprehension, Similarities, and Vocabulary subtests; and *sequencing,* composed of the Digit Span, Arithmetic, and Coding subtests) and later added a fourth (*acquired knowledge,* composed of the Arithmetic, Information, and Vocabulary subtests). He reported that retarded readers tend to have high scores on the spatial subtests and low scores on the sequential subtests. Essentially the same subtest profile was reported by Rugel (1974) and Smith et al. (1977a, 1977b). These results are also consistent with those of Keogh and Hall (1974), who, although they labeled their three categories differently, included the same subtests in a field analytic category that Bannatyne included in his spatial category, and the same subtests in their attention-concentration category that Bannatyne had included in his sequencing category. In the Keogh and Hall (1974) study, educationally handicapped boys received their highest scores on field analytic subtests and their lowest scores on attention-concentration subtests; the educationally handicapped girls' scores on the three categories did not differ, however.

Rather consistently, the subtest profile studies have shown that relatively good performance on Picture Completion, Block Design, and Object Assembly subtests in conjunction with relatively poor performance on Arithmetic, Digit Span, Coding, and Information subtests is characteristic of groups of learning disabled children. However, these same studies have also shown that few individuals conform to this group pattern and that no single profile is characteristic of all learning disabled children. In fact, the research of Vance and colleagues (Blaha & Vance, 1979; Vance, Gaynor, & Coleman, 1976; Vance & Singer, 1979; Vance, Wallbrown, & Blaha, 1978) suggests that at least five profiles are required to adequately characterize the learning disabled population.

The usefulness of WISC-R profiles for purposes of diagnosis and/or remediation has been questioned (Huelsman, 1970; Kaufman, 1976; Vance & Singer, 1979). Because individual profiles often do not conform to group findings, the diagnostic validity of the group findings is minimal. Because the relationship between the abilities tapped by the subtests and those involved in school achievement is unclear in most cases, the delineation of a characteristic profile lends little direction to remediation. Despite these shortcomings for purposes of diagnosis and remediation, IQ scores derived from these standardized tests remain our most valid and reliable indicators of general ability or potential; thus, they will no doubt continue to be used as measures of ability in determining the existence of a discrepancy between ability and achievement.

Selective Attention and Verbal Rehearsal

The research of Hallahan and colleagues at the University of Virginia Learning Disabilities Research Institute (Hallahan, 1978) on the selective attention problems of learning disabled children is clearly based upon the earlier theories and research of Strauss, Werner, Cruickshank, and others associated with the study of perceptual and motor disorders. Although distractibility is viewed as distinct from selective attention today (Hallahan & Reeve, 1980), these early theorists' studies of distractibility and hyperresponsiveness provided fertile soil from which a variety of studies of attention problems grew (Tarver & Hallahan, 1974). Selective attention, in particular, has been investigated widely and is theorized to play a central role in the learning disabilities syndrome (Ross, 1976).

As defined by Hallahan and Reeve (1980), selective attention is the "ability to focus on relevant stimuli and ignore irrelevant stimuli that are relatively close to the relevant stimuli themselves" (p. 1). While they initially studied selective attention only (Hallahan, Kauffman, & Ball, 1973, 1974), they later incorporated verbal rehearsal into their research (Dawson, Hallahan, Reeve, & Ball, 1980; Hallahan, Tarver, Kauffman, & Graybeal, 1978; Tarver, Hallahan, Cohen, & Kauffman, 1977; Tarver, Hallahan, Kauffman, & Ball, 1976). Among the general conclusions drawn from their research (Hallahan & Reeve, 1980) were

1. Children identified as learning disabled generally demonstrate about a two-to-three-year developmental lag in the ability to attend selectively.
2. One of the primary reasons learning disabled children do poorly on tasks of selective attention is that they are deficient in the application of strategies to learn. In particular, compared to normal peers, they often do not apply verbal rehearsal strategies to tasks requiring selective attention.
3. The deficiency in the use of verbal rehearsal strategies can be overcome by specific training in these skills. In other words, when instructed to rehearse verbally, the selective attention performance of learning disabled children equals that of normal controls. (p. 142)[6]

Further evidence of a developmental lag in selective attention was reported by Pelham and Ross (1977). A deficit in the application of veral rehearsal strategies was documented by several investigators using a variety of serial memory tasks (Bauer, 1977a, 1977b; Swanson, 1977; Torgeson, 1978–1979).

Oral and Written Language Characteristics

A review of the literature related to the oral and written language problems of learning disabled children led Tarver and Ellsworth (1981) to conclude that

---

[6]Reprinted with permission from Hallahan, D. P., & Reeve, R. E. Selective attention and distractibility. In B. K. Keogh (Ed.), *Advances in special education* (Vol. 1). Greenwich, Conn.: JAI Press, 1980.

Learning disabled children are more deficient in nonmeaningful, than meaningful, aspects of language. The acquisition of decoding skills primarily involves nonmeaningful learning; the acquisition of vocabulary-concept knowledge (i.e., single word meanings) primarily involves meaningful learning. The learning disabled are deficient in decoding; they are not deficient in vocabulary-concept knowledge. (p. 507)[7]

These decoding deficiencies were further linked to failure to automatize decoding skills (Bateman, 1979; LaBerge & Samuels, 1974), and deficiencies in phonological awareness and/or segmentation (Rozin & Gleitman, 1977). Automaticity of decoding skills (i.e., rapid, automatic processing that does not require conscious attention) is deemed to be an essential prerequisite to reading comprehension because this allows the reader to direct attention to meaning rather than to the decoding process itself. A conscious awareness of the segmentability of our phonological system is an essential prerequisite to the ability to segment spoken sentences into words and words into syllables and phonemes. Phonemic segmentation, in turn, is an essential prerequisite to the acquisition of phoneme-grapheme associations.

Regarding the oral language characteristics of learning disabled children and adolescents, Wiig, Lapointe, and Semel (1977) posited two distinct syndromes, one characterized by reductions in the knowledge and the use of morphology and syntax and the other characterized by deficiencies in speed and accuracy of word retrieval (i.e., dysnomia). Consistent with the previously mentioned findings of McKinney and Feagans (1980) regarding deficiencies in expression, but not comprehension, of oral language, are the findings of Newcomer, Magee, and Adelman (1978). These authors found that learning disabled children's performance on receptive subtests of the Test of Language Development (Newcomer & Hammill, 1977) was similar to that of their nondisabled peers, whereas their performance on the expressive subtests was lower than that of their nondisabled peers.

In attempting to explain how spoken language problems, written language problems, and cognitive processing deficits of learning disabled children may be interrelated, Tarver and Ellsworth (1981) wrote:

The evidence presents a picture of the learning disabled child as one whose core problem is that of acquiring rapid, automatic decoding skills. Difficulties with this aspect of written language can be linked to deficiencies in oral language and cognitive processing. The processes of attention and verbal labeling/rehearsal are involved in the acquisition of decoding skills. Deficiencies in both of these cognitive processes have been documented in learning disabled children. . . . Word retrieval problems, a major oral language deficiency of the learning disabled, may represent the linguistic counterpart of the cognitive verbal labeling/rehearsal problem. . . . Awareness, i.e., access to the linguistic systems, may represent the linguistic or metalinguistic counterpart of the cognitive process of attention. The evidence also suggests that *speed* . . . is an important element of the learning disability syndrome. Slowness of processing and/or retrieving language units could account for the extreme difficulties experienced by these children in acquiring rapid, automatic decoding skills. (p. 506)[8]

---

[7]From Tarver, S. G., & Ellsworth, P. S. Written and oral language for verbal children. In J. M. Kauffman & D. P. Hallahan (Eds.), *Handbook of special education*. Englewood Cliffs: Prentice Hall, 1981. Reprinted by permission of Prentice-Hall, Inc., Englewood Cliffs, New Jersey.

[8]From Tarner, S. G., & Ellsworth, P. S. Written and oral language for verbal children. In J. M. Kauffman & D. P. Hallahan (Eds.), *Handbook of Special Education*. Englewood Cliffs: Prentice-Hall, 1981. Reprinted by permission of Prentice-Hall, Inc., Englewood Cliffs, New Jersey.

Social and Affective Characteristics

Studies conducted by Tanis and James Bryan and their colleagues at the Chicago Institute for Learning Disabilities (T. Bryan & Eash, 1978) provided a great deal of information about the social and affective characteristics of learning disabled children—their interactions with peers and teachers, their self-concepts, and their causal attributions. In summarizing the results of some of their studies, T. Bryan stated that

> . . . the studies support the hypothesis that learning disabled children experience difficulties in social development, interpersonal relationships, and perceiving and understanding others' affective states. It is also quite clear that teachers, peers, and even strangers make negative evaluations of these children. The source of difficulty for LD children's interpersonal problems seems to rest in their comprehension of nonverbal communication, their affective involvements with others, and their expressive language ability—what they say and how they say it. (p. 115)[9]

T. Bryan's (1974a, 1974b, 1976) findings that learning disabled children are less socially accepted and more unpopular than their peers are consistent with those of other studies (Bruininks, 1978a, 1978b; Siperstein, Bopp, & Bak, 1978; Siperstein & Gottlieb, 1977). Several possible sources of this rejection have been suggested:

1. Learning disabled children's inaccurate comprehension of nonverbal communication (T. Bryan, 1977) can lead to rejection by others. Wiig and Semel (1976) also attributed learning disabled children's poor social perception to deficiencies in the interpretation of everyday expressions of affect and attitudes through facial expressions, gestures, caresses, or touches.
2. Learning disabled children's expression of nonverbal communication may also contribute to their rejection. J. H. Bryan, Sherman, and Fisher (1980) found that their smiling and looking behaviors differed from those of their peers and J. H. Bryan and Perlmutter (1979) found that learning disabled children were devalued by strangers after only a few minutes of observation.
3. Learning disabled children's poor verbal skills may also elicit rejection. This is suggested by findings that the learning disabled, relative to their nondisabled peers, make more nasty statements to peers (T. Bryan & J. H. Bryan, 1978a); make fewer helpful and considerate statements (T. Bryan, Wheeler, Felcan, & Henek, 1976); and fail to modify the form and content of their speech in accordance with what the listener is presumed to know (T. Bryan & Pflaum, 1978).
4. Learning disabled children's inferior role-taking skills (Wong & Wong, 1980) (i.e., their difficulties in putting themselves in another's place and seeing things from a perspective different from their own) may lead to rejection by others. Bachara (1976) also found learning disabled children to lack empathy.
5. Learning disabled children's abilities in areas other than academics may interact with their "smartness" to determine their social acceptability. Siperstein and Gottlieb (1977) found that learning disabled children who were viewed as

---

[9]Reprinted with permission from Bryan, T. Social relationships and verbal interactions of learning disabled children. *Journal of Learning Disabilities*, 1978, *10*, 115.

good athletes had a greater chance of being accepted socially. Conversely, it may be that poor athletic ability exacerbates the learning disability.

6.   Learning disabled children's school placement may have an affect upon self-concept, which, in turn, may affect popularity. Ribner (1978) compared the self-concept scores of learning disabled children in full-day special classes to those of learning disabled children in full-day regular classes who had been recommended for, but not yet placed in, special classes. The scores of the children in the regular classes were significantly lower than those of the children in self-contained special classes. Smith, Dokecki, and Davis (1977) found that the self-concept scores of learning disabled children in self-contained classes were equivalent to those of nondisabled children in regular classes, providing further support for the view that special class placement has a positive effect on learning disabled children's self-concepts. However, subsequent placement of the learning disabled children in a half-day mainstream condition increased their self-concept scores. A simulated full-day mainstream condition produced lower self-concept scores than the half-day condition.

Regarding their studies of self-concepts and causal attributions of learning disabled children, T. Bryan and Pearl (1979) stated that

> Learning disabled children are more likely than nondisabled children to have negative self concepts and to make causal attributions likely to lead to "learned helplessness." In addition, teachers and mothers hold little expectation that these children will improve academically across time. It appears that not only do learning disabled children have to cope with their own negative feelings about failure, the persons who provide important feedback about their performance are also likely to judge them as doing badly. (p. 226)

Individuals with an internal locus of control view their successes or failures as contingent upon their own behaviors, whereas those with an external locus of control view their successes or failures as dependent upon factors external to themselves, e.g., fate, luck, chance. The T. Bryan and Pearl suggestion that children with learning disabilities are more likely to show learned helplessness is supported by studies showing that learning disabled children have an external locus of control (Hallahan, Gajar, Cohn & Tarver, 1978; Pearl, T. Bryan, & Donahue, 1980) and accept responsibility for their failures, but not their successes (Pearl et al., 1980).

REFERENCES

Ackerman, P., Peters, J., & Dykman, R. Children with specific learning disabilities: WISC profiles. *Journal of Learning Disabilities*, 1971, *4*, 150–166.

Anderson, M., Kaufman, A., & Kaufman, N. Use of the WISC-R with learning disabled population: Some diagnostic implications. *Psychology in the Schools*, 1976, *13*, 381–386.

Bachara, G. H. Empathy in learning disabled children. *Perceptual and Motor Skills*, 1976, *43*, 541–542.

Bannatyne, A. Diagnosing learning disabilities and writing remedial prescriptions. *Journal of Learning Disabilities*, 1968, *1*, 28–35.

Bannatyne, A. Diagnosis: A note on the recategorization of the WISC scaled scores. *Journal of Learning Disabilities*, 1974, *7*, 272–273.

Bateman, B. Teaching reading to learning disabled children: A fourth approach. In L. B. Resnick & P. A. Weaver (Eds.), *Theory and practice of early reading: Research issues* (Vol. 1). New York: Lawrence Erlbaum

Press, 1979.

Bauer, R. H. Memory processes in children with learning disabilities: Evidence for deficient rehearsal. *Journal of Experimental Child Psychology*, 1977, *24*, 415–430. (a)

Bauer, R. H. Short-term memory in learning disabled and nondisabled children. *Bulletin of the Psychonomic Society*, 1977, *10*, 128–130. (b)

Bender, L. Specific reading disability as a maturational lag. *Bulletin of the Orton Society*, 1963, *13*, 25–44.

Blaha, J., & Vance, H. The hierarchical factor structure of the WISC-R for learning disabled children. *Learning Disabilities Quarterly*, 1979, *2*, 71–75.

Blatt, B. Bandwagons also go to funerals. *Journal of Learning Disabilities*, 1979, *12*, 222–224, 288–291, 360–361.

Bruininks, V. L. Actual and perceived peer status of learning-disabled students in mainstream programs. *Journal of Special Education*, 1978, *12*, 51–58. (a)

Bruininks, V. L. Peer status and personality characteristics of learning disabled and non-disabled students. *Journal of Learning Disabilities*, 1978, *11*, 484–489. (b)

Bryan, J. H., & Perlmutter, B. Female adults' immediate impressions of learning disabled children. *Learning Disability Quarterly*, 1979, *2*, 80–88.

Bryan, J. H., Sherman, R. E., & Fisher, A. Learning disabled boys' nonverbal behaviors within a dyadic interview. *Learning Disability Quarterly*, 1980, *3*(1), 66–72.

Bryan, T. Learning disabled children's comprehension of nonverbal communication. *Journal of Learning Disabilities*, 1977, *10*, 501–506.

Bryan, T. An observational analysis of classroom behaviors of children with learning disabilities. *Journal of Learning Disabilities*, 1974, *7*, 35–42. (a)

Bryan, T. Peer popularity of learning disabled children. *Journal of Learning Disabilities*, 1974, *7*, 621–625. (b)

Bryan, T. Peer popularity of learning disabled children. A replication. *Journal of Learning Disabilities*, 1976, *9*, 307–311.

Bryan, T. Learning disabled children's comprehension of nonverbal communication. *Journal of Learning Disabilities*, 1977, *10*, 501–506.

Bryan, T. Social relationships and verbal interactions of learning disabled children. *Journal of Learning Disabilities*, 1978, *10*, 107–115.

Bryan, T., & Bryan, J. H. Social interactions of learning disabled children. *Learning Disability Quarterly*, 1978, *1*, 33–38. (a)

Bryan, T., & Bryan, J. H. *Understanding learning disabilities* (2nd ed.). Sherman Oaks, California: Alfred Publishing, 1978. (b)

Bryan, T., & Eash, M. Chicago Institute for Learning Disabilities: Project CHILD. *Learning Disability Quarterly*, 1978, *1*, 71–72.

Bryan, T., & Pearl, R. Self concepts and locus of control of learning disabled children. *Journal of Clinical Child Psychology*, 1979, *8*, 223–226.

Bryan, T., & Pflaum, S. Social interactions of learning disabled children: A linguistic, social and cognitive analysis. *Learning Disability Quarterly*, 1978, *1*, 70–79.

Bryan, T., Wheeler, R., Felcan, J., & Henek, T. Come on, dummy: An observational study of children's communications. *Journal of Learning Disabilities*, 1976, *10*, 661–669.

Bush, W. J., & Giles, M. T. *Aids to psycholinguistic teaching*. Columbus, Oh.: Charles E. Merrill, 1969.

Clements, S. D. *Minimal brain dysfunction in children: Terminology and identification, Phase one of a three-phase project*. NINDB Monograph No. 3, Washington, D.C.: U.S. Department of Health, Education and Welfare, 1966.

Cohen, S. A. Dyspedagogia as a cause of reading retardation: Definition and treatment. In B. Bateman (Ed.), *Learning disorders* (Vol. 4). Seattle: Special Child Publications, 1971.

Cruickshank, W. M. (Ed.). *The teacher of brain-injured children*. Syracuse, N.Y.: Syracuse University Press, 1966.

Cruickshank, W. M. William M. Cruickshank. In J. M. Kauffman & D. P. Hallahan (Eds.), *Teaching children with learning disabilities: Personal perspectives*. Columbus, Oh.: Charles E. Merrill, 1976.

Cruickshank, W. M., Bentzen, F. A., Ratzeburg, F. H., & Tannhauser, M. T. *A teaching method for brain-injured and hyperactive children*. Syracuse, N.Y.: Syracuse University Press, 1961.

Cruickshank, W. M., Bice, H. V., & Wallen, N. E. *Perception and cerebral palsy*. Syracuse, N.Y.: Syracuse University Press, 1957.

Cruickshank, W. M., & Paul, J. L. The psychological characteristics of brain-injured children. In W. M. Cruickshank (Ed.), *Psychology of exceptional children and youth* (3rd ed.). Englewood Cliffs: Prentice-Hall, 1971.

Danielson, L. C., & Bauer, J. N. A formula-based classification of learning disabled children: An examination of the issues. *Journal of Learning Disabilities*, 1978, *11*, 163–176.

Dawson, M. M., Hallahan, D. P., Reeve, R. E., & Ball, D. W. The effect of reinforcement and verbal rehearsal on selective attention in learning disabled children. *Journal of Abnormal Child Psychology*, 1980, *8*, 133–144.

deHirsch, K. Psychological correlates of the reading process. *Bulletin of the Orton Society*, 1963, *13*, 59–71.

Engelmann, S. E. Sequencing cognitive and academic tasks. In R. D. Kneedler & S. G. Tarver (Eds.), *Changing perspectives in special education*. Columbus, Oh.: Charles E. Merrill, 1977.

Gajar, A. Educable mentally retarded, learning disabled, emotionally disturbed: Similarities and differences. *Exceptional Children*, 1979, *45*, 470–472.

Gillingham, A., & Stillman, B. *Remedial training for children with specific disability in reading, spelling, and penmanship*. Cambridge: Educators Publishing Service, 1956.

Goldstein, K. *The organism*. New York: American Book, 1939.

Grossman, H. J. (Ed.). *Manual on terminology and classification in mental retardation, 1973 revision*. Washington, D.C.: American Association on Mental Deficiency, 1973.

Hallahan, D. P. University of Virginia Learning Disabilities Research Institute. *Learning Disability Quarterly*, 1978, *1*, 77–78.

Hallahan, D. P., & Cruickshank, W. M. *Psychoeducational foundations of learning disabilities*. Englewood Cliffs: Prentice-Hall, 1973.

Hallahan, D. P., Gajar, A. H., Cohen, S. B., & Tarver, S. G. Selective attention and locus of control in learning disabled and normal children. *Journal of Learning Disabilities*, 1978, *11*, 231–236.

Hallahan, D. P., & Kauffman, J. M. *Introduction to learning disabilities*. Englewood Cliffs: Prentice-Hall, 1976.

Hallahan, D. P., & Kauffman, J. M., Labels, categories, behaviors: ED, LD, EMR reconsidered. *Journal of Special Education*, 1977, *11*, 139–149.

Hallahan, D. P., & Kauffman, J. M. *Exceptional children*. Englewood Cliffs: Prentice-Hall, 1978.

Hallahan, D. P., Kauffman, J. M., & Ball, D. W. Selective attention and cognitive tempo of low achieving and high achieving sixth grade males. *Perceptual and Motor Skills*, 1973, *36*, 579–583.

Hallahan, D. P., Kauffman, J. M., & Ball, D. W. Developmental trends in recall of central and incidental auditory material. *Journal of Experimental Child Psychology*, 1974, *17*, 409–421.

Hallahan, D. P., & Reeve, R. E. Selective attention and distractibility. In B. K. Keogh (Ed.), *Advances in special education* (Vol. 1). Greenwich, Conn.: JAI Press, 1980.

Hallahan, D. P., Tarver, S. G., Kauffman, J. M.,

& Graybeal, N. L. A comparison of the effects of reinforcement and response cost on selective attention of learning disabled children. *Journal of Learning Disabilities*, 1978, *11*, 430–438.

Hobbs, N. (Ed.). *Issues in the classification of children* (Vols. 1 & 2). San Francisco: Jossey-Bass, 1975.

Huelsman, C. B. The WISC subtest syndrome for disabled readers. *Perceptual and Motor Skills*, 1970, *30*, 535–550.

Johnson, D. J., & Myklebust, H. R. *Learning disabilities: Educational principles and practices*. New York: Grune & Stratton, 1967.

Kaufman, A. A new approach to the interpretation of test scatter in the WISC-R. *Journal of Learning Disabilities*, 1976, *9*, 160–168.

Keogh, B. K., & Hall, P. J. WISC subtest patterns of educationally handicapped and educable mentally retarded pupils. *Psychology in the Schools*, 1974, *11*, 296–300.

Kephart, N. C. *The slow learner in the classroom* (2nd ed.). Columbus, Oh.: Charles E. Merrill, 1960.

Kephart, N. C. *The slow learner in the classroom*. Columbus, Oh.: Charles E. Merrill, 1971.

Kirk, S. A. Samuel A. Kirk. In J. M. Kauffman & D. P. Hallahan (Eds.), *Teaching children with learning disabilities: Personal perspectives*. Columbus, Oh.: Charles E. Merrill, 1976.

Kirk, S. A., & Elkins, J. Characteristics of children enrolled in the child service demonstration centers. *Journal of Learning Disabilities*, 1975, *8*, 630–637.

Kirk, S. A., McCarthy, J. J., & Kirk, W. D. *Illinois test of psycholinguistic abilities* (experimental ed.). Urbana: University of Illinois Press, 1961.

LaBerge, D., & Samuels, S. J. Toward a theory of automatic information processing in reading. *Cognitive Psychology*, 1974, *6*, 293–323.

Larsen, S. Learning disabilities and the professional educator. *Learning Disability Quarterly*, 1978, *1*(1), 5–12.

Lavine, S. B. The paired comparisons method of identifying developmental discrepancies with the ITPA. *Journal of Learning Disabilities*, 1978, *11*, 506–510.

Mayron, L. W. Ecological factors in learning disabilities. *Journal of Learning Disabilities*, 1978, *11*, 495–505.

McIntosh, D. K., & Dunn, L. M. Children with major specific learning disabilities. In L. M. Dunn (Ed.), *Exceptional children in the schools: Special education in transition* (2nd ed.). New York: Holt, Rinehart and Winston, 1973.

McKinney, J. D., & Feagans, L. *Longitudinal studies of learning disabled children.* Paper presented at the annual meeting of the Association for Children with Learning Disabilities, Milwaukee, Wis., February 1980.

McLeod, J. Educational underachievement: Toward a defensible psychometric definition. *Journal of Learning Disabilities,* 1979, *12,* 322–330.

Minskoff, E. H., Wiseman, D. E., & Minskoff, J. C. *The MWM program of developing language abilities.* Ridgefield, N.J.: Educational Performance Associates, 1973.

Myklebust, H. R. *Auditory disorders in children: A manual for differential diagnosis.* New York: Grune & Stratton, 1954.

National Advisory Committee on Handicapped Children. *Special education for handicapped children.* First Annual Report. Washington, D.C.: U.S. Department of Health, Education and Welfare, January 31, 1968.

Newcomer, P. L., & Hammill, D. D. *The Test of Language Development.* Austin, Tex.: Empiric Press, 1977.

Newcomer, P. L., Magee, P. A., & Adelman, M. *A comparison of the performance of learning disabled and mentally retarded children on a test of oral language abilities.* Paper presented at the national conference of the Council for Exceptional Children, Kansas City, Mo., April 1978.

Orton, S. T. *Reading, writing, and speech problems in children.* New York: Norton, 1937.

Owen, F. W., Adams, P. A., Forrest, T., Stolz, L. M., & Fisher, S. Learning disorders in children: Sibling studies. *Monographs of the Society for Research in Child Development,* 1971, *37* (4, Serial No. 144).

Pearl, R., Bryan, T., & Donahue, M. Learning disabled children's attributions for success and failure. *Learning Disability Quarterly,* 1980, *3*(1), 3–9.

Pelham, W. E., & Ross, A. O. Selective attention in children with reading problems: A developmental study of incidental learning. *Journal of Abnormal Child Psychology,* 1977, *5,* 1–8.

Ribner, S. The effects of special class placement on the self-concept of exceptional children. *Journal of Learning Disabilities,* 1978, *11,* 319–323.

Ross, A. O. *Psychological aspects of learning disabilities and reading disorders.* New York: McGraw-Hill, 1976.

Rourke, B. P., Dietrich, D. M., & Young, G. C. Significance of WISC verbal–performance discrepancies for younger children with learning disabilities. *Perceptual and Motor Skills,* 1973, *36,* 275–282.

Rourke, B. P., & Finlayson, M. A. Neuropsychological significance of variations in patterns of academic performance: Verbal and visual-spatial abilities. *Journal of Abnormal Child Psychology,* 1978, *6,* 121–133.

Rourke, B. P., Young, G. C., & Flewelling, R. W. The relationship between WISC verbal–performance discrepancies and selected verbal, auditory-perceptual, visual perceptual, and problem solving abilities in children with learning disabilities. *Journal of Clinical Psychology,* 1971, *7,* 475–479.

Rozin, P., & Gleitman, L. The reading process and the acquisition of the alphabetic principle. In A. S. Reber and D. Scarborough (Eds.), *Toward a psychology of reading.* Hillsdale, N. J.: Lawrence Erlbaum Associates, 1977.

Rugel, R. P. WISC subtest scores of disabled readers: A review with respect to Bannatyne's recategorization. *Journal of Learning Disabilities,* 1974, *7,* 48–62.

Schere, R. A., Richardson, E., & Bialer, I. Toward operationalizing a psychoeducational definition of learning disabilities. *Journal of Abnormal Child Psychology,* 1980, *8,* 5–20.

Senf, G. M. Implications of the final procedures for evaluating specific learning disabilities. *Journal of Learning Disabilities,* 1978, *11,* 124–126.

Siperstein, G., Bopp, M., & Bak, J. Social status of learning disabled children. *Journal of Learning Disabilities,* 1978, *11,* 98–102.

Siperstein, G. N., & Gottlieb, J. Physical appearance and academic performance as factors affecting children's attitudes toward handicapped peers. *American Journal of Mental Deficiency,* 1977, *5,* 455–462.

Smith, M. D., Coleman, J. M., Dokecki, P. R., & Davis, E. Intellectual characteristics of school labeled learning disabled children. *Exceptional Children, 1977, 43,* 352–357. (a)

Smith, M. D., Coleman, J. M., Dokecki, P. R., & Davis, E. Recategorized WISC-R scores of learning disabled children. *Journal of Learning Disabilities,* 1977, *10,* 437–443. (b)

Smith, M. D., Dokecki, P. R., & Davis, E. E. School-related factors influencing the self-concepts of children with learning problems. *Peabody Journal of Education,* 1977, *54,* 185–195.

Strauss, A. A., & Kephart, N. N. Behavior differences in mentally retarded children as measured by a new behavior rating scale. *American Journal of Psychiatry,* 1940, *96,* 1117–1123.

Strauss, A. A., & Lehtinen, L. E. *Psychopathology and education of the brain-injured child.* New York: Grune & Stratton, 1947.

Strauss, A. A., & Werner, H. Disorders of conceptual thinking in the brain-injured child. *Journal of Nervous and Mental Disease,* 1942, *96,* 153–172.

Swanson, H. L. Nonverbal visual short-term memory as a function of age and dimensionality in learning disabled children. *Child Development,* 1977, *48,* 51–55.

Tabachnick, B. Test scatter in the WISC-R. *Journal of Learning Disabilities,* 1979, *12,* 626–628.

Tarver, S. G., & Ellsworth, P. S. Written and oral language for verbal children. In J. M. Kauffman & D. P. Hallahan (Eds.), *Handbook of special education.* Englewood Cliffs: Prentice-Hall, 1981.

Tarver, S. G., & Hallahan, D. P. Attention deficits in children with learning disabilities: A review. *Journal of Learning Disabilities,* 1974, *7,* 560–569.

Tarver, S. G., & Hallahan, D. P. Children with learning disabilities: An overview. In J. M. Kauffman & D. P. Hallahan (Eds.), Teaching children with learning disabilities: Personal perspectives. Columbus, Oh.: Charles E. Merrill, 1976.

Tarver, S. G., Hallahan, D. P., Cohen, S. B., & Kauffman, J. M. The development of visual selective attention and verbal rehearsal in learning disabled boys. *Journal of Learning Disabilities,* 1977, *10,* 491–500.

Tarver, S. G., Hallahan, D. P., Kauffman, J. M., & Ball, D. W. Verbal rehearsal and selective attention in children with learning disabilities: A developmental lag. *Journal of Experimental Child Psychology,* 1976, *22,* 375–385.

Torgeson, J. K. Performance of reading disabled children on serial memory tasks: A selective review of recent research. *Reading Research Quarterly,* 1978–1979, *14,* 57–87.

United States Office of Education. Assistance to states for education of handicapped children: Procedures for evaluating specific learning disabilities. *Federal Register,* 1977, *42,* 65082–65085.

United States Office of Education. Education of handicapped children. Assistance to states: Proposed rulemaking. *Federal Register,* 1976, *41,* 52404–52407.

Vance, H. B., Gaynor, P., & Coleman, M. Analysis of cognitive abilities for learning disabled children. *Psychology in the Schools,* 1976, *13,* 477–483.

Vance, H. B., & Singer, M. G. Recategorization of the WISC-R subtest scaled scores for learning disabled children. *Journal of Learning Disabilities,* 1979, *12,* 487–491.

Vance, H. B., Wallbrown, F., & Blaha, J. Determining WISC-R profiles for reading disabled children. *Journal of Learning Disabilities,* 1978, *11,* 657–661.

Waldrop, M. F., & Halverson, C. F. Minor physical anomalies and hyperactive behavior in young children. In J. Hellmuth (Ed.), *Exceptional infant: Studies in abnormalities* (Vol. 2). New York: Brunner/Mazel, 1971.

Wepman, J. M., Cruickshank, W. M., Deutsch, C. P., Morency, A., & Strother, C. R. Learning disabilities. In N. Hobbs (Ed.), *Issues in the classification of children* (Vol. 1). San Francisco: Jossey-Bass, 1975.

Werner, H., & Strauss, A. A. Pathology of figure-background relation in the child. *Journal of Abnormal and Social Psychology,* 1941, *36,* 236–248.

Wiederholt, J. L. Historical perspectives on the education of the learning disabled. In L. Mann & D. Sabatino (Eds.), *The second review of special education.* Philadelphia: Journal of Special Education Press, 1974.

Wiig, E. H., Lapointe, E., & Semel, E. M. Relationships among language processing and production abilities of learning disabled adolescents. *Journal of Learning Disabilities,* 1977, *10,* 292–299.

Wiig, E., & Semel, E. *Language disabilities in children and adolescents.* Columbus, Oh.: Charles E. Merrill, 1976.

Wong, B. Y. L., & Wong, R. Role-taking skills in normal achieving and learning disabled children. *Learning Disability Quarterly,* 1980, *3*(2), 11–18.

Ysseldyke, J., Shinn, M., McGue, M., & Epps, S. *Performance of learning disabled and low achieving students on the Wechsler Intelligence Scale for Children—Revised and the Tests of Cognitive Abilities from the Woodcock-Johnson Psycho-educational Battery.* Paper presented at the Annual Meeting of the Association for Children With Learning Disabilities, Milwaukee, Wis., February 1980.

Zingale, S. A., & Smith, M. D. WISC-R patterns for learning disabled children at three SES levels. *Psychology in the Schools,* 1978, *15,* 199–204.

Stephen S. Strichart
Jay Gottlieb

3

Characteristics of Mild Mental Retardation

Socialization is the process by which children learn the rules and values of the larger society into which they ultimately will become assimilated. The home and the school are the two most prominent socializing agents affecting child development.

Glidewell, Kantor, Smith, and Stringer (1966) provided an excellent conceptualization of the issues inherent in the socialization of children. This conceptualization is equally applicable to the socialization of children who are mildly mentally retarded (i.e., educable mentally retarded [EMR]). Glidewell et al. (1964) observed that children strive to fulfill three basic needs: (1) to have a sense of personal competence; (2) to be emotionally accepted by others in their environment; and (3) to have influence over the behavior of others. Since emotional acceptance—being liked—is conceptually related to power (that is, being liked by people who themselves are well liked), the number of basic needs that motivate children in the classroom can be reduced from three to two: *competence* and *liking*. To the extent that mentally retarded children feel competent and sense that they are well liked by others, they will have healthy social and emotional development. If, on the other hand, mildly retarded children feel incompetent and believe that they are not well liked by their peers, there could be some difficulty in their socioemotional development.

COGNITIVE COMPETENCE OF MILDLY RETARDED CHILDREN

The literature in the field of mental retardation as it pertains to cognitive abilities is careful to distinguish capacity from performance (Bortner & Birch, 1970). Cognitive capacity refers to the child's potential to learn, while cognitive performance refers to the level of ability that the child actually demonstrates in the circumscribed conditions in which he or she is asked to perform. This distinction should be kept in mind both for studies of learning characteristics (in which

37

principles of learning are deduced from laboratory studies) and for studies of academic achievement (in which mentally retarded children's performance is examined under actual classroom conditions).

To illustrate: the fact that most mentally retarded children seldom attain a classroom grade equivalent reading score exceeding 4.0 (Semmel, Gottlieb, & Robinson, 1979) does not at all imply that if the presentation of the material were made more conducive to their learning style, they would not achieve at a higher level. A reading score of 4.0, for example, simply indicates that when the material was presented in a certain way, mentally retarded children performed at a grade equivalent of 4.0. In other words, the children's performance was 4.0; their capacity may have been considerably more.

LEARNING CHARACTERISTICS

In its basic sense, learning refers to changes in behavior due to experience or practice. It is often said that mentally retarded children are slow and inefficient learners (Baumeister, 1967; Bruininks & Warfield, 1978; Macmillan, 1977; Robinson & Robinson, 1976). Hallahan and Kauffman (1978) stated that the most obvious characteristic of retarded children is their reduced ability to learn. This is most apparent when considering the relationship between cognition and intelligence. Brown (1980) observed that deficits in all basic cognitive processes have been demonstrated for the retarded, at least when they have been compared with nonretarded individuals of the same chronological age.

Trends and Issues in Research on Learning Characteristics

It is difficult to succinctly discuss research on the learning characteristics of mildly retarded children. This is because of the sheer quantity and range of studies that have occurred since the mid 1950s. Leaving issues of quality aside, the quantity is staggering. Dunn (1973) pointed out that more data on the behavioral characteristics of mildly retarded children have been gathered than for any other group of exceptional children. Discernible trends have been discussed by various workers. Payne, Polloway, Smith, and Payne (1977) indicated that statements about a general learning deficiency for the retarded no longer suffice. Rather, experimental inquiry has increasingly focused on specific aspects of learning. Early attempts to answer practical questions through applied research have been supplanted by the investigation of theoretical and applied concepts derived from general psychology (Macmillan, 1977). In examining the history of work with retarded people, Robinson and Robinson (1976) observed a shift of emphasis from grand theories to more specific ones and from simple forms of learning to more complex ones. Their analysis indicated that research prior to the 1950s was conducted by theorists who sought to test the universal characteristics of learning processes. In their efforts, individual differences among retarded subjects were of little interest. Recent research, however, considers retarded people as of interest in their own right, as reflected by studies seeking to characterize the learning of retarded as opposed to nonretarded persons.

A caveat is necessary at this point. Haywood (1979) reported a significant trend away from studies on mildly and moderately retarded persons in favor of an increasing number of studies on severely and profoundly retarded persons, and has in fact demonstrated this statistically. Haywood attributed this shift to the realization that severely and profoundly retarded individuals were neglected for many years both in research and service; a backlash, supported by funding and legislation, inevitably occurred. Haywood's alarm related to the broad implications of reduced attention to the needs of mildly and moderately retarded learners. It seems that research efforts over the past few years regarding the learning characteristics of the mildly retarded have not greatly advanced the knowledge base with respect to the delivery of effective classroom-based instructional programs. Haywood issued an important imperative when he wrote, ". . . let us rediscover mild and moderate retardation and invest in these levels renewed research interest and the necessary public support to sustain good research . . . "(p. 431).

Determining the learning characteristics of mildly retarded children is not a straightforward matter. The general observation that they have less than normal learning ability obviously must be qualified. Baumeister (1967) observed that the learning deficiency of mildly retarded persons is related to only certain aspects of the learning situation. In fact, as will be shown, their learning is not deficient at all, under certain conditions. In a related vein, Bryan and Bryan (1979) specified that the learning of the retarded has been assessed in many different ways using many different tasks. As a consequence, the difference between the learning of retarded and nonretarded subjects often is a partial function of how learning is measured and how the learning task is presented to the subjects. Within the variability, however, there has been a basic consistency of experimental design. For the most part, experimental studies have employed either of the first two of Denny's three basic designs (1964). Some studies use nonretarded subjects matched on mental age (MA) with retarded subjects; the nonretarded subjects have a higher IQ and a lower chronological age (CA). Where the performance of retarded subjects is found to be inferior, a low-IQ deficit is identified. In a second paradigm, nonretarded subjects are matched on CA with retarded subjects, with inferiority on the part of the retarded here called a low-MA–low-IQ deficit. Denny proposed the use of a third design in which there are two groups of nonretarded subjects, one matched with the retarded subjects for CA, and the other for MA, thereby allowing the researcher to determine whether there is a low-MA–low-IQ deficit, a low-IQ deficit, or no deficit at all, as well as whether a deficit is independent of CA (Denny, 1964). Because of its expensive logistics, this approach is infrequently used.

These alternative experimental designs have facilitated two ways of looking at retarded cognitive development. MacMillan (1977), borrowing from earlier formulations, identified the two approaches as developmental orientation and difference orientation. The developmental approach assumes that the cognitive processes used by mildly retarded persons are the same as those used by nonretarded persons, except that there is slower progression through developmental stages, and a lower ceiling on ultimate level of development. It follows that when retarded subjects are matched with normals on the basis of MA, no difference in learning will be apparent. The difference approach assumes that differences in IQ in and of themselves produce (or are reflective of) qualitative differences in learning between retarded and nonretarded persons. In this formulation, studies using an MA match should still show poorer retarded performance. MacMillan noted a bifurcation of the latter position; the *defect* orientation maintains that the differences occur only below an IQ cutoff of 50. This implies that the mildly retarded are developmentally delayed in learning when compared to nonretarded persons, but are not different. MacMillan asserted that research has borne this out; that is, that the mildly retarded are slower at mastering tasks than are persons of average intelligence. Differences in retarded and normal performance then are quantitative, not qualitative. This finding has optimistic connotations, including well-designed training increasing the learning rates of mildly retarded persons.

The importance of research on learning characteristics of retarded individuals is obvious. As Baumeister (1967) noted, knowledge of the circumstances in which the retarded child performs best points the way to optimally effective education and training programs. Similarly, MacMillan (1977) pointed out that if teachers know the difficult areas of learning for retarded children, they can anticipate likely problems as they formulate their instructional plan. Unfortunately, MacMillan also observed that despite the great amount of theoretical material available regarding learning by the retarded, there is a minimum of practical information available. Thus, there is little empirical research that clearly identifies effective techniques for teaching the retarded.

Limitations of the Research

The failure of research to generate sufficient practical information germane to teaching is due to the laboratory nature of the research, according to MacMillan (1977). MacMillan pointed out that the research tasks typically employed are not directly relevant to the learning of basic academic subjects such as reading and mathematics, thereby rendering classroom extrapolations speculative if not tenuous. This is a point of view echoed by Baumeister (1967), who reasoned that the manipulations that produce certain effects in the controlled laboratory setting may not produce the same effects in more natural settings where there are uncontrolled variables. Baumeister cogently discussed a number of other problems concerning research on the learning characteristics of retarded subjects. One is that what an experimenter defines as learning may be quite different from what the practitioner views as learning. While researchers may go out of their way to use tasks uncontaminated by the previous experience and learning of subjects, teachers systematically build on prior experience and learning. Furthermore, Baumeister observed the contrasting ways in which researchers and teachers regard individual differences. While the researcher treats these as error and attempts to minimize them, the teacher is committed to recognizing and adapting to them, if not philosophically, then legally (i.e., because of the Individualized Education Program [IEP] requirement of PL 94-142). The points raised by Baumeister serve to further explain the observation that practical information is not an abundant product of research efforts to date.

Baumeister (1967) also suggested that the retarded subjects used in typical learning experiments are frequently unrepresentative of the general retarded population. The variation among many dimensions within the retarded population was emphasized by Dunn (1973) and by Mercer and Payne (1975). Also, Robinson and Robinson (1977) highlighted the wide number of potentially relevant variables that must be taken into account if one is to discover anything more novel than the fact that retarded persons typically are not as proficient as normal persons in most learning tasks and situations. The need to account for CA, MA, and IQ has already been seen. Robinson and Robinson added the necessity of equating subject groups on background factors such as social class and educational experience, and on psychophysiological factors such as central nervous system integrity. While they realized that equating groups for all relevant factors is an unrealizable ideal, they also pointed out that to the degree this is not done, generalizability of results is attenuated.

The problems cited do not mean that the learning research fails to generate or permit educational implications. But, they do imply that these implications must be drawn cautiously.

Research in Developmental Areas

The typical progression of development from the perspective of psychology involves passing through motor, perceptual, language, and cognitive stages. These have not received equal attention in experimental studies with the mentally retarded. Language development has unquestionably received the greatest attention, while perceptual development, an area of considerable study with the learning disabled, has not been emphasized. While studies involving the retarded often include consideration of cognitive variables such as the use of mediation and generalization of learning, the study of cognitive development directly, as in problem solving, for example, is recent and incomplete. Motor development has received a steady, albeit not exhaustive, emphasis. Consequently, language and motor development will be the two areas addressed here. Perceptual and cognitive aspects, however, will be included within the consideration of learning processes and forms.

Language Development

It is appropriate to consider language first, since, as noted by Kirk and Gallagher (1979), delayed and retarded language is a common characteristic of mentally retarded people. MacMillan (1977) observed that the fact that retarded individuals display language problems is to be expected, given the definition of mental retardation, while Dunn (1973) pointed out that a close relation exists between language and intellectual development. Overall, the majority of studies concerning the language characteristics of retarded individuals have focused more on speech than on language (Bryan & Bryan, 1979).

Keane (1972), reviewing the literature on speech and language problems in the mentally retarded, formulated several conclusions of present interest. He found significant documentation for a higher than normal incidence of speech disorders in the mentally retarded population. Institutionalized retarded individuals showed higher speech problem incidence than did noninstitutionalized retarded people, and special school retarded children had more problems than public school retarded children. These findings suggest that speech difficulties are less problematical for the mildly retarded; there is general evidence that the lower the IQ, the greater the likelihood of speech difficulties. These data do not suggest, however, that mildly retarded children do not suffer from speech and language deficits. Spradlin (1963) found that articulation of speech sounds was related to intelligence test scores. Further conclusions drawn by Keane (1972) were that articulation, voice, and stuttering difficulties are the speech problems most often found with the retarded, and that of these, articulation disorders were the most prevalent; the evidence for more frequent than normal stuttering was far from conclusive. Whle retarded individuals have a greater incidence of problems in speech than normal individuals, their problems are of the same qualitative nature (MacMillan, 1977). Dunn (1973) noted that retarded children generally profit from speech therapy.

In their review of speech and language characteristics of the retarded, Webb and Kinde (1967) concluded that language delay, less abstraction, shortened sentence length, syntax disproportion, and restricted vocabulary size typify this population. MacMillan (1977), in addition to noting differences in grammatical structure, found limited vocabulary among mentally retarded people. Dunn (1973) pointed out that oral language development becomes an increasingly serious problem for mildly retarded children as they mature. Kirk and Gallagher (1979) identified the ability to use complex clauses and subject elaboration as the retarded child's greatest deficiency. They observed that this presents a significant communication problem since it limits the kind and amount of information that the retarded child can communicate to others, especially when sequences of activities are required.

An interesting line of research is that of Semmel, Barritt, Bennett, and Perfetti (1968). They analyzed word associations of mildly retarded and nonretarded children on the basis of syntagmatic and paradigmatic responses. *Syntagmatic responses* are in a developmentally early language class representing a sequential-associative strategy. Thus, for example, a syntagmatic response to the word *eat* might be *breakfast*. In contrast, paradigmatic responses represent a more mature, hierarchical language strategy. Here, associations to words are alike in their grammatical form class, as for example, the response *bed* to *chair*. Semmel et al. (1968) found retarded children less likely to respond paradigmatically than nonretarded children of the same age. This finding reinforces the observation that the language of retarded individuals is less abstract than that of nonretarded counterparts.

Dunn (1973) reported that oral language stimulation appears to be modestly effective with mildly retarded children. On the whole, however, there is surprisingly little documentation of efforts to improve language functioning of the retarded. Reasons for this advanced by Webb and Kinde (1963) are largely still applicable: They noted that language training is infrequent because of the long, time-consuming nature of the task, personnel shortages, and the general antipathy of speech and language therapists towards working with the retarded. Consequently, the prognosis for language improvement of retarded individuals is not clearly known. As an overall statement regarding language development of the retarded, MacMillan's (1977) conclusion is appropriate: with the exception of the profoundly retarded, the differences in the language of retarded and nonretarded persons is of a quantitative (i.e., developmental) rather than qualitative (i.e., different) character.

Motor Development

Many tasks employed in experiments involve retarded subjects in some sort of motor response. But, as clarified by Baumeister (1967), an experiment qualifies as a study of motor learning only when the actual motor movements themselves are the criterion of learning. The particular importance of studies of motor skill of the retarded was addressed by Baumeister, who reasoned that the fulfillment of the major goal of vocational adequacy for the mildly retarded is highly dependent upon their motor development. Research findings have consistently indicated that the retarded come closer to nonretarded functioning in motor development than in other developmental spheres. Basically, there is evidence for a positive but low correlation between intelligence and motor skills among mildly retarded people (Baumeister, 1967; Dunn, 1973). While not as great as in other areas of learning, deficiencies in motor skills do exist for the retarded.

Baumeister (1967) pointed out that the relationship between mental ability and motor proficiency is dependent on the particular motor ability in question. Evidence from pursuit motor experiments, wherein a subject is given a stylus and asked to keep it on a revolving target, indicates that retarded subjects demonstrate most of the same effects on the task as do nonretarded subjects. On the other hand, Baumeister reported that retarded subjects are inferior in reaction speed when the required response is complex. The primary problem for the retarded occurs where there is a requirement for precision of movement. In general, the simpler the motor task, the less the retarded are at a disadvantage.

Bruininks and Warfield (1978) regarded the assumption that the retarded are not as deficient in motor development as in intellectual areas as being somewhat applicable to mildly retarded persons. They summarized work by Bruininks that showed that mildly retarded children are significantly below nonretarded children in all areas measured by the Bruininks-Oseretsky Test of Motor Proficiency. The mildly retarded peoples greatest deficiencies in skill areas include complex motor responses requiring coordination of both sides of the body, visual-motor coordination, and fine motor precision where speed and balance are involved. Bruininks and Warfield speculated that these deficiencies may at least partly result from limited opportunity for motor skills development and practice in school physical education programs and out-of-school peer activities. The finding that the retarded benefit from motor training supports this possibility (Bruininks & Warfield, 1978; Kirk & Gallagher, 1979). Baumeister (1967) stressed the substantial benefits of motor training for retarded individuals, finding improvement to be both rapid and lasting. Furthermore, he observed that the improvements transfer to motor tasks related to the training tasks. He concluded that with the proper training methods, the moderately retarded individual (and thereby the mildly retarded individual) can learn many complex and intricate motor skills. Overall, it is apparent that the motor development area is relatively intact in mildly retarded individuals.

Research in Learning Processes and Forms

Analysis of learning studies with the mentally retarded reveals particular areas of emphasis, including discrimination learning (subsuming attentional processes), memory (subsuming organizational processes), and paired-associate learning (subsuming mediational processes). While these areas do not represent the totality of research regarding learning characteristics and behavior of retarded individuals, they do provide a substantial view of the whole.

Discrimination Learning

The relationship between discrimination learning and attention is almost implicitly obvious when each is defined. Thus, Mercer and Payne (1975) defined discrimination learning as occurring when an individual responds to a specific stimulus in a specific manner. Attention may be viewed as referring to the ability of an individual to orient to the relevant dimensions of stimuli (Payne et al., 1977). The apparent requirement of effective attention for efficient discrimination learning was clearly established by Zeaman and House (1963) in their classic series of experiments with mentally retarded individuals. Their methodology involved the use of the Wisconsin General Test Apparatus to present retarded subjects with two-choice visual discrimination tasks. In the basic experimental paradigm, a subject was required to select from two stimuli presented on a sliding tray. For example, the two stimuli might be a yellow triangle and a blue circle. The subject had to choose the correct one on the basis of feedback about the correctness of his or her choices on previous trials. If the correct stimulus dimension to attend to was *color,* with *yellow* being the correct distinctive feature, the subject would be reinforced with a piece of candy for selecting the yellow triangle. Results indicated that two learning responses were required. First, a subject had to attend to the relevant dimension (e.g., color), and then the subject had to learn which aspect along that dimension was correct (e.g., yellow). Zeaman and House (1963) characterized these response stages as an *initial attention stage* followed by a *learning (acquisition) stage*.

In plotting learning curves, Zeaman and House (1963) found an initial relatively long horizontal segment followed by a steep slope segment. Their interpretation was that the flat portion of the curve represented a stage during which a subject predominantly attended to irrelevant stimulus dimensions, consequently making little progress in mastering the discrimination task. Once, however, the subject began to attend to the relevant dimension, mastery of the task occurred rapidly, resulting in the steep ascent of the learning curve. Their major finding about the learning of retarded subjects was that the length of the flat portion of the curve was a function of intelligence; lower MA subjects required more trials in the attention stage than higher MA subjects. However, once the discrimination was learned, there was no difference in the acceleration slope as a function of MA. As Zeaman and House put it, the difference between fast and slow learning was not the rate at which improvement occurred, but how long it took for learning to start. It seems clear that the learning deficiencies of the lower MA children resulted from a deficiency in attention, and not from a deficit in instrumental discrimination learning. Put more broadly, it appears that an attentional deficit may be at the root of the learning problems of retarded individuals. While further elaborations have been made in this theory, it is the Zeaman and House (1963) model that has been used as the basis for many discrimination learning experiments involving retarded subjects.

It is important to note that the Zeaman-House work involved subjects functioning below the mildly retarded range (with IQs in the 30–40 range). However,

Mercer and Snell (1977) reviewed a sizable group of experiments stemming from the Zeaman-House model, many of which have involved mildly retarded subjects. Of 11 such studies, six clearly supported the Zeaman-House formulation, four provided equivocal support, and one study clearly provided opposing data. While the data in support of the attention deficit construct are apparent, they are neither consensual nor extensive. MacMillan's caution (1977) not to generalize the Zeaman-House work to mildly retarded individuals should be kept in mind. Bryan and Bryan's summary statement (1979) is apt. They concluded that by and large, most studies prior to and following the Zeaman-House research have found that retarded individuals show inferior learning in discrimination tasks compared with normal individuals. Furthermore, the severity of retardation is associated with the learning process; the greater the degree of retardation, the less the individual is capable of mastering the discrimination task.

A number of workers have considered ways by which the discrimination learning of retarded individuals could be facilitated. Baumeister (1967) presented a number of strategies. He observed that, in general, procedures that lead to increased distinctiveness of the stimuli to be discriminated are helpful. This can be achieved by either increasing the number of relevant cues or by increasing the differences between the stimuli. Specifically, Baumeister noted that multidimensional stimulus displays are more effective than unidimensional ones. For example, he suggested that learning is more efficient if a distinction can be made on the basis of size and pattern, as opposed to pattern or size alone. Other effects noted by Baumeister are (1) that object discrimination is better than pattern discrimination and pattern is better than color as a cue; (2) that presenting the objects in their depth dimension of space improves performance; and (3) that novelty improves the rate of learning. Baumeister also noted findings suggesting that retarded subjects perform better when a perceptual rather than a verbal solution is required. However, he observed that teaching retarded individuals to verbally identify the stimuli that are to be discriminated is an effective technique, particularly where the stimuli are initially ambiguous and meaningless.

Finally, Baumeister added that language need not be a necessary precondition for the use of mediation in discrimination learning in light of evidence that cue distinctiveness can be attained by requiring the subject to make a specific motor response in relation to each cue. Robinson and Robinson (1976) suggested making the relevant dimension one to which the retarded individual naturally attends more readily. Similarly, Bryan and Bryan (1979) noted the effectiveness of using familiar objects rather than pictures, and of reducing the time between the subject's correct response and reinforcement. Also, in the same vein, MacMillan (1977) suggested the use of attention-getting devices, sequencing the task so that it progresses from easy to more difficult, and structuring it so that the child avoids failure.

It is not difficult to see how these suggestions may be used in classroom adaptations with the retarded. Mercer and Payne (1975) suggested a number of instructional implications:

1. Use stimulus displays with only a few relevant dimensions.
2. Assist the child to form associations for stimuli used in the instructional setting.
3. Avoid presentation of irrelevant information.

4. Remove extraneous stimuli from the immediate area.
5. Use novelty and reward to foster attention to assigned tasks.
6. Use easy-to-difficult instructional sequences, with variation among cue properties already learned to increase transfer and facilitate progress.
7. Prevent wrong responses in order to minimize associations and attention to irrelevant stimuli.
8. Provide immediate feedback for correct responses.

Memory

Memory (the storage and retrieval of sensations and perceptions that have been experienced) appears to be the most heavily studied learning characteristic of mentally retarded individuals. The considerable emphasis given to its study is understandable in light of the significance of memory for learning and behavior. Baumeister (1967) regarded learning and memory as inseparable in that the only possible way to demonstrate what someone has learned is to measure his or her retention of that material. Learning is inextricably bound to memory. If one is to profit from past experience, memory of prior events is a prerequisite (Robinson & Robinson, 1976). What has been learned does us little good if we are unable to remember it.

As MacMillan (1977) observed, mentally retarded people as a group have traditionally been characterized as having poor memory. This impression is based on research lacking theoretical support and using superficial memory measures (notably the number of items that could be recalled; Robinson & Robinson, 1976). Thus, it has been found that when asked to remember lists of words or sounds or groups of pictures that have been presented a few seconds previously, retarded individuals do poorly as compared with nonretarded individuals (Hallahan & Kauffman, 1978). That is, it is clear that the retarded have a deficit in short-term memory. This was shown by Spitz (1973), who found that while the digit span capacity for normal individuals is 5 to 7 digits, for retarded individuals it is 3 to 4 digits. As Robinson and Robinson (1976) observed, however, the research did little to suggest why this was the case.

Research findings on long-term memory are quite different. Generally, studies do not indicate a long-term memory deficit for retarded individuals (Bryan & Bryan, 1979; Hallahan & Kauffman, 1978; MacMillan, 1977). Once material has been learned, the ability of retarded people to retain the information is comparable to that of nonretarded people. It must be kept in mind, however, that this statement does not suggest that the retarded learn as well as the nonretarded, nor that they apply what they learn as well. Baumeister's analysis (1967) of the long-term memory of retarded individuals is incisive: "Apparently, if the material is meaningful, and if the learning is reinforced by additional practice, if the materials are programmed appropriately, and if the learner is not profoundly retarded, he will remember as well as the normal individual over fairly long intervals" (p. 187).

Recent research has shifted from a focus on the product of memory (i.e., the number of items recalled) to consideration of the process (i.e., what a person does as he or she tries to remember) (MacMillan, 1977; Robinson & Robinson, 1976). Campione and Brown (1977) discussed this shift in terms of structural features and control processes. *Structural features* are defined as invariant components of the system, and are seen as unmodifiable. *Control processes* are viewed as optional strategies that an individual can bring to bear on memory tasks, and are susceptible to training. The extent to which short-term memory deficits of retarded individuals are of a structural or processing nature may be deduced from the effects of training. If a memory deficiency responds to training, control processes are implicated. If, on the other hand, training is unsuccessful, structural differences are apparently involved.

This shift in research emphasis is clearly exemplified in the work of Ellis (1963). Ellis originally explained the short-term memory deficit of retarded individuals in structural terms. Specifically, he theorized that retarded people are susceptible to rapid deterioration of the stimulus trace, a hypothesized neural circuit activated in the brain in response to stimuli reception. Ellis theorized that low IQ is associated with a lack of neural integrity, lowering the amplitude and direction of a stimulus trace, causing it to fade rapidly, and thereby inhibiting memory. The poor memory of the retarded then was viewed in terms of the failure of stimuli to sufficiently register their impact neurally. Where stimuli were presented sufficiently long or strongly enough, the stimuli trace deficit was overcome, and long-term memory was then accomplished. Ellis's model clearly focused on the compensating effect of careful stimulus presentation as a facilitator of memory in retarded people, but did not consider the role the learner could play. His physiological construct has not been proven and Ellis himself, like other workers, has looked to the possibility that the short-term memory deficit of retarded individuals has more to do with their failure to effectively employ memory strategies than with some structural deficit.

Thus, in his later work, Ellis (1970) focused on the role of the subject in memory experiments. With a number of colleagues, Ellis conducted a series of 14 experiments using a probe serial-recall task. In this paradigm, subjects are shown a random series of numbers exposed one after the other, from left to right. After exposure of the ninth position, the probe is presented; the subject's task is to press a key at the position where the probe number was seen. This procedure permits important aspects of the task to be varied, including item-exposure duration, inter-item interval, interval between last item and probe, and stimulus materials (numbers, letters, pictures, etc.). Ellis found that whereas nonretarded subjects characteristically are most likely to remember initial and final items, retarded subjects had difficulty remembering initial items, thus demonstrating a recency effect. Ellis reasoned that the failure of retarded subjects to remember early items suggested their failure to spontaneously adopt a rehearsal strategy. That is, while the final items could be recalled on the basis of their immediacy, in order for initial items to be remembered, some active attempt to keep them in memory by the subject was required. Further, Ellis found that nonretarded subjects benefitted from increased time between stimulus items, indicating that they used this time to rehearse items. A similar benefit did not occur for retarded subjects, suggesting that they did not use the time to rehearse items. Ellis speculated that retarded individuals try to rehearse but do not employ appropriate or effective strategies for remembering material. This conclusion obviously is different from his earlier one and generates significantly distinct implications for educational training of the retarded. As pointed out by Robinson and Robinson (1976), Ellis's reformulation implies that training retarded individuals to rehearse should reduce, if not eliminate, differences between their memory performance and that of nonretarded individuals. Considerable research attention has been deployed to study the use of rehearsal and other memory strategies by the retarded.

Campione and Brown (1977) extensively analyzed this line of research, and concluded that developmental or comparative differences for retarded people are obtained only when some kind of strategic intervention is required. Research has focused on three major strategy forms: rehearsal, organization, and elaboration. As already indicated, Ellis (1970) found that retarded subjects fail to spontaneously rehearse material to be learned, and additional evidence has since been accummulated. While it is not accurate to say that retarded learners never rehearse, it is clear that they are much less likely to employ an efficient rehearsal strategy than their CA counterparts. Importantly, Campione and Brown reported that training the retarded to rehearse results in improved levels of performance and in patterns of performance similar to those of nonretarded counterparts of equal CA. In fact, they said that the resulting improvements were dramatic, with long-lasting effects evident. Transfer effects, however, are restricted to what Campione and Brown called maintenance of a trained strategy. *Maintenance* applies to situations where the tasks used in the training and transfer situations are the same. There is little evidence of generalization effects, i.e., transfer of training where the transfer task differs from the training task.

Organizational efforts by retarded individuals have been comprehensively studied, notably by Spitz (1966). The approach used most often in this research is associative clustering. Here, words (or pictures or objects) representing several categories or concepts (e.g., animals, household furniture, toys) are randomly ordered and presented to a subject with no mention that they fall into certain categories. The subject is then asked to recall as many items as possible. Normal individuals are typically found to spontaneously cluster the items recalled into categories. Thus, they recall animals in a group, and so on. This represents organizing or structuring the stimuli, thereby facilitating recall. Spitz found that retarded individuals are deficient in organization of sensory input. Rather than systematically organizing stimuli on lists, Spitz found retarded subjects to appear to use rote memory. He also found, though, that these subjects could be induced to cluster through two means. One successful technique was to present the list already clustered, a technique Spitz termed the *presented clustered* method. A second successful procedure was termed the *requested clustered* method. Here, the words were presented normally, but the subject was asked to "Tell me all the animals you remember from the list," etc. Spitz concluded, "It is quite clear that presenting the words in an already organized state induces clustering and significantly raises recall. Inducing the retarded learners to organize the material, by whatever means, has a facilitative effect on recall" (p. 44). Campione and Brown (1977) reported some evidence for a maintenance transfer effect of these techniques, but only where training was extensive. In reviewing the question of organizational strategies, MacMillan (1977) concluded that, while retarded individuals acquire spontaneous concepts that they can use to advantage in organizing material to be remembered, without external prompting they resort to inefficient organizational strategies, or none at all.

Elaboration has been the least studied of the major strategy forms. Campione and Brown (1977) indicated that providing retarded individuals with verbal or visual elaborations, or instructing them in their use, clearly improves memory performance. Retarded learners, then, are apparently capable of efficiently using mediators that are provided, and, with training, can provide some of their own, albeit not of the quality of those produced by their nonretarded peers. As with rehearsal and clustering, there is evidence of a maintenance effect.

Overall, the retarded person has a control process deficiency in the use of a variety of mnemonic strategies. Training results in considerable improvement, and maintenance can be achieved with a sufficient amount of training, although generalization is elusive. However, Campione and Brown cautioned that it should not be concluded that no structural differences exist between the retarded and nonretarded. Their feeling is that differences could be identified using a more powerful theoretical framework and more sophisticated experimentation.

The emphasis on control processes is compatible with the recent emphasis on metacognition in studying children's cognitive development. *Metacognition* refers to that level of understanding in which an individual becomes aware of his or her own thinking in terms of cognitive processes and products (Loper, 1980). When applied specifically to memory, the concept is called *metamemory* and refers to an individual's awareness and control of his or her memory processes, including the ability to estimate task difficulty and to evaluate the current strength or desirability of what is remembered (Campione & Brown, 1977). One of the possibilities Campione and Brown considered is that retarded individuals fail to realize that a task is difficult and thus do not attempt to use goal-directed mnemonic strategies. Robinson and Robinson (1976) stressed the importance of such introspective knowledge because unless an individual realizes that a particular memory task is difficult, there is no reason for him or her to do anything extra to help remember. The sparse research available led Campione and Brown to conclude that mildly retarded children have difficulty estimating their own memory performance. Robinson and Robinson pointed out that even if retarded persons were trained to deliberately use strategies, and the necessary strategies were understood, a major problem would remain. This would be the problem of inducing the retarded person to decide which strategy to use on a particular task, that is, to use executive control. *Executive control* is a process requiring the individual to evaluate the demands of a specific task, choose an appropriate strategy, and then monitor its execution and effectiveness, changing strategies as needed. As with metamemory, Campione and Brown reported that initial evidence shows the retarded to be deficient in executive control. While more research is clearly needed, there is an increasing tendency to regard the retarded as what Torgesen (1977) called *inactive learners,* that is, individuals who possess the capacity to use strategies to solve problems, but who for various reasons are not predisposed to do so. The problem thus becomes one of appropriately activating the retarded learner.

Numerous educational principles for use with retarded students have been derived from memory research. The following are derived from a number of sources (Bruininks & Warfield, 1978; Bryan & Bryan, 1979; MacMillan, 1977; Mercer & Payne, 1975; Payne et al., 1977):

1. Train the use of strategies such as verbal labeling, associations, and rehearsal.
2. Organize stimuli to be remembered into meaningful parts.
3. Provide a structured instructional environment.
4. Use materials of high interest.

5. Use meaningful stimuli.
6. Provide overlearning in a variety of contexts.
7. Provide repetition, drill, and review.
8. Provide distributed practice.
9. Present stimuli to be remembered at a reasonable pace.
10. Provide incentives for remembering.

Paired-Associate Learning

The typical paired-associate task is one in which a subject is shown a pair of stimuli (e.g., pictures or words) with one of each pair designated the stimulus item and the other the response item. On the initial trial, both items are shown. On subsequent trials, only the stimulus items are shown, with the subject being required to indicate the matching response items. The key cognitive ability apparently tapped by this task is the use of verbal mediation (Payne et al., 1977). Payne et al. (1977) described *verbal mediation* as verbalizations by the subject that are elicited by the stimulus and help to formulate the response. There is considerable research evidence that suggests that retarded individuals do not spontaneously employ verbal mediators in the paired-associate task, or that if they do, the mediators are insufficient (Baumeister, 1967; MacMillan, 1977; Payne, et al., 1977; Robinson & Robinson, 1976). Consequently, studies reporting inferior performance on the part of retarded subjects are those that use abstract or conceptually confusing materials (Baumeister, 1967). In contrast, retarded subjects have considerably less difficulty when the stimulus materials are concrete, familiar, meaningful, and easily mediated (Baumeister, 1967), and when the stimulus pairs are easily associated (MacMillan, 1977).

There is evidence that the associative learning performance of retarded individuals improves when they are first taught to mediate cues with distinctive labels (Baumeister, 1967). However, they do not appear to benefit as much as nonretarded individuals. Where the paired-associates are presented in a meaningful context, as in the form of a sentence, performance of retarded subjects is further heightened. MacMillan (1977) reported that retarded people are able to use verbal mediators to advantage when the experimenter provides them. Further, performance is facilitated when the experimenter simply requires retarded subjects to make up their own mediators (Payne et al., 1977). However, the mediators produced under these circumstance are not as effective as those provided by the experimenter (MacMillan, 1977), nor are they of the quality produced by nonretarded individuals (Robinson & Robinson, 1976). Interestingly, however, it does not appear to be the quality of the mediators that is significant, but the act of producing them. Robinson and Robinson (1976) noted that when retarded subjects are instructed to generate mediators, they perform as well on the paired-associate task as they do when the experimenter provides better-quality mediators. Unfortunately, Robinson and Robinson further observed that retarded individuals do not appear to transfer the strategy of producing verbal mediators to other tasks. This suggests that the poor performance of retarded subjects, where no training in verbal mediation is provided, is due to failure to adopt a mediator strategy rather than ineffective ability to produce mediators. In addition to the use of verbal mediators, MacMillan (1977) noted that imagery and verbal elaboration are successful techniques for improving paired-associate learning by retarded individuals.

Overall, the situation regarding the paired-association of retarded learners is analogous to memory research. That is, the basic problem seems to be not one of reduced ability but one of inefficient use of ability. Thus, Robinson and Robinson (1976) concluded that the poorer performance of retarded individuals compared with that of nonretarded individuals is not due to an inability to use mediators, but to the failure to habitually produce them. It is appropriate to translate this conclusion into the terms employed by Flavell (1970) in describing learning deficiencies—mediation deficiency and production deficiency. A *mediation deficiency* refers to the inability to use a mediational strategy even when instructed to do so. In contrast, a *production deficiency* refers to the failure to produce such a strategy in the face of the capability of producing and using it. Seen in this context, the problem of mildly retarded individuals is of a production nature.

Based upon paired-associate research with retarded subjects, Payne et al. (1977) provided the following educational implications:

1. Provide the retarded individual with mediation strategies.
2. Draw on the retarded individual's own experiences, reinforcing success by allowing him or her to utilize previously learned associates.
3. Keep the content meaningful.
4. Emphasize the concrete, avoid the abstract.

General Implications

The preceding sections have listed specific instructional implications for retarded learners derived from selected learning research. Several workers have summarized specific procedures based upon the totality of research endeavors with this group (Bruininks & Warfield, 1978; Dunn, 1973; Kirk & Gallagher, 1979) and the reader is encouraged to consult these as resources. Rather than summarize their suggestions—many of which have been indicated throughout this section of the chapter—general considerations will be broached.

MacMillan (1977) introduced two important general issues. One is the importance of not assuming that retarded individuals have learned things incidentally, an admonition echoed by Kirk and Gallagher (1979). Thus, as MacMillan put it, the retarded child's maturation may have to be guided. The implication for teachers is that they must not assume that a retarded student has learned certain prerequisite facts or skills on his or her own as have nonretarded students. Consequently, MacMillan advised that it is frequently necessary for the teacher to confirm whether a retarded child has acquired certain knowledge commonly acquired incidentally by normal children. If the child has not, then the teacher will need to directly teach these prerequisites prior to the intended lesson. Kirk and Gallagher emphasized the need for systematic instruction without too much reliance on incidental learning. It must be cautioned, however, that after a review of the literature, Hardman and Drew (1975) questioned the typical assumption that the retarded are poor incidental learners, observing that the research supporting this view was relatively sparse and poorly designed. MacMillan's suggestion that teachers assess acquisition of prerequisite skills remains pedagogically sound, although it may not pertain to the retarded significantly more than it does to any other group of students.

A second issue discussed by MacMillan (1977) is the differing implications that emerge from adherence to the developmental view of retardation as opposed to the difference view. He noted that if the developmental model is essentially correct, then teachers of mildly retarded children should employ similar cognitive strategies as do teachers of younger normal children. In contrast, support for the difference model would imply that teachers must use unique teaching methods in order to compensate for the retarded students inefficiencies in learning. MacMillan's position was that the trend of research provides more support for the developmental position, a conclusion shared by these authors. There is a need to more forcefully expect and require mildly retarded children to think and learn. This need was eloquently stated by Winschel and Ensher (1978), who believed that special education has failed to emphasize the development of the intellectual skills of this category of students. Citing the research findings that teaching retarded individuals strategies for learning substantially improves their learning efficiency, Winschel and Ensher called for a new curricular approach for mildly and moderately retarded children, emphasizing the processes of intellectual development and opportunities for learning and discovery. They contended that education for retarded children must concentrate on developmental acquisitions with a de-emphasis on specific experiences that contribute to some growth in knowledge but have little impact on the ability to learn. Thus, their position is that curricula must be designed to encourage retarded children to demonstrate more of the capacities they possess.

As MacMillan (1977) wrote, "the fact that they are capable of improving their performance if certain strategies are provided makes the outlook for teaching retarded children an optimistic one" (p. 360).

ACADEMIC ACHIEVEMENT

The review until this point has focused on laboratory research of the learning strategies employed by retarded children. A relevant issue now is how well the experimental laboratory research coincides with the more practical concern of educating mentally retarded children in the classroom. Is there much application of the information gained in laboratory research into the learning of subject matter? Unfortunately, there is not. There appears to be relatively little overlap in the research literature on basic concerns of how children learn in laboratory situations and how children learn in the classroom. It is immediately obvious that learning in the laboratory and learning in the classroom, although they share certain commonalities, also have substantial differences. One important difference is that, unlike most laboratory research in which the child is studied individually, learning in the classroom invariably involves the presence of other children. These other children can serve as distractors, motivators, sources of anxiety, or sources of rewards, depending upon the specific child or group of children in whose presence the retarded individual is required to perform.

A second major difference between learning in the laboratory and learning in the classroom is in the material that is to be learned. In the laboratory, the researcher has control over the situation and usually confines the experimental paradigm to a circumscribed and homogeneous set of material that is to be learned. In the classroom, on the other hand, the material to be learned is far more variable, requires a variety of learning strategies, and can seldom be presented in as consistent a fashion as it is in the laboratory.

The third difference is in the objectives that are established. Laboratory research aims to understand basic principles of learning; classroom instruction aims to prepare mentally retarded children to lead useful and independent lives. Although the two goals are not mutually exclusive, they do differ in the demand that is placed on the mentally retarded learner.

RESEARCH IN THE CLASSROOM

In reviewing studies and descriptions of the academic skills of mildly retarded children, Quay (1963) observed that the basic educational objectives for this category, including occupational adequacy, social competence, and personal adequacy, all seem to involve academic achievement. From this vantage point, it is surprising, and dismaying, to discover that the academic performance of mildly retarded students has been investigated rather lightly, and relatively nonsystematically. What empirical literature exists is almost exclusively in reading and arithmetic, particularly the former. Consequently, this consideration of the academic characteristics of the mildly retarded is restricted to these two basic skills.

Reading

Kirk (1940) provided the following guidelines for the level of reading achievement demonstrated by mildly retarded students: first- to third-grade levels for the IQs of 50–59; second- to fourth-grade levels for IQs of 60–69; and third- to seventh-grade levels for IQs of 70–79. More recently, Kirk and Gallagher (1979) stated that educable mentally retarded children are usually capable of learning to read somewhere between second- and fifth-grade level and are capable of using reading in their adult life. Gillespie and Johnson (1974) observed that by the age of 16, a retarded student with an IQ of 70 should be able to read at approximately a fifth-grade level. In actuality, Phelps (1956) found that a group of 163 retarded individuals, having a median IQ of 60.6, read at a median grade level of 3.9 on leaving school.

The reliance on IQ level to predict reading level is a derivative of Kirk and Johnson's position (1951) that mental age (MA) is probably the most important single factor of reading capacity. Kirk, Kliebhan, and Lerner (1978) reported that the majority of mentally retarded children in special classes are below their MA in reading achievement. MacMillan (1977) stated that if reading disability is defined as a discrepancy between actual and expected level of achievement, then reading disabilities are at least as serious a problem with mentally retarded students as with nonretarded students. Dunn (1954) suggested that with special attention given to reading, mildly retarded children are capable of reading at or above their MA—a suggestion that is supported by Kirk's (1964) review of remedial reading intervention.

Another consideration is when to begin reading instruction with mildly retarded students. Kirk et al. (1978) noted that the results of investigations of the

minimum MA required for beginning reading instruction for the retarded are neither clear-cut nor decisive. Gillespie and Johnson (1974) pointed out that early
guidelines that a child must have a minimum MA of 6.6 in order to learn to read
have been questioned. On the other hand, they cited research to indicate that
retarded children learn more rapidly when reading instruction is delayed until an
MA of 8 or so, and that this delay does not attenuate long-range achievement.
Gillespie and Johnson suggested that an advantage of delaying formal reading
instruction for retarded children is the alleviation of failure and frustration that
occurs when reading is introduced earlier.

Dunn (1973) summarized the literature on the reading characteristics of the
mildly retarded. The most noteworthy of his conclusions are that (1) in oral reading, the retarded are inferior to nonretarded of the same mental age in word attack
skills, making more faulty vowel and omission of sound errors, and requiring that
more words be pronounced for them; (2) the retarded are more retarded in reading
comprehension than in any other school subject, being inferior to nonretarded of
the same mental age in locating relevant facts, recognizing main ideas, and drawing inferences and conclusions; (3) the retarded are inferior in the use of context
clues; and (4) retarded girls tend to be superior readers to retarded boys and less
variable in their performance. Levitt (1972) found that older retarded children
(mean CA of 139 months) made more morphological errors than normal first-grade
children, and made heavy use of ideographic responses as opposed to genuine
decoding based on sound-symbol relationships. Gillespie and Johnson (1974)
noted reports that the educable mentally retarded child reads less and sometimes
has preferences that are immature for his or her CA, but that are more mature than
those of younger children of the same MA. Further, the retarded child has essentially the same reading interests as the nonretarded child. These characteristics
are derived from comparisons of retarded and nonretarded readers.

Shepherd (1967) divided special class mentally retarded students into
matched groups of adequate readers (reading age above MA) and inadequate readers (reading age below MA). Mean CA and IQ for the two groups were 11-10 and
72.05 for the adequate readers, and 12-2 and 69.65 for the inadequate readers.
Based on an extensive battery of tests, Shepherd found the inadequate readers to
make significantly more vowel and consonant errors, reversals, omissions of
sounds, and word substitutions. They also required the examiner's aid significantly more often. The adequate readers made better use of context clues. Shepherd observed that while the adequate readers attempted to draw relationships
between words, the inadequate readers appeared to be more concerned with ver-
balizing words than with comprehending content. Shepherd's approach and findings are an important reminder to resist making overgeneralizations regarding the
reading abilities of mildly retarded students.

Two of the problem areas noted by Dunn (1973) have received particular
attention: comprehension and use of context. Hurley (1969) reviewed the literature regarding reading comprehension skills of the mentally retarded and found
there to be little substantive work. Hurley concluded that almost all reading comprehension skills are, and should be, taught to educable mentally retarded students, although for some skills (e.g., literary criticism and dictionary skills) the
question of degree surfaces. Furthermore, he found that there is close correspondence between the age at which curriculum experts say a comprehension skill

should be taught to retarded students and the age at which at least 60 percent of the students can learn the skill. Finally, Hurley observed that not much progress has been made in identifying comprehension skills to be taught to the retarded or in putting these skills in some sort of logical sequence. L. J. Jordan (1969) commented that if comprehension work is held off until reading mechanics are mastered, up to 3–6 years can pass for educable mentally retarded children, with the result that they might become very dependent on memorization, not comprehension. Her point is strengthened by Belch's finding (1978) that the reading comprehension of secondary-level retarded students is significantly improved as a result of relating their reading to higher-order questions calling for evaluating, synthesizing, reading for the main idea, and predicting outcomes. The implication is clear— rather than wait for the retarded child to reach readiness to comprehend what is read, we need to challenge and assist retarded children to use their cognitive abilities effectively in gaining meaning from their reading activities. The contrast with the philosophy of Gillespie & Johnson (1974), described earlier, is noteworthy.

Streib (1976–1977) reviewed research literature related to the use of context as an aid to word identification among educable mentally retarded children. In four of six studies comparing context utilization by nonretarded and retarded subjects, nonretarded children were found to make more effective use of context than retarded children; two studies found no difference. In one study using just retarded subjects, there was evidence that retarded children are able to respond to contextual cues beyond the sentence boundaries. All of the studies used a cloze procedure. Streib cautioned, however, that the relationship between performance on a cloze task and the use of context in ordinary reading has not been explored. Because of this methodological limitation, Streib concluded that clear-cut evidence as to how retarded children utilize context in a natural situation is lacking. However, tentative suggestions do emerge, all of which require more careful study. Based on her analysis of the research, Streib offered the following impressions: (1) retarded children might be less likely than nonretarded children to produce word substitutions that fit the context when the clues are not strong enough to determine the exact response; (2) when the contextual constraints are sufficiently strong to determine the exact response, retarded children may be as likely as nonretarded children to predict correctly from context; (3) like nonretarded children, retarded children do better at evaluating hypotheses concerning the identity of words to be predicted from context than they do at generating acceptable hypotheses; and (4) differences in context utilization between retarded and nonretarded children may be quantitative rather than qualitative in nature. Streib concluded that provided it is established that retarded children make less than optimal use of context, instructional focus should be on ways to facilitate this important skill.

Various workers have agreed that there is no evidence for the superiority of a particular reading technique for the retarded (Cegelka & Cegelka, 1970; Dunn, 1973; Kirk, 1964; MacMillan, 1977). Dunn (1973) suggested that the method is not as important as the teacher. Kirk (1964) emphasized that retarded children can learn by various modes of presentation, and MacMillan (1977) wrote that the teaching methods used with normals are equally applicable to educable mentally retarded students. Cegelka and Cegelka (1970) believed that the primary difference among the various methods employed with retarded children lies in some gimmick or unusual feature; they felt that the problem of selecting a reading approach is one of matching the gimmick with the child.

Arithmetic

According to Kirk and Johnson (1951), it is a commonly accepted fact that most mentally retarded students will achieve between third- and fifth-grade level in their arithmetic abilities. This was borne out by Phelp's finding (1956) that mildly retarded children attained an average arithmetic grade level of 4.3 upon leaving school. The research clearly indicates that mildly retarded individuals achieve at or close to their MA in arithmetic computation, but below MA expectancy in arithmetic reasoning and problem solving (Kirk & Gallagher, 1979; Mac-Millan, 1977; Nofsinger, 1970; Peterson, 1973; Vitello, 1976).

The mildly retarded have been found to have typical characteristics in learning arithmetic (Dunn, 1973; Kirk & Gallagher, 1979; Kirk & Johnson, 1951), including

1. Immature habits such as counting on the fingers
2. Poorer performance in multiplication and division than in addition and subtraction
3. Difficulty grasping advanced and complicated concepts
4. Inferior ability to solve abstract and verbal problems as compared with solving concrete problems
5. Poor understanding of the processes to be used in solving problems
6. Careless errors in working out problems
7. Tendency to guess when faced with problems they cannot solve
8. Tendency to be confused by superfluous data
9. Limited arithmetic vocabulary, particularly for abstract terms involving space, time, and quantity
10. Little conception of sequence and time concepts
11. Better performance by girls than boys

Peterson (1973) observed that much of the research has employed a group of nonretarded children of comparable MAs to test for similarities and differences. At least one systematic line of research has occurred seeking to understand the arithmetical processes of mentally retarded children rather than focusing on a comparison with nonretarded children. Goodstein and his colleagues (Goodstein, 1973; Goodstein, Bessant, Thibodeau, Vitello, & Vlahakos, 1972; Goodstein, Cawley, Gordon, & Helfgott, 1971) found retarded children of intermediate-school age to have difficulty dealing with distractors and extraneous information, and to have a tendency to solve problems by adding all of the numbers in a problem. It appears that retarded subjects do not carefully read word problems, but rather, select all numbers contained in the problem and perform rote computations. Goodstein and colleagues concluded that mildly retarded children use a scanning strategy as opposed to a comprehension strategy in dealing with problems. That is, they tend to scan the format of the problem for key words or other structural cues that suggest the operation to use, demonstrating little comprehension for the meaning of the total problem. Since these scanning strategies interfere with conceptualization of the problem-solving process when employed in rote fashion, these workers recommend that retarded students be taught to carefully process the information requirements of problems. Thus, they must be led to understand that problems are defined by the interaction of the question with the information contained in the narrative body of the problem.

Vitello (1976) reached a similar conclusion. He pointed out that deficiencies in the ability to reason have been used to explain the difficulties in understanding basic mathematical concepts and problem solving. Yet, as he further noted, mildly retarded individuals frequently reach the concrete operational stage, indicating that they are capable of thinking logically and abstractly and of reversing their thought process. These abilities would enable retarded children to understand mathematical concepts, rules, and problems. Vitello suspected that the poor arithmetic problem-solving performance of the retarded is mainly the result of the absence of appropriate instruction in concept learning and problem solving. He recommended that the curriculum for the mildly retarded be expanded to include conceptual mathematical learning as well as rote arithmetical learning.

New Directions

It is apparent that the reading and arithmetic characteristics of mildly retarded students have been fairly well established over a period of years. Further studies merely seeking to describe these academic behaviors are likely to add little practical or conceptual nature to what is already known. Two studies are presented as exemplars of the type that can move our knowledge and application base forward considerably.

Blackman, Bilsky, Burger, and Mar (1976) investigated the interrelationships among 12 cognitive skills and their relationship to the performance of educable mentally retarded adolescents on standardized measures of reading and arithmetic achievement. The subjects were 67 males and 48 females selected from junior high school special classes, with a mean CA of 177.86 months and a mean IQ of 62.44. Academic achievement was measured by the Wide Range Achievement Test (WRAT). Digit recall and paired-associate learning were significantly related to WRAT–Reading. Blackman et al. (1976) regarded both of these learning tasks as representing memory variables, with the tasks containing embedded structures providing obvious opportunities for the utilization of conceptual strategies for reducing memory load. They suggested that among the prerequisites for acquiring reading skills is the capacity to be sensitive to strategy-relevant structure embedded in stimuli. The tasks associated with WRAT–Arithmetic were oddity learning and digit recall, particularly the former. In this study, oddity learning was a task requiring a subject to identify one of several stimulus elements not subsumable within one or more conceptual sets that related to the other elements. The relationship with arithmetic scores was apparently explained by the frequent inability of subjects to maintain a consistent focus on the arithmetic operation required to achieve problem solution. For example, a common error in a two- or three-digit addition problem was to add the first set of numbers but then ignore the plus symbol and subtract the second set of numbers. Blackman et al. reasoned that a similar loss in operational focus could also adversely affect oddity performance.

They concluded that cognitive processes responsible for generating or being sensitive to strategies are related to initial acquisition of reading and arithmetic skills by the mildly retarded.

Mason (1978) investigated the role of strategies in the reading performance of 24 persons living in a residential setting, three of whom were adults, with the remainder 12–16 years old. The subjects had a mean MA of 8, and a mean IQ of 63. As part of the study, subjects were asked to pronounce sets of words sorted according to vowel complexity, vowel regularity, word length, word frequency, and concreteness. The success rate of the retarded subjects was equivalent to that of normal second-graders, but the pattern of errors differed considerably. The retarded subjects were strongly affected by word frequency in that common words were readily pronounced while uncommon words were usually mispronounced. They were also affected by vowel complexity and regularity. Errors reflected reliance on common words rather than on letter–sound pattern information. Frequent errors included turning a word into a familiar word (*skip* for *skimp*), reading only a common shorter word that was embedded in the common word (*yes* for *yeast*), incorrect word endings (*seem* for *seep*), and misreading of consonant clusters (*class* for *clash*). Mason concluded that the retarded subjects overgeneralized, typically using a recognition strategy of memorizing whole words, relying on short common word patterns, and, in the process, discounting vowel and consonant information. This, of course, represents an immature and poor reading strategy—especially considering the irregularities of many common words, which render them a poor basis for generalization. Mason, therefore, advocated strategy training for improving the ability of retarded people to read effectively.

These studies, along with the work of Goodstein and his colleagues, are noteworthy in their attempt to relate cognitive abilities and strategies to academic attainment by mildly retarded persons.

ACCEPTANCE OF MENTALLY RETARDED CHILDREN

The study of retarded children's learning characteristics and academic achievement also addresses the competence aspect of socialization. It is clear from the evidence presented that the learning strategies that mildly retarded children employ are less adaptive than the strategies employed by their nonretarded peers. It should come as no surprise, then, that mildly retarded children also achieve at lower levels than their nonretarded counterparts.

Competence is only one of the three aspects of socialization, the other two being power and acceptance. As discussed earlier, the conceptual relationship of acceptance to power permits focus on the dynamics of acceptance alone. How well are the mildly retarded accepted by other children? Before this area is explored, a brief point must be made. Competence and acceptance are themselves not unrelated. As a general rule, competent individuals tend to be better accepted (Gottlieb, Semmel, & Veldman, 1978). Competence and acceptance are separate here simply because the two aspects of socialization often tend to be treated separately in the literature.

The history of special education in this country has been characterized, in part, by the desire to protect mentally retarded children from the barbs and taunts of others. As children who were not able to achieve at a normal rate, they were not well accepted by their smarter peers. The intent of the first special classes was partially to offer slow-learning children an environment that would shield them from the competition with other children.

It was not until 1950, however, when Johnson conducted a sociometric study of the social relationships of the regular classroom that the plight of mentally retarded was highlighted in a scientifically precise way. Johnson (1950) studied the social position of 698 elementary school children, of whom 39 were found to be educable mentally retarded (EMR) on the basis of IQ testing. The results of the sociometric research indicated that the EMR children were rejected more often and chosen as friends less often than the nonretarded children. When the nonretarded peers were asked the reasons for their rejection of the other children, they reported that perceived misbehavior by the children was the primary reason for their rejecting ratings. The fact that the EMR children were not academically competent did not influence rejection ratings, according to the nonretarded raters.

The results of Johnson's study (1950) of the social position of EMR children in regular classes were essentially replicated in later research studies by Johnson and Kirk (1950) and by Heber (1956). It is important to consider that each of the studies cited was conducted in regular classes where the EMR children were not identified prior to the onset of the research.

There has been considerable controversy in the field of special education as to the effects of the label ''mentally retarded.'' One school of thought has suggested that labels tend to stigmatize children and lead to low self-esteem and possibly social rejection (e.g., Dunn, 1968). Another school of thought has suggested the possibility that the label may actually shield the individual from overt rejection (Guskin, Bartel, & MacMillan, 1975). The question of whether the label helps or hurts retarded children is a difficult one to untangle, because, in addition to the label possibly affecting the extent to which retarded children are liked, the amount and intensity of exposure that nonretarded children have with their retarded peers also plays an important role. That is, in school situations nonretarded children vary in the amount of experience they have with special education youngsters. The trend presently is to encourage mentally retarded children to have as much contact with nonretarded peers as is possible.

In the 1950s, when the early sociometric research was conducted, there was little pressure on schools to identify children as mentally retarded. Today, the ''child-find'' provisions of Public Law 94-142, which was passed in 1975, are designed to ensure that all handicapped children who may require special services are identified and receive the services to which they are entitled. Consequently, there is less likelihood today that handicapped children would go undetected in the schools.

As indicated earlier, sociometric research conducted in the 1950s suggested that unidentified EMR children tended to be sociometrically rejected far more frequently than nonretarded classmates. Other research indicated that EMR children who attended special classes tended to be sociometrically accepted more frequently than EMR children who attended regular classes (A.M. Jordan, 1959). At face value, it seems that everyone would agree that special classes were appropriate vehicles for fostering improved social acceptance of EMR children. But this was not the case. Indeed, there was considerable dissatisfaction with special classes for EMR children. The dissatisfaction stemmed from several sources.

First, a substantial amount of data suggested that EMR children in special classes did not achieve more than EMR children who remained in regular classes. This was disturbing because special classes were far more expensive to maintain. Also, children who were enrolled in these classes were labeled as mentally retarded, and it was widely assumed that the label was harmful to the children. The issue of labeling also took on legal weight when a number of lawsuits were filed asserting that certain children had been labeled as mentally retarded on the basis of culturally biased IQ testing. The claim was that the children—mostly members of minority groups—were never mentally retarded and should not have been placed in special classes, which were viewed as being "deadends" (*Larry P. v. Riles,* 1970).

Society's concern for protecting the civil rights of disenfranchised segments of society was mirrored in the narrower concern with the civil rights of handicapped persons. The philosophy of normalization was advanced, advocating treating handicapped people as much as possible like nonhandicapped people (Wolfensberger, 1972). Normalization propelled special educators to move away from special classrooms where mentally retarded children had only minimal opportunities to interact with nonretarded peers. The subsequent placement of handicapped children with nonhandicapped peers was referred to as mainstreaming. When Public Law 94-142 was passed in 1975, the new mandate, legal extension of the already-existing philosophy, was to educate children in the least-restrictive environment, in contact with nonhandicapped peers to the maximum extent that this was appropriate to the needs of the handicapped child.

The implicit assumption underlying both mainstreaming and the least-restrictive environment was that handicapped children, including mentally retarded children, would benefit from being placed among their nonhandicapped peers. One aspect of the benefit was thought to be in the area of social acceptance; mainstreamed mentally retarded children were assumed to be better accepted socially than retarded children who were confined to special classes. In 1972, a series of studies had been done to determine whether the assumption was correct.

Goodman, Gottlieb, and Harrison (1972) studied the sociometric acceptance of EMR children who attended special classes and EMR children who were placed in regular classes. The status of both mainstreamed and segregated EMR children were compared to the social status of nonretarded children. Forty nonretarded children were asked to indicate their liking of ten mainstreamed and eight segregated EMR children, as well as a of sample of nonretarded children. Briefly, the results indicated that nonretarded children were liked significantly better than either mainstreamed or segregated EMR children, and that male raters liked the segregated EMR children more than they did the mainstreamed children. No significant differences in girls' ratings of mainstreamed and segregated children were evident.

These findings were quite unexpected insofar as they suggested not only that contact between retarded and nonretarded children did not improve the former group's social acceptance, but that, among boys, contact between retarded and nonretarded children resulted in less social acceptance. The study conducted by Goodman et al. (1972) was subsequently replicated with a larger sample by Gottlieb and Budoff (1973), with similar results; mainstreamed EMR children occupied a lower sociometric status than EMR children in special classrooms. The latter study was of interest because it was conducted in a school with open architecture;

that is, there were no interior walls and all children had maximum exposure to all other children. The combined results of the studies by Goodman et al. (1972) and Gottlieb and Budoff (1973) suggest that the more visible EMR children are to their nonretarded peers, the less likely they are to be accepted. A more conservative conclusion is that mainstreaming, per se, does not result in greater social acceptance of EMR children. This is not a surprising conclusion and has also been voiced with regard to the integration of black children (Riordan & Ruggiero, 1980) and socially unacceptable children who were not classified as handicapped (La-Greca & Santogrossi, 1980).

The general conclusion that contact between retarded and nonretarded does not automatically result in superior acceptance of retarded children was also found by Gottlieb, Cohen, and Goldstein (1974), Gottlieb and Davis (1973), and Iano, Ayers, Heller, McGettigan, & Walker (1974). The point of view expressed by Riordan and Ruggiero (1980) in their discussion of racial integration applies equally to the integration of retarded children: "Both studies, conducted five years and 3000 miles apart, demonstrate the futility of attempting to reduce interracial hostilities through contact *without* an organized plan of intervention" (p. 135).

Fortunately, several organized plans of intervention are available that have been found to result in improved sociometric acceptance of EMR children when properly applied. Many of these techniques have been reviewed in detail by Gottlieb and Leyser (1981). The common elements of these various techniques involve structuring situations that allow retarded and nonretarded children to work together in a cooperative manner on tasks on which the retarded child is capable of performing satisfactorily. Examples of such tasks are the production of class plays (Chennault, 1967) and multimedia skits (Ballard, Corman, Gottlieb, & Kaufman, 1977). It should be pointed out, however, that even when interventions are successful in significantly improving the social acceptance of retarded children, they are still not as socially accepted as the typical nonretarded child. At the present time, interventions that are capable of improving the sociometric status of retarded children to the level of nonretarded children are not available. However, it should also be noted that not all retarded children occupy an inferior sociometric status. Approximately one retarded child in six is as well-accepted as the average nonretarded child (Ballard et al., 1977).

Why do EMR children occupy an inferior sociometric status in their peer group? Is it because they cannot achieve as well as their nonretarded classmates, or is it because they exhibit inappropriate social behavior that their peers find offensive? This question was investigated by Gottlieb et al. (1978), who studied the sociometric status of 300 mainstreamed EMR children. The researchers asked nonretarded classmates to indicate the extent to which they liked and/or disliked retarded children in their classes. Approximately 8000 classmates rated the sociometric status of 300 EMR pupils. Then, the investigators asked both the EMR pupils' classmates and teachers to fill out a questionnaire that measured perceptions of EMR pupils' academic competence and social behavior. The results of the study indicated that when EMR children were not accepted by their classmates, they tended to be viewed by the same classmates as being academically incompetent. When EMR children were overtly rejected by their peers, they were perceived as having behavior problems. This investigation points out the need to be especially sensitive to the specific kind of sociometric improvement desired. If the aim is to increase social acceptance, focus should be on improving children's academic ability; to reduce rejection, focus should be on improving EMR children's social behavior.

CONCLUSIONS

Despite the fact that mildly mentally retarded children have difficulty with academic material and interpersonal behavior, there are many studies that indicate that as adults they assume normal lifestyles (Goldstein, 1964). It is not clear why they function as normal adults. One possibility is that EMR people still lead marginal lives as adults even though they are no longer officially classified as mentally retarded. A second possibility is that they take jobs where the cognitive demand is not so pronounced as it is in school, and consequently their limitations are not as easily exposed.

We believe that in the next few years the EMR classification will change substantially from what it has been in the past. EMR as a diagnostic category will be reserved for children whose IQ scores are in the low 60s and below. Children whose IQ scores are above the mid-60s will be classified differently, probably as learning disabled, or perhaps in a new diagnostic category not yet developed. Regardless of what the children will be called, one fact remains. There will be children whose cognitive abilities will not allow them to progress at the same rate as mentally average children. These slow-learning children will require help from the schools in order to take their rightful place in the mainstream of our culture. Our hope is that the schools will be prepared for that responsibility.

REFERENCES

Ballard, M., Corman, L., Gottlieb, J., & Kaufman, M. J. Improving the social status of mainstreamed retarded children. *Journal of Educational Psychology,* 1977, *69,* 605–611.

Baumeister, A. Learning abilities of the mentally retarded. In A. Baumeister (Ed.), *Mental retardation.* Chicago: Aldine, 1967, pp. 181–211.

Belch, P. J. Improving the reading comprehension scores of secondary level educable mentally handicapped students through selective teacher questioning. *Education and Training of the Mentally Retarded.* 1978, *13,* 385–389.

Blackman, L. S., Bilsky, L. H., Burger, A. L., & Mar, H. Cognitive processes and academic achievement in EMR adolescents. *American Journal of Mental Deficiency,* 1976, *81,* 125–134.

Bortner, M., & Birch, H. G. Cognitive capacity and cognitive competence. *American Journal of Mental Deficiency,* 1970, *75,* 735–744.

Bruininks, K. H., & Warfield, G. The mentally retarded. In E. Meyen (Ed.), *Exceptional children and youth.* Denver: Love, 1978, pp. 162–216.

Bryan, J. H., & Bryan, T. H. *Exceptional children.* Sherman Oaks, California: Alfred, 1979.

Campione, J. C., & Brown, A. L. Memory and metamemory in educable retarded children. In E. V. Kail & J. W. Hagen (Eds.), *Perspectives on the development of memory and cognition.* Hillsdale, N.J.: Lawrence Erlbaum Associates, 1977, pp. 367–406.

Cegelka, P. A., & Cegelka, W. J. A review of research: Reading and the educable mentally handicapped. *Exceptional Children,* 1970, *37,* 187–200.

Chennault, J. Improving the social acceptance of unpopular mentally retarded pupils in special classes. *American Journal of Mental Deficiency,* 1967, *72,* 455–458.

Denny, M. R. Research in learning and performance. In H. A. Stevens & R. Heber (Eds.), *Mental retardation*. Chicago: University of Chicago Press, 1964, pp. 100–142.

Dunn, L. M. A comparison of reading processes of mentally retarded and normal boys of the same MA. *Monographs of the Society for Research in Child Development*, 1954, *19*, 7–99.

Dunn, L. M. Special education for the mildly retarded—Is much of it justifiable? *Exceptional Children*, 1968, *35*, 5–22.

Dunn, L. M. Children with general learning disabilities. In L. M. Dunn (Ed.), *Exceptional children in the schools* (2nd ed.). New York: Holt, Rhinehart and Winston, 1973, pp. 125–188.

Ellis, N. R. The stimulus trace and behavioral inadequacy. In N. R. Ellis (Ed.), *Handbook of mental deficiency*. New York: McGraw-Hill, 1963, pp. 134–158.

Ellis, N. R. Memory processes in retardates and normals. In N. R. Ellis (Ed.), *International review of research in mental retardation* (Vol. 4). New York: Academic Press, 1970, pp. 1–32.

Flavell, J. H. Developmental studies of mediated memory. In H. W. Reese & L. P. Lipsitt (Eds.), *Advances in child development and behavior* (Vol. 5). New York: Academic Press, 1970.

Gampel, D. H., Gottlieb, J., & Harrison, R. H. A comparison of the classroom behaviors of special class EMR, integrated EMR, low IQ, and nonretarded children. *American Journal of Mental Deficiency*, 1974, *79*, 16–21.

Gillespie, P. H., & Johnson, L. *Teaching reading to the mildly retarded child*. Columbus, Oh.: Charles E. Merrill, 1974.

Glidewell, J. C., Kantor, M. B., Smith, L. M., & Stringer, L. A. Socialization and social structure in the classroom. In L. W. Hoffman & M. L. Hoffman (Eds.), *Review of child development research* (Vol. 2). New York: Russell Sage Foundation, 1966.

Goldstein, H. Social and occupational adjustment. In H. A. Stevens & R. Heber (Eds.), *Mental retardation*. Chicago: University of Chicago Press, 1964.

Goodman, H., Gottlieb, J., & Harrison, R. H. Social acceptance of EMR's integrated into a nongraded elementary school. *American Journal of Mental Deficiency*, 1972, *76*, 412–417.

Goodstein, H. A. The performance of educable mentally retarded children on subtraction word problems. *Education and Training of the Mentally Retarded*, 1973, *8*, 197–202.

Goodstein, H. A., Bessant, H., Thibodeau, G., Vitello, S., & Vlahakos, I. The effect of three variables on the verbal problem solving of educable mentally handicapped children. *American Journal of Mental Deficiency*, 1972, *76*, 703–709.

Goodstein, H. A., Cawley, J. F., Gordon, S., & Helfgott, J. Verbal problem solving among educable mentally retarded children. *American Journal of Mental Deficiency*, 1971, *76*, 238–241.

Gottlieb, J., & Budoff, M. Social acceptability of retarded children in non-graded schools differing in architecture. *American Journal of Mental Deficiency*, 1973, *78*, 15–19.

Gottlieb, J., Cohen, L., & Goldstein, L. Social contact and personal adjustment as variables relating to attitudes toward EMR children. *Training School Bulletin*, 1974, *71*, 9–16.

Gottlieb, H., & Davis, J. E. Social acceptance of EMRs during overt behavioral interaction. *American Journal of Mental Deficiency*, 1973, *78*, 141–143.

Gottlieb, J., & Leyser, Y. Friendship between retarded and nonretarded children. In S. R. Asher & J. M. Gottman (Eds.), *The development of children's friendship*. New York: Cambridge University Press, 1981.

Gottlieb, J., Semmel, M. I., & Veldman, D. J. Correlates of social status among mainstreamed mentally retarded children. *Journal of Educational Psychology*, 1978, *70*, 396–405.

Guskin, S. L., Bartel, N. R., & MacMillan, D. L. The perspective of the labeled child. In N. Hobbs (Ed.), *Classification of exceptional children*. San Francisco: Jossey-Bass, 1975.

Hallahan, D. P., & Kauffman, J. M. *Exceptional children*. Englewood Cliffs: Prentice-Hall, 1978.

Hardman, M. L., & Drew, C. J. Incidental learning in the mentally retarded: A review. *Education and Training of the Mentally Retarded*, 1975, *10*, 3–9.

Hayward, H. C. What happened to mild and moderate retardation? *American Journal of Mental Deficiency*, 1979, *83*, 429–431.

Heber, R. F. The relation of intelligence and physical maturity to social status of children. *Journal of Educational Psychology*, 1956, *47*, 158–162.

Hurley, O. L. Reading comprehension skills vis-a-vis the mentally retarded. *Education and Training of the Mentally Retarded*, 1969, *4*, 132–140.

Iano, R. P., Ayers, D., Heller, H. B., McGettigan, J. F., & Walker, V. S. Sociometric status of retarded children in an integrative program. *Exceptional Children*, 1974, *40*, 267–271.

Johnson, G. O. A study of social position of mentally handicapped children in the regular grades. *American Journal of Mental Deficiency*, 1950, *55*, 60–89.

Johnson, G. O., & Kirk, S. A. Are mentally handicapped children segregated in the regular grades? *Exceptional Children*, 1950, *17*, 65–68, 87–88.

Jordan, A. M. Personal social traits of mentally handicapped children. In T. Thurstone (Ed.), *An evaluation of mentally handicapped children in special classes and regular grades*. U.S. Office of Education Cooperative Research Program. Project #OE-SAE-6452. Chapel Hill: University of North Carolina, School of Education, 1959.

Jordan, L. J. Promoting reading comprehension. *Education and Training of the Mentally Retarded*, 1969, *4*, 132–140.

Keane, V. E. The incidence of speech and language problems in the mentally retarded. *Mental Retardation*, 1972, *10*(2), 3–8.

Kirk, S. A. *Teaching reading to slow learning children*. Boston: Houghton Mifflin, 1940.

Kirk, S. A. Research in education. In H. A. Stevens & R. Heber (Eds.), *Mental retardation*. Chicago: University of Chicago Press, 1964, pp. 57–99.

Kirk, S. A., & Gallagher, J. J. *Educating exceptional children* (3rd ed.). Boston: Houghton Mifflin, 1979.

Kirk, S. A., & Johnson, C. O. *Educating the retarded child*. Cambridge: Houghton Mifflin, 1951.

Kirk, S. A., Kliebhan, Sr. J. M., & Lerner, J. *Teaching reading to slow and disabled learners*. Boston: Houghton Mifflin, 1978.

Kolstoe, O. P. *Mental retardation*. New York: Holt, Rinehart and Winston, 1972.

LaGreca, A. M., & Santogrossi, D. A. Social skills training with elementary school students: A behavioral group approach. *Journal of Consulting and Clinical Psychology*, 1980, *48*, 220–227.

Larry P. v. Riles, Civil Action No. C-71-2270 343 F. Supp. 1306 (N. D. Cal., 1970).

Levitt, E. Higher-order and lower-order reading responses of mentally retarded and nonretarded children at the first-grade level. *American Journal of Mental Deficiency*, 1972, *77*, 13–20.

Loper, A. B. Metacognitive development: Implications for cognitive training. *Exceptional Education Quarterly*, 1980, *1*(1), 1–8.

MacMillan, D. L. *Mental retardation in school and society*. Boston: Little, Brown, 1977.

Mason, J. M. Role of strategy in reading by mentally retarded persons. *American Journal of Mental Deficiency*, 1978, *82*, 467–473.

Mercer, C. D., & Payne, J. S. Learning theories and their implications. In J. M. Kauffman & J. S. Payne (Eds.), *Mental retardation*. Columbus, Oh.: Charles E. Merrill, 1975.

Mercer, C. D., & Snell, M. E. *Learning theory research in mental retardation*. Columbus, Oh.: Charles E. Merrill, 1977.

Nofsinger, T. Teaching arithmetic to educable mentally retarded children. *The Journal of Educational Research*, 1970, *64*, 177–184.

Payne, J. S., Polloway, E. A., Smith Jr., J. E., & Payne, R. A. *Strategies for teaching the mentally retarded*. Columbus, Oh.: Charles E. Merrill, 1977.

Peterson, D. L. *Functional mathematics for the mentally retarded*. Columbus, Oh.: Charles E. Merrill, 1973.

Phelps, H. R. Post-school adjustment of mentally retarded children in selected Ohio cities. *Exceptional children*, 1956, *23*, 58–62.

Quay, L. C. Academic skills. In N. R. Ellis (Ed.), *Handbook of mental deficiency*. New York: McGraw-Hill, 1963, pp. 664–690.

Riordan, C., & Ruggiero, J. Producing equal status interracial interaction: A replication. *Social Psychology Quarterly*, 1980, *43*, 131–136.

Robinson, N. M., & Robinson, H. B. *The mentally retarded child* (2nd ed.). New York: McGraw-Hill, 1976.

Semmel, M. I., Barritt, L. S., Bennett, S. W., & Perfetti, C. A. A grammatical analysis of word associations of educable mentally retarded and normal children. *American Journal of Mental Deficiency*, 1968, *72*, 567–576.

Semmel, M. I., Gottlieb, J., & Robinson, N. M. Mainstreaming: Perspectives on educating handicapped children in the public schools. In D. Berliner (Ed.), *Review of research in education* (Vol. 7). Washington, D. C.: American Educational Research Association, 1979.

Shepherd, G. Selected factors in the reading ability of educable mentally retarded boys. *American Journal of Mental Deficiency*, 1967, *71*, 563–570.

Spitz, H. H. The role of input organization in the learning and memory of mental retardates. In N. R. Ellis (Ed.), *International review of research in mental retardation* (Vol. 2). New

York: Academic Press, 1966. pp. 29–56.

Spitz, H. H. Consolidating facts into the schematized learning and memory system of educable retardates. In N. R. Ellis (Ed.), *International review of research in mental retardation* (Vol. 6). New York: Academic Press, 1973, pp. 149–168.

Spradlin, J. E. Language and communication of mental defectives. In N. R. Ellis (Ed.), *Handbook of mental deficiency*. New York: McGraw-Hill, 1963, pp. 149–168.

Streib, R. Context utilization in reading by educable mentally retarded children. *Reading Research Quarterly*, 1976–1977, *12*(1), 33–53.

Torgeson, J. K. The role of nonspecific factors in the task performance of learning disabled children: A theoretical assessment. *Journal of Learning Disabilities*, 1977, *10*, 27–34.

Vitello, S. J. Quantitative abilities of mentally retarded children. *Education and Training of the Mentally Retarded*, 1976, *11*, 125–129.

Webb, C. E., & Kinde, S. Speech, language, and learning of the mentally retarded. In A. Baumeister (Ed.), *Mental retardation*, Chicago: Aldine, 1967.

Winschel, J. F., & Ensher, G. L. Educability revisited: Curricular implications for the mentally retarded. *Education and Training of the Mentally Retarded*, 1978, *13*, 131–138.

Wolfensberger, W. *Normalization*. Toronto: Canadian Association for Retarded Children, 1972.

Zeaman, D, & House, B. J. The role of attention in retardate discrimination learning. In, N. R. Ellis (Ed.), *Handbook of mental deficiency*. New York: McGraw Hill, 1963.

Michael H. Epstein
Douglas Cullinan

4

Characteristics of Mild Behavioral Disorders

BACKGROUND

From information available on ancient civilizations around the Mediterranean, the roots of biological and psychological conceptions of behavior disorders, as well as treatments based on these conceptions, can be explored. For instance, the Greek philosopher–physician Hippocrates held that behavior disorders were produced by imbalances in the body's humors (fluids), and recommended treatment included laxatives, bloodletting, and brain surgery as well as therapeutic bathing and massage, exercise, and pleasant rehabilitative environments. Other ancient ideas of maladjustment emphasized that unfortunate life events or excessively strong emotions caused mental breakdowns. Proponents of this view recommended problem-oriented discussions, extended rest, and temperance in desires and behaviors.

With the growth of the church in Europe, these ideas were superceded by the doctrine that behavior disorders are caused by intervention or possession by the devil, requiring exorcism to save the individual's soul. Treatment included prayers, penitence, and potions if the possessed person was lucky, and torture and death if not. Although these practices fell into disfavor with the coming of the Renaissance and its emphasis on reason and human worth, behaviorally disordered persons were still likely to be driven away from home or imprisoned. And, although there is very little information prior to the 18th century on behaviorally disordered children, the indications are that prevailing concepts and treatments held for children as well as adults (Achenbach, 1974).

By the end of the 17th century, Renaissance concepts of human nature began to be translated into humane treatment for the behaviorally disordered. Imprisonment gave way to "moral treatment," provided at retreats emphasizing family-like living, sympathy for the individual's problems, and firm insistence on positive change through education and work. Early 18th-century American crusaders for moral treatment forced states to provide asylums for poor persons with maladaptive behavior; these asylums soon became "mental hospitals" run by physicians specializing in the fledgling discipline of psychiatry. Unfortunately, this set the stage for a flood of "mental patients" who could rarely be provided with much more than custodial care, a situation that changed little until the middle of the 20th century.

The beginning of the 18th century also saw some progress toward differentiating behaviorally handicapped children and adults. The 18th century produced descriptions of children with severe behavior disorders and/or retardation, statements on the role of parental failure in producing maladjustment in children, and recommendations against harsh discipline and for kind treatment and adequate education of deviant children (Kauffman, 1976). Outstanding educators such as Itard and Seguin utilized sound methods for teaching the severely handicapped, laying the groundwork for teaching systems that are widely used even today. Special classes for "incorrigible," "mentally defective," and non-English-speaking immigrant children were established in the larger American cities, and these classes became widespread as compulsory school attendance laws began to be enforced. During the 19th century, a philosophy of juvenile justice evolved for delinquent and neglected youngsters emphasizing the need for protection of the youngster, along with education and rehabilitation to change his or her life direction. These developments helped set the stage for 20th-century events that shaped contemporary special education for behaviorally disordered pupils.

The Twentieth Century

Three trends stand out from among the many that molded contemporary special education for the behaviorally disordered: the child study movement, the mental hygiene movement, and the development of modern psychological theories of behavior disorders.

Child Study

The turn of this century saw rapidly increasing awareness of the importance of studying intellectual, behavioral, and emotional development of children. Pioneering psychologist G. Stanley Hall conducted research on what children think and know at various ages, and offered a theory of how youngsters develop and adapt to their environments. Binet developed and standardized a test of the learning abilities of pupils, and his concepts were adopted and amplified by American psychologists interested in the measurement of intelligence. During the 1920s, several studies of the long-term development of children's physical, social, emotional, and intellectual behavior patterns were undertaken with large samples of children in order to learn how early behavioral characteristics predicted later ones. During the same time, Piaget was developing a biological-experiential theory of children's cognitive development, based on continuing and highly intensive study of a few children. The growth in knowledge about children's psychological development has continued to this day, and child development is a major area within the field of psychology. Understanding the development of normal children is highly relevant to understanding and treating behavior disorders in several ways: information on normal development strongly affects judgment of what constitutes abnormality, plays a critical role in meaningful assessment of pupils with behavior disorders, and has far-reaching implications for the establishment of intervention goals.

Mental Hygiene

Also in the early 1900s, influential psychologists and psychiatrists began to emphasize the importance of needed reforms in mental health care, particularly those relevant to the prevention of behavior disorders, thus initiating a "mental hygiene movement" in this country. There was a diminishing of the earlier search for biological causes for the majority of behavior disorders; the importance of family, neighborhood, and other environmental factors was emphasized. The newly formed National Committee on Mental Hygiene was oriented to the study of children's mental health, early detection and prevention of childhood behavior disorders, and efforts to increase psychological, educational, and related resources for children. The committee was influential in initiating and promoting child guidance clinics that utilized professionals from psychology, social work, psychiatry, and other disciplines; these clinics worked closely with schools and juvenile courts. By the 1950s, child mental health services had become available in or near many communities in America.

Modern Psychological Theories

Two of the most influential developments in the area of children's behavior disorders are the psychodynamic model and the behavioral model (Corsini, 1977; Hall & Lindzey, 1978).

Between about 1890 and 1930, Sigmund Freud developed the prototypic psychodynamic model, psychoanalysis, as a result of his professional training, interaction with other thinkers, and therapeutic practice with behaviorally disordered adults. Psychoanalysis is (1) a theory of normal psychological development through life stages; (2) a theory of how emotional disorders originate; and (3) a method of treating such disorders. Freud believed that disturbance originates when a child fails to psychologically progress from stage to stage or within a stage, due primarily to traumatic, overly indulgent, frustrating, or otherwise faulty parenting practices. As a result, the individual thinks, feels, and behaves immaturely under stress; functioning regresses to the stage at which development was arrested. Stressful situations may also lead to the use of defense mechanisms, which are behavior patterns that temporarily reduce anxiety but are maladaptive in the long run and usually mark the individual as deviant. These disorders of functioning stem from memories and motivations of which the individual is not aware because they operate at the unconscious level. Psychoanalytic therapy consists of discussions and other activities designed to make the developmental origins of the unconscious motivations apparent so that the individual is more aware of the reasons for his disordered reactions.

Many disciples of Freud modified psychoanalysis in varying degrees, so that now the psychodynamic model includes not only psychoanalysis, but also minor variations, major revisions, and hybrid concepts that draw both on psychoanalysis and totally unrelated psychological principles. Prominent among these psychodynamic variations are ego psychologies, especially Erikson's psychosocial theory; humanistic-phenomenological theories, particularly C. R. Roger's client-centered theory; and the here-and-now, goal-oriented therapies such as transactional analysis and reality therapy.

Ego psychologies. In pychoanalysis, the ego is a mental faculty that operates to satisfy basic wishes and drives in ways that will not endanger the person. To do this, the ego utilizes various psychological capacities: perceiving, remembering, thinking, acting, reasoning, creating, etc. Ego psychologists (e.g., Erikson, 1963; Anna Freud, 1965; Hartmann, 1964) have concerned themselves with details of how the ego develops and operates, and how ego dysfunctioning leads to behavior disorders. Erikson's psychosocial theory holds that a person's ego capacities "unfold" according to an inborn sequence. As each new ego capability comes into play, the person is thrust into a new stage of development where she must struggle with and master an increasingly complex physical and social world. An individual's personality reflects what has gone before, so if the struggles of one stage are not properly resolved there will be personality maladjustments in later stages.

Humanistic-phenomenological theories. The philosophy of phenomenology holds that objective facts and unconscious mental operations are not important in and of themselves; what is important is how the individual perceives such things. Everyone perceives events in subjective ways that differ from individual to individual, so each person can be understood only in terms of his unique perceptions and representations of reality. Humanistic psychologies additionally propose that every person is born with a constructive, self-enhancing motivation to achieve ever-higher levels of pleasure, consciousness, and personal growth.

In the client-centered theory of Carl Rogers (1951), for example, each child is born with an actualizing tendency that motivates her to develop all her capacities in positive ways that maintain or enhance her. A feedback system exists to indicate whether or not a particular phenomenological experience is compatible with the actualizing tendency or interferes with it. Additionally, there is a universal need for positive regard—to be loved, respected, accepted, given warmth and sympathy, and so on—that can best be satisfied by parents, friends, and other significant persons. Unfortunately, this need for positive regard can trap a person, because the thoughts and behaviors generated by the actualizing tendency can clash with cultural, religious, or other taboos, and not be given positive regard. As a result, the individual comes to distort or deny some of the thoughts, feelings, or behaviors that she knows will not be worthy of positive regard. This is a very unhealthy development: It makes for psychological tension, confusion, and estrangement from one's true human nature—which is called being in a state of incongruence. Incongruence exists in nearly all of us, but in more extreme cases it produces severe unhappiness and disruptions of appropriate functioning. Client-centered therapy attempts to reduce the incongruence, providing the individual with positive regard "unconditionally," that is, no matter what she says or does. In this way, the individual becomes able to risk consciously experiencing all the feelings and behaviors generated by her actualizing tendency, and learns to accept these feelings as a natural part of her self.

Here-and-now therapies. Transactional analysis and reality therapy are two modern extensions of the psychodynamic tradition. In transactional analysis (TA) (Berne, 1961, 1964), psychodynamic principles are presented in terms of concepts relevant to everyday life. There are a few basic motivations, such as the "hunger" for recognition, intimacy, and excitement. According to a life script that is determined early in life, the person adopts consistent roles (games) designed to achieve specific feelings (stamps); his particular pattern of games and stamps defines his racket. If he cannot find another player for the game, or if he tires of his racket, he will probably feel and act maladjusted. The object of TA therapy is to achieve insight into one's own games and rackets, to be specific about what changes need to be made, and to rewrite one's life script accordingly.

Reality therapy (Glasser, 1965, 1969) holds that maladjusted and unsuccessful individuals have failed so often that they have adopted a "failure identity," cannot accept responsibility for their own lives, and therefore have trouble loving themselves and others. They have an inadequate sense of their selves, question their own work, are unsure about their values, and experience difficulty relating to others as equals. Reality therapy attempts to remedy these maladaptive characteristics by an insistence that the person take responsibility for her own behaviors and their consequences; it teaches her to set feasible goals, carefully plan how each goal will be achieved, and avoid rationalizations or excuses for nonperformance and failure. Both TA and reality therapy rely on teaching the behaviorally disordered person to make responsible commitments for specific behavior changes.

The psychodynamic model owes a great debt to Freud's formulation of psychoanalysis, as well as to the other theorists and therapists who have enriched this model through modifications and extensions. In fact, today's teachers of behaviorally disordered children usually find that the psychologists, psychiatrists, social workers, or other clinical professionals that they contact draw freely on a variety of psychodynamic conceptionalizations to explain and treat pupil problems. But even more important are the adaptations that have facilitated the use of the psychodynamic approach to educational situations for behaviorally disordered children. Advocates of the psychodynamic approach who have worked with such youngsters found that they had to modify the application of psychodynamic principles in response to the realities of educational and other rehabilitative situations. This led to the evolution of contemporary psychoeducational approaches to educating pupils with behavior disorders.

Psychoeducational approach. Early applications of psychodynamic principles to the education of the behaviorally disordered children closely adhered to psychoanalytic therapy, particularly in their emphasis on permitting children to "act out" their fantasies and unconscious drives. In his work with juvenile delinquents, for example, Aichhorn (1965) believed that maladaptive behavior is a symptom of unresolved mental conflict, and that its resolution depends upon establishing a warm and understanding relationship with the disturbed youngster. Boys were allowed to act out their inner conflicts with essentially no pressure to conform to staff expectations: the motto of Aichhorn's school was, "As far as possible, let the boys alone" (p. 172). In 1944, the Sonja Shankman Orthogenic School, under the direction of Bruno Bettelheim, was opened for the treatment of children with severe behavior disorders. Bettelheim (1950, 1967) believed that behavior disorders stemmed from grossly improper parenting (particularly deprivation of affection) during the early years of life. Within the Orthogenic School's "therapeutic milieu," the children were encouraged to relive earlier life phases in order to achieve the gratification of impulses that was formerly denied to them. Bettelheim believed that only through total acceptance of the child's wishes could a positive therapeutic relationship to adults come into existence, and that it is this relationship that is the necessary ingredient in remediation of the disturbance (Bettelheim & Sylvester, 1948).

One of the most important developments in the evolution of the psychoeducational approach took place in 1946 when Fritz Redl opened Pioneer House, a residential treatment center for severely aggressive disturbed boys—the "children who hate" (Redl & Wineman, 1951). Treatment at Pioneer House involved program activities especially chosen to develop adaptive ego functioning; there was complete acceptance of and affection for the children even when they misbehaved, but the boys were made to understand that although misbehavior would be tolerated insofar as possible, the staff would help them improve their behavior. Also, episodes of behavioral and emotional disturbance were utilized in treatment by providing on-the-spot therapeutic interviews. This practice was gradually expanded into an intervention procedure called the life space interview (Redl & Wineman, 1952), which remains a major psychoeducational intervention strategy. Redl also developed the concept and practice of "managing surface behavior" through a set of classroom management techniques that have been further refined by others (e.g., Long & Newman, 1976). But these contributions sprang from Redl's recognition of the need to adapt psychodynamic principles to educational needs: he was fully willing to provide acceptance and sympathetic understanding for disordered behavior, but he believed it unwise to allow total permissiveness; the children were consistently made aware of his long-term expectation that their behavior would change.

Redl's work influenced a number of other persons associated with the psychoeducational interpretation of children's social and emotional disorders that is called the conflict cycle. The conflict cycle (Long, 1974) is a framework by which the teacher can understand a child's behavior disorders; it provides insights into how such behaviors can be altered. The conflict cycle assumes that each child has a personality structure that is formed early in life. Psychological conflicts arise as the child tries to fulfill her own basic needs and the social expectations of parents; if the parental expectations interfere with basic needs, she is likely to develop a negative or inferior self-image. Such a child will perceive her interpersonal world negatively (e.g., as hostile, incompetent, and infantile) and behave accordingly, bringing these perceptions and behaviors to the school setting. At school, typical academic and social demands create stress for the pupil; she becomes highly anxious and begins to employ defense mechanisms and engage in immature expressions of feelings. These behavior patterns represent temporary solutions to the child's overwhelming anxiety, and they also provoke negative reactions from teachers and peers that add new sources of anxiety. In turn, the pupil's awareness of these negative reactions of others perpetuates her own maladaptive behavior and creates a self-fulfilling prophecy.

Psychoeducational intervention.   The basic goal of psychoeducational intervention is to alter a child's perceptions of herself and her environment; it is assumed that positive behavior changes will thereby be facilitated. Some of the methods for achieving this goal include life space interviewing (Redl, 1959); expressive therapies (Michielutte, 1974); play therapy (Axline, 1947); crisis intervention (Caplan, 1961); guided group interaction (Empey & Lubeck, 1971); the self-control curriculum (Fagen, Long, & Stevens, 1975); and developmental therapy (Wood, 1972, 1975).

The behavioral model is a major 20th-century development that has had enormous impact on special education for behaviorally disordered pupils. Many of the concepts of the behavioral model have been used intuitively for a long time by those wishing to change children's behavior (see Kazdin, 1978). Early in the 20th century, psychologists such as E.L. Thorndike, John Watson, and Ivan Pavlov published research and position papers arguing for an explanation of behavior in terms of the environmental stimuli that precede and/or follow it. In the first half of this century, however, therapeutic and educational applications of behaviorism to children's behavior disorders were relatively rare. Behaviorism as a model for understanding and treating human behavior disorders really received its impetus from the laboratory research on operant conditioning of B. F. Skinner and his students during the 1950s and early 1960s.

Skinner's operant conditioning theory makes a discrimination between two classes of behaviors: respondents and operants. Respondents are behaviors that are almost invariably produced by certain environmental or internal stimuli. For instance, loud, unexpected sounds almost invariably produce reflexive muscular contraction respondents. Some respondents are subject to learning in that stimuli that ordinarily do not elicit a respondent can acquire the power to do so by repeatedly being paired with the natural eliciting stimulus.

Skinner was far more concerned with the second type of behavior, operants. Most human behaviors are not automatically elicited by stimuli; they are emitted by people in response to circumstances. The likelihood that an operant behavior will be emitted again in similar future circumstances is determined by the consequences for that particular operant. Reinforcing consequences increase the chance that the operant will occur again; punishing consequences decrease the probability that it will recur.

Based on a massive amount of research in laboratories and practical situations, behaviorists have come to believe that most human behaviors and behavior changes can be understood in terms of the principles of operant conditioning, and that these principles can be used to teach a person to behave more adaptively, competently, and appropriately. Five of the major operant conditioning principles that account for behavior development and change, and that may be used as teaching procedures to improve children's behavior, are as follows:

1. Positive reinforcement is a procedure in which a specific behavior is followed by a reward, with the result that that behavior is more likely to occur in the future. For example, if a pupil accurately completes an assigned task within a specified time limit and receives free play time as a result, she is more likely to accurately complete future assignments.

2. Negative reinforcement, also a procedure designed to increase behavior, involves removing aversive stimuli following the performance of a specific behavior. For instance, if a boy politely asks a peer to refrain from loudly tapping his pencil during study time and the peer stops making the noise, the response of asking politely would be negatively reinforced by the removal of

the aversive pencil tapping, and the boy would be more likely to request politely in the future.

3. Punishment is a process in which an operant is followed by some aversive consequence and is therefore less likely to recur in the future. If an angry pupil throws books and trash on the classroom floor and as a consequence is required to clean up her mess and straighten the room in general, the angry behavior may be less likely to occur in the future.

4. Negative punishment includes procedures for decreasing a behavior by either removing a specific amount of reward (response-cost procedure) or removing access to rewarding events for a specific period of time (time-out procedure) when the inappropriate behavior occurs. For instance, unpermitted talking in class can result in the removal of a privilege or the loss of a specific amount of recess time; in either case, the goal is to utilize a negative punishment procedure to decrease the talking.

5. Extinction can also be used to decrease behavior that formerly has been reinforced. For instance, if a teacher believes she has been positively reinforcing a pupil's noisy disruptions by consistently talking things over with him when he disrupts, she may withhold her attention (the positive reinforcer) by totally ignoring the pupil's disruptions. This strategy is extinction if it succeeds in reducing or eliminating the intended behavior.

A basic concept in the behavioral model is that most human behavior is learned. The existence of emotions, thoughts, and feelings is recognized by behaviorists, but these phenomena are not considered important determinants of behavior. What is emphasized is the back-and-forth interplay and reciprocal influence of a person's behaviors and the environments they occur in. In the behavioral view, then, behavior disorders originate and are perpetuated through the operation of the same principles that regulate other behaviors—especially reinforcement, punishment, and extinction. For example, if incompetent, antisocial, bizarre, immature, or otherwise disordered behaviors are reinforced, they will begin to occur frequently and/or in more severe degrees. Research has shown that teachers unfortunately tend to pay a lot of attention to inappropriate child behavior patterns such as classroom aggression, disruption, disobedience, and so on; at the same time they largely ignore children whose behavior is industrious, quiet, or otherwise prosocial (Walker & Buckley, 1973). While teacher attention to disturbing behavior takes a variety of forms (e.g., reprimands, rule reminders, discussions about the propriety of rules, or public ridicule), each of these teacher reactions shares one important property: providing attention from an adult as a consequence of the disordered behavior. Thus, teachers can unwittingly encourage behavior disorders by misallocating their attention (Becker, Madsen, Arnold, & Thomas, 1967).

Another way in which children can unintentionally be taught to behave deviantly is through exposure to deviant models (Bandura, 1969). Especially if a child lives in a home, school, or community in which many individuals exhibit illegal, highly aggressive, bizarre, or otherwise maladjusted behavior, observational learning of such behavior patterns is quite likely. Additionally, films, television, and verbal and written acounts of deviant behavior provide additional sources of information on how to behave inappropriately.

In classroom methods and programs, behavioral interventionists often combine the basic teaching procedures—reinforcement, punishment, and extinction—into behavior-modification treatment packages. For instance, the token economy (Kazdin, 1977) is commonly utilized with the behaviorally disordered; it may involve some combination of positive reinforcement, extinction, and other behavior-modification procedures. Behavioral contracting utilizes several basic behavioral procedures along with a written specification of the relationships between desired behaviors and their consequences. Behavioral self-control procedures are becoming widely employed in schools; in this type of intervention, the pupil herself is responsible for observing, instructing, and/or reinforcing herself in order to change her own behavior (Thoresen & Mahoney, 1974). Behavioral techniques may also be applied within group-oriented contingencies (Litow & Pumroy, 1975), in which a group of pupils may jointly experience certain consequences depending on the behavior of one or more of its members. Detailed presentations of behavioral theory, intervention techniques, and school applications are widely available (e.g., Bandura, 1969; Cullinan, Epstein, & Kauffman, in press; Kazdin, 1980; O'Leary & O'Leary, 1977).

Applications of operant techniques with behaviorally disordered children gradually emerged in the early 1960s. First, these were individual applications to mildly or severely disordered children (e.g., Allen, Hart, Buell, Harris, & Wolf, 1964; Ferster & DeMyer, 1962; Hewett, 1964; Lovaas, 1966; Patterson, 1965; Wolf, Risley & Mees, 1964), but they soon became fully developed programs.

Perhaps the first behaviorally oriented public school program for disturbed children was the Arlington Project implemented by Haring and Phillips (1962). The primary features of the project were to provide a structured educational program through such procedures as controlling distracting stimuli; assigning small amounts of academic work at a time; giving clear, specific directions and instructions; communicating expectations that the student would perform appropriately; and providing predictable consequences for behavior. Although these specific procedures were not evaluated, class gains appeared to be quite favorable.

Very likely, the most widely known application of behavioral principles to educating children with behavior disorders was the engineered classroom by Hewett (1968, 1974) as featured in the Santa Monica Project. Hewett devised a hierarchy of educational goals that featured seven major levels (attention, response, order, exploratory, social, mastery, and achievement) through which children needed to progress. In the engineered classroom, an assessment system was devised to determine the extent to which each pupil had or had not achieved these educational goals. Behavior management and instructional activities designed to facilitate pupil progress included carefully structured daily activities, physical arrangement of the classroom into task centers, and a token reward system. Based on the evaluation data, the engineered classroom was effective in improving on-task behavior and improving some aspects of academic functioning (Hewett, 1968).

The value of a behaviorally oriented resource room program for improving the school functioning of disturbed pupils was evaluated by Quay and his associates (Quay, Glavin, Annesley, & Werry, 1972). Pupils assigned to the resource room program were of elementary school age, evidenced either extreme conduct problems or overly withdrawn behaviors, and, except for a few exceptions, evidenced poor academic achievement. The resource program was segmented into four 15-minute work periods. During the first three segments, pupils earned token reinforcers for starting work, continuing to work on, and finishing assigned academic tasks. In the final time period, pupils could use their tokens to buy access to a free-time area or save them for a higher valued item. The social behavior and academic achievement of the resource-room pupils improved substantially, but some of these improvements did not generalize to the pupil's regular classrooms.

In the 1970s, the Center at Oregon for Research in Behavioral Education of the Handicapped (CORBEH), a research and demonstration center funded by the Bureau of Education for the Handicapped, began to develop, evaluate, and disseminate educational packages for handicapped pupils. Although not specifically designed for children with behavior disorders, several "packaged" interventions have been very successful for children who evidence particular learning and behavior problems. Among the programs applicable for use with disturbed pupils in public school settings are (1) contingencies for learning, academic, and social skills (CLASS), designed for regular classroom teachers to modify disruptive pupil behaviors (Hops, Beickel & Walker, 1976); (2) the program for academic survival skills (PASS), developed to allow teachers to increase such educational readiness skills as attending to tasks, following directions, and working on assignments (Greenwood, Hops, Delquadri & Walker, 1974); (3) the procedures for establishing effective relationship skills (PEERS), an intervention to facilitate adaptive skills and interactions for socially withdrawn children (Hops, Guild, Fleischman, Paine, Street, Walker, & Greenwood, 1978); and (4) reprogramming environmental contingencies for effective social skills (RECESS), a program designed to improve the school and playground behavior of young children (Walker, Street, Garrett, & Crossen, 1978). Clearly these programs focus on some of the more common problems that confront teachers, and were designed for use in regular and special class settings. Also, these programs are chiefly noted for their adherence to behavioral principles; including the high degree of environmental structure, the specificity of defining and observing target behaviors, and the use of positive environmental contingencies to improve behavior.

In a sense, the behavioral model has come of age as an acceptable, highly appropriate educational treatment for disturbed children (Cullinan et al., in press). In addition to its uses in special education, applications of the behavioral approach have been described for use in other disciplines involved in helping behavior-disordered children, including counseling (Krumboltz & Thoresen, 1976); social work (Tharp & Wetzel, 1969; Thomas, 1974); psychotherapy (Agras, 1978); psychiatric nursing (O'Neil, McLaughlin, & Knapp, 1977); and medicine (Williams & Gentry, 1977). Presently, the behavioral model appears to be the most widely used approach for school intervention with behaviorally disordered children and youth (see Fink, Glass, & Guskin, 1975).

Other Models of Behavior Disorder

Two other models, the biological model and the ecological model, have also been developed in recent years. These models have not yet had as much direct impact as the psychodynamic and the behavioral models, but they contribute substantially to our understanding of behavior disorders of children.

Biological model.   The biological model includes a number of ideas about the origins and treatment of behavior disorders. Cattell (1950) grouped biological factors in development into four classes: hereditary, innate, congenital, and constitutional. Hereditary and innate factors are those that originate prior to or at conception; normal genetic processes are involved in hereditary contributions to development and deviance, while genetic or chromosomal errors from various causes would constitute innate factors. Congenital factors refer to physical trauma, toxins, infections, maternal malnutrition, and other circumstances that can result in unfortunate consequences for the developing individual in utero. Finally, constitutional factors refer to similar factors that have biological consequences to the individual postnatally. One possible consequence of such biological factors is brain damage or dysfunctioning, which obviously can have substantial effects upon the individual's abilities and performance in the home, school, and other environments. Biological influences upon behavior disorders have been reviewed by Achenbach (1974) and Cullinan, Epstein, and Lloyd (in press). In general, like all of the available models, the biological model proposes numerous interesting and suggestive links with behavior disorders, but few definite cause-and-effect relationships. There is substantially greater reason to accept biological disorders as causing the rarer severe behavior disorders than the much more common mild and moderate behavior disorders.

While educators usually play little or no role in the administration of treatments developed from the biological model, they need to be aware of some of these treatments along with the controversial issues involved. For example, drug therapy for children with behavior disorders is not only an unresolved professional issue (e.g., Adelman & Compas, 1977; Connors & Werry, 1979), but it has also become a public controversy (Hentoff, 1970; Schrag & Divoky, 1975). Other biological interventions, such as massive doses of vitamins (Cott, 1972) and dietary restrictions (Feingold, 1975) are also controversial. The biological model also suggests preventive strategies such as genetic assessment, counseling (or even manipulation), and improvement in the medical and nutritional care of pregnant mothers and young children. Desirable as these strategies may be, it is not yet clear what effects they can have on the overall problem of behavior disorders.

Ecological model.   In the past 20 years, the ecological model has begun to capture the attention of educators of behaviorally disordered pupils. This model stems from the research and writing of professionals in diverse fields—including ethology (e.g., Lorenz, 1965); anthropology (Benedict, 1934); and psychology (Barker, 1968; Barker & Wright, 1955; Willems, 1965)—all of which are concerned with a more inclusive view of behavior and environment. The ecological model assumes that the interaction of an individual with his social and physical environment over time is more than the sum of its parts; in other words, if this behavioral ecology system is broken down and its components are studied in isolation, the result will be a fragmented and misleading picture.

In its application as a model for understanding children's behavior disorders, the ecological model provides more of an orientation than a coherent theory at the present time. In this orientation, the major focus is upon behavior ecosystems, which are patterns of interaction between an individual's behavior and the social and physical environment. When this behavior is more or less in harmony with environmental restrictions, demands, and expectations, there is "goodness-of-fit." A behavior disorder is the lack of "goodness-of-fit"; it is not a property of any particular child, but a disturbance in the patterns of interchange between the individual and the environment. When goodness-of-fit is disturbed, however, the environment (usually, authoritative individuals such as parents, teachers, or legal personnel) sets in motion the process of "labeling" (Des Jarlais & Paul, 1978). Labeling locates the source of disturbance in the individual perceived as having initiated disturbances in "goodness-of-fit" in that ecosystem.

Ecological treatment recommendations mainly consist of general orientations rather than specific practices. One major ecological recommendation is that treatment goals should include needed modifications in the environment as well as changes in the child's functioning (Rhodes, 1970a). It is also emphasized that any localized ecosystem (e.g., the classroom or school) almost certainly is linked subtly, but importantly, to other environmental settings (e.g., the home or community), so real intervention demands looking beyond the immediate problem for larger solutions. As a consequence, proponents of the ecological model have insisted that the traditional role of the teacher be redefined and expanded to produce increased impact beyond the boundaries of the school (Hobbs, 1966; Rhodes, 1970b).

Summary of Models

Attempts to determine the origins of behavior disorders have provoked lively debate and research, but scientific investigations to substantiate any of the positions have as yet not been forthcoming. Indeed, the available evidence indicates that there are many potential causes of children's behavior disorders. At present, no one model—psychoanalytic, behavioral, biological, or ecological—can thoroughly explain the origins of behavior disorders. In fact, if the source of behavior disorders is actually determined at some future date, it will very likely represent a synthesis or interaction of the various models.

DEFINITIONS

To define something is to identify exactly its nature, distinguishing characteristics, and boundaries. By this yardstick, many important human relationship phenomena, including "behavior disorders," defy definition. Still, there is no shortage of attempts to define behavior disorders.

Despite their problems, definitions of behavior disorders carry important implications. First, because they frequently reflect how an individual, district, or agency views behavior disorders, definitions may indicate important information about services: which interventions will be utilized; how a treatment program will be communicated to the child, parents, community, and other individuals involved; and so on. Second, definitions serve as a basis for estimates of prevalence, thus helping to determine who will receive special services. Third, definitions impact legislative, administrative, and advocacy-group decisions related to education for behaviorally disordered pupils, including such issues as teacher preparation, research and development grants, and state and local funding levels. Finally, definitions are critical in the continuing research effort to understand behavior disorders. Unfortunately, it is not unusual that potentially important findings of one research study may be of no use to other investigators because of questions about the characterisitics of the behaviorally disordered children involved.

Definitions of behavior disorders are intended to serve various purposes, and there are several types of definitions. Three types of definitions are relevant to the study of children's behavior disorders: research, authoritative, and administrative definitions.

Research Definitions

The function of a research definition is to clarify the external validity of a research study by indicating the population of children or behavior disorders to which the findings are applicable. Effective research definitions help other researchers to integrate new research findings with existing ones and to duplicate critical or controversial studies. These definitions can also help special educators, clinicians, and other practitioners to determine whether the outcome of a study has any application to the children with whom they deal. One of the main problems with research definitions is that there is no consensually agreed-upon classification system for children's behavior disorders to which research definitions could be keyed. Until such time as an agreeable system emerges, practitioners must judge research definitions on the basis of how clearly they define the children studied, so that each practitioner can make an individual judgment about the value of the findings to his or her professional needs.

Authoritative Definitions

Authoritative definitions are statements that reflect the professional training, experience, philosophy, and/or theoretical orientation of the individual or group that constructs them. Authoritative definitions are often intended to structure a text or other discussion of behavior disorders, or occasionally to provide an innovative analysis or provoke consideration of some position. Some authoritative definitions have had much influence on special education for the behaviorally disordered.

Figure 4-1 presents some of the numerous authoritative definitions of behavior disorders. Note that one can find definitions oriented to biological, psychodynamic, behavioral, ecological, and eclectic viewpoints. Although these definitions and the numerous additional ones compiled by others (e.g., Hewett & Forness, 1974) are far from compatible, some areas of common concern can be seen.

Administrative Definitions

The purpose of administrative definitions as found in rules, regulations, and pronouncements of local, state, or federal governmental organizations are a third type of definition of children's behavior disorders. Administrative definitions guide the delivery of appropriate educational services to children with behavior disorders. For example, the United States Office of Education's definition, as contained in Public Law 91-230, is found in many papers disseminated by the Bureau of Education for the Handicapped (BEH). Interestingly, the BEH defini-

Biological. "A biogenic mental disorder is a severe behavior disorder that results solely from the effects of biological factors, including both gene action and the effects of the physical-chemical environment" (Rimland, 1969, p. 706).

General psychiatric. "An emotionally disturbed child is one whose progressive personality development is interfered with or arrested by a variety of factors so that he shows impairment in the capacity expected of him for his age and endowment: (1) for reasonably accurate perception of the world around him; (2) for impulse control; (3) for satisfying and satisfactory relations with others; (4) for learning; or (5) any combination of these" (Reprinted with permission from the Joint Commission on Mental Health of Children. *Crisis in Child Mental Health*. New York: Harper & Row, 1969, p. 253).

Ecological. "In the community participation analysis of emotional disturbance, the problem is seen as . . . a reciprocal condition which exists when intense coping responses are released within a human community by a community member's atypical behavior and responses. The triggering stimulus, the rejoinder of the microcommunity, and the ensuring transactions are all involved in emotional disturbance" (Reprinted with permission from Rhodes, W. C. A. community participation analysis of emotional disturbance. *Exceptional Children*, 1970, *37*, 311 (a)).

Behavioral. "A psychological disorder is said to be present when a child emits behavior that deviates from a discretionary and relative social norm in that it occurs with a frequency or intensity that authoritative adults in the child's environment judge, under the circumstances, to be either too high or too low" (Ross, 1974, p. 14).

Educational. "The emotionally handicapped child demonstrates one or more of the following characteristics to a marked extent and over a period of time: (1) an inability to learn which cannot be explained by intellectual, sensory or health factors; (2) an inability to build or maintain satisfactory interpersonal relations with peers and teachers; (3) inappropriate types of behavior or feelings under normal conditions; (4) a general pervasive mood of unhappiness or depression; and (5) a tendency to develop physical symptoms, pains, or fears associated with personal or school problems (From Bower, E. M. *The Early Identification of Emotionally Handicapped Children in School*, (2nd ed.), 1969. Courtesy of Charles C Thomas, Publisher, Springfield, Illinois, pp. 22–23).

Fig. 4-1. Selected authoritative definitions of behavior disorders.

tion is virtually identical to the one given by Bower (1969), which appears in Figure 4-1, except that the BEH version excludes pupils who are merely "socially maladjusted."

State educational agencies also provide definitions of behaviorally disordered children that are presumably designed to help state and local services find such pupils. Most obviously, a state definition identifies the behavioral, social, and other characteristics of those pupils who are eligible for specialized services; at least theoretically, this strongly influences whether or not a specific pupil will be served. Because of the important role that administrative definitions play in the education of handicapped pupils, several investigators have recently reviewed state definitions (Morse, Cutler, & Fink, 1964; Schultz, Hirshoren, Manton, & Henderson, 1971). More recently, Epstein, Cullinan, and Sabatino (1977) surveyed how behavior disorders were defined by state law, rule, or regulation. They concluded that (1) there was definitely a lack of agreement as to what constitutes a behavior disorder; (2) the terms that were used were too vague and difficult to measure accurately; and (3) obsolete medical-psychiatric viewpoints were common. These findings are in agreement with earlier reports by Schultz et al. (1971) and Morse et al. (1964).

Problems with Definitions

Clearly, one of the most obvious problems with definitions of children's behavior disorders is that no consensus has yet been achieved. Shortcomings in the existing research, authoritative, and administrative definitions can be readily found. Additionally, the very notion of defining behavior disorders has been questioned because of implications about the potential harmful effects of labeling pupils (Lilly, 1979; MacMillan, Jones, & Aloia, 1974); the overlapping nature of mild handicaps (Hallahan & Kauffman, 1976; Kauffman, 1977); and the confusion over terminology (T. L. Miller & Epstein, 1979).

At the heart of the problem is that most of the terms and ideas put forward in definitions have not lent themselves to being "operationally defined"—i.e., clearly stated in ways that can be adequately measured. Some of these terms will remain difficult to operationally define, particularly those concerned with a pupil's attitudes, feelings, and internal states of mind. The instruments developed to measure such concepts are questionable because of validity and reliability problems. However, other important constructs such as severity and chronicity appear to be amenable to operational definition and careful measurement, given sufficient effort and care.

Proposed Definition

We offer the following proposal in the belief that a definition of behavior disorders of pupils is important, and that as special educators we can profit from the strengths and weaknesses of past definitional efforts. This definition, presented by Cullinan et al. (in press) is an attempt to incorporate objective features into a definition insofar as possible:

> Behavior disorders of a pupil are behavior characteristics that deviate from educators' standards of normality and impair the functioning of that pupil or others. These behavior characteristics appear as: (1) environmental conflicts and/or (2) personal conflicts, and are usually accompanied by learning disorders.

There are several features in this definition that deserve expanded discussion. For instance, the term "behavior characteristics" indicates that educators are concerned most about what the pupil does (e.g., movements) and the effects these behaviors have on objects and people in the environment. Additionally, the phrase "deviate from educators' standards" acknowledges that behavior is labeled disordered when it departs from some environmental standard and becomes unacceptable to the perceiver (i.e., teacher, parent, or psychologist). Experience has provided us all with expectations about what is typical in day-to-day situations, and these situational expectations also take into account the pupil's age, sex, and other characteristics. Furthermore, behavior disorders often involve behavior patterns that are not rare or unique, but that create concern because the frequency or intensity is either too much or too little. Educators are also likely to tolerate mild behavior problems for awhile, but become disturbed about maladaptive situations that last too long. Taken together, these qualifiers may be used to differentiate transient, setting-specific, or mild behavior problems (those that do not require specialized services) from problems that are obviously of a severe or chronic nature.

The behavior characteristics identified in the definition acknowledge that children labeled as behavior disordered manifest behaviors that are directed outward, creating disturbances in the environment and/or are directed inward, creating problems for the individual himself. Additionally, these pupils usually manifest learning disorders, including some degree of handicap in general or specific learning abilities, as well as academic or other skill deficits.

Definitions of pupil's behavior disorders are clearly deserving of concern, attention, and study on the part of special education practitioners, researchers, and other individuals involved with school children with behavior disorders. Our definition's recommendations, general and ambitious as they are, suggest one way in which steps can be taken toward a more relevant and useable definition of behavior disorders.

PREVALENCE

The term *prevalence* refers to the number of instances of something during a specific period of time (Graham, 1979). Prevalence information on behaviorally disordered pupils is important to those who head special education programs and need to predict funding, personnel, and other requirements to provide special services to behaviorally disordered pupils. Prevalence data can also indicate how a behavior disorder varies according to area, time, sex, age, socioeconomic status, and so on; therefore, prevalence has implications for understanding causes and treatment of behavior disorders. But actually determining prevalence is difficult, because prevalence figures are dependent on the definition used (Hallahan & Kauffman, 1976), and how it is operationalized (Wood & Zabel, 1978). Because there are many different ways to define and measure behavior disorders, prevalence figures often vary from study to study.

In one of the first major attempts to estimate prevalence, C. R. Rogers (1942) studied over 1500 elementary school pupils in Columbus, Ohio. He reported that if mild disturbances were included, one of every three children would be identified as behavior disordered. In a large-scale study in California, Bower (1969) found that, on the average, about three children in every classroom (roughly 10 percent) were experiencing substantial maladjustment. White and Harris (1961), from a review of six prevalence studies, determined that about 4–7 percent of the school-aged population may be considered in need of specialized educational services. Glidewell and Swallow (1968) analyzed 27 prevalence studies published between 1925 and 1967; despite great differences in the measurement procedures and populations involved, the authors concluded that approximately 30 percent of elementary school children present some deviant behavior, 10 percent display enough disordered behavior to justify special attention, and 4 percent experience behavior disorders severe enough to justify referral to psychological or special treatment services.

Prevalence estimates from state departments of special education also vary considerably. In their national survey, Schultz et al. (1971) noted that 18 states used a prevalence estimate of 2 percent, 7 states estimated 3 percent, 6 states cited 5 percent, and 7 states offered no estimates. The federal administrative agency for special education, the Bureau of Education for the Handicapped (reorganized in

1980 as the Office for Special Education and Rehabilitative Services of the Department of Education), estimates prevalence at 2 percent of the school population. This estimate is influential, since it is used in formulas for funding special education for these children. However, it is considerably more conservative than most of the estimates derived from actual surveys of behavior disorders of pupils. Credible prevalence information will probably remain elusive until common definition and measurement problems are resolved.

CLASSIFICATION

In any area of study, progress is facilitated when the things under study can be described and classified. Classification is "the act or process of arranging or grouping objects or facts by classes, based on similar attributes or relations; the process may involve the gathering together of similar things in classes or the splitting of general groups into more specific divisions" (Prugh, Engel & Morse, 1975, p. 272). The classification of behavior disorders has implications for decisions as to what is wrong in a particular child's case, what the sources of the problem are, what treatments will be beneficial, and what is the prognosis (Achenbach, 1974). To make a classification, information must be collected about various child characteristics; depending on the particular classification system used, such characteristics may include behavior, behavior problems, mental abilities, personality patterns, medical information, personal life history, or some combination of these.

There have been two major approaches to classifying behavior disorders of children—the clinical-deductive approach and the inductive approach.

Clinical-Deductive

Clinical-deductive classification begins with an overall theory or collection of ideas that suggests what categories of maladjustment ought to be found among behaviorally disordered individuals. Although clinical-deductive classification systems for adult disturbances have been available since the late 1800s, childhood disorders were essentially ignored until very recently. Most clinical-deductive systems are substantially based on the psychodynamic model, and adopt a medical orientation to behavior disorders in that (1) the disorder is viewed as only a symptom of some underlying internal dysfunction; (2) the disorder resides within the individual; and (3) the disorder is similar in nature to medical diseases (Phillips & Dragnus, 1971).

The American Psychiatric Association has published several editions of its *Diagnostic and Statistical Manual of Mental Disorders*, the official classification system for emotional and behavior disorders. The second edition, published in 1968, used one of its ten categories exclusively for disorders of childhood and adolescence. This system was widely criticized for its lack of specificity in describing symptoms and the limited range of childhood disorders included (Achenbach, 1974; Phillips & Dragnus, 1971). The third revision (DSM-III), published in 1980, seems to have addressed some major criticisms by providing more categories for the diagnosis of childhood and adolescent disorders; also, there are more specific operational criteria for diagnostic purposes, and a severity rating is included to differentiate degrees of disturbance (Quay, 1979). Whether these revisions make DSM-III actually more useful and sound than its predecessors remains to be seen. Other clinical deductive systems include ones put forward by the Group for Advancement of Psychiatry (1966), the World Health Organizations' Multiaxial Classification System (Rutter, 1969), and the Developmental Profile (Freud, 1965).

Inductive Classification

Dissatisfied with traditional deductive classification, some mental health professionals have investigated the inductive (also called dimensional or statistical) approach. This strategy begins not with established theories or other preconceptions, but with data on behaviors and other characteristics of children. Then, statistical methods are applied to the data to identify those behaviors that tend to occur together. Such a collection of behaviors is often called a factor or dimension; usually two or more factors are found in this type of study, and these are the categories of an inductive classification system. However, these categories are patterns of behavior disorder, whereas in the clinical-deductive approach, categories are types of person.

Several inductive classification systems have been developed (e.g., Achenbach, 1966; Patterson, 1964). Perhaps the most widely known example is based on the Quay–Peterson behavior problem checklist (Quay & Peterson, 1975). Based on a considerable amount of research (see Quay, 1977), four dimensions of behavior disorders were identified.

1. A conduct disorder is a collection of verbally and physically aggressive behaviors toward peers and adults. Characteristics typical of this pattern are disobedience, uncooperativeness in a group, showing off, bullying, hyperactivity, and temper tantrums.
2. A personality disorder encompasses behaviors or attitudes that involve withdrawal from interactions with the environment. Feelings of inferiority, fear, anxiety, and unhappiness are characteristics associated with this dimension.
3. Immaturity–inadequacy represents behaviors that are inappropriate to the age of the child; some of the associated behaviors are sluggishness, lack of interest, and being easily led by others.
4. Socialized delinquency is often found among adolescents, especially juvenile delinquents. This dimension involves characteristics such as stealing and participating in gang activities.

These behavior problem checklist dimensions are found among groups of nondisturbed as well as disturbed children; the latter, however, are typically much more extreme (high-scoring) on these dimensions (Cullinan, Epstein, & Dembinski, 1979).

Much more research is needed on classification of children's behavior disorders. The available evidence offers little support for clinical-deductive systems, but many professionals believe that the DSM-III will be more satisfactory than earlier guidelines. On the other hand, clinical-inductive systems satisfy many requirements of a useful classification system for children's behavior disorders and have relevance for special educational efforts.

CHARACTERISTICS

What characteristics identify a child as behaviorally disordered? A simple answer to this straightforward question is not possible for several reasons. As described previously, there are many problems with describing and measuring the social, emotional, and learning characteristics of these behaviorally disordered pupils. Also, there is no typical behavior problem that characterizes all behaviorally disordered children; their problems are varied, and like all children, each is a unique individual. Further complicating the issue is the fact that the study of characteristics of behaviorally disordered children is closely intertwined with the concept of normality. Identifying a child or a behavior as disordered means there is some variance from normalcy, but no absolute criteria exist to differentiate between normal and abnormal. The judgment of a characteristic as disordered must involve some degree of subjectivity.

Several authorities have prepared lists of the most common problematic behaviors that disturbed children are thought to show. A representative sample of these characteristics appears in Figure 4-2. Most behaviorally disordered children will confront teachers with one or more of these behaviors, and sooner or later the special education teacher may see all of them, but no one disturbed pupil will display all these characteristics. All-inclusive lists do not and cannot provide easy answers regarding the outstanding characteristics of the disturbed. However, the

Acts out	Inattentive
Achieves poorly	Incoherent
Aggressive	Inflexible
Aloof	Irresponsible
Anxious	Isolated
Attention-seeking	Jealous
Behaves oddly	Lazy
Boisterous	Moody
Clumsy	Negative
Cries easily	Nervous
Daydreams	Oppositional
Destructive	Overly shy
Depressed	Passive-aggressive
Dislikes school	Preoccupied
Disobedient	Repeats self frequently
Disruptive	Restless
Distractible	Reticent
Enuretic	Self-conscious
Excitable	Sluggish
Fidgety	Steals
Fights	Swears
Hyperactive	Tense
Hypersensitive	Throws temper tantrums
Hypoactive	Truant
Hypochondriacal	Uncooperative
Immature	Understands self poorly
Impertinent	Unmotivated
Inadequate	Withdrawn

Fig. 4-2. Frequently cited behavioral characteristics of disturbed children.

results of a variety of research studies—on prevalence, classification, prognosis, and other issues—have suggested which characteristics are most central to children's behavior disorders.

Research in clinics and schools with children identified as disturbed has provided some fairly consistent results that can help organize a meaningful discussion of behavioral characteristics. Although the instruments (e.g., parent rating or teacher rating), settings (e.g., clinics or schools), age, geographical locales (e.g., urban, rural, or suburban), and other demographic factors varied from study to study, certain general patterns of behavior disorder repeatedly emerged. Additionally, within each pattern certain more specific problems tended to account for much of the overall area. There appear to be three major patterns of behavior disorders, which could be labeled environmental conflicts, personal conflicts, and learning disorders. Environmental conflicts are patterns of behavior disorder directed toward the external environment, especially people in the environment. The specific behavior problems found within this pattern are aggression–disruption, hyperactivity, and social maladjustment. Personal conflicts are patterns of behavior disorders that seemingly are directed inward, creating or perpetrating problems for the individual himself. Anxiety and social withdrawal are behavior problems characteristic of such a pattern. Learning disorders are characteristics that many behaviorally disordered children exihibit, which interfere with their chances of profiting from academic instruction and other educational tasks. The more specific problems associated with this pattern are academic problems and learning aptitude disabilities.

As suggested by some of the research on inductive classification (e.g., Quay, 1979), it must be remembered that the characteristics attributed to disturbed children are in many respects similar to those of normal children. In fact, prevalence studies (e.g., Lapouse & Monk, 1958; MacFarlane, Allen, & Honzik, 1954; Oliver, 1974; Roberts & Baird, 1972) have often reported a relatively high degree of behavior disorders in the child population in general. What distinguishes the behavior of disturbed and nondisturbed pupils is very likely a difference in the amount, duration, and intensity of their behavior problems. For instance, many young children cry occasionally; an older child who cries frequently would probably be considered abnormal. Many pupils fidget for a small portion of the day, but those who are fidgety throughout much of the school day are considered abnormal. Many youngsters talk in a subdued voice now and again, but those whose speech is so soft as to virtually never be heard are considered abnormal. Thus, a judgement of behavior disorder is likely to be made not solely on the basis of a particular behavior, but because the amount, duration, and/or intensity with which the behavior occurs is unusual.

Aggression – Disruption

Aggression–disruption is commonplace in our (and nearly every) society; in fact, some aggression is tolerated and even encouraged in children. Assertiveness in pursuing goals, standing up for one's rights, and so on, are admired by parents and teachers. Conversely, behavior patterns that are destructive, or inflict pain or discomfort on others, irritate and disturb adults and children alike. In schools, aggression may be manifest in many forms, including physical and verbal abuse of others, destruction of school property, and disobedience of rules and regulations. Teachers frequently find these patterns among the most disturbing and difficult to manage in classrooms (Bullock & Brown, 1972). Children who persistently exhibit these behavior patterns are likely to be labeled as "conduct disordered," "acting-out," or "aggressive."

Although we all "know it when we see it," aggression is not easy to define. It has been characterized in many different ways. Labeling of a behavior as aggressive involves a judgment based on criteria including the type and intensity of the behavior, the degree of pain or injury inflicted, the intentions attributed to the aggressor, and characteristics of the aggressor and the labeler (Bandura, 1973).

Along with academic problems, aggression is one of the most common reasons for referring a pupil to special education classes and mental health clinics. Between 20 and 30 % of child referrals to mental health clinics by teachers and parents are for aggression and related conduct problems (e.g., Gilbert, 1957; Patterson, 1964). Aggressive behavior is generally listed by teachers as the pupil behavior problem of greatest concern (e.g., Bullock & Brown, 1972; Morse et al., 1964; Wickman, 1928).

Aggression, especially in severe degrees, does not "go away." It has been found that aggression manifested in the preschool and primary grades persists well into adolescence (Kagan & Moss, 1962). Childhood aggression is related to adult behavior patterns such as anger and aggressive retaliation (Feshbach, 1970); consistently over-aggressive children are at increased risk for juvenile delinquency and various forms of adult maladjustment (Kohlberg, LaCrosse, & Ricks, 1972; Robins, 1979). Milder degrees of aggression, however, are not strongly predictive of adult maladjustment (Kohlberg et al., 1972).

Hyperactivity

Excessive motor movements, failure to sit still, disruptive behavior, and flightiness make the hyperactive child stand out from others at home and school. Persistent hyperactivity is likely to cause concern among parents, teachers, siblings, and peers. Yet a great deal of confusion surrounds the term. It is sometimes used to refer to excessive movement of the child's limbs or whole body. However, research has shown that any judgment that movement is or is not excessive varies according to the type of situation (e.g., classroom or playground), the child's age and sex, observer characteristics, and other important factors (e.g., Ross & Ross, 1976). Hyperactivity is also used to refer to a collection of problems, including mild deficits in attention, learning disabilities, impulsiveness, emotional problems, and uncertain ("soft") signs of brain disorder, as well as excessive movement. Other terms for this collection of problems are hyperkinetic syndrome, minimal brain dysfunction, or attention-deficit disorder. The broad meaning of hyperactivity is controversial (see Werry, 1979). Some researcher's maintain that all of these problems are caused by subtle, difficult-to-detect brain disorders (Strauss & Lehtinen, 1947; Wender, 1971), but other authorities dispute this or point out that the available evidence does not permit such a firm conclusion (Werry, 1979).

Hyperactivity is a common behavior problem of childhood. Teachers judge between 15 and 30 percent elementary school-aged children as restless and disruptive (Miller, Palkes, & Stewart, 1973; Werry & Quay, 1971), and approximately 50 percent of the referrals to clinics are for hyperactivity. Typically, hyperactivity is noted at around 6 or 7 years of age. The disorder also tends to be persistent: while individuals identified early as hyperactive may not show excessive activity in adolescence, they do tend to show various problems of learning, school behavior, and vocational adjustment (Weiss, Hechtman, & Perlman, 1978; Weiss, Minde, Werry, Douglas & Nemeth, 1974).

Social Maladjustment

Social maladjustment refers to actual violations of law and other antisocial acts that break school or other regulations. Recent statistics on juvenile delinquency, along with media reports and the everyday experience of many people, indicate that there is an "epidemic" of juvenile delinquency in many areas; even these unpleasant statistics underestimate the size of the problem in terms of unreported crimes against person and property, lost instructional time, teacher "burnout," and other unfortunate side effects of social maladjustment.

Like many other problem characteristics, social maladjustment is troublesome to define. The term juvenile delinquency has been defined in many ways—a superego deficiency, a moral flaw, a brain disorder, a personality problem. There are also purely legal definitions (Wirt & Briggs, 1965). On the behavior problem checklist (Quay & Peterson, 1975), the "socialized delinquency" factor includes such problems as "belongs to a gang," "truancy from school," "has bad companions," and "steals in company with others."

Social maladjustment would seem to put the youngster at high risk for maladjustment in older adolescence and adulthood. Robins (1966) found that children and youth referred to mental health clinics for socially maladjusted and delinquent behaviors were likely to show many kinds of adult maladjustment: high arrest rates, poor health conditions, high divorce rates, low occupational status, alienation from family and friends, extensive use of social and welfare services, and excessive alcoholism. Their children also seem to have behavior problems. Admission to a correctional institution is an especially strong predictor of continuing maladjustment (Robins, 1979). Glueck and Glueck (1968) also found the prognosis for socially maladjusted children to be grim.

Social Withdrawal

Children who are withdrawn do not create overt disturbances and generally are not listed as the most severe problems for teachers. Indeed, because teachers are confronted with more overt problems from other children, withdrawn children may be quite easy to forget in the school setting. Still, in many classrooms, there will be children who show social withdrawal. Their behavior often causes teachers to infer that they are self-conscious, uncommunicative, shy, sad, and moody, and they usually fail to participate in school activities.

Greenwood, Walker, and Hops (1977) delineated two types of withdrawal: social withdrawal and social isolation or rejection. Social withdrawal affects children who never or almost never initiate social interactions; the problem is generally due to undeveloped social skills or fear of personal interactions. Social isolation or rejection, on the other hand, applies to children who initiate social interactions, but are ignored or rarely reciprocated by others.

The prevalence of withdrawal, while significant, appears to be lower than that of the various problems of externalizing. Research indicates that about 15 percent of all child clinic referrals are for withdrawal (Gilbert, 1957; M. E. Rogers, Lilenfield, & Pasamanick, 1955). Referrals are greatest for children between 6 and 10 years of age.

Withdrawal alone does not appear to be a clear-cut predictor of later maladjustment (see Kohlberg et al., 1972; Strain, Cooke, & Apolloni, 1976). This may mean that children "outgrow" withdrawal and that it is easily treated through the everyday understanding and help that teachers and parents ordinarily give to withdrawn youngsters, or it may mean that measures of adult maladjustment are not sensitive to the mild or subtle problems that are experienced by the withdrawn child. At any rate, positive social interaction is an important, desirable feature of growing up, and withdrawal may deprive the child of significant learning opportunities (Bijou, 1966). Teachers cannot afford to hope that withdrawn children will eventually become "ready" to interact; they are well-advised to take action to help children do so (Strain et al., 1976).

Anxiety

Highly anxious children present problems that can test even the best of teachers. Mischel (1971) identified three common aspects of anxiety: the individual experiences a conscious feeling of fear and anticipated danger; undergoes physiological arousal, bodily discomfort, and in some cases, physical changes; and may experience disorganization in cognitive and problem-solving skills. Anxiety may be evidenced in children who predict dreadful results when given a test, become nervous and irritable when presented with an academic task, refuse to come forward when asked to take their turn speaking in front of the class, or become ill when it is time to leave for school. Anxious children are also described as fearful, nervous, tense, overly sensitive, and lacking in self-confidence. These and other behaviors indicative of anxiety, especially a chronic pattern of anxiety, may not always create classroom disturbances but frequently frustrate and alarm teachers. The fact that feelings of anxiety are common to most of us complicates the problem of deciding the point at which anxiety exceeds the boundaries of normality.

The nature of anxiety is controversial: for example, psychodynamic theorists view anxiety as a basic cause of most behavior disorders of children, while operant behaviorists do not give it an important place in explanations of behavior disorders. These positions are obviously contradictory to one another. However, both are compatible with the statement that anxious children often develop a variety of behavior patterns that are frequently viewed as disordered and that seem to produce personal unhappiness, impaired social and intellectual functioning, and a vicious cycle of maladaptive behavior.

Prevalence research on fears and worries of normal children indicate that at least this type of anxiety is fairly common among children. Lapouse and Monk (1959) found that over 40 percent of elementary school-aged children show a large number of fears and worries. With increasing age, the number of fears lessened. Interestingly, the authors also reported that children with many fears and worries were *not* particularly likely to show other problems that might be logically associated with anxiety, such as nightmares, bed-wetting, nail-biting, thumb-sucking, and so on. According to national data on persons using outpatient psychiatric clinic services in the United States, about 4 percent of boys and girls aged 5 to 17 were diagnosed as having "anxiety reactions" (Rosen, Bahn, & Kramer, 1964). Lahey and Ciminero (1980) estimated that 2 or 3 percent of children show disorders of anxiety and withdrawal.

The prognosis for anxiety disorders is generally much more favorable than for other types of disorders. The rate of improvement for untreated anxiety disorders is fairly high (Rutter, Tizard, Yule, Graham, & Whitmore, 1976) treatments for severe fears can be highly successful (Miller, Barrett, Hampe & Noble, 1972), and anxiety disorders of childhood do not usually portend serious adult maladjustment of any kind (Kohlberg et al., 1972; Robins, 1979). On the other hand, anxiety disorders are undoubtedly disturbing to the child, family, and classroom during the time they exist, and therefore, must be targeted for school intervention.

Academic Problems

Behaviorally disordered pupils perform significantly more poorly than normal students on reading, arithmetic, and spelling achievement tests (Glavin & DeGirolamo, 1970; Kitano, 1959; Motto & Wilkins, 1968; Stone & Rowley, 1964). In a national study of educational programs for the behaviorally disordered, Morse et al. (1964) found that most teachers perceived academic retardation to be an important accompaniment of behavior disorders. These and other studies support a position taken by Bower (1969) that poor academic achievement is a most significant characteristic of behaviorally disordered children.

There are many ideas as to why children in general, and behaviorally disordered pupils in particular, often fail to achieve academically: biological, home, community, and other factors have been implicated. However, it must be acknowledged that schools themselves may contribute to educational failure. Kauffman (1977) noted five possible ways in which this may occur: (1) insensitivity of educators to children's individuality; (2) inappropriate (particularly inappropriately low) teacher expectations; (3) inconsistent classroom management; (4) instruction in nonfunctional skills; and (5) improper methods of reinforcement. It is unclear whether behavior disorders result in academic problems, or academic problems result in behavior disorders, or both behavior and academic problems are caused by some other factor(s); in all probability, individual children could be found to illustrate all of these possibilities.

Poor school achievement, by itself, is probably not a good predictor of maladjustment in adulthood (Kohlberg et al., 1972), but poor school performance rarely occurs in isolation. Children who show both academic problems and severe externalizing behavior disorders (aggression, hyperactivity, social maladjustment) are at high risk for becoming criminal, alcoholic, severely disturbed, and otherwise maladjusted in adulthood (Kauffman, 1977; Robins, 1979).

Learning Aptitude Disabilities

Children with mild behavior disorders often show some degree of disability in general learning aptitude and in certain specific abilities. Surveys of measured intelligence of these children indicate that their IQs can range from 70, or even lower, to high levels of intellectual giftedness; however, the bulk of evidence also indicates that most of these IQs fall a little below normal, perhaps in the 80–100 IQ range (see Kauffman, 1977). Because IQ is closely linked to educational, social, and personal adjustment (Kohlberg et al., 1972), the lower general intellectual ability of many behaviorally disordered pupils is probably closely connected to their academic problems, and it may be related to their tendency toward other behavior problem characteristics.

Behaviorally disordered children also show deficits in certain specific aptitudes related to learning, including problems usually associated with learning disabled pupils. Hallahan and Kauffman (1976) proposed that "learning disabilities" is a collection of learning problems that frequently characterizes educationally handicapped pupils, regardless of which category ("learning disability," "behavior disorder," "educable mental retardation") they have been assigned for the purposes of special education. Clearly, the behaviorally disordered may show important learning disabilities, including problems in attention and in solving problems.

Any child who is inattentive to teacher instructions, distracted by events irrelevant to learning, or cannot concentrate for long periods, will often fail in educational situations. Pioneering educational programs for behaviorally disordered pupils (e.g., Haring & Phillips, 1962; Hewett, 1968) assigned a high priority to providing the proper structure and training to increase pupils' attention to learning tasks. There is some research evidence suggesting that attention problems are likely to be found among pupils with behavior and learning problems (Keogh & Margolis, 1976), especially those showing persistent hyperactivity (Denton & McIntire, 1978). Also, the fact that many behavior-modification studies with behaviorally disordered pupils have concentrated on increasing their attention to assigned tasks (e.g., Broden, Hall, Dunlap, & Clark 1970; Meichenbaum, Bowers & Ross, 1968) further supports the impression that problems of attention are an important concomitant of behavior disorders.

As their teachers can often verify, children with behavior disorders commonly fail to carefully consider alternative solutions to questions or problems, rapidly respond with erroneous answers or solutions, and otherwise appear to have impulsive problem-solving styles. These behavior patterns are related to the issue of "cognitive tempo" or "reflection-impulsivity." For a number of years, psychologists and special educators have been interested in reflection-impulsivity, especially as it applies to children with educational problems (see Kagan & Kogan, 1970; Messer, 1976; Epstein, Hallahan, & Kauffman, 1975). Whereas the reflective child tends to consider the appropriateness of alternative hypotheses or solutions to a problem, taking his time and making few inappropriate responses, the child with impulsive cognitive tempo is prone to respond thoughtlessly and rapidly to problems and make many errors. It has been found that children with behavior disorders are more likely to show the impulsive tempo than normals (Brown & Quay, 1977; Firestone & Martin, 1979). Because there is much research linking impulsive-cognitive tempo to poor performance on various tasks of perceptual and cognitive skills and to poor academic achievement (see Digate, Epstein, Cullinan, & Switzky, 1978; Messer, 1976), impulsivity has to be an important concern for teachers of the behaviorally disordered.

Attention problems and impulsive cognitive tempo seem to characterize many children with behavior disorders. Future research may identify others, and perhaps indicate how teaching techniques designed to correct such specific learning disorders can help normalize pupils with behavior disorders.

Discussion of Characteristics

At present, it is uncertain how the various behavior disorder characteristics are related to one another, although it is not difficult to speculate about possible linkages between various ones. For instances, it might be suggested that attention problems and impulsive cognitive tempo are closely tied to hyperactivity among the behaviorally disordered. There could be important relationships between withdrawal and learning aptitude disabilities, with logical arguments advanced as to how either could cause the other. Academic problems and learning aptitude disabilities seem to be strongly associated with social maladjustment (Murray, 1976), but it is unknown whether and how one contributes to the other.

It must be reiterated that the behavior disorder characteristics discussed should not be taken to mean types of children; rather they describe dimensions or varieties of problems most often encountered by those who work with behaviorally disordered pupils. Any individual pupil may show—in fact, is likely to show—more than one of these characteristics. While other characteristics could have been described, the ones selected represent those that most commonly must be dealt with by educators. As such, they have important implications for the professional preparation of teachers of children with behavior disorders.

SUMMARY

The study of behavior disorders, as we have pointed out, is a relatively new area of special education. Consequently, many important issues such as definition, classification, and causation have not been resolved. The central issues involved in each of these areas were reviewed in this chapter. More recently, behavioral scientists have identified the varieties of behavior problems often encountered by teachers and other educational personnel that work with children with behavior disorders. A teacher who works with these children needs to be prepared to modify and improve these behaviors. Several chapters in this book deal with different treatment approaches to improve social and academic skills.

REFERENCES

Achenbach, T. M. The classification of children's psychiatric symptoms: A factor analytic study. *Psychological Monographs*, 1966, *80* (Whole No. 615).

Achenbach, T. M. *Developmental psychopathology.* New York: Ronald Press, 1974.

Adelman, H. S., & Compas, B. E. Stimulant drugs and learning problems. *Journal of Special Education*, 1977, *11*, 377–416.

Agras, W. S. *Behavior modification: Principles and clinical applications* (2nd ed.). Boston: Little, Brown, 1978.

Aichhorn, A. *Wayward youth.* New York: Viking Press, 1965.

Allen, K. E., Hart, B. M., Buell, J. S., Harris, F. R., & Wolf, M.M. Effects of social reinforcement on isolate behavior of a nursery school child. *Child Development*, 1964, *35*, 511–518.

Axline, V. *Play therapy.* Boston: Houghton-Mifflin, 1947.

Bandura, A. *Principles of behavior modification.* New York: Holt, Rinehart & Winston, 1969.

Bandura, A. *Aggression: A social-learning anal-*

ysis. Englewood Cliffs: Prentice-Hall, 1973.

Barker, R. G. *Ecological psychology: Concepts and methods for studying the environment of human behavior*. Palo Alto: Stanford University Press, 1968.

Barker, R. G., & Wright, H. F. *Midwest and its children*. New York: Harper & Row, 1955.

Becker, W. C., Madsen, C. H., Arnold, C. R., & Thomas, D. R. The contingent use of teacher attention and praise in reducing classroom behavior problems. *Journal of Special Education*, 1967, *1*, 287–307.

Benedict, R. F. Anthropology and the abnormal. *The Journal of General Psychology*, 1934, *10*, 59–80.

Berne, E. *Transactional analysis in psychotherapy*. New York: Grove Press, 1961.

Berne, E. *Games people play*. New York: Grove Press, 1964.

Bettleheim, B. *Love is not enough*. New York: Free Press, 1950.

Bettleheim, B. *The empty fortress*. New York: Free Press, 1967.

Bettleheim, B., & Sylvester, E. A therapeutic milieu. *American Journal of Orthopsychiatry*, 1948, *18*, 191–206.

Bijou, S. W. A functional analysis of retarded development. In N. R. Ellis (Ed.), *International review of research and mental retardation*. New York: Academic Press, 1966.

Bower, E. M. *The early identification of emotionally handicapped children in school* (2nd ed.). Springfield, Il.: Charles C. Thomas, 1969.

Broden, M., Hall, R. V., Dunlap, A., & Clark, R. Effects of teacher attention and a token reinforcement in a junior high school special education class. *Exceptional Children*, 1970, *36*, 341–349.

Brown, R. T., & Quay, L. C. Reflection-impulsivity in normal and behavior-disordered children. *Journal of Abnormal Child Psychology*, 1977, *5*, 457–462.

Bullock, L. M., & Brown, R. K. Behavioral dimensions of emotionally disturbed children. *Exceptional Children*, 1972, *38*, 740–742.

Caplan, G. *Prevention of mental disorders in children*. New York: Basic Books, 1961.

Cattell, R. B. *Personality*. New York: McGraw-Hill, 1950.

Conners, C. K., & Werry, J. S. Pharmacotherapy. In H. C. Quay & J. S. Werry (Eds.), *Psychopathological disorders of childhood* (2nd ed.). New York: John Wiley & Sons, 1979.

Corsini, R. J. (Ed.). *Current personality theories*. Itasca, Il.: F. E. Peacock Publishers, 1977.

Cott, A. Megavitamins: The orthomolecular approach to behavioral disorders and learning

disabilities. *Academic Therapy*, 1972, *7*, 245–258.

Cullinan D., Epstein, M. H., & Dembinski, R. J. Behavior problems of educationally handicapped and normal pupils. *Journal of Abnormal Child Psychology*, 1979, *7*, 495–502.

Cullinan, D., Epstein, M. H. & Kauffman, J. M. The behavioral model and children's behavior disorders: Foundations and evaluation. In R. L. McDowell, F. Wood, & G. Admanson (Eds.), *Current issues in educating behaviorally disordered children*. Boston: Little, Brown, in press.

Cullinan, D., Epstein, M. H., & Lloyd, J. *Behavior disorders of children*. Englewood Cliffs: Prentice-Hall, in press.

Des Jarlais, D., & Paul, J. L. Labelling theory: Sociological views and approaches. In W. C. Rhodes & J. L. Paul (Eds.), *Emotionally disturbed and deviant children*. Englewood Cliffs: Prentice-Hall, 1978.

Denton, C. L., & McIntire, C. W. Span of apprehension in hyperactive boys. *Journal of Abnormal Child Psychology*, 1978, *6*, 19–24.

Digate, G., Epstein, M. H., Cullinan, D., & Switzky, H. N. Modification of impulsivity: Implications for improved efficiency in learning for exceptional children. *Journal of Special Education*, 1978, *12*, 459–468.

Empey, L. T. & Lubeck, S. *Silverlake experiment: Testing delinquency theory and community intervention*. Chicago: Aldine, 1971.

Epstein, M. H., Cullinan, D., & Sabatino, D. A. State definitions of behavior disorders. *Journal of Special Education*, 1977, *11*, 417–425.

Epstein, M. H., Hallahan, D. P., & Kauffman, J. M. Implications of the reflectivity-impulsivity dimension for special education. *Journal of Special Education*, 1975, *9*, 11–25.

Erikson, E. H. *Childhood and society* (2nd ed.). New York: Norton, 1963.

Fagen, S. A., Long, N.J., & Stevens, D. J. *Teaching children self-control*. Columbus, Oh.: Charles E. Merrill, 1975.

Feingold, B. *Why your child is hyperactive*. New York: Random House, 1975.

Ferster, C. B., & DeMyer, M. K. A method for the experimental analysis of the behavior of autistic children. *American Journal of Orthopsychiatry*, 1962, *32*, 89–98.

Feshbach, S. Aggression. In P. H. Mussen (Ed.), *Carmichael's manual of child psychology* (Vol. 2; 3rd ed.). New York: Wiley, 1970.

Fink, A. H., Glass, R. M., & Guskin, S. L. An analysis of teacher education programs in behavior disorders. *Exceptional Children*, 1975, *42*, 47.

Firestone, P., & Martin, J. E. An analysis of the hyperactive syndrome: A comparison of hyperactive, behavior problem, asthmatic, and normal children. *Journal of Abnormal Child Psychology*, 1979, *7*, 261–274.

Freud, A. *Normality and pathology in childhood*. New York: International Universities Press, 1965.

Gilbert, G. M. A survey of "referral problems" in metropolitan child guidance centers. *Journal of Clinical Psychology*, 1957, *13*, 37–42.

Glasser, W. *Reality therapy*. New York: Harper & Row, 1965.

Glasser, W. *Schools without failure*. New York: Harper & Row, 1969.

Glavin, J. P., & DeGirolamo, G. Spelling errors of withdrawn and conduct problem children. *Journal of Special Education*, 1970, *4*, 199–204.

Glavin, J. P., Quay, H. C., Annesley, F. R., & Werry, J. S. An experimental resource room for behavior problem children. *Exceptional Children*, 1971, *38*, 131–137.

Glidewell, J., & Swallow, C. *The prevalence of maladjustment in elementary school*. Chicago: University of Chicago Press, 1968.

Glueck, S. & Glueck, E. *Delinquents and nondelinquents in perspective*. Cambridge: Harvard University Press, 1968.

Graham, P. J. Epidemiological studies. In H. C. Quay & J. S. Werry (Eds.), *Psychopathological disorders of childhood*. New York: John Wiley, 1979.

Greenwood, C. R., Hops, H., Delquadri, J., & Walker, H. M. *PASS (program for academic survival skills): Group management of academic related behaviors: Manual for consultants*. Eugene, Or.: Center at Oregon for the Behavioral Education of the Handicapped, 1974.

Greenwood, C. R., Walker, H. M., & Hops, H. Issues in social interaction: withdrawal assessment. *Exceptional Children*, 1977, *43*, 490–501.

Group for the Advancement of Psychiatry. *Psychopathological disorders in childhood: Theoretical considerations and a proposed classification*. New York: Group for the Advancement of Psychiatry, 1966.

Hall, C. S., & Lindzey, G. *Theories of personality* (3rd ed.). New York: Wiley, 1978.

Hallahan, D., & Kauffman, J. *Learning disabilities: A psycho-behavioral approach*. Englewood Cliffs: Prentice-Hall, 1976.

Haring, N. G., & Phillips, E. L. *Educating emotionally disturbed children*. New York: McGraw-Hill, 1962.

Hartmann, H. *Essays on ego psychology*. New York: International Universities Press, 1964.

Hentoff, N. The drugged classroom. *Evergreen Review*, 1970, *14*, 31–33.

Hewett, F. M. Teaching reading to an autistic boy through operant conditioning. *The Reading Teacher*, 1964, *18*, 613–618.

Hewett, F. M. *The emotionally disturbed child in the classroom*. Boston: Allyn & Bacon, 1968.

Hewett, F. M. Frank M. Hewett. In J. M. Kauffman & C. D. Lewis (Eds.), *Teaching children with behavior disorders: Personal perspectives*. Columbus, Oh.: Charles E. Merrill, 1974.

Hewett, F. M., & Forness, S. R. *Education of exceptional learners*. Boston: Allyn & Bacon, 1974.

Hobbs, N. Helping disturbed children: Ecological and psychological strategies. *American Psychologist*, 1966, *21*, 1105–1115.

Hops, H., Beickel, S. L., & Walker, H. M. *Class: Contingencies for learning academic and social skills*. Eugene, Or.: Center at Oregon for Research in the Behavioral Education of the Handicapped, 1976.

Hops, H., Guild, J. J., Fleischman, D. H., Paine, S. C., Street, A., Walker, A. S., & Greenwood, C. R. *Peers: Procedures for establishing effective relationship skills*. Eugene, Or.: Center at Oregon for Research in the Behavioral Education of the Handicapped, 1978.

Joint Commission on Mental Health of Children. *Crisis in child mental health*. New York: Harper & Row, 1969.

Kauffman, J. M. Nineteenth century views of children's behavior disorders: Historical contributions and continuing issues. *Journal of Special Education*, 1976, *10*, 335–349.

Kauffman, J. M. *Characteristics of children's behavior disorders*. Columbus, Oh.: Charles E. Merrill, 1977.

Kagan, J., & Kogan, N. Individuality and cognitive performance. In P. H. Mussen (Ed.), *Carmichael's manual of child psychology*. New York: Wiley, 1970.

Kagan, J., & Moss, H. A. *Birth to maturity*. New York: Wiley, 1962.

Kazdin, A. E. *The token economy: A review and evaluation*. New York: Plenum, 1977.

Kazdin, A. E. *History of behavior modification*. Baltimore: University Park Press, 1978.

Kazdin, A. E. *Behavior modification in applied settings* (2nd ed.). Homewood, Il.: The Dorsey Press, 1980.

Keogh, B. K., & Margolis, J. Learn to labor and to wait: Attentional problems of children with learning disorders. *Journal of Learning Disabilities*, 1976, *9*, 276–286.

Kitano, H. L. Reversals and illegibilities in the spelling errors of maladjusted children. *Journal of Educational Psychology*, 1959, *50*, 129–131.

Kohlberg, L., LaCrosse, J., & Ricks, D. The predictability of adult mental health from childhood behavior. In B. B. Wolman (Ed.), *Manual of child psychopathology*. New York: John Wiley, 1972.

Krumboltz, J. D., & Thoresen, C. E. (Eds.). *Counseling methods*. New York: Holt, Rinehart and Winston, 1976.

Lapouse, R., & Monk, M. A. An epidemiologic study of behavior characteristics of children. *American Journal of Public Health*, 1958, *48*, 1134–1144.

Lapouse, R., & Monk, M. Fears and worries in a representative sample of children. *American Journal of Orthopsychiatry*, 1959, *29*, 803–818.

Lilly, M. S. *Children with exceptional needs: A survey of special education*, New York: Holt, Rinehart and Winston, 1979.

Litow, L., & Pumroy, D. K. A brief review of classroom group-oriented contingencies. *Journal of Applied Behavior Analysis*, 1975, *8*, 341–347.

Long, N. J. Nicholas J. Long. In J. M. Kauffman & C. D. Lewis (Eds.), *Teaching children with behavior disorders: Personal perspectives*. Columbus, Oh.: Charles E. Merrill, 1974.

Long, N. J., & Newman, R. G. Managing surface behavior in children in school. In N. J. Long, W. C. Morse, & R. G. Newman (Eds.), *Conflict in the classroom: The education of emotionally disturbed children* (3rd ed.). Belmont, Ca.: Wadsworth Publishing, 1976.

Lovaas, O. I. A program for the establishment of speech in psychotic children. In J. K. Wing (Ed.), *Early childhood autism: Clinical, educational and social aspects*. New York: Pergamon, 1966.

Lorenz, K. Z. *Evolution and modification of behavior*. Chicago: University of Chicago Press, 1965.

MacFarlane, J. W., Allen, L., & Honzik, M. P. *A developmental study of the behavior problems of normal children between twenty-one months and fourteen years*. Berkeley: University of California Press, 1954.

MacMillan, D. L, Jones, R. L, & Aloia, G. F. The mentally retarded label: A theoretical analysis and review of research. *American Journal of Mental Deficiency*, 1974, *79*, 241–261.

Meichenbaum, D. H., Bowers, K., & Ross, R. R. Modification of classroom behavior of institutionalized female adolescent offenders. *Behaviour Research and Therapy*, 1968, *6*, 343–353.

Messer, S. B. Reflection-impulsivity: A review. *Psychological Bulletin*, 1976, *83*, 1026–1052.

Michielutte, R. The use of music with exceptional children. In L. Mann & D. Sabatino (Eds.), *The second review of special education*. Philadelphia: JSE Press, 1974.

Miller, L. C., Barrett, C. L., Hampe, E., & Noble, H. Comparison of reciprocal inhibition, psychotherapy and waiting list control for phobic children. *Journal of Abnormal Psychology*, 1972, *79*, 269–279.

Miller, R. G., Palkes, H. S., & Stewart, M. A. Hyperactive children in suburban elementary schools. *Child Psychiatry and Human Development*, 1973, *4*, 121–127.

Miller, T. L, & Epstein, M. H. State terminology of behavioral disorders. *Psychology in the Schools*, 1979, *16*, 224–229.

Mischel, W. *Introduction to personality*. New York: Holt, Rinehart and Winston, 1971.

Morse, W. C., Cutler, R. L., & Fink, A. H. *Public school classes for the emotionally handicapped: A research analysis*. Washington, D.C.: Council for Exceptional Children, 1964.

Motto, J. J., & Wilkins, G. S. Educational achievement of institutionalized emotionally disturbed children. *Journal of Educational Research*, 1968, *61*, 218–221.

Murray, C. A. *The link between learning disabilities and juvenile delinquency: Current theory and knowledge*. Washington, D.C.: U.S. Government Printing Office, 1976.

O'Leary, K. D., & O'Leary, S. G. (Eds.). *Classroom management: The successful use of behavior modification* (2nd ed.). New York: Pergamon Press, 1977.

Oliver, L. I. *Behavior patterns in school of youths 12–17 years*. (National Health Survey, Series 11, No. 139, U.S. Department of Health, Education and Welfare). Washington, D.C.: U.S. Government Printing Office, 1974.

O'Neil, S. M., McLaughlin, B. N., & Knapp, M. B. *Behavioral approaches to children with developmental delays*. St. Louis: C. V. Mosby, 1977.

Patterson, G. R. An empirical approach to the classification of disturbed children. *Journal of Clinical Psychology*, 1964, *20*, 326–337.

Patterson, G. R. An application of conditioning techniques to the control of a hyperactive child. In L. P. Ullmann & L. Krasner (Eds.), *Case studies in behavior modification*. New York: Holt, Rinehart and Winston, 1965.

Phillips, L., & Dragnus, J. G. Classification of the behavior disorders. *Annual Review of Psychology*, 1971, *22*, 447–482.

Prugh, D. G., Engel, M., & Morse, W. C. Emotional disturbance in children. In N. Hobbs (Ed.), *Issues in the classification of children* (Vol. 1). San Francisco: Jossey-Bass, 1975.

Quay, H. C. Measuring dimensions of deviant behavior: The behavior problem checklist. *Journal of Abnormal Child Psychology*, 1977, *5*, 277–287.

Quay, H. C. Classification. In H. C. Quay & J. S. Werry (Eds.), *Psychopathological disorders of childhood* (2nd ed.). New York: Wiley, 1979.

Quay, H. C., Glavin, J. P., Annesley, F. R., & Werry, J. S. The modification of problem behavior and academic achievement in a resource room. *Journal of School Psychology*, 1972, *10*, 187–198.

Quay, H. C., & Peterson, D. R. *Manual for the behavior problem checklist*. Unpublished, 1975.

Redl, F. The concept of the life space interview. *American Journal of Orthopsychiatry*, 1959, *29*, 1–18.

Redl, F., & Wineman, D. *Children who hate*. New York: Free Press, 1951.

Redl, F., & Wineman, D. *Controls from within*. New York: Free Press, 1952.

Rhodes, W. C. A community participation analysis of emotional disturbance. *Exceptional Children*, 1970, *37*, 309–314.(a)

Rhodes, W. *The emotionally disturbed student and guidance*. New York: Houghton Mifflin, 1970.(b)

Rimland, B. Psychogenesis versus biogenisis: The issues and the evidence. In S. C. Plog & R. B. Edgerton (Eds.), *Changing perspectives in mental illness*. New York: Holt, Rinehart, & Winston, 1969.

Roberts, J., & Baird, J. T. *Behavior patterns of children in school* (DHEW Publication No. (HSM) 72-1042). Washington, D.C.: U.S. Government Printing Office, 1972.

Robins, L. N. *Deviant children grown up: A sociological and psychiatric study of sociopathic personality*. Baltimore: Williams & Wilkins, 1966.

Robins, L. N. Follow-up studies. In H. C. Quay & J. S. Werry (Eds.), *Psychopathological disorders of childhood* (2nd ed.). New York: Wiley, 1979.

Rogers, C. R. The criteria used in a study of mental health problems. *Educational Research Bulletin*, 1942, *81*, 29–40.

Rogers, C. R. *Client-centered therapy*. Boston: Houghton Mifflin, 1951.

Rogers, M. E., Lilenfield, A. M., & Pasamanick, B. *Prenatal and paranatal factors in the development of childhood behavior disorders*. Baltimore: Johns Hopkins University Press, 1955.

Rosen, B. M., Bahn, A. K., & Kramer, M. Demographic and diagnostic characteristics of psychiatric clinic outpaitents in the U.S.A., 1961. *American Journal of Orthopsychiatry*, 1964, *34*, 455–468.

Ross, A. O. *Psychological disorders of children: A behavioral approach to theory, research, and therapy*. New York: McGraw-Hill, 1974.

Ross, D., & Ross, S. *Hyperactivity: Research, theory, action*. New York: Wiley, 1976.

Rutter, M., Lebovici, S., Eisenberg, L., Snevnevskij, A. V., Sadoun, R., Brooke, E., & Lin, T. Y. A triaxial classification of mental disorders in childhood. *Journal of Child Psychology and Psychiatry*, 1969, *10*, 41–61.

Rutter, M., Tizard, J., Yule, W., Graham, P., & Whitmore, K. Isle of Wight studies, 1964–1974. *Psychological Medicine*, 1976, *6*, 313–332.

Schrag, P., & Divoky, D. *The myth of the hyperactive child*. New York: Random House, 1975.

Schultz, E. W., Hirshoren, A., Manton, A. B., & Henderson, R. A. Special education for the emotionally disturbed. *Exceptional Children*, 1971, *38*, 313–320.

Stone, F. & Rowley, V. N. Educational disability in emotionally disturbed children. *Exceptional Children*, 1964, *30*, 423–426.

Strain, P. S. Cooke, T. P. & Apolloni, T. *Teaching exceptional children: Assessing and modifying social behavior*. New York: Academic Press, 1976.

Strauss, A. A., & Lehtinen L. E. *Psychopathology and education of the brain-injured child*. New York: Grune & Stratton, 1947.

Tharp, R. G., & Wetzel, R. J. *Behavior modification in the natural environment*. New York: Academic Press, 1969.

Thomas, E. J. *Behavior modification procedure: A sourcebook*. Chicago: Aldine, 1974.

Thoresen, C. E., & Mahoney, M. J. *Behavioral self-control*. New York: Holt, Rinehart and Winston, 1974.

Walker, H. M., & Buckley, N. K. Teacher attention to appropriate and inappropriate classroom behavior: An individual case study.

Focus on Exceptional Children, 1973, *5*, 5–11.

Walker, H. M., Street, A., Garrett, B., & Crossen, J. *Recess: Reprogramming environmental contingencies for effective social skills.* Eugene, Or.: Center at Oregon for Research in the Behavioral Education of the Handicapped, 1978.

Weiss, G., Hechtman, L., & Perlman, T. Hyperactives as young adults: School, employer, and self-rating scales obtained during a ten-year follow-up evaluation. *American Journal of Orthopsychiatry,* 1978, *43,* 438–445.

Weiss, G., Minde, K., Werry, J. S., Douglas, V., & Nemeth, E. Studies on the hyperactive child: VIII. Five-year follow-up. *Archives of General Psychiatry,* 1971, *24,* 409–414.

Wender, P. H. *Minimal brain dysfunction in children.* New York: Wiley, 1971.

Werry, J. S. Organic factors. In H. C. Quay & J. S. Werry (Eds.), *Psychopathological disorders of childhood* (2nd ed.). New York: John Wiley & Sons, 1979.

Werry, J. S., & Quay, H. C. The prevalence of behavior symptoms in young elementary school children. *American Journal of Orthopsychiatry,* 1971, *4,* 136–143.

White, M. A., & Harris, M. *The school psychologist.* New York: Harper, 1961.

Wickman, E. *Children's behavior and teacher's attitudes.* New York: Commonwealth Fund, 1928.

Willems, E. P. An ecological orientation in psychology. *Merrill-Palmer Quarterly,* 1965, *11,* 317–343.

Williams, R. B., & Gentry, W. D. (Eds.). *Behavioral approaches to mental treatment.* Cambridge: Ballinger, 1977.

Wirt, R. D., & Briggs, P. F. The meaning of delinquency. In H. C. Quay (Ed.), *Juvenile delinquency: Research and theory.* Princeton: Van Nostrand, 1965.

Wolf, M. M., Risley, T. R., & Mees, H. Application of operant conditioning procedures to the behavior problems of an autistic child. *Behavior Research and Therapy,* 1964, *1,* 305–312.

Wood, M. M. (Ed.). *The Rutland Center model for treating emotionally disturbed children* (2nd ed.). Athens, Ga.: Rutland Center Technical Assistance Office, 1972.

Wood, M. M. (Ed.). *Developmental therapy.* Baltimore: University Park Press, 1975.

Wood, F. H., & Zabel, R. H. Making sense of reports on the incidence of behavior disorders/emotional disturbance in school-aged populations *Psychology in the Schools,* 1978, *15,* 45–51.

PART II

Psychoeducational Similarities and Differences

David A. Sabatino

5

Cognitive Development of Mildly Handicapped Children and Adolescents

The dictionary definition of cognition is "any mental operation by which we become aware of objects, thought, or perception" (Webster's Unabridged, 1979). While the human newborn cannot be described as displaying cognitive qualities by even this simplified definition, the search for activity, if not familiarity, is taking place within the visual world of the child within days of birth. By three weeks, firm fixations occur more regularly than the out-of-control blinking noted in the first two weeks. Within the following three weeks, visual tracking occurs smoothly with increased control over fixations and eye movements. Thus, observation of infant development during the first four months clearly identifies the progress of visual activity in response to the information-seeking behaviors of children.

Beginning with perception, cognition is a developmental act in which the mental processes that comprise it grow in capacity to gather and interpret sensory stimuli. Denied information, mental processes seem to slow down or stop. Sensory delays, even in normally developing children, inevitably alter the development of behavioral and physiological responses to the processing and assimilation of information by the central nervous system. The result is a disruption of the evolvement of cognition. Clearly, perception and cognition, although difficult to define, develop in reciprocal fashion. Thus, cognition may be accepted as the placing of language concepts on perceptual units, a process that permits abstract thinking and the eventual communication of high-order symbol systems. Simultaneously, cognitive learning is the utilization of these mental processes. This involves reception of symbolic information perceptually, associating the distinctive features of symbolic properties by assigning conceptual meaning, and mediating abstract conceptual units to enhance understanding of the information in the environment.

In actuality, cognitive development occurs as a theoretically formulated set of mental processes or functions, which (while performing the act of learning) are not directly observable and are therefore assumed. The search for understanding of these mental processes is dependent upon the particular theoretical structure's explanation of how information is processed. Usually, the names given a specific information-processing behavior describe the traits they are felt to identify in terms of the function performed. For example, the mental process of discriminating the distinctive features of visual symbols is known as *visual perceptual discrimination.* Accordingly, *cognitive development,* as used in this chapter, represents the mental processes used to learn or the ''how'' of learning.

WHAT IS LEARNED: PRODUCT LEARNING

Product learning is the observable result of information processing and cognitive development. Any willful, directed act is the result of cognitive functioning. Learning to read, write, and perform arithmetic calculations are all examples of product learning, and most manual-motor or vocal-motor responses in the school setting result in product learning in its simplest form. Product learning is somewhat distinct from cognition though the former is often taken as evidence of the latter. Where products are not observable, cognition is presumed to be the process by which humans interact with their environment, by receiving sensory information as perceptual experiences, ordering that information, and assigning it meaning by providing symbols. As noted, cognition is never actually seen, so the most common manner of observing cognitive development in children is measuring it by administering various aptitudinal (perceptual-language) and academic achievement tests. Aptitudes are clusters of traits, i.e., reasonably well-defined information-processing behaviors. Occasionally, such learner aptitudes may be referred to as personalogical variables because they are unique to the individual. Personalogical variables (aptitudes) may be very complex. For example, consider the ''simple'' motor response of pointing to a picture stimulus upon verbal command. The aural (auditory) reception of information is one aptitude, the visual-motor response is another, and processing a word as a central language concept may be a third. Additional aptitudes may include the visual discrimination of the correct picture (i.e., the one that matches the aural stimulus signal) and the manual-motor coordination to complete the pointing response. Should any of these aptitudes be faulty, the completed response will be less than fully appropriate.

How many cognitive traits and aptitudes are there? There is no answer to this question. There are few studies directed at pinpointing specific traits or aptitudes. There are even fewer studies validating a particular trait to determine if it exists in reality. Thus, traits and aptitudes are operationally defined for the most part—they exist because someone assumed they do and gave them a name.

HISTORICAL CONCEPTUALIZATIONS OF COGNITIVE DEVELOPMENT

History is often viewed as an irrelevant collection of worn-out happenings that do not cover the current scene. In special education this is simply not true, especially in cognitive training. Cognitive training is very much in effect in special education instruction in the forms of sensori-motor training, perceptual-motor activities, perceptual discrimination, perceptual memory, and many language-intervention strategies. Cognitive training is not necessarily academic achievement remediation since cognitive activities may not directly apply to academic achievement, skill acquisition, or academic product learning. Even so, instructional objectives can be written with a focus on word-recognition development, or study methods, i.e., events that include cognitive training. Mann (1974), made the following observations:

> Cognitive training is very much a part of the current educational scene, and it is not just limited to training programs specifically intended to train cognitive processes. Many curricular approaches also boast of their potential for developing cognitive skill, or as having been developed on the basis of cognitive principles . . . It is true that there has been a general renaissance of interest in cognitive training during the past fifteen years in education, and that preschool, general and higher education as well as special education have participated in it. Nevertheless, no other group has as earnestly dedicated itself to the evaluation and training of inner "processes," or abilities, including those of cognition, as has special education. (p. 83)[1]

There are several reasons for this affinity with cognitive processes. Mann noted that special education maintains a unique relationship with psychology, more so than most other areas of education. Additionally, there is a tedium engendered from teaching handicapped children, and teaching mental processes provides the special educator an alternative. Finally, it has been viewed as conceptually possible that the training of mental processes might offset the inability to show sufficient progress in more traditional remedial approaches. But all has not proven well in these efforts for, "the tide has now turned. The perceptual trainers have had their turn on stage and been found wanting" (Mann, 1974, p. 83). So, in some quarters of special education, cognitive processes are now eschewed for more direct instruction.

Despite this decided trend, a recent resurgence of effort (Mann, 1980; Sabatino, Miller & Schmidt, 1981) suggests that an interest in cognitive development has continued. But this is not an uncommon occurrence, for cyclical interest in cognitive training and the study of the process of cognition has been a recurrent historical theme. Perhaps the earliest speculation on these topics can be traced to the Socratic-Platonic ideas that targeted study upon the powers, capacities, or facilities of the mind. Earlier Greek philosophies had promoted sensationalistic thinking, which held that knowledge was built from the sensory experiences (sensory energy) that it received. The sensationalistic position paved the way for the Sophists, who believed in learning to improve the capacity of meeting the demands of daily living. It was Socrates who broke with the sensation-dependent experiences and the amoral everyday information and knowledge required for successful, practical living offered by the heuristic philosophers. Socrates and Plato introduced the belief that the mind went beyond the senses and was capable of experiences, knowledge, and truths that were not tied to the practical eye-motor tools needed for everyday living. Eventually, cognitive training, or the development of mental processes, was advanced by Plato and Socrates; in fact, the famous English cognitive psychologist, Spearman, credits Plato with a doctrine that divided the mind into sensory-dependent learning and the drive for intelligent human reasoning.

After a period of disrepute, cognitive training resurfaced in the 16th century

---

[1]Reprinted with permission from Mann, L. *Cognitive training: A look at the past and some concerns about the present.* A paper presented at the National Regional Resource Center Conference, Reston, Va., 1974.

(Mann, 1980) Richard Mulcaster (Campagnac, 1925) announced in his work that the purpose of cognitive training was to help nature to her perfection. He considered the three main powers of the mind to be "wit to take, memory to keep, and discretion to discern." Building in part upon the work of Mulcaster, the eloquent 17th-century spokesman John Locke (1961) was in favor of cognitive training:

> We are born with faculties and powers capable of almost anything, . . . such at least as would carry us farther than can easily be imagined; but it is only the exercise of those powers which gives us ability and skill in anything.

By the 18th century, a new "science" had arrived to study mental processes. This "science," phrenology, gave proof of the desire to measure relationships between mental processes and performance. Phrenology survived to almost the middle of the 20th century, and under the guiding hands of various popularizers such as Spurzheim in Europe and the Fowler brothers and Coombe in this country, the depressions and protrusions on the skull were thought to be the first outward manifestations of what might be taking place in the brain. Phrenology promised scientific improvements of humans and had particular appeal to educators. As Mann (1974) wrote,

> Famous educators swore by the doctrine and guided their educational practices by it . . . The fervor of modern special educators, enthusiastic over a new approach . . . simply does not compare with the assurety of nineteenth century psychoeducational practitioners who knew that they could assess *abilities* and *disabilities* via head proportions and remediate accordingly! (p. 91)[2]

Montessori, Decroly, and Descoeudres, all believed in cognitive or mental process training although there were different degrees of purity in their beliefs and positions on this subject. Itard assumed a position closely associated with the sensationalist concepts he inherited from Locke and Rousseau. Seguin, despite a faculty psychology orientation, seems to have kept his eye firmly on utilitarian pragmatic goals. Montessori seems to have less critically accepted the classical faculty conceptions of her time. All, however, were committed to training mental processes, in part to modify academic learning, but also for the sake of improving the process, trait, or ability as an entity.

The major source of contemporary support was yet to come. It arrived as a development of the mental-measurement movement that appeared toward the close of the 19th century. As Galton noted in Mann (1980), "one of the most important objects of measurement . . . is to obtain a general knowledge of the capacities of man by sinking shafts, as it were, at a few critical points" (p. 420). Even Alfred Binet, despite his fame as the creator of a global intelligence test, was in reality a faculty psychologist who should be credited with tying the final knot in the relationship between handicapping condition and process training through psychometric testing. His work was carried on by a variety of other psychologists and educators who, in essence, created the beginnings of the diagnostic prescriptive training movement as it is now known in special education. In short, these psychometric pioneers continued and expanded the traditions of mental process

---

[2]Reprinted with permission from Mann, L., *Cognitive training: A look at the past and some concerns about the present.* A paper presented at the National Regional Resource Center Conference, Reston, Va., 1974.

training, although they were often simultaneously dealing with abilities, capabilities, powers, aptitudes, or traits.

The post-World War II years heralded a new emphasis on cognitive process assessment and training. The work of Strauss, Kephart, Wepman, Kirk, Frostig, Meeker, Myklebust, and Cruickshank evidenced great interest in cognitive psychology; all of these special educators were interested in the capability of mental training with so-called minimally brain-damaged children. This legacy continues in numerous ways; for example, the very definition of learning disabilities, as an outgrowth of minimal brain injury, is tied to the basic psychological processes deficit factor proposed in cognitive psychology. Thus, special education remains, from a great many perspectives, intrinsically entwined with the conceptualizations developed in the quest of understanding cognitive development.

COGNITIVE DEVELOPMENT: A COMPONENT DEFINITION

Modern day theorists approaching the development of human learning from a number of standpoints have contributed to the understanding of the processes by which the mind works. Important to that understanding has been the construction of models upon which a theoretical framework for research has proceeded. Piaget's genetic epistemology (1970); Bruner's instrumental conceptualization (Bruner, Oliver, & Greenfield, 1966); the information theory of Newell and Simon (1972); Davis's creative problem solving (1973); Gagne's cumulative learning (1970); and Guilford's structure of intellect (1967) have all had decided impact on the study of cognition.

An example of model construction and theory building, taken from work by Klausmeier (1976), addresses the issue of concept attainment by normally developing children. The model details acquiring and remembering names of concepts at four levels: concrete, identity, classification, and formal. Attaining a concept at the concrete level requires having had experiences with it. Those tasks involved in concrete learning are attending, discriminating the distinctive features to be learned, representing the features internally as an image or trace, and retaining that representation through memory. A child may learn the concept *ball* by attending to the physical characteristics of a ball, discriminating its features, obtaining a mental image, and recognizing the ball when experiencing it later. A simplified model represents, then, a flow of cognitive processes at the concrete level:

1. Attending to the ball—a realistic experience in nature
2. Discriminating the ball—learning its characteristics
3. Remembering the ball—memory for the critical features of the ball
4. Acquiring the name ball—learning the word
5. Remembering the name *ball*—matching it to that object and to other objects with the same physical characteristics

At the identity level, the child must generalize between two or more objects, discriminating and naming the ball; however, the real object may now be a form or a picture of a ball. Likewise, at the classification level, the child must generalize between classes of objects, things, and symbols. At the formal level, the child must discriminate the attributes of the symbol or concepts. The process can be accomplished indirectly by breaking the code and reapplying the rules to identify the attributes or components of something, thus inferring the concept. Deductively, an assimilation of the concept may take place, permitting the child to identify examples, and nonexamples, of the concept (i.e., what it is or isn't) from the sum of what is known about its parts, functions, and characteristics.

MODELS OF COGNITIVE DEVELOPMENT

It is important to understand many models of cognitive development before choosing one to use as a basis for teaching. One model of cognitive abilities was developed specifically to provide greater accessibility to the structure of intellect (SOI) by practicing educators. Guilford's SOI model of intellectual aptitudes or learning characteristics (1966) was designed to teach students *how* to learn. The impetus was quite simple: there is too much information in the world to be learned in a rote manner and the nature of human intelligence, at least as it is measured, requires the integration of human abilities. This view forces a shift away from the traditional requirement of many schools, i.e., the rote learning of specific academic tasks. Meeker (1969) wrote,

> One goal of cognitive therapy is the realization of a student's learning potential, and the process requires some measure of his abilities and some concrete means of exploiting his strengths and developing his weaknesses . . . . Cognitive Therapy, for all its practical *saliency* and patently direct approach, is not a generally well-developed practice in the educational system. (pp. 6–7)

Guilford's work has been validated by a host of researchers using factor analytic methods. In his model, a number of operational by-products are recognized; thus, every intellectual activity may be characterized in terms of the type of operation that is employed, the content involved, and the product that results. Figure 5-1 provides the three categories that organize the structure of intellect, and the subclasses within each category, as a cube. It is important to note that each intellectual act requires one cell from all three categories. Hence, in the dimension of operation, cognition (C) may be figural (F) but it could also be symbolic, semantic, or behavioral in the contents or dimension. In the dimension of products, cognition could be identified under units, classes, relations, systems, information, or implications.

Complete characterization of an intellectual ability is achieved in terms of the possible subclass differentiation five ways: memory, cognition, evaluation, divergent production, and covergent production. Figure 5-2 demonstrates the breaking apart of the major slices (operations) of the matrix cube. Contents and products are identical components in each of the major operations. Contents is differentiated by four subclasses: figural, symbolic, semantic, and behavioral. Products is differentiated by six subcategories: units, classes, relations, systems, transformations, and implications. The complete schema is represented by a three-dimensional array of 120 predicted cells or categories of intellectual abilities. The task for the special educator then is to develop unused or poorly used cells or to assist a student to overcome the persistent failure of a task by utilizing strategies that

OPERATIONS
Cognition
Memory
Divergent Production
Convergent Production
Evaluation

PRODUCTS
Units
Classes
Relations
Systems
Transformations
Implications

CONTENTS
Figural
Symbolic
Semantic
Behavioral

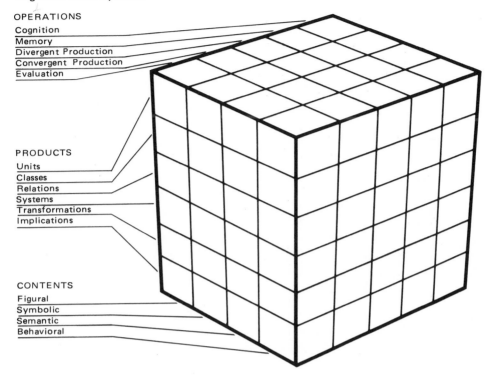

Fig. 5-1. The Guilford (1965) model of the structure of intellect. (Reprinted with permission from Guilford, J. P. Intelligence: 1965 model. *American Psychologist,* 1966, *21*(1), 21.)

draw upon other, better developed cells. To some extent, this appears to be a feasible enterprise although the techniques are not fully defined (Meeker, 1969).

The oldest cognitive classification structure in education is based on cognitive-learning task analysis: Bloom's six-level hierarchically ordered cognitive taxonomy (1956). The six levels represented in the taxonomies are knowledge, comprehension, application, analysis, synthesis, and evaluation. In practice, the cognitive taxonomy has been used primarily as a model for curriculum planning and design. The reason for this is that a taxonomy is more an analysis of the interaction of child and learning task than of the purely cognitive structures synonymous with learning characteristics, traits, or aptitudes. However, the cognitive tasks outlined by Bloom have been used to prepare instructional objectives and in planning enabling steps. Figure 5-3 provides a list of the six major components and subcomponents in the taxonomy developed by Bloom.

Another approach to understanding cognition was proposed by Valett. In Valett's conceptualization (1968), cognition begins on level 3, and includes levels 4 and 5 (Fig. 5-4). The structure proposed by Valett may be viewed as a systematic means of planning remediation for learning disabled children. It is developmental, beginning with gross motor activity in level 1 and continuing through conceptual skills in level 5. Moreover, it provides the diagnostician with a map of activities and a structure for ascertaining sensory, perceptual, and cognitive functioning, with some attention paid to social skill development.

Sabatino's model (1968) is based on a simplified view of how information is

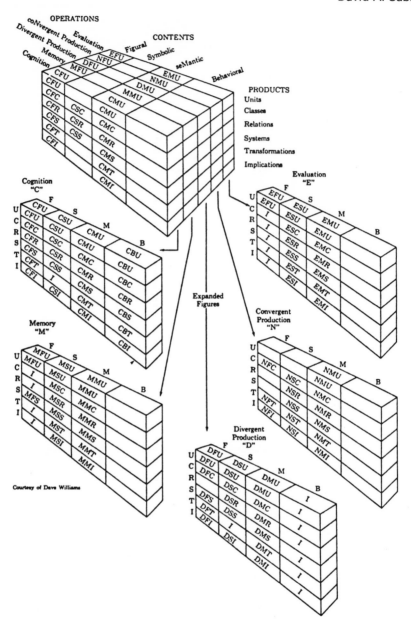

Fig. 5-2. Operations, contents, and products of Guilford and Hoepfner's structure (1966). (Reprinted with permission from Meeker, M. N. *The structure of the intellect: Its interpretation and uses.* Columbus: Charles E. Merrill, 1969.)

processed by the human nervous system. The model has three major parameters (Fig. 5-5). The first parameter, sensation, or the reception of environmental information by the peripheral sensory end organs of vision (eye) and hearing (ear), is *not* a cognitive function. It is only the reception of sensory information and the coding of that sensory information for transmission from the peripheral sensory end organs to the brain. Sensation is important to the extent that accurate representations of occurrences, objects, or things are being received and neurally co-

The Cognitive Taxonomy

- *Knowledge,* including the ability to
  recall, remember
  recognize a given object or idea when it is presented
- *Comprehension,* including the ability to
  predict
  generalize
  interpret
- *Application,* including the ability to
  apply or use ideas in appropriate ways
- *Analysis,* including the ability to
  detect fallacies
  detect interrelations
  detect cause and effect
- *Synthesis,* including the ability to
  create
  propose new solutions
- *Evaluation,* including the ability to
  judge on the basis of criteria

Fig. 5-3. Bloom's taxonomy of cognitive skills.

ded for transmission to the higher learning centers of the central nervous system.

The second parameter of the Sabatino model is perception. While it is true that there is disagreement as to the inclusion of perception in the cognitive structures, this model does not consider perception to be a cognitive function. Instead, perception is defined as the accurate and rapid interpretation of neurally coded information as a symbol system. In short, perception is that function that translates people, places, and things occurring in the environment into symbolic components as discriminated by the nervous system. The symbols used are based on experience, and therefore there may be as few, or as many, individual units within a classification as experience permits. Perception can further be classified according to the two major sensory systems, auditory and visual. Both visual and auditory perceptual systems contain at least three functions. The first two functions are used to discriminate and retain information; i.e., the task is to describe information on the basis of its distinctive features (discrimination) and retain it for very short periods of time. The information that is unwanted is filtered from the system and is lost to the retention process. The third perceptual function is sequencing, which is the long-term storage of symbols that provides order to perceptual information according to experience, logic, or previous learning.

The final parameter of Sabatino's model is cognition, considered in this case to be the association, mediation, and expressed use of perceptual symbols by assigning concept to them. In short, cognition represents the use of language as a means of examining, relating to, and explaining the environment.

From a practical standpoint, the information-processing model developed by Sabatino (1968) results in a systematic assessment procedure using a descriptor system. The purpose of the descriptor system is to insure that most academic and nonacademic behaviors that can be described, are described. The basic description may suggest that the behavior is within the normal range for that particular child's age, or that it is inhibiting the child's function in that and related areas of performance.

Basic Learning Abilities

Level 1: Gross motor development

- Rolling (controlled)
- Sitting (erect)
- Crawling (smoothly)
- Walking (coordinated)
- Running (course)
- Throwing (accurately)
- Jumping (obstacles)
- Skipping (alternately)
- Dancing (eurythmy)
- Self-identification (name awareness)
- Body localization (part location)
- Body abstraction (transfer, generalization)
- Muscular strength (sit-ups, leg-ups, bends)
- General physical health (significant history)

Level 2: Sensory-motor integration

- Balance and rhythm (games, dance)
- Body-spatial organization (mazes)
- Reaction-speed dexterity (motor accuracy)
- Tactile discrimination (object identification)
- Directionality (right-left, etc.)
- Laterality (hand-eye-foot)
- Time orientation (lapse and concept)

Level 3: Perceptual-motor skills

Auditory

- Acuity (functional hearing)
- Decoding (following directions)
- Vocal association (initiative response)
- Memory (retention)
- Sequencing (patterning)

Visual

- Acuity (Snellen chart)
- Coordination and pursuit (tracking)
- Form discrimination (association)
- Figure-ground (differentiation)
- Memory (visual recall)

Visual-motor

- Memory (designs)
- Fine muscle coordination (designs)
- Spatial-form manipulation (blocks)
- Speed of learning (coding)
- Integration (Draw-A-Man)

Level 4: Language development

- Vocabulary (word knowledge)
- Fluency and encoding (use and structure)
- Articulation (initial, medial, final)
- Word attack skills (phonic association)
- Reading comprehension (understanding)
- Writing (expression)
- Spelling (oral, written)

Level 5: Conceptual skills

- Number concepts (counting)
- Arithmetic processes ($+$, $-$, $\times$, $+$)
- Arithmetic reasoning (problem solving)
- General information (fund of knowledge)
- Classification (relationships)
- Comprehension (commonsense reasoning)

Level 6: Social skills

- Social acceptance (friendship)
- Anticipatory response (foresight)
- Value judgments (ethical-moral sense)

Fig. 5-4. The critical features of Valett's system. (Reprinted with permission from Valett, R. E. *Developing cognitive abilities: Teaching children to think.* St. Louis: C. V. Mosby, 1978, p. 37.)

The psychoeducational diagnostician using the Sabatino (1968) system or a similar system should view it as a pilot does the preflight of his aircraft. Research to date (Ryckman & Wiegerink, 1969; Sabatino, 1968; Sabatino & Hayden, 1970a, 1970b) suggests that there are at least four areas that must be described in this checkoff: visual perception, auditory perception, perceptual integration, and receptive expressive language. Since these four information-processing behavioral complexities must be addressed with a stimulus input even though the exact nature of the component traits of each complex behavior is not clear, a stimulus-response descriptor system has been developed to assist the diagnostician classify

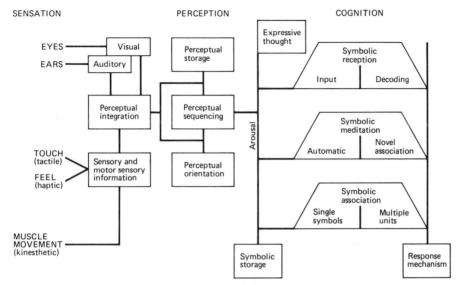

Fig. 5-5. Sabatino's model (1968) of information-processing behaviors.

learner characteristics. As a result, the learner characteristic system has four major classifications:

1. Motor training (sensorimotor)
2. Perceptual training (visual and auditory)
3. Language, related to nonacademic and academic learning
4. Academic remediation of achievement areas, e.g., reading, math, and handwriting

These four factors were selected because they make it possible to classify learner characteristics systematically, using learner characteristics as a means for instructional interventions. Of the four, motor training is the most basic and has the poorest transfer to academic achievement. Perceptual training may show some transfer to academic learning, but it primarily provides for the discrimination of perceptual information and for the storage and integration of visual or auditory symbols. Language learning is directly related to academic learning, for without language there is no basis for learning academic subject matter; however, language training does not automatically mean that language skills will also increase. Finally, direct academic remediation of achievement skills provides the richest increase in academic skill growth, but does not improve coordination, balance, perception, and, possibly, new language learning. In short, educational prescriptions can provide the bases for training a specific academic or nonacademic behavior, but the professional judgment of the educator is required to determine the behavior that needs attention.

It may be seen that cognitive theorists have generally used models as concrete explanations, permitting greater examination of the component parts, aptitudes, traits, or learner characteristics represented in a theory. Yet it is important to remember that most explanations of cognition are based on either a theoretical view of how information is processed or on how the human nervous system interacts with a task to be learned. The practitioner must be willing to accept speculation and some ambiguity as any cognitive model is accepted and placed into the instructional procedure.

COGNITIVE TRAITS AND ACADEMIC PERFORMANCE

There is a voluminous body of research literature examining the relationship between specific cognitive mental processes and subsequent academic achievement. Many mildly handicapped children have difficulty associating word meaning with perceptually received symbolic information (McGinnis, 1963), and children with so-called central language problems are frequently unable to consistently name objects, recall words, and/or interpret environmental or language stimuli. Some children are able to learn nouns and verbs and employ their usage well, but are unable to use verbs denoting past or future tense, adverbs, and adjectives. Generally, the more abstract the stimuli, the greater the difficulty in using that concept meaningfully. One example is that many mildly handicapped children can interpret one word or one sentence, but are unable to understand multiple words or multiple sentences. Wiig and Semel (1973) noted that learning disabled adolescents have difficulty in comprehending logical operations in even single sentences and perform poorly on measures of syntax and language comprehension. Thus, a vicious circle is born: delays in learning syntactical rules reduce the ability to comprehend the language fully, and the inability to comprehend language diminishes subsequent verbal rule learning. Therefore, much of the diagnostic and management training associated with central language difficulties in mildly handicapped students are caught in this cyclic interdependence. One of the resulting problems is the extreme difficulty in diagnostically differentiating expressive and receptive language deficits.

Theoretically, it should be easy to distinguish differences in the ability to receive meaningful speech and the ability to express it. In some cases, as with children who are unable to form word units motorically (apraxia), the expressive language problem appears obvious. However, some children may have word deafness, failing to develop expressive language because of a complete inability to know the meaning of words. One of the more common difficulties frequently experienced by children with expressive language difficulties is that they reauditorize words for spontaneous speech (Bryant, 1972). Reauditorization refers to a disturbance in retrieving words, even though the meaning of the word is known. Some children are unable to organize words and phrases; therefore, their use of language shows a struggle for production. It is not uncommon for older children to develop monotone speech as a result of "feeling" their words with tongue and teeth. On the one hand, children with expressive disorders may read better than they speak, or they may not read well at all. On the other hand, it is not unusual for children with receptive problems to read words far beyond their expected grade level. Their dependence on the visual world forces them to begin to read (by themselves) at age 3 or so, and it is not unusual to see these children, with very confused speech and an inability to comprehend auditory language signals, recognize words at the third- to fifth-grade level at age 5.

Wiig, Semmel, and Crouse (1973) obtained data suggesting that mildly handicapped children with central language problems have difficulty with the third person singular, singular and plural possessives, and meaningful inflections. Seligman (1972–1973) analyzed the speech of four mildly handicapped children and found an overdependence on single declarative sentences and sentences that did not express ideas in a logical sequence; these children confused present and past tense verbs, often using them inappropriately. Moran and Byrne (1977) noted that learning disabled children were frequently unable to use the morphological rules regulating verb tense.

Fry, Johnson, and Merehl (1970) found good readers to possess better verbal story-telling capabilities, including greater fluency and larger speaking vocabularies, than poor readers. Vogel (1977) and Denckla (1974) both found poor readers to evidence greater syntactical and morphological errors than good readers. That inability to grasp the suprasegmental structures of language is summarized in the work with learning disabled children by Wiig and Roach (1975). Their observations were focused by the fact that learning disabled subjects relied heavily upon sentence meaning to aid in their recall of words or sentences. Memory for sentences was not difficult for this group of academic underachievers even when there was a minimum of semantic cues.

Memory for words, digits, and sentences has been investigated as a cognitive variable relating to academic achievement. Different outcomes suggest that there are several different types of memory functions. Long-term, short-term, rote, perceptual memory, memory for words, and memory for digits all appear to require a relationship between performance on auditory memory tasks and reading achievement for first- and third-grade low socioeconomic, academic high-risk children. B. Witkin (1969) and Berry and Eisenson (1956) observed memory difficulties associated with reading and spelling errors in mildly handicapped children. These children shared an inability to cluster words or pictures into meaningful information units and to assign, in turn, a conceptual category to that cluster. In short, insufficient memory for word units definitely interferes with forming new language concepts, and the inability to form concepts for clusters of words interferes with memory. The relationship between memory, intelligence, language output, and language learning remains a strong one.

Connors, Kramer, and Guerra (1969) compared the dichotic listening performance (memory for single words) of children achieving academically with those underachieving and found no significant differences. Yet the word-synthesis ability of the underachieving children was markedly impaired. Menyuk and Looney (1976) found word memory for normal children to be influenced by the child's age (older children had better memories), how the voice was presented, and the nature of the word. Multisyllabic words were easier to remember than single-syllable words. A rich history of research with mildly mentally retarded children (Ellis, 1971) reveals that brain-damaged children frequently evidence memory deficits. Rarely does a retarded child's memory exceed his or her mental age, although memory may be one of the strongest traits for many mildly retarded persons.

Language development is related to academic achievement performance. Diagnostically isolating the specific expressive, central, and receptive components of language function is most difficult. One of the more common problems associated with language learning is memory. Memory is in every sense an aspect of cognition. Yet clear patterns of memory deficit are rarely identified in students, and few teaching materials are directed toward emphasizing memory training for the mildly handicapped. This is unfortunate, since memory can be improved in most mildly handicapped children. Similarly, despite the fact that language relates well to academic achievement, it is heartbreaking to note that few interventions structure and control the use of language, either as a mechanism for teaching other traits, i.e. perceptual skills, or as a major intervention effort in itself. Language, the epitome of cognition, is, like cognition itself, poorly planned as a teaching effort with the mildly handicapped.

COGNITION AND THE THREE MILDLY HANDICAPPED GROUPS

In considering the concept of cognitive similarities and differences among the mildly handicapped groups—the mildly mentally retarded, the behaviorally disordered, and the learning disabled—it is important to note that there are few commonalities among the cognitive development of any two children, so much so that a set of definite cognitive rules of learning is not possible at this time. One person may have a rare talent for music, another for mathematics, and a third for spatial design as manifest in mechanical aptitude. Siblings may vary greatly. Cognitive characteristics within any culture, ethnic group, religious sect, or race vary just as greatly as between any two cultural groups. The differences accepted in the physical attributes of the people of the world may even be greater for learning characteristics. Therefore, any discussion concerning the between-group comparisons of children in the high-incidence handicapped classifications (learning disabled, mildly mentally retarded, and behaviorally disordered) has an added dimension: while it is obvious that differences exist among people who are not "handicapped," add to those differences a "handicapping condition" and the noticeable amount of difference vastly increases.

What do the classifications of mildly mentally retarded, behaviorally disordered, and learning disabled have in common? It has been difficult to attain professional agreement on each of the three definitions. Mild mental retardation (or educational mental retardation) is defined on the basis of cognitive functioning—in particular, intelligence and adaptive behaviors as measured or described using standardized assessment procedures. A behavioral disorder is rarely described on cognitive measures, and while some interferences in cognitive function may result from a behavioral disorder, it is generally regarded as an affective or inter/intrapersonal disturbance. A person with a learning disability is usually defined as being developmentally in the normal range of intelligence, or above, while evidencing the presence of a discernible basic psychological process deficit in one or more of the principle information-processing behaviors. That is, a learning disability is a condition wherein there is a noticeable difference between intelligence (or the ability to form language concepts) and the reception or expression of symbolic conceptual-perceptual language.

Briefly, then, mild mental retardation is a general depression of cognitive capability, resulting primarily in the lack of the capability to formulate language concepts and use them abstractly. Behavioral disorders may interfere in the utilization of cognitive abilities already developed, and, in fact, a cognitive learning problem may be secondary to the behavioral disorder itself, thereby interfering in further affective development. Learning disabilities are thought to be perceptual-cognitive disabilities. According to the commonly accepted definition, the manner in which information is processed and/or expressed by the central nervous system in relationship to language formation capability explains the presence of a learning disability. Theoretically, the three high-incidence handicapped groups are not alike, given age differences, language-formation differences, and type and amount of any specific cognitive deficit (Table 5-1).

Generally speaking, children with mild behavioral disorders display a high frequency of disruptive behaviors (as contrasted to children with serious behavioral disorders), attention getting, and inappropriate behavioral responses, while manifesting normal language reception, concept formation, language usage, and expressive skills, with no memory or spatial ability deficits. The mildly retarded represent suppressed cognitive skills; frequently, the expressive, concept forma-

Table 5-1
Characteristics Identified with Mild Mental Retardation, Behavior Disorders, and Learning Disabilities

	Mild Mental Retardation	Behavioral Disorders	Learning Disabilities
Perception	Visual and auditory perception develops more slowly than CA, but is frequently equivalent to MA.	Perceptual distortions are inconsistent and project the interference of anxieties in how the world is perceived.	Perception is usually less well developed than MA level of language usage.
Language reception	Generally developed at level equivalent to MA and 2–3 years less than CA.	No deficit. Listening problems are associated with manipulation of persons in the environment.	Frequent difficulty in understanding meaning of words or sentences.
Language concept formation	Language learning is generally confined to concrete concept formation.	Language concept formation is not normally influenced unless the behavioral disorders are severe.	Language concept formation proceeds normally.
Language association	Symbol-to-concept association is delayed 2–3 years.	Symbol-to-concept association is generally normal.	Symbol-to-concept formation is source of great difficulty.
Language mediation	Mediation of abstract language is very difficult. Reading and language comprehension is limited to immediate perceptual experiences maintained at a concrete operational level.	Not normally impaired. Child or adolescent may be overdependent upon language to control anxieties or manipulation.	Usually not a problem, except for children with so-called central language deficits.

(continued)

Table 5-1 (continued)

	Mild Mental Retardation	Behavioral Disorders	Learning Disabilities
Language expression	Generally slow to develop, usually equivalent to MA.	Dependence on gang or social values or fear producing words may be exaggerated.	Frequently not equivalent to language reception or usage capability.
Learned behaviors	Social adjustment related to MA. Child may experience rejection as a result of immature social-personal behaviors.	These children are often antisocial. They frequently display inappropriate behaviors, such as daydreaming, poor school adjustment, inability to accept help. They are destructive, rigid, and difficult to modify.	These children perseverate, and may be hyperactive, hypoactive, impulsive, overemotional, and distractible.
Short-term memory	Equivalent to MA or language-concept level. Dicholic and short-term memory may be trained to high degree.	Generally not impaired except under conditions of extreme anxiety.	Inconsistent: good some days, poor on others—usually not well developed.
Long-term memory	Generally very inadequate and below MA. Day-to-day recall of new verbal learning is extremely difficult.	Generally not impaired, except under conditions of extreme anxiety.	Depending upon the child, memory ranges from excellent in remembering language concepts or symbols, to very poor in recalling language units.
Spatial abilities	Generally equivalent to MA.	Generally unimpaired.	May be seriously impaired, representing a significant deficit.

116

tion, and receptors of language are somewhat developed. Memory and spatial abilities may be developed at the language level, but rarely exceed it. In contrast, behavior-disordered children display difficulty in displaying behavior appropriate to a particular social order and its rules. Rarely do these children display severe memory, language learning, or spatial difficulties. Learning disabilities seemingly has the foggiest definition. The entity is supposedly characterized by poor information-processing behaviors in the presence of normal intelligence. Motivation and self-concept are generally quite low in contrast to the other groups.

There are real differences in the cognitive development capabilities of these three groups of handicapped children—if one is permitted to generalize about the diagnostic categories, and is not asked to reference a specific case in any of three groups. But it should always be kept in mind that handicapped children seldom read professional textbooks, and therefore feel little call to think or behave as we expect them to. Therefore, we may wish to speculate that some differences are more theoretical than actual.

CAN COGNITIVE DIFFERENCES AMONG THE MILDLY HANDICAPPED BE DIAGNOSED?

Asking if the mildly handicapping conditions can be diagnosed is not the same as asking if theoretical, category-specific differences exist. Theoretically, differences do exist, especially between two children of the same age, free of any behavioral disorder, one with mild mental retardation, and one with learning disabilities. But, there are very few studies that contrast the cognitive development of the three groups comprising the mildly handicapped condition.

Unfortunately a substantial problem surfaces immediately: there is still confusion as to what constitutes a cognitive measure. Much of that confusion results from the rigid dependence on product or output measurement, i.e., IQ scores or grade-level equivalents. The scores may indeed be derived from cognitive tasks, but a global score such as an IQ constitutes only a summation of interindividual comparisons. Therefore, tests that offer scores other than a composite IQ have been used in the bulk of investigations of cognition. Of available tests, the Wechsler Intelligence Scale for Children (WISC) has been the most commonly used. Indeed, this test has been used in the majority of studies examining the consistencies of cognitive patterns in children of specific diagnostic classifications.

Wechsler developed the Wechsler Intelligence Scales for Children in 1949 (Sabatino & Miller, 1979). No other standardized instrument used in an educational setting has been subjected to more rigorous empirical investigation. A wealth of studies generated by the WISC consistently demonstrate its powerful psychometric properties. Twenty-five years after its publication, the WISC was revised (WISC-R; Wechsler, 1974). Seventy-two percent of the WISC items were retained in the WISC-R. However, the WISC-R was standardized on a stratified sample of white and nonwhite American children representative of data from the 1970 United States Census.

With the WISC-R has come new research interest in the diagnostic applications of WISC. Verbal IQ–performance IQ discrepancies, scaled-score scatter, factor structures, and subtest patterns for special populations are of concern to the psychologist and educator who seek to use the WISC-R for differential diagnosis and educational programming.

While earlier studies such as those by Burks and Bruce (1955), Altus (1956), Robeck (1960, 1964), Pattera (1963), and Birch and Belmont (1966), showed considerable promise, the results of more recent studies are discouraging in their efforts to report a single, clear-cut pattern of WISC subtest scores. Ackerman, Peters, and Dykman (1971) concluded that: "There are not, so far as the authors can determine, any characteristic WISC patterns which single children with learning disabilities out of a school population" (p. 163). Waugh and Bush (1971), Matarazzo (1972), and Bannatyne (1971, 1974) suggested that intersubtest scatter has diagnostic relevance for selected kinds of pathology, i.e., minimal brain dysfunction and learning disabilities. In a recent study of 200 learning disabled students (Smith, Coleman, Dokecki, & Davis, 1977), distinct scaled-score patterns consistent with those hypothesized by Bannatyne (1971) were found. In contrast, two reviews of research on the original WISC, covering the years 1950–1960 (Littell, 1960) and 1960–1970 (Zimmerman & Woo-Sam, 1972) indicated that prediction based upon subtest scales and score patterns was speculative and not empirically supported.

As in the measurement of all cognitive abilities, theoretical views abound. For example, Witkin, Dyk, Faterson, Goodenough, and Kays (1962) proposed that WISC subtests fall into three major categories that tap relatively independent functions: (1) The verbal-comprehension segment is composed of information, vocabulary, and comprehension subtests; (2) the analytic-field-approach segment is made up of object assembly, block design, and picture completion subtests; and (3) the attention-concentration segment is composed of arithmetic, digit span, and coding subtests. Witkin et al. proposed that this factor-score approach would offer diagnostic information of importance in understanding the learning problems of specific children being assessed, thus enhancing the usefulness of the WISC-R in psychoeducational evaluation. Few studies support this, although some recent studies have found significant differences in performance factors by clinically defined samples of hyperactive and learning disabled children and by pupils in public schools classified as educationally handicapped and educably mentally retarded (Keogh & Hall, 1974; Keogh, Wetter, McGinty, & Donlon, 1973).

Anderson, Kaufman, and Kaufman (1976) administered the WISC-R to 41 learning disabled children. Despite the facts that (1) the learning disabled children scored about one standard deviation below the normative mean on the WISC-R, and (2) there were no characteristic strengths and weaknesses in the group profile, the learning disabled children did not show a consistent subscale (subtest) pattern. The researchers estimated that 30 percent of all children with normal intelligence have discrepancies as large or larger than learning disabled children.

Bannatyne (1968) categorized the WISC subtest scaled scores into three main areas for diagnostic purposes: (1) spatial; (2) conceptual; and (3) sequential. The spatial score was derived from three performance subtest scaled scores: object assembly, block design, and picture completion. These subtests do not involve sequencing, but require the ability to manipulate objects in multidimensional space either symbolically or directly, according to Smith et al. (1977). The conceptual score was obtained from three verbal subtest scores: vocabulary, comprehension, and similarities, which together represent general verbal fluency. Digit span, coding, and picture arrangement subtests are contained within the sequential category. These subtests usually require short-term memory storage and retrieval of sequences of auditory and verbal stimuli.

This suggested tripartite recategorization of WISC-R subtest scores possess greater diagnostic value than the traditional verbal versus performance dichotomy, according to Smith et al. (1977). Using 208 learning disabled and educably mentally retarded children, they reported that the subjects manifested spatial-sequential subtest patterns for both low- and high-IQ learning disabled groups, but not for educable mentally retarded children.

An interesting profile paradigm of WISC-R scores for reading disabled children was presented by Vance, Wallbrown, and Blaha (1979). Five meaningful profiles were obtained by these researchers: distractibility, perceptual organization, language disability–automatic, language disability–pervasive, and behavioral comprehension and coding. Most students (75 percent) had WISC-R profiles that showed considerable similarity to one of these ability patterns (syndromes). The profiles of some students (14 percent) tended to split evenly between syndromes or showed only minimal similarity to any of the five syndromes. These findings suggest that WISC-R profiles often provide useful information for generating remedial hypotheses, although this is not always the case. The study further suggests that the WISC-R profiles for 78 of the 128 students originally included in the sample present enough similarity to be useful in generating remedial strategies.

Jackson, Farley, and Zimet (1979) investigated the effects of five alternative administrative procedures for the WISC-R on 100 low- and high-impulsive, emotionally disturbed children. The tests were: (1) reinforcing attention; (2) reward for success; (3) self-vocalization; (4) feedback; and (5) standard conditions. Low-impulsive students ranked highest with the feedback and standard administrative procedures and lowest on the self-vocalization procedure on a consistent basis across IQ scales. The reinforcing attention and reward for success were ranked as the next most effective conditions. For high-impulsive subjects, reward for success and reinforcing attention were ranked as the two most effective administrative procedures. As with low-impulsive children, the self-vocalization procedure produced the lowest scores. The feedback and standard administrative conditions were ranked third and fourth. These rank orders were consistent for full-scale, verbal, and performance IQ scores for the high-impulsive group.

Hart (in press) examined verbal IQ–performance IQ discrepancies and scaled-score scatter with 477 elementary school-aged ("high-risk") students who were diagnostically classified as educably mentally retarded, learning disabled, emotionally handicapped, slow learner, culturally different, and no significant problems. No differences were reported by Hart in the verbal IQ–performance IQ discrepancy scores and in the subtest range and deviation scores among any of the six "high-risk" groups. The author noted that the verbal–performance discrepancies and scaled-scored scatter for the six groups of students were very similar to the discrepancies and scatter reported for the WISC-R standardization sample. Similarly, Wolf (1965) found emotionally disturbed adolescents to be similar in IQ scores on intelligence tests to nonemotionally disturbed youths, while Rowley (1961) demonstrated no significant differences between a group of emotionally disturbed children and a group of brain-injured children on intelligence test profiles.

Is there a consistent cognitive difference among various "high-risk" groups?

If there is, it apparently is not captured by one of the most common diagnostic instruments used to sample several different assumed cognitive functions. Yet, on the other hand, the study of cognitive processes is frequently not observed or reported. If indeed it were, two phenomena would be noted: (1) intraindividual comparisons would result, and (2) the observations of the interaction of learner with the information to be learned would remain the detailed content of any reports. In short, cognition generally is not studied or reported by most diagnosticians as a specific function. The result is that the measures of cognition are summaries, influenced by many test-taking and test-administration variables. Indeed, variance in scores has been recognized and attributed to test instructions (Swineford & Miller, 1953), test-sensitivity of the child (Baurer, 1977), and test anxiety and dependence proneness (Yamamoto & Davis, 1966). Given this, it may be concluded that there simply is not a great amount of sophistication in assessing or interpreting measures of specific cognitive processes. The result is that any conclusions stating that the three mildly handicapped groups are similar or dissimilar in cognitive development are probably faulty.

PROGRAMMATIC AND INSTRUCTIONAL CONSIDERATIONS

The use of cognitive differences in the provision of instruction and program development is cloudy. Differences in the development and function of cognitive performance should exist between the three groups of handicapped children from a definitional standpoint. If the categories are in fact valid, differences in the development of mental processes should be apparent, and applicable to programming. But as we have seen in our examination of diagnostic practices, the commonly used WISC seldom shows a distinct category-specific subscale profile. Instead, the three groups of high-incidence handicapped children often demonstrate considerable intragroup overlap as well as considerable similarity with the normal population. While one could then easily conclude that no differences exist, several factors must be considered. First, standard diagnostic procedures reflect learned products, not learning-process orientations. This means that formal tests generally request responses asking what one has learned, now how the mental processes work in learning a given dimension. Second, commonly used tests (WISC/WISC-R, Illinois Test of Psycholinguistic Abilities, etc.) have failed to demonstrate adequate reliability or validity for the specific tasks purported to be ascertained. Therefore, we cannot be certain of the meaning and accuracy of these results. Finally, most instructional goals are directed at learning to read, write, manipulate mathematics, learn social studies, etc., with the assumption that cognitive development proceeds from those experiences. For these reasons, at least, the past decade has seen a rejection of cognitive measurement and training; hence, new procedures have largely not been developed or tested in wide-scale practice. Therefore, if we consider cognitive development from the standpoint of the mildly handicapped, what conclusions can be reached? The following seem most likely.

1.   Instructionally, the same noncognitive-specific teaching methods and materials appear to be equally applicable to all three handicapped groups.

2. A goodly number of mildly mentally retarded and learning disabled children have behavioral disorders that must be managed appropriately before instructional intervention can begin (Christoplos, 1973).
3. Many of the behavioral management techniques—shaping, modeling, operant conditioning procedures—are equally applicable to all three groups of high-incidence handicapped children (Gardner, 1977).
4. Perceptual-motor training benefits children only in the early years (Cratty, 1971) and does not transfer to the higher cognitive traits (Keogh, 1973).
5. Language training does provide transfer to memory training (Semmel & Bennett, 1970) and academic achievement growth (Goodman, 1970), but is rarely practiced as a specific training procedure. Instead, it is frequently linked to vocabulary training, reading vocabulary, and academically related language usage and not to critical problem solving through the structured language-learning stages derived from the developmental and functional use of language under normal conditions (Graham, 1976). In fact, in a national survey (Fristoe, 1976) of 187 language-intervention programs used with mentally retarded children, it was found that 39 of the language-intervention programs are published in kit form; 31 are in journals and books; 66 are in experimental phase, and 51 are currently available only to researchers. Furthermore, most of the approaches to language intervention were, according to Fristoe (1976) "equally applicable for use with other types of developmental disability" (p. 50). It is quite paradoxical, then, that the one most effective cognitive training area is often ignored, perhaps in large part because of a lack of available data at the consumer level.

CONCLUSION

The best practice interventions for handicapped students potentially reside in information concerning a profile of the cognitive learning style. Such instructional and behavioral management plans are rarely helped by formal test results, seldom relate to categorical labels, and are difficult to formulate based on informal task-oriented diagnostic prescriptive approaches (Reger, Schroeder, & Uschold, 1968). Cognitive training results from these interventions. Functional improvement is sought for those specific traits that constitute the mental processes required to successfully perform a task. In some respects, cognitive training is developmental; it is process-learning as opposed to product-learning information. We support the supposition advanced by Kirk (1962) that handicapped children have discrepancies in growth, which, in turn, tend to aid in their classification into some category of exceptionality. In this view, the principle discrepancies between normal and handicapped learners are cognitive growth factors influenced by the pathology that causes the disability. But since there is only an indirect relationship between disability and etiology, there is at best only an indirect relationship between type of cognitive deficit (strength and weakness) and either the etiology or pathology. Therefore, it is the educator's responsibility to decide if cognitive development should be trained before other behavioral and/or instructional programs can be successful in reaching the set product-learning objectives.

REFERENCES

Ackerman, P. T., Peters, J. E., & Dykman, R. A. Children with specific learning disabilities: WISC profiles. *Journal of Learning Disabilities*, 1971, *4*, 150–166.

Altus, G. T. A WISC profile for retarded readers. *Journal of Consulting Psychology*, 1956, *20*, 155–156.

Anderson, M., Kaufman, A. S., & Kaufman, N. L. Use of the WISC-R with a learning disabled population: Some diagnostic implications. *Psychology in the Schools*, 1976, *13*, 381–386.

Bannatyne, A. Diagnosing learning disabilities and writing remedial prescriptions. *Journal of Learning Disabilities*, 1968, *1*, 242–249.

Bannatyne, A. *Language, reading, and learning disabilities: Psychology, neuropsychology, diagnosis and remediation*. Springfield, Il.: Charles C Thomas, 1971.

Bannatyne, A. Diagnosis: A note on recategorization of the WISC scaled scores. *Journal of Learning Disabilities*, 1974, *7*, 272–273.

Baurer, R. H. Memory processes in children with learning disabilities: Evidence for deficient rehearsal. *Journal of Experimental Child Psychology*, 1977, *24*, 415–430.

Berry, M. F., & Eisenson, J. *Speech disorders*. New York: Appleton-Century-Crofts, 1956.

Birch, H. G., & Belmont, I. The intellectual profile of retarded readers. *Perceptual and Motor Skills*, 1966, *22*, 787–816.

Bloom, B. (Ed.). *Taxonomy of educational objectives, the classification of educational goals. Handbook 1: Cognitive domain*. New York: McKay, 1956.

Bruner, J., Oliver, R., & Greenfield, P. *Studies in cognitive growth: A collaboration at the Center for Cognitive Studies*. New York: Wiley, 1966.

Bryant, N. C. Subject variables: Definition, incidence, characteristics, and correlates. In N. D. Bryant & C. Kass (Eds.), *Final report: LTI in Learning Disabilities*, (Vol. 1). (USOE Grant No. OE6-0-71-4425-604, Project No. 127145). Tucson, Arizona: University of Arizona, 1972.

Burks, H. F., & Bruce, P. The characteristics of poor and good readers as disclosed by the WISC. *Journal of Educational Psychology*, 1955, *46*, 488–493.

Campagnac, E. T. *Mulcaster's elementarie*. London: Clarendon Press, 1925.

Christoplos, F. Keeping exceptional children in regular class. *Exceptional Children*, 1973, *39*, 569–572.

Connors, C. K., Kramer, K., & Guerra, F. Auditory synthesis and dichotic listening in children with learning disabilities. *Journal of Special Education*, 1969, *3*, 163–170.

Cratty, B. *Active learning: Games to enhance academic abilities*. Englewood Cliffs: Prentice-Hall, 1971.

Davis, O. *Psychology of problem solving: Theory and practice*. New York: Basic Books, 1973.

Denckla, M. B. *Naming of pictured objects by dyslexic and non-dyslexic MBD children*. Paper presented at the Academy of Aphasia, 1974.

Ellis, N. R. (Ed.) *Handbook on mental deficiency*. New York: McGraw-Hill, 1971.

Fristoe, M. Language intervention systems: Programs published in kit form. *Journal of Children's Communication Disorders*, 1976, *1*, 49–54.

Fry, M. A., Johnson, C. A., & Merehl, S. Oral language production in relation to reading achievement among select second grades. In D. V. Bakker & P. Satz (Eds.), *Specific reading disability*. Rotterdam, Netherlands: Rotterdam University Press, 1970.

Gagne, R. Instructional variables and learning outcomes. In M. Wittrock & D. Wiley (Eds.), *The evaluation of instruction: Issues and problems*. New York: Holt, Rinehart & Winston, 1970.

Gardner, W. *Learning and behavior characteristics of exceptional children and youth*. Boston: Allyn & Bacon, 1977.

Goodman, K. S. Reading a psycholinguistic guessing game. *International Reading Association Conference Papers*, 1970, *14*, 259–272.

Graham, L. W. Language programming and intervention. In L. Lloyd (Ed.), *Communication assessment and intervention strategies*. Baltimore: University Park Press, 1976.

Guilford, J. P. *Fields of psychology*. Princeton: Van Nostrand, 1966.

Guilford, J. P. Intelligence: 1965 model. *American Psychologist*, 1966, *21* (1), 21.

Guilford, J. P. *The nature of human intelligence*. New York: McGraw-Hill, 1967.

Hart, D. H. *WISC-R test performance of "high-risk" students who are classified according to six diagnostic groups*. Salt Lake City: University of Utah, in press.

Jackson, A., Farley, G., & Zimet, S. Optimizing the WISC-R test performance of low- and high-impulse emotionally disturbed children. *Journal of Learning Disabilities*, 1979, *12*, 56–59.

Keogh, B. Perceptual and cognitive styles: Implications for special education. In L. Mann & D. Sabatino (Eds.), *The first review of special education* (Vol. 1). Philadelphia: JSE Press, 1973.

Keogh, B. K., & Hall, R. J. WISC subtest patterns of educationally handicapped and educable mentally retarded pupils. *Psychology in the Schools,* 1974, *11,* 296–300.

Keogh, B. K., Wetter, J., McGinty, A., & Donlon, G. Functional analysis of WISC performance of learning disordered, hyperactive, and mentally retarded boys. *Psychology in the Schools,* 1973, *10,* 178–181.

Kirk, S. A. *Educating exceptional children.* Boston: Houghton Mifflin, 1962.

Klausmeier, H. J. Individually guided education: 1966–1980. *Journal of Teaching Education,* 1976, *27,* 199–207.

Littell, W. M. The WISC—A review of a decade of research. *Psychological Bulletin,* 1960, *57,* 132–162.

Locke, J. *An essay concerning human understanding.* London: J. M. Dent, 1961.

Mann, L. *Cognitive training: A look at the past and some concerns about the present.* A paper presented at the National Regional Resource Center Conference, Reston, Va., 1974.

Mann, L. *On the trail of process.* New York: Grune & Stratton, Inc., 1980.

Matarazzo, J. D. *Wechsler's measurement and appraisal of adult intelligence.* Baltimore: Williams & Wilkins, 1972.

McGinnis, M. *Aphasic children: Identification and education by the association method.* Washington, D.C.: Volta, 1963.

Meeker, M. N. *The structure of the intellect: Its interpretation and uses.* Columbus: Charles E. Merrill, 1969.

Menyuk, P., & Looney, P. L. A problem of language disorder: Length versus structure. In D. M. Morehead & A. E. Morehead (Eds.), *Normal and deficient child language.* Baltimore: University Park Press, 1976.

Moran, M. R., & Byrne, M. C. Mastery of verb tense markers by normal and learning disabled children. *Journal of Speech and Hearing Research,* 1977, *20,* 529–542.

Newell, A., & Simon, H. *Human problem solving.* Englewood Cliffs: Prentice-Hall, 1972.

Pattera, M. E. A study of thirty-three WISC scattergrams of retarded readers. *Elementary English,* 1963, *40,* 394–405.

Piaget, J. *Science of education and the psychology of the child.* New York: Orion Press, 1970.

Reger, R., Schroeder, W., & Uschold, K. *Special education: Children with learning problems.* New York: Oxford University Press, 1968.

Robeck, M. C. Subtest patterning of problem readers on WISC. *California Journal of Educational Research,* 1960, *11,* 110–115.

Robeck, M. C. Intellectual strengths and weaknesses shown by reading clinic subjects on the WISC. *Journal of Developmental Reading,* 1964, *7,* 120–129.

Rowley, V. N. Analysis of the WISC performance of brain damaged and emotionally disturbed children. *Journal of Consulting Psychology,* 1961, *25,* 553.

Ryckman, D. B., & Wiegerink, R. Factors of the Illinois test of psycholinguistic abilities: A comparison of 18 factor analyses. *Exceptional Children,* 1969, *36,* 107–113.

Sabatino, D. A. The information processing behaviors associated with learning disabilities. *Journal of Learning Disabilities,* 1968, *1,* 440–450.

Sabatino, D. A., & Hayden, D. L. Information processing behaviors related to learning disabilities and mental retardation. *Exceptional Children,* 1970, *37,* 21–29. (a)

Sabatino, D. A., & Hayden, D. L. Variation in information processing behaviors. *Journal of Learning Disabilities,* 1970, *3,* 404–412. (b)

Sabatino, D. A., & Miller, T. L. *Describing learner characteristics of handicapped children and youth.* New York: Grune & Stratton, 1979.

Sabatino, D. A. Miller, T. L., & Schmidt, C. *Learning disabilities.* Rockville Md.: Aspen Systems Corporation, 1981.

Seligman, J. Speech pathology progress report. In *Symbol communication research project, progress report 1972–3.* Toronto: Ontario Crippled Children's Center.

Semmel, M. I., & Bennett, S. W. Effects of linguistic structure and delay on memory span of EMR children. *American Journal of Mental Deficiency,* 1970, *74,* 674–680.

Smith, M. D., Coleman, J. M., Dokecki, P. R., & Davis, E. E. Intellectual characteristics of school labeled learning disabled children. *Exceptional Children,* 1977, *43,* 352–357.

Swineford, F., & Miller, P. M. Effects of directions regarding guessing on items statistics of a multiple-choice vocabulary test. *Journal of Educational Psychology,* 1953, *44,* 129–140.

Valett, R. A. *A psychoeducational inventory of basic learning abilities*. Palo Alto, Ca.: Fearon, 1968.

Valett, R. A. *Developing cognitive abilities: Teaching children to think*. St. Louis: C. V. Mosby, 1978, p. 37.

Vance, H., Wallbrown, F. H., & Blaha, J. Developing remedial hypotheses from ability profiles. *Journal of Learning Disabilities, 1979, 12,* 557–561.

Vogel, S. A. Morphological ability in normal and dyslexic children. *Journal of Learning Disabilities, 1977, 10,* 35–43.

Waugh, K. W., & Bush, W. J. *Diagnosing learning disorders*. Columbus, Oh.: Charles E. Merrill, 1971.

Webster unabridged dictionary. New York: American Book Company, 1979.

Wechsler, D. *Manual for the Wechsler Intelligence Scale for Children (revised)*. New York: Psychological Corporation, 1974.

Wiig, E. H., & Roach, M. A. Immediate recall of semantically varied "sentences" by learning disabled adolescents. *Perceptual and Motor Skills, 1975, 40,* 119–125.

Wiig, E. H., & Semel, E. M. Comprehension of linguistic concepts requiring logical opera-tions by learning disabled children. *Journal of Speech and Hearing Research, 1973, 16,* 627–636.

Wiig, E. H., Semel, E. M., & Crouse, M. A. The use of English morphology by high-risk and learning disabled children. *Journal of Learning Disabilities, 1973, 6,* 457–465.

Witkin, B. Auditory perception: Implications for language development. *Journal of Research and Development in Education, 1969, 3,* 53–71.

Witkin, H. A., Dyk, R., Faterson, H., Goodenough, D. R., & Kays, S. *Psychological differentiation*. New York: Wiley, 1962.

Wolf, M. G. Emotional disturbance and school achievement. *Journal of School Psychology, 1965, 4,* 16–18.

Yamamoto, K., & Davis, O. L. Test instructions, test anxiety, and dependence proneness in relation to children's performance on tests of intelligence. *Psychology in the Schools, 1966, 3,* 167–170.

Zimmerman, I. L., & Woo-Sam, J. Research with the Wechsler Intelligence Scale for Children: 1960–1970. *Psychology in the Schools, 1972, 9,* 232–271.

Carol Lynn Waryas

6
Language Development of Mildly Handicapped Children and Adolescents

Language poses multiple problems for education because it is both curriculum content and learning environment, both the object of knowledge, and a medium through which other knowledge is acquired. (p. 135)

The foregoing quote by Cazden (1973) summarizes the complex role of language and its development in the educational process; in Marshall McLuhan's words, it might be said of language that "the medium is the message"—in a very real sense. First, an appropriate, fully developed, shared system of communication is a sine qua non of all effective and efficient interactions with others in the environment. The lack of such a system often serves as one of the primary, defining characteristics of many handicapping conditions, including, in particular, mental retardation, emotional disturbances, and learning disabilities. Also, language has been termed "the primary means of socialization by the environment" (Olson, 1970, p. 273), and thus can be seen as the primary mode of all instruction, academic or otherwise. Even the most basic stimulus-response (S-R) interaction can be seen to consist of a communicative exchange between the subject and the trainer. Furthermore, language deficits do not exist in a vacuum. Regardless of etiology, deficient communication may result in other deficits in behavior (particularly in the areas of cognitive and social-affective development), which in turn serve to depress communicative functioning even further. Thus, the study of language development, disorders, and remediation is vital to an understanding of the educational process for the handicapped student; communication is the basis of education, and perhaps *is* the educational process itself.

The terms *language* and *communication* have been used interchangeably here, not because they mean exactly the same thing, but because it is important to view language as the vehicle for communication, rather than an end in itself. This deliberate ambiguity reflects the current conceptualization of language as comprised of more than just the parameters of phonology, morphology, syntax, and semantics—the traditional divisions of grammar. If language is seen only as grammar, the structure of language assessment and remediation procedures assumes a different form than structures that begin with a broader view of language as a

125

formalized system of communication consisting of interlocking aspects of structure, function, and meaning. Bloom and Lahey's definition (1978) of language encompasses all three aspects: "A language is a code whereby ideas about the world are represented through a conventional system of arbitrary signals for communication" (p. 4). Thus, according to this definition, communication is the purpose that gives rise to the need for the system of language. Proceeding from this perspective, an examination of language development and disorders begins not with the code itself, but with the process—communication—that it carries out. Viewed in this light, it is less important to determine whether an individual can manipulate given aspects of grammar—such as past tense markings, passive voice, and other such structures, which comprise the majority of traditional analysis procedures—than to determine what the communicative demands of the environment actually are and how well his or her language skills conform to them (Gruenwald & Yoder, in press).

This is not to suggest that the acquisition of grammatical rules is an unimportant factor in language development. It is vital, in order for communicative functions to be carried out, that these rules be acquired. However, as Ervin-Tripp (1967) wrote, "To qualify as a native speaker . . . one must learn . . . rules. . . . This is to say, of course, that one must learn to behave *as though one knew the rules*" (p. x). Before considering the nature of these rules, it is important to place them in the perspective of the process of communication itself; how the language system is viewed has a profound effect upon what is presumed to be acquired in the process of language development, how it is acquired, what the nature of language deficiency is, and how it may be remediated. There is also a vital difference in teaching someone rules and teaching someone to behave as though he or she knew them.

THE NATURE OF THE LANGUAGE SYSTEM

The study of language development, viewed by those not directly concerned with this investigation, must often seem like the story of the blind men of Hindustan who set out to describe an elephant, one feeling the leg and calling it a tree, another approaching the trunk and calling it a hose, and so on. It is not surprising that the study of such a complex phenomenon has forced investigators to such partial descriptions in order to begin to understand its parameters; however, the danger in such fractionation lies in the potential failure to reunify the "elephant" from its component parts. Investigations of language development have tended to parallel the theoretical approaches to the study of the language system within the field of linguistics since the early 1960s, and, thus, results have been largely colored by the prevailing assumptions of linguistic theory (Waryas, 1978a). This explains the reorientation in focus that is apparent from early studies of language development, which focused largely on phonology or vocabulary development (McCarthy, 1954; Templin, 1957); to studies of syntax in child language following the introduction of N. Chomsky's transformational grammar (Braine, 1963; N. Chomsky, 1957, 1965; McNeill, 1966); to the "semantic revolution" of the early 1970s, reflecting renewed linguistic investigations into the meaning component of language (Bloom, 1970; Bowerman, 1973a, 1973b); to current research interest in the functions of language, inspired by the study of pragmatics (Dore, 1974; Halliday, 1970).[1] It is easy for observers of this restructuring of language research to become frustrated by what seems to be a lack of unanimity among language investigators concerning even what they are investigating, and to elect either to ignore these seemingly divergent issues or to adopt simplistic or static models of language for their particular purposes. However, as Rees (1978) pointed out, language researchers are not just replacing one view of language with another—one does not stop considering syntax, for example, to look for semantics. Rather, new approaches to the study of language development add to and supplement each other, creating a multidimensional approach to language. In light of the past, current formulations of the components of the language system and their interrelationships can be appreciated, bearing in mind that the multidimensional model is neither a rejection of all previous conceptualizations nor the final answer to the question of what is language.

Bloom and Lahey (1978) proposed a three-dimensional view of language, based on their previously cited definition: "Language consists of some aspect of *content* or meaning that is coded or represented by linguistic *form* for some purpose or *use* in a particular context" (p. 11). This model has been visually represented as a set of three interlocking circles, representing the assumed synergy between the components in normal development. The form component is probably most familiar to those acquainted with previous studies of language, since it is the form of language that has been most studied and that, in fact, is often erroneously assumed to *be* language. The form of language comprises those aspects of a communication system that give rise to its structure of expression. At least five subcomponents of form can be identified: syntax, morphology, phonology, prosodic features, and kinesics and proxemics. (In this chapter, language is discussed as a spoken system, since the aural-oral modality is primary in all human communication, with all written and most manual systems derived from it.)

Syntax can be defined as the rules for ordering words and morphemes into gramatical utterances, both of sentence formation and transformation. Morphology refers to the rules for the formation of words and the modification of words into other words by the processes of derivation (*farm–farmer*) or grammatical modulation (*see* + past tense = *saw*). Phonology refers to the system of sounds of the language and the rules for their combination. Syntax, morphology, and phonology together define the basic structure of an utterance with prosodic features—those aspects of voice that give rise to the intonation patterns of speech and that provide a second channel of communication that may emphasize or modify the form of the utterance. Body language, or the parameters of kinesics and proxemics, is an additional mechanism for further modifying or emphasizing the structure. Any utterance may be described from the perspective of any one or all of these parameters, as illustrated by the analysis of a question of a teen-ager to her father: "I can have the car tonight, can't I?"

In terms of its surface syntactic structure, this utterance could be described in the following way:

---

[1]Further discussion of the evolution of language development research is provided in McLean and Snyder-McLean (1978), Waryas and Stremel-Campbell (1978), Waryas and Crowe (in press), and Bloom and Lahey (1978).

Pronoun + modal verb + main verb + article + noun +
adverb + modal + negative + pronoun.

Alternatively, it could be described as a declarative sentence with an attached tag question.

In order to convey this same information, a simpler utterance that maintained the meaning-bearing words of the main clause of the utterance could have been used, such as "I have car tonight?" However this would violate the "code" of adult language usage because of omission of function words. Total lack of word ordering principles—"Car I tonight have?"—might even result in a loss of intended meaning. Thus, the rules of syntactic formation are necessary to encode meaning in an acceptable form.

The tag question of the utterance "I can have the car tonight, can't I?" is constructed from the main clause by a process of transformation. Stated in terms of rules, this process involves the following steps:

1. Identify the subject and pronominalize it if it is not a pronoun. (Note that if the word *John* had been used in the main clause, *he* would have been used in the tag question.)
2. Check that the auxiliary or modal verb is present; if it isn't, insert the verb *do*. (Note the structure: "John likes ice cream, *doesn't* he?")
3. Invert the order of the pronoun and the modal verb ("I can" becomes "can't I").
4. Change the sign of the verb from positive to negative (or vice versa, as in "He *isn't* here, *is* he?").

The application of these rules occurs automatically in speech, and it is uncommon for someone to even be able to describe what he or she does to construct a tag question. Thus, syntatic rules are considered to be a form of covert or tacit knowledge, comprising a relatively small set capable of describing or generating the infinite number of grammatical sentences in a language.[2]

At other levels of analysis, the same sentence consists of a string of morphemes, which are in turn comprised of phonemes. For example, this utterance consists of the morphemes, *I, can, have, the, car, -n't*. Five of these can occur in isolation (free morphemes), and one, the negative marker, is a bound morpheme and must be attached to another word. Phonologically, the utterance is composed of sound units that obey the rules of English (for example, the consonant combination /nt/ is permissible at the end of a word, but not at the beginning).

In addition, this utterance could be said with a variety of stress patterns, each of which would modify the structure (e.g., "*I* can have the car . . ." versus "I can have the *car* . . .": the first implies "as opposed to *someone* else" and the second implies "as opposed to *something* else"). In addition, facial expression and gestures (kinesics) and position of body in space (proxemics) would greatly affect the spoken form of the utterance. For example, if a negative response were feared, the teen-ager might position herself further from her father, avert her gaze, and chew on her lip.

---

[2]For a comprehensive view of syntactic rules and their operations, see Langacker (1968), Streng (1972), Dale (1976), Hargis (1977), or Fromkin and Rodman (1974).

Just as there are rules for syntax, morphology, and phonology, there are conventions for use of prosodic features and body language, although these are less clearly understood. Their existence is attested to, however, by the fact that we recognize their misuse or their deviations from expected patterns, such as in the case of an individual who speaks in a monotonous fashion or maintains an inappropriate personal distance from his listener. It is clear that people must learn to behave in accordance with these rules.[3]

The second component of Bloom and Lahey's model (1978) is content. Content refers to the meaning of words, both singly (lexical semantics) and in relation to each other (relational semantics). Lexical semantics is the aspect of meaning that is assessed in tests of vocabulary; it refers to the topics of communication, but it has less to do with the total meaning of utterances than the relationships between words. For example, the utterances

> Tom eats ice-cream.
> Sue hit Tom.
> Sue likes ice-cream.

are similar in syntactic structure but differ in the roles that the words play. Assuming that all three utterances refer to the same two individuals, then the lexical meanings of *Sue* and *Tom* are the same in each sentence. In the first sentence, *Tom* plays the role of agent, (or the person conducting the action) of the verb *eat*, while in the second, *Tom* is the recipient of the action. Also in the second, *Sue* is the agent of the action *hit*. In the third sentence, *like* cannot be considered an action since Sue's liking affects her, not the ice-cream. Thus, in the third sentence, the role of Sue may be considered that of person affected by the action. In this regard, Bloom and Lahey suggested that the content of language (semantic concepts such as objects, actions, relations, possession, attributes, and location) are common across all speakers, from the earliest stages of language development through adulthood, while the topics (lexical concepts) discussed will vary widely depending on age, environment, and other factors. Thus, there is a semantic continuity between the infant pointing to the countertop and saying "cookie" and the teen-ager requesting use of the car.[4]

The third component of the model—use—hearkens back to deLaguna's contention (1927) that language exists for the purpose of establishing and maintaining social relationships and providing symbolic representation of one's perceptions and cognitions. In other words, if content refers to the meaning of words, then use (or pragmatics) refers to the meaning of the speaker. Halliday (1970) suggested that three major types of functions are apparent in adult language: the ideational, which serves to express the speaker's perception of the world and his or her experiences with it; the interpersonal, which serves to establish and maintain social relationships; and the textual, which serves to relate language to itself and to the context of use. Integral to appropriate use of language, then, is the speaker's perception of his or her relationship to the listener, the intended effect, the listen-

---

[3]For further reading on morphology, phonology, prosodic features, and body language, see Dale (1976), Wood (1976), Crystal (1969), and Fromkin and Rodman (1974).

[4]A thorough discussion of relational semantics is provided in Brown (1973) and Bloom (1970, 1974). Dale (1976) has provided introductions to the study of word meanings.

er's knowledge, and the linguistic and nonlinguistic communicative demands of the environment. In the pragmatic realm, as well, there are rules of appropriate usage. Some of these rules specify certain conventions or tacit agreements between individuals about what they may expect of each other. Such conversational postulates specify, for example, that a speaker will be clear, that he or she will not provide or ask for unnecessary information, and that he or she will tell the truth. Deliberate violations of these rules indicate that the speaker intends something other than what the content of the utterance indicates. Consider the following utterances:

> Do you know the time?
> You look terrific!
> Eschew obfuscation.

In the first example, it is apparent to the listener that the speaker is not really interested in whether the listener knows what time it is since this would be unnecessary information—except that it would be a necessary condition for being able to tell the speaker what the time is. Thus, the expected answer is "4:00," not "yes." In the second example, the illocutionary force of the utterance (that is, how the speaker intends the utterance to be taken by the listener) will differ depending on the context. Said to one's date for the prom, it has an entirely different force than if said to a friend who has just come in out of the rain. The third example indicates its meaning (that of avoiding ambiguity) by deliberately violating its own principle.

In order to have the intended effect on a listener, a speaker must be able to both (1) take the listener's point of view (in terms of what the speaker presupposes the listener's knowledge to be) and (2) encode more than one intent at a time. To illustrate the first point: The rules of pronominalization require that the speaker be sensitive to the listener's knowledge of an intended referent. Thus, the utterance "He really is nice" can be appropriately used only after first establishing who "he" is. If the speaker is mentioning a variety of males, it is necessary to periodically refer to them by name so that ambiguity will be avoided. In regard to the second point: there is a vast difference between saying "I want some candy" and "That fudge sure looks good." The latter form, called an indirective, has the same intent—that of obtaining candy—as the first, but it also has the added intent of being polite. (In this regard, Bates (1976) provided an excellent discussion of pragmatic theory.)

These examples indicate the effect of pragmatic factors on the form of language. Returning to our teen-ager, let us consider variations on her utterance.

> I can have the car tonight, can't I?
> I can't have the car tonight, can I?
> Can I have the car tonight?

Each utterance is a request for permission, but only the third leaves the expected answer in doubt. Obviously, the first anticipates and prompts a positive response, and the second expects a negative one. Thus, as Bruner (1974–1975) suggested, "utterances are used for different ends and use is a powerful determinant of rule structures" (p. 283).

McLean and Snyder-McLean (1978) suggested an alternative to Bloom and Lahey's interlocking circle model of form, content, and use that captures the effect of use and content on form in comprehension and production. In their model, the pragmatic component (comprised of the speaker's social history and immediate interpersonal context) and the semantic component (representing the speaker's cognitive-sensorimotor history and immediate physical context) jointly determine the operation of the "referencing mechanisms" (the form components) in the process of language production. In comprehension, a "referent-decoding mechanism" is proposed as the first step, since decoding of form is obviously required for correct interpretation of both the speaker's semantic meaning and pragmatic intent. In this process, the listener does not have access to the speaker's meaning and intent directly, but instead must make reference to his or her own past cognitive and social experiences and perception of the present physical and social-communicative context to determine the intended effect of what has been said.

THE ROLE OF LANGUAGE IN DEVELOPMENT

The interaction of the form, content, and use components of language was neatly summarized in the contention of J. Miller and Yoder (1972) that in order to talk, the speaker must have something to say, a way to say it, and a reason for saying it. This reinforces the assumption that considerations of content and use are at least as important as form in the development of language. There is little need to have a way to say something if there is nothing to say or no reason to say it.

Mahoney (1975) suggested that the communication system exists before the child even begins to acquire the formal components of language. A variety of pragmatic intents are apparent prior to the development of syntactic structures. Dore (1975) identified a set of "primitive speech acts" that can be identified at the one-word stage of development on the basis of the phonemic and prosodic structure of the utterance, the child's nonlinguistic behavior (gestures and body actions), contextual factors, and adult response. Bates and Johnston (1977) even suggested that communicative functions (in terms of effects on the listener) may be perceived in the infant's earliest vocalizations. Thus, the use component of language can be found prior to content or form in the course of development, and it could be inferred that it is this component that provides the motive force for the entire process of language development. Halliday (1975) wrote of the process of language development as "learning how to mean," and Dore (1975) suggested that the child's attempts to "get different things done with words" directs him or her to "the appropriate devices and conventions" (or form components).

With interpersonal functions providing the initial motivation, the child's course of language development consists, in broad terms, of learning about the world of people, objects, events, attributes, and the relationships among them, on one hand, and of learning how to "map" or represent them symbolically through language, on the other. McLean and Snyder-McLean (1978) saw this last process as being accomplished via a "transactional" association between the child and the mature language users in the environment. As Lyons (1966) suggested, by 18 months the child already possesses the concepts of "things," "properties," and "situations." The child has the conceptual base for developing language, given that he or she is then provided with "primary linguistic data" by language users in the environment. In a similar fashion, MacNamara (1972) suggested that it is only because the infant already understands the concepts that language encodes that he or she is able to acquire it, or, in MacNamara's terms (1972) to "crack the code" of language, since "the infant uses meaning as a clue to language, rather than language as a clue to meaning" (p. 1). Bruner (1974-1975) suggested that "to master a language a child must acquire a complex set of broadly transferable or generative skills—perceptual, motor, conceptual, social, and linguistic—which when appropriately coordinated yield linguistic performances" (p. 256). The "transactional model" of McLean and Snyder-McLean (1978) suggests that the child acquires the cognitive and social bases of language from perceptual-motor interactions with the environment. McLean and Snyder-McLean (1978) suggested that the "specific linguistic code is acquired through the child's participation in a dynamic partnership with the mature language users in his environment" (p. 111).

The process of language development appears to rest on four synergistic aspects of development or interaction.

1. Interactions with the language environment
2. Social-affective development
3. Cognitive development
4. Neurological maturation

While it has been contended that form, use, and content are natural outgrowths of linguistic, social, and cognitive interactions, respectively (McLean & Snyder-McLean, 1978), it is apparent that linguistic interactions depend heavily on social interaction, and that both require cognitive development (in the sense that both learning the language and learning how to interact with others require cognitive abilities and organization). Also, since cognitive development must surely depend on neurological maturation and organization, this comprises the substrata for all three aspects of development (Waryas & Crowe, in press).

The course of language development in the domains of form, content, and use provides both a means of gauging the child's linguistic, social, and cognitive maturity in interactions with the environment and a set of feedback or regulatory mechanisms for determining the course of further interactions (Waryas & Crowe, in press). As the child matures, the environment increases both the challenges it presents (as seen in the increased linguistic complexity it provides) and, its mental demands—what Sigel and Cocking (1977) called "distancing behaviors," which are conveyed through the use of language. In other words, language provides both the content and primary modality of environmental interactions and instruction. The child who fails to acquire language skills at the expected age begins to be increasingly "out of sync" with the environment—socially, cognitively, and linguistically—and this difference, in turn, begins to affect the course of further environmental interactions.

The specifics of the process of language development have been investigated by countless researchers and from numerous perspectives; a venture into the literature often leaves one with the feeling that the field is more replete with theories than with data. It is particularly difficult to emerge from a casual review of the literature with a clear picture of when particular language skills emerge, and in relationship to what other factors.

The majority of research has focused on children between birth and 5 years old. Educators dealing with older populations (that is, students in the formal school years) might well wonder if developmental information is relevant to their specific problems. In fact the question "What can I expect of the junior high student in terms of language skills?" is often asked. More explicitly, educators ask, "How do I apply this infant research to the language deficits of my students, anyway?" The answers to such questions lie in the fact that children older than 5, for the most part, are assumed to be essentially linguistically mature. This does not suggest that all language development has been accomplished prior to the start of schooling. For example, vocabulary development constitutes a lifelong process. Moreover, C. Chomsky (1969), in an investigation of the acquisition of several complex linguistic constructions such as "ask/tell," found an increase in comprehension up to age 10. In a similar fashion, certain forms of technical communication require increasing levels of linguistic sophistication in adult life, as any graduate student writing a thesis will attest. However, it is generally assumed that the basic components of form, content, and use are established early, with only further minor modifications necessary to reach the skills of an adult. Thus, one should expect a junior high student to be a linguistically mature adult, with no essential deviations from adult usage. It is interesting to note the perplexity of beginning speech and language clinicians in assessing the speech and language skills of older children and adolescents because "there aren't any norms for them!" A moment's reflection will indicate that if, for example, a 6-year-old is expected to make no errors on a given test according to norms, the same would be expected of a 16-year-old. In such cases, standardized tests become, in essence, criterion-referenced tests (i.e., the number of correct responses is compared against the criterion that all should be correct) of the skills assessed.

There is evidence to suggest that failure to appropriately develop early linguistic foundations has serious impact on the older child. In reference to a study by de Ajuriaguerra, Jaeggi, Guignard, Kocher, Maquard, Roth, and Schmid (1976), Morehead and Morehead (1976) suggested that "the failure to develop an adequate linguistic system appears to have its most serious repercussions during early adolescence in nonlinguistic areas of development, such as intelligence and social behavior" (p. 345). Lack of appropriate language development at this point appears to preclude the development of formal operations and adult thought. Formal porpositional thinking, according to Wood (1976), comprises the abilities to (1) think logically in propositions that can be stated and tested against personal experiences; (2) understand causal and syllogistic reasoning; (3) develop hypotheses about relationships; and (4) draw inferences from appropriate data.

In regard to a directly relevant concern for school-aged populations—reading—Vellutino (1977) provided a thorough analysis of theories of reading failure and presented compelling evidence for a relationship between reading problems and deficits in phonological, syntactic, and semantic development. As he (Vellutino, 1977) stated,

> . . . children who lag behind their peers in general language ability—for example, those who have difficulty with grammatic transformational rules, who are unable to make morphophonemic generalizations, who cannot perceive the syntactic invariants and redundancies characteristic of all natural languages—can be expected to have difficulty in one or more aspects of reading. (p. 349).

Thus, the relevance of information regarding the normal course of language development, albeit at preschool ages, has relevance for the educator in several respects—first, as a description of the linguistic competence that a child entering school should possess; second, as a description of the interrelatedness of the multiple aspects of the system called language, which interrelated across time; and third, as a guideline for curriculum development in cases of spoken and/or written language disorders.

It is apparent from the abundance of research on language development that there is no single outline of the sequential stages of the development of form, content, and use. No single investigator could possibly hope to be able to describe the entire process, which is only slightly less complex than the study of human behavior itself. It is even difficult to summarize the findings of other investigators into a common framework; investigations differ in whether they use chronological age, level of cognitive development, or level of linguistic development as their yardsticks. These differing approaches result from differences in the underlying assumptions regarding the primary factors correlated with changes in the language system:

1. Chronologically based analyses rest on the assumption that because the majority of children studied seem to exhibit a given behavior at a specific age, this constitutes the norm. This, of course, is the underlying assumption of standardized tests, However, recent research in language development suggests that although there is a virtual invariance in the sequential stages of language development, there is a wide variation in the chronological emergence of these skills in the normal child. In regard to this, Crystal, Fletcher, and Garman (1976) wrote "Whatever the facts, we advocate caution and flexibility in using these age ranges, and would suggest that each age range be viewed as a mean. A spread of ± 6 months is quite tolerable within the notion of normal age range" (p. 84).
2. Brown's intensive analysis of children's grammatical development (1973) showed that while age is not a good indicator of language development, many aspects of language appear to be correlated with children's mean length of utterance (MLU) or average length of utterance in morphemes. As MLU emerges, certain predictable complexities of development emerge. Brown termed the period beginning with the first multiword utterances "stage I," representing an MLU of 1. 1–2.0. Stages II–V are defined at successive increments of 0.5 to the MLU. It should be noted that after an MLU of 4.0 is reached, it ceases being a good predictor of development because children acquire procedures for reducing utterance length, e.g., "He is," as an elliptical form of the utterance "The boy is going," may be used to answer a question. It is linguistically more complex, although shorter in length.
3. Recent research examining the relationship between language development and levels of cognitive development as defined by the work of Piaget (Chapman & Miller, 1981) has indicated a high degree of correlation between the two, particularly in evaluation of language-deficient children.

Tables 6-1–6-4 present a summary of sources of information regarding developmental sequences of receptive and expressive processes (Table 6-1); form (Ta-

Table 6-1
Summary Charts of Language Development—Receptive and
Expressive Processes

	Parameter or Aspect	Basis and Range	Source
Receptive processes	Receptive linguistic development	Chronological age, 0–36 mo	McLean and Snyder-McLean (1978, p. 88)
	Phonemic and para-linguistic comprehension	Chronological age, 0–10 mo	McLean and Snyder-McLean (1978, p. 90)
	Lexical-semantic comprehension	Chronological age, 0–30 mo	McLean and Snyder-McLean (1978, p. 94)
	Syntactic-grammatical comprehension	Chronological age, 30–48 mo	McLean and Snyder-McLean (1978, p. 96)
	Comprehension (lexical)	Cognitive level, 8–27 mo	Chapman and Miller (in press, Table 1)
	Comprehension (lexical)	Cognitive level, 2–3½ yr	Chapman and Miller (1981, Table 5)
	Comprehension (lexical)	Cognitive level, 4–11 yr	Chapman and Miller (1981, Table 6)
	Metalinguistic awareness	Brown's stages	Dale (1976, p. 128)
Expressive processes	Structure development	Chronological Age, 0–36 mo	McLean and Snyder-McLean (1978, p. 98)
	Production	Cognitive level, 8–24 mo	Chapman and Miller (in press, Table 2)
	Production—syntactic processes	Cognitive level, Brown's stages, 2–7 yr	Chapman and Miller (in press, Table 3)
	Production—seman-tics	Cognitive level, 2–7 yr	Chapman and Miller (in press, Table 4)
	Production patterns	Chronological age, 18–36 mo	Trantham and Pedersen (1976, p. 31–33)

ble 6-2); content and use (Table 6-3); and methods of linguistic analysis utilized in the study of these parameters of the language system (Table 6-4). An excellent overview of the entire system, by Prutting (1979), contains parallel charts for pragmatics, syntax and semantics, and phonology. The drawback to Prutting's charts, however, is that because of their breadth of coverage they miss some of the finer analysis provided by other sources that are included in the tables.

Table 6-2
Summary Charts of Language Development—Form

Parameter or Aspect	Basis and Range	Source
Syntax	Brown's stages	Muma (1978)
	Successive stages	Wood (1976, pp. 129, 148)
	Stage 0–adult	Prutting (1979, p. 25)
Syntactic constructions and transformations	Brown's stages	Morehead and Ingram (1973, Appendices B and E)
	Stage 0–6+	Crystal, Fletcher, and Garman (1976, p. 85)
Negatives	Age, 18–36 mo	Trantham and Pedersen (1976, p. 76)
Conjunctions	Age, 18–36 mo	Trantham and Pedersen (1976, p. 93)
Verb development	Age, 18–36 mo	Trantham and Pedersen (1976, p. 67–69)
Pronouns	Age, 18–36 mo	Trantham and Pedersen (1976, pp. 45–47)
Questions	MLU	Dale (1976, p. 107)
	Age, 18–36 mo	Trantham and Pedersen (1976, p. 83)
Morphology	Chronological age, 12 mo–6+ yr	Wood (1976, p. 125)
	Relative order	McLean & Snyder-McLean (1978, p. 108)
Phonology	Chronological age, 1½–8½ yr	Ingram (1976)
Prosody	Chronological age, 0–8 yr	Menyuk (1972)
Prosody	Chronological age, 4 mo–12+ yr	Wood (1976, p. 214)
	Stage 0–adult	Prutting (1979, p. 26)
Proxemics	Chronological age, 0–7+ yr	Wood (1976, p. 239)

In general terms, what emerges from these sources is a view of a multidimensional system of communication with development occurring simultaneously on all fronts. The "referencing mechanisms" appear to have received the most study as indicated by the number of references, and aspects of use the least, but this represents more an artifact of the history of investigations of language development, rather than relative importance. As Feldman (1977) wrote "the meaning-determining rules of language can only be understood by reference to the function of communication" (p. 293).

Table 6-3
Summary Charts of Language Development—Content and Use

	Parameter/Aspect	Basis and Range	Source
Content	Vocabulary size	Age, 8 mo–6 yr	Dale (1976, p. 174)
	Relational semantics	Stage 0–adult	Prutting (1979, p. 25)
	Word categories	Age, 12–24 mo	McLean and Snyder-McLean (1978, p. 99)
	Minor lexical categories	Brown's stages	Morehead and Ingram (1973, Table 2)
	Categorization	Developmental periods	Wood (1976, p. 143)
	Thinking-word meanings	Stage 0–11 + yr	Wood (1976, pp. 154, 156)
Use	Pragmatics	Stage 0–adult	Prutting (1979, p. 24)
	Developmental functions	Successive phases	Halliday (1975, p. 158)

Table 6-4
Methods of Linguistic Analysis

Factor	Source
Semantic categories	Muma (1978, pp. 86–87, Appendix B)
Primitive speech acts	Dore (1975, p. 33)
Phrase structure rules	Muma (1978, Appendix B)
Transformational rules	Muma (1978, Appendix B)
Procedures for calculating MLU and Brown's stages	Dale (1976, pp. 19–20)
Consonant phonemes	Bolinger (1975)
Vowel phonemes	Bolinger (1975)
Communicative functions	McLean and Snyder-McLean (1978, p. 55)
MLU and age	Brown, Cazden, and Bellugi-Klima (1969)
Requirements of nonvocal systems	Chapman and Miller (in press, Table 7)
Developmental sentence analysis	Lee (1974)
Distancing strategies	Sigel and Cocking (1977, pp. 210–211)
Piaget's developmental stages	Muma (1978, pp. 37–38)

LANGUAGE DEVELOPMENT AND THE HANDICAPPED STUDENT

Three main approaches to the study of language disorders are apparent in current practices, each with its own assumptions regarding the nature of disorders, procedures for determining deviance from presumed normality, and procedures for remediation. These orientations can be generally defined as the linguistic-behavioral, the etiologic, and the specific-abilities approaches.

The specific-abilities approach rests on the theoretical assumption that "first, there are certain abilities that are required for language and, second, these abilities can be identified, measured, and remediated" (Bloom and Lahey, 1978, p. 529). Specific-abilities approaches are based on models of the cognitive operations that are assumed to occur between input signals and responses. Bloom and Lahey (1978) presented an analysis of such approaches, noting that most models include (1) a perceptual component; (2) a conceptual or representational component; and (3) an output component. The first component involves the processing of inputs; the second, meaning and symbolic thinking; the third, planning and command of motor responses. Visual and auditory modalities are assumed to be independent, and processing is generally assumed to be a linear phenomenon. The types of language processes that are the focus of such approaches—for example, auditory sequential memory, temporal factors in processing, and the processing of multisensory input—logically would appear on the surface to be necessary for language functioning; a great deal of research has been conducted to determine the relationship between dysfunctions in specific abilities (primarily utilizing the Illinois Test of Psycholinguistic Abilities; Kirk, McCarthy, & Kirk, 1968) and clinical categories, particularly the learning disabled and the emotionally disturbed. In regard to such studies, Bloom and Lahey (1978) wrote "Whenever units of language are used as the stimuli to be perceived, the question arises as to whether perceptual dysfunction, identified by response to such stimuli, is a cause or a reflection of a language disorder" (p. 532). They presented a summary of research on the utility of such approaches and concluded that the specific abilities assumed to underlie language have not been demonstrated to be isolated from one another in the process of normal acquisition; are not necessarily improved through remediation procedures; and, most importantly, do not appear to be prerequisite to language learning. To cite one example, "sound-blending" tasks run counter to what is known about the processes of speech perception and production, since acoustic signals are not segmentable into phonemes in actual speech.

In summary, Bloom and Lahey (1978) suggested that the primary problem of the language disabled child is the meaningful use of language for problem solving and communication, not deficits in presumed underlying abilities. Specific-abilities approaches may be useful in determining modalities of language training, but should not comprise the goals of intervention. For example, a child who shows visual deficits might learn better through the auditory mode, but the goal of intervention should be to remediate the deficits in the language system, not in visual processing itself.

Specific abilities are considered to be causative factors by those who espouse that orientation, and, as such, constitute etiological classifications, since etiology means study of the cause. The etiological approach, per se, rests on the assumption that it is clinically useful to identify an individual in terms of syndromes or patterns of behavior that define clinical diagnostic categories, since there are common needs and deficits for all children so categorized. This process of categorization by manifest behavioral similarities or differences is termed "differential diagnosis" and leads to the development of remedial education programs for the mentally retarded child, or the learning disabled child, and so on.

In regard to language disorders, Bloom and Lahey (1978) indicated that language learning seems to require the following: (1) an intact peripheral sensory system; (2) an intact central nervous system; (3) adequate mental abilities; (4) emotional stability; and (5) exposure to language. Deficits in these areas are related, respectively, to the categories of (1) hearing impairment; (2) aphasia (and learning disabilities); (3) mental retardation; (4) emotional disturbances; and (5) environmental deprivation. Central to most such etiological classifications is the existence of a deficit in language functioning. For example, the American Association on Mental Deficiency (AAMD) definition of mental retardation (Grossman, 1977) requires both depressed measured intelligence and depressed adaptive functioning as criteria for classification. As Waryas and Waryas (1979) wrote,

> Not only are the majority of I.Q. tests verbal in nature, requiring that one be able to hear, understand language, and speak, but communication skills (or their lack) can severely depress one's ability to interact adaptively with one's environment. It should not be surprising, therefore, that there is an extremely high incidence of communication problems among the retarded. This is not to suggest that communication problems *cause* retardation but rather that they comprise part of the symptom complex defined as retardation.

In a similar fashion, language disorders are a part of the definition of childhood psychosis (Creak et al., cited in Bloom & Lahey, 1978). Among the diagnostic signs is found:

> Loss of, lack of, or late development of speech, possibly accompanied by confusions in the use of personal pronouns, echolalia, and other mannerisms of use and diction—as when words and phrases are uttered but convey no sense of meaningful communication. (p. 515).

In regard to learning disabled children, numerous investigators have identified language and communication deficits—including verbal and nonverbal communication, reception and production, and social interaction—in this population. Of these deficits, Wiig and Semel (1976) stated, "Clinical observations and research suggest that the language and communication problems exhibited by learning disabled youngsters are multi-faceted, defying unitary description" (p. 23). The statement underscores the weakness of the etiological approach as a clinically useful basis for language intervention. While it is true that categorical designation of children may be useful as a shorthand system of description, specific language behaviors that are common to all children within a diagnostic category, and that serve to differentiate between categories are nonexistent. Moreover, as Bloom and Lahey (1978) suggested,

> . . . what an aphasic child needs to learn is the same as what the mentally retarded, deaf, or emotionally disturbed child needs to learn. In fact, what the child with a language problem needs to learn is precisely what the normal child needs to learn at some point in development. The model language is the same for all. At present, there is no reason to suspect that the sequence in which that model is achieved does, or should differ, for different groups of children (p. 524).[5]

---

[5]Reprinted with permission from Bloom, L., & Lahey, M., *Language development and language disorders*. New York: Wiley, 1978.

This brings us, then, to the linguistic-behavioral approach. The conjunction of these two terms may seem quixotic to some, since linguists and behaviorists rarely find themselves on the same side of the fence concerning language-intervention procedures (despite what can be a very fruitful marriage of the approaches) (Waryas, 1978a, 1978b; Waryas & Stremel-Campbell, 1978). As opposed to the specific-abilities and the etiological approaches, this approach focuses on the language behavior itself as the determinant of the existence of a problem, and as the target of training. The point of divergence between developmental linguists and behaviorists revolves around the issue of the utilization of information regarding the normal course of development in language-intervention programming. As Rees (1971) noted, "The assumption that the normal sequence is somehow that 'right' sequence for the language disordered child to follow has not been proved, but neither has it been seriously challenged" (p. 289). Waryas (1978a, 1978b) provided a further discussion of this issue, as well as a rationale for a developmental approach.

The application of a linguistic approach to the language problems of the handicapped student does not imply that no differences will be found among children who have been differentially categorized based on etiology. Rather, it suggests that such differences should play an ancilliary role in planning language-remediation procedures. For example, it would be expected that mentally retarded children might show a slower rate of learning than learning disabled children, with the latter able to "jump steps" in programming. Clinical experience with such children following the same language-training curriculum substantiates this. In a similar fashion, emotionally disturbed children may show major deficits in the use of language, being only able to produce language structures inappropriately, while retarded children may demonstrate communicative functions that surpass their skills in the realm of form, as is seen in the elaborate pantomime of some Down's symdrome children. The goal for these children, however, is the same—to bring the use and form components of the language system into synchrony.

The adoption of a linguistic approach to the language deficiencies of handicapped students, regardless of their diagnostic category, approaches the ideal of "individualized educational programming" for each student, since just as there is no such thing as a "typical" mentally retarded student, there is no "retarded intervention program."

The utilization of a linguistic approach, incorporating information regarding the course of normal language development, is most appropriate when dealing with the mildly handicapped student, since the emphasis of training with such a student should be on the fact that he or she is more similar to, than different from, nonhandicapped peers. Issues such as whether the student should be considered "language delayed" or "language disordered" or whether the differences noted between the handicapped student and nonhandicapped peers are "quantitative" or "qualitative" in nature have been the target of much investigation (Waryas & Crowe, in press). However, Siegel and Spradlin (1978) aptly summarized the secondary importance of such concerns to the intervention process:

> For most of the children seen in educational programs or speech and language programs, the condition exists as the expression of some unknown mixture of biological and environmental influences, and the best predictions concerning the child's devel-

opmental potential can be derived by analyzing the child's previous accomplishments and his response to therapy. (p. 379)[6]

This statement suggests that the goal for any student who demonstrates a language disorder should be to evaluate his or her current level of linguistic functioning, in light of both that of nonhandicapped peers and of the communicative demands being faced, and to institute procedures for reducing the discrepancies that are found. In practice, this approach requires a firm background on the part of the special educator and the speech-language pathologist in the structure of language and its development, in all its myriad facets; an ability to evaluate assessment instruments and training programs in the area of language to determine whether they are congruent with this approach and meet the unique needs of each child; and a willingness to work in a team effort to provide the student with the language skills necessary to meet the demands of academic and postschool settings.

REFERENCES

Bates, E. *Language and context: The acquisition of pragmatics*. New York: Academic Press, 1976.

Bates, E., & Johnston, J. *Pragmatics in normal and deficient child language*. A short course presented at the American Speech and Hearing Association Annual Convention, Chicago, November 1977.

Bloom, L. *Language development: Form and function in emerging grammars*. Cambridge: MIT Press, 1970.

Bloom, L. Talking, understanding, and thinking. In. R. L. Schiefelbusch & L. L. Lloyd (Eds.) *Language perspectives: Acquisition, retardation, and intervention*. Baltimore: University Park Press, 1974.

Bloom, L., & Lahey, M., *Language development and language disorders*. New York: Wiley, 1978.

Bolinger, D. *Aspects of language*. New York: Harcourt Brace Jovanovich, 1975.

Bowerman, M. *Early syntactic development: A cross-linguistic study with special reference to Finnish*. Cambridge: Cambridge University Press, 1973. (a)

Bowerman, M. Structural relations in children's utterances: Syntactic or semantic? In T. Moore (Ed.), *Cognitive development and the acquisition of language*. New York: Academic Press, 1973. (b)

Brown, R. *A first language: The early stages*. Cambridge: Harvard University Press, 1973.

Brown, R., Cazden, C., & Bellugi-Klima, U. The child's grammar from I to III. In J. P. Hill (Ed.), *Minnesota symposia on child psychology* (Vol. 2). Minneapolis: University of Minnesota Press, 1969.

Braine, M. The otogeny of English phrase structure: the first phrase. *Language*, 1963, *39*, 1–13.

Bruner, J. S. From communication to language: A psychological perspective. *Cognition*, 1974-1975, *3*, 255–287.

Cazden, C. Problems for education: Language as curriculum and learning environment. *Daedalus*, 1973, *102*, 135–148.

Chapman, R., & Miller, J. Analyzing language and communication in the child. In R. Schiefelbusch (Ed.), *Nonspeech language intervention*. Baltimore: University Park Press, 1981.

Chomsky, C. *The acquisition of syntax in children from 5 to 10*. Cambridge: MIT Press, 1969.

Chomsky, N. *Syntactic structures*. The Hague: Mouton, 1957.

Chomsky, N. *Aspects of the theory of syntax*. Cambridge: MIT Press, 1965.

Crystal, D. *Prosodic systems and intonation in English*. London: Cambridge University Press, 1969.

Crystal, D., Fletcher, P., & Garman, M. *The grammatical analysis of language disability*. New York: Elsevier, 1976.

---

[6]Reprinted with permission from Siegel, G., & Spradlin, J. Programming for language and communication therapy. In R. Schiefelbusch (Ed.), *Language Intervention Strategies*. Baltimore: University Park Press, 1978.

Dale, P. *Language development.* New York: Holt, 1976.

de Ajuriaguerra, J., Jaeggi, A., Guiganard, F., Kocher, F., Maguard, M., Roth, S., & Schmid, E. The development and prognosis of dysphasia in children. In D. Morehead & A. Morehead (Eds.), *Normal and deficient child language.* Baltimore: University Park Press, 1976.

deLaguna, G. A. *Speech: Its function and development.* Bloomington: Indiana University Press, 1927.

Dore, J. A pragmatic description of early language development. *Journal of Psycholinguistic Research,* 1974, *3*, 343–350.

Dore, J. Holophrases, speech acts, and language universals. *Journal of Child Language,* 1975, *2*, 21–40.

Ervin-Tripp, S. In D. Slobin (Ed.), *A field manual for cross-cultural study of the acquisition of communicative competence.* Berkeley: University of California, 1967.

Feldman, C. Two functions of language. *Harvard Educational Review,* 1977, *47*, 282–293.

Foss, D., & Hakes, D. *Psycholinguistics.* Englewood Cliffs: Prentice-Hall, 1978.

Fromkin, V., & Rodman, R. *An introduction to language.* New York: Holt, 1974.

Grossman, H. (Ed.). *Manual on terminology and classification in mental retardation.* Washington, D.C.: American Association on Mental Deficiency, 1977.

Gruenwald, L., & Yoder, D. Severely handicapped hearing-impaired considerations for curriculum development and implementation. In C. Campbell (Ed.), *Development of programmatic services for the severely handicapped student,* in press.

Halliday, M. Language structure and language function. In J. Lyons (Ed.), *New horizons in linguistics,* Baltimore: Penguin, 1970.

Halliday, M. *Learning how to mean: Explorations in the development of language.* London: Arnold, 1975.

Hargis, C. *English syntax.* Springfield: Charles C Thomas, 1977.

Ingram, D. *Phonological disability in children.* London: Arnold, 1976.

Kirk, S., McCarthy, J., & Kirk, W. *The Illinois Test of Psycholinguistic Ability.* Urbana: University of Illinois Press, 1968.

Langacker, R. *Language and its structure: Some fundamental linguistic concepts.* New York: Harcourt, 1968.

Lee, L. *Developmental sentence analysis.* Evanston, Il.: Northwestern University Press, 1974.

Lyons, J. General discussion to D. McNeill's paper, "The creation of language." In J. Lyons & R. Wales (Eds.), *Psycholinguistic papers.* Edinburgh: Edinburgh University Press, 1966.

MacNamara, J. Cognitive basis for language learning in infants. *Psychological Review,* 1972, *79*, 1–13.

Mahoney, G. An ethological approach to delayed language acquisition. *American Journal of Mental Deficiency,* 1975, *80*, 139–148.

McCarthy, D. Language development in children. In P. Mussen (Ed.), *Carmichael's manual of child psychology.* New York: Wiley, 1954.

McLean, J., & Snyder-McLean, L. *A transactional approach to early language training.* Columbus, O.: Charles E. Merrill, 1978.

McNeill, D. Developmental psycholinguistics. In F. Smith & G. A. Miller (Eds.), *The genesis of language: A psycholinguistic approach.* Cambridge: MIT Press, 1966.

Menyuk, P. *The development of speech.* Indianapolis: Bobbs-Merrill, 1972.

Miller, J., Chapman, R., & Bedrosian, J. Defining developmentally disabled subjects for research: The relationship between etiology, cognitive development and language communicative performance. *New Zealand Speech Therapist's Journal,* 1978.

Miller, J., & Yoder, D. A syntax teaching program. In J. McLean, D. Yoder, & R. Schiefelbusch (Eds.), *Language intervention with the retarded: Developing strategies.* Baltimore: University Park Press, 1972.

Miller, W., & Ervin, S. The development of grammar in child language. In U. Bellugi & R. Brown (Eds.), *The Acquisition of Language.* Monographs of the Society for Research in Child Development, 1964, *29*.

Morehead, D., & Ingram, D. The development of base syntax in normal and linguistically deviant children. *Journal of Speech and Hearing Research,* 1973, *16*, 330–352.

Morehead, D., & Morehead, A. (Eds.), *Normal and deficient child language.* Baltimore: University Park Press, 1976.

Muma, J. *Language handbook: Concepts, assessment, and intervention.* Englewood Cliffs: Prentice-Hall, 1978.

Olson, E. Language and thought: Aspects of a cognitive theory of semantics. *Psychological Review,* 1970, *77*, 257–273.

Prutting, C. Process: The action of moving forward progressively from one point to another on the way to completion. *Journal of Speech and Hearing Disorders,* 1979, *44*, 3–30.

Rees, N. Bases of decision in language training. *Journal of Speech and Hearing Disorders,* 1971, *36,* 283–304.

Rees, N. Pragmatics of language: Applications to normal and disordered language development. In R. L. Schiefelbusch (Ed.), *Bases of language intervention.* Baltimore: University Park Press, 1978.

Siegel, G., & Spradlin, J. Programming for language and communication therapy. In R. Schiefelbusch (Ed.), *Language intervention strategies.* Baltimore: University Park Press, 1978.

Sigel, I., & Cocking, R. Cognition and communication: A dialectic paradigm for development. In M. Lewis & L. Rosenblum (Eds.), *Interaction, conversation, and the development of language.* New York: Wiley, 1977.

Stremel, K., & Waryas, C. A behavioral-psycholinguistic approach to language training. In L. McReynolds (Ed.), *Developing systematic procedures for training children's language.* American Speech and Hearing Association Monograph #18, 1974.

Streng, A. *Syntax, speech, and hearing.* New York: Grune & Stratton, 1972.

Templin, M. *Certain language skills in children.* Minneapolis: University of Minnesota Press, 1957.

Trantham, C., & Pedersen, J. *Normal language development.* Baltimore: Williams & Wilkins, 1976.

Vellutino, F. Alternative conceptualizations of dyslexia: Evidence in support of a verbal-deficit hypothesis. *Harvard Educational Review,* 1977, *47,* 334–354.

Waryas, C. Language intervention programming as a revolutionary activity. *Human Communication,* 1978, *3,* 31–81. (a)

Waryas, C. Response to Guess, Baer, and Sailor. *Human Communication,* 1978, *3,* 85–87.

Waryas, C., & Crowe, T. Language delay. In N. Lass, L. V. McReynolds, J. L. Northern, & D. E. Yoder (Eds.), *Speech, language and hearing.* Philadelphia: Saunders, in press.

Waryas, C., & Stremel-Campbell, K. Grammatical training for the language deficient child: A new perspective. In R. L. Schiefelbusch (Ed.), *Language intervention strategies.* Baltimore: University Park Press, 1978.

Waryas, C., & Waryas, P. Mental retardation. Unpublished manuscript, University of Mississippi, 1979.

Wiig, E., & Semel, E. *Language disabilities in children and adolescents.* Columbus, Oh.: Charles E. Merrill, 1976.

Wood, B. *Children and communication.* Englewood Cliffs: Prentice-Hall, 1976.

David A. Sabatino
Ann C. Sabatino

7

Perceptual-Motor Development of the Mildly Handicapped

The history of psychology and, to lesser extent, education is tightly interwoven with the study of perception and perceptual-motor activity. Perception is a receptive process, one in which information is received by the central nervous system (CNS). It may be viewed as an interpretation of what happens when sensory information is received by one of the two primary sensory-receiving mechanisms (i.e., eyes or ears) and communicated to the central nervous system where it can become a language-related symbol or, in fact, a language concept.

Perception has often been seen as critical to the formulation of cognition. From this vantage point the German gestalt psychologists in the late 1800s explained cognition as a summary by the nervous system of information received. The emphasis derived from the gestalt school of psychology persisted well into the current century and was an early contributor to the assessment and training practices of special education. Although an emphasis on perceptual assessment/training was a predominant practice well into the 1960s, recent critiques surrounding common procedures such as the Frostig Developmental Test of Visual Perception (Hammill, 1972) and the Illinois Test of Psycholinguistic Ability (Sedlak & Weener, 1973) have discouraged many special educators from placing emphasis upon perceptual development. Indeed, the entire perceptual process is now only rarely used to explain educational events and individual differences. Still, it is important to note that the earliest conceptualizations of learning disabilities posited perceptual differences as a source of the disorder; perceptual deficits, as a part of the phrase "basic psychological processes," is retained within the 1968 NACHC definition adopted by Public Law 94-142. Furthermore, theories of cognition virtually always are concerned with perceptual development as a foundation for cognition, and some behavioral disorders are linked to perceptual dysfunction. It is clear then, that special education for the mildly handicapped cannot ignore the importance of perception.

Motor development has been a concern of philosophers and educators since the beginning of recorded history. Education entails instruction of the *whole* person and cannot be divided into a physical and mental aspect. There are no such arbitrary boundaries in nature, the mind cannot function without the body and the

145

body cannot perform without the mind. Certainly the concept of instructional "wholeness" of the person, dating from the Greeks, suggests that people are only as strong as their weakest function. Yet, while the early Greeks wished to blend a sound mind with a sound body, emphasis during the Middle Ages was placed on the development of the mind at the expense of the body. In the rebirth of learning that occurred during the Renaissance, importance was again attached to the development of mind *and* body. Montague, Locke, and Comenius all believed in health and physical training, although they failed to understand the esthetic and social values of motor behavior. None of these early theorists explored their views systematically, but during the latter part of the 19th century muscular movement was scientifically investigated. After World War II, and again after President John F. Kennedy's emphasis on physical fitness, physical education was actively promoted for all children, especially the handicapped. It was only at this juncture that motor training was fully recognized as a basic survival skill necessary in order that normalization could occur. That observation, and the fact that physical attractiveness and social competence are judged in large part by motor movement, led to the requirement of adaptive physical education in PL 94-142.

THE ART OF MOVEMENT

Humans begin practicing movement before they are born. The early primitive movements of the human embryo are limited but have great importance. The fetus learns what movements are available to it and what sensory stimuli these movements create. The primitive nervous system receives stimuli triggered by bones and muscles through biochemical action. A series of actions, interrelated and interdependent, provide the developing child with information. Biological feedback from these activities provides the nervous system with the first information promoting learning and growth.

Postnatally, elemental sensorimotor development has many additional opportunities for development. As the environment changes, the child has more reason to move, and every movement causes new responses to the environment. Before birth, the environment was consistent; the postnatal environment is composed of inconsistencies: new noises, more space, different textures, brightness instead of darkness, and new temperatures are available to adjust to and learn from. The world is full of fascinating opportunities to move and explore, and each movement promotes learning.

During most of the first 18 months, an infant learns how to move and how to refine movements with greater fluidity. Developmentally, the first challenge is to learn the art of movement; i.e., how to move the arm and the leg. The first step in the development of the nervous system requires interpretation of sensorimotor information; i.e., when to move the arm, with how much force, and in which direction. Soon, locomotion provides the senses with an orientation to the environment and to space. Logically, a child cannot gain skill in locating herself spatially unless the child can move; if, for some reason the child is not permitted movement, physical development and orientation to space are slowed. Physical handicaps, mental retardation, emotional disturbance, and other handicaps may limit the child from basic movements; even if others assist in movements for practice and to provide an opportunity to learn orientational judgments, there will still be a major deficiency of perception (Getman, Kane, Halgren, & McKee, 1968). Movement ultimately brings about the opportunity for making judgments. "Where did this movement take me?" "Where am I?" "How far did I go?" "How much more must I move to reach my toy?" Curiosity is created by movement, and curiosity fosters new learning; therefore, movement is the basis for much initial learning.

PHASES OF MOTOR DEVELOPMENT

Most early motor-learning experiences occur in a sequential manner. The patterning theory of neurological organization (Doman & Delacato, 1959); the sensory-integration theory (Ayres, 1973); the theory of movigenics (Barsch, 1968); and the visuomotor theory (Getman, 1965) are all based on an organized hierarchy of developmental steps or physical achievements. Each succeeding plateau is only as strong and supportive as the one preceding it, and there are several observable stages or phases in the child's motor development.

The rudimentary first movements, between birth and about 2 years, serve as a critical basis for the development of future motor patterns. According to Bloom (1964), achieving the greatest possible change in an attribute will occur when modification is attempted at the point where perceptual-motor change occurs in children. According to Cratty (1969), this is usually before age 7, so the importance of early identification and efforts to aid children develop motorically can easily be seen. If the child evidences aberrant motor development at birth, the pediatrician may identify the problems early. Neurologists can identify a child with minimal motor control by the end of the first year of life. All too often, however, subtle motor deficits are overlooked in preschool children, and valuable interventions are not begun. Unfortunately, later efforts have much less likelihood for success.

In the second phase of motor development (age 3–7 years), fundamental movement patterns are explored and practiced. Generality of movement, not skill, is stressed as children learn the movement potentials of their bodies. All children should experience success within their abilities, including a wide variety of fundamental movements: rolling, waving, squatting, running, walking, reaching, kicking, pushing, pulling, etc. By kindergarten age, children can be compared with their peers, and children with motor ineptitudes usually become painfully obvious to the teacher, who often categorizes them as clumsy. Finishing last in drawing and writing, spilling juice, using scissors poorly, and failing to catch balls are motor behaviors frequently observed in mildly handicapped children.

General movement is the third phase of motor development (third to eighth grade). During this phase, accuracy, form, and skilled performance are expected. Motor learning is product oriented (i.e., hit the pitched ball), with a de-emphasis on the process learning of basic skills. Concern with product and not process can cause the general movement skills of the mildly handicapped to stand out as poorly developed. If the teacher jumps rope and the student models the motor behavior, the closer his attempt to the model the greater his feeling of success—and the further his attempt from the model, the greater the sense of failure. Such a behavior is more than a failure in motor skills. How does a student who fails to jump rope *feel* when he steps on the rope, flailing his arms, kicking his legs, contorting his face, and falling to the floor entangled in the rope? What cognitive and affective processes come into play?

The fourth phase of motor development is specialized skill development (14 years old +). It is similar to general skill development, except that specific skills are isolated, practiced, and perfected for high levels of performance (e.g., as in interscholastic athletics). Too often, the child who has not developed a basis for rudimentary or fundamental movement patterns is dropped by the wayside, never to achieve the specialized skill development necessary for sports. In our society, the attitude of living in a competitive society stresses that all children must learn to compete. That attitude neglects the development and refinement of many motor performance skills useful for life in mildly handicapped children.

Movement is the center of life for most preschool and primary school children, normal or handicapped. The self-concept a child develops may partially reside in how she evaluates her performance in movement activities. The child who cannot run, dodge, or kick a ball will not be on a team at recess, and likely will not be among the children chosen for other physical, social, or academic activities.

MOTOR LEARNING

The primary characteristic of motor learning, in contrast to other types of learning, is movement. Muscle movement results in motor behavior. But, what stimulates muscles to react to arousal? Generally, the body recognizes and interprets stimuli received by the brain from the sense organs (Fait, 1978). These data provide information on changing conditions in the environment and what must be done to adapt. Next, the sensory system receives stimuli which are transmitted as electrical signals through sensory neurons. But, before the central nervous system can attend, perceive, or judge the appropriate motor behavior, the stimuli must be restructured into electrical energy (Sabatino, 1979). The amazing quality of the transducers (nerve cells) is their ability to change a specific kind of stimulus (i.e., visual, tactile, or auditory) to the common transmission (electrical impulse) necessary for muscles to move for motor behavior. Without the transmission of mechanical stimuli to electrical impulse, there would be no muscle movement.

A perceptual-motor movement is a chain of events—input, process, output. It begins with a sensory stimulus, then is dependent upon congitive processes (attending, perceiving, judging, retrieving), and results in a self-directed motor behavior. The movement skills that should be mastered for everyday living—crossing the street, climbing stairs, stepping off curbs—are complex and involve detection, evaluation, and decision-making. Therefore, motor behavior is an actual response to an entire act after perception (information gathering). Performing any motor behavior requires many facets of the learning process and cannot be separated from the intelligent behaviors displayed by the person. In short, it is impossible to separate perceptual and the motor processes in children.

There is much confusion as to what the perceptual processes are, as well as to how they manifest themselves for measurement or description. The distinction between where sensation (vision and hearing) ends and cognition (visual and auditory perception) begins is blurred. There is also a total absence of clarity concerning the distinction between perceptual symbolization and language conceptualization. Many psychologists merely lump all perceptual and language functions together in a cognitive complex. However, there seem to be two distinctly separate perceptual functions, visual perception and auditory perception, even though there is a cross-model interaction between the two, referred to as "perceptual integration." This suggests that information may be received simultaneously by the two perceptual processes, or received by one in order to obtain meaning in the other.

There is evidence to suggest that within each perceptual function (vision or auditory) at least two distinct functions can be isolated: (1) perceptual discrimination and (2) perceptual memory. Perceptual discrimination is the act of distinguishing the critical features (distinctive feature differences) between visual and auditory sensory information. Perceptual memory appears to be the short-term storage function, whenever sensory material is scanned for meaning, or filtered as being unusable. Could it be that the filtering function, when defective, results in hyperactivity? In essence, irrelevant information maintained in the central nervous system is seemingly related to hyperactivity.

Assessment of Perceptual Function

There are several problems associated with the measurement of perceptual function. First, and foremost, it must be remembered that any mental process or trait, e.g., visual or auditory perception, is named for the function it is assumed to perform. That means a test used to measure a particular trait may indeed be measuring that trait, but it could also be ascertaining any number of related functions. The measuring instrument used most commonly to describe the state of a child's visual-perceptual discrimination is the Bender Visual-Motor Gestalt Test (BVMGT). The BVMGT began as a laboratory measurement of gestalt function (Wertheimer, 1923) and was adopted for clinical work with children in 1938. The purpose of the test was to determine the presence of brain damage (Bender, 1938). In 1958, Koppitz established developmental norms for the BVMGT with children aged 5 to 11. These norms reflected the developmental status achieved (or developmental age equivalent) for any child being administered the test. The test stimuli are geometric designs, the very rudiments of most perceptual tests. Nonlanguage meaningful stimuli were used to maintain a measure of the perceptual level, which is a sublinguistic trait.

Diagnostic problems begin with the test administration, which requires the child to draw nine designs on an unlined $8\frac{1}{2}'' \times 11''$ space of paper. The examiner may assume that visual-perceptual discrimination is being ascertained, but, in fact, the measurement of visual-perceptual discrimination may be influenced by the manual-motor response. Therefore, it is possible that what the child perceives may be offset by how well he can draw through manual-motor expression. In addition, many examiners have used tests of visual-motor-perceptual development to determine intelligence (Armstrong & Hauck, 1961) and diagnose brain damage (Shaw & Cruickshank, 1956) and emotional difficulties (Clawson, 1959), as well as to understand the perceptual process and its relationship to academic achievement deficits (Koppitz, 1964).

Secondly, most perceptual tests have low test-retest reliability. The number of test items may have a profound influence on reliability, and most perceptual tests have few items or stimuli. Generally speaking, a reliability of less than .90 is considered inadequate for educational decision making. The reliability of most perceptual tests ranges from about .35 to about .80.

The third problem associated with assessing perceptual deficits is the fact that test authors construct an instrument to ascertain a trait that they think they observe being performed. Available research data that imply the tests do measure what they purport to measure are very limited, and there are very few perceptual tests developed from accepted models, paradigms, and theoretical constructs of how processes function. In short, construct validity, or the ability of a test to measure what it purports to, is low or nonexistent.

But the phenomena that created the most controversy are the operational definitions applied to those traits reasoned to represent a process. There is little disagreement that at least two distinct perceptual processes exist, one visual and one auditory (Sabatino & Hayden, 1970). The disagreement begins with the identification of components that comprise the perceptual skill, for just what are the visual-perceptual and auditory-perceptual specific functions that can be described, observed, and measured? As noted earlier, there is some evidence to support at least two specific perceptual processes: perceptual discrimination and memory. There is also evidence to suggest that a sequencing component also exists. Yet many tests now exceed these known limits. For example, the Frostig Developmental Test of Visual Perception (DTVP; Frostig & Horne, 1964) claims to measure five essential processes of the visual-perceptual behavioral complex. As a result, any discussion limiting the possibilities of visual perceptual traits to give specific functions, if they exist in nature or not, is to tell only a partial truth.

Auditory Perception

Auditory perceptual development appears to be far more complex than visual perception and is relatively unexplored. The reason for the complexity of the auditory process is that sound is a more multidimensional stimulus than light. Consequently, the physiological aspects of the auditory-receiving system appear to be more complex than the visual aspects in the sense that it is more difficult to know where the sensory function of hearing begins and where it ends, and it is more difficult to know where auditory perception stops and language-learning begins. What then, is the auditory-perception process?

Usually, auditory-perceptual development is viewed as a process of change in the ability to differentiate characteristics of, and impose structure on, auditory stimuli. The development of these parallel processes of differentiation and structuring, along with the development of memory processes, makes up the three major components of the process of auditory perception. Components refer to behavioral constructs rather than anatomical units, since the recent trend in the field has been to provide a psychological rather than physiological interpretation of auditory perception. In most models, incoming sensory stimuli are received from the external auditory receptors in a short-term storage unit labeled echoic memory (Neisser, 1967). Auditory stimuli are stored here for very brief periods of time in an undifferentiated form; if the contents of this unit are not attended to shortly after stimulation they are lost through a process of rapid decay. The storage unit is, in a sense, passive, because no structuring or organizing influences act on it. The duration of echoic memory most likely increases with maturation in early childhood.

The discriminative filter abstracts the distinctive features of the incoming auditory stimuli, and "attends" or "tunes;" this process results in the active focusing on a limited amount of the available stimuli. The selective filter is the mechanism that accepts some incoming stimuli and rejects or strongly attenuates all other stimuli, thus preventing an overloading of the subsequent perceptual mechanisms. The filter is set, or tuned, by a central control unit that is influenced by events stored in active auditory memory and by other knowledge in long-term storage. Developmentally, the child learns to discriminate among the various characteristics that define auditory stimuli—pitch, intensity, phonemic distinctions, spatial direction, voice quality, and so forth—and to focus on only that part of the available auditory stimuli that is relevant. Auditory-perceptual learning may be defined at this stage as a process of abstracting many different dimensions from auditory stimuli and making increasingly finer differentiations within each of the abstracted dimensions. The developing ability to abstract this information is paralleled by an increase in the capacity to focus on a subset of the total auditory stimuli and to ignore the remainder.

The active auditory memory is a unit in which active organization occurs. Through a process of integration, the incoming stimuli are grouped and recoded into larger units. Research has indicated that these larger units are based on the acoustic and linguistic properties of the stimuli. Acoustic properties such as rhythm and pitch patterns serve as a basis for the construction of larger units. Word composition, phrase structures, and sentence structures are derived from linguistic knowledge—an important basis for integration. The amount of material that can be held in active auditory memory is a function of the integrative process that draws on the perceiver's past experiences and relates them to the potential structural characteristics of the incoming stimuli. As a child learns the structural features of language-based auditory stimuli, the unit size that can be held in active auditory memory increases.

In addition to the development of the ability to structure incoming auditory stimuli, the sheer size of the storage unit also increases with age. As Miller (1956) pointed out in his classic paper, the amount of auditory stimuli that can be held in active auditory memory depends on the number of units available as well as on the richness or compactness of the units. Miller notes that previous studies of memory span, immediate memory, or short-term memory were measures of active auditory memory. However, most previous research failed to take into account the integrative and structuring activities of the short-term perceptual memory unit. The definition of the unit as "active and integrative" implies that its functioning can best be studied using stimuli that vary in acoustic and linguistic structure.

In comparison with active auditory memory, the long-term memory unit is passive rather than active, has almost infinite (rather than limited) capacity, and provides permanent (rather than transient) storage. Although the processes involved in storage and retrieval in long-term memory are experimentally intriguing, their study would go beyond the scope of a project on auditory perception. Long-term memory is important because of the influence of stored information on attention, discrimination, and integration.

Some of the commonly used tests of auditory perception are sound-recognition tests, such as the Wepman Auditory Discrimination Test (Wepman, 1958), the PERC test (Drake, 1965), and the Boston University Speech Sound Discrimination Picture Test; these tests have speech-sound discrimination tasks that require the child to respond to a pair of words by indicating whether they sound the same or different. In their research review of central-processing dysfunctions in children, Chalfant & Scheffelin (1969) made the following comment:

> The chief difference between the two tests is that the child is required to say "same" or "different" . . . on the Wepman, whereas he is required to say "same" or "not the same" on the PERC. (p. 13)

Several researchers have commented on the difficulty posed by having only two response alternatives (Coltheart & Curthoys, 1968), since a subject has a 50 percent chance of getting the correct response by random guessing. Furthermore, inconsistency in examiners' speech patterns, children's phonetic competence and vocabulary familiarity, test conditions (e.g., extraneous environmental noise), and cultural biases can easily influence the test results. Snyder & Pope (1970) could not confirm the norms published by Wepman. They found, for example, that 67 percent of their subjects exceeded the cutoff score for auditory discrimination problems, as given in the test manual. Snyder & Pope (1970) believed, however, that with refinements at the age levels with which they were working (6-year-old subjects), the Wepman test could be a useful device for the assessment of auditory discrimination, "but the test user should consider discrepancies with norms in arriving at a realistic understanding of his test data" (p. 1010).

Possibly, criterion cutoff scores, or any scores that differentiate one group from another or categorize a child as being deviant, are not necessary. Flower (1968) suggested focusing on individual differences and believed that certain educational strategies might be more effective than others when the particular subskills, strengths, or weaknesses of a child were known. Sabatino (1979) noted that a number of workers in the field try to specify the type of speech-sound discrimination difficulty a child has, rather than hypothesizing an organic impairment or merely noting that there is a failure to perform at a level equal to that of others of the same age.

Redegeair and Kamil (1970) reviewed the literature on the Travis and Rasmus Test (1931) and the work of Templin (1957) and Wepman (1958); they also reported a study by Skeel, Calfee, and Venesky (1969), who tested the efficacy of discrimination of fricatives in preschool children. Redegeair and Kamil (1970) concluded that the correlation between poor articulation ability and poor discrimination was significant, but an item analysis found that the articulation-error pattern differed from the discrimination-error pattern. Redegeair and Kamil believed that such results were related to a third factor, i.e., general language-processing ability. To test this hypothesis, they conducted two experiments. In the first, nonsense syllables were used with 12 first-grade and 12 kindergarten children. Mixed lists of repeated-contrast pairs, initial-contrast pairs, and final-contrast pairs were presented by tape recorder; each list was presented for six days. In the second experiment, the real-word items from the Wepman were used.

The results showed that repeated-contrast pairs were easier to discriminate than either initial- or final-contrast pairs, and that there was no difference between initial- and final-contrast pairs. Performance on the first day was significantly poorer than on all other days; there was no difference among the other five days. According to the researchers, the results have two major implications: (1) that repeated testing is necessary with young children and (2) that with repeated-contrast pairs, a more complete assessment of phonological discrimination ability in children may be obtained.

Tests of auditory discrimination such as the Templin's and Wepman's are useful in determining whether a child can distinguish similarities between syllables or words, but they do not identify children whose primary disability is with sound perception within words. Since so many different kinds of auditory disturbances interfere with reading, it is necessary to explore a child's ability in many areas: in hearing similarities and differences in words; in distinguishing similar parts of words; in following an auditory sequence; in blending sounds into words, and in dissecting word wholes into syllables or individual sounds. Although there seems to be agreement among authorities that all these auditory discrimination skills are essential to reading, especially beginning reading, there has been relatively little pertinent research other than correlational studies (Evans, 1969).

No discussion of the assessment of perception of the mildly handicapped could be complete without examining the characteristics of a typical assessment. In this vein, Gallagher (1970) noted that auditory perception, in contrast to visual perception, is rarely measured. Wepman's (1958) study of the frequency of test administration reported that the Bender Visual-Motor Gestalt Test is the most commonly used of all clinical instruments; not even one auditory-perceptual test ranked among the top 10 most frequently administered instruments. Paradoxically, almost all the predictive and correlational work reported in the literature indicates that auditory perception relates more significantly to school failure (Dystra, 1966; Sabatino & Hayden, 1970a, 1970b; Vernon, 1971), language development (Morency, Wepman, & Hass, 1970; Parnell & Korzeniowski, 1972; Van Atta, 1973), the diagnosis of brain injury (Eisenson, 1954; Myklebust, 1965), and reading-spelling achievement (Gibson, 1967; Goetzinger, Dinks, & Baer, 1960; Lloyd, 1968; Tikofsky & McInish, 1968) than does visual perception. There are two reasons that may explain why emphasis is on visual perception despite the importance of auditory perception. First, visual perception is regarded by many (Frostig, 1972) to be the most dominant perceptual channel. Secondly, visual perception is less complex (and therefore easier to understand) and possesses many more theoretical models and developed tests. It is unfortunate that these factors may dictate our assessment practices.

The clinician attempting to isolate perceptual traits from either description or measurement faces certain bewilderment. Perceptual theorists (Lashley, 1950; Magnoum, 1969; Penfield, 1951; Pribram, 1971; Wepman, 1958) have disagreed about the component traits comprising the perceptual hierarchy. Yet Gollin and Moody (1973) declared the information-processing approach to perception as being "characterized by a level and component analysis of information reduction" (p. 127). Brindley (1970) noted that visual perception is comprised of perception of form and size, visual constancy, perception of direction and location, figure-ground relationships, relationships of position in space, and spatial sequences.

Others (e.g., Frostig, Lefever, Whittlesey, & Maslow, 1966) noted that visual perception is composed of five factors, although only two perceptual traits are distinctly measured in large-scale factors of tests that operationally measure perception. In short, the isolation of specific subcomponents of perception is always bound to a specific theory and is never simple to accomplish.

MEASUREMENT OF VISUAL AND AUDITORY DISCRIMINATION IN CONTRAST TO VISUAL AND AUDITORY MEMORY

If the Bender Visual-Motor Gestalt Test measures visual perception discrimination of geometric forms, and the Auditory Discrimination Test (Wepman, 1958)) measures auditory perceptual discrimination, what tests measure perceptual memory? The answer lies in the improvisation on the part of the clinician who, by administering tests designed and normed under discrimination conditions, attempts to measure short-term perceptual memory. Ironically, almost all the predictive work with poor readers showed perceptual memory to be more important than perceptual discrimination (Gibson, 1967; Van Atta, 1973).

Auditory-perceptual memory (or at least a model of its possible dimensions) is frequently comprised of two distinct functions. One is a short-term storage unit labeled echoic memory, after Neisser (1967). The echoic-memory unit is similar to the mechanism that was described by Hull (1952) and Peterson (1963) as the stimulus trace mechanism. Auditory stimuli are stored there for very brief periods of time in an undifferentiated form. If the contents of the unit are not attended to shortly after stimulation, they are lost through a process of rapid disintegration. The short-term storage is passive, as it fails to respond to any structuring or organizing influences. In contrast, the long-term active memory unit organizes information into language units for long-term storage. As noted earlier, the amount of information that can be held in active auditory memory depends on the number of units as well as the richness or compactness of the units. In short, the active memory process holds integrated information for two purposes: (1) to overlay the short-term memory process, providing recognition of similarities or previously learned material that is different in either context or stimulus presentation and (2) to retain symbolic perceptual information useful until language conceptualization is achieved. Short-term memory, like the echoic memory, is temporal and passive, needing either external or internal triggering (which is the role of the active memory process).

DEPENDENCE UPON DATA OBTAINED FROM INSTRUMENTS LACKING ADEQUATE RELIABILITY

Table 7-1 shows the highest test-retest reliabilities for several commonly administered auditory or visual perception tests. It is interesting that some authors fail to report data on test-retest reliability, and it is also noteworthy that the information on test stability reported from test manuals is generally higher than corresponding reliability measures reported in the literature. Although reliability mea-

Table 7-1
Test-Retest Reliability

Test	Study	Highest Test-Retest Reliability Reported
Auditory Discrimination Test	Wepman (1958)	.91
Goldman-Fristoe-Woodcock Test of Auditory Discrimination	Goldman, Fristoe, & Woodcock (1970	.87 (quiet) .81 (noise)
Test of Auditory Discrimination	Risko (1975)	NA*
Screening Test for Auditory Perception	Kimmel & Wahl (1969)	.80
Kindergarten Auditory Screening Test	Katz (1971)	NA*
Bender Visual-Motor Gestalt Test	Bender (1938)	.55–.69
Motor-Free Visual-Perceptual Tests	Colarusso & Hammill (1972)	.81
Southern California Figure-Ground Visual Perceptual Test	Ayers (1973)	.37–.53
Frostig Developmental Test of Visual Perception (3rd ed.)	Frostig, Lefever, Whittlesey, Maslow (1969)	.84
Developmental Test of Visual Motor Integration	Beery & Buktenica (1967)	.83–.87
Dennis Visual Perception Scale	Dennis & Dennis (1969)	NA*
Benton Visual Retention Test	Benton (revised 1974)	.76

*NA = not available.

sures vary considerably, it should be noted that the reported highest test-retest stability factors are generally in the .80s. It has generally been recognized that test-retest reliability measures should be .50 to .60 for research purposes; however, to make decisions about children, a reliability coefficient of .90–.95 should be considered the desired standard (Nunnally, 1967). Obviously, very few of the heavily utilized perceptual tests offer the necessary test-retest reliability.

PERCEPTUAL DEVELOPMENT AND THE MILDLY HANDICAPPED

There is almost a total absence of research relating to the perceptual development of the mildly handicapped. Specific problems include the following: (1) Auditory perception has received little attention, so any discussion relating to auditory perceptual differences among the three populations is extremely limited; (2) There is little research on trait-test validation; therefore, a description of the perceptual development of one of the mildly handicapped groups, as opposed to another, is impossible; and (3) There is very little information on perceptual memory, and what data do exist were ascertained using instruments with low reliability. However, it remains certain that perceptual-processing errors almost certainly exist among the mildly mentally retarded, the mildly behaviorally disordered, and the learning disabled. Indeed, as noted previously, perceptual deficits are part of the definition of learning disabilities. But, beyond this, it is virtually certain that perceptual deficits make a considerable difference in the nature of special programs. While the type and amount of perceptual errors present are not easily discernible, they are important.

In the mildly retarded, the level of perceptual error is generally developmentally equivalent to the child's language age, but significantly delayed relative to the chronological age. Perceptual memory is generally slower to develop than immediate perceptual discrimination. The result is that the child is highly dependent upon immediate perceptual experience, as opposed to building skills to replace the perceptual experiences, even into the adult years. The inability of the mildly mentally retarded child to generalize and abstract the use of language forces him to remain highly dependent upon what he sees and hears. Another difficulty is that the retarded child is also dependent upon being in the physical presence of a stimulus when he needs information from it. An absence of care in helping the retarded child build perceptual memory skills and learn to differentiate key features, while learning to use limited language as a replacement for perceptual experiences, can limit the child's learning.

Children with behavioral disorders seemingly distort their perceptual world, thus receiving unrealistic perceptual information. This is critical in the diagnosis of children with behavioral disorders, because the developmental age-level difference between perceptual performances on any two given days may indicate the amount of regression being experienced. Allen (1969) considered this phenomenon to be developmental lag and viewed it as a critical factor in the diagnosis and treatment of the child. It was believed that the developmental level achieved on any given day was crucial in the treatment, and it was recommended that the therapist's language or level of relationship not exceed the developmental level indicated by the perceptual function.

The need for diagnosis and critical use of perceptual training as the key to intervention planning occurs with learning disabled children, particularly those under 12 years of age. A child with learning disabilities should have considerably better language skills than are indicated by the performance on behavior perceptual tests. There is also evidence (Sabatino & Hayden, 1971) to indicate that learning disabled children may perform significantly better in one area of perceptual development as opposed to another. All of the difficulties associated with concepts of perception, diagnosis, and treatment seemingly coalesce at the diagnostic category of learning disabilities. Despite disagreement (Hammill, 1972; Mann, 1971), perceptual deficiencies are believed to lie at the core of the concept of learning disabilities; therefore, it would be erroneous to delete the construct from criticisms of past assessment and training procedure. The real value of contemporary criticisms lies in their capacity to avoid the premature acceptance of conclusions and to promote the continued exploration of perceptual capacities.

PERCEPTUAL-MOTOR DEVELOPMENT AND THE MILDLY HANDICAPPED

Kinesthetic information, movement experiences, and audio and visual integration seemingly contribute to perceptual development. The physically, mentally, and emotionally impaired are limited in perceptual ability and require perceptual training beyond that found in regular classrooms. Mildly retarded children have had limited success in motor experiences and therefore have not developed the kinesthetic awareness of movement abilities. Minimally brain-injured children or slow learners (Kephart, 1971) often display deficits in the perceptual development of sensorimotor feedback.

In order to master higher-order perceptual-motor skills, primary perceptual-motor experiences must be mastered. Early perceptual learning is provided through differential movement experiences (Ayres, 1973; Getman, 1965; Piaget, 1967). As children move physically, they gain mobility, strength, and experience, come to recognize shapes and sizes of objects, and develop the capacity to interpret positions in space.

Each new perceptual experience encourages the child to search out greater experiences. Limited motor activity, on the other hand, contributes to static or lag in perceptual development due to the lack of new developmental experiences. Thus, "handicapped children who lag in early development may be afflicted with abnormal development in the social and emotional spheres" (Wundelich, 1969). Perceptual development involves storage and retrieval of movement experiences as needed. The failure to develop "milestone" skills such as walking is an example of an early developmental lag of the behavior disordered. Other motor problems include difficulty moving through space, resistance to change, aversion to physical activity, and poor body image. Without proper body image, imitation is difficult. Schilder (1935) and Bender (1938) emphasized the importance of body image as necessary for the imitation of movement.

A child may fail to master a skill because of (1) an inability to interpret current stimulation, e.g., speed or direction; (2) inappropriate last experience, e.g., having never jumped rope; (3) a lack of physical prerequisites to make a response, e.g., being physically unable to jump, lacking in strength; (4) an inability to interpret the desired response through inappropriate feedback (i.e., the child who doesn't understand a task is likely to make the same mistake twice); and (5) any combination of the above (Ainheim, Auxter, & Crowe, 1977). It is important to know *why* she failed in order to help the child experience success. Task analysis of the skill is vital, but, despite theoretical differences, categorically unique perceptual problems do not yet seem capable of affecting the course of instruction. However, research generated from the study of movement has established the following basic generalities for all mildly handicapped children.

Growth and maturation influence motor skill learning. Children learn specific motor skills when they achieve the actual physical growth and development required to accomplish the movement. Motor readiness is affected by physical size and level of maturation of the neuromuscular system, and it may be useful to compare the motor achievements of the handicapped youngsters and normal youngsters of the same chronological age. A child's psychological age, reflective of the neuromuscular system, more frequently approximates the mental rather than the chronological age. Sensitivity to the child's reaction to motor movement and awareness of his limitations are important considerations.

Performance of motor skills is dictated by mechanical and physiological principles of movement. The movement educator must be aware of Isaac Newton's three laws of motion—the law of inertia, the law of acceleration, and the law of action and reaction—and be able to apply these to the moving problems of the handicapped. Maintaining balance requires a sense of center of gravity, line of gravity, and size of the base of support. The learning disabled, behaviorally disordered, and the mentally retarded must be taught principles of movement, and the physical educator must be aware of methods to guide handicapped children and help them explore movement skills using the principles of movement to their best advantage.

New motor skills are learned through reinforcement and repetition. Immediate goals should be stressed, and reinforcement must be immediate. For many children, knowing that certain efforts produce a desired result is a reinforcement, but some children are unable to understand the intrinsic consequence of an act; therefore, extrinsic reinforcement is essential at each step in any sequence of activities.

Children learn different activities at different rates. Even children having achieved similar neuromuscular status do not learn the same motor skill with equal speed. Determine the learning pace of the student and consider that pace when developing motor goals for individualized education programs. There is a high positive relationship between speed of learning and intelligence when the IQ falls below 70, with an even sharper rise in that relationship when the IQ falls below 60. Some emotionally disturbed children are extremely bright and capable of learning, but the vast majority are not. Indeed, most disturbed children are somewhat below average in IQ, and the more severely disturbed tend to have even lower IQs (Kauffman, 1979). It is important that individual learning rates be taken into consideration.

Social-personal behaviors affect the process of motor learning. During the time a motor skill is being learned, social-emotional factors may be detrimental to learning. For this reason, extreme care is required in introducing motor learning to behaviorally disordered children. These children are often distressed by movement patterns and feel pressure to perform. They may develop physical symptoms such as stomachaches because of their aversion to physical activity. Slow exposure and much encouragement is paramount for the individual in the program. Short-term goals, individual free play, and immediate success are necessary for behaviorally disordered children.

Learning one motor skill does not necessarily improve performance in another. Cratty and Martin (1969) found that when children are informed about how a skill from one motor task may be applicable to performance in another, a transfer may be expected. They noted that transfer of training is more critical with handicapped children. Teaching movements in a natural pattern ensures longer retention than teaching them in isolation; e.g., teach the hop in relation to a skip (Fait, 1978).

Motor learning for the mildly handicapped should be fun.   A child needs to know when she has been successful and that her effort is appreciated. Mildly handicapped children experience competition in the classroom, responding to academic performance under pressure through joy or frustration. Physical education need not be an area of competition; movement can be a fulfilling, self-gratifying experience for the mildly handicapped to enjoy. Being in control of one's body, feeling the movement become easier, and knowing success is fun. There need be no pressure to perform or opportunity to fail, for movement is beneficial and will lead to self-enjoyment and pride. Physical education offers the mildly handicapped child a chance to create, explore, and expand her own potential.

Fatigue detracts from the motor learning processes.   Fatigue is a factor in learning for the physically handicapped, behaviorally disordered, learning disabled, and mildly mentally retarded. Mildly handicapped children will tire more easily from physical exertion than children developing normally, even when they share similar neuromuscular ages.

An over-learned motor skill will be retained for a long period of time.   Over-learning is essentially the process of repeating a task until performance is automatic. The point at which a skill is over-learned varies with each individual. The mentally retarded require many more repetitions in performing a skill to reach this point than nonretarded persons.

Understanding techniques to improve motor abilities for the mildly handicapped is important. Emotional deficits can be a result of poor gross or fine motor development. As previously discussed, the mildly handicapped child judges himself in terms of his movement ability as compared to his peers. Repeatedly being left out of group games is socially devastating. Physical inadequacies can establish the basis for social withdrawal; the mildly handicapped child must not develop an expectation of failure in attempting motor skills.

EMOTIONAL DEFICITS AS A RESULT OF POOR FINE MOTOR BEHAVIOR

Children with mild-to-moderate perceptual-motor problems will evidence different kinds of behavioral deficits: speech and vision may be poor and problems in reading, writing, arithmetic, and spelling may appear. Special aid for children with fine movement difficulties is justified for several reasons. A child with hand–eye coordination problems will often be unable to transmit her thoughts on paper, resulting in a negative attitude toward writing. Children with problems of large muscle control will usually be less acceptable to potential friends.

Social acceptance is generally associated with academic success; if a child's social status with a class is low, his academic performance suffers. Other outlets for success and approval are needed. Physical education and the benefits derived from improvement in movement skills can offer him an alternative. Children with movement problems frequently suffer from concomitant problems involving emotional adjustment. Learning disabled children evidence a high prevalence of withdrawal from physical education (as do the behavior disordered). While the mildly handicapped may not be stars physically, structured motor activities applied correctly may exert a powerful influence on their motivation to achieve all things. Leisure time activities and recreational skills offer relaxation and self-fulfillment without the pressure to perform competitively. Planned skill development is not the solution to all learning or behavioral disorders; however, movement training, especially in the preschool and early school years, can improve the perceptual-motor capacities of children, and should play an increasingly important role in educating the mildly handicapped child.

THE LAW (PL 94-142) AND PERCEPTUAL-MOTOR PROFICIENCY

The Education for All Handicapped Children Act, PL 94-142, provides support for motor development. Those who framed the law recognized the importance of motor proficiency by mandating a physical education curriculum for every handicapped child. PL 94-142 defines physical education clearly and concisely as including (1) development of physical and motor fitness; (2) development of fundamental motor skills and patterns; (3) development of skills in aquatics, dance, and individual and group games and sports; and (4) special physical education, adapted physical education, movement education, and motor development.

Children with handicapping conditions *can* attain realistic physical and motor goals, and this is especially true for the mildly handicapped. Movement and motor proficiency are important ends, worth achieving. Furthermore, some physical educators claim that motor behaviors can enhance the academic, intellectual, social, and personal development of handicapped children. In one study involving 132 learning disabled students (6–15 years old), the efficacy of an individualized structured physical education program for learning disabled students was supported (Elstein, 1977). Hopkins (1976) reported that children doing yoga (slow, controlled movement and breathing) were noticeably more relaxed and controlled than other children. Kirshner (1973) reported a program of motor and kinesthetic games that was developed to decrease the print phobia of 20 dyslexic boys. The program, lasting 4 weeks with four 45-minute lessons each week, involved freezing in the body alphabet positions and racing, tracing, and throwing activities. The 10 passive children in the study showed no improvement, and one child became more disruptive (Kirshner, 1973). In a study (Rosenborough, 1963) of 20 problem readers (5–17 years old), which emphasized the relationship of physical fitness to reading problems, improved use of the eyes, increased reading, and improved school work were noted after therapy. It was discovered that all 20 students were suffering from physical handicaps—*not one* could pass the Kraus-Weber Tests for physical education. After a program of visual training and body dynamics, physical fitness and academic work improved.

An investigation of motor proficiency, mental age, school attainment, sociometric status, and classroom behavior of 31 educably mentally retarded boys and girls indicated that motor proficiency was related in varying degrees to *all* the areas investigated, even when the factors of chronological age and mental age were statistically eliminated (Hofmeister, 1969). A perceptual-motor curriculum in body image and in space and directionality produced significant effects for kindergarteners identified as potentially perceptual-motor disabled (Sunal, 1978). PL 94-142 and PL 93-112 both support physical education as contributing to physical growth, physical proficiency, and motoric skill development for children with handicapping conditions.

In short, the law requires that the needs of handicapped children must be translated into specific goals and objectives. There must be opportunities for the learning disabled, behavior disordered, and mildly mentally retarded to observe, participate, associate, and be reinforced in physical activities. To engage in exploratory movements, aquatics, rhythms, tumbling, and individual sports is essential for the mildly handicapped (Stein, 1979).

REFERENCES

Ainheim, D. D., Auxter, D., & Crowe, W. C. *Principles and methods of adapted physical education and recreation* (3rd ed.). St. Louis: C. V. Mosby, 1977.

Allen, R. M. The mental age—Visual perception issue assessed. *Exceptional Children,* 1969, *35,* 748–749.

Armstrong, R. G., & Hauck, P. A. Sexual identification and the first figure drawn. *Journal of Consulting Psychology,* 1961, *25,* 51–54.

Ayres, A. J. *Sensory integration and learning disorders.* Los Angeles: Western Psychological Services, 1973.

Barsch, R. *Perceptual-motor curriculum.* Seattle: Special Child Publications, 1968.

Beery, K., & Buktenica, N. *Developmental test of visual motor integration.* Chicago, Il.: Follet Publishing, 1967.

Bender, L. A. A visual motor gestalt test and its clinical use. *American Orthopsychiatric Association Research Monthly.* Research Monograph Number 3, 1938.

Bender, L. *Psychopathology of children with organic brain disorders.* Springfield, Il.: Charles C. Thomas, 1956.

Benton, A. L. *Benton visual retention test* (Rev.) New York: Psychological Corporation, 1974.

Bloom, B. S. *Stability and change in human characteristics.* New York: Wiley, 1964.

Brindley, G. S. *Physiology of the retina and visual pathway.* London: Edward Arnold, 1970.

Chalfant, J., & Schefflin, M. *Central processing dysfunctions in children: A review of research.* (NINDS Monograph No. 9, Task Force III.) Bethesda, Md.: U.S. Department of Health, Education and Welfare, 1969.

Clawson, A. The Bender Visual Motor Gestalt Test as an index of emotional disturbance in children. *Journal of Projection Technology,* 1959, *23,* 198–206.

Colarusso, L., & Hammill, D. *Motor-free visual motor perceptual tests.* San Rafael, Ca.: Academic Therapy Publication, 1972.

Coltheart, M., & Curthoys, I. Short-term recognition memory for pitch: Effect of a priori probability on response times and error roles. *Perception and Psychophysics,* 1968, *4,* 85–89.

Cratty, B. J. *Movement behavior and motor learning.* Philadelphia: Lea & Febiger, 1969.

Cratty, B. J., & Martin, M. M. *Perceptual-motor efficiency in children.* Philadelphia: Lea & Febiger, 1969.

Dennis, R., & Dennis, M. *Dennis visual perception scale.* Los Angeles: Western Psychological Services, 1969.

Doman, R. J., & Delacato, C. H. *The treatment and prevention of reading problems: The neuro-psychological approach.* Springfield, Il.: Charles C. Thomas, 1959.

Drake, C. *PERC Auditory Discrimination Test.* Sherborn, Mass.: PERC Educational and Research Center, 1965.

Dykstra, R. Auditory discrimination abilities and beginning reading achievement. *Reading Research Quarterly,* 1966, *3,* 2–34.

Eisenson, J. *Examining for aphasia.* New York: Psychological Corporation, 1954.

Elstein, A. E. *Effects of physical education on the physical fitness, social adjustment and self-concept of learning disabled students.* Temple University. (University Microfilms International, Ann Arbor, MI, Catalogue No. 77-13, 505), 1977.

Evans, J. R. Auditory and auditory-visual integration skills as they relate to reading. *The Reading Teacher*, 1969, *22*, 625–629.

Fait, H. F. *Special physical education: adapted, corrective, developmental* (4th ed.). Philadelphia: Saunders, 1978.

Flower, R. The evaluation of auditory abilities in the appraisal of children with reading problems. In A Figurel (Ed.), *Perception and reading*. Newark, Del.: Intentional Reading Association, 1968.

Frostig, M. Visual perception, integrative functions and academic learning. *Journal of Learning Disabilities*, 1972, *5*, 1–15.

Frostig, M., & Horne, D. *The Frostig program for the development of visual perception*. Chicago: Follett, 1964.

Frostig, M., Lefever, D. W., Whittlesey, J. R. B., & Maslow, P. *Frostig developmental test of visual perception*. Palo Alto, Ca.: Consulting Psychologists Press, 1966.

Gallagher, C. E. *Federal involvement in the use of behavior modification drugs on grammar school children of the right to privacy inquiry*. Paper presented to a hearing before a Subcommittee on Government Operational Operations, House of Representatives, Ninety-first Congress, Second Session. L. No. 52–268. Washington, D.C.: U.S. Government Printing Office, 1970.

Getman, G. N. *Visualmotor complex in the acquisition of learning skills*. Seattle: Special Child Publication, 1965.

Getman, G. N., Kane, E. R., Halgren, M. R., & McKee, P. W. *Developing learning readiness*. St. Louis: McGraw-Hill, 1968.

Gibson, E. J. *Principles of perceptual learning and development*. New York: Meredith, 1967.

Goetzinger, C. P., Dinks, D. D., & Baer, C. J. Auditory discrimination and visual perception in good and poor readers. *Annals of Otology, Rhinology and Laryngology*, 1960, *69*, 121–136.

Goldman, R., Fristoe, M., & Woodcock, R. *Test of auditory descrimination*. Minnesota: American Guidance Service, 1970.

Gollin, E. S., & Moody, M. Developmental psychology. In P. H. Mussen & M. R. Rosenzweig (Eds.), *Annual review of psychology* (Vol. 24). Palo Alto, Ca: Annual Review, 1973.

Hammill, D. D. Training visual perceptual processes. *Journal of Learning Disabilities*, 1972, *5*, 552–555.

Hofmeister, A. Motor proficiency and other variables in educable mentally retarded children. *American Journal of Mental Deficiency*, 1969, *74*, 264–268.

Hopkins, L. J., & Hopkins, J. T. Yoga in psychomotor training. *Academic Therapy*, 1976, *7*, 461–465.

Hull, C. L. *A behavior system: An introduction to behavior theory concerning the individual organism*. New Haven: Yale University Press, 1952.

Katz, J. *Kindergarten auditory screening test*. Chicago, Il.: Follett Educational Corporation, 1971.

Kauffman, J. Emotional disorders in young children. In S. G. Garwood (Ed.), *Educating young handicapped children: A developmental approach*. Germantown, MD: Aspen Systems, 1979.

Kephart, N. C. *The slow learner in the classroom* (2nd ed.). Columbus, Oh.: Charles E. Merrill, 1971.

Kimmel, G. M., & Wahl, J. *Screening test for auditory perception* (Experimental ed.). San Rafael, Ca.: Academic Therapy Publications, 1969.

Kirshner, A. J. A cause of poor reading is poor reading. *Special Education in Canada*, 1973, *47*, 13–19, 22–25.

Koppitz, E. M. *The Bender Gestalt Test for Young Children*. New York: Grune & Stratton, 1964.

Lashley, K. S. In search of the engram. In F. A. Beach, D. O. Hebb, C. T. Morgan, & H. W. Nissen (Eds.), *The neuropsychology of Lashley*. New York: McGraw Hill, 1960.

Lloyd, B. A. Helping the disabled reader at the elementary level. *International Reading Association Conference Proceedings*, 1968, *1*, 171–175.

Magnoum, H. W. Advances in brain research with implications for learning. In K. H. Pribram (Eds.), *On the biology of learning*. New York: Harcourt, Brace and World, 1969.

Mann, L. Perceptual training revisited—the training of nothing at all. *Rehabilitation Literature*, 1971, *32*, 322–335.

Miller, G. A. The magical number seven, plus or minus two: Some limits on our capacity for processing information. *Psychological Review*, 1956, *63*, 81–97.

Morency, A. S., Wepman, J. M., & Hass, S. T. Developmental speech inaccuracy and speech therapy in the early school years. *El-*

ementary School Journal, 1970, *70*, 219–224.

Myklebust, H. *The psychology of deafness* (2nd ed.) New York: Grune & Stratton, 1965.

Neisser, V. *Cognitive psychology.* New York: Appleton-Century-Crofts, 1967.

Nunnally, J. *Psychometric theory.* New York: McGraw-Hill, 1967.

Parnell, P., & Korzeniowski, R. Auditory perception and learning, Part II. *Remedial Education*, 1972, *4*, 20–22.

Penfield, W. *Epileptic seizure patterns.* Springfield, Il.: Charles C. Thomas, 1951.

Peterson, L. R. Immediate memory: Data and theory. In C. N. Cofer & B. S. Musgrave (Eds.), *Verbal behavior and learning.* New York: McGraw-Hill, 1963.

Piaget, J. *The psychology of intelligence.* Totowa, N.J.: Littlefield, Adams, 1967.

Pribram, K. H. *Language of the brain.* Englewood Cliffs: Prentice-Hall, 1971.

Redegeair, R. E., & Kamil, M. L. *Assessment of phonological discrimination in children.* (Technical Report No. 118, March, 1970. Wisconsin Research and Development Center for Cognitive Learning, the University of Wisconsin, Contract OE 5-10-15-4.) Washington, D.C.: U.S. Office of Education, Department of Health, Education, and Welfare.

Risko, V. *Test of auditory discrimination.* San Rafael, Ca.: Academic Therapy Publications, 1975.

Rosenborough, P. M. *Physical fitness and the child's reading problem.* New York: Exposition Press, 1963.

Sabatino, D. A. A review of diagnostic and classification antecedents in special education. In D. A. Sabatino & T. L. Miller (Eds.), *Describing learner characteristics of handicapped children and youth.* New York: Grune & Stratton, 1979.

Sabatino, D. A., & Hayden, D. L. Information processing behaviors related to learning disabilities and educable mental retardation. *Exceptional Children*, 1970, *37*, 21–29. (a)

Sabatino, D. A., & Hayden, D. L. Psychoeducational study of selected behavioral variables with children failing the elementary grades, Part I. *The Journal of Experimental Education*, 1970, *38*, 40–57. (b)

Sabatino, D. A., & Hayden, D. L. Variations in information processing behaviors as related to age differences for children failing the elementary grades. *Journal of Learning Disabilities*, 1970, *3*, 404–412.

Schilder, P. *The image and appearance of the human body.* New York: International Universities Press, 1935.

Sedlak, R. A., & Weener, P. Review of research on the Illinois Test of Psycholinguistic Abilities. In L. Mann & D. Sabatino (Eds.), *The first review of special education,* (Vol. 1). Philadelphia: JSE Press, 1973.

Shaw, M. G. II, & Cruickshank, W. M. Use of the Bender Gestalt Test with epileptic children. *Journal of Clinical Psychology*, 1956, *12*, 192–193.

Skeel, M., Calfee, R. C., & Venesky, R. L. *Perceptual confusions among fricatives in preschool children.* (Technical Report No. 73, Research and Development Center for Cognitive Learning.) The University of Wisconsin, Madison, 1969.

Snyder, R. J., & Pope, P. New norms for and an item analysis of the Wepman Test at the first grade six-year level. *Perceptual and Motor Skills*, 1970, *31*, 1007–1010.

Stein, J. Education unlimited. *Educational Resource Center*, 1979, *1*, 31–33.

Sunal, C. S. Training program for kindergarten children identified as potentially perceptual motor disabled. *Reading Improvement*, 1978, *15*, 208–214.

Templin, M. C. *Certain language skills in children: their development and interrelationships. Institute of Child Welfare Monograph*, 1957, No. 26, University of Minnesota Press.

Tikofsky, R. S., & McInish, J. R. Consonant discrimination by seven year olds. *Psychometric Science*, 1968, *10*, 61.

Travis, L. E., & Rasmus, B. The sound discrimination ability of cases with functional disorders of articulation. *Q J Speech*, 1931, *17*, 217–226.

Van Atta, B. A comparative study of auditory skills (sensitivity, discrimination, and memory span) of dyslexic and normal speaking children in grades 1–3. *Aviso*, 1973, *4*, 1–7.

Vernon, M. D. *Reading and its difficulties.* New York: Cambridge University Press, 1971.

Wepman, J. M. Relationship between self-correction and recovery from aphasia. *Journal of Speech and Hearing Disorders*, 1958, *23*, 302–305.

Wertheimer, W. Studies in the theory of gestalt psychology. *Psychologische Forscherung*, 1923, *4*, 132–136.

Wundelich, R. C. Learning disorders. *Physical Therapy*, 1969, *47*, 700–708.

Melinda Parrill-Burnstein

8

Social-Cognitive and Affective Development

Social-cognitive and affective development are concomitant parts of a child's general cognitive development. Social competence is one product of the social-cognitive process. It is the ability to interact appropriately with others and to interpret people's behavior accurately (Parrill-Burnstein & Baker-Ward, 1979). The relationship between social competence and social cognition is depicted in Figure 1 and is described in detail elsewhere (see Parrill-Burnstein, 1981). Affect is the emotional response to internal and/or external stimuli, such as other persons, situations, or events (Yarrow, 1979).[1] Social perception reflects attention to social and affective cues, cues that provide information about the beliefs, attitudes, and feelings of others (Flavell, 1977). Social perception is inferred from a child's social interactions. These interactions are problem-solving situations in which the child must use acquired social and affective skills to respond appropriately.

DEVELOPMENT

The development of affect and social cognition are interrelated; the development of one affects the development of the other. Research trends suggest that the child is an active participant in his or her social affective development (Parke, 1979); during social-affective development, the child influences and is influenced by others. Because the child exists in the context of more than one social system (e.g., family, school; Hartup, 1979), the individual learns skills specific to each social system, as well as skills appropriate across social systems. Social affective patterns and competencies differ within different cultures and are influenced by social policy (Parke, 1979).[2]

Hoffman's summary (1979) of early development of empathy and prosocial behavior emphasized the development of a cognitive sense of others. Empathy

---

[1]For purposes here, affect is studied within the context of interactions with other people.

[2]For comprehensive reviews see Shantz (1975) and Lewis and Rosenblum (1978).

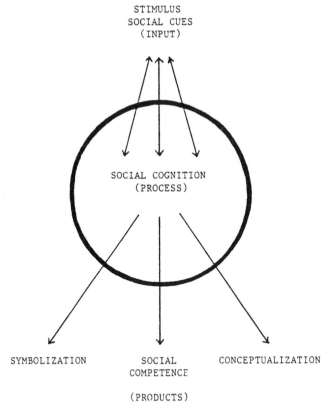

Fig. 8-1. An analysis of the components involved in the social-cognitive process. (Reprinted with permission from Parrill-Burnstein, M. *Problem solving and learning disabilities:
An information processing approach.* New York: Grune &
Stratton, 1981, p. 177.)

was defined by Hoffman as a vicarious emotional response to another person,
which is a function of both the level and ability to understand others. Hoffman's
summary of the development of empathy is applicable to the development of other
affective states. Within a cognitive sense of others, one learns to accurately evaluate and interpret the actions of oneself and others (Yarrow, 1979).

Hoffman (1979) proposed four stages in the development of a cognitive sense
of others. Stage one, birth to 1 year, is a fusion of self and others. Awareness of
others as distinct and differentiated physical entities is achieved by 11– 12 months.
Stage two, 2–3 years, marks the beginning of role-taking skills. The child recognizes that others have independent states, but is not able to act on that information. In stage three, 8– 12 years, the child's cognizance of others becomes more
sophisticated since the child is aware that others have unique identities and that
experiences persist beyond the immediate situation. These latter skills are further
elaborated and defined in adolescence and throughout adulthood.

Shantz (1975) and Chandler (1977) summarize social-cognitive development.
Their focus, and the focus taken here, is on the skills of perspective-taking, person-perception, and role-taking. Perspective-taking is the ability to take another

person's physical perspective through imagery (Hardwick, McIntyre, & Pick, 1976). Person-perception is the ability to describe and categorize the behaviors of others (Shantz, 1975). Role-taking is the ability to take another's social-cognitive perspective simultaneously with one's own social-cognitive perspective (Flavell, 1977). Perspective-taking skills are limited before the age of 6 years; other people's physical perspectives are recognized but not understood. Between the ages of 6 and 10 years, the child develops two skills: (1) the ability to take another's perspective through imagery; and (2) the ability to understand the reciprocal relationship between self and others. Perspective-taking, person-perception, and role-taking skills continue to develop throughout life.

Social-cognitive and affective development are interrelated, and the development of skills, such as role-taking and person-perception, reflects both social-cognitive and affective knowledge. Prerequisites to these skills are mastered early and form the foundation for later learning of more complex social and affective behaviors.

RELATIONSHIP BETWEEN SOCIAL COGNITION AND AFFECT

Interpretations of social interactions reflect social-cognitive and affective skills. Social cognition is the cognitive strategy of social behaviors while affect is the emotional reaction, the feeling underlying the problem-solving process. Social interactions provide situations in which social problems are posed.

Social interactions may involve the family, peers, or schoolmates. Family relationships, which are usually the first relationships established, underlie social relationships (Hartup, 1979). Peer relationships, which have received increased attention, consist of complex social structures that change with age (Hoffman, 1979). Fewer data are available about the school as a social system affecting the social competencies of the individual (Hartup, 1979). These relationships between social systems (peer, family, and school) are described by conjunctive-, single-, or dual-process models. A conjunctive-process model describes the connections between social systems, rather than focusing on the development of an individual social system (Hartup, 1979). The single-process model poses that social competencies evolve in family interactions and are extended and elaborated in peer interactions. In a dual-process model, social competencies for each system develop independently (Hartup, 1979).

As in the conjunctive model, the development of social and affective skills may be viewed as interrelated or connected (Yarrow, 1979). The influence of affect and social cognition is bidirectional (Yarrow, 1979), since states of affect influence the processing of stimulus cues, as does cognition. For example, when feeling sad, attention is directed to different cues, which are, in turn, interpreted differently than when feeling happy. Cognitions influence emotions at many different levels, as well. For example, the ability to discriminate influences what is perceived at higher levels; cognitions are related to past experiences and are symbolized and integrated with other perceptions and processed information (Yarrow, 1979).

A proposed relationship between social cognition and affect is shown in Fig-

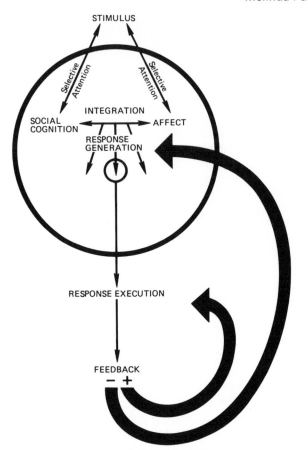

Fig. 8-2. A proposed relationship between social cognition
and affect.

ure 8-2, which represents an application of hypothesis-testing theory (Levine,
1975; Parrill-Burnstein, 1978) to this area of problem solving. The inside of the
circle represents covert responses; the outside of the circle represents overt responses. Analysis of cognitive processing of social and affective information occurs at all levels. Initially, the stimulus, a social interaction, is encountered (external stimulus) or evoked (internal stimulus). In response to the stimulus, social and
affective cues are perceived, separately and simultaneously (level-selection attention). The processor actively seeks information, which both influences and is influenced by what is perceived from the original stimulus. Once perceived, these
social-cognitive and affective cues are integrated and processed with immediate,
past, and inferred information (level-integration process).

   Once integrated, a social problem is posed, and possible appropriate social
options or responses are generated (level-response generation). From the set of
responses generated, a specific option is selected and tested (level-response execution). Once the child tests a response, feedback is given that allows an evaluation of the response. Based on feedback, the response is either modified, eliminated, or retained as appropriate. An appropriate response is one that is

consistent with feedback and relevant to the problem-solving situation. After positive feedback, the reinforced response is repeated, though not necessarily immediately. If delayed, the appropriate social response is stored and later retrieved in the same or a similar social situation.[3] If feedback is negative, the child samples a new response from those generated initially.

To further clarify application of the analysis shown in Figure 8-2, the following example is provided: A child encounters a group of children playing baseball. The child observes seven youngsters on the playground, one at each base, a pitcher, a catcher, and a coach (level-selective attention). She sees the coach walking up and down the field shaking hands with the players. The child processes information about facial expressions, body perceptions, which are social perceptions. An affective perception is to attend to the coach's smile and interpret the smile as a feeling of enthusiasm and joyfulness. Social-cognitive and affective cues are integrated and interpreted as "the coach is pleased with the players." Ultimately, the child wants to join the team (problem posed) and decides possible responses: (1) ask the coach to play; (2) walk onto the field; or (3) walk away (level-response generation). The child decides and walks onto the field (level-response execution). When the child walks onto the field, she is told to get off by another player (level-feedback, negative). The response of walking onto the field is eliminated. The child selects another response (samples from initial responses generated) and approaches the coach (response execution). The coach points to a part of the field. The child walks onto the field and is welcomed by fellow players (level-feedback, positive). This response will be repeated in a similar situation.

The relationship between social cognition and affect is not clear-cut, and it is proposed that perception of social interactions has both social-cognitive and affective components. These components interact at various levels of processing and result in overt social behaviors. Problems in selective attention, integration, response generation, response execution, and responding appropriately to feedback disrupt this problem-solving process.

PERCEPTIONS OF OTHERS REGARDING THE MILDLY HANDICAPPED CHILD

The most frequently used measures of the perceptions of others regarding the mildly handicapped are the rating-scale and sociometric techniques. Usually, the child's teacher or parent is asked to rate a child's problem behaviors. Peers are sometimes asked to rate the popularity of their classmates, including mildly handicapped children.

Teacher Impressions

When evaluating social and affective behavior, most researchers use a modification of the Quay–Peterson Behavior Problem Checklist (Quay & Peterson, 1967) with teachers as informants. In general, the scale consists of some 50 items

---

[3]An application to similar social situations would represent generalization.

describing various overt behaviors categorized as conduct disorders, personality disorders, and immaturity. Examples of behaviors associated with these categories include (1) conduct disorder: aggression and hostility; (2) personality problems: anxiety, withdrawal, and introversion; and (3) immaturity: preoccupation, lack of interest, and daydreaming (Quay, Morse, & Cutler, 1966).

Gajar (1979) used a modification of the Quay–Peterson Behavior Problem Checklist with teachers as raters. Gajar's subjects were 378 children in special education classes. Of these children, 122 were identified as emotionally disturbed, 135 were identified as having learning disabilities, and 121 were identified as educably mentally retarded. Children with educable mental retardation were distinguished from those in other groups by lower IQ scores. Children with learning disabilities were distinguished by significantly lower reading scores, while those with emotional disturbances had significantly lower scores in math.

Results indicated that children with emotional disturbances had significantly more conduct problems than either the retarded children or the children with learning disabilities. Emotionally disturbed children also had more personality problems and were more immature. The children with learning disabilities had fewest behavior problems. These results suggested that the main problem with the emotionally disturbed children was acting-out behavior.

Cullinan, Epstein, and Dembinski (1979) used a modification of the Behavior Problem Checklist with teachers as raters. Characteristics of four populations were studied. Children ranged in age from 6 to 13½ years and were classified as behavior disordered, mentally retarded, having learning disabilities, or without learning problems. Results indicated that children with behavior disorders were rated as having significantly greater behavior problems than children in the other groups. Children with behavior disorders also scored highest on the personality items (higher scores reflected greater disturbances). Significant differences were obtained when the mildly handicapped as a group were compared to the normals. Mentally retarded children were significantly rated as more immature than children without learning problems. These results were consistent with Gajar (1979) and McCarthy and Paraskevopoulas (1969).

McCarthy and Paraskevopoulas (1969) used the Behavior Problem Checklist (Quay & Peterson, 1967) to evaluate teacher impressions of children between the ages of 5 and 15 years who were diagnosed as having learning disabilities, emotional disturbances, or average learning abilities. Emotionally disturbed children had significantly more conduct problems than children with learning disabilities, who had significantly more problems than those without learning problems. On the personality and immaturity items, behavior-disordered children also scored significantly higher, although personality and immaturity behaviors occurred with less frequency than conduct problems.

On the whole, using variations of the Quay–Peterson Behavior Problem Checklist, researchers noted that teachers differentiated students within the multiply handicapped categories. Retarded children were differentiated by lower IQ scores; children with learning disabilities were differentiated by academic failure; and children with behavior disorders were differentiated by conduct problems. Of these three groups, children with learning disabilities had the fewest behavior problems.

Researchers have also analyzed teacher–student interactions and actual verbal behavior of children with learning disabilities. Teachers and peers interacted as frequently with children with learning disabilities as with those without learning problems, but the quality of the interactions was different (Bryan 1978). With children with learning disabilities, there was less socializing and more helping behavior. Analysis of verbal behavior indicated that children with learning disabilities made more negative and competitive statements than children without learning problems.

Peer Impressions

To assess peer impressions, sociometric data were gathered. Usually, the procedures involved asking children in a class to rate the popularity or behavior status of their classmates, including mildly handicapped children. For the most part, available data were with children with learning disabilities.

Siperstein, Bopp, and Bak (1978) asked 177 children, (22 of whom were receiving itinerant help for learning disabilities and 155 of their classmates who did not have learning problems) to name the child who (1) was most liked; (2) was the best athlete; (3) was the smartest; and (4) was the most attractive. Results showed that children with learning disabilities were rated as less popular than children without learning problems. Children with learning disabilities were selected less frequently in all categories than children without learning problems; however, these same children were not significantly isolated within the class.

Bryan (1974b) used sociometric techniques with 84 children with learning disabilities and 84 children without learning problems in grades three through five. The children were asked to select (1) three friends; (2) the children they did not want to sit next to in class; (3) the child they thought had the most difficulty sitting in class; and (4) the child who was the most physically attractive. Results indicated that children with learning disabilities received more votes of rejection, particularly white females with learning disabilities. In a later study, Bryan (1976) replicated these results.

Bruininks, Rynders, and Gross (1974) studied social acceptance of the mildly retarded in resource and regular classrooms. A sociometric questionnaire, the peer acceptance scale, was administered to 1234 nonretarded peers and 65 elementary-school-aged mildly retarded children from urban and suburban schools. The peer acceptance scale required all children to rate every child in the class as to the degree of perceived friendship. Results indicated that when same-sex ratings were examined, urban district retarded children were rated as more popular than nonretarded peers. In the suburban schools, the retarded children were rated as less popular than nonretarded peers. When data from the urban and suburban mentally retarded groups were combined and compared to data from nonretarded children, no significant differences were obtained. Combining these two groups masked the differences within this mentally retarded population. An implication was for further differentiation within the mildly retarded population.

The few available studies suggest that children with learning disabilities are penalized most in peer ratings, while mentally retarded children are penalized least.

Parent Impressions

Parents have also been asked to rate behaviors of the mildly handicapped. Doleys, Cartelli, and Doster (1976) observed parent–child interaction and asked parents to rate the severity of presenting behavior problems. They found that parents of noncompliant children rated their children as more disruptive. Children with learning disabilities were rated as less disruptive, though they still had more problems than those without learning problems.

Strag (1972) compared behavior ratings of parents of severely retarded children, children with learning disabilities, and children without learning problems. Parents rated children with learning disabilities as significantly more depressed, less considerate of others, having difficulty receiving affection, and clumsier than children without learning problems. When children with learning disabilities were compared to the retarded group, children in the latter group were considered significantly less depressed.

An examination of these data indicates that children with behavior disorders were rated as having more severe behavior problems than either mildly retarded children or children with learning disabilities by both teachers and parents. Peers consistently differentiated children with learning disabilities but not necessarily retarded children; children with learning disabilities were rated as less popular children, though not isolated. Studies of peer impressions of behavior-disordered children were unavailable.

SELF-PERCEPTION OF THE MILDLY HANDICAPPED

Self-perception of the mildly handicapped is inferred from how children organize responses to sets of stimuli, notably declarative self-statements and card sorts (i.e., when asked to sort a series of cards into groups). Stimuli used to elicit role-taking behaviors include stories and drawings.

Self-Concept

How the child feels about himself or herself is referred to as self-concept. Self-concept is inferred from what a child does with information provided by the examiner. Three self-concept measures are pertinent to this discussion: the Piers-Harris Children's Self-Concept Test; a modified version of the Coopersmith Self-Concept Inventory; and the Children's Personality Questionnaire. Only limited data are available, particularly with regard to the child with behavior disorders.

The Piers-Harris Children's Self-Concept Test consists of 80 declarative statements. Half of the statements are worded positively, such as, "I am a happy person," and half are worded in a negative fashion, such as, "I behave badly at home." The children's task is to indicate whether or not each statement describes the way they feel about themselves.

Black (1974) and Smith (1979) used the Piers-Harris Children's Self-Concept Test with children with reading and learning disabilities. Black (1974) worked with 50 elementary school-aged children, 25 with delays in reading achievement and 25 achieving normally in reading. The mean age was approximately 11 years. Black found that the self-concept of delayed readers was lower than that of normal readers. A significant negative correlation was found between self-concept and age, as well as between school grade and achievement. The correlation between IQ and self-concept was not significant.

Smith (1979) administered the Piers-Harris Children's Self-Concept Test to 147 children with learning disabilities between the ages of 7 and 12 years (mean age, 9 years, 11 months). Smith found that verbal IQ, performance IQ, and reading achievement did not correlate significantly with self-concept. Word knowledge, math performance, and socioeconomic status (SES) did correlate significantly with self-concept. Furthermore, children with learning disabilities from higher SES had lower self-concepts than children with learning disabilities from lower SES. As in Black's study (1974), IQ and self-concept were not significantly related.

Porter (1965) used the Children's Personality Questionnaire, which is based on factor analysis and personality theory, to measure the self-concept of mildly mentally retarded children. Porter found that the characteristics of retarded children differed from the available data regarding normal children. As a group, retarded students were less intelligent, more submissive, and more phlegmatic than children without learning problems. With respect to this study, intelligence was a key characteristic that differentiated retarded children from those children without learning problems.

Larsen, Parker, and Jorjorian (1973) studied differences in self-concept of 30 normal children and 30 children with learning disabilities. Each child's task was to sort 28 statements from Coopersmith's Self-Concept Inventory (Coopersmith, 1967) into two categories—real self and ideal self. Children with learning disabilities demonstrated a greater discrepancy between real self and ideal self than those without learning problems.

In summary, academic problems (Black, 1974; Smith, 1979) and below average IQ (Porter, 1965) affected self-concept. For children with learning disabilities, differences in expectations (Smith, 1979) and actual achievement (Larsen et al., 1973) affected self-concept.

Role-Taking

Role-taking is the ability to recognize and coordinate thoughts, feelings, and beliefs of self and others during a social interaction (Feffer, 1970). The development of role-taking skills is associated with changes in cognitive development when children without learning problems are studied. Selman and Byrne (1974) summarized the relationship between the development of role-taking and changes in cognitive structure proposed by Piaget. Changes in role-taking are observed at four levels: egocentric role-taking; subjective role-taking; self-reflective role-taking; and mutual role-taking. Egocentric role-taking is associated with an inability to differentiate others' points of view. Subjective role-taking is evident when different perspectives are differentiated but not related. Self-reflective role-taking occurs when the child can evaluate his or her actions from another's point of view but not from two points of view; perceptions are related but not simultaneously. Mutual role-taking occurs when the child is able to relate and process the perspectives of self and others simultaneously; third-party perspectives are also possible.

Different types of stimuli were used to document changes in role-taking ability. Some emphasized moral development (Selman & Byrne, 1974); others emphasized social communicative skills (Flavell, 1977); and still others evaluated performance on projective-type tasks (Feffer & Gourevitch, 1960).

Role-Taking and Mentally Retarded Children

Affleck (1975a, 1975b, 1976) contributed substantially to the study of role-taking skills with the mentally retarded. In the first study (Affleck, 1975a), subjects were 16 young adult males with a mean age of 22 years selected at random from a larger group at a sheltered workshop. Two role-taking tasks were presented. The first involved figure and background stimuli, and the task was to construct a scene and tell a story about it. Then, each subject was asked to relate the story told from the perspective of each of the figures in the scene. The subject's ability to refocus the description while being consistent with the initial story was evaluated. The second task involved presenting a conflict situation where the subject was assigned one of two roles to act out. A nonretardate adult acted out the second role. Criteria included (1) conceptualization of the conflict; (2) recognition of others' feelings and intents; and (3) understanding the consequences of the solution.

Results showed a significant relationship between the two types of role-taking tasks. Nonsignificant correlations were obtained between the role-taking tasks and chronological age, as well as between chronological age and IQ. Unlike the lack of relationship between IQ and self-concept, I.Q. was significantly related to both role-taking tasks. Affleck concluded that role-taking was related to interpersonal conflict among retarded adults.

In a second study, Affleck (1975b) studied role-taking ability and interpersonal competencies of retarded children. Mean age was approximately 13 years, with a mean IQ of 66.58. The procedure involved two tasks. The story-telling task described in the first Affleck study was employed here. In addition, the child played a two-person game. Briefly, this two-person game involved two children sitting facing each other. Each child was given a set of four cards with pennies and arrows printed on each card. The arrows pointed either to that child or the other child. Each child took turns selecting particular cards that revealed the child's intent (e.g., either egocentric or reciprocal-giving choices). Children designated as having higher role-taking abilities earned more pennies than those with lower scores on the role-taking task. A significant positive correlation between role-taking performance and mental age was obtained. Role-taking and chronological age were not significantly correlated.

In the third study, Affleck (1976) studied role-taking ability and the interpersonal tactics of 50 mentally retarded children. The mean chronological age of the children was 12.96 years, mean mental age was 8.60, and mean IQ was 66.58. Two role-taking tasks were presented. The first role-taking task was the same as that used in the preceding studies: the child was asked to construct a scene, tell a story, and then tell the story from the perspective of each figure. In the second task, the child was presented with a social problem and asked how to solve the problem. Again, results indicated a positive correlation between role-taking and mental age, but not between role-taking and chronological age. Children who performed better on the story role-taking task also stressed mutual advantage when solving the verbal problems. Affleck suggested that role-taking ability was specifically associated with interpersonal control.

In summary, Affleck found a significant and positive correlation between role-taking ability and mental age, but not with chronological age, when retarded children were studied. With retarded adults, role-taking and chronological age were not related either; rather, role-taking skills reflected actual levels of social functioning. Affleck also suggested a relationship between role-taking ability and the ability to understand and use inferred information about others—that is, to make mutually advantageous decisions. He suggested that this ability was impaired or delayed in the mentally retarded population.

Blacher-Dickson and Simeonsson (1978) worked with 31 mildly or moderately retarded children between the ages of 6 and 12 years (mean age, 10 years, 3 months), with mental ages (according to the Peabody Picture Vocabulary Test) between 5 and 9 years and a mean IQ of 61 (also according to the Peabody Picture Vocabulary Test). Children did not differ significantly on any of these variables,[4] thus, a major difference between Affleck's work and these authors was procedural.

Blacher-Dickson and Simeonsson presented the children with two role-taking tasks involving two drawings, one of which was a completed figure and one of which was a partial, unrecognizable outline of a figure. On the first role-taking task, the children were required to describe each drawing and then state what a friend would describe if he or she saw the partial figure and not the completed figure. Depending on performance on this task, the children were grouped into three levels: egocentric, intermediate, and decentered. Those at the egocentric level were considered socially less sophisticated than those at the intermediate level, who, in turn, were less sophisticated than those at the decenterd level. On the second role-taking task, the children were shown the ambiguous or incomplete figure without seeing the completed figure and then asked to describe it. This was referred to as the shared-experience task in that the child experienced only what the friend would. The procedure described for the first role-taking task was repeated.

In addition to the two role-taking tasks, both the children and their parents were asked to fill out a behavior rating scale, the Predicted Behavior Scale, which provided a measure of social competency. The results of the study indicated that when the children were classified prior to the rating, (that is after the first role-taking task), and were then contrasted, their performance differed both on that task as well as the second role-taking task. A significant difference on the first role-taking task was expected in that the children were classified based on different performance on that task. On the second role-taking task, children in the decentered group differed significantly from those in the egocentric group. Children in the intermediate group differed significantly from those in the egocentric group as well, but children in the decentered and intermediate groups did not differ significantly. Children at the transitional or intermediate level improved role-taking skills after being placed in the friend's perspective, that is, after having shared the experience.

---

[4]It should be noted that both mental age and IQ were computed on the same raw score and therefore were not independent measures.

With respect to the Predicted Behavior Scale, neither the responses of the children nor of the parents differentiated the children assigned to the three groups. The responses of the parents and the children did not differ significantly, although a significant and positive relationship between the children's responses and mental age was obtained. The relationship between the parents' responses and mental age was not significant. These results were interpreted as suggesting variability in the levels of role-taking skills of retarded children of approximately the same mental ages. Because of the individual differences, and the lack of significant correlations between mental age and role-taking performance on both tasks, mental age as an accurate predictor of role-taking performance by retarded children was questioned. It was suggested that characteristics that differentiated within the population with similar mental ages be further examined.

Monson, Greenspan, and Simeonsson (1979) assessed social competencies, role-taking skills, and referential communication of retarded children. Their subjects were 32 retarded children between the ages of 8 years, 5 months and 18 years, 1 month (mean age, 13 years, 7 months) and with IQ scores between 38 and 83 (mean IQ, 56.4). Mental ages were not reported. To evaluate social competency, two teacher-rating scales were employed that were appropriate for children with these mental ages. The Kohn Social Competency Scale was used to measure teacher ratings of social competency. The Predicted Behavior Scale was used to measure teacher and child judgments of social competencies. The role-taking task was identical to that described by Blacher-Dickson and Simeonsson (1978). To evaluate referential communication, the children were presented with eight cans, which varied in size, color, and location. The child was to place a small object under one of the cans and then verbalize to the experimenter, who had left the room when the small object was placed, where the small object was.

Using criteria, results indicated significant correlations between teacher ratings and teacher judgments of social competencies, as well as between teacher and child judgment of social competencies. A significant relationship between role-taking tasks and measures of social competencies supported the relationship between social competencies and social skills. The referential communication task was significantly related to teacher judgments but not teacher ratings. Children's judgments of social competencies and referential communication were significantly related to IQ. Role-taking performance was not significantly correlated with IQ.

Implications of these findings were that both the teachers and children provided information about social competencies but from different frames of reference. Role-taking performance was significantly correlated with social competencies but not IQ, while referential communication was significantly related to both IQ and social competencies. These findings were interpreted as indicating differences in skills measured. IQ may have been related to referential communication because of the verbal nature of the task.

Taken together, these five studies suggest a relationship between role-taking and social competencies when the responses of mentally retarded youngsters are examined using a variety of tasks. The relationship between role-taking skill, referential communication, social judgment, and ratings differs with respect to mental age and IQ. Researchers consistently found a significant relationship between IQ and role-taking (Affleck, 1975a) and between role-taking and mental age (Affleck,

1975b, 1976). Blacher-Dickson and Simeonsson (1978) found a great deal of variability with children with similar mental ages and questioned whether or not mental
age is a good predictor of role-taking skill. Significant correlations between role-
taking and chronological age were not obtained in any of the studies reported.

PERCEPTIONS OF THE MILDLY HANDICAPPED
REGARDING OTHERS

Few studies are available that concern the perceptions of the mildly handicapped regarding others. In the studies reported, visual stimuli were used and
verbal responses required. Social and affective perception were inferred. Subjects
in these studies were children with learning disabilities. In one of the studies, the
learning-disabilities population was equated on IQ and achievement age. In this
way, the two groups were further delineated into younger and older children.
Normal comparison groups were included in these experiments.

Affective Perceptions

Bachara (1976) worked with 50 boys, 25 with learning disabilities and 25 without learning problems. The children ranged in age from 7 to 12 years and were
identified as having visual-perceptual problems and learning disabilities. The procedure involved presenting the children with the Borke Scales for Empathy. The
stimuli were 16 stories, presented either verbally or verbally with pictures. On
each trial, the child was to identify the appropriate emotion of the main character.
Children with learning disabilities identified significantly fewer correct emotions
than children without learning problems. Results were interpreted as indicating
the importance of intact social perception in the appropriate development of affect.

Social Perception and Cognition

Parrill-Burnstein and Baker-Ward (1979) differentiated within the category of
learning disabilities. Initially, their differentiation was based on the two schools'
descriptions of the types of students they accepted. One school focused on children with verbal learning disabilities and the other worked with a more heterogeneous group (Parrill-Burnstein, 1979). However, further statistical analysis indicated that the children within these two educational settings did not differ with the
type of learning disability; rather, when equated on achievement level, these children differed on the basis of age. That is, children in the first school who were
achieving at the same achievement level as those in the second school were significantly younger (Parrill-Burnstein, 1980). Results presented here are based on the
second analysis.

Their subjects were 118 children in grades one through five who were equated
on IQ and academic achievement. Thirty-nine of the children were diagnosed as
younger children with learning disabilities and 37 were older children with learning disabilities who were achieving at the same grade levels. Forty-two children
did not have learning problems.

The procedure used involved presenting the child with a picture depicting both foreground and background in terms of inside-outside scenario. In each of the four corners of the picture was an object that was obviously separate from the pictured theme. The child was asked to tell a story about the picture, and responses were recorded and later transcribed verbatim. Oral expression was scored according to a modification of Myklebust's criteria for his Picture Story Language Test, which was developed to analyze written language (Myklebust, 1965). Three aspects of language were considered: (1) productivity: how much was spoken; (2) syntax: sentence structure; and (3) the ability to abstract or infer an idea. In addition, attention to irrelevant information was evaluated by monitoring responses to the four peripheral objects.

Results showed that children with learning disabilities performed similarly to those without learning problems when productivity and syntax were scored. Significant differences between groups were obtained when children were scored according to levels of abstraction, attention, and integration of the peripheral items. Younger children with learning disabilities did not differ from those without learning problems when levels of abstraction were evaluated. However, those from the older group of children with learning disabilities, who were performing at the same achievement levels as the younger children with learning disabilities, obtained significantly lower abstract scores than those in the other group with learning disabilities and those without learning problems. This was interpreted as indicating differences in social cognition.

Attention and integration of the peripheral items were used as measures of social perception. Older children with learning disabilities mentioned the peripheral items significantly more often than the younger children with learning disabilities who were performing at the same achievement levels. Children in the two learning-disabilities groups did not differ from those without learning problems. Qualitative differences were noted in terms of whether or not the individual items were integrated into the story. The individual items were integrated into the story by 56 percent of the children without learning disabilities; 32 percent of the children with learning disabilities; and 30 percent of the younger children with learning disabilities performing at the same achievement levels. Implications in terms of social perception were that perception and integration problems were observed with the older children with learning disabilities. The younger children with learning disabilities did not differ significantly from those without learning problems. The importance of age and achievement level on nonverbal processing when the stimulus was visual was suggested.

The authors of these studies suggested the importance of intact perception and integration. Children who performed differently either had perceptual problems or were older, yet attaining at the same achievement levels as the younger children with learning disabilities. Younger and older children with learning disabilities, when equated on achievement, said as much and used appropriate syntax as frequently as children without learning problems. Ideation, or the ability to abstract and infer from visual social stimuli, differentiated those in the older group from those without learning problems and from younger children with learning disabilities who were performing at the same achievement levels.

These findings imply the importance of (1) further differentiation within the categories of learning disabilities, behavior disorders, and mild mental retardation; and (2) nonverbal processing in social and affective perception and cognition.

SUMMARY

Others' impressions regarding the mildly handicapped were different and varied as a function of the type of problem. Teachers, peers, and parents regard the mildly mentally retarded child as having a lower IQ (Gajar, 1979), and behaving more immaturely than children with behavior disorders or learning disabilities (Cullinan et al., 1979). Children with behavior disorders were differentiated as having more conduct and personality problems (Gajar, 1979; Cullinan et al., 1979). Children with learning disabilities were differentiated as having more problems than children without learning problems, but also as having significantly fewer conduct and behavior problems than those identified as having behavior disorders (McCarthy & Paraskevopoulas, 1969). In terms of responses elicited by children with learning disabilities, teachers spent significantly more time helping these children than those without learning problems (Bryan, 1974a).

Peer impressions also differentiated children with learning disabilities from those without learning problems. When sociometric techniques were used, it was found that children with learning disabilities were not rated among the most popular or desirable. However, these same children were not regarded as more isolated (Siperstein et al., 1978). Bryan (1974b, 1978) found that children with learning disabilities received more votes of rejection by peers, particularly by white females.

Peer ratings of mildly mentally retarded children in resource and regular classrooms indicated that when same-sex children were considered, the mentally retarded were discriminated less in urban school districts than in suburban school districts (Bruininks et al., 1974). In general, children with learning disabilities were less desirable than the mentally retarded child. Data regarding the behaviorally disordered child were not available.

Parents also differentiated within the category of mildly handicapped (Doleys et al., 1976; Strag, 1972). Noncompliant children were more disruptive than children with learning disabilities, who had more behavior problems than those without learning problems (Doleys et al., 1976). Parents also rated children with learning disabilities as being more depressed, less considerate, and clumsier than children without learning problems (Strag, 1972).

In general, when the perceptions of others were evaluated, it was found that children with learning disabilities, behavior disorders, and mild mental retardation were differentiated by people with whom they came into contact. The reasons for these differentiations varied as a function of the person interacting. In other words, unexpected or inappropriate behavior of those children within the mildly handicapped category were responded to differently by teachers, peers, and parents, due to differences in the perceptions of the teachers, peers, and parents. These perceptions, therefore, reflected differences in responses attended to, elicited, and emitted by the heterogeneous group of children.

With respect to the self-perceptions of the mildly handicapped, it was found that self-concept and role-taking tasks were related to social competencies. The relationship between role-taking and self-concept was different. Role-taking was correlated with IQ and mental age while self-concept was not correlated with IQ. This suggests that role-taking and self-concept consist of different skills, though both are necessary in social cognitive and affective development.

Black (1974) found that self-concept was lower in delayed readers when compared to those achieving normally. He also found that there was not a significant relationship between IQ and self-concept. This latter finding was confirmed by Smith (1979) when working with children with learning disabilities.

Mentally retarded children have also been examined with respect to self-concept. Porter (1965) found that children who were labeled mentally retarded were more submissive, less intelligent, and less phlegmatic when compared to normal data. The implication of these findings was that the level of functioning accounted for this relationship, not IQ.

With respect to role-taking, data available were with children with mental retardation. Affleck (1975a, 1975b, 1976) did not find a significant correlation between role-taking and chronological age or between chronological age and IQ. However, unlike work on self-concept, IQ was significantly related to role-taking. Blacher-Dickson and Simeonsson (1978) and Monson et al. (1979) confirmed these findings. The implication is that those children with lower IQ have poor role-taking performance due to an inability to attain more complex skills; this supports a relationship between cognitive levels of functioning and the development of role-taking skills. It was also found within one of these studies (Blacher-Dickson & Simeonsson, 1978) that experience in role-taking improved role-taking skills of children who were at a transitional cognitive stage.

The perceptions of the mildly handicapped about others were examined in two studies dealing with children with learning disabilities. Perceptions of affect (Bachara, 1976) and social perception and cognition were studied (Parrill-Burnstein & Baker-Ward, 1979). In general, children with different types of learning disabilities and with similar achievement levels but of differing ages differed from each other and a normal comparison group when the tasks required different skills. This research suggested the importance of further differentiating, not only the learning disabilities category, but within the behavior disordered and educably mentally retarded categories as well. This would enable a better understanding of the variability in performance reported for children in all three categories.

In conclusion, it is suggested that differences between those children identified as being mildly handicapped are perceived by those with whom they come into contact. It is also suggested that their perceptions and integration of information may be different from those without learning problems.

IMPLICATIONS

Remediation is planned and implemented to improve learned behavior. Appropriate social-cognitive and affective responses are learned and are deficient in many mildly handicapped children. The category of mildly handicapped is homogeneous; however, as indicated in the literature review, parents, teachers, and peers respond differently to children within specific categories.

Implications for classroom management focus on the child's overt behavior in dealing within the class structure, including with classmates and teachers. Mildly handicapped children do not behave as expected in the class; their overt behaviors are different and elicit different responses from others. Children with learning disabilities are differentiated by academic problems; children with behavior disorders are differentiated by conduct and personality problems, though academic failure is present; and children with mild mental retardation are differentiated by lower IQ.

These results may be interpreted as suggesting that the primary deficits match each group as follows: psychological: behavior disorders; academic failure: learning disabilities; and generalized delays: mildly retarded. This is not to suggest, for example, that children with learning disabilities do not have behavior problems; rather, these behaviors are a reflection and not the core of their learning deficits. The implication of this interpretation is that different classroom management techniques would be effective in modifying inappropriate social and affective behaviors of children in the three groups.

Available data support this interpretation, but are too few to substantiate it. For example, (1) encounter groups were effective in deterring maladaptive behavior with behavior-disordered children (Garner, 1974); (2) teaching social-cognitive and affective responses through modeling, explicit instruction, and social praise facilitated sharing behavior, smiling behavior, positive physical contact, and complimentary behavior with children with learning disabilities (Cooke & Apolloni, 1976); and (3) exposure to similar experiences enabled some mentally retarded children to take another's cognitive perspective (Blacher-Dickson & Simeonsson, 1978). The effects of these three remedial procedures were not evaluated across the three populations, which limits the generalizations.

With respect to instruction, two positions emerge: (1) educational remediation as a function of the level of deficit; and (2) educational remediation as a function of the learning strategies employed. With respect to the first position, it is proposed that children at the same levels of functioning be educated using the same procedures (e.g., Neisworth & Greer, 1975). This implies similar learning strategies as reflected in similar levels of functioning. This position is supported by data substantiating significant positive correlations between mental age and role-taking and self-concept, and the lack of a significant correlation between self-concept and IQ. This position is not supported when data regarding variability *within* categories is reported (e.g., Blacher-Dickson & Simeonsson, 1978; Parrill-Burnstein & Baker-Ward, 1979).

The alternative position, suggesting differences in learning strategies as a function of the type of learning problem, takes a very different approach. Educational remediation is implemented depending on present and potential learning strategies, not only on levels of involvement or types of problems (see, for example, Johnson & Myklebust, 1967). In addition, variables such as rate of processing and rate of learning should influence how and what is taught to children with similar learning strategies that are reflected in similar overt behaviors. Research data regarding this position are lacking. Regardless of which position is adhered to, teaching strategies, rather than skills, is proposed.

In terms of the feasibility of the noncategorical approach to special education, Garrett and Brazil (1979) reviewed categories currently used for the identification and education of exceptional children. Questionnaires were sent to each of 50 state Departments of Education to assist in determining current practice. Garrett and Brazil concluded that there appeared to be an increase in the use of categories, suggesting further differentiation and delineation within the type of learning problem. This trend is consistent with the data reviewed here.

The most pronounced and consistent finding was that regarding variability. Children within the regular classroom who evidenced a great deal of variability in behavior did not benefit from traditional or standard instruction. The noncategorical approach assumes that because these children do not learn within this context, they are a homogeneous group. Not so! Variations in performance within categories, as well as a lack of consistency in the quality of performance between categories, has been substantiated in study after study. The implication is for further differentiation within the broad categories of behavior disordered, learning disabilities, and mild retardation.

REFERENCES

Affleck, G. G. Role-taking ability and interpersonal conflict resolution among retarded young adults. *Journal of Mental Deficiency,* 1975, *80*(2), 233–236.(a)

Affleck, G. G. Role-taking ability and the interpersonal competencies of retarded children. *Journal of Mental Deficiency,* 1975, *80*(3), 312–316. (b)

Affleck, G. G. Role-taking ability and the interpersonal tactics of retarded children. *American Journal of Mental Deficiency,* 1976, *80*(6), 667–670.

Bachara, G. Empathy in learning disabled children. *Perceptual and Motor Skills,* 1976, *43,* 541–542.

Blacher-Dickson, J., & Simeonsson, R. J. Effects of shared experience on role-taking performance of retarded children. *American Journal of Mental Deficiency,* 1978, *83*(1), 21–28.

Black, W. Self-concept as related to achievement and age in learning disabled children. *Child Development,* 1974, *45,* 1137–1140.

Bruininks, R. H., Rynders, J. E., & Gross, J. C. Social acceptance of mildly retarded pupils in resource rooms and regular classes. *American Journal of Mental Deficiency,* 1974, *78,* 377–383.

Bryan, T. An observational analysis of classroom behaviors of children with learning disabilities. *Journal of Learning Disabilities,* 1974, *7*(1), 26–34. (a).

Bryan, T. Peer popularity of learning disabled children. *Journal of Learning Disabilities,* 1974, *7*(10), 621–625.

Bryan, T. H. Peer popularity of learning disabled children: A replication. *Journal of Learning Disabilities,* 1976, *9*(5), 307–311.

Bryan, T. Social relationships and verbal interactions of learning disabled children. *Journal of Learning Disabilities,* 1978, *11*(2), 58–66.

Chandler, M. J. Social cognition: A selective review of current research. In W. F. Overton & J. M. Gallagher (Eds.), *Knowledge and development* (Vol. 1). New York: Plenum Press, 1977.

Cooke, T. P., & Apolloni, T. Developing positive social-emotional behaviors: A study of training and generalization effects. *Journal of Applied Behavior Analysis,* 1976, *9*(1), 65–78.

Coopersmith, S. *The antecedents of self-esteem.* San Francisco: W. H. Freeman & Company, 1967.

Cullinan, D., Epstein, M. H., & Dembinski, R. J. Behavior problems of emotionally handicapped and normal pupils. *Journal of Abnormal Child Psychology,* 1979, *7*(4), 495–502.

Doleys, D. M., Cartelli, M., & Doster, J. Comparison of patterns of mother-child interaction. *Journal of Learning Disabilities,* 1976, *9*(6), 371–375.

Feffer, M. Developmental analysis of interpersonal behavior. *Psychological Review,* 1970, *77*(3), 197–214.

Feffer, M., & Gourevitch, V. Cognitive aspects of role-taking in children. *Journal of Personality,* 1960, *28,* 383–396.

Flavell, J. H. *Cognitive development.* Englewood Cliffs: Prentice-Hall, 1977.

Gajar, A. Educable mentally retarded, learning disabled, emotionally disturbed: Similarities and differences. *Exceptional Children,* 1979, *45*(6), 470–472.

Garner, H. G. Mental health benefits of small group experiences in the affective domain.

Journal of School Health, 1974, *44*(8), 314–318.

Garrett, J. E., & Brazil, N. Categories used for identification of exceptional children. *Exceptional Children*, 1979, *45*(4), 291–292.

Hardwick, D. A., McIntyre, C. W., & Pick, H. L. The content and manipulation of cognitive maps in children and adults. *Monographs of the Society for Research in Child Development*, 1976, *4*(3, Serial No. 166).

Hartup, W. W. The social worlds of childhood. *American Psychologist*, 1979, *34*(10), 944–950.

Hoffman, M. L. Development of moral thought, feeling, and behavior. *American Psychologist*, 1979, *34*(10), 958–966.

Johnson, D. J., & Myklebust, H. *Learning disabilities: Educational principles and practices*. New York: Grune & Stratton, 1967.

Larsen, S. C., Parker, R., & Jorjorian, S. Differences in self-concept of normal and learning disabled children. *Perceptual and Motor Skills*, 1973, *37*, 510.

Levine, M. *A cognitive theory of learning: Research on hypothesis testing*. Hillsdale, N.J.: Lawrence Erlbaum Associates, 1975.

Lewis, M., & Rosenblum, L. *The development of affect*. New York: Plenum Press, 1978.

McCarthy, J., & Paraskevopoulas, J. Behavior patterns of learning disabled, emotionally disturbed, and average children. *Exceptional Children*, 1969, *35*, 69–74.

Monson, L. B., Greenspan, S., & Simeonsson, R. J. Correlation of social competence in retarded children. *American Journal of Mental Deficiency*, 1979, *83*(6), 627–630.

Myklebust, H. R. *Development and disorders of written language: Picture Story Language Test* (Vol. 1). New York: Grune & Stratton, 1965.

Neisworth, J. T., & Greer, J. G. Functional similarities of learning disability and mild retardation. *Exceptional Children*, 1975, *42*(1) 17–21.

Parke, R. D. Emerging themes for social-emotional development: Introduction. *American Psychologist*, 1979, *34*(10), 930–931.

Parrill-Burnstein, M. Teaching kindergarten children to solve problems: An information processing approach. *Child Development*, 1978, *49*(3), 700–706.

Parrill-Burnstein, M., & Baker-Ward, L. Learning disabilities: A social cognitive difference. *Learning Disabilities: An Audio Journal for Continuing Education*, 1979, *3*, 10.

Parrill-Burnstein, M. *Social cognition and learning disabilities: A re-analysis*. Unpublished manuscript, Emory University, Ga., 1980.

Parrill-Burnstein, M. *Problem solving and learning disabilities: An information processing approach*. New York: Grune & Stratton, 1981.

Piers, E. V., & Harris, D. B. Age and other correlates of self-concept in children. *Journal of Educational Psychology*, 1964, *55*(2), 91–95.

Porter, R. B. A comparative investigation of the personality of educable mentally retarded children and those of a norm group of children. *Exceptional Children*, 1965, *31*, 457–463.

Quay, H. C., Morse, W. C., & Cutler, R. L. Personality patterns of pupils in special classes for the emotionally disturbed. *Exceptional Children*, 1966, *32*, 297–301.

Quay, H. C., & Peterson, D. R. *Manual for the behavior problem checklist*. Champaign, Il.: Children's Research Center, University of Illinois, 1967.

Selman, R. L., & Byrne, D. F. A structural-developmental analysis of levels of role-taking in middle childhood. *Child Development*, 1974, *45*, 803–806.

Shantz, C. U. The development of social cognition. In E. M. Hetherington (Ed.), *Review of child development research* (Vol. 5). Chicago: University of Chicago Press, 1975.

Siperstein, G. N., Bopp, M. J., & Bak, J. J. Social status of learning disabled children. *Journal of Learning Disabilities*, 1978, *11*(2), 49–53.

Smith, M. D. Prediction of self-concept among learning disabled children. *Journal of Learning Disabilities*, 1979, *12*(10), 664–669.

Strag, G. A. Comparative behavioral rating of parents with severe mentally retarded, special learning disability, and normal children. *Journal of Learning Disabilities*, 1972, *5*, 631–635.

Yarrow, L. J. Emotional development. *American Psychologist*, 1979, *34*(10), 951–957.

The Assessment of the Mildly Handicapped

George B. Helton
Edward A. Workman

9

Considerations in Assessing the Mildly Handicapped

The assessment of students experiencing school difficulties proceeds in terms of a number of factors. Assessment specialists are required to decide how they will address issues within each factor and how decisions within these several factors should be blended in the assessment process, for the cumulative effects of these decisions determine the quality of the assessment product.

FACTORS RELEVANT TO THE ASSESSMENT OF MILDLY HANDICAPPED STUDENTS

Among the factors that should be considered in devising assessment systems for mildly handicapped (or any other) students are (1) the goals of assessment; (2) assessment models; (3) legal requirements; (4) procedural safeguards; (5) ethical considerations; (6) situational constraints; and (7) existing assessment techniques. Quality assessment depends on an adequate "fit" among decisions made about these factors.

Goals of Assessment

Coulter and Morrow (1978) indicated that assessment processes may be directed toward the functions of (1) classification of handicapped students and/or (2) programming for such students. The classification function of assessment involves assigning a categorical handicapping-condition label to students ("mentally retarded," "emotionally disturbed," etc.) who may receive special education services as a consequence of the label. The programming function of assessment involves pinpointing deficits in educational functioning and determining remedial procedures appropriate to those deficits. Coulter (1980) noted that most psychoeducational assessment techniques were designed primarily to accomplish only one of these functions, while Helton, Morrow and Yates (1977) suggested that the traditional focus of assessment in special education has been on the classification function. Hallahan and Kauffman (1976), however, argued strongly that the emphasis in assessment *should be* on the programming function.

While we agree philosophically with Hallahan and Kauffman (1976), we also feel that assessment in special education must *currently* be directed toward *both* classification and programming functions. For a number of reasons, we see no present alternative to our position. For one, we agree with Hobbs's argument (1975) that some sort of classification mechanism is necessary in order for handicapped students to receive needed educational services. Hobbs (1975) of course proposed classification mechanisms that make special education services available to students on the basis of educational deficits and needed remedial services rather than on the basis of categorical handicapping-condition labels. When such classification mechanisms are sufficiently developed and institutionalized in appropriate laws and regulations, then very similar assessment procedures will be involved in both the classification and programming functions of assessment. Unfortunately, however, that day has not yet arrived: Public Law 94-142 requires classification decisions according to categorical handicapping-condition labels and programming decisions as operationalized in individualized education programs. Given these simultaneous statutory requirements, no alternative to the assessment process serving both classification and programming functions is now available. Our regret is that these assessment functions cannot currently be combined in terms of a major emphasis on programming—a step that could be taken were special education services available solely on the basis of educational deficits and needed remedial services (rather than on the basis of educational need *and* a handicapping-condition label).

It should be added that our regret has more than a philosophical base: As Bardon and Bennett (1974) noted, categorical labels imply more than may be true of students, tell us too little about how best to teach them, may set up negative self-fulfilling prophecies, and may be applied incorrectly to students in the first place. Nevertheless, such labels are required by law and, therefore, should be applied to students as carefully and as correctly as possible. Imprecision in the labels cannot, legally or ethically, constitute a legitimate reason to assign them carelessly (a point that will be discussed later).

Our regret is also based on the fact that assessment will inevitably take longer to accomplish when both classification and programming functions are served. Increased length of assessment time would not be a problem if resources for assessment were unlimited. Such, however, is not the case; assessment time is limited, which means that neither function of assessment may be served to the degree that would be desirable. To illustrate, state Department of Education personnel in Georgia estimate that each *initial* assessment (including report writing) of an educable mentally retarded, learning disabled, or mildly behaviorally disordered student requires a minimum of 6–9 hours (Kicklighter & Bailey, Note 1).

Making this picture somewhat more complicated are the provisions in PL 94-142 requiring that "Testing and evaluation materials and procedures used for the purposes of evaluation and placement of handicapped children must be selected and administered so as not to be racially or culturally discriminatory" (*Federal Register,* August 23, 1977, p. 42496). While we certainly have no quarrel with this requirement, we believe that one of the central issues in nondiscriminatory assessment is usually defined in terms of the disproportionate assignment of categorical handicapping-condition labels to ethnic minority students. Attempts to rectify this situation usually involve increased attention to the classification function of assessment. For instance, the System of Multicultural Pluralistic Assessment (SOMPA; Mercer, 1979b) presents a rationale and a set of techniques that may be used to eliminate the disproportionate assignment of ethnic minority students to the mental retardation category. While we view this as a desirable goal, use of the SOMPA will often require additional assessment time (Oakland, 1979). Since the emphasis of the SOMPA is on the classification function of assessment, its use may result in lessened attention to the programming function.

Assessment Models

The quality of assessment work performed by assessment personnel will also be affected by their understandings of, and abilities to utilize, various assessment models. In this context, a number of models must be considered. Psychometric models, which are concerned with stable traits, are particularly helpful in terms of the classification function, for "Psychometric tests rank student performance compared with a normative population, utilize standard scores, and provide information useful in making placement decisions" (Mercer, 1979a, p. 90). Edumetric tests are more relevant to the programming function, since they are designed to measure characteristics, often educational, which are thought to be teachable. "Edumetric measures focus on specific academic areas, compare the student's performance with criteria linked to a particular curriculum, utilize raw scores, and provide information useful in planning educational programs" (Mercer, 1979a, p. 90). Since we propose that assessment serve both classification and programming functions, we view the psychometric-edumetric distinction to be one that assessment personnel need to understand. In keeping with this orientation, the assessment strategy we shall propose includes both psychometric and edumetric measures.

Assessment personnel also need to understand medical, social system, and pluralistic assessment models (Mercer, 1979b). Each of these three models incorporates different assumptions and decision rules. The models are best used for different purposes but can be combined when appropriate to the welfare of the students being assessed. Utilizing the models incorrectly and/or combining them in inappropriate ways may result in errors in classification and/or programming.

The medical model of assessment assumes that students are abnormal when they exhibit biological symptoms (such as deficient vision). Measurement devices within the medical model, therefore, are designed to detect such biological symptoms. When operating within the medical model, data that suggest but do not prove a biological abnormality should be tentatively regarded as indicating abnormality until the absence of abnormality can be clearly demonstrated. This decision rule prevents us from ignoring and thereby failing to treat problems in students which are responsive to medical interventions.

The social systems model of assessment, on the other hand, assumes that students are abnormal when their behaviors fail to conform to the expectations of the social systems in which they function. In the public school setting, failure to make passing grades would be construed as abnormal behavior (since the great majority of students pass). Measurement devices within the social systems model are designed to detect deviation from social system norms. Social systems model data that suggest only moderate deviation from norms should be regarded as evidence of acceptable normality, while abnormality should be defined as only gross deviations from social norms. This decision rule prevents us from assigning categorical handicapping-condition labels to students and placing them in special education programs in the absence of compelling reasons to do so.

The pluralistic model of assessment assumes that students are abnormal when their behaviors are deviant from the behavioral norms for their particular subcultural groups. From this perceptive, Black English would not be considered abnormal when used by a Black child residing in an urban ghetto. Measurement devices within the pluralistic model are designed to detect deviation from subcultural norms. Pluralistic model data that suggest only moderate deviation from subcultural norms should be regarded as evidence of acceptable normality, while abnormality is presumed only when gross deviations from subcultural norms occur. This decision rule prevents us from assigning categorical handicapping-condition labels to students and placing them in special education programs when their behaviors are deviant from that of ''mainstream culture peers'' but not from that of subcultural peers.

At this point, it should be noted that the assumptions and decision rules associated with these three assessment models have been most thoroughly operationalized in the SOMPA (Mercer, 1979b). We acknowledge that there is considerable controversy surrounding this assessment system (e.g., J. F. Goodman, 1979; Mercer, 1979a). But whether or not assessment specialists agree with the system's assumptions and decision rules, and/or choose to use the system in assessment, they should be cognizant of the three models when making assessment decisions. Errors in classification decisions, in particular, have too often been made because of a lack of understanding of the issues involved in the use of these models. Such errors violate at least the spirit of PL 94-142 (particularly in terms of its requirement of nondiscriminatory evaluation and placement). Such errors have also led to a number of successful court challenges to disproportionate representation of ethnic minority students in educational programs for the handicapped (Reschly, 1979).

Two other models with relevance for the assessment process are the psychoeducational process model and the task-analysis model described by Mercer and Ysseldyke (1977). While the medical, social systems, and pluralistic assessment models described above have particular import for classification decisions, the psychoeducational process model and the task-analysis model are crucial in terms of programming decisions.

One of the important distinctions between the psychoeducational process model and the task-analysis model involves their different assumptions about what student characteristics should be assessed. The psychoeducational process model assumes that students have difficulty learning because of deficits in what might be called ''processing skills'' (such as visual perception). From this perspective, it becomes important to identify these ''processing-skill deficits'' and then to develop these deficit areas in students. It is assumed that adequate processing skills are a prerequisite to academic success.

The task-analysis model, on the other hand, assumes that students have difficulty learning because of their failures to master lower-level skills in a learning task hierarchy. An example of such an assumption is that students must learn to discriminate the letters of the alphabet from one another before learning the sounds associated with each letter. From this perspective, it becomes important to identify which specific lower-level skills have not been mastered and to help students master such skills. It is assumed that the acquisition of academic skills in a sequential fashion will best facilitate academic success and that remediation of "processing-skill deficits" is less clearly relevant to improving students' academic performances.

Assessment emphases and procedures within each of these models are consistent with their differing assumptions about how to facilitate student learning. Appropriate measures within the psychoeducational process model tend to be psychometric tests designed to assess student strengths and weaknesses in cognitive, perceptual, psycholinguistic, and psychomotor areas (Mercer & Ysseldyke, 1977). Appropriate measures within the task-analysis model tend to be edumetric tests designed to assess skill hierarchy development within each subject matter area.

It is a truism that how assessment personnel define a problem dictates how they will assess that problem. In turn, their assessment procedures to some degree dictate what kinds of programming recommendations they will include in individualized educational programs. Thus, it is extremely important for assessment specialists to understand the psychoeducational process and task-analysis models. Their primary orientation to one or the other model will strongly influence the kinds of programming recommendations they make.

Several additional considerations are also important. One is that the definition of learning disability found in PL 94-142 implies the use of a psychoeducational process model, at least in making classification decisions (*Federal Register,* August 23, 1977):

> "Specific learning disability" means a disorder in one or more of the basic psychological processes involved in understanding or using language, spoken or written, which may manifest itself in an imperfect ability to listen, think, speak, read, write, spell, or to do mathematical calculations. (p. 42478)

This definition may influence assessment specialists to assess students with suspected learning disabilities in terms of psychoeducational process model measures and to make classification and programming decisions compatible with this model. Assessment specialists with a primary orientation to the task-analysis model may feel compelled to classify according to the psychoeducational process model but to program in terms of the task-analysis model. This situation is disheartening to some assessment specialists in that they view their classification assessment work as being divorced from their programming assessment work. An inability to combine assessment functions within a single model is not only frustrating on logical grounds but also requires additional assessment time when such time is scarce.

Earlier, we indicated our philosophical agreement with Hallahan and Kauffman's (1976) position that assessment should be mainly focused on its programming function. It is appropriate that we now also express our agreement with their position that the task-analysis model represents a more useful framework for assessment and programming than does the psychoeducational process model. It should be remembered, however, that we shall present an assessment strategy that serves both classification and programming functions. Because we view some classification decisions as implying the use of psychoeducational process measures, our strategy will include such measures as well as measures appropriate to the task-analysis model.

Legal Requirements

While assessment specialists must make decisions in terms of both assessment goals and assessment models, they must also decide how to respond to legal requirements in assessment. The importance of decisions in this area is suggested by Monroe's (1979) statement that assessment specialists "have been profoundly influenced by litigation and legislation dealing with special children" (p. 39).

Our exclusive focus on legislative influences on assessment is based on the assertions by Bersoff (Note 2) and Reschly (1979) that legislation tends to follow litigation. What this means is that principles and procedures included in legislation often are based on previous court decisions. This being the case, our discussion of pertinent legislation touches on many of the issues addressed in litigation and provides a basic (but not comprehensive) orientation to legal requirements in assessment.

PL 94-142 is the latest, most detailed, and most comprehensive piece of legislation governing the assessment and education of handicapped students, but Section 504 of the Rehabilitation Act of 1973 (*Federal Register,* May 4, 1977) also impacts assessment practice. Since these two federal laws "provide almost identical guidelines for the assessment and placement of handicapped children" (Reschly, 1979, p. 228), we shall focus exclusively on the more comprehensive of the two, PL 94-142.

An important feature of PL 94-142 is its status as a funding statute (Bersoff, Note 2). Specifically, it provides federal funds for the assessment of and the provision of a free, appropriate public education for, handicapped students between the ages of 3 and 21. State and local education agencies, however, are not required to provide special education services to preschool-aged children if such provision is in conflict with a state law or court order nor are agencies required to abide by the provisions of the law if they elect to decline funds provided under the law. However, Section 504 of the Rehabilitation Act of 1973 (*Federal Register,* May 4, 1977) provides for loss of *any* federal funds provided to state and local education agencies if they are found to be engaged in practices discriminatory to handicapped persons. Since Section 504 of the Rehabilitation Act of 1973 requires steps similar to those found in PL 94-142, state and local education agencies are obligated to abide by most of the provisions of PL 94-142 unless they accept no federal aid at all (Bersoff, Note 2).

The inclusion of the right to a free, appropriate public education has a number of implications for assessment specialists. One is the need to become familiar with assessment techniques appropriate to young children. Another is the need to augment current assessment skills with techniques appropriate for severely and multiply handicapped students (as all students have a right to an education, regardless of severity of handicap). Since many assessment specialists were trained prior to the implementation of PL 94-142, extensive inservice training in these areas will be needed.

As has been noted, PL 94-142 also mandates nondiscriminatory assessment and placement practices. In this context, the law requires that assessment procedures be administered in the student's native language. Further, tests must be administered by qualified personnel (appropriately certified within each state), and all tests used for classification purposes must have been validated for the specific purposes for which they are being used. Additionally, classification decisions must be based on more than a single source of information (i.e., an IQ score by itself does not suffice). In fact, assessment must be conducted "in all areas related to the suspected disability, including, where appropriate, health, vision, hearing, social and emotional status, general intelligence, academic performance, communicative status, and motor abilities" (*Federal Register,* August 23, 1977, p. 42497). In reviewing these data, assessment specialists are not to draw inferences about limited aptitude or achievement in students when test scores actually reflect impaired sensory, manual, or speaking skills (rather than limited aptitude or achievement). Data on adaptive behavior of students are also to be considered in making judgments about them. Finally, assessment procedures must identify areas of specific educational need (including, when appropriate, prevocational and vocational training).

It is clear from the above that PL 94-142 requires careful and comprehensive assessment of handicapped students. These requirements must be blended with decisions made in the areas of assessment goals and assessment models in order to arrive at useful and legally defensible assessment processes.

But the scope of PL 94-142 extends beyond the completion of an initial assessment. Classification and programming decisions are to be made by a multidisciplinary team, a group that includes the student's regular teacher, special education personnel, personnel knowledgeable of assessment procedures, one or both of the student's parents, the student (if appropriate), and other persons at the discretion of the parents or the school. This team must consider all relevant data on the student and document the bases for its decisions. The decisions made by the team include whether or not to assign a categorical handicapping-condition label to the student, where to place him in the school program so as to meet his educational needs while keeping him maximally in contact with nonhandicapped peers (least-restrictive environment), and what goals and activities to include in his individualized educational program.

We view the individualized educational program as the vehicle for operationalizing programming decisions. Well-constructed and implemented programs promote optimum student development, while poorly constructed or implemented programs do not. PL 94-142 (*Federal Register,* August 23, 1977) defines an adequate individualized educational program as a plan that includes

(a) A statement of the child's present levels of educational performance; (b) a statement of annual goals, including short-term educational objectives; (c) A statement of the specific special education and related services to be provided to the child, and the extent to which the child will be able to participate in regular educational programs; (d) The projected dates for initiation of services and the anticipated duration of the services; and (e) Appropriate objective criteria and evaluation procedures and schedules for determining, on at least an annual basis, whether the short-term instructional objectives are being achieved. (p. 42491)

Again, assessment processes should assist in making appropriate programming decisions to be included in individualized educational programs.

Section (c) above refers to "related services." According to PL 94-142 (*Federal Register,* August 23, 1977) "related services" include

> transportation and such developmental, corrective, and other supportive services as are required to assist a handicapped child to benefit from special education and includes speech pathology and audiology, psychological services, physical and occupational therapy, recreation, early identification and assessment of disabilities in children, counseling services, and medical services for diagnostic or evaluation purposes. The term also includes school health services, social work services in schools, and parent counseling and training. (p. 42479)

In terms of assessment serving a programming function for handicapped students, the implication that assessment should identify areas of needed related services seems clear.

PL 94-142 also requires that each individualized educational program be reviewed and, if needed, modified at least once a year. Further, each handicapped student receiving special education services must be reassessed at least once every 3 years (more often if circumstances warrant or if requested by the student's teacher or parent). The 3-year (or more frequent) reassessments must meet the same standards as initial assessments. Such review and reassessment requirements are for the purpose of determining which students continue to be eligible for and require special education services. As such, the requirements help prevent students from continuing in special education programs when such programs are no longer appropriate. While we support this goal, it should also be noted that the 3-year reassessment requirement further strains the time and other resources needed for assessment activities.

Procedural Safeguards

PL 94-142 also requires rather extensive procedural safeguards in assessment-related activities. These procedural safeguards involve informed parental consent for certain actions, parental rights to prior notice of certain actions to be taken by school personnel, parental right to appeal certain decisions, parental access to educational records, and parental consent to release educational records to other persons and agencies. While PL-94-142 contains most of the procedural safeguards available to handicapped students and their parents, those interested in a more comprehensive understanding of this topic should familiarize themselves with Section 504 of the Rehabilitation Act of 1973 (*Federal Register,* May 4, 1977) and the Family Rights and Privacy Act (*Federal Register,* June 17, 1976).

Under PL 94-142, parents must give written informed consent for their child to be initially assessed to determine eligibility for special education services and areas of specific educational need. While this requirement appears to be a rather straightforward one, Bersoff (Note 2) suggested that any parental consent should meet the legal requirements of knowledge, voluntariness, and capacity. In other words, parental consent should involve sufficient knowledge of the activities to be undertaken, freedom from coercion, and parental ability to make a rational choice. School personnel (including assessment specialists) should provide enough information to parents to allow them to decide whether or not to give consent, and should refrain from subtly (or otherwise) coercing consent. In this context, PL 94-142 requires that information be provided to parents in their native language and acknowledges the right of parents to revoke their previously given consent. The law also requires that consent be obtained from a parent surrogate when a legal guardian cannot be located or when the child is a ward of the state.

Parental consent is also required by PL 94-142 for the initial placement of a student in a special education program of any sort. As already noted, such placements (and other components of the individualized educational program) should be decided upon by a multidisciplinary team including the affected student's parents. Again, consent for initial placement must be in writing and must adhere to the other requirements for parental consent mentioned in the previous paragraph. If informed and written parental consent for initial assessment and for initial placement is appropriately secured, the classification and programming process is proceeding smoothly.

PL 94-142 also provides for procedures to resolve conflicts that develop between the schools and parents. A basic right of parents (and also schools) embodied in the law is the right to call for a due process hearing. Such hearings must be conducted in a timely manner, must be presided over by a hearing officer who is not employed by the school district involved in the conflict, and must result in timely decisions on the part of the hearing officer. If either party to the hearing is not satisfied with the decision of the hearing officer, the decision may be appealed for review to the state education agency, and the state education agency must render its judgment in a timely manner. After state education agency review, the decision may be appealed by civil suit filed in federal court.

In the initial due process hearing (and in state education agency review of a decision), PL 94-142 provides for both parties to be represented by legal counsel, to present evidence, to call and to cross-examine witnesses, to prohibit the introduction of evidence not submitted to the other party 5 days in advance of the hearing, to receive a written record of the hearing proceedings, and to receive the written findings of the hearing officer. Prior to the decision of the hearing officer, the affected child must be allowed to enter school or to remain in his regular educational program unless both parties agree otherwise.

One of the bases for the conflicts that result in due process hearings may be parental lack of confidence in assessment data and conclusions generated by school personnel. If such is the case, parents may request a second assessment from a private practitioner or another community agency, and this second assessment must be paid for by the school. The school, however, may request a due process hearing if the school believes the request for a second assessment at public expense to be unwarranted. PL 94-142, however, does stipulate that assessment data generated by nonschool personnel must be considered by the multidisciplinary team in its decision-making role.

The law also requires that written notice be provided parents prior to the school's initiating or changing the identification, evaluation, or educational placement of the child or the provision of a free appropriate public education to the child. Such notice must also be given when the school refuses a parental request to perform any of these activities. The prior notice requirement is intended to provide parents sufficient time and information to agree with or contest school decisions that do not require parental consent. Parents might, for example, decide to contest such decisions by requesting a due process hearing. It should be remembered that in spite of the extensive procedural safeguards found in PL 94-142, the law requires parental consent only for initial assessments, for initial special education placements of students, and for release of educational records to parties outside the school system.

In addition to the previously mentioned procedural safeguards provided by PL 94-142, the law guarantees parents the right of access to their child's educational records. This means that school officials cannot prevent parents from reviewing such records. Furthermore, parents have the right to request that school officials amend those portions of their child's educational records that, in the parents' judgment, are inaccurate or misleading. If school officials refuse such requests, the parents may request and receive a hearing on the matter. If the hearing is decided in favor of the school, the parents still have the right to insert their written objections into the child's educational records. Once such objections are added to the records, they must be retained and transmitted with the records.

Finally, PL 94-142 requires parental consent for the release of their child's records to parties outside the school system. This consent must be in reference to specific portions of the records to be released and must indicate specific persons or agencies to receive the records. "Blanket" release forms are thus not in compliance with the requirements of the law.

The procedural safeguards found in PL 94-142 mandate a number of cautions on the part of assessment personnel. For instance, students should not be initially assessed without parental consent, parents should not be coerced into accepting special education placements for their children, etc. Furthermore, assessment personnel may be required to testify in due process hearings and should honor parental rights relative to access and release of records.

Ethical Considerations

Many assessment specialists belong to professional organizations that have developed codes of ethics to guide the professional behaviors of their members. We believe that the relevant provisions of the various ethical codes should be honored when assessment specialists are engaged in assessment (and other professional) activities. In this context, we here present what we believe to be the relevant provisions of the Ethical Principles of the American Psychological Association (APA, 1981) and the Principles for Professional Ethics of the National Association of School Psychologists (NASP, 1978). While this strategy does not encompass all the ethical codes adhered to by assessment specialists by virtue of their various professional memberships, the discussion should highlight a number of ethical considerations in assessment. It should also be noted that ethical conduct does not, in and of itself, guarantee that all aspects of practice will meet all legal requirements of practice (Bersoff, 1975). Thus, assessment personnel should be familiar with both legal and ethical requirements relevant to the performance of their duties.

Both the Ethical Principles of the American Psychological Association (APA, 1981) and the Principles for Professional Ethics of the National Association of School Psychologists (NASP, 1978) state that professional competence is a necessary condition of ethical practice. Principle 2e of the Ethical Principles (APA, 1981) indicates that competent utilization of assessment procedures requires adequate understanding of measurement principles, test validation problems, and other test research. Principle IIb of the Principles for Professional Ethics (NASP, 1978) requires that school psychologists choose assessment techniques that are appropriate to the client being assessed. An adequate knowledge base is clearly required to abide by such provisions. This knowledge base should include a detailed understanding of areas of personal competence and incompetence since, ethically, professionals should not use procedures they are unfamiliar with, even if they are legally entitled to use them. Instead, referrals to other professionals should be made.

The Ethical Principles and the Principles for Professional Ethics also require that assessment data be presented objectively and that reservations about the accuracy of test results be clearly stated. We believe that these requirements preclude any alterations of test scores or diagnostic conclusions in order to qualify students for special education placements. Again, our position is that the imprecision of the handicapping-condition labels does not justify assigning them to students in imprecise ways. While some may view this interpretation of the ethical codes as even more unethically denying certain students special education services, we believe that services outside of special education programs should be developed for such students. In addition, it is sometimes assumed too quickly that students benefit more from special education placements than from regular education placements. Definitive data to support such an assumption are lacking (Mercer, 1979a).

Another area of ethical conflict experienced by assessment specialists is addressed by the Ethical Principles and the Principles for Professional Ethics: both ethical codes require that psychologists prevent their assessment results from being misused by other professionals. If misuse of assessment results is taking place in, for example, the classification and/or programming activities of multidisciplinary teams, psychologists should intervene to stop such misuse. This is not to say that psychologists should display professional discourtesy in the process, but that the process itself should be undertaken. Steps such as this are in keeping with both codes' identification of the clients of the organization (i.e., students) as the persons deserving (at least in most instances) the psychologist's primary allegiance.

A number of the provisions of the Ethical Principles and the Principles for Professional Ethics are similar to those embodied in the legal requirements and procedural safeguards of PL 94-142. For example, both codes indicate that psychologists should avoid undue invasion of client privacy, should inform consumers of the purpose and nature of assessment activities, and should fully explain assessment results and recommendations based on the results. Explanations are to be phrased in language that is understandable to the consumer.

A more general feature of the Ethical Principles (APA, 1981) is the proposal that psychologists are responsible, *as individuals,* to the highest standards of the profession. This obligation, when combined with the primary allegiance to the client required by both codes, establishes an ethical mandate for psychologists to resist organizational pressures that run counter to client needs. It follows that psychologists and other assessment specialists who embrace this reasoning may sometimes be in conflict with their employing organizations. Such conflicts, however, represent opportunities to focus organizational attention on better ways of serving client needs. As such, they should be entered into (albeit constructively and tactfully) rather than avoided.

Situational Constraints

We have already noted that time pressures represent a major situational constraint faced by school assessment specialists. We have also stated that assessments should be conducted so as to adhere to legal requirements, procedural safeguards, and ethical considerations. Assessments done in keeping with these guidelines require more time than is sometimes allotted by school administrators unfamiliar with the intricacies of assessment. Assessment specialists, at a minimum, should take time to work constructively with their bureaucratic superiors in an effort to promote better understanding of these time requirements.

A partial solution to time problems involves the team approach to assessment mentioned in PL 94-142, in which school psychologists, school counselors, school social workers, school nurses, regular teachers, and special education personnel share the assessment load. A team approach, however, must ethically utilize professionals of different types in ways that are appropriate to their areas of competence. Such an approach must also involve a spirit of cooperation among team members—a situation that does not automatically occur.

Sharing the assessment load in terms of a team approach to assessment may not totally solve the time problems encountered by assessment specialists. Sometimes individual members of assessment teams complain that they are so caught up in assessment that they have too little time for other role-appropriate activities. For example, school psychologists may not have sufficient time to consult, guidance counselors may lack time to counsel, and resource teachers may find themselves slighting the teaching function. If such is the case, the assessment team may need to request additional resources from the school administration. Such additional resources may involve adding assessment personnel to the district's payroll. This step may be difficult to implement in the context of an increasingly tight economy. If so, the assessment team and school administrators will face some hard choices in terms of how best to achieve their assessment and other goals. Nevertheless, these issues must be addressed and solved to the best of our ability to do so.

In this context, we should mention that we find the "solution" of giving a minimum battery of tests to all students, regardless of referring problem, to be an inadequate option. While a minimum standard battery reduces assessment time, it will, for many students, be inappropriate in terms of the legal requirements, procedural safeguards, and ethical considerations already discussed. Such a battery may also be ineffective in helping make adequate classification and programming decisions. Failure to make adequate decisions in these areas will violate the spirit (and perhaps the letter) of PL 94-142 and will also be ethically questionable.

ASSESSMENT TECHNIQUES

For purposes of clarity and organization, assessment instruments can be classified in terms of the matrix model shown in Figure 9-1. The core dimensions of this model include (1) criterion-referenced versus norm-referenced instruments

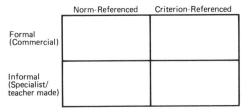

Fig. 9-1. Matrix model for classifying assessment techniques.

and (2) formal (commercially available) versus informal (specialist/teacher-made) instruments.

Health Conditions

Screening students for hearing, vision, and other health problems is an important part of the assessment process for a number of reasons. For one, serious errors in classification and programming can and do occur when this step is neglected. Horror stories involving students who are actually hard-of-hearing but who are classified, and programmed for, as mentally retarded surface from time to time. As a preventive measure, PL 94-142 requires that students be assessed in all areas related to their suspected disabilities, that limited aptitude not be surmized when poor test performance is actually a result of impaired sensory and other skills, and that related services needed by handicapped students be identified. These statutory requirements simply cannot be met without always screening for hearing and vision problems, and sometimes screening for other health problems. Such screening falls within the medical model of assessment. Medical model assessment techniques are designed to detect biological pathology (such as deficient vision). The decision rule in this model calls for referrals for further diagnosis and possible treatment even when pathology is suspected rather than proven.

School personnel have traditionally administered screening programs for vision and hearing deficits in students because the impact of such deficits on school learning is self-evident. However, as indicated previously, such deficits go undetected in some students, sometimes with serious consequences. While we advocate diligence in screening for vision and hearing problems in all students, we also believe that screening for other health problems should be routinely conducted, when possible for most children, but certainly in all individual cases in which such screening is clearly relevant.

A rather comprehensive set of medical model assessment procedures is found in the SOMPA (Mercer, 1979b). The SOMPA uses traditional procedures to screen students for hearing and vision problems but contains additional measures to screen for other health problems. Each of these procedures in the SOMPA results in students being identified as "at risk" or "not at risk." If students obtain one or more "at risk" scores across the procedures, consideration should be given to referring them for further diagnosis and possible treatment. All the medical model measures in the SOMPA are norm-referenced and formal (commercially available).

The SOMPA's procedure for screening for vision problems is the standard Snellen Test. Students are classified in terms of visual acuity using the standard

Snellen notation (20/20, 20/30, etc.). It should be noted that the Snellen Test assesses distance vision only. Mercer (1979b) recommended that near-vision abilities also be assessed whenever possible.

Screening within the SOMPA for auditory problems is done in terms of pure tone audiometric measurement. Specifically, auditory acuity in each ear at five different frequencies (250, 500, 1000, 2000, and 4000 cycles per second) is assessed. "If the child wears a hearing aid, both corrected and uncorrected hearing are recorded" (Mercer, 1979b, p. 73).

The SOMPA also contains four less traditional assessment procedures to screen for other health problems. These additional procedures are the Physical Dexterity Tasks, the Bender-Gestalt Test, the Health History Inventories, and Weight by Height. Each procedure is described briefly below.

The Physical Dexterity Tasks require the student to perform a number of physical activities (such as walking a line). Performances on the various activities are judged in terms of factors involved in each activity. These factors are ambulation, equilibrium, placement, fine motor sequencing, finger-tongue dexterity, and involuntary movement. "The Physical Dexterity Tasks provide a series of tests of the intactness and capability of the motor and sensory pathways that are involved in the performance of the exercises" (Mercer, 1979b, p. 60).[1]

The Bender-Gestalt Test (full name, Bender Visual-Motor Gestalt Test) requires the student to copy a series of geometric designs using paper and pencil. Bender-Gestalt Test performance is evaluated in the SOMPA according to the scoring system developed by Koppitz (1975). High error scores are interpreted as indicating probable difficulties in perceptual-motor integration. Mercer (1979b) warned, however, that the Bender-Gestalt Test is not a "pure type" medical model measure and that poor Bender-Gestalt Test scores should not be overinterpreted as indicating biological pathology. This caution is particularly appropriate when the poor Bender-Gestalt Test score "is the only 'at risk' score in the medical model profile" (Mercer, 1979b, p. 72). (The Bender-Gestalt Test will be discussed more thoroughly later in this chapter.)

The Health History Inventories are administered to the student's mother or other knowledgeable adult in an interview. The structured questions asked of the mother deal with the student's prenatal and postnatal well-being, history of physical trauma, past diseases and illnesses, and perceived vision and hearing abilities. Raw scores and standard scores are computed for each of these five factors. The Health History Inventories are designed to provide systematic "health histories of individual students that will assist in identifying high-risk children" (Mercer, 1979b, p. 76). High-risk children are considered to be those who have experienced a greater than average number of negative health events and who, as a consequence, are more likely than average children to be experiencing current health problems.

The purpose of the Weight by Height measure is to detect students who are under- or overweight in relation to other children of the same sex and height. The

---

[1]From Mercer, J. R. *Technical manual: System of multicultural pluralistic assessment.* New York: Psychological Corporation, 1979(b). Reproduced by permission from the System of Multicultural Pluralistic Assessment Technical Manual. Copyright © 1979 by the Psychological Corporation, New York, New York. All rights reserved.

SOMPA contains "conversion tables for both sexes from which scaled scores for each height by weight can be obtained" (Mercer, 1979b, p. 74). Students whose scaled scores represent underweight or overweight conditions are referred for physician evaluation.

The medical model measures found in the SOMPA represent one set of procedures for screening for vision, hearing, and other health problems. Other sets of procedures could be used in identifying these problems in students. The crucial task is to insure that *some* adequate system for detecting such problems in students is implemented as part of the total assessment process. It is also important to act in terms of the medical model decision rule of referring students with suspected health problems for further diagnosis and possible treatment. Finally, students should not be assessed further until additional diagnosis and/or treatment has taken place. Failure to defer further assessment pending completion of the needed diagnosis and/or treatment could lead to errors in classification and programming decisions.

General Intellectual Functioning

Traditionally, the primary measures of overall intellectual functioning have included such instruments as the Wechsler Intelligence Scale for Children–Revised (WISC-R; Wechsler, 1974), and the Stanford-Binet Intelligence Scale (Terman & Merrill, 1973). Quite clearly, both of these instruments fall within the norm-referenced and formal dimensions of the matrix model.

The primary use of measures of general intelligence has involved classification of handicapping conditions (Anastasi, 1976). Such measures have played a particularly significant role in the classification of mental retardation (Hallahan & Kauffman, 1976). Typically, children with IQ scores falling below a specific level (e.g., 70) are considered to be intellectually deficient (i.e., retarded). Various schemes have been developed to differentiate between levels of mental retardation. For example, the American Association on Mental Deficiency (Grossman, 1973) described four levels of mental retardation based on Stanford-Binet IQ scores. These levels are (1) mild retardation: IQ scores between 52 and 68; (2) moderate retardation: IQs between 36 and 51; (3) severe retardation: IQs between 20 and 35; and (4) profound retardation: IQs of 19 or below.

Although measures of general intelligence are primarily used for classification purposes, attempts have been made to enhance their diagnostic usefulness. For example, Valett (1965) developed a method for analyzing Stanford-Binet results into six separate factors: (1) general comprehension; (2) visual-motor ability; (3) arithmetic reasoning; (4) memory and concentration; (5) vocabulary and verbal fluency; and (6) judgment and reasoning. The purpose of this method is to view a student's overall Stanford-Binet test results in terms of that individual's strengths and weaknesses across each area of functioning measured. Although this method allows for the "diagnosis" of gross areas of strength and weakness, it does not indicate the usefulness of Stanford-Binet test results for programming since no specific procedures for remediation are tied directly to the identified areas of weakness.

In terms of diagnostic usefulness, the WISC-R (and, for that matter, all Wechsler Intelligence Scales) yields three IQ scores and a number of subtest scaled scores. The latter may be interpreted in terms of strengths and weaknesses. While Wechsler (1974) indicated that subtest scaled scores can be analyzed for strengths and weaknesses, he also noted that the WISC-R was designed primarily as a measure of general intelligence. Attempts have been made to develop remediation/programming procedures tied directly to specific subtest deficits (Banas & Wills, 1977; 1978). Unfortunately, no clear empirical data are provided (Banas & Wills, 1977; 1978) to suggest that these remediation/programming procedures have any measurable effect on either subtest performance or academic performance in the classroom.

Attempts have been made to measure intellectual development from a Piagetian perspective. Those interested in programming for students in terms of Piaget's model of intellectual development should find such assessment approaches of interest (DeAvila & Havassy, 1975; Elkind, 1969). Attempts have also been made to assess intellectual development in terms of Guilford's Structure of the Intellect model (Guilford, 1967). Those interested in assessing and programming for students in terms of this model should consult Meeker (1973).

Information Processing Skills

Information processing skills are defined here as the ability of a child to receive a sensory stimulus input, internally "process" (e.g., associate) the received stimulus input, and respond to the stimulus input overtly. Several measures have been developed to assess students' information processing skills. Some of these attempt to measure a wide range of information processing skills, while others focus exclusively on one specific type of skill. The measures, as a group, are similar in that they fall within the norm-referenced and formal categories of the matrix model. Examples of such tests include the Illinois Test of Psycholinguistic Abilities (ITPA; Kirk, McCarthy, & Kirk, 1968); the Visual Aural Digit Span Test (VADS; Koppitz, 1977); the Bender-Gestalt Test (BGT; Bender, 1946); and the Developmental Test of Visual Perception (DTVP; Frostig, Lefever, & Whittlesey, 1964).

The ITPA is an example of a test that attempts to measure an extremely wide variety of information processing areas. Twelve subtests (10 primary and 2 supplementary subtests) are included in the ITPA, each of which, according to the authors, measures an aspect of how children process psycholinguistic information (Kirk et al., 1968). Of the 10 primary subtests, two purport to measure stimulus reception skills (in visual and auditory reception), two measure short-term memory skills (visual and auditory memory), two measure association skills (visual and auditory association), and two measure expressive skills (verbal and manual skills). The two remaining subtests are purported to measure two automatic language processing skills—visual closure and grammatic (auditory) closure.

In practice, the ITPA is used in both classification and programming. Its usefulness in classification is based on the common learning disability category definition involving the student exhibiting a deficit in a basic psychological process that influences learning. Many practitioners use the ITPA subtest profile (or, in some cases, the overall psycholinguistic age score) to determine if a student has such a deficit in a critical area, and, if so, the student may (depending upon other information) be classifiable as a learning disabled student.

In terms of programming, the ITPA is designed to yield a profile of strengths and weaknesses in information processing areas. Diagnosis with the ITPA could be construed as a process of identifying weak areas that are in need of programming. For such purposes, Kirk and Kirk (1971) developed a manual of remediation procedures for each ITPA subtest. Unfortunately, their discussion of remediation procedures does not include clear empirical research which indicates that the procedures have a significant effect on subtest scores or a child's school functioning. Vance (1975) also provided descriptions of remediation strategies based on the ITPA, but, again, no reference is made to research indicating effectiveness. In order to evaluate the effectiveness of "psycholinguistic training" based on ITPA results, Hammill and Larsen (1974) reviewed the studies that evaluated the effects of such procedures. Their conclusions were far from optimistic; they saw no clear indication that the procedures have beneficial effects. These conclusions were challenged by Lund, Foster, and McCall-Perez (1978) but reaffirmed by Hammill and Larsen (1978). Our own conclusion is that the efficacy of "psycholinguistic training" has not, to date, been clearly demonstrated.

The VADS is similar to the ITPA in its orientation toward measuring a relatively wide range of information processing skills. However, the VADS purports to measure different types of short-term memory (STM) skills. Specifically, the VADS subtests include visual-oral STM, visual-written STM, aural-oral STM, and aural-written STM. In addition to these scores, various combination scores are available, such as aural input (overall scores on subtests involving auditory presentation across oral and written response modalities) and oral expression (overall scores on subtests with oral expression, measured across visual and auditory presentation tasks).

The use of the VADS for classification is analogous to the use of the ITPA for this purpose. That is, a significant deficit in a basic STM process as measured by the VADS might warrant a child's classification as learning disabled. In addition, the VADS could conceivably be used for programming purposes by developing remediation procedures that are specific to a child's pattern of STM deficits on the VADS. Recently, behavioral researchers have developed operant conditioning procedures that can enhance a child's STM in both visual and auditory areas (Farb & Throne, 1978). Should a child exhibit deficits in a given STM area, such operant procedures could be integrated into the child's program in order to remediate the deficits. Although operant procedures have been demonstrated to be effective in strengthening STM skills, the ultimate demonstration of the programmatic usefulness of STM measures such as the VADS would entail a demonstration that increased STM skills are functionally related to increased skills in academic areas. Obviously, further research is needed to rigorously assess the programmatic usefulness of the VADS by addressing the effect of STM remediation on academic skill areas.

The BGT and the DTVP are more restricted measures of information processing variables in that both focus exclusively on visual-motor integration processes. Many practitioners simply refer to such processes as "eye-hand coordination" (Hallahan & Kauffman, 1976). That is, visual-motor integration tests require the ability to coordinate eye movements and visual stimulus input with hand movements. Tests such as the BGT and DTVP are most frequently used for classification purposes in a manner analogous to the classification use of the ITPA or

VADS. In other words, if a student has deficits in visual-motor integration, and the assessment specialist makes the assumption that this process is basic to learning, then under certain circumstances the student might be classified as learning disabled.

The BGT and DTVP, as well as various other tests of visual-motor integration, have been used rather widely as instruments to suggest remedial programming. As Hallahan and Kauffman (1976) indicated, procedures involving perceptual-motor training are frequently prescribed for children who exhibit deficits in visual-motor integration. If such procedures are effective in improving both visual-motor integration and academic skills, then the programmatic usefulness of the BGT, DTVP, and other visual-motor tests would be indicated. However, Hammill (1972) reviewed the published literature involving empirical evaluations of the effects of perceptual-motor training on perceptual skills (e.g., visual-motor integration) and found that only 2 of 13 studies demonstrated a consistent positive effect of training. In a similar review of 16 studies, Goodman and Hammill (1973) found no evidence that perceptual-motor training was any more effective than control procedures in improving academic or perceptual-motor skills. These reviews do not support the usefulness of tests such as the BGT and DTVP in designing remedial programs for handicapped children.

Academic Achievement

Measures of academic achievement fall within three classes in the matrix classification model. These classes include norm-referenced—formal, criterion-referenced—formal, and criterion-referenced—informal.

Representative achievement measures in the norm-referenced—formal class include the Peabody Individual Achievement Test (PIAT; Dunn & Markwardt, 1970) and the Wide Range Achievement Test (WRAT; Jastak & Jastak, 1978). The PIAT is a broad-based achievement measure, which includes subtests in mathematics, reading recognition, reading comprehension, spelling, and general information. The instrument can be used for students in grades K–12. The WRAT includes subtests in mathematics, reading (recognition), and spelling. The instrument can be used with students in grade K through college.

Both the PIAT and WRAT allow for the conversion of raw scores into grade equivalents and scaled scores. As with all norm-referenced tests, these scores allow for the comparison of a given student's score on a specific subtest with the scores of students in the normative sample. On the basis of such comparisons, a student's degree of deficit in a given academic skill area can be established. Such data can be used in making classification decisions about the student. For example, if a student is significantly delayed in math and reading, and has substantial deficits in one or more information processing skills (which are logically related to the academic skill deficits), then the student might be classified as learning disabled.

Since norm-referenced tests such as the PIAT and WRAT provide only global comparative information about a student's academic skills, the use of these tests in programming is relatively restricted. The primary programming information obtainable from these tests is a statement that suggests the level at which the student should be instructed in a given subject area. The tests do not indicate the specific academic skills (e.g., specific types of math skills) in which the student is weak; therefore, they provide the teacher with little information with which to develop an individualized program.

Representative achievement measures in the criterion-referenced—formal class include the Criterion Tests of Basic Skills (CTBS; Lundell, Brown & Evans, 1976) and the Brigance Diagnostic Inventory of Basic Skills (BDIBS; Brigance, 1976). The CTBS includes two basic batteries: one for math skills (CTBS-M) and one for reading skills (CTBS-R). The CTBS-M includes several problems within each of the following areas: numbers and numerals (e.g., reading numerals), addition, subtraction, multiplication, and division. Each of these areas is further divided into sub-areas, which involve cumulatively learned skills. For example, the subtraction sub-areas include problems in subtraction with one-digit numbers, two- and three-digit numbers (without regrouping), and two- and three-digit numbers (with regrouping). Five optional skill areas are included, covering skills such as using money, understanding measurement, telling time, and using fractions and decimals.

The CTBS-R is also designed with skill areas and sub-areas placed in a cumulative learning sequence. The primary skill areas include letter recognition; letter sounding, blending, and sequencing; special sounds (e.g., vowel digraphs); and sight words. An optional skill area is writing letters of the alphabet.

The BDIBS measures basic academic readiness skills, in addition to skills within the areas of reading, language arts, and math. The tasks in the readiness section involve academic precursor skills such as visual discrimination, visual memory, sentence memory, and fine motor skills. The reading section includes word recognition tasks (broken into sub-areas such as basic sight vocabulary, abbreviations, and contractions); oral reading and reading comprehension; word analysis skills (broken into an impressively wide range of sub-areas such as initial consonant sounds, ending sounds, initial clusters, and suffixes); and vocabulary (with sub-areas such as classification, analogies, and antonyms). The language arts section includes handwriting, grammar mechanics, spelling tasks, and reference skills (e.g., outlining). The math section includes numbers (e.g., counting objects), operations (e.g., addition, subtraction), measurement (e.g., money, time, liquids, weight), and geometry.

The usefulness of the CTBS and BDIBS for classification purposes would appear to be limited due to their inability to yield information about a student's functioning relative to that of other students. Current classification systems are oriented primarily toward norm-referenced concepts of handicap or deficit. However, the CTBS and BDIBS appear to have substantial potential for use in programming. Since these measures allow for the precise specification of a student's academic deficits, they provide information that can be translated directly into programs designed to remediate these deficits.

The third class of academic achievement measures involves criterion-referenced—informal procedures. These are actually sets of guidelines that allow the assessment specialist to design assessment procedures that directly address a student's academic problems. All of these guidelines are oriented toward providing programming information that clearly describes the skills a student needs in order for a deficit to be remediated. These guidelines are based to a great extent on the tradition of task analysis (Hallahan & Kauffman, 1976). As indicated earlier, task analysis refers to an orientation that conceptualizes academic skills as cumulative in nature, with more complex skills being sequentially built upon more simple, precursor skills. Task analysis also involves breaking a given skill into its component parts (sub-skills), and assessing a student's performance on each sub-skill of the overall skill in which she is deficient. Through such analyses of skills, the assessment specialist can isolate the "gaps" in a sequence of sub-skills that aggregate to yield the overall skill deficit. The "gaps" in sub-skills are seen as being responsible for the overall skill deficit.

Dickinson (1978, 1980) developed a task analytic approach to assessment called direct assessment. This approach combines task-analysis procedures with the conceptual framework of applied behavior analysis. There are a number of steps in direct assessment. The first step is pinpointing the student's problem in terms of observable behaviors (e.g., Johnny doesn't carry numbers from the first to second set of digits when completing two-digit addition problems with regrouping). This step entails performing a detailed criterion assessment to isolate those tasks on which a student has difficulty. The second step is determining whether the appropriate behavior is in the student's behavioral repertoire (e.g., Does Johnny ever regroup appropriately?). If the correct behavior *is* in the student's repertoire, the third step is determining what events set the occasion for (i.e., serve as cues for) the incorrect behavior. For example, Johnny might sometimes covertly verbalize an incorrect regrouping rule, which sets the occasion for an incorrect regrouping response. This type of "setting event" could be determined by having Johnny "think aloud" as he works through a problem (Dickinson, 1980). If the correct behavior is in the child's repertoire, then setting events can be modified so as to increase the likelihood of the correct behavior (rather than the incorrect behavior) occurring. If the correct behavior is *not* in the child's repertoire, the fourth step is a task analysis of the student's "entering" level of behavior (vis-à-vis the task). For example, if Johnny can never perform two-digit addition regrouping problems correctly, then this task would be broken down into its component parts, and the assessment specialist would determine which of the component parts Johnny could or could not perform correctly. The most complex subtask component that Johnny could perform correctly would be his entering level of behavior. Suppose that Johnny could correctly perform two-digit addition problems without regrouping, but not those with regrouping. The former would represent his entering level of behavior. A skill "gap" would be present between his entering level and the terminal skill (i.e., two digits with regrouping). Remediation procedures would be directed toward teaching Johnny those skills between his entering level and the task in question.

In addition to Dickinson's direct assessment (1978, 1980) approach, Resnick and Ford (1978) described rational and empirical task analyses for a variety of academic behaviors (e.g., math and reading). Rational task analyses are essentially detailed descriptions (in terms of components) of *ideal* task performances. That is, models are constructed of the ideal steps involved in performing various tasks. Empirical task analyses essentially involve descriptions of the steps in task performance that have been observed to occur in children performing a given task. The specific task analyses that Resnick and Ford (1978) provided (as well as the generalized approach to task analysis that they described) could be used in conjunction with the fourth step of Dickinson's direct assessment (1980) approach.

It should be clear that informal task-analytic approaches, like formal criterion-referenced procedures, have limited usefulness in the classification of handicapping conditions. However, these procedures would appear to be extremely useful for programming purposes. Specifically, they clearly indicate what skills the student needs to learn, and they also address the cumulative *sequence* in which skills should be taught.

Social-Emotional Functioning

Instruments that allow the assessment specialist to evaluate a student's social-emotional behaviors basically fall into three classes of our matrix: norm-referenced—formal, criterion-referenced—formal, and criterion-referenced—informal.

Within the class of norm-referenced—formal procedures are a wide range of behavior checklists, which allow for the comparison of a given student's behavior to that of a particular norm group. Representative examples of this type of assessment instrument include the Walker Problem Behavior Identification Checklist (WPBIC; Walker, 1976), Burks Behavior Rating Scale (BBRS; Burks, 1977), and the Behavior Rating Profile (BRP; Brown & Hammill, 1978).

The WPBIC is a behavior checklist completed by a student's parent or teacher. This checklist allows the student to be normatively evaluated on the following dimensions: (1) acting out; (2) withdrawal; (3) distractibility; (4) disturbed peer relations; and (5) immaturity.

The BBRS is also a checklist that is completed by a student's teacher or parent. The checklist offers a wide range of dimensions on which the student can be normatively evaluated, including excessive anxiety, excessive withdrawal, poor impulse control, and poor anger control. A common feature of both the WPBIC and the BBRS is that they assess students' social-emotional adjustment in terms of *several* specific areas of social-emotional functioning.

Unlike both the WPBIC and BBRS, the BRP provides a *global* normative measure of the student's adjustment across several environments. This instrument includes behavior checklists completed by one or more of the student's teachers; behavior checklists completed by one or both of the student's parents; a behavior checklist completed by the student, including self-ratings of behavior in home, school, and peer settings; and a sociogram completed by the student's peers. The BRP allows for a child to be compared to the normative group in terms of overall behavior as measured by *each* of the above components. This instrument, therefore, allows for a relatively detailed ecological analysis of a student's overall adjustment.

These three representative instruments are clearly useful in the classification of students in that they allow for the *severity* of a social-emotional disorder to be evaluated on a normative basis. In terms of programming, however, information regarding relative severity of a social-emotional problem is of limited value. Statements of severity do not clearly describe what specific social-emotional behaviors need to be changed. For programming purposes, additional procedures that allow for precise "target behavior" specification are needed.

The Ecological Assessment of Child Problem Behaviors, a particularly comprehensive criterion-referenced—formal system for assessing specific social-emotional behaviors, was developed by Wahler, House, and Stambaugh (1976). This is a formal behavioral observation system, which allows for the systematic, simultaneous observation of 19 different student behaviors and 6 social stimulus events that are frequently related to various student behavior patterns. The 19 specific student behaviors represent five basic classes of behavior: compliance-opposition, autistic, play, work, and social behavior. The stimulus events involve instructions from adults, attention from adults, and attention from peers. The observational data derived from this system allow for (1) the specification of which of a student's behaviors needs programming (as indicated by excessively low or high rates of the behavior), and (2) a functional analysis of each behavior in terms of relationships between the behaviors and the stimulus events.

An alternative to the use of a formal observation system such as that of Wahler et al. (1976) is the use of a "homemade" observation system designed to assess *only* those behaviors targeted as problematic during interviews with a student's teacher (or parent). Such criterion-referenced—informal procedures generally fall into three basic categories: (1) frequency counts, during which the observer simply counts the number of times each day that the student emits a particular behavior(s); (2) duration procedures, during which the observer records the total *amount of time* a student spends engaging in a given behavior(s); and (3) interval assessment, in which the observer records the presence or absence of a given behavior during each of a number of intervals (Kazdin, 1980).

Like the Wahler et al. (1976) system, informal observation systems can provide program-relevant information regarding the specific student behaviors that are in need of change. Furthermore, both types of procedures allow the assessment specialist to monitor the student's behaviors over time (i.e., through periodic sequential observation) in order to evaluate the effectiveness of programming. Although observational systems currently have limited classification usefulness, this weakness could be dealt with by combining such systems with the use of behavior checklists. The behavior checklists could be used to derive normative severity data for use in classification, and to *suggest* possible behaviors to be observed during systematic observation.

We have intentionally omitted a discussion of "projective" techniques (such as the Thematic Apperception Test and the Rorschach) as measures of students' social-emotional problems. The primary reason for this omission is that such instruments have been found to have questionable validity for the purposes of assessing the presence of social-emotional problems in students (O'Leary, 1972; Bardon & Bennett, 1974). In other words, such procedures yield results that may have little, if any, relationship to a student's current behavioral functioning. As such, they have limited usefulness in both classification and programming areas.

Adaptive Behavior

Adaptive behavior, in our judgment, most appropriately refers to a student's level of social functioning in home and neighborhood environments. At issue in measures of adaptive behavior is the question of how well the student has adapted to the survival requirements of nonacademic (i.e., nonschool) environments in which she is placed. Although measures of adaptive behavior may be required as general components of an assessment battery, such measures are specifically required when a student is suspected to be mentally retarded. This classification category not only requires verification of "deficient" intellectual functioning, but also requires demonstration that these intellectual deficiencies have resulted in retardation in adaptive behavior. In other words, the student must be "retarded" in terms of both (1) how she functions at school vis-à-vis academic/intellectual tasks, and (2) how she functions at home and in the neighborhood in terms of "everyday" survival-related tasks.

In this context, we shall not discuss a number of adaptive behavior measures that are completed by or in conjunction with teachers. Our position is that the assessment of adaptive behavior is most appropriately conducted with parents so as to maximize our understanding of the student's out-of-school functioning. Such understanding should lead to more accurate classification of students as mentally retarded.

Developing remedial programs for deficient nonacademic behavior in school can proceed on the basis of data from the criterion-referenced—formal and criterion-referenced—informal procedures discussed in the section on social-emotional functioning. These same procedures can also be used in developing corrective programs for problem behaviors occurring at home. Thus, our discussion of representative measures of adaptive behavior is confined to those that fall within the norm-referenced—formal class and are, therefore, primarily used for classification purposes. Additionally, all the instruments discussed are best completed in conjunction with the parents of the students being assessed, as all focus on home and neighborhood behaviors.

Representative measures of adaptive behavior in the home and neighborhood include the Vineland Social Maturity Scale (VSMS), the Preschool Attainment Record (PAR), and the Adaptive Behavior Inventory for Children (ABIC). All of these measures involve structured interviews with a student's parent in order to ascertain his level of social adaptive functioning. As noted, all can be classified within the norm-referenced—formal class. The VSMS (Doll, 1965) is a measure of adaptive behavior in individuals of all ages. Categories of adaptive behavior included in this measure are self-help (general, eating, and dressing), locomotion, occupation, communication, self-direction, and socialization. The VSMS yields a social age equivalent score and an overall social quotient.

The PAR (Doll, 1966) is an adaptive behavior measure for use with preschool students. Categories of behavior measured include ambulation, manipulation, rapport, communication, responsibility, information, ideation, and creativity. Like the VSMS, the PAR also yields a social age equivalent score and an "attainment quotient."

The ABIC (Mercer, 1979b) is an adaptive behavior measure for use with students 5–11 years old. It yields five scaled scores reflecting the adequacy of the student's role performances in family, community, peer relations, nonacademic school (e.g., relations with teachers and classmates), and earner/consumer roles. It also yields a sixth scaled score, which reflects the adequacy of the student's self-maintenance skills across all his social roles. A "veracity scale" is included, and the score on this scale is useful in determining whether parents are accurately reporting the level of functioning of their child. An average scaled score, reflecting overall level of adaptive behavior, is also determined.

Vocational and Prevocational Needs

As mandated by PL 94-142, handicapped students should be provided the same types of educational services as nonhandicapped students. This requirement would apparently include vocational guidance and self-exploration activities, since such experiences are a regular component of most students' educational programs. Traditionally, vocational guidance has focused on vocational interest and aptitude measurement (Anastasi, 1976). A particularly common measure of vocational interests in high school students is the Strong-Campbell Interest Inventory (SCII; Campbell, 1974). This instrument is a norm-referenced—formal device that allows measurement of interests within the areas of realistic, investigative, artistic, social, enterprising, and conventional realms. In addition to these broad interest scales, occupational scales are included which normatively plot students' levels of interest in each of a large number of specific occupations.

A vocational-interest measure, which is designed for use with students in grades 6–12, is the Kuder General Interest Survey (KGIS; Kuder, 1966). This measure provides for normative plotting of students' levels of interests in each of several broad occupational areas (e.g., outdoor, mechanical, artistic, etc.).

It would seem that vocational interest measures, when combined with data regarding a student's strengths and weaknesses, could be used for programming purposes. That is, such data could provide a basis for vocational-counseling programs as well as occupational-exploration programs for handicapped and nonhandicapped students.

Readers interested in other assessment instruments and procedures should consult other chapters in this book and texts such as Salvia and Ysseldyke (1978).

SELECTION OF APPROPRIATE ASSESSMENT MODELS AND TECHNIQUES

Our proposed model attempts to address the issues of (1) time considerations, and (2) the need for a broad-based, multifactored assessment of students' needs. In order to both minimize assessment time *and* assess a variety of factors, we suggest the utilization of a *branching assessment model,* which allows for the inclusion of only those instruments that are highly relevant to the referral problem. This branching model is shown schematically in Figure 9-2.

The stationary aspects of this model include health screening and a referral-source interview. The former allows the assessment specialist to determine whether sensory or health factors may contribute to a student's difficulty and serves as a data base for referral to health specialists. The referral-source interview allows the assessment specialist to conceptualize the referral problem as involving academic behavior problems, or social-emotional behavior problems, or, in some cases, both. Detailed instructions for conducting such interviews may be found in Bergan (1977). Once the referral problem is classified as *primarily*

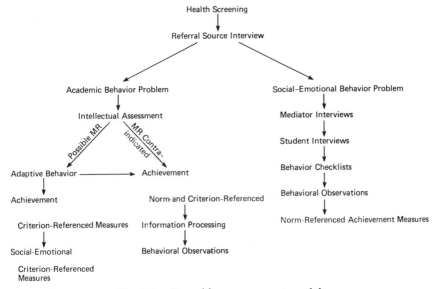

Fig. 9-2. Branching assessment model.

involving academic or social-emotional problems, the assessment specialist can proceed to the appropriate "branch" of the model. At this point, the assessment specialist can administer only those assessment instruments that will allow for classification and programming in regard to *either* academic problems (with possible classification categories including mental retardation and learning disability) or social-emotional problems (with the possibility of a classification of seriously emotionally disturbed). The assessment procedures within each branch are included to provide information useful for *both* classification and remedial programming.

Academic Behavior Problems

If interview data have "branched" the specialist into the academic behavior area of the model, the next step entails individual intellectual assessment with an instrument such as the WISC-R or Stanford-Binet. The purpose of this step is to provide an estimate of overall intellectual functioning, as required by classification guidelines. Under the mental retardation (MR) classification guidelines, a global measure of intellectual functioning is required to ascertain the existence of serious cognitive deficits, whereas the learning disabilities (LD) guidelines require a measure of intellectual functioning from which expected achievement level is predicted.

If the intellectual assessment indicates intellectual retardation, the assessment specialist is further "branched" into assessment procedures that are required to determine the appropriateness of an MR classification. The primary assessment procedure for this purpose would be a measure of adaptive behavior (e.g., VSMS, PAR, or ABIC). If the measure of adaptive behavior (which primarily serves a classification function) indicates subnormal functioning, our model would involve measures that provide programming information. Within our model, programming information would be provided by criterion-referenced achievement measures (e.g., CTBS or BDIBS). These measures would allow for the specification of academic skills a child is to be taught during a given interval of time. Programming needs relative to poor school, home, and/or neighborhood nonacademic functioning could be ascertained with criterion-referenced measures of social-emotional functioning such as the Ecological Assessment of Child Problem Behaviors (Wahler et al., 1976) or the informal observation systems described by Kazdin (1980).

If either the intellectual assessment or the adaptive behavior assessment contraindicate the MR classification, the specialist would be "branched" into procedures required for a classification of LD. These measures would include normative- and criterion-referenced achievement tests, measures of information processing, and observations of behavior in a classroom environment.

Norm-referenced measures (such as the PIAT or WRAT) would be used to determine the severity of academic deficits (as required by classification guidelines), while criterion-referenced measures (such as the CTBS or BDIBS) would be used to specify academic skills to be strengthened. Measures of information processing skills (such as the ITPA, VADS, BGT, and/or the DTVP) would allow for the specification of information processing strengths and weaknesses as suggested by LD classification regulations. In addition, a student's weak information processing skills could be targeted for remediation. Another possibility would be the specification of areas of strength, which could be used to design programs that "tap" a student's strong information processing areas, while bypassing areas of weaknesses (Hallahan & Kauffman, 1976).

In addition to the above procedures, the assessment specialist would perform behavioral observations of the student in the classroom setting. These observations would focus primarily on attending behaviors, on-task behaviors, and disruptive behaviors. The purpose of such observations is twofold. As required by federal regulations, systematic behavioral observations must be performed on a student classified as LD. The regulations indicate the need to relate classroom behaviors to the child's learning problems. A second purpose of the observations is to determine if the student has behaviors that interfere with appropriate learning (e.g., disruptive behaviors or inadequate attention). If such behaviors are present, observational data could be used to design intervention programs to change them.

The above procedures for assessing children with academic behavior problems attempt to provide information for *both* classification and programming. It should be noted that this model does not clearly specify what specific instruments should be used for assessment within a given branch of the model. The model simply attempts to delineate sequential steps in the assessment process, while allowing each assessment specialist to choose specific measures with which to assess a particular area of functioning.

It should be noted at this point that some students referred for special education services will not qualify for such services. In order to receive special education services, a student must be found (via the assessment process) to merit a categorical handicapping-condition classification (such as MR or LD) that is accompanied by deficits in educational performance. As previously indicated, students should not be so classified unless there is clear evidence that they are actually handicapped. Furthermore, the determination of whether a student is handicapped or not must be made in reference to the definitions of the various categorical handicapping conditions.

We illustrate this point by describing a hypothetical student who has been judged subnormal in terms of general intellectual functioning but does not appear subnormal in terms of adaptive behavior. She should be "branched" into the MR contraindicated section of the assessment model following the finding of adequate adaptive behavior (Fig. 9-2). This student may or may not ultimately be judged to be learning disabled. The LD classification regulations (*Federal Register,* December 29, 1977) require that students not be judged to be LD unless there is a significant discrepancy between expected academic achievement and actual academic achievement. Given this student's low level of general intellectual functioning, her expected level of academic achievement might also be low. Unless actual academic achievement is significantly below this already low level of expected achievement, she could not be classified as LD. Students such as this are often described as "slow learners" and found ineligible for any type of special education services. Those interested in the specific definitions of the various categorical handicapping-condition classifications should consult the issues of the *Federal Register* dated August 23, 1977 and December 29, 1977. As has been stated earlier (and illustrated above), assessment for classification purposes is an intricate and complex process requiring much professional judgment.

Social-Emotional Behavior Problems

If the referral source interview indicates social-emotional behavior problems (e.g., deficient social interaction, excessive disruptive behavior), the model "branches" the assessment specialist into procedures designed specifically for these types of problems. This branch includes (1) mediator and student interviews; (2) the use of behavior checklists; (3) ecological behavioral observations; and (4) norm-referenced achievement testing.

The mediator and student interviews involve systematic discussions with a student and his teachers and parents. The purposes of such interviews are to (1) clearly delineate the specific behaviors that are problematic (e.g., behavior excesses or deficits); (2) ascertain the relevant history of the problem behaviors, including types of interventions that have been attempted; (3) describe the functional relationships between the problematic behaviors and current environmental events (e.g., setting events and consequences); and (4) delineate student perceptions and affective states that may be functionally related to the problematic behaviors (Bergan, 1977; Dickinson, 1978).

The behavior checklists (such as the WPBIC or the BBRS) can serve primarily to determine the normative *severity* of the problematic behaviors for classification purposes. However, if individual items are analyzed, behavior checklists can also serve as validity checks for information derived from the interviews. In addition, information derived from checklists can be used to structure the interview. For example, the specialist can probe the mediator or student extensively on those items or areas that the checklists identify as particularly problematic or central to the overall problem.

The behavioral observations (such as those described in the section on social-emotional functioning) involve direct observations of the student in the settings (e.g., the classroom) in which the problem behaviors occur (Bergan, 1977). Such observations can be taken by either the specialist or mediators trained by the specialist (e.g., teachers). These observations allow for (1) measurement of the static frequency (rate) of the problem behaviors across time, and (2) a more detailed analysis of functional relationships between environmental events and the problematic behaviors. Measures of static frequency across time not only serve as validity checks for severity data from behavior checklists, but, more importantly, allow for the subsequent evaluation of the effectiveness of programming efforts; that is, continued monitoring of the relevant student behaviors will clearly indicate whether programming efforts have the desired effect on the rate of those behaviors. The use of observational data to explore and verify interview-derived hypotheses regarding functional relations between the problem behavior and environmental events has particular significance for programming efforts. Once clear functional relationships have been observed, empirical data are available to guide those aspects of programming that involve restructuring the student's environment in order to increase appropriate and/or decrease inappropriate behavior (Dickinson, 1978).

The final aspect of the assessment of social-emotional behavior problems involves the use of norm-referenced achievement tests (e.g., the PIAT or WRAT). The purpose of such testing is to determine whether academic skill deficits accompany social-emotional behavior problems. Frequently, children with certain types of behavior problems (e.g., excessive disruptive behavior) may develop academic skill deficits due to the incompatability between the problem behaviors and appropriate academic performance (Williams & Anandam, 1973). In such cases, the level of instruction to which the student is exposed should be altered to that compatible with his entering skill level. This may prevent the student from falling farther behind and becoming more and more frustrated with school experiences. It may also serve as a context for the further development of appropriate behaviors which may be incompatible with inappropriate problematic behaviors (Allyon & Roberts, 1978). Data derived from normative achievement testing can provide an empirical basis for modifying the level of a student's instructional program to make it compatible with that student's skill level.

ASSESSMENT IN NONCATEGORICAL SPECIAL EDUCATION PROGRAMS

At this point it is appropriate to restate our agreement with Hobbs's (1975) proposal that eligibility for special education services be made contingent on identified educational deficits and needed remedial services rather than on categorical handicapping-condition classifications assigned to some students with such deficits. We do not take this position because we believe that the conditions described by the classifications fail to exist. Some students are, for example, *truly* mentally retarded and will be so throughout their lives. Instead, we take this position because we believe that categorical handicapping-condition classifications can be stigmatizing to students and are sometimes misapplied to them. In addition, we believe that assessment to determine both students' special education classifications and their programming needs represents inefficient use of scarce assessment resources. Furthermore, such assessment often is less effective than it should be as a result of a disproportionate emphasis on classification. Were special education services contingent only on identified educational deficits and needed remedial services, assessment for classification and programming would be largely synonymous and, therefore, both more efficient and more effective in positively impacting students' lives.

Factors Influencing the Adoption of Noncategorical Assessment

The delivery of educational and related services to students is heavily influenced by social policy as operationalized in laws and regulations. PL 94-142 has done much to promote access to educational services for handicapped students, and these gains should not be lost. PL 94-142, however, has also helped institutionalize assessment designed, in part, to determine categorical handicapping-condition classifications.

While we advocate a noncategorical classification system, we also believe that establishing such a system will involve some difficulties. Several factors should be addressed in order to minimize these difficulties. To be adopted, a noncategorical classification system must satisfy a number of functional requirements. Such a system must, for instance, incorporate a clear and administratively feasible procedure for allocating funds for special services to students experiencing educational problems. While several strategies are possible, the system may need to include mechanisms for determining whether an educational or related deficit is of sufficient severity to warrant the allocation of special service funds. Judgments of severity of deficits will most likely require norm-referenced assessments of academic achievement and social-emotional functioning. The norm-referenced—formal assessment instruments described earlier could be used for this purpose. Also, the system must incorporate mechanisms for determining the amount of additional funds to be allocated. Judgments in this area may require criterion-referenced assessments of academic achievement (functioning) and social-emotional functioning as such procedures yield information relevant to the design of specific educational programs. The criterion-referenced—formal and/or informal assessment instruments described earlier could be used for this purpose.

A noncategorical classification system must also be found acceptable in terms of political, legal, and attitudinal factors. For instance, such a system must be compatible with statutory law. For this to occur, laws institutionalizing categorical classification systems must be amended or replaced with new laws to allow for noncategorical allocations of special service funds. Amendment or replacement of these laws will require legislative action, and such action occurs in a political context. Thus, groups (such as parent advocacy groups) that supported the passage of these laws must provide political support for the new legislation required by a noncategorical classification system. Since some of these groups may be fearful of losses of services for some students as a consequence of new legislation, these fears must be clearly addressed in the drafting of new legislation. New legislation, in turn, should not be introduced if the political climate might result in losses of services to students.

Finally, a noncategorical classification system (or any new classification system) must be acceptable in terms of practitioner attitudes to insure intitial political support and effective implementation (Cromwell, Blashfield, & Strauss, 1975). Since acceptance is at least partially predicated on understanding, sufficient effort must be devoted to assisting current practitioners in understanding the new legislation. Problems involving changes in practitioner roles which may result from the new legislation must also be resolved for the legislation to gain widespread practitioner support.

The barriers to the adoption of a noncategorical classification system may be formidable. Readers interested in more detailed analyses of the prospects for changes in special education classification systems should consult Hobbs (1975) and Gallagher, Forsythe, Ringelheim, and Weintraub (1975).

The Noncategorical Assessment Model

We envision four types of student descriptors in a noncategorical classification system. One of the types of descriptors would be a general term that would release funds for special services for students experiencing educational problems. Gallagher et al. (1975) found that the general classification term of "children with special problems and special needs" (p. 458) was acceptable to most state directors of special education, and this term is acceptable to us as well. The second type of descriptor would indicate degree of educational deficit (such as 2 years delayed in math). The third type of descriptor would indicate specific educational skills that the student needs to acquire (such as addition of two-digit numbers with regrouping, and interacting without fighting on the playground). The fourth type of descriptor would describe the service options most appropriate to the degree of educational deficit and to the skills to be acquired (such as 1 hour each day in the resource room plus individual behavioral counseling). While there would be four descriptor types, each "student with special problems and special needs" might have several different degrees of educational deficit, a number of specific skills in need of acquisition, and several service options. Thus, most of the descriptor types could be responded to with multiple entries for an individual student.

One anticipated advantage of such a noncategorical classification system would be the replacement of highly stigmatizing classification terms (such as mentally retarded) with less stigmatizing classification terms. While we recognize that any term that denotes poor educational performance may be somewhat stigmatizing, we believe that classification terms under the proposed system will be less stigmatizing than the current categorical classifications. A second anticipated advantage of the proposed classification system would be that descriptors of degree of deficit, needed skills, and appropriate service options provide more guidance in designing an individualized educational program for a student than does classifying her as mentally retarded, etc.

A third anticipated advantage of the proposed system would be fewer errors in classification. Concluding that a student is 2 years delayed in math, needs to learn two-digit addition with regrouping, and needs 1 hour each day in the resource room requires less difficult inferences than does concluding that the student is MR or LD. The first type of conclusion requires only descriptions of a student's performances and needed services while the second type of conclusion requires a global inference about the student himself. Both types of conclusions, however, require the exercise of professional judgment.

A fourth anticipated advantage of the proposed system would be more efficient assessment. Efficiency can be judged in terms of total time spent on assessment or in terms of value received per given unit of assessment time. While we are not sure that assessment in terms of a noncategorical classification system will take less time than is currently allocated, we do believe that such a system will be more efficient in terms of value per unit of assessment time. We are defining value in terms of the degree to which assessment promotes effective remedial programming for students.

Our belief that this noncategorical classification system will result in more value per unit of assessment time is based on how we see assessment proceeding under such a classification system. In a noncategorical classification system, we see the techniques dealing with health conditions, academic achievement, and social-emotional functioning as necessary to the assessment process. Techniques falling under the other classes of assessment domains could be used *as needed* in conducting an assessment which is ethically and legally appropriate.

We have already argued that screening for health problems is essential in the assessment of a referred student. We believe that such screening is also essential under a noncategorical classification system. Screening for hearing and vision problems is particularly important but, again, screening for other health conditions is recommended as a routine procedure if such is feasible. The medical model measures of the SOMPA could be used in the screening process. The important point is that *some* set of procedures be used for health conditions screening and that the decision rule appropriate to the medical model be applied.

We have noted that norm-referenced—formal measures of academic achievement may be needed in a noncategorical classification system. We have also stated that criterion-referenced—formal and/or informal measures of academic achievement may also be needed. We are particularly concerned that criterion-referenced measures of academic achievement be utilized since such measures pinpoint students' "gaps" in learning task hierarchies within various curricular areas. Knowledge of these "gaps" should be very helpful in developing the specific remedial strategies for individualized educational programs. Our emphasis in this area stems from our primary commitment to the task-analysis model of assessment and programming; we see this model as resulting in the most effective remedial strategies for students. As in screening for health problems, the choices of instruments and procedures should be left to assessment specialists. However, we see the CTBS, the BDIBS, and direct assessment as useful approaches in the context of the task analysis model.

We have also noted that norm-referenced—formal and criterion-referenced—formal and/or informal measures of social-emotional functioning may be needed in a noncategorical classification system. Again, we are hopeful that criterion-referenced measures of social-emotional functioning will be used to pinpoint particular problematic behaviors so that specific remedial strategies to deal with such behaviors can be incorporated in individualized educational programs. While we see the choices of instruments and procedures as being made by assessment specialists, we view the Ecological Assessment of Child Problem Behavior (Wahler et al., 1976) and the informal observation systems described by Kazdin (1980) as helpful approaches.

As we have indicated, measures of general intellectual functioning, information processing skills, adaptive behavior, and vocational and prevocational needs may be useful, but probably not required, in terms of a noncategorical classification system. Our position is that measures in these assessment domains should be used only as needed in conducting an ethically and legally appropriate assessment. We cannot speculate about what would constitute legally appropriate assessment in terms of a noncategorical classification system; as indicated earlier, the statutory framework for such a system does not currently exist (at least at the federal level). From an ethical perspective, however, we would hope that assessment specialists would not ignore other assessment domains if measures in those domains would be useful in promoting student welfare. We also hope that assessment of students in nonschool settings (home and neighborhood) would be done (whether required or not in terms of a noncategorical classification system) if such assessments promote student welfare. In this context, we believe that students will benefit maximally when school personnel and parents are working as partners on their behalf. Assessment of nonschool behaviors done in conjunction with parents might promote such partnership, and many of the assessment techniques described in the sections on social-emotional functioning and adaptive behavior do measure behaviors in the home and neighborhood. Additionally, the criterion-referenced—formal and informal measures of social-emotional functioning can be used to design programs to remediate nonproductive student behaviors occurring in the home and neighborhood.

We have stressed the need for more effective remedial programming throughout this chapter. At this point, we should mention that more effective programming has been a point of contention in lawsuits stemming from disproportionate representation of ethnic minority students in special education programs (Reschly, 1979). Detailed analyses of the impact of litigation on assessment techniques may be found in Oakland & Laosa (1977), Reschly (1979), and Bersoff (1980). Hopefully, less stigmatizing and more accurate classification, when combined with procedural safeguards in determining effective remedial programming strategies in the least restrictive environment, will represent a helpful and defensible response to such lawsuits.

In conclusion, we hope that the information provided in this chapter has been helpful and that the opinions expressed represent "food for thought." While we are aware that other professionals may disagree with our opinions, we see a need for continuing dialogue on the issues within special education. While these issues can be vexing, their resolution will result in improved services to students.

REFERENCES

Allyon, T., & Roberts, M. Eliminating discipline problems by strengthening academic performance. *Journal of Applied Behavior Analysis*, 1978, *7*, 71–76.

Anastasi, A. *Psychological testing*, New York: MacMillan, 1976.

American Psychological Association. Ethical principles of psychologists. *American Psychologist*, 1981, *36*, 633–638.

Banas, N., & Wills, I. Prescriptions from WISC-R patterns. *Academic Therapy*, 1977, *13*, 241–246.

Banas, N., & Wills, I. Prescriptions from WISC-

R patterns. *Academic Therapy*, 1978, *13*, 365–370.

Bardon, J., & Bennett, V. *School psychology*. Englewood Cliffs: Prentice-Hall, 1974.

Bender L. *Bender motor gestalt test: Cards and manual of instructions*. New York: American Orthopsychiatric Association, 1946.

Bergan, J. *Behavioral consultation*. Columbus, Oh.: Charles E. Merrill, 1977.

Bersoff, D. Professional ethics and legal responsibilities: On the horns of a dilemma. *Journal of School Psychology*, 1975, *13*, 359–376.

Bersoff, D. *P. V. Riles:* Legal perspective.

School Psychology Review, 1980, *9,* 112–122.

Brigance, A. *Brigance diagnostic inventory of basic skills.* Woburn, Mass.: Curriculum Associates, 1976.

Brown, L., & Hammill, D. *Behavior rating profile: An ecological approach to behavioral assessment.* Austin, Tex.: Pro-Ed, 1978.

Burks, H. *Burks behavior rating scales.* Los Angeles: Western Psychological Services, 1977.

Campbell, D. *Manual for the Strong-Campbell interest inventory.* Stanford, Ca.: Stanford University Press, 1974.

Coulter, W. A. Adaptive behavior and professional disfavor: Controversies and trends for school psychologists. *School Psychology Review,* 1980, *9,* 67–74.

Coulter, W. A., & Morrow, H. W. A contemporary conception of adaptive behavior within the scope of psychological assessment. In W. A. Coulter & H. W. Morrow (Eds.), *Adaptive Behavior: Concepts and measurements.* New York: Grune & Stratton, 1978.

Cromwell, R., Blashfield, R., & Strauss, J. Criteria for classification systems. In N. Hobbs (Ed.), *Issues in the classification of children* (Vol. 1). San Francisco: Josey-Bass, 1975.

DeAvila, E., & Havassy, B. Piagetian alternative to IQ: Mexican-American study. In N. Hobbs (Ed.), *Issues in the classification of children* (Vol. 2). San Francisco: Josey-Bass, 1975.

Dickinson, D. Direct assessment of behavioral and emotional problems. *Psychology in the Schools,* 1978, *15,* 472–477.

Dickinson, D. The direct assessment: An alternative to psychometric testing. *Journal of Learning Disabilities,* 1980, *13,* 472–476.

Doll, E. *Vineland social maturity scale.* Circle Pines, Minn.: American Guidance Service, 1965.

Doll, E. *Preschool attainment record: Research edition.* Circle Pines, Minn.: American Guidance Service, 1966.

Dunn, L., & Markwardt, F. *Peabody individual achievement test: Manual.* Circle Pines, Minn.: American Guidance Service, 1970.

Elkind, D. Piagetian and psychometric conceptions of intelligence. *Harvard Educational Review,* 1969, *39,* 171–189.

Farb, J., & Throne, J. Improving the generalized mnemonic performance of a Down's Syndrome child. *Journal of Applied Behavior Analysis,* 1978, *11,* 413–417.

Federal Register. Privacy rights of parents and students. Regulations implementing Family Rights and Privacy Act of 1974. June 17, 1976, pp. 24670–24675.

Federal Register. Nondiscrimination on basis of handicap. Regulations implementing Section 504 of the Rehabilitation Act of 1973. May 4, 1977, pp. 22676–22702.

Federal Register. Education of handicapped children. Regulations implementing Education for All Handicapped Children Act of 1975. August 23, 1977, pp. 42474–42518.

Federal Register. Procedures for evaluating specific learning disabilities. December 29, 1977, pp. 65082–65085.

Frostig, M., Lefever, D., & Whittlesey, J. *The Marianne Frostig developmental test of visual perception.* Palo Alto, Ca.: Consulting Psychologists Press, 1964.

Gallagher, J., Forsythe, P., Ringelheim, D., & Weintraub, F. Funding patterns and labeling. In N. Hobbs (Ed.), *Issues in the classification of children* (Vol. 2). San Francisco: Josey-Bass, 1975.

Goodman, J. F. Is tissue the issue? A critique of SOMPA's models and tests. *School Psychology Digest,* 1979, *8,* 47–62.

Goodman, L., & Hammill, D. The effectiveness of Kephart-Getman activities in developing perceptual motor and cognitive skills. *Focus on Exceptional Children,* 1973, *4,* 1–9.

Grossman, H. (Ed.). *Manual on terminology and classification in mental retardation.* Washington, D.C.: American Association on Mental Deficiency, 1973.

Guilford, J. P. *The nature of human intelligence.* New York: McGraw-Hill, 1967.

Hallahan, D. P., & Kauffman, J. M. *Introduction to learning disabilities: A psycho-behavioral approach.* Englewood Cliffs: Prentice-Hall, 1976.

Hammill, D. Training visual perceptual processes. *Journal of Learning Disabilities,* 1972, *5,* 552–559.

Hammill, D., & Larsen, S. The effectiveness of psycholinguistic training. *Exceptional Children,* 1974, *41,* 5–14.

Hammill, D., & Larsen, S. The effectiveness of psycholinguistic training: A reaffirmation of position. *Exceptional Children,* 1978, *44,* 402–417.

Helton, G., Morrow, H., & Yates, J. Grouping for instruction: 1965, 1975, 1985. *The Reading Teacher,* 1977, *31,* 28–33.

Hobbs, N. *The futures of children.* San Francisco: Josey-Bass, 1975.

Jastak, J., & Jastak, S. *Wide range achievement test.* Wilmington, Del.: Guidance Associates of Delaware, 1978.

Kazdin, A. *Behavior modification in applied settings.* Homewood, Il.: Dorsey Press, 1980.

Kirk, S., & Kirk, W. *Psycholinguistic learning disabilities: Diagnosis and remediation.* Urbana, Il.: University of Illinois Press, 1971.

Kirk, S., McCarthy, J., & Kirk, W. *Illinois test of psycholinguistic abilities.* Urbana, Il.: University of Illinois Press, 1968.

Koppitz, E. *The Bender-Gestalt test for young children: Research and application, 1963–1973* (Vol. 2). New York: Grune & Stratton, 1975.

Koppitz, E. *The visual aural digit span test.* New York: Grune & Stratton, 1977.

Kuder, G. *Kuder occupational interest survey: General manual:* Chicago: Science Research Associates, 1966.

Lund, K., Foster, G., & McCall-Perez, F. The effectiveness of psycholinguistic training: A reevaluation. *Exceptional Children,* 1978, *44,* 310–321.

Lundell, K., Brown, W., & Evans, J. *Criterion test of basic skills.* Novato, Ca.: Academic Therapy Publications, 1976.

Meeker, M. Individualized curriculum based on intelligence test patterns. In R. Coop & K. White (Eds.), *Psychological concepts in the classroom.* New York: Harper & Row, 1973.

Mercer, J. R. In defense of racially and culturally nondiscriminatory assessment. *School Psychology Digest,* 1979, *8,* 80–115.(a)

Mercer, J. R. *Technical manual: System of multicultural pluralistic assessment.* New York: Psychological Corporation, 1979.(b)

Mercer, J., & Ysseldyke, J. Designing diagnostic-intervention programs. In T. Oakland (Ed.), *Psychological and educational assessment of minority children.* New York: Brunner-Mazel, 1977.

Monroe, V. Roles and status of school psychology. In G. D. Phye & D. J. Reschly (Eds.), *School psychology: Perspectives and issues.* New York: Academic Press, 1979.

National Association of School Psychologists. Principles for professional ethics. In *Membership directory.* Washington, D.C.: National Association of School Psychologists, 1978.

Oakland, T. O. Research on the adaptive behavior inventory for children and estimated learning potential. *School Psychology Digest,* 1979, *8,* 63–70.

Oakland, T., & Laosa, L. Professional, legislative, and judicial influences on psychoeducational assessment practices in schools. In T. Oakland (Ed.), *Psychological and educational assessment of minority children.* New York: Brunner-Mazel, 1977.

O'Leary, D. The assessment of psychopathology in children. In H. Quay & J. Werry (Eds.), *Psychopathological disorders of childhood.* New York: John Wiley & Sons, 1972.

Reschly, D. J. Nonbiased assessment. In G. D. Phye & D. J. Reschly (Eds.), *School psychology: Perspectives and issues.* New York: Academic Press, 1979.

Resnick, L., & Ford, W. The analysis of tasks for instruction: An information-processing approach. In C. Catania & T. Brigham (Eds.), *Handbook of applied behavior analysis: Social and instructional processes.* New York: Irvington, 1978.

Salvia, J., & Ysseldyke, J. *Assessment in special and remedial education.* Boston: Houghton Mifflin, 1978.

Terman, L., & Merrill, M. *Manual for the third revision of the Stanford-Binet intelligence scale (Form L-M).* Boston: Houghton Mifflin, 1973.

Valett, R. *A profile for the Stanford-Binet.* Palo Alto, Ca.: Consulting Psychologists Press, 1965.

Vance, H. Instructional strategies with the ITPA. *Academic Therapy,* 1975, *11,* 223–230.

Wahler, R., House, A., & Stambaugh, E. *Ecological assessment of child problem behavior.* New York: Pergamon Press, 1976.

Walker, H. *Walker problem behavior identification checklist.* Los Angeles: Western Psychological Services, 1976.

Wechsler, D. *Manual: The Wechsler intelligence scale for children-revised.* New York: Psychological Corporation, 1974.

Williams, R., & Anandam, K. *Cooperative classroom management.* Columbus, Oh.: Charles E. Merrill, 1973.

REFERENCE NOTES

1. Kicklighter, R., & Bailey, B. *Memorandum to school psychological services personnel.* Atlanta: Georgia Department of Education, March 21, 1980.

2. Bersoff, D. *Legal issues in the practice of psychology.* Workshop presented at the joint convention of the Kentucky Psychological Association, the Tennessee Psychological Association, and the Tennessee Association for Psychology in the Schools, Nashville, Tenn., October 31, 1979.

John Salvia
Paul T. Sindelar

10

Aptitude Testing and Alternative Approaches to Maximizing the Effects of Instruction

Human performance is variable. Often, particular variations are unwelcome in specific social situations and especially in the public schools. Schools have explicit and implicit standards to which all students are expected to conform. When pupils fail to meet enough of these standards or fail to meet one critical standard, the schools begin to look for reasons to explain the failure. Although several explanations are available, they are all either of two types. First, events or conditions outside the child may be responsible. For example, the child's teacher may be incompetent and not teach any of the children in the class effectively, or the community may have provided inadequate financial support so that classrooms are overcrowded and materials are lacking. More likely, however, is the assumption that the children themselves are damaged. And, because the children are imperfect, the schools are exonerated of any blame and can adopt the position of therapeutic agents rather than the causative factor. As anchors for concepts of imperfection, the schools have looked at extremely deviant individuals, severely retarded, psychotic, psychopathic, or dyslexic.[1] Although such extremely deviant persons have been excluded from the schools until recently, educators have adopted a position that assumes that there are continua for several deviations that range from extreme (e.g., profound mental retardation) to mild manifestations. Thus, humanity is conceptualized on a continuum of relative perfection that ranges from severe impairment through no visible impairment through superior functioning (e.g., retarded, normal, and gifted, respectively).

---

[1]Dyslexic is used in the strictest sense and refers to the very few individuals who are psychologically incapable of decoding visual symbols.

ASSESSMENT OF ABILITIES

Assessment by the schools usually follows this sequence:

1. Problem confirmation: Pupils are assessed to ascertain if their achievements in reading are really significantly discrepant from anticipated achievements.[2]
2. Diagnosis: A cause for the lack of achievement is sought. If it does not seem likely that the cause is external, then the search for the internal cause begins. For mildly handicapped pupils, this generally comes to deciding if a pupil is mildly retarded, mildly disturbed, or learning disabled (LD).
3. Therapeutic intervention: After pupils are diagnosed and classified as handicapped, an appropriate course of action is recommended. Three fundamental courses of action are available. First, the schools can attend to the goals of instruction. For example, they could attempt to bring the pupil up to the standards expected of most pupils. Such attempts involve either more intensive application of traditional approaches to instruction or "special" approaches. On the other hand, the schools can change their goals and adopt a set of standards and expectations more in line with the perceived capabilities of the pupil. For example, the schools may give up the objective of independent reading and adopt objectives of daily living skills. The second course of action is for the schools to attend to the presumed cause of poor performance. Such attention would entail some balance between ameliorating the cause (e.g., ability training) or compensation (e.g., stressing a different modality for learning). The third course is a combination of the first two. Here, a pupil would receive instruction, for example, in learning to pay closer attention and in phonics.

Aptitude or ability testing is important because test results are used in decisions of classification and in decisions of treatment. Thus, certain psychological constructs—abilities and aptitudes—play central roles in theories of educational deviance as well as theories of intervention. Special education has been especially influenced by inferred abilities and processes—constructs—that are believed to underlie surface behavior. Special educators have used intelligence, minimal cerebral dysfunction, perception and perceptual motor integration, psycholinguistic abilities, locus of control, and attention, etc., as a basis upon which to classify or to treat pupils. Definitions contained in federal laws and regulations clearly substantiate this assertion. Table 10-1 contains relevant excerpts from definitions for Public Law 94-142 (*Federal Register,* August 23, 1977, p. 42478), which imply that intelligence and various basic psychological processes must be assessed in order to classify pupils as handicapped.

When definitions of handicapping conditions are couched in terms of abilities, and when these definitions are used to determine eligibility for educational services, several assumptions are implicit. The most fundamental of these are (1) the abilities (or lack thereof) cause the disorder; (2) the abilities can be reliably and validly assessed; (3) pupils can be reliably and validly sorted on the basis of the

---

[2]Note that what is anticipated varies.

Table 10-1
Relevant Definitions from 94-142

---

(4) "Mentally retarded" means significantly subaverage general intellectual functioning existing concurrently with deficits in adaptive behavior and manifested during the developmental period, which adversely affects a child's educational performance.

(8) "Seriously emotionally disturbed" is defined as follows:

(i) The term means a condition exhibiting one or more of the following characteristics over a long period of time and to a marked degree, which adversely affects educational performance:

(A) An inability to learn which cannot be explained by intellectual sensory, or health factors. . . .

(9) "Specific learning disability" means a disorder in one or more of the basic psychological processes involved in understanding and using language, spoken or written, which may manifest itself in an imperfect ability to listen, think, speak, read, write, spell, or to do mathematical calculations. . . . The term does not include children who have learning problems which are primarily the result of visual, hearing, or motor handicaps, of mental retardation, or of environmental, cultural, or economic disadvantage.

---

assessed abilities; and (4) classification of pupils on the basis of abilities (as opposed to surface behavior) results in efficacious treatment.

Hypothetical Abilities Cause Handicaps

To view aptitudes or abilities as a cause of behavior is common. Yet such a view rests on a tautology. Several writers have pointed out the error. Neisworth (1969) argued the distinction between abilities as a convenient description and abilities as an explanation. A number of observations (e.g., works for 5 seconds, regularly loses place while reading, forgets which word to spell on the quiz, fails to finish tasks, wanders around room) may be summarized (e.g., inattentive, distractable). Similarly, if pupils consistently earn poor grades and low scores on standardized achievement tests, they may be described as slow learners. Skinner (1953) argued that such summaries or descriptions become nouns (e.g., distractability or learning ability), and these nouns become the cause of the behaviors that were initially described. "The label that serves only to describe the behavior becomes the instrument of a very deceptive and fallacious explanation" (Neisworth, 1969, p. 34). The label becomes the cause.[3] Thus, pupils wander around the classroom, lose their places, etc., because they lack attention; they earn poor grades because they lack learning ability or academic aptitude.

Tests of ability or aptitude only describe a pupil's performance by comparing that performance to the performances of other pupils of similar demographic characteristics. Thus, tests of ability make norm-referenced comparisons, which offer a numerical description. No test of ability explains the behavior described because descriptive statements cannot cause themselves. Thus, tested abilities do not cause handicaps although they may well describe them.

---

[3]Technically, this error is called reification.

Abilities Can Be Reliably and Validly Assessed

Intelligence

Intelligence plays a key role in the classification of mildly handicapped pupils. State education codes often specify that intelligence quotients must be below some point (usually between 85 and 68 or one or two standard deviations below the mean) on individually administered tests before a pupil can be considered mentally retarded and above that point before a pupil may be considered eligible for categorical services for the learning disabled or emotionally disturbed. Thus, valid measurement should be of high priority.

There are several problems in measuring intelligence accurately. For example, there are substantial differences in how intelligence is conceptualized, and these differences are apparent in various theories of intelligence. Some theorists (e.g., Spearman, 1923) ascribe to a "g" theory of intelligence—an undifferentiated ability that is reflected in a variety of tasks. Others ascribe to dualistic theories of intelligence: crystalized-fluid (Cattell, 1971), process-product (Newland, 1980); and level I and level II (Jensen, 1969). Still others subscribe to multifactor models (Guilford, 1967; Thurstone, 1938). Finally, there are developmental theories of cognitive development of which Piaget's (1950) and Bruner's (1964) probably receive the most citations and greatest lip service. There is no generally accepted theory of intelligence, although the "g" theory appears passé.

A second related problem is that the tests used to measure intelligence are not interchangeable either in the behaviors sampled or in their technical adequacy. Unfortunately, most tests of intelligence are designed to assess "g" (e.g., the Stanford-Binet, the Pictorial Test of Intelligence, the Wechsler Scales), but they assess it in different ways. Salvia and Ysseldyke (1978, pp. 222–229) describe 13 types of items that appear on tests of intelligence: discrimination, generalization, motor behavior, general information, vocabulary, induction, comprehension, sequencing, detail recognition, analogies, abstract reasoning, memory, and pattern completion. As they noted, no test of intelligence consistently samples all the types of items, and some assess only one type. In the *Eighth Mental Measurement Yearbook,* Buros (1978) lists 235 published tests of intelligence. No two contain the same mix of items; no two measure intelligence in quite the same way. This disparity in behavior samples is not trivial. Scores from two of the most widely used tests of intelligence, the Wechsler Intelligence Scale for Children–Revised (WISC-R) and the Stanford-Binet (1972 norms edition) correlate only .7. The tests cannot be used interchangeably because children earn scores on them that are quite different. The various tests also differ quite a bit in the adequacy of their normative samples and estimates of their reliability. It is widely believed that test authors and publishers should provide potential users with information about their tests' technical characteristics. A joint committee of the American Psychological Association, the American Education Research Association, and the National Council for Measurement in Education (1974) viewed this as an essential requirement for all tests. Yet, some prominent tests of intelligence (e.g., the 1972 Stanford-Binet) report no applicable estimates of reliability. Other tests report reliability estimates that indicate inadequate levels of accuracy (e.g., the quick test). A few report excellent reliability (e.g., WISC-R).

Perceptual Development

Tests of perceptual development are routinely used in the classification of mildly handicapped pupils to diagnose the presence of brain damage, emotional disturbance, or specific learning disabilities. All of the tests that are currently available have very serious shortcomings that should restrict or preclude their use. Perhaps the most serious flaw is that of the general applicability of test results. Humans vary considerably on perceptual tasks, but their variability is highly task specific. Performance is affected by such factors as task requirements, stimuli (e.g., size, complexity, familiarity), and setting (Cruickshank, Bice, Wallen, & Lynch, 1965; Flavell, 1977; Rubin, 1969). Thus, the results of perceptual tests are generalizable neither to the same skill measured under different conditions nor to different skills. While modern theorists have duly noted the tremendous importance that the method of measurement has in the results obtained from perceptual testing (Flavell, 1977), current devices have not taken such effects into consideration.

A related issue is the limited conceptualization of visual perception used by test developers. With the exception of the Purdue Perceptual Motor Survey, the most commonly used tests require only copying designs (e.g., Bender Visual-Motor Gestalt Test; Memory for Designs Test; Development Test of Visual Motor Integration) or some form of drawing (e.g., Developmental Test of Visual Motor Perception). Tests of visual perception used in the school seldom directly assess (1) the perception of motion, patterns, figure-background relationships, or depth; (2) pursuit, the following of a moving object (although tracking an object with the eye may be assessed); (3) complex perceptual-motor integrations; or (4) perceptual speed. In essence, the content validity of the tests used in schools must be questioned.

The last fundamental shortcoming of these tests is their technical inadequacy. The norm samples appear to be unrepresentative, and test reliabilities tend to be poor (see Salvia & Ysseldyke, 1978, pp. 463–465). Thus, even if the content validity were acceptable, the inadequate norms and reliability should preclude the use of these tests in applied settings.

Psycholinguistic Abilities

The importance of psycholinguistic abilities in the diagnosis of mildly handicapped pupils dates primarily from the development of the Illinois Test of Psycholinguistic Abilities (ITPA). In many ways, ITPA and psycholinguistic abilities are interchangeable in special education, although other procedures are available for less formal assessment of language (e.g., Carrow Elicited Language Inventory or the Northwestern Syntax Screening Test). Critical reviews of the ITPA are available elsewhere (e.g., Salvia & Ysseldyke, 1978), but three aspects of the ITPA are noteworthy. First, the obtained reliabilities for each subtest (the unit recommended for diagnostic purposes) are inadequate. Nine of 96 estimates of internal consistency exceed .9, while none of the 96 estimates of stability exceed .86. Second, the norms are not representative. They were developed on normal children only; handicapped children were systematically excluded. Moreover, the children in the normative groups were selected only from Illinois and Wisconsin. Third, content validity is lacking. A simple illustration is the grammatic closure subtest. Designed to assess a pupil's competence in using the correct grammatic form automatically, the test fails to assess relative or demonstrative pronouns, auxiliary verbs, adverbs, articles, descriptive adjectives, linguistic transformations, imperatives, or subjunctive mood, among others. Stress is placed on irregular morphology (e.g., one sheep, two sheep; leaf, leaves).

DIFFERENTIAL DIAGNOSIS

The basic issue of differential diagnosis is whether school personnel can accurately sort pupils into various categories of handicap; specifically, whether the school personnel charged with classifying pupils can tell if a student is retarded, learning disabled, maladjusted, disturbed,[4] or perhaps brain injured,[4] using the typical psychometric batteries.

Tests of intelligence are used in differential diagnosis in two ways. First, they are used to distinguish educable mentally retarded individuals from other handicapped pupils with normal intelligence (e.g., learning disabled students). While some overlap in scores earned by groups of educable mentally retarded (EMR) pupils and groups of pupils with other handicaps would be expected since retardation requires more than just low scores on intelligence tests, we should find marked mean differences overall. Gajar (1979) compared the performances of 122 emotionally disturbed pupils, 135 learning disabled pupils, and 121 mentally retarded pupils. She found significant mean differences in IQ among the three groups; as expected, EMRs earned lower IQs than did learning disabled pupils and emotionally disturbed (ED) pupils. Using different methodology, Peterson and Hart (1978) found similar results: WISC-R full-scale IQ discriminated among groups of mentally retarded pupils, children with learning disabilities, emotionally disturbed pupils, culturally disadvantaged students, and slow learners. While mean differences do shed light on how intelligence test scores separate groups of students, they do not provide much information on how useful such scores are in making decisions for individual students. In 1972, Hoffmann studied the extent to which IQ actually predicted classification of pupils as educable mentally retarded and their subsequent placement in special education. Using a stratified random sample of 113 school districts in Iowa, he analyzed data from 4335 pupils who attended public school and were being assessed for the first time. He found correlations of .4 between the psychologists' recommendations and pupil IQ and between actual placement and pupil IQ. Hoffmann also provided some interesting frequency counts. At the time he collected data in Iowa, the cutoff score for mental retardation was an IQ of 80; a score of 79 or less indicated eligibility for placement as educable mentally retarded. He found 424 pupils with IQs of 79 or less; 199 were recommended for placement while 225 were not. Hoffman also found that 17 pupils with IQs above 80 were recommended for placement.

A second way intelligence is used in classification is less direct. Many theorists believe that uneven performance on the subtests of measures of intelligence indicates pathology. The phenomenon, generally termed "scatter," is believed by

---

[4]A state may require a physician or specialist (i.e., psychiatrist or neurologist) to make the official diagnosis for these classifications.

many to indicate brain damage (e.g., Clements, 1971) or learning disability (e.g., Bannatyne, 1968). The diagnostic utility of scatter has been rebuked on statistical grounds (Cronbach, 1960; Salvia & Ysseldyke, 1978) and on conceptual grounds (Yates, 1954). Still, its attraction lingers on. Recently, Kaufman (1976) analyzed the standardization sample of the WISC-R and found that about two thirds of the children in the norm groups had subtest scores that differed from about two to three standard deviations (i.e., 5–9 scale score points). Despite the great variability in normal populations, it appears that school personnel still rely on scatter as an indication of pathology. For example, Gajar (1979) found that children diagnosed as learning disabled had greater WISC-R scatter than pupils diagnosed as either emotionally disturbed or mentally retarded. Salvia and Ysseldyke (1978, p. 410) summed up the situation when they stated that many handicapped individuals

[O]ften exhibit large intraindividual differences on a profile. . . . The difficulty is that persons who are brain-injured, disturbed, or disadvantaged sometimes do not exhibit scatter while normal individuals occasionally do exhibit scatter. Thus, while profile scatter may distinguish groups of individuals, it does not typically distinguish individuals (Dunn, 1968; Yates, 1954).

It must be noted that tests of intelligence have not been useful with groups of children euphemistically labeled as culturally disadvantaged/deprived. The difficulties in discriminating between ignorance and stupidity are generally well known and have been discussed at length (e.g., Mercer, 1979; Oakland, 1977). Most introductory texts recount the injustices that result from inappropriately testing ethnically or racially different and/or poor children as well as the court cases involving the testing of minority students: *Arreola v. Santa Ana Board of Education: Diana v. California State Board of Education; Stewart et al. v. Philips et al.; Larry P. v. Riles.* Most readers are familiar with federal laws and regulations requiring nonbiased assessment of handicapped pupils such as Section 504 of PL 93-112 and PL 94-142. It is unfortunate that the laws demanding nondiscriminatory assessment offer no tests or procedures whereby such assessments may be achieved.

The Bender Visual-Motor Gestalt Test has been used frequently through the years to compare various groups of handicapped persons. Koppitz (1963) reviewed and summarized most of these comparisons. She noted that children with learning disabilities and educational handicaps scored lower than normal students. There are *key indicators* used in scoring the Bender-Gestalt, which are particular responses that are more highly associated with particular disorders than age scores or number of errors. Key indicators for minimal brain damage can discriminate groups of normal or disturbed pupils from those with brain damage. Key indicators for emotionality can distinguish groups of disturbed pupils from normals.

Less research is available on psycholinguistic abilities. Kirk and Kirk (1971) reviewed several studies that documented different profiles for various exceptionality patterns of strengths and weaknesses within profile types.

The major problem with all research showing mean differences or profile differences is overlap. As shown in Figure 10-1, two groups may have different means but still have considerable overlap. Just because there are mean differences on previously diagnosed groups does not allow one to infer that a person can be

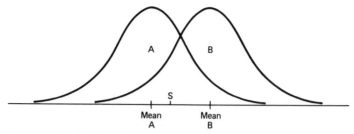

Fig. 10-1. Overlapping distributions can result in incorrect classification of a person despite significant differences between group means.

reliably classified on the basis of a score on the test. For example, in Figure 10-1, if a person earns a score, S, on the test, in which group does the person belong? One cannot tell. Although it is more probable that the person belongs in distribution A, it is still very likely that he or she could belong to distribution B. Thus, a finding that a test will produce statistically significant differences between established groups does not lead to the conclusion that the test is useful in diagnosing individual cases.

EFFICACIOUS TREATMENTS

The assumption that classification by abilities results in efficacious treatments is multifaceted. It can be dealt with as a "state of the field" issue. Given the status of ability assessment and current classification systems, can special educators use data from ability tests to affect instruction positively? Essentially, this is a question of aptitude-by-treatment interaction (ATI). The basic presumption in special education is that while handicapped pupils do not exhibit satisfactory

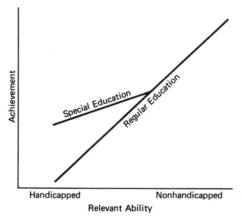

Fig. 10-2. The aptitude-by-treatment that special educators hope for.

achievement under traditional or regular educational arrangements, they can progress satisfactorily under "special" arrangements. As shown in Figure 10-2, if left in regular education, pupils with low ability (e.g., intelligence or perception, etc.) will have low achievement; however, if given special education, the students will achieve significantly higher.

Several reviews of research are available that shed light on this question. Kirk (1964), Guskin and Spicker (1968), and Sindelar and Deno (1978) reviewed the research on the education of the mentally retarded. To date, there is really no research that supports the notion that either self-contained classes or resource rooms for the educable mentally retarded offer any academic benefits above regular classrooms. Hirshoren, Schultz, Manton, and Henderson (1970) reviewed the research on the education of the emotionally disturbed. Although there are methodological problems, the results of these studies suggest that special education is helpful academically and socially. Finally, Sindelar and Deno (1978) examined the efficacy of resource-room programming for learning disabled and emotionally disturbed pupils. Their conclusions support resource room programming.

When considering special education within an ATI framework, the particular abilities involved as aptitudes are seldom consistent within handicaps. For example, a pupil may be learning disabled because of impulsivity, inattentiveness, faulty perception, or inadequate psycholinguistic development. Research examining the efficacy of special education does not allow the precise examination of ATI because various aptitudes are lumped together. Similarly, the treatments in ATI research are seldom comparable to each other, but are often lumped together as "special education" or "a phonics approach." Consequently, it is difficult to ascertain which aptitudes are critical for which treatments. Fortunately, there are several fine-grained reviews that summarize the research on particular ATIs.

The most extensive examination of ATIs was conducted by Cronbach and Snow (1977) who wrote that "Instead of finding general intellectual/mental abilities irrelevant to schooling, we find nearly ubiquitous evidence that general measures predict amount learned or rate of learning on both" (p. 496). The types of instructional interventions that interact with general ability have some relevance for special education but one should not expect direct application to handicapped pupils.

Even though abilities such as memory or spatial ability have not typically produced meaningful interactions within the normal population (Cronbach & Snow, 1977), special educators have been more concerned with splinter or fractional abilities such as form perception or particular psycholinguistic abilities. The most recent comprehensive review of ATI research involving these abilities was conducted by Arter and Jenkins (1979) who noted that attempts to train such abilities have not been successful.

> [D]ifferential diagnosis is said to reveal individual learning styles which, in turn, determine special instructional methodologies and materials. To date, there are 14 reported efforts to improve beginning reading by matching instructional materials and procedures to children's modality strengths. In none of these was reading instruction improved. . . . (p. 547)

Summary

Using test-identified abilities to classify mildly handicapped students is a widely accepted practice. Yet, upon careful examination there is little to recommend it. The assumptions underlying this practice are seldom met. There are difficulties with the logic of treating abilities and aptitudes as entities capable of causing handicaps. With the notable exception of tests of intelligence, tests of ability and aptitude generally lack validity. Moreover, the tests are not capable of discriminating individuals as handicapped or normal although they can regularly discriminate between groups that are already classified. In special education, the treatment component of ATI has often appeared to be aimed at groups of children rather than individual pupils. Program adjustments on the basis of individual progress are seldom discussed. Pupil outcome (e.g., achievement) is used to evaluate the magnitude of the ATI rather than to fine-tune individual programs. In short, in ATI research in special education, the emphasis has been on abilities. In contrast to this approach is one in which programs are regarded as hypotheses (Deno & Mirkin, 1977), and attempts are made to validate the hypotheses. Assessment in this alternative approach focuses on program validation and not program prescription. The results of teaching programs are operationalized, and frequent assessment of performance is made to determine if the teaching program is having the desired effect upon the child's behavior. This process, unlike the ATI approach, allows for the refinement and modification of the teaching program, based upon performance, until the data show that the child has mastered the skill or is making adequate progress toward mastery. Precision teaching and data-based modification are two recently developed techniques that focus on *post hoc* program validation, since programs are validated on the basis of pupil change. These techniques are potentially quite important, for there is little evidence to support the current implicit beliefs in ATI as applied in special education.

PRECISION TEACHING

According to Gaasholt (1970), precision teaching involves five essential steps, of which the final three constitute a process for maximizing the effects of a teaching program. These steps are (1) pinpointing behavior; (2) obtaining a daily record of the behavior; (3) recording teacher behavior as it relates to student performance; (4) analyzing data to decide what changes in teacher behavior might affect pupil performances; and (5) making one change at a time, then re-evaluating.

Pinpointing Behavior

To pinpoint a behavior, three pieces of information are necessary: the movement, the cycle, and the direction. Movement is a precise description of the behavior involved. Thus, reading aloud becomes saying words; solving arithmetic problems becomes writing numbers; and spelling becomes writing letters. Cycle refers to the direct object of the movement. In the first example *words* are the cycle of the pinpoint "saying words." In the same way, *numbers* and *letters* are the cycles in the two pinpoints, "writing numbers" and "writing letters." Direction refers to the acceleration or deceleration of change. The three examples above are acceleration targets; direction is indicated by adding the word *more* to the movement cycle. To improve reading, the pinpoint is "says words more;" to improve arithmetic, the pinpoint is "writing numbers more." For inappropriate social behavior and errors in academic performance, deceleration pinpoints are written by adding the word *less*. For a child who talks out of turn too frequently, the "says words" acceleration pinpoint may be rewritten as "says words less."

In addition to specifying the movement, cycle, and direction, pinpoints must meet three other criteria. First, the pinpoint must contain movement. While the pinpoint "says words" obviously does contain movement, the pinpoint "sits still" does not. Consequently, "sits still" is not considered an appropriate pinpoint. Second, the movement must be under the child's control. So, while "says words" is controllable, "dilates pupils" usually is not and cannot be considered an appropriate pinpoint. Third, movements must be repeatable. "Says words" is repeatable; "sits still" is not since it lacks a precise beginning and ending point. In summary, movement cycles must contain movement, be under the child's control, and be repeatable in order for the pinpoint to be properly specified.

Daily Recording of Behavior

Once a movement cycle is pinpointed, a daily sample of the performance is taken and a record is maintained. All behaviors are expressed as rates (or frequencies, in the language of precision teaching) and displayed on the Standard Behavior Chart (SBC). Precision teachers believe that frequency is a behavior "compare-all" (Lindsley, 1972) in the sense that all behaviors have frequency and that any two behaviors can be compared using frequency. Frequency, of course, is calculated by dividing the number of behaviors by the number of minutes during which the behavior was observed. Assuming that an individual is awake for roughly 1000 minutes each day, the lowest possible frequency is 1/1000 or .001. The highest frequency of any human behavior, saying sounds in fluent speech, is 1000 movements per minute. The SBC, designed to accomodate any frequency of human behavior, ranges from 1000 Movements/minute (M/m) to .001 M/m, through six logarithmic cycles.

Since precision teachers regard frequency as the behavioral compare-all, change in frequency serves as the measure of behavioral change. In order for equal changes in frequency to appear as equal distances on the chart, a ratio scale is used on the Standard Behavior Chart. The scale of the SBC is logarithmic; consequently, the SBC is sometimes called six-cycle paper or, in the language of precision teachers, "multiply-divide" paper. A modified version of the SBC is shown in Figure 10-3. On the SBC, the distance from 10 to 20 is equivalent to the distance from 100 to 200, since the ratios—10:20 and 100:200—are the same. In fact, the distance between any two numbers in a 1:2 ratio is the same, regardless of where the numbers appear on the chart. The same is true of any pairs of numbers with equivalent ratios. Thus, doubling (or tripling or quadrupling) a frequency produces the same amount of change regardless of the original frequency. In this way, equivalent changes in rate appear as equal distances.

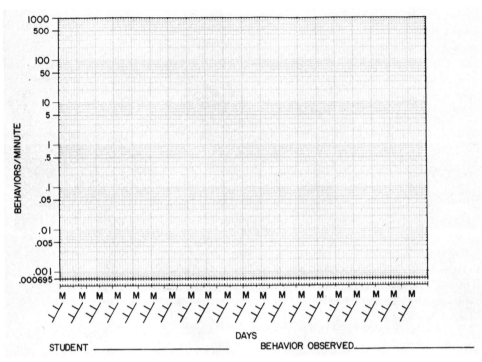

Fig. 10-3. Six-cycle "multiply-divide" paper.

Recording Teacher Behavior in Relation to Pupil Behavior

Once a baseline of behavior has been established, an instructional program is introduced and assessed by comparing baseline frequency to the frequency obtained during the instructional phase. From this perspective, instructional programs are conceptualized as best-guesses or hypotheses (Deno & Mirkin, 1977) and not as unquestionable and proven solutions. Bijou (1972) described the attitude with which precision teachers approach their work as the "let's try doing something else kind of thing." When data suggest that an instructional program has not produced the anticipated rate of change, modifications are required. Precision teaching allows for these judgments by relating modifications in teaching programs to the effects they produce on the child's behavior.

The precision-teaching technology includes specific recommendations about the kinds of changes that should be made when data indicate that a child's performance has not been improving adequately. In such cases, pinpoints are sliced into component skills, and instruction is continued at the level of component skills until these have been mastered. For example, if a child were experiencing difficulty in learning addition facts, sums less than 10, this pinpoint could be sliced into its components: +1 facts, sums less than 10; +2 facts, sums less than 10; +3 facts, sums less than 10; and so forth. The child's performance is then assessed on each of these component pinpoints, and instruction begins on those she or he has not mastered. When the child masters all of the component skills, assessment (and instruction, if necessary) would be conducted again on the original pinpoint.

It should be emphasized at this point that the effect of any modification in the child's instructional program can be assessed in much the same way. Although precision teachers advocate the task-analytic slicing of pinpoints, slicing is by no means the only modification amenable to assessment. For example, the effects of a modification as simple as changing the schedule of reinforcement can be evaluated in this way. When the initial data indicate that the child is not making adequate progress, the frequency of reinforcement may be increased (or a new reinforcer chosen). If the change proves effective, then data points collected subsequent to the change will show a steeper slope than the slope of the data points in the first instructional phase.

Prompting and the fading of prompts are two important and frequently used instructional strategies. The essential question with regard to prompting is whether the prompt can be faded without disrupting the child's performance. Data collected after the first step in a fading procedure is begun can be compared to the data during the original phase. If the rate of improvement is similar in the two phases, then the first step is considered successful: the child has maintained his or her growth even though a less pronounced prompt has been used. If, on the other hand, the rate of improvement decreases, it may be concluded that too large a step has been taken and that an intermediate step is required.

The effects of overlearning are well known: transfer and generalization are facilitated, and retention is improved. These effects can also be assessed with precision-teaching techniques. After an initial criterion on a particular skill has been reached, performance checks can be conducted to determine the extent to which the child has maintained performance level. When performance has not been maintained, additional instruction beyond the initial level of mastery is required. Continuous feedback from performance checks allows a determination of the adequacy of the overlearning strategy in maintaining the child's proficiency on a particular skill. The amount and the nature of overlearning necessary for maintenance can be empirically determined in this manner.

Generalization is another illustration of an important educational outcome that may be evaluated using precision-teaching techniques. Strategies for promoting generalization include instruction on a variety of stimuli, instruction in many different contexts or with many different teachers, and modification of the training environment so that it is as similar as possible to the environment in which the response is intended to occur. The effect of these procedures is essentially the same: there is increased likelihood that the response will occur in noninstructional settings or in response to stimuli that were not part of the instructional set. The effects of these strategies for promoting generalization may be assessed by obtaining measures of the child's performance not only in the instructional environment but also in the environments to which the behavior is intended to generalize. When growth is evident in the data from both environments, it may be concluded that generalization has occurred and that the strategy has been effective. On the other hand, when growth is evident in the training environment but not in the generalization environment, then the use of a different strategy for generalization is indicated.

Some teaching programs involve response generalization in the sense that instruction on some items in the instructional set facilitates the acquisition of other items. Teaching basic arithmetic facts illustrates what is meant by response generalization. Addition facts may be organized in pairs, so that each pair has the same two addends. The algorithms 2 + 4 and 4 + 2 represent one such pair. Teaching the 2 + 4 = 6 fact does not guarantee that the child will automatically respond correctly to the 4 + 2 = 6 fact (or to the $\frac{\begin{array}{r}2\\ +4\end{array}}{6}$ algorithm, for that matter), but he or she may. Teaching an operation (Becker, Englemann, & Thomas, 1971), in this case the commutative property of addition, increases the likelihood that the child will generalize from 2 + 4 = 6 to 4 + 2 = 6. To assess the extent of response generalization, performance from two domains, the instructional and the generalization, must be sampled. If performance has improved on both sets after instruction on half of the items, then generalization has occurred. If, on the other hand, performance improves on the instructional set only, generalization has not occurred; a tactic such as teaching the operation is indicated.

These examples are not meant to exhaust the kinds of strategies that may be assessed using precision-teaching techniques. Rather, they are intended to illustrate how these techniques may be used with strategies other than slicing pinpoints. The effects of these same strategies and others are also amenable to assessment with data-based teaching techniques.

It must be emphasized that thinking about teaching programs as hypotheses does not free the teacher from the responsibility of developing well-conceptualized instructional programs. Also, data suggesting that a program has not produced the desired rate of improvement do not imply that the entire program must be abandoned. Such variables as placement, amount of instruction, pupil–teacher ratio, or schedule of reinforcement may be manipulated with the intention of producing desired rates of change. In any case, the intent of this process is to relate changes in teacher behavior to changes in pupil performance. Application of this process will presumably result in successive refinements and modifications of teaching programs until a satisfactory rate of improvement is achieved. The assessment of aptitudes and the search for aptitude-by-treatment interactions presently offers no such guarantee.

Analyzing Data

Improvement over baseline frequency may be assessed in one of two ways. First, a line may be drawn to represent the trend of the data using either the split-middle trend estimation technique (White, 1971) or the freehand procedure (Pennypacker, Koeing, & Lindsley, 1972). (Because variability is reduced when points are plotted on the SBC, lines drawn with the freehand method approximate the lines drawn with the split-middle estimation procedure.) A trend line may be extended into the treatment phase to predict subsequent performance. White (1971) documented the predictive validity of lines drawn with the split-middle procedure; the frequency of behavior during subsequent phases may be compared to the baseline projection to determine whether change has occurred and whether the change is in the desired direction.

The second strategy for assessing change over baseline involves establishing a goal and projecting a line from the baseline data to the goal, representing an idealized course of progress. Two dimensions of a goal must be specified: the desired frequency and the anticipated length of time for the change to occur. On the SBC, the intersection of the desired frequency and the anticipated date of completion represents the goal or aim. Points falling above a line from a measure of current performance to an aim indicate adequate progress for an acceleration target; points below the line signal the possible need for program change. (The opposite relationship holds for a deceleration target.) The advantage of using an aim over projecting the baseline trend is that behavior change is assessed against an absolute criterion, the goal, while the trend-projection procedure fails to address the question, "How much change is enough?" and consequently involves assessment against a relative criterion. One disadvantage in using aims is the difficulty involved in establishing appropriate and realistic goals. Although researchers are accumulating information about appropriate *levels* of performance (Starlin & Starlin, 1973, for academic tasks; Patterson, Reid, Jones, & Conger, 1975, for social behaviors, for example), less is known about anticipated time for goal attainment. Consequently, data points falling below the progress line of an acceleration target may indicate either an inappropriate goal or an inadequate program.

It must be emphasized here that when a change is made in an initial program, the process of data collection and analysis must continue. However, to assess changes in the initial program validly, the original trend projections or aim lines are no longer useful and must be redrawn. The trend during an instructional phase may be drawn using the same procedures as described above and projected into a new instructional phase for the purpose of evaluating change. Alternately, a new aim line may be drawn, parallel to the original aim, from the data in the first instructional phase. In this way, expectation about rate of improvement is unchanged. The effects of all subsequent modifications are consequently evaluated against the original criterion.

Making One Change at a Time

Precision teachers advocate making only one change in an instructional program at a time. When only one change is made, changes in the child's performance presumably reflect the effects of that modification. In this way, teachers are afforded precise information about the effects of particular manipulations. As data on program modifications accumulate, teachers develop an empirical base that they may use to determine a generalized set of effective strategies. On the other hand, when confronted with a difficult and persistent instructional or management problem, teachers may be more concerned with eliminating the problem than with determining the elements of the program that produced the change. In that case, the importance of making one change at a time is secondary to the need to eliminate a demanding, time-consuming, and taxing problem.

The Unique Features of Precision Teaching

The unique features of precision teaching include its emphasis on frequency as an outcome measure, the use of the Standard Behavior Chart, and the projection of baseline trends with the split-middle trend estimation technique for the purpose of assessing program effectiveness. However, precision teaching is not the only technique available that allows for *post hoc* program validation. Data-based program modification (Deno & Mirkin, 1977), or data-based teaching (DBT), is designed to accomplish this same goal, without relying exclusively on a single measure of behavior or one particular strategy for displaying data.

Data-Based Teaching

Deno and Mirkin (1977) described the procedures of DBT as they apply to the entire process of special education intervention in considerable detail. Three features differentiate DBT from precision teaching: the measurement of performance on terminal objectives, so that the dependent measure remains constant throughout an instructional program; the measurement of progress (as opposed to performance) through an instructional program or curriculum; and the application and validation of a standard decision-making rule.

Dependent measures.   Rate of responding is as important a dependent measure in DBT as it is in precision teaching. However, in DBT, rate is not the exclusive measure of performance nor is the SBC the only method for displaying the data. However, the most critical difference between DBT and precision teaching is the behavior (or behaviors) from which rates are obtained. Typically, in precision teaching, a global skill is task analyzed, and measures are obtained on each of the component skills. For example, in a reading curriculum in which words are introduced with each new section, precision teachers would obtain frequencies for each set. Consequently, the sample of words from which the rate measures are obtained changes as the child masters or reaches his or her aim on the individual sets. No overall measure of the child's growth on the universe of items is obtained.

In DBT, on the other hand, the child's growth may be measured by assessing performance on the entire universe of items and not on individual sets of words. In this way, the dependent measure with which the instructional program is assessed does not change during the course of treatment. The overall pattern of growth on a particular skill is displayed, and program effects are not confounded with changes in the dependent measure. Deno and Mirkin (1977) refer to this assessment strategy as the measurement of vital signs or performance on the terminal objective.

Another example may help to illustrate the significance of this strategy: in measuring the effects of a program to increase oral reading fluency, samples from individual stories or sections of the curriculum would reflect not only the improvement the child makes, but also the increasing difficulty of the material from which the child reads. Consequently, growth would not appear as clearly as it would if the difficulty of the material were controlled. By defining a terminal objective, readability would be controlled and improvement would not be confounded with increasing difficulty of the reading material. The reading fluency of a second-grader may be assessed by using passages from stories at the end of the second-grade reader. Since difficulty would be controlled, changes in fluency would represent increased skill. The source of the passages is important for a second reason: performance in the last few stories of a second-grade reader represents the terminal objective of the second-grade reading program. Throughout the year, instruction is designed to increase the child's fluency in the material from which the assessment is made.

Unlike precision teaching, DBT sometimes focuses on progress through an

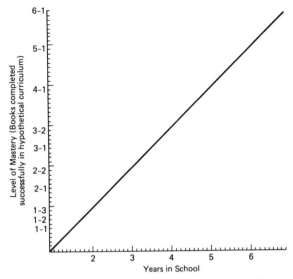

Fig. 10-4. Progress chart with idealized course of progress through curriculum.

instructional program or curriculum. Progress charting is illustrated by the chart that appears in Figure 10-4. On the ordinate of the chart, books from a hypothetical reading curriculum serve as the unit of measurement; along the abscissa, the 6 years, divided into month-long units, of an elementary school program are shown. The diagonal line across the chart represents the idealized course of progress a student would follow to complete or master each step in the curriculum on time. The spacing of the books up the left side of the chart reflects the hypothesized amount of time required to complete or master each, as implied by the organization of the curriculum. Thus, by January of the first grade, book 1-1 should be mastered; by March, book 1-2; and by May, book 1-3.

A progress chart like the one in Figure 10-4 permits a comparison of a child's progress against the progress required for the successful mastery of the curriculum. Points falling below the line indicate unsatisfactory progress; if persistent, they may signal the need for special education intervention. Points falling on or above the line suggest that the child is making adequate progress and that the objectives of the curriculum will be mastered by the end of the sixth grade without special or supplementary instruction. On a progress chart, each data point indicates level of mastery; jumps indicate the mastery of new objectives. Mastery may be operationalized in many ways, though reaching a fluency aim in a particular story or section of the curriculum is commonly used (Haring, Lovitt, Eaton, & Hanson, 1978).

The relationship between the task-analytic or objective-specific measurement of precision teaching and the progress measurement of DBT should now be clear. While precision teachers focus on the attainment of individual objectives, data-based teachers are more likely to focus on the overall pattern of attainment through the entire curriculum. Where attainment of specific aims may be critical to the assessment of programming for remedial students, it affords no overall look at the child's progress through the entire curriculum. Progress recording, as in the illustration above, may be used as a vital sign to signal the need for special or supplementary instruction or, for that matter, the need to terminate a special program.

Progress recording may be used with individual instructional programs when those programs are arranged as a sequence of instructional objectives. For example, the steps in a program designed to teach children to brush their teeth may be listed on the ordinate of a progress chart. When the child masters a particular step, his or her data point jumps up a unit to indicate mastery. When the anticipated length of the program can be specified, a line representing an idealized course of progress can be drawn. The line would represent the skill attainment of a hypothetical child who would master all of the component skills in the desired amount of time. The effects of the training program can then be assessed by contrasting actual progress through the skill sequence with this idealized course of progress.

Decision making. In DBT, whether performance or progress is used as the dependent measure, growth is assessed against an expected-progress line (EPL) connecting a measure of current performance (or level of progress) with the idealized level of performance (or level of progress). The EPL of DBT is essentially the same as the aim line in precision teaching. (Consequently, it suffers from the same limitations, most notably, the necessity of specifying a desired length of time for program completion.) Deno and Mirkin developed a decision rule that is used in conjunction with the EPL: for an acceleration target, three consecutive data points below the EPL signals the need for program change. (Of course, for a deceleration target, the points must fall above the EPL in order to suggest the need for change.) When a program change is made, the EPL is redrawn parallel to the original, from the last point in the preceding phase. Bohannon (1975) and Mirkin and Deno (1979) have validated the usefulness of this (or similar) decision rules.

CONCLUSIONS

Measures of various aptitudes play an important role in the classification of persons as handicapped. Since federal and state regulations that pertain to the education of the handicapped explicitly require assessment of aptitudes, new tests of intelligence, perception, and psycholinguistic abilities will be necessary in the foreseeable future. Their utility beyond ensuring that local educational agencies are eligible for money is negligible. There are both logical and technical problems in measuring aptitudes presumed to cause handicapping conditions. Moreover, the scores from tests of various aptitudes have not proved useful in developing education interventions.

Alternatives to aptitude testing, such as precision and data-based teaching, allow for the validation, though not for the prescription, of teaching programs. Currently, program validation is the preferred approach although considerable research and evaluation are necessary before the practicality of these strategies can be known. Furthermore, the fact that ATI research to date has not yielded aptitude measures that interact with treatments or treatments that interact with aptitude measures does not imply that it will not do so in the future. Moreover, should instructionally valid ATIs be found, there will always be a need to modify treatments because of individual variation. Program prescription may be coupled with program validation to maximize the likelihood that children will benefit from special education programming. Thus, ATI and data-based alternatives are not mutually exclusive. ATI just is not useful *now*.

REFERENCES

American Psychological Association, American Education Research Association, and National Council on Measurement in Education. *Standards for educational and psychological tests*. Washington, D.C.: APA, 1974.

Arter, J. A., & Jenkins, J. R. Differential diagnosis-prescriptive teaching: A critical appraisal. *Review of Educational Research*, 1979, *49*, 517–555.

Bannatyne, A. Diagnosing learning disabilities and writing remedial prescriptions. *Journal of Learning Disabilities*, 1968, *1*, 28–34.

Becker, W. C., Engelmann, S., & Thomas, D. R. *Teaching: A course in applied psychology*. Chicago: Science Research Associates, 1971.

Bijou, S. J. These kids have problems and our job is to do something for them. In J. B. Jordan & L. S. Robbins (Eds.), *Let's try doing something else kind of thing: Behavioral principles and the exceptional child*. Arlington, Va.: Council for Exceptional Children, 1972.

Bohannon, R. *Direct and daily measurement procedures in the identification and treatment of reading behaviors of children in special education*. Unpublished doctoral dissertation, University of Washington, 1975.

Bruner, J. S. The course of cognitive growth. *American Psychologist*, 1964, *19*, 1–15.

Buros, O. K. (Ed.). *The eighth mental measurements yearbook*. Highland Park, N.J.: Gryphon Press, 1978.

Cattell, R. B. *Abilities: Their structure, growth and action*. Boston: Houghton Mifflin, 1971.

Clements, S. D. *Minimal brain dysfunction in children*. Columbus, Oh.: Charles E. Merrill, 1971.

Cronbach, L. *Essentials of psychological testing*. New York: Harper, 1960.

Cronbach, L. J. & Snow, R. E. *Attitudes and instructional methods*. New York: Irvington, 1977.

Cruickshank, W. M., Bice, H. V., Wallen, N. E., & Lynch, K. S. *Perception and cerebral palsy: Studies in figure-background relationship*. Syracuse, N.Y.: University Press, 1965.

Deno, S. L., & Mirkin, P. K. *Data-based program modification: A manual*. Reston, Va.: Council for Exceptional Children, 1977.

Federal Register. Education of handicapped children. Regulations implementing Education for All Handicapped Children Act of 1975. August 23, 1977, pp. 42474–42518.

Flavell, J. H. *Cognitive development*. Englewood Cliffs: Prentice-Hall, 1977.

Gaasholt, M. Precision techniques in the management of teacher and child behaviors. *Exceptional Children*, 1970, *37*, 129–135.

Gajar, A. Educable mentally retarded, learning disabled, emotionally disturbed: Similarities and differences. *Exceptional Children*, 1979, *45*, 470–472.

Guilford, J. P. *The nature of human intelligence*. New York: McGraw-Hill, 1967.

Guskin, S. L., & Spicker, H. H. Educational research in mental retardation. In N. R. Ellis (Ed.), *International review of research in mental retardation* (Vol. 3). New York: Academic Press, 1968.

Haring, N. G., Lovitt, T. C., Eaton, M. D., & Hansen, C. L. *The fourth R: Research in the classroom*. Columbus, Oh.: Charles E. Merrill, 1978.

Hirshoren, A., Schultz, E., Manton, A., & Henderson, R. *A survey of public school special education programs for emotionally disturbed children*. (ERIC Document Reproduction Service No. ED050540), 1970.

Hoffman, A. *Functional determinants for special education in the Iowa testing and referral program*. Unpublished doctoral dissertation, University of Illinois, 1972.

Jensen, A. R. How much can we boost intelligence and academic achievement? *Harvard Educational Review*, 1969, *39*, 1–123.

Kaufman, A. S. Scatter on WISC-R for normal children. *Journal of Learning Disabilities,* 1976, *9*(3), 33–41.

Kirk, S. A. Research in education. In H. A. Stevens & R. Heber (Eds.), *Mental retardation, a review of research.* Chicago: University of Chicago Press, 1964.

Kirk, S. A., & Kirk, W. D. *Psycholinguistic learning disabilities, diagnosis and remediation.* Urbana, Il.: University of Illinois Press, 1971.

Koppitz, E. *The Bender Gestalt test for young children.* New York: Grune & Stratton, 1963.

Lindsley, O. R. From Skinner to precision teaching: The child knows best. In J. B. Jordan & L. S. Robbins (Eds.), *Let's try doing something else kind of thing: Behavioral principles and the exceptional child.* Arlington, Va.: Council for Exceptional Children, 1972.

Mercer, J. *System of multicultural pluralistic assessment: technical manual.* New York: Psychological Corporation, 1979.

Mirkin, P. K., & Deno, S. L. *Formative evaluation in the classroom: An approach to improving instruction* (Research Report No. 10). Minneapolis: University of Minnesota, Institute for Research on Learning Disabilities, August, 1979.

Neisworth, J. T. The educational irrelevance of intelligence. In R. M. Smith (Ed.), *Teacher diagnosis of educational difficulties.* Columbus, Oh.: Charles E. Merrill, 1969.

Newland, T. E. Psychological assessment of exceptional children and youth. In W. M. Cruickshank (Ed.), *Psychology of exceptional children and youth* (4th ed.). Englewood Cliffs: Prentice-Hall, 1980.

Oakland, T. (Ed.) *Psychological and educational assessment of minority children.* New York: Bruner/Mazel, 1977.

Patterson, G. R., Reid, J. B., Jones, R. R., &

Conger, R. E. *A social learning approach to family intervention. Families with aggressive children.* (Vol. 1). Eugene, Or.: Castalia, 1975.

Pennypacker, H. S., Koenig, C. H., & Lindsley, O. R. *Handbook of the standard behavior chart.* Kansas City, Ks.: Precision Media, 1972.

Petersen, C. R., & Hart, D. H. Use of multiple discriminant function analysis in evaluation of a state-wide system for identification of educationally handicapped children. *Psychological Reports,* 1978, *43,* 734–755.

Piaget, J. *The psychology of intelligence.* New York: Harcourt, Brace, 1950.

Rubin, S. A reevaluation of figure-ground pathology in brain-damaged children. *American Journal of Mental Deficiency,* 1969, *74,* 111–115.

Salvia, J., & Ysseldyke, J. E. *Assessment in special and remedial education.* Boston: Houghton Mifflin, 1978.

Skinner, B. F. *Science and human behavior.* New York: Macmillan, 1953.

Sindelar, P. T., & Deno, S. L. The effectiveness of resource programming. *Journal of Special Education,* 1978, *12,* 17–28.

Spearman, C. *The nature of "intelligence" and the principles of cognition.* London: Macmillan, 1923.

Starlin, C., & Starlin A. *Guides for continuous decision making.* Bemidji, Mn.: Unique Curriculums, Unlimited, 1973.

Thurstone, L. L. *Primary mental abilities.* Chicago: University of Chicago Press, 1938.

White, O. R. *A pragmatic approach to the description of progress in the single case.* Unpublished doctoral dissertation, University of Oregon, 1971.

Yates A. J. The validity of some psychological tests of brain damage. *Psychological Bulletin,* 1954, *51,* 359–379.

Libby Goodman
Randy Elliot Bennett

11

Use of Norm-Referenced Assessment for the Mildly Handicapped: Basic Issues Reconsidered

If assessment is important to the instructional process for normal children, it is critical to the instructional process for the handicapped. At the outset, assessment provides the data with which decision makers identify the child as exceptional or nonexceptional and determine the type and nature of the handicapping condition. Continual evaluation of learning progress helps the teacher set the direction and pace for instructional activity and suggests student learning characteristics, which are the basis for individualization of the instructional program. Also, assessment provides data relevant to mastery or nonmastery of learning goals and thereby helps determine the student's readiness for the next curricular step.

While the need for assessment information is indisputable, there is not general agreement among educators as to the manner of assessment or the types of tools to be used. Many considerations (e.g., content area, developmental areas to be evaluated, age of student, type of exceptionality, etc.) affect the decisions made regarding assessment instruments, approaches, and procedures. One of the major issues related to the use of assessment tools is the debate over norm- versus criterion-referenced tests. For some years now, criterion-referenced testing approaches have gained increasing professional and lay support, while the advocates of standardized norm-referenced tests and procedures have been forced to respond to a growing chorus of critics. This controversy forms the backdrop for the discussion of norm-referenced approaches to the assessment of academic achievement in mildly handicapped students.

NORM- VERSUS CRITERION-REFERENCED MEASUREMENT

An extended discussion of formal academic tests must begin with a clear definition of standardized tests and norm- and criterion-referenced measurement. Standardization refers to the extent to which a measure possesses a fixed and explicit set of administrative and scoring procedures that allow the measure to be given in the same way from one occasion to the next and from one examinee to the next (Cronbach, 1970). Norm- and criterion-reference refer to measures that have been constructed so as to facilitate a particular type of interpretation. Norm-referenced measures are constructed to allow comparison of the performance of an individual to some relevant reference group. Criterion-referenced measures are constructed to permit interpretation of performance relative to a specific domain of behaviors measuring an objective or skill (Popham, 1975). Norm-referenced tests must be standardized if they are to permit precise comparisons among individuals; criterion-referenced tests may or may not be standardized.

In recent years, the use of norm-referenced tests with exceptional and minority group children has been variously reviewed, discussed, condemned, and, in some cases, even prohibited by court mandate.[1] Professionals of various disciplines have taken sides on this issue, and the debate has coalesced with the larger antitesting debate, which has already affected educational testing. Among the many criticisms that have been directed at norm-referenced testing, the issue of instructional utility seems to be at the center of the controversy. Critics denounce norm-referenced tests for the absence or almost total lack of diagnositc and instructionally useful data. This issue surely is of pressing importance to educators in general, and special educators in particular, who know beforehand that regular curricular programs will not meet the needs of their students. As modifications and adjustments in instructional programming are the rule and not the exception in special education, the instructional and diagnostic information derived from evaluation instruments is of critical importance to teachers of exceptional children. In order to "individualize" instructional programs, diagnostic information is essential; the assertion that norm-referenced tests have little or no diagnostic value, therefore, takes on added importance, for it is diagnostic information that forms the basis for instructional analysis and design.

In a recently published debate, two notable spokespersons for opposing sides of the norm-referenced versus criterion-referenced test controversy, Robert Ebel and W. James Popham, set forth their views on the subject. In defense of norm-referenced tests, Ebel (1978) maintained that norm-referenced tests are important educational tools, which fulfill certain purposes, namely summative evaluation of learning outcomes and assessment of the student's mastery of broad, general levels of knowledge that reflect commonly held goals of learning. Criterion-referenced tests, on the other hand, are more suited to formative evaluation of specific, distinct skills. Ebel contended that "there is a difference in the level of attainment that each type of test is best adapted to measure" (p. 3). Popham (1978) did not advocate the use of norm-referenced achievement tests under any circumstances and wrote that "for purposes of instruction or evaluation, norm-referenced achievement tests are essentially worthless" (p. 6). Popham based his rejection of norm-referenced tests on (1) the mismatch between test content and curriculum;

---

[1]In the *Larry P. v. Riles* (1979) case, the court for the Northern District of California imposed severe restrictions on the use of standardized tests, particularly IQ tests, for black children. Interestingly, and in contrast to the *Larry P.* case, which was expected to become the overriding precedent for the country at large, District Judge John F. Grady, in a case involving the use of intelligence tests in the Chicago Public School System, ruled that the Stanford-Binet, WISC, and WISC-R are not inherently biased against minority children (IQ Tests, 1980). Also, standardized criterion-referenced tests have not been untouched by the controversy. In *Debra P. v. Turlington*, for example, the court dealt with the fairness of minimum competency tests (*Debra P. v. Turlington*, 1979).

(2) the lack of information derived from norm-referenced tests that would give teachers relevant information for instruction; and (3) the emphasis on performance variance, a key feature of norm-referenced tests, but not of criterion-referenced tests, which leads to elimination of many test items that represent important learning outcomes but that do not add to the ability of the test to differentiate among individuals.

Ebel noted that comparisons to some norm group are involved in the interpretation of criterion-referenced tests also. Even when using criterion-referenced tests, the criterion of mastery must be based on something, most likely a perception of what performance is normal for some age or grade group. Interestingly, Popham (1978) did not view the question of interpretation of student test scores as a major distinguishing characteristic of criterion-referenced tests. Rather, he believed that this point has been overemphasized to the neglect of the more important issue, namely that criterion-referenced tests measure well-defined classes of behavior. Popham's point, however, needs to be tempered by the fact that criterion-referenced measures are constructed to include well-defined classes of behavior for the sole purpose of allowing individual student performance to be interpreted relative to those classes of behavior.

It appears that the conflict ultimately revolves about the question of educational utility. The conflicting perceptions of norm-referenced and criterion-referenced tests and their usefulness for educational purposes may well represent inherent values and beliefs as to the purpose of education. Haney (1980), writing about the current testing controversy, articulated this crucial point very well:

> Rather the differences [in opinion] derive from deeper underlying assumptions about the relative rights and prerogatives of individuals versus those of state agencies and institutions about the different social functions served by standardized testing, and, at root, from underlying differences in educational and social philosophies. (p. 646)

When the conflict results from differing basic values, can solutions to surface questions be resolved? Ebel (1973) posed the question "What do educational tests test?" If we concede that criterion-referenced and norm-referenced tests measure different levels of educational outcome, it may be more productive to understand what norm-referenced tests can and cannot do and the educational use to which this type of test should be applied. This chapter will explore the purpose and application of these tests as well as future avenues for development. The chapter is organized around two major topics: (1) the use of norm-referenced tests with atypical populations and (2) the educational utility of norm-referenced tests.

THE USE OF NORM-REFERENCED TESTS WITH ATYPICAL POPULATIONS

Discussions about the use of standardized norm-referenced tests with handicapped children have emphasized the obstacles inherent in the design and administration of such tests for use with this population. A recurring theme is that norm-referenced tests emphasize limitations or disabilities and concomitantly underestimate true achievement or potential. Undoubtedly, there is some validity in this criticism. But it must be discerned if the limitations attributed to these tests stem primarily from the tests themselves or rather from factors related to professional use and/or judgment.

Tests themselves possess basic statistical and structural characteristics that describe the utility of the instrument for a particular purpose with a particular population. These basic characteristics are reliability, validity, and reference frame (i.e., how scores are given meaning—which, for the purposes of this discussion, is done through norms). It should be noted that these three characteristics are essential for all types of assessment procedures and not just standardized tests (*Standards*, 1974).

The interpretability of test results is dependent in large measure upon the degree to which an instrument adequately possesses these basic characteristics. The American Psychological Association's *Standards for Educational and Psychological Tests* clearly articulates the requirements for appropriate tests and testing procedures.[2] Almost every text on measurement and evaluation in education, educational psychology, special education, etc., covers or mentions these basic topics.

A second basic requirement for assessment (i.e., besides the existence of technically adequate tools), is professionally competent and responsible use of tools. Competent and responsible use includes the selection of tests that are technically adequate and appropriate for the purposes of assessment and the populations being assessed; administration and scoring according to the instructions specified by the producer; and interpretation of results using basic principles of measurement and test interpretation. With regard to test selection, evidence has been presented to suggest that professionals involved in the assessment of the handicapped tend to select and use tests that are not appropriate to the purposes of assessment or populations to be assessed (Thurlow & Ysseldyke, 1979; Ysseldyke, Algozzine, Regan, & Potter, 1980). Research has likewise documented a tendency among professionals to make errors in administrative and scoring procedures, resulting in inaccurate test scores (C. Miller & Chansky, 1972; C. Miller, Chansky, & Gredler, 1970; Warren & Brown, 1973). Evidence has also been presented to show that many professionals do not possess the basic competencies necessary to allow accurate and meaningful interpretations of test results (Bennett, 1980a, 1980b; Bennett & Shepherd, in press). In a synthesis of the literature on professional proficiency and assessment, Bennett (in press, a) concluded that "serious problems exist with regard to the competence of professionals involved in the educational and psychological assessment of exceptional children" (p. 15). If it is indeed the case that tests are not being properly selected, administered, scored, and interpreted, the problem may not be the adequacy of tests, but rather the manner in which they are used. In sum, both the technical characteristics of tests and the competencies of professionals must be considered in evaluating the use of tests with atypical populations.

---

[2]The APA standards are not mandatory and there is no clearing-house that sanctions certain tests and rejects others. The *Mental Measurement Yearbook* (Buros, 1978) is an invaluable compendium of third-party information on formal assessment instruments. There are many other sources of information on testing, such as the ERIC Clearinghouse on Tests, Measurement and Evaluation, and the Test Collection, both at Educational Testing Service (Princeton, New Jersey), as well as publishers' catalogues, journal articles, etc. (It is distressing to note how little use test users make of the information that is available to them.)

Technical Characteristics

Reliability

Reliability, in the simplest terms, refers to the precision or accuracy with which a test or assessment procedure measures a particular skill, ability, or trait. Like other statistical characteristics of assessment tools, reliability is not an inherent characteristic, but rather is a result of an interaction between the test and a particular group of examinees. This means that tests are not reliable in the abstract, but are reliable (or unreliable) for use with a particular population. It is entirely possible for specific tests or other assessment tools to be reliable for use with one population and relatively unreliable for use with another population. (Take, for example, a common wooden ruler, which is relatively accurate for measuring the length of a person's foot, but undoubtedly innaccurate for measuring the length of an amoeba's body.) Finding that a test is reliable for use with normal first-grade students, then, does not mean that the test is necessarily reliable for use with handicapped students of the same grade.

Because there are several sources of error in measurement, there are several types of reliability (Livingston, 1980). Each type of reliability refers to a specific error source or to a combination of error sources. Three major sources of measurement error are those resulting from (1) selection of a particular sample of questions for a test (assessed through split-half, internal consistency, and alternate-forms studies); (2) the time of testing (assessed through test-retest and alternate forms studies); and, for some types of tools, (3) those who grade or score the results (assessed through inter-rater studies). Knowledge of the extent to which each of these error sources affects a particular test permits different generalizations about the dependability of test results. Clearly, in order to generalize test results across the greatest range of situations, one must have estimates of the extent to which all three types of error are present for a given procedure when it is used with a particular population.

Estimates of a test's reliability are commonly expressed in two ways. The reliability coefficient indicates the extent to which a particular error source or combination of sources is present in a given procedure; a high coefficient signifies a low degree of error and a low coefficient signifies a high degree of error. As there is an inverse relationship between measurement error and the magnitude of the reliability coefficient, high reliability coefficients are desirable. The reliability coefficient is most useful for comparing the accuracy of one test or assessment tool with that of another.

A second way in which a test's reliability can be expressed is through the standard error of measurement. Expressed in the same score units as the test, the standard error of measurement is an average that tells the degree to which scores obtained through testing are likely to vary around a student's hypothetical "true" score. The standard error of measurement, both added to and subtracted from the student's obtained score, may be thought to indicate the range within which the student's "true" score is likely to fall. As there is an inverse relationship between reliability and the standard error of measurement, the smaller the standard error, the greater the reliability of the test, and vice versa. The standard error of measurement, because it is expressed in the same units as the test, is often not useful for comparing the accuracy of different tests. The major use of the standard error is in the interpretation of individual scores. Because no test (or any other assessment procedure, for that matter) is perfectly reliable, the standard error of measurement should always be considered in interpreting and reporting the scores of individual students.

With regard to both the standard error of measurement and the reliability coefficient, it needs to be emphasized that neither statistic is meaningful unless the sources of error (or the methods used to derive them) are explicit. Without such information, appropriate generalizations about the accuracy of the test simply cannot be made.

How reliable must a procedure be before it is used with a particular population? This question can be answered in a variety of ways. One way is to state that a procedure should be as close to perfect in terms of precision as possible. The closer an instrument is in approximating perfect accuracy, the greater the trust that can be placed in the results of assessment with that instrument.

A second way to answer the question of how reliable an instrument should be, is to say that it should be more reliable than any other instrument or procedure available for fulfilling the same measurement purpose. Decisions made about the identification and programming of handicapped children are made on the basis of information gathered through a variety of means. The procedures used to gather that information, whether they be tests, observations, or opinions, must be the most reliable (and valid) ones available. If procedures are used that are not the most reliable available, then decisions will be made on the basis of information that is not of the highest possible accuracy.

A third way to deal with the question of reliability is to recognize that the level of reliability required is in part a function of the nature of the decision to be made. If decisions made on the basis of assessment results have far-reaching consequences or are difficult to reverse (e.g., classification), reliability must be relatively high. If incorrect decisions are easy to reverse or have only slight consequences, reliability need not be as high.

A final way to address the question of minimal reliability is to specify a set of standards, albeit somewhat arbitrarily, for judging reliability. As a rule of thumb, Salvia and Ysseldyke (1981) recommended that .60 be the minimum reliability desirable for group data or decision making; that a minimum of .90 be the standard for individual assessment that is to be the basis for important educational decisions; and that .80 be the standard for screening purposes. The standards recommended by Salvia and Ysseldyke are, in general, consistent with the numeric reliability values recommended by other authorities. The considerable gap between the minimal reliability level for individual testing as compared to the reliability suggested for group decision making emphasizes a point upon which most authorities agree: reliability standards for procedures used in individual decision making must be more stringent than those used for group evaluation purposes (Guilford, 1954; Mehrens & Lehmann, 1975; Sax, 1974).

Test users cannot casually assume that all commercial tests have adequate reliability for particular populations. Reliability data should be provided in accompanying test manuals, but it is the responsibility of the practitioner to review the reliability data on a particular test prior to its use. If the information is not available for the population of interest, the value of the test for that population should be seriously questioned; if the information is provided but ignored, then the practitioner is to blame.

Table 11-1 lists the reliabilities and standard errors of measurement for three commonly used special education tests and their subtests; the table illustrates a number of points with regard to reliability. First, note that different types of reliability are reported. The Peabody Individual Achievement Test (PIAT), for example, reports test-retest reliability, which tells the degree to which the test is free from error associated with the time of testing. For the Woodcock Reading Mastery Tests, both test-retest estimates and split-half reliabilities are listed, which gives an indication of the extent to which the test is free from error associated with the time of testing and error related to the particular sample of items used. Inter-rater reliability estimates are not listed for any of the tests; for tests that use objective item formats (and these tests do for the most part), error due to different examiners is usually negligible.

The table also shows that test reliability is a function of both the test and the population tested. This can be clearly seen by examining the test-retest reliabilities for the Woodcock Letter Identification subtest. The subtest is fairly reliable for use with the younger population but clearly unreliable for use with the older group.

A third point of interest relates to the differences in total test and subtest reliabilities for the various tests. The total test reliabilities meet Salvia and Ysseldyke's suggested rule of thumb in most cases, but the same cannot be said for the subtest reliabilities. In fact, there is considerable variation for the reliabilities reported for subtests, and the vast majority of reliabilities fall below the recommended standard of .90. This obvious difference in reliability levels for total tests and subtests brings out a very important point about the nature of reliability—reliability is very much a function of length. For example, if every possible item relevant to a particular skill was used in a test, the test would contain no error resulting from using only a sample of items. Likewise, if the test was infinitely long, there would be no need to worry about error resulting from the particular time of testing since the test would continue to be given across time.

It is a fact that subtests are shorter in length than total tests and hence will generally be less reliable than total tests. However, isn't it possible to raise the reliabilities of the subtests to meet the standards specified earlier by simply lengthening the subtests? The answer to this question is a qualified "Yes." In simplest terms, this is a trade-off situation involving precision and time. If more precise measurement is wanted, more time must be devoted to assessment. Yet generally more time cannot be devoted to assessment because there are waiting lists for evaluation, longer assessment is more costly, and time spent in assessment is time taken away from instruction.

Given this situation, two pieces of adivce are helpful. First, when test, subtest, or procedure reliabilities appear low or are unknown, be wary of assessment results and use caution in interpretation. Second, if more time is available, use it to raise the precision of assessment by repeating assessment (Bennett, in press, b; Salvia & Ysseldyke, 1981), corroborating results by using other measuring devices that tap the same skills (Farr, 1969), contrasting test performance with classroom behavior, or all three.

Table 11-1

Total Test and Subtest Reliabilities
for Three Popular Achievement Tests

Test		Reliability	SEM*
		Test-Retest Reliability	
PIAT Individual	Total Test	.82–.92	6.5–16.3
Achievement	Math	.52–.84	2.63–5.38
Test: Grades	Reading Recognition	.81–.94	1.66–4.54
K, 1, 3, 5	Reading Comprehension	.61–.78	2.48–7.39
8, and 12	Spelling	.42–.78	3.16–6.38
	General Information	.70–.88	2.40–5.71
		Split-Half Reliability	
Woodcock	Total Test	.97–.99	2.1–5.3
Reading Mastery	Letter Identification	.02–.96	0.6–1.9
Tests: Grades	Word Identification	.96–.99	0.9–2.7
1.2, 1.9, 2.9,	Word Attack	.94–.97	1.6–2.4
4.9, 7.9, and	Word Comprehension	.83–.96	1.4–2.9
10.9	Passage Comprehension	.90–.97	1.9–2.7
		Test-Retest Reliability	
Grades 2.9	Total Test	.97 and .83	NR†
and 7.9	Letter Identification	.84 and .16	NR
	Word Identification	.94 and .93	NR
	Word Attack	.90 and .85	NR
	Word Comprehension	.90 and .68	NR
	Passage Comprehension	.88 and .78	NR
		Internal (Consistency)	
Key Math	Total Test	.94–.97	3.3
Diagnostic	Numeration	.68–.78	1.2
Arithmetic	Fractions	.36–.89	0.8
Test: Grades	Geometry and Symbols	.28–.84	0.8
1–4, 6, and 7	Addition	.44–.79	0.8
	Subtraction	.33–.84	0.7
	Multiplication	.52–.84	0.7
	Division	.23–.83	0.6
	Mental Computation	.55–.81	0.9
	Numerical Reasoning	.67–.90	0.8
	Word Problems	.37–.67	0.9
	Missing Elements	.67–.90	0.7
	Money	.63–.75	1.0
	Measurement	.66–.88	1.3
	Time	.51–.85	1.2

*Note that standard errors of measurement (SEM) are generally not comparable across tests.
†NR = not reported.

In addition to the reliabilities of total test scores and individual subtest scores, the reliability of one other type of score must frequently be considered. Very often teachers and diagnosticians rely most heavily upon difference scores and derive individual diagnoses from differences in test or subtest scores.[3] The child's performance on one test or subtest is contrasted with his or her performance on another test or subtest. If differences in test performance are found, it is often interpreted as evidence of a deficit or disability. But, when contrasting test or subtest scores, the diagnostician *must* take into account the fact that differences between sets of scores may be due to measurement error and may not represent real differences in a child's abilities. It is essential, therefore, that reported difference scores be accompanied by the standard error of measurement or the reliability for differences—"at least for those differences upon which most interpretation and weight are placed" (Guilford, 1954, p. 394).

Information on the standard error of measurement for difference scores is rarely provided by test manufacturers for intra-test differences. Newland and Smith (Sattler, 1974) determined the magnitude of difference between various combinations of WISC subtest scores and IQ scales needed for statistical significance at both the .05 and .01 confidence levels. Comparable tables for the WISC-R, as well as the Newland and Smith tables, are available in Sattler (1974). The WISC and WISC-R tables are cited as unusual examples

In the arena of academic achievement testing, information on the standard error of measurement for intra-test difference scores is relatively rare; reliability information across or among various test instruments is rarer still. The Peabody Individual Achievement Test (Dunn & Markwardt, 1970) provides the "standard errors of measurement for differences between pairs of subtest raw scores to provide a guide for evaluating the meaning of differences between subtest scores" (p. 45). The PIAT also provides intercorrelations for itself and the Peabody Picture Vocabulary Test, which can be used to calculate standard error.

It is obviously difficult for test manufacturers to provide reliability comparisons: The potential number of different test or subtest comparisons which could be made is almost limitless, as the specific comparisons of interest fluctuate from one child to another and from one testing situation to another. Yet, without knowledge of the reliability (or the standard error of measurement) of each test and the correlation between the tests,[4] the standard error for differences cannot be precisely computed.

Fortunately, some short-cut methods for determining the extent to which a particular observed difference can be trusted exist. One such method is a conservative formula for the standard error of measurement for differences recommended by Thorndike and Hagen (1977). The formula is conservative in that it will usually result in a standard error of measurement for differences slightly larger than that

---

[3]A demonstrable discrepancy between achievement and expected achievement in one or more of seven areas is a requirement under PL 94–142, in order to identify the learning disabled (*Federal Register,* December 29, 1977).

[4]Statistically, the standard error of measurement for differences is a function of the standard deviations of the tests, their average reliabilities, and their intercorrelation. Comparability of norm groups is a judgmental factor that does not contribute to the statistical calculation, but that needs to be considered by the test user in the interpretation of difference scores.

obtained through more comprehensive formulae. The formula is

$$\text{SEM difference} = \sqrt{\text{Sm}_1{}^2 + \text{SM}_2{}^2}$$

where Sm_1 and Sm_2 are the standard errors of measurement for the two tests expressed on the same standard score scale.

A second short-cut method is through use of a set of tables provided by Thorndike (1973), which allow the user to determine, for *any* pair of scores, the likelihood that a real difference exists. To use Thorndike's tables, one must have estimates of the reliabilities of the tests and their intercorrelation, and be able to express the differences between the scores in standard deviation units.

The calculations involved in determining the standard error for difference scores are not difficult, though they may be time-consuming. Test manufacturers should provide as much information relevant to the reliablity of differences among various tests as possible. But, if the information is lacking, is it reasonable to expect teachers, clinicians, and/or psychologists to undertake the necessary statistical work? We believe that it is. Making decisions that affect children's lives is part of the educator's daily work. Ultimately, we are, and should be, held accountable for the decisions made. Skills in assessment and diagnosis, including critical analysis of assessment instruments and the ability to perform basic statistical calculations, must be in the repertoire of all special education teachers and clinicians. For exceptional or thought-to-be exceptional children for whom assessment is an individualistic process with direct bearing on classification, placement, and programming, it is imperative that interpretation of standardized tests and other assessment tools, and the decisions which result, be tempered with knowledge of the limitations of measurement.

Validity

Validity refers to the adequacy and appropriateness of a test for particular interpretations and uses (Messick, 1980). From this definition of validity, it can be seen that validity speaks to the question of what a test measures and what meaning or inference can be drawn from the results of applying the procedure. Clearly, validity is a concept that relates directly to the purposes for which a procedure should or should not be used.

As with reliability, a test cannot have validity in and of itself. A test possesses validity only with regard to a particular population of examinees (*Standards*, 1974). This concept can be illustrated by the case of a paper and pencil test, which is valid for assessing normal children's command of basic addition facts but which is clearly not valid for assessing those same skills in a blind population.

In general, the important question for special educators is, "Is this test valid for assessing children with specific handicapping conditions?" To answer this question for a particular test, the examiner should first consult the instrument manual to see if it presents data to support the validity of the test for use with the population in question. If such data are not presented, the next step is to examine the professional literature concerning the test. In the complete absence of data (which for many tests is the case), the user should try to determine from logical analysis if the response mode of the test demands physical or sensory abilities that the child does not possess. If it does, the user should assume that the test is not valid for use with that population. If the test does not appear to make physical and sensory demands beyond the child's capabilities, the examiner may use the test but should interpret and report results with caution and with explicit reference to the fact that validity data for use of the test with such children are not available.

Also related to validity, and of particular importance to the evaluation of achievement, is the notion of content relevance or content validity (Messick, 1980). Content relevance can be conceived of as the extent to which a test's content is related to the curriculum or the objectives of instruction; a test of mathematics would be expected to contain items reflecting important aspects of the math curriculum or the objectives of instruction.

The notion of content relevance is especially important to the testing of achievement at two particular times. The first of these is during the test development process. In the course of test development, manufacturers usually take great pains to build tests that will be relevant in terms of content to the greatest number of test users. This is done through surveys of school curricula, analysis of popular instructional programs, interviews with teachers, use of advisory committees composed of subject matter experts, and repeated reviews of test items to ensure their match with curricular content. The advantageous result of this process is a test that contains a common core of content—that is, content held to be important across a large number of schools and districts. The disadvantageous result of the process is that the content of the test will probably not be perfectly relevant for any one school or district.

Content relevance is also important in test selection. The extent of content overlap between a standardized achievement test and the goals of instruction for a child or group of children should always be assessed before a test is selected for use. As there are no standard statistical procedures for expressing content relevance, it should be assessed judgmentally by comparing curricula and instructional goals and objectives directly with test content. If such an analysis is omitted from the test selection process, then only the practitioner can be held to blame if a test with irrelevant content is used in assessment.

Norms

Validity lends meaning to test results by specifying what ability is reflected by the results and how results can be used. An additional level of meaning must be lent test scores, however, if sense is to be made of them individually. This additional level of meaning is given to individual test scores by comparing them to external referents, such as prespecified standards, instructional goals, or the test scores of others.

Comparison of an individual's performance to that of a particular norm group allows two types of inferences. First, normative comparison allows decision makers to estimate the individual's status in the larger population (which the norm group represents) with regard to a particular trait or ability. Second, such comparisons allow for contrasting performance across skill or content areas. For example, it can be said that a child is doing poorly in math only if usual math performance for other children of the same age or grade is known.

Authorities agree that two key questions concerning the use of norms are the degree to which the norm group accurately represents the population it claims to represent, and the degree to which the norm group is relevant to the purpose for which the student is being evaluated (Seashore & Ricks, 1950). A norm group is relevant if it answers the question(s) that are posed as the purpose(s) for assessment. For example, if the purpose is to estimate an individual's likelihood of competing academically in a school attended primarily by low socioeconomic status (SES) children, the relevant norm group, regardless of our student's SES, would be one representative of low SES students of the type attending that school. If, on the other hand, the purpose is to estimate the student's likelihood of competing in a school attended primarily by high SES students, the norm group of choice, again regardless of the SES of our student, would be one representative of high SES students like the ones attending the school of interest. These examples illustrate a very important point about the concept of relevance of norms: This is that relevance is *not* necessarily a function of the extent to which a student is like the members of a particular norm group, but rather the extent to which the particular norm group is relevant for the purpose for which the student is being assessed.

Once we have stated the purpose for assessment, specified a population to which to compare a student, and found a test with norms that claim to represent that population, we should try as best we can to evaluate the credibility of this claim. The importance of this analysis is that if we err in our evaluation we will be vulnerable to the possibility that we have compared our student to some other population than the one intended and have, as a consequence, answered an evaluation question other than the one originally posed.

Traditionally, norm groups for standardized instruments have been developed to represent populations with broad characteristics, such as the population of children in particular school grades across the nation. As purposes for assessment have changed, and as social and political beliefs about the nature and make-up of American society have shifted, the use of more narrowly defined norms has become more widespread. One type of "special" norm, the local norm, allows comparison of a student to others in the same locale, a comparison that is clearly more relevant for some purposes of assessment than comparison to national norms. Other types of special norms include norms attempting to represent various populations of handicapped individuals. Examples of standardized instruments with such norms are (1) the AAMD Adaptive Behavior Scale (normed on institutionalized retardates); (2) the Blind Learning Aptitude Test (normed on blind children); (3) the Nebraska Test of Learning Aptitude (normed on deaf children); and (4) the TARC[5] (normed on severely/profoundly mentally retarded children).

Obviously, the use of such tests is restricted to particular purposes. Handicapped group norms, like local norms, enhance the relevance of tests for particular assessment purposes and have meaning limited to the local or special group represented.

In addition to tests developed with single sets of local or special norms, tests developed with multiple sets of norms are becoming more widespread. The purpose of multigroup norms is to provide, within the same test, the means for making comparisons relevant to a wider variety of assessment purposes. Multigroup norms organized around grade and age groups have been available for some time.

---

[5]TARC refers to the Topeka Kansas Association for Retarded Citizens, which cooperated in the development of the instrument.

It is only recently, however, that tests have become available with multiple norms organized around such variables as ethnic and socioeconomic status. At the forefront of this trend appears to be the System of Multicultural Pluralistic Assessment (SOMPA; Mercer & Lewis, 1979). The SOMPA provides multiple norms that permit the WISC-R performance of English-speaking white, black, and Hispanic children to be interpreted along sociocultural and ethnic lines.

One final important point is that the meaningful comparison of a student's performance to some relevant norm group presumes that the student took the test under essentially the same conditions as the norm group. This means that adaptations in testing procedures to accommodate the needs of the handicapped render questionable the use of the reported test norms; in such cases, interpretation of test results should be limited to qualitative rather than quantitative judgments (Salvia & Ysseldyke, 1981). The practice of the Educational Testing Service (ETS; Princeton, N.J.) may be enlightening: Some testing programs currently administered by ETS have provided special accommodations for handicapped students as a matter of policy since 1939 (Educational Testing Service, 1979). The Admissions Testing Program sponsored by the College Board, for example, offers special arrangements for students with visual, physical, hearing, or learning disabilities. Accommodations to the Scholastic Aptitude Tests and Achievement Tests include braille, large-type, and cassette editions and extended testing time periods. Responses may be recorded on large block-answer sheets. If warranted, a reader, manual translator, or amanuensis may be used. However, changing the conditions under which a student takes the test makes it difficult to meaningfully compare that student's performance to the performance of those who took the test under the usual conditions. The student's reported score therefore includes the designation NON-STD ADMIN (nonstandard administration). Regarding interpretation, the College Board (ETS, 1979) maintains that it is not able to provide interpretive data for scores earned in nonstandard administrations, and advises that test scores are only one factor in the assessment of a student's academic potential. This is good advice for all diagnosticians.

With the mildly handicapped, where physical or sensory disabilities are absent or pose only minor impediments to test-taking ability, evaluators must recognize the importance of adherence to standard procedures if they plan to interpret results in the standard way. If standard procedures are put aside or altered, then interpretability of test results is altered as well.

THE INSTRUCTIONAL UTILITY OF
NORM-REFERENCED TESTS

How can the instructional utility of norm-referenced tests be judged? Armstrong (1976) espoused a functional view of assessment and test information and maintained that the utility of a test should be gauged by the degree of inference involved in the application of the data to instructional decisions. Based on this premise, Armstrong categorized possible data sources as low-, medium-, or high-inference data.

According to Armstrong (1976), low-inference data sources are samples of a learner's work which are viewed directly by the instructional decision maker and relate closely to skills, knowledge, or attitudes needed for success on a new in-structional task. Work samples and checklists of pertinent behaviors are two ex-amples of low inference data sources.

Medium-inference information consists of samples of learner's work which are not directly related to the upcoming curricular task demands or which involve judgments about the learner's skills, knowledge, or attitudes made by someone other than the instructional decision maker. Grades, anecdotal records, and inter-est inventories given by someone other than the instructional decision maker are examples of medium-inference data sources.

When judgments about the learner's skills, knowledge, and attitudes are ren-dered by someone other than the instructional decision maker on information about learner characteristics that appear only marginally, if not totally, irrelevant to the task situation, a situation of high inference exists.

Armstrong believes that low-inference information sources are to be pre-ferred to intermediate- or high-inference information sources since low-inference data have the highest diagnostic value. Within Armstrong's framework, norm-referenced achievement tests fare badly: they are judged to be high-inference data with little if any diagnostic value—the information source of last resort. In consid-ering Armstrong's views, however, it is well to emphasize a number of points. First, different tests will overlap to different degrees with the educational goals and curricula held important in any one local situation. The responsibility for ensuring a high degree of content relevance therefore rests with the professional who chooses to use a particular test. If achievement tests are *properly* selected, a situation of "high inference" should rarely exist. Situations in which a test with minimal content relevance is used are more accurately referred to as "low compe-tence" rather than "high inference." Second, Armstrong's standard may prove to be too constricting for the totality of the assessment process even as it applies to day-to-day instructional decision making, for not all instructional decisions are task specific. Ultimately, the purpose of education for the mildly handicapped is not to teach specific isolated bits of content or splinter skills, but rather to develop generalized competencies or abilities for use in the wide range of situations chil-dren will encounter in their lives. While much assessment activity involves imme-diate curricular decisions, assessment serves many purposes, e.g., screening, placement, program evaluation, program planning, and assessment of individual progress (Salvia & Ysseldyke, 1981). As there are many purposes for testing, day-to-day instructional utility cannot be the one standard by which all tools are judged. The purpose for which a source of information is to be used may in fact dictate the selection of high-inference tools rather than low-inference proce-dures—to use Armstrong's terms. There are testing situations, involving assess-ment of achievement, which expressly call for the use of tools that present tasks different from those on which the student has been instructed. We need to guard against too-narrow conceptualizations that limit our assessment and educational alternatives.

Can the instructional utility of standardized norm-referenced tests be en-hanced? Popham (1978) asserted that criterion-referenced tests can, if properly designed, fulfill the functions heretofore ascribed to both criterion-referenced and norm-referenced tests. Nitko (1980), in a recent discussion of the varieties of crite-rion-referenced tests, graphically portrayed a combined criterion-referenced and norm-referenced elementary mathematics test of addition skills (Fig. 11-1).

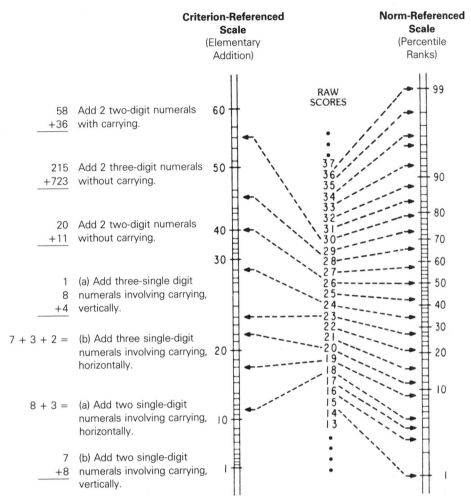

Fig. 11-1. Hypothetical example of two ways to reference test scores: criterion referencing and norm referencing. (Reprinted with permission from Nitko, Anthony J., "Distinguishing the Many Varieties of Criterion-Referenced Tests." *Review of Educational Research*, Fall, 1980, Vol. 50, no. 3, 461–464).

There are many indications that the major test manufacturers are attempting to place more emphasis on developing tools that respond to needs for both norm- and criterion-referenced information. For example, the Woodcock Reading Mastery Tests allow for the "joint norm-referenced criterion-referenced interpretations" of students' performance which "describe a person's competency with a given task compared to others on the same task" (Woodcock, 1973, p. 25). The Iowa Tests of Basic Skills (Hieronymous, Lindquist, & Hoover, 1978) and the Tests of Achievement and Proficiency (Scannell, Haugh, Schild, & Ulmer, 1978) both provide norm-referenced and criterion-referenced assessment of student achievement. These tests are designed for (1) determining students' developmental status; (2) identifying student strengths and weaknesses; (3) identifying readiness for instruction; (4) providing data for grouping students; (5) evaluating group strengths and weaknesses; and (6) evaluating individual pupil progress (Salvia & Ysseldyke, 1981).

Another approach to enhance the diagnostic value of a test involves increasing the range of content sampled and organizing the items into subtests and performance areas that roughly parallel instructional activity in the typical classroom. The Key Math Diagnostic Arithmetic Test (Connolly, Nachtman, & Pritchett, 1976) displays these structural refinements; the test provides diagnostic information for the total test performance, area performance, subtest performance, and item performance. The latest edition of Metropolitan Achievement Tests (Prescott, Balow, Hogan & Farr, 1978) also has been adapted by the authors to meet the expanding and varied needs of test users. The MAT now encompasses both survey and diagnostic tests. The survey test provides norm-referenced and criterion-referenced interpretation of achievement in reading comprehension, mathematics, language, social studies, and science. The MAT for instructional diagnosis incorporates these instructional batteries for reading, mathematics, and language, and is designed as "an instructional planning tool that provides detailed prescriptive information on the educational performance of individual pupils in terms of specific instructional objectives" (Prescott, Balow, Hogan & Farr, 1978, p. 2).

These tests are surely harbingers of the new type of test we can expect in the foreseeable future. The pressing need for such testing devices will create the economic incentive for test manufacturers to insure that the demand is met. The utility of these new tests will likely come to light through their use by practitioners in the field.

Norm-Referenced Tests and Curriculum

The similarity of content found across standardized norm-referenced tests reflects common test development procedures used by test manufacturers. These procedures are expressly designed to elucidate a common core of educational values, objectives, and content. This consistency of content makes possible comparisons in achievement across students, programs, schools, and geographic locations. Many persons, however, view this commonality as one of the shortcomings of standardized instruments because achieving such commonality necessarily results in the loss of some degree of content-relevance for any one local situation. The degree of overlap of test content and curricular content therefore varies from one classroom to the next and from one program to the next.

This lack of perfect relevance or overlap with any one particular curriculum or instructional program reflects on what standardized norm-referenced tests are intended and designed to do—provide educators with a means for assessing the status of individual students relative to their peers (or a group of students relative to other groups) with regard to a conventional set of educational goals. Such information is useful in making judgments about the general progress of individual students and about the adequacy of programs.

Two important points about norm-referenced achievement tests need to be re-emphasized: (1) such tests measure progress through comparison with the progress of others, and (2) they measure progress not in any one curriculum but in those areas held important across curricula. These facts have very important implications for what norm-referenced tests are *not* designed or intended to do. Because they generally are not designed for use with any one particular curriculum, and because they focus on determining a student's status relative to others, norm-referenced achievement tests should not be expected to be valid for the purpose of assessing a student's progress at specified absolute points in instructional programs. It should be obvious that to satisfy such a purpose, separate tests would need be developed for each individual instructional program, and scores would need to be referenced, not directly to the performance of others, but to levels within the specified instructional program.

The utility of standardized norm-referenced tests for placing children in reading curricula has been the subject of empirical study. Jenkins and Pany (1978) looked at the degree of overlap of test and curricular content for five elementary-level tests and five basal-reading programs. They concluded from their investigation that "bias" exists between achievement tests and reading curricula, and cautioned educators about the effects of such "bias" on curricular placement decision. Jenkins and Pany proved a known and obvious (but important) point: standardized norm-referenced achievement tests are not useful for purposes for which they are not intended or designed.

Looking at Performance Differences

Far more important than the fact that a student has received a particular test or subtest score is how scores differ from one another and from those of some relevant peer group. Intra-individual differences (which depend on norms for meaning) are used diagnostically (1) to establish the existence of significant discrepancies between actual performance and expected levels of performance, (a prerequisite for diagnosing learning disabilities), and (2) to identify strengths and/ or weaknesses in specific skills or aptitudes by comparing performance across skill or academic areas. Inter-individual differences, on the other hand, are used diagnostically (1) to distinguish the handicapped from the nonhandicapped; (2) to distinguish among different handicapping conditions; and (3) to identify subgroups of handicapped students within categories of exceptionality. The process involved in the examination of performance differences is generally referred to as differential diagnosis, of which profiling is one of the tools.

Profiling

A profile is a graphic display of test (or subtest) scores that highlights intra-individual, inter-individual, or group differences. Profiles facilitate test interpretation and communication among professionals and between professionals and non-professionals. Capability for profiling is provided for by many manufacturers of standardized tests, and is a very effective device used by diagnosticians. However, there are some guidelines that should be observed whenever profiles are employed for diagnostic purposes.

All scores plotted on a profile must be expressed in the same units of measurement. The most adequate units of measurement for such purposes are standard or percentile scores. It is also necessary that all scores included in the profile be based either on the same norm group or on norm groups representative of the same population. Differences in norm groups for different tests are one plausible explanation for observed differences in a student's performance on two tests. While it is difficult to determine if discrepancies are due to norm group differences, the more evidence one can provide for two norm groups as accurate representations of the same population, the less likely it is that observed differences in an individual's performance are due to differences in the two groups.

Along with the actual scores, a profile should always include an index of error, which enables the decision maker to determine if the differences are real or simply due to measurement error. Bearing in mind that the reliability of difference scores is generally lower than the reliabilities of the tests from which the difference was derived, we can see that it is imperative to know the standard error of measurement for difference scores for the particular test or subtest differences of interest. As has been mentioned, a conservative estimate of this statistic can be made from knowledge of the standard errors for each of the tests on which performance is being compared.

Profiling is a practice so common that it is distressing to question the value of profiles for educational purposes. However, the value of profiles—and the use made of them—has indeed been scrutinized, and there are serious differences of opinion.

Kaufman (1976) examined the scatter on the WISC-R for the test's standardization population and developed normative tables of intra-test variability. The two indices of test variability he used were (1) the magnitude of the difference between the highest and lowest scaled score and (2) the number of subtests deviating by three or more points from the child's own mean scaled score. The degree of subtest variability within a population of normal students was most noteworthy and inconsistent with the "flat profile stereotype" which many educators hold for normal children and against which they gauge the "irregular" profiles of atypical children. Kaufman's data provide a "basal level for comparison" of normal and exceptional children's test profiles and a basis for interpretation and decisions. These data highlight the fact that test results may be misinterpreted due to limited knowledge of how normal children behave. More work of this sort is needed on a wider range of test instruments.

Vance, Wallbrown and Blaha (1978) reported the identification of subgroups of reading-disabled children on the basis of WISC-R profiles. Factor analysis of the WISC-R performance of 104 children referred to a clinic for reading difficulties yielded five reading disability syndromes. The profile for each syndrome in conjunction with other assessment data and clinical/diagnostic information was used to develop brief descriptions of each diagnostic grouping. Remedial strategies for each of the five syndromes were offered in a subsequent publication (Wallbrown, Vance, & Blaha, 1979). The authors concluded that the WISC-R is a useful instrument for describing the patterns of reading disability for many disabled children. However, they cautioned that a substantial number of the profiles reviewed did not adhere to any of the five reading disability clusters.

M. Miller (1980), in a review of the research reported by Vance, Wallbrown, and Blaha, emphasized the critical weakness in profile analysis and pointed out that standards for individual decision making are more stringent than those for groups:

Findings from group data were a fluke. If, therfore, a particular pattern were found for groups, there is no assurance that it would relate to individuals, and one remediates individuals. (p. 339)

In their rejoinder to Dr. Miller, Wallbrown, Blaha, and Vance (1980) characterized the reading syndromes as "clinical hypotheses." But Miller emphasized that the number of children who fell outside the five categories suggests caution in interpretation. The existence of "profiles" for groups of children does not automatically translate to useable findings or a basis for decision making for individual children.

Finally, in a most recent report of WISC-R analysis, Stevenson (1980) portrayed another approach to profile development and analysis. Suspecting that WISC-R IQ scores (full-scale, verbal, and performance) masked much diagnostic and evaluative data, she regrouped the WISC-R subtests along three process dimensions she believed to tap relatively independent functions: verbal comprehension, analytic-field approach, and attention-concentration (dimensions suggested by Witkin, Dyk, Paterson, Goodenough, & Karp, 1962). The deviation IQ scores for 55 children were derived to reflect their relative standing on the three process functions. Differences in the deviation scores suggested that attentional difficulties were prevalent for this sample of children and contributed to their learning difficulties. As Stevenson provided no data on the magnitude of differences among the various deviation IQ scores, nor any assurance that the differences were statistically significant, further discussion of her findings is precluded. Rather, the study is useful for its approach to profile analysis rather than for its findings per se.

Profile analysis is a technique, facilitated by the use of norm-referenced tests, that may be useful in the assessment of handicapped children. But the diagnostician must be aware of the shortcomings of profile analysis in order to put the technique to best use. Attention to the technical characteristics of the tests used, and development of profiles that account for the unreliability of difference scores, will enhance the interpretability of test results. Extension of profiles derived from subgroup research to individual diagnosis and evaluation should be very cautiously done. At best, profile analysis, in this instance, can only lead to a diagnostic hypothesis to be corroborated by other evidence.

CONCLUSION

Our defense of norm-referenced standardized tests for use with the mildly handicapped reflects our belief that the level of accomplishment of nonhandicapped students is the reference point against which the achievement of the mildly handicapped student is judged. In working with various populations of mildly handicapped students (the learning disabled, the educable mentally retarded, the emotionally disturbed or socially maladjusted) as well as individuals with mild to moderate physical or sensory impairments, we strive to overcome the social and/or academic gaps that separate the handicapped from the nonhandicapped. "Normalization" is the goal on which our educational efforts are focused. Within the myriad details and nuances of daily instruction for the individual, specific skills, small social accommodations, and modest increments in achievement are necessarily our concern, but all of these intermediate achievements and accomplishments must be part of a cohesive and purposeful plan toward some essential goal. With the mildly handicapped, it is undeniable that the goal is to integrate these students into the mainstream of education and, later, adult life. Within this context, comparisons of the handicapped to the nonhandicapped are unavoidable. When such comparisons are to be made, norm-referenced tests are the instruments of choice. Rather than avoiding such comparisons and evaluations, they should be incorporated appropriately into the decision-making process.

The polarity that has evolved between the advocates of norm-referenced tests and the advocates of criterion-referenced tests hinges on the perceived educational utility of the two types of educational test instruments, but opposing points of view are tied to inherent personal and philosophical values. The distance between the two camps may diminish as tests designed for both norm-referenced and criterion-referenced evaluation are developed—which clearly appears to be a trend for the future. An evolving evaluation technology, and an increase in the availability of testing instruments for various academic subjects and skills, places an increasing burden on the classroom teacher and the diagnostician to keep abreast of new developments and products in order to make informed selections and to use tests in the most professional manner. To these ends, we believe that minimal competencies for teachers and diagnosticians in the area of assessment must be upgraded. Required competencies should include basic statistical concepts, application of basic concepts to test selection and interpretation, test administration, and sufficient knowledge of categories of test instruments and their uses and limitations, to ensure the meaningful and sensible use of assessment tools in the decision-making process.

REFERENCES

Armstrong, G. A framework for determining the value of diagnostic information for instructional decision-making. *Educational Technology*, 1976, *16*, 30–34.

Bennett, R. *Basic measurement competence in special education teacher diagnosticians.* Doctoral dissertation, Teachers College, Columbia University, 1979. (Dissertation Abstracts International, 1980, *40*, 4996A; University Microfilms No. 8006792.) (a)

Bennett, R. *The special education teacher diagnostician: Professional training needs.* Paper presented at the International Conference of the Association for Children with Learning Disabilities, Milwaukee, Wis., February 1980. (b)

Bennett, R. Professional competence and the assessment of exceptional children. *Journal of Special Education*, in press. (a)

Bennett, R. Cautions in the use of informal measures in the educational assessment of ex-

ceptional children. *Journal of Learning Disabilities*, in press. (b)

Bennett, R., & Shepherd, M. Basic measurement proficiency of learning disability specialists. *Learning Disability Quarterly*, in press.

Buros, O. (Ed.). *The eighth mental measurement yearbook.* Highland Park, N.J.: Gryphon Press, 1978.

Connelly, A. J., Nachtman, W., & Pritchett, E. M. (Eds.). *Key math diagnostic arithmetic test: Manual.* Circle Pines, Mn.: American Guidance Service, 1976.

Cronbach, L. J. *Essentials of psychological testing* (3rd ed.). New York: Harper & Row, 1970.

Debra, P. v. Turlington, Federal Supplement, 1979, *464,* 244. (DCMD Florida, Tampa Division).

Dunn, L. M., & Markwardt, F. C. *Peabody Individual Achievement Manual.* Circle Pines, Mn.: American Guidance Service, 1970.

Ebel, R. L. What do educational tests test? *Educational Psychologist*, 1973, *10*, 76–79.

Ebel, R. L. The case for norm-referenced measurements. *Educational Researcher*, 1978, *7*, 3–5.

Educational Testing Service. *Information for students*. Princeton, N.J.: College Entrance Examination Board, 1979.

Farr, R. *Reading: What can be measured?* Newark, De.: International Reading Association, 1969.

Federal Register. Assistance to states for education of handicapped children: Procedures for evaluating specific learning disabilities. December 29, 1977, pp. 65082–65085.

Guilford, J. P. *Psychometric methods* (2nd ed.). New York: McGraw-Hill, 1954.

Haney, W. Trouble over testing. *Educational Leadership*, 1980, *37*, 640–650.

Hieronymous, A., Lindquist, E., & Hoover, H. *Iowa tests of basic skills*. Boston: Houghton-Mifflin, 1978.

IQ tests not biased against blacks, judge rules. *Education of the Handicapped*, 1980, *6*, 3–4.

Jenkins, J. R., & Pany, D. Standardized achievement tests: How useful for special education? *Exceptional Children*, 1978, *44*, 448–453.

Kaufman, A. S. A new approach to the interpretation of test scatter on the WISC-R. *Journal of Learning Disabilities*, 1976, *9*, 160–168.

Larry, P. v. Riles. Opinion, U.S. District Court for Northern District of California (No. C-712270 RFP), October 11, 1979.

Livingston, S. Reliability and "error of measurement." In Educational Testing Service (Ed.), *Issues in testing*. Princeton, N.J.: Educational Testing Service, 1980.

Mehrens, W. A., & Lehmann, I. J. *Standardized tests in education* (2nd ed.). New York: Holt, Rinehart and Winston, 1975.

Mercer, J., & Lewis, J. *System of multicultural pluralistic assessment*. New York: Psychological Corporation, 1979.

Messick, S. Test validity and the ethics of assessment. *American Psychologist*, 1980, *35*, 1012–1027.

Miller, C., & Chansky, N. Psychologists' scoring of WISC protocols. *Psychology in the Schools*, 1972, *9*, 144–152.

Miller, C., Chansky, N., & Gredler, G. Rater agreement on WISC protocols. *Psychology in the Schools*, 1970, *7*, 190–193.

Miller, M. On the attempt to find WISC-R profiles for learning and reading disabilities (A response to Vance, Wallbrown, and Blaha). *Journal of Learning Disabilities*, 1980, *13*, 338–340.

Nitko, A. J. Distinguishing the many varieties of criterion referenced tests. *Review of Educational Research*, 1980, *50*, 461–485.

Popham, W. J. *Educational evaluation*. Englewood Cliffs: Prentice-Hall, 1975.

Popham, W. The case for criterion-referenced measurements. *Educational Researcher*, 1978, *7*, 6–10.

Prescott, G., Balow, I., Hogan, T., & Farr, R. *Metropolitan achievement tests: Teachers manual for administering and interpreting*. New York: Psychological Corporation, 1978.

Salvia, J., & Ysseldyke, J. *Assessment in special and remedial education* (2nd ed.). Boston: Houghton Mifflin, 1981.

Sattler, J. M. *Assessment of children's intelligence*. Philadelphia: Saunders, 1974.

Sax, G. *Principles of educational measurement and evaluation*. Belmont, Ca.: Wadsworth, 1974.

Scannell, D., Haugh, O., Schild, A., & Ulmer, G. *Tests of achievement and proficiency*. Boston: Houghton-Mifflin, 1978.

Seashore, H., & Ricks, J. *Test service bulletin 39*. New York: Psychological Corporation, 1950.

Standards for educational and psychological tests. Washington, D.C.: American Psychological Association, 1974.

Stevenson, L. P. WISC-R analysis: Implications for diagnosis and intervention. *Journal of Learning Disabilities*, 1980, *13*, 346–349.

Thorndike, R. Dilemmas in diagnosis. In W. MacGinite (Ed.), *Assessment problems in reading*. Newark, De.: International Reading Association, 1973.

Thorndike, R., & Hagen, E. *Measurement and evaluation in psychology and education*. New York: Wiley, 1977.

Thurlow, M., & Ysseldyke, J. Current assessment and decision-making practices in model LD programs. *Learning Disability Quarterly*, 1979, *2*, 15–24.

Vance, H., Wallbrown, F. H., & Blaha, J. Determining WISC-R profiles for reading disabled children. *Journal of Learning Disabilities*, 1978, *11*, 657–661.

Wallbrown, F. H., Blaha, J. & Vance, B. A reply to Miller's concerns about WISC-R profile analysis. *Journal of Learning Disabilities*, 1980, *13*, 340–345.

Wallbrown, F. H., Vance, H., & Blaha, J. Developing remedial hypotheses from ability profiles. *Journal of Learning Disabilities*, 1979, *12*, 557–561.

Warren, S., & Brown, W. Examiner scoring errors on individual intelligence tests. *Psychology in the Schools,* 1973, *10,* 118–122.

Witkin, H. A., Dyk, R., Paterson, H., Goodenough, D., & Karp, S. *Psychological differentiation.* New York: John Wiley, 1962.

Woodcock, R. W. *Woodcock Reading Mastery Tests: Manual.* Circle Pines, MN: American Guidance Service, 1973.

Ysseldyke, J., Algozzine, B., Regan, R., & Potter, M. Technical adequacy of tests used by professionals in simulated decision making. *Psychology in the Schools,* 1980, *17,* 202–209.

Robert A. Sedlak
Cecelia Steppe-Jones
Denise Sedlak

12

Informal Assessment: Concepts and Practices

Informal assessment utilizes evaluation procedures that the teacher can use in the classroom every day in order to plan instruction. It refers to the process of determining the behaviors and/or subject matter that a student does and does not possess, and determines how to best instruct the student. It also represents an essential link between formal assessment procedures and direct instruction. While formal assessment provides valuable information in regard to a student's functioning level relative to peers, it does not provide a direct match with instructional objectives and procedures. Such is the role of informal assessment, for informal assessment does more than tell the teacher which objectives the learner has and has not mastered. It also provides guidance on the optimal instructional strategies to use with the youngster. These principles may be applied equally well to the informal assessment of the learning disabled, the mildly retarded, or the mildly behaviorally disabled.

ACHIEVEMENT VERSUS DIAGNOSTIC TESTING

In determining a learner's present level of functioning for the purpose of programming, a process often referred to as diagnostic testing is used. A differentiation should be made between the assessment of achievement in academic subject areas and the diagnostic assessment process. In most cases, a battery of tests is given (either criterion- or norm-referenced), and the results are summarized into a profile or a checklist, and suggested teaching objectives are specified. The testing is often done individually or in a structured situation. Testing procedures are carefully adhered to so that the results can be considered reliable and valid. In most cases, this type of diagnostic testing results in a good indication of a learner's achievement, i.e., what the learner has or has not mastered. Norm-referenced tests also show how a youngster compares to chronological age peers in different areas such as comprehension, computation, reasoning, vocabulary, spelling, and grammar, while criterion-referenced measures show how each item missed is linked to a behavioral objective and becomes the basis for instruction. This type of information is usually adequate for making an instructional decision regarding

263

what to teach, but will not be a sufficient basis for programming a learner with serious academic problems. In contrast to the achievement task, the diagnostic task is aimed at answering the questions "Why hasn't the learner mastered this skill?" "What is he or she doing wrong?" "What can be done to correct the problem?" Teacher observation and informal assessment procedures can be carried out by the classroom teacher on a daily basis as a part of the instructional process to determine the answers to these questions.

THE INFORMAL ASSESSMENT PROCESS

An informal evaluation is usually undertaken by a teacher or an educational diagnostician. It is the essential step in the assessment process that verifies, probes, or discards the conclusions and recommendations of the formal assessment and leads to the formulation of a remedial program for the learner.

The process of informal evaluation is dynamic rather than static, involving the use of paper and pencil criterion-referenced tests, analysis of the student's errors, behavioral observations, checklists, and analysis of the student's responses to various instructional tasks. Informal assessment does not take place within a set period of time, but rather is a total part of the teaching process.

In order to effectively do an informal assessment, the classroom teacher needs to possess a wide variety of skills. Among these are the ability to (1) construct a criterion-referenced test; (2) do an error analysis; (3) separate behavior from subject matter content; (4) use dimension control; (5) use observation/recording skills; and (6) use task analysis for evaluation purposes.

Criterion-Referenced Measures

Norm-referenced and criterion-referenced tests are both used for the purpose of determining a starting point for instruction. At the present time, criterion-referenced tests and inventories are quite popular among special educators. Such tests are designed to measure the specific knowledge or content a student has and has not learned, in contrast to norm-referenced tests, which compare an individual's performance to that of a norm group (Kelly & Vergason, 1978).

Most criterion tests and inventories are linked directly to a particular curriculum or have a mechanical or manual cross-referencing retrieval system for the purpose of linking the objectives on the test to specific page numbers in a variety of commercially available programs and textbooks. Some of the tests have diagnostic bases from which they operate, providing not only a summary of correct and incorrect responses for a learner, but an elementary error analysis as well.

Popham (1978) wrote probably the single most comprehensive handbook to date on the construction of criterion-referenced measures. He noted that in order to prepare an adequate criterion-referenced measure, the test developer must have an adequate description of the content base about which the items are to be written. Several factors mentioned by Popham are needed for the construction of criterion-referenced measures: (1) an adequate description of the domain to be measured; (2) an adequate number of items for each measured behavior; (3) a test

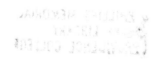

sufficiently limited in scope so that performance information is useable; (4) a good match between items and the content domain; (5) reliability; and (6) validity.

The fact that a test has correlated objectives does not in and of itself make the test a good criterion-referenced measure. Many of the commercially available criterion-referenced tests are nothing more than tests with objectives and lack an adequate sampling of behavior within a domain. In fact, quite a few tests do not even define the behavioral domain from which the items were sampled. Sedlak & Fitzmaurice (1981) called these tests diagnostic screeners because, while they cannot provide a comprehensive analysis of a student's skills, they do represent a starting point in the diagnostic process. Examples of these diagnostic screener systems include Diagnosis: An Instructional Aid (*Diagnosis*, 1973); Fountain Valley Teacher Support Systems in Mathematics and Reading (Zweig, 1974); Mathematics Concept Inventory Levels I–IV (Cawley, Goodstein, Fitzmaurice, Lepore, Sedlak, & Althaus, 1976; 1977); and System Fore (Los Angeles Public Schools).

The teacher who wishes to develop a criterion-referenced assessment system should follow these steps:

1. Determine the goals of the program by curriculum area.
2. List a sequence of sub-skills within each curriculum domain.
3. List a sequence of objectives within each sub-skill area, based upon a developmental or behavioral analysis of the sub-skill.
4. Develop procedures that adequately assess sub-skill objectives, using a paper and pencil test, an obserational checklist, or a performance-rating scale.
5. Cluster items on the test or scale that measure a common concept or objective in order to facilitate an error analysis of the learning performance.

Error Analysis

The teacher's ability to do an analysis of a student's errors and to identify consistent patterns of errors is an extremely valuable dimension of the informal assessment process. While error analysis is not the preferred means of assessment (since it allows a student to practice her errors), it is a common means of determining a persistent problem or skill deficit. Error analysis works particularly well in skill areas such as reading, spelling, math, and grammar.

To conduct an error analysis requires that the student perform the academic task. Preferably, this task results in a permanent product of his work so that an analysis can be made of the errors. The teacher examines the items on the test that are wrong and attempts to identify commonalities of the incorrect responses. Once some of these commonalities are identifed, the teacher verifies the existence of the error pattern by requiring the student to take a test composed of a parallel set of items. If a similar error pattern exists, the teacher can then target the rule or skill that needs correcting. Some examples of error patterns and alternative explanations for the errors are presented in Figures 12-1 and 12-2. The process of error analysis, then, becomes an exercise in hypothesis testing. In some cases, it is valuable to have the student orally work through the problem or complete the assignment as he is writing it.

46	32	38	49	50	43
+26	+46	+11	+12	+13	+27
612 X	*78*	*49*	*511* X	*63*	*610* X

Possible explanations: (1) Student adds from left-to-right.
(2) Student does not understand place value.
(3) Student does not regroup.

56	43	68	45	26	23
+14	+67	+27	+48	+19	+18
61 X	*11* X	*95*	*93*	*45*	*41*

Possible explanations: (1) Student does not understand place value.
(2) Student does not understand zero as a place holder.
(3) Student does have a concept of zero and believes that it stands for nothing and therefore disregards it.

Fig. 12-1. Sample error analysis in arithmetic.

In order to minimize time spent in doing the error analysis, it is important for the teacher to construct the test in such a way that each group of problems has a unique set of dimensions that differentiate the evaluation item from another. An example of this differentiation is shown in Figures 12-3 and 12-4. In these two examples, the items are differentiated by a single dimension. (In a later section on dimension control, the use of a matrix to control for several dimensions simultaneously is discussed.)

In the error-analysis process, any aspect of the problem can create difficulty for the learner. The learner's error could be conceptual in nature, represent a skill deficit, or merely be the result of the presentation of the problem in an unfamiliar format. Format includes such aspects as a math problem being presented vertically rather than orally. Conceptual errors deal with the use of incorrect rules and are

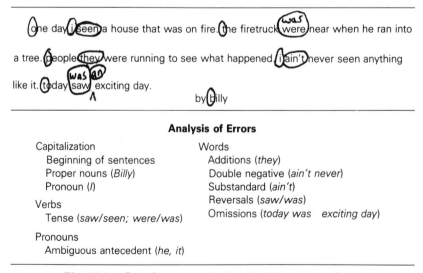

One day i seen a house that was on fire. the firetruck were (was) near when he ran into a tree. people they were running to see what happened. i ain't never seen anything like it. today saw (was an) exciting day.
                                                         by Billy

Analysis of Errors

Capitalization
  Beginning of sentences
  Proper nouns (*Billy*)
  Pronoun (*I*)

Verbs
  Tense (*saw/seen; were/was*)

Pronouns
  Ambiguous antecedent (*he, it*)

Words
  Additions (*they*)
  Double negative (*ain't never*)
  Substandard (*ain't*)
  Reversals (*saw/was*)
  Omissions (*today was   exciting day*)

Fig. 12-2. Sample error analysis of written expression.

Skill	Examples of Tasks				
Sum of two one-digit numbers < 10	4 +5	6 +2	2 +1	4 +3	7 +2
Sum of three one-digit numbers < 10	4 2 +1	3 3 +3	2 1 +1	1 2 +1	1 1 +4
Sum of two one-digit numbers <10 horizontal format	4 + 2 = 5 + 3 =		6 + 2 = 5 + 4 =		2 + 1 =
Sum of two one-digit numbers < 20	8 +7	6 +8	5 +9	7 +7	8 +4
Sum of two two-digit numbers with regrouping	27 +17	46 +17	49 +24	42 +29	37 +35

Fig. 12-3. Sample math test with items organized by dimensions.

generally the result of incomplete concept formation resulting from poor instruction. A teacher who is sensitive to the critical dimensions of a task can be assured that incomplete concept formation is not caused by using examples of the rule *and its exceptions* as a part of the teaching process. Skill deficits are usually easily recognized. Examples of skill deficits include nonmastery of basic math facts and nonmastery of basic vocabulary.

Behavior versus Content

Behavioral objectives are the foundation of criterion-referenced testing. Since behavioral objectives always specify both observable behavior (how the student is to respond) and the content (subject matter), a student's mastery or nonmastery of the objective can be assessed reliably. The problem encountered

Skill	Example of Task				
	Direction: Teacher pronounces word and student writes and spells orally				
-*at* family	pat	mat	rat	fat	sat
-*et* family	pet	met	let	bet	set
-*ing* suffix with final consonant doubled	running	sitting	hitting	swimming	petting
-*ing* suffix with final consonant not doubled	kicking	fighting	jumping	writing	walking
final *e* silent: one-syllable words	bite	rate	late	pale	mute

Fig. 12-4. Sample spelling test with items organized by dimensions.

when directly applying the notion of behavioral objectives to mildly handicapped learners, and subsequently constructing criterion-referenced tests, is that *by definition* mildly handicapped learners have behavioral deficits. If a student fails the criterion-referenced assessment, the examiner (teacher) still does not know if the failure is attributable to a lack of knowledge of the subject matter or to the manner in which the objective was assessed. In order to solve this problem, content must be separated from behavior in the objective, and a range of behavioral response options for demonstrating mastery of the subject matter must be specified.

An example of this problem might help to clarify the dilemma. Given the behavioral objective "from written directions the student will write in order the names of the last five presidents of the United States with 100 percent accuracy," the teacher may find that a handicapped student can fail this objective for a variety of reasons, none of which have to do with knowledge of the subject matter (history). For example, at least two nonhistory behaviors could interfere. The first behavior requires that the learner be able to read and interpret the printed word. The second requires that the learner be able to spell and write the names. A learner who is not competent in writing and/or spelling would not be able to successfully pass the objective even though the student might know the names of the last five presidents. A sensitivity on the part of the teacher is needed in order to discern whether the lack of mastery is attributable to a content or behavioral deficit.

The teacher who finds that the learner has failed certain items needs now to explore behavioral-response options in order to pinpoint the source of the difficulty. Several procedures can be undertaken at this point. The first is to consider the objective as a terminal objective that has subunits or subcomponents, commonly referred to as target objectives. The teacher can list the target objectives and assess the student's mastery of each. A second procedure would be to assess the student's knowledge by varying the behavioral demands. This second procedure would involve asking the student to tell you the names of the last five presidents, to spell aloud (or in written form) their names as they are dictated to her, or to name the presidents from pictures.

The Interactive Unit

One model that has been used successfully in a math curriculum for the handicapped and separates the behavioral demands of the task from the content is the interactive unit (Cawley et al., 1976, 1977). The model (Fig. 12-5) is composed of eight cells, four of which identify teacher behaviors and four of which identify learner responses. There are 16 possible behavioral interactions. The model allows either the teaching or the assessment of a concept through one or all of the behavioral combinations. A nonacademic situation may help to explain the model. Suppose that you wished to assess if someone knew the steps required to change the tire on a car. Working backwards within the model, you might (1) give a paper and pencil test with the written instruction, "list the steps needed to change a tire" (graphically symbolize–graphically symbolize); (2) instruct the student to "tell me the steps needed to change a tire" (state–state); (3) show the student a scrambled sequence of pictures and ask him to identify or put into correct order the steps needed to change a tire (present–identify); or (4) demonstrate for the

| Teacher | Construct (C) | Present (P) | State (S) | Graphically symbolize (GS) |
| Learner | Construct (C) | Identify (I) | State (S) | Graphically symbolize (GS) |

Construct (C): teacher manipulates or uses objects to demonstrate a math concept, and the learner uses objects to demonstrate understanding.

Present (P): teacher presents the learner with a fixed visual displayed composed of pictures or prearranged objects.

Identify (I): teacher asks learner questions with multiple-choice answers.

State (S): spoken instructions, questions, and/or responses are used.

Graphically symbolize (GS): written or draw symbolic sets of materials, nonpictorial worksheets, and computational worksheets are used. Learner responds by writing.

Fig. 12-5. The interactive unit.

student how to change a tire on a car and then ask him to do it (construct–construct). Table 12-1 shows all 16 possible ways to assess if the student knows the steps required to change the tire on a car.

Behavior Resource Guide

A system that has been found helpful in identifying relevant organizational patterns of content is the Behavior Resource Guide (BRG) by Cawley, Calder, Mann, McClung, Ramanauskas, and Suiter (1973). The BRG is a compendium of 266 behaviors, which define the channel of stimulus presentation (auditory or visual), the type of response required (e.g., verbal or pointing), and the organization or the subject matter (e.g., a sequence, list, picture, paragraph, or objects). The entire listing of behaviors is content free. Such a system allows a great many options for assessing a given content domain and also allows a great deal of dimension control. The system also has a section of behaviors in the social-emotional domain that can be used to assess problems in that area.

The 266 behaviors listed in the BRG are referred to as desired learner outcomes (DLOs). Each DLO has a code, a standard, and a learner response. The code helps the user identify whether the set of DLOs being used is visually presented, aurally presented, or in the social-emotional domain. Examples of DLOs in the visual (V), aural (A), and social-emotional (S) areas are presented in Table 12-2.

The BRG system and the interactive unit have common characteristics. The major difference between the two is that the BRG offers a greater degree of specificity, especially in regard to the organization of the material. Both systems allow the assessment of strengths and weaknesses across subject matter while keeping behavior constant. For example, in the DLO coded AGR-1 (Table 12-2), the word in the standard could be from science, history, or even auto mechanics. By holding a behavior constant, the teacher can determine content deficits, and by reversing the process, the teacher can determine behavioral deficits.

Table 12-1
Sample of 16 Interactions on the Same Task

Assessment Procedure	Interaction
1. The teacher demonstrates the steps needed to change the tire on a car and then asks the student to do it.	Construct/Construct
2. The teacher demonstrates the steps needed to change the tire on a car and then asks the student to arrange or identify a sequence of pictures representing the act.	Construct/Identify
3. The teacher demonstrates the steps needed to change the tire on a car and then asks the student to tell the steps that were taken.	Construct/State
4. The teacher demonstrates the steps needed to change the tire on a car and then asks the student to write the steps that were taken.	Construct/Graphically Symbolize
5. The teacher presents the student with a sequence of pictures in correct order showing a person changing a tire. The student is asked to actually change the tire.	Present/Construct
6. The teacher presents the student with a scrambled set of pictures of a person changing a tire. The student is to put them into the correct order.	Present/Identify
7. The teacher presents the student with a sequence of pictures in the correct order and says to the student, "Tell me the steps needed to change a tire." The student states the steps.	Present/State
8. The teacher presents a sequence of pictures in the correct order and tells the student to write the steps in changing a tire.	Present/Graphically Symbolize
9. The teacher tells the student the steps necessary to change a tire and asks the student to demonstrate these steps.	State/Construct
10. The teacher tells the student the steps necessary to change a tire and asks the student to arrange or identify a sequence of pictures representing the act.	State/Identify
11. The teacher says to the student, "Tell me the steps needed to change a tire." The student is to state the steps.	State/State
12. The teacher says to the student, "Tell me the steps needed to change a tire." The student is to write the steps.	State/Graphically Symbolize
13. The teacher writes the steps needed to change a tire and asks the student to demonstrate the steps needed to change a tire.	Graphically Symbolize/ Construct

Table 12-1 (*continued*)

Assessment Procedure	Interaction
14. The teacher writes the steps needed to change a tire and asks the student to arrange or identify a sequence of pictures representing the act.	Graphically Symbolize/ Identify
15. The teacher writes the steps needed to change a tire. The student is asked to state the steps that would be taken.	Graphically Symbolize/ State
16. The teacher writes the steps needed to change a tire and the student is then asked to write them.	Graphically Symbolize/ Graphically Symbolize

Dimension Control

In the development of an informal assessment procedure, the teacher needs to be fully aware of the dimensions of the task that influence performance. One dimension already mentioned is the behavioral response required and the manner in which the material is presented. A second aspect of dimension control revolves around the organization of the subject matter. Listing and sequencing (a list used in a particular order) are examples of two dimensions that deal with the organization of the subject matter. The task requirement can be made more or less difficult by the arrangement of the material. In the example on writing the names of the last five presidents in order, the sequencing factor makes the objective slightly more difficult than just requiring a student to list them in any order.

The section on error analysis provided two examples of test items written according to different dimensions, but each set of item clusters only isolated a

Table 12-2
Sample of DLOs from the Behavior Resource Guide

Code	Standard	Learner Response
VDS-2	A picture of real object and two or more choices	Identify picture that is same as object
VCN-6	A set of pictures of objects	Orally state common characteristics of each group
ARG-1	A word	Identify from two or more choices the picture that represents the meaning of the word
ACM-3	Descriptive characteristics of an object(s)	Name the object
SCN-3	An opportunity to work independently to construct an object(s) of the student's own design and choosing	Work independently to construct an object of own design and choosing
SCN-7	The responsibility to organize a group of learners in the construction of an object	Organize a group of learners in the construction of an object

1. The tall man with the grey beard ate 5 frankfurters in the contest. The tall man without a beard ate 3 frankfurters in the contest. The short man with the grey beard ate 2 frankfurters in the contest. How many frankfurters did the men eat?	2. A tall man ate 5 frankfurters. Another tall man ate 3 frankfurters. A short man ate 2 frankfurters. How many frankfurters did the men eat?
3. The tall man with the grey beard ate 12 frankfurters in the contest. The tall man without a beard ate 9 frankfurters in the contest. The short man with the grey beard ate 8 frankfurters in the contest. How many frankfurters did the men eat?	4. A tall man ate 12 frankfurters. Another tall man ate 9 frankfurters. A short man ate 8 frankfurters. How many frankfurters did the men eat?
5. The tall man with the grey beard ate 12 frankfurters in the contest. The tall man without a beard ate 9 frankfurters in the contest. The short man with the grey bead ate 8 frankfurters in the contest. How many frankfurters did the tall men eat?	6. A tall man ate 12 frankfurters. Another tall man ate 9 frankfurters. A short man ate 8 frankfurters. How many frankfurters did the tall men eat?

Fig. 12-6. Sample word problems.

single-dimension difference. Figure 12-6 is an example of math-word problems that shows that a variety of dimensions can be controlled simultaneously when problems are written. The dimensions around which these problems were written are (1) syntactic complexity level of the information statements; (2) vocabulary level; (3) presence or absence of extraneous information; (4) computational difficulty; and (5) set complexity language in the question. There may be other factors within these problems, but these five illustrate a number of points.

Syntactic complexity refers to sentence structure. Word problems containing prepositional phrases, clauses, negations, and embedded structures are more difficult to comprehend than simple declarative sentences (kernels). It is obvious that problems 1 and 2 in Figure 12-6 differ in syntactic complexity. It should be noticed, however, that in both problems computational difficulty is the same, the question statement is the same, the information load is the same, and the vocabulary level is about the same. The problems only differ on one variable—syntax. If a student missed number 1 and solved number 2 correctly, syntactic complexity might be suspected as the dimension interfering with the correct solution to the problem.

An examination of problems 1 and 3 reveals that they also differ on only one dimension—computational difficulty. All other dimensions of the problem are the same. A student missing number 3, but solving problem 1 correctly might have difficulty with computation.

Problems 5 and 6 differ from problems 3 and 4 in only one way. Do you see the difference? If you said that the two differ on set complexity you would be wrong. The correct difference is that 5 and 6 have extraneous information. Congratulations if you spotted it. To change the set complexity level of the questions in each of the problems, you would ask, "How many pieces of food did the people eat?" By asking this question you would have also eliminated the extraneous information in problems 5 and 6.

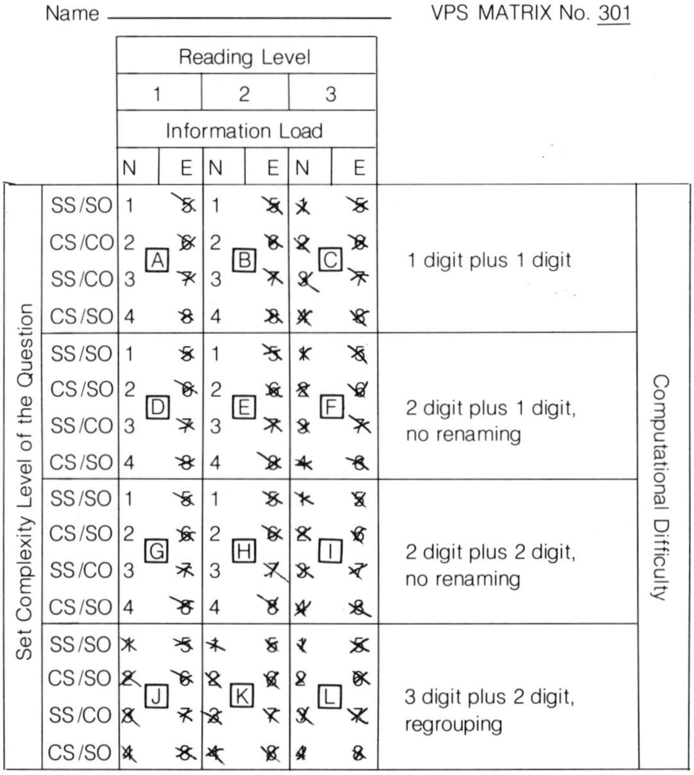

Name _____ VPS MATRIX No. 301

Fig. 12-7. Portion of an addition word problem matrix.

The key to understanding the concept of dimension control in an informal assessment procedure is to realize that minor changes in the presentation and organization of the material affects the learner's response; in order to control for the different dimensions, the examiner should only change one variable at a time. For organizational purposes, a matrix listing the different dimensions of a task in the rows and columns is helpful. An example of such an organizational schema is shown in Figure 12-7.

Each number within this matrix represents a problem with different identifiable characteristics. Problems 1, 2, 3, and 4 on all worksheets have no extraneous information. Worksheets A, B, and C all are at a common computational level. The same is true for the sets of worksheets "D-E-F," "G -H-I," and "J-K-L." The problems the student got wrong have been crossed out on the worksheets. All problems on worksheets C, F, I, and L were missed by the student. What is the variable common to this set of problems? All problems on worksheets J, K, and L were missed. What is the variable common to this set of problems? Problems 5, 6, 7, and 8 on all worksheets were missed. What is the variable common to this set of problems? After answering these questions you might suspect that this student cannot do problems with extraneous information, cannot do problems requiring regrouping (carrying), and seems to have problems with third grade vocabulary.

According to the patterns of errors, the teacher can formulate hypotheses regarding the primary problem impeding performance. The use of a matrix in the construction of criterion-referenced tests is an excellent technique since it helps to isolate the variables affecting performance.

RECORDING PROCEDURES

Beside using systems that rely heavily on paper and pencil types of diagnoses, the informal assessment process also relies on systematic observational/recording skills. Far more than just the act of looking is required in systematic observation. The observer must have a specific behavior or behaviors (targets) to look for and a means of recording the occurrence or nonoccurrence of these behaviors during a specified period of time. The systematic observation procedure may also require that the observer record what events or behaviors preceded the target behavior (antecedents) and what behaviors or events followed the behavior (consequences). Observational techniques are most commonly used to informally assess social-personal behaviors, although it is quite possible and appropriate to apply them to measures of academic performance. There are a variety of recording procedures. Among these are anecdotal recording, frequency recording, interval recording, and time sampling.

The first step in the observation process (frequency, interval, or time-sample records) is to define the behavior(s) of concern. The process is commonly referred to as targeting a behavior. Repp (1979) indicated that a definition of a target behavior should

> (a) describe the behavior in objective terms, (b) include the conditions under which it will be rewarded, (c) be complete, providing appropriate information on what should and should not be included, and (d) describe the behavior so that it can be measured. (p. 98)

The second step in the process is to determine the manner in which the behavior is to be measured. Event, interval, duration, and time-sample recording are the four procedures that the teacher will need to select from.

Anecdotal Records

Behavior can be recorded or documented in a variety of ways, one of which is anecdotal records. An anecdotal record is a written description of an event, describing the behaviors exhibited during the event, the persons present during the event, any antecedents to the behavior, and the reaction of others in the environment to the event. It is normally written in an informal style, and is objective in tone. An example of an anecdotal record appears in Figure 12-8.

Anecdotal records are generally not written on a regularly scheduled basis, but rather are written upon the occurrence of unusual events. It should be noted that the regular use of anecdotal records is the preferred method, but, realistically, these records are not kept systematically. For reliability, anecdotal records should be written as soon as possible after the event has occurred to minimize the influence of errors in recording the events. In addition, inferential statements should be minimized and clearly labeled. The best anecdotal record contains only factual behavioral observations.

Two major shortcomings of anecdotal records are (1) they generally are not kept in a systematic fashion, and (2) analysizing these records is a time-consuming task. If records are not kept in a systematic fashion, the resulting data may be highly biased. This particular shortcoming is not unique to the use of anecdotal records, but anecdotal records are most typically abused in this manner. Analysis

Student	Denise M.
Sept. 8	9:00 a.m. Denise got up from her desk and ran into the hall crying as we were beginning our spelling lesson. I went after her and asked what was wrong. She shook her head and didn't say anything and then walked back into the room.
Sept. 17	2:30 p.m. Denise hit Joey in the stomach while they were in line to get a drink of water. Joey said he didn't do anything. Denise just looked at Joey and didn't say anything. I asked her what happened but she wouldn't talk.
Sept. 25	10:30 a.m. Denise came running into the classroom during recess time and sat down at her desk and cried. I asked her what was wrong. She said "Nothing. Leave me alone."
Sept. 26	Denise was accused by Linda of taking her lunch money. Denise said it wasn't true. Linda said that she didn't see Denise take the money but that she was pretty sure that she had.

Fig. 12-8. Sample anecdotal record.

of anecdotal records is time consuming because each recorded event may deal with totally different behaviors in totally different environments. Quantifying these data is not a fruitful activity.

An advantage of anecdotal records *(when done properly)* is that they can help identify (1) possible problem areas needing closer scrutiny, and (2) consequences of specific behavioral events (which in turn can help the teacher in planning an intervention strategy).

Anecdotal records are generally not kept for academic behavior, but are used in describing inappropriate social behaviors. This is quite unfortunate because it shows a limited use of the technique.

Frequency Recording

Event or frequency recording is probably the most useful and least time-consuming method of measuring a behavior; it is a count of the occurrences of the target behavior in each observational session. In order to use frequency record-ing, there are two conditions that should be met (Kazdin, 1980). First, the re-sponse should have distinct starting and stopping points, such as catches made, words spoken, or pushups completed. Second, the target behavior should last a relatively constant period of time. Tantruming or screaming might not be best measured using a frequency recording strategy because the period of time for which they last varies. A student may only scream one or two times a day, but for an extended period. In order to be sensitive to changes in that behavior, a time-related system of measurement might be better utilized.

Comparisons of frequency data from day to day or session to session can be made only if the length of observation time each day or session is the same. If the length of the observation period is not the same, the information can be trans-formed to a rate of response, which gives comparable data across observation periods. The rate of response is computed by dividing the number of occurrences by the amount of time observed in each observational period.

$$\text{Rate} = \frac{\text{Frequency}}{\text{Time}}$$

Interval Recording

During interval-recording, each observation session is divided into a number of continuous intervals of equal length (usually 5–30 seconds). Interval recording is commonly used to measure behaviors which do not have discrete start or stop times and which vary in length. The observer records a + during each interval of time that a behavior occurred and a − during the intervals of time that a behavior did not occur. The data are summarized by dividing the number of intervals during which the target behavior was observed by the total number of intervals.

Kazdin (1980) described an interval-recording procedure in which several children in a classroom can be observed over the same period of time. The first child is observed during the first interval, the second child during the second, and so on, until all children have been observed.

Time Sampling

Time sampling is a method similar to interval recording in that its observation period relies on divided intervals of time that are usually fairly long in length. Using this method, the observer picks a few seconds randomly throughout the interval or at the end of the interval to observe the behavior. This method of observation just samples behavior at various times of intervals (in contrast to interval recording in which the interval is observed continuously). Thus, the observer might observe for a period of 3 seconds randomly throughout, or at the end of, every 60-second interval to see whether the child is screaming. If the child is actively screaming during the 3 seconds, a screaming response is recorded. If the child is not screaming in that 3-second period, even though he may have been seconds before and after the time-sample period, a screaming response cannot be recorded. A question that the observer may ask herself to clarify if she is using time-sample recording is "Was behavior observed during a sample of time in which the observation periods did not follow one another continuously?"

Graphing Behavior

To a large extent, evaluative data have greatest worth when summarized. The summary process is an important one, for it is through this process that the problem becomes clear. It is also at this point of summarization that progress toward the goal can be depicted most dramatically. A common method for summarizing data is graphing. Objectives that have been task analyzed provide data on student progress that can be easily graphed. In addition, information such as the number of problems worked, the percentage of words spelled correctly, and the number of words read per minute can be displayed in a graph.

While graphing is generally not seen as being a complicatd process, there are some basic rules to follow in creating a graph. Rule 1 is to be sure that the performance data are in a common base or unit. Only performance data that have a common base can be graphed. For example, the percentage of words spelled correctly, the number of steps in a task analysis done correctly, and the number of states named are all examples of performance data in a common base. It simplifies matters considerably if tests are prepared with a common number of items or a

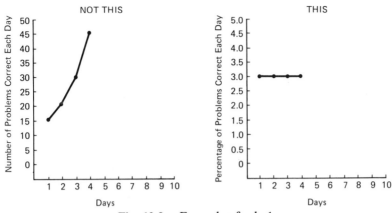

Fig. 12-9.   Example of rule 1.

common time limit so that the data base each day is consistent. In cases where the base differs from day to day or session to session, the data must be converted to a common base. For example, if a student is given 12 problems to work on Monday, 8 on Tuesday, 10 on Wednesday, and 10 on Thursday, and each day he solves 5 problems correctly, the information cannot be graphed before the data are converted to a common base. In this case, the common base would be determined by dividing the number of problems worked correctly by the number attempted each day to get a percentage. The resultant percentages would be 42%, 62%, 50%, and 50%, respectively. Another example of this data conversion process is the following: A student correctly solved 15 problems in a 5-minute period; 21 problems in a 7-minute period; 30 problems in a 10-minute period; and 45 problems in a 15-minute period. Correctly graphing these data requires that the number of problems per minute be determined, because the amount of time the student had available to her influenced the number of problems she did each session—which could lead the observer to conclude that her performance was increasing. However, by converting the information to a common base, it can be seen that her actual rate of doing the problems did not change; she did three problems per minute (Fig. 12-9). Understanding rule 1, finding the common base, is important to understanding the graphing process.

Rule 2 (Fig. 12-10) is to label the horizontal line and to be sure that there is

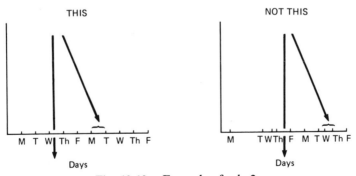

Fig. 12-10.   Example of rule 2.

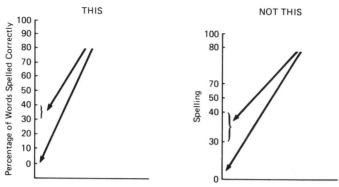

Fig. 12-11.   Example of rule 3.

equal spacing between the markings. This line should designate a time dimension, e.g., days, sessions, or periods.

Rule 3 (Fig. 12-11) is to label the vertical line and to be sure that there is equal spacing between the markings, as with the horizontal line. The label for this line should represent student performance information such as number of questions answered correctly, number of steps completed in a task analysis, percentage of words spelled correctly, or number of completions in a set period of time (rate). In numbering the vertical line, it is important that the lowest level of performance, "0", should not meet the horizontal line. If the "0" level of performance is put on the horizontal line, the graph is much harder to read.

Rule 4 (Fig. 12-12) is to put the student's name and the class from which the data are being summarized on the graph. Rule 5 (Fig. 12-12) is to title the graph. Rules 4 and 5 are important because a graph should convey information quickly to the reader. Rule 6 (Fig. 12-12) involves labeling the baseline and training phases of the graph and separating the phased with a vertical dotted (phase) line. The convention of using a broken vertical line to separate these phases quickly transmits to the reader the student's performance level before intervention and immediately after intervention. The phase line should be between the markings on the horizontal line.

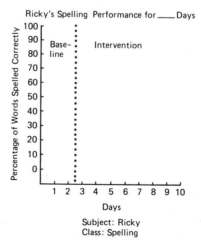

Fig. 12-12.   Example of rules 4, 5, and 6.

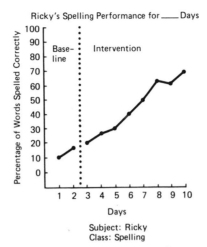

Fig. 12-13. Example of a complete graph.

Rule 7 (Fig. 12-13) is to place the dots representing the performance data on the intersecting lines and to connect the dots for each phase but not the dots between phases. A line connecting dots across a phase line should never be drawn.

Once these data have been summarized and graphed, it is possible to determine if the behavior in question is accelerating, decelerating, or remaining constant. Based upon the conclusion reached, the lesson plan may need to be revised or the evaluation may need to be made more precise. One method of measuring more precisely is to do a task analysis of the skill and evaluate the learner's functioning level.

Task Analysis

Task analysis is a very useful process to understand and use in the informal assessment process. It is defined as the process of identifying the sequential steps to be followed by the learner in the successful completion of a task. The process involves defining a skill or instructional objective, breaking that skill or objective into its component parts, and then sequencing these subtasks in a logical order. There are many advantages to using task analysis:

1. Evaluation is easily implemented when objectives are written into statements that describe observable behavior.
2. Task analysis provides a basic diagnosis by determining what a student can and can not do.
3. Reporting progress to parents is easier.
4. A more efficient basis for lesson planning and instruction is usually evolved.
5. Task analysis enhances the probability that the student will acquire the skill.

Observable Steps

Having observable substeps allows the teacher to choose a measurement system that best represents the behavior. Words and phrases such as "picks up," "writes," and "points to" can be recorded by an event recording procedure. The use of words that are behavioral replaces terms that are not susceptible to precise measurement (e.g., "knows how," "appreciates"). The behavioral nature of each step directs the observer's attention to the actual nature of the task.

Level of Functioning

Pinpointing the exact steps that are interfering with a student's mastery of a skill is a valuable use of the task-analysis process. By identifying the exact nature of the deficiency, the teacher can either teach the sub-skill or provide a prosthesis to achieve the sub-skill, so that the goal can be achieved. Teaching the sub-skill is a matter of showing and telling the student the aspect of the task that he is not demonstrating. A deficit in one sub-skill may be inhibiting a learner's use of a skill that has as many as 15 or 20 sub-skills. A prosthesis is used whenever the teaching of the sub-task is an unachievable goal in a reasonable period of time. The prosthesis may take the form of having the student use a calculator to solve word problems when the student can reason the problem through but is unable to consistently compute the answer mentally; it may be using a tape-recorded copy of a history test for the student who cannot read the test, but knows the historical facts; or it may be an analog computer for the blind student who needs to measure chemicals in a science laboratory but cannot see the markers on the measurement beakers.

Reporting Progress to Parents

Evaluative information about children should be in a positive form that is easily conveyed to professionals as well as parents. The use of a task analysis provides an optimistic goal-directed evaluation of a student's skills. Rather than saying that a learner cannot do long division problems, the teacher might say that the learner can consistently do 75 percent of the steps in the long division process correctly without help. The student still cannot do long division problems, but the statement reflects progress toward the goal. It also reflects a success-oriented sensitivity on the part of the teacher.

Lesson Planning and Efficient Instruction

Once a student's baseline behavior is determined, the task analysis acts as a means of measuring progress or nonprogress toward the goal. Based upon the information obtained each day, the teacher can modify the lesson plan for the subsequent day's instruction. Trend lines can be used to predict where a student should be in a week using 3 or 4 days of data. If, in a week, the student has not met the projection, a change in the teaching procedure may be in order. Also, having done a task analysis, the teacher is aware of the critical steps needed by the student to perform a task correctly. As the student attempts to perform the required behavior, the teacher can interrupt incorrect actions (errors) so that the learner is only required to exhibit correct behaviors.

Enhancing Skill Acquisition

By breaking a task into its component parts, the achievement of the objective is made easier: "Life is hard by the yard, but a cinch by the inch." Accordingly, an objective may seem unobtainable by a learner who has repeatedly experienced failure, but given small, easily obtainable steps directed toward that goal, the learner may find the task considerably easier to attain.

Ready Diagnosis

The steps in the task analysis are sequenced in the order they are to be executed. If a student fails to follow one of the steps, the teacher can immediately note the error and intervene to correct it. Analyzing a task into its component parts is a valuable skill that each teacher should possess. Such analysis helps the teacher pinpoint specific observable problems, which can be translated directly into behavioral objectives, and ultimately into a plan for remediation.

CONCLUSION

The authors have discussed graphing, task analysis, dimension control, matrices and a number of other strategies in the chapter. Each of these is tied heavily to a data-based model for instruction. The reader who implements the ideas expressed in this chapter in their assessment model with mildly handicapped students should be cautioned not to become so enamored with the brilliance of the data and the graphs that he/she loses sight of the primary objective: to identify problems *and* provide an appropriate program for the learner. The ultimate criteria of our success should be measured by the test of "interocular significance." Interocular significance refers to the fact that the improvement in a student's performance is so dramatic that it "hits you between the eyes." All the graphs and task analyses and sophisticated evaluation techniques are worthless if a program based upon the results has not been effective in changing the behavior of the learner in a positive meaningful fashion.

REFERENCES

Cawley, J. F., Calder, C. R., Mann, P. H., McClung, R. M., Ramanauskas, S., & Suiter, P. *Behavior resource guide*. Wallingford, Cn.: Educational Sciences, 1973.

Cawley, J. F., Goodstein, H. A., Fitzmaurice, A. M., Lepore, A., Sedlak, R. A., & Althaus, V. *Project MATH: Mathematics activities for teaching the handicapped: Level I and II.* Tulsa, Ok.: Educational Process Corp., 1976.

Cawley, J. F., Goodstein, H. A., Fitzmaurice, A. M., Lepore, A., Sedlak, R. A., & Althaus, V. *Project MATH: Mathematics activities for teaching the handicapped: Levels III and IV.* Tulsa, Ok.: Educational Process Corp. 1977.

Diagnosis: An instructional aid—mathematics. Chicago, Il.: Science Research Associates, 1973.

Kazdin, A. *Behavior modification in applied settings*. Homewood, Il.: Dorsey Press, 1980.

Kelly, L. J., & Vergason, G. A. *Dictionary of special education and rehabilitation*. Denver: Love Publishing Company, 1978.

Los Angeles Public Schools. *System fore.* North Hollywood, Ca.: Foreworks, no date available.

Popham, W. J. *Criterion-referenced measurement*. Englewood Cliffs, N.J.: Prentice-Hall, 1978.

Repp, A. Describing and monitoring behavior. In D. A. Sabatino & T. L. Miller (Eds.), *Describing learner characteristics of handicapped children and youth*. New York: Grune & Stratton, 1979.

Sedlak, R. A., & Fitzmaurice, A. Teaching arithmetic. In J. M. Kauffman & D. P. Hallahan (Eds.), *Handbook of special education*. Englewood Cliffs, N.J.: Prentice-Hall, 1981.

Zweig, R. L. *Fountain Valley teacher support system in mathematics and reading*. Huntington Beach, Ca.: Richard L. Zweig, Associates, 1974.

Edward Earl Gotts

13

Assessment of Affective Development

OBJECTIVES AND STRATEGIES OF AFFECTIVE ASSESSMENT: AN OVERVIEW

Objectives

There are four essential objectives that underlie classroom affective assessment: (1) understanding; (2) predicting; (3) planning; and (4) relating.

Understanding

Teachers assess to understand their students—not just to understand about them as a group, but to understand them as individual people. Such understanding is a uniquely human capacity, which derives, first, from people's knowledge of themselves as persons (Polanyi, 1958). That is, people are enabled to know others' identities as persons in the same *sense* that they have come to know themselves as persons (Erikson, 1963, chap. 7). Second, through a continuing process of getting to know other persons in face-to-face situations, people's human nature is refined to the point that they internalize rules or standards by which they can understand what each interpersonal encounter means both to them and to their fellow participants (Goffman, 1967, chap. 1). Third, people apply these standards, which they have internalized about their own and others' behavior, whenever they make judgments (attributions) about the behaviors. Moreover, behavior is judged in terms of perceptions of what "can be done" as well as in terms of what "should be done" (de Charms, 1968, chap. 9; Heider, 1958). Finally, the process of "knowing" others is enriched, as people mature into adulthood, by a deepening of feelings for others and an ability to think more objectively (that is, less "egocentrically") about others as persons (Piaget, 1967, chap. 1).

The capacity to understand students as individual human beings: (1) is a complex capacity made up of many skill components; (2) results from a series of developmental processes which people experience personally over their lifetimes; and yet, (3) is normally exercised automatically and informally as a part of life, with little conscious effort or thought about how people are able to "know" others.

283

This last fact highlights both a danger and a possibility. The danger is that people may rely too exclusively on the informal use of this capacity, which leaves them at the mercy of potential biases of both oversight and misperception. The possibility is that teachers can know their students more comprehensively and, therefore, more accurately, if they will turn to formal assessment procedures that can fill in the gaps and correct the misperceptions they may have.

None of the remaining three objectives of classroom assessment can be achieved fully unless this first objective of understanding students is achieved; the teacher's understanding of the student is the foundation for the entire assessment process. When working with the mildly handicapped, this includes understanding some of the more fundamental areas of affective development with which these students need help.

Mildly handicapped students need help in (1) knowing who they are as persons; (2) internalizing the rules or standards by which interpersonal encounters are assigned meanings; (3) making inferences or attributions about behavior in terms of particular circumstances; and (4) deepening their feelings for others while also increasing their ability to think more objectively about others.

Predicting

The second objective of affective assessment is prediction. Teachers do not usually think of themselves as needing to make predictions about students, so it is fair to ask, "In what areas do teachers *need* to make such predictions?"

Teachers need to make predictions about whether students possess the affective resources to handle a mainstream placement versus a special class placement. Teachers are periodically called on to discuss whether the placement is still appropriate. Furthermore, teachers may initiate the process of re-evaluation of placement. With the mildly handicapped student, decisions about placement must usually be based on more than intellectual and academic performance—hence the requirement for an assessment of such affective characteristics as social maturity, independence, and degree of academic motivation.

Questions will also be raised by parents and the school special-services unit regarding the child's long-range prospects for achieving social and economic independence. Predictions of these long-range outcomes must rely heavily on indications in the child's affective development.

Some parents solicit the teacher's opinion about whether particular experiences outside of school may be beneficial to their child. These questions may be raised in a comparative form, i.e., asking which of two or more available experiences should be sought. On such occasions, the teacher can assist in this decision-making process by helping parents to clarify how well each experience might complement the child's development.

Planning

The process of developing an individualized educational plan (IEP) is the most notable example of formal planning. Planning the IEP depends not only on appraising a child's current needs but also on predicting what kinds of experiences will be most beneficial over the school year. The IEP is usually planned by a team, which estimates what can and should be accomplished next in various areas; predicts what will probably occur and in what sequence; and sets goals to match the individual student's needs.

IEPs use a relatively long-term perspective. Planning, however, is also necessary on a week-to-week basis within the general framework provided by the IEP. For such shorter-range planning, assessment is also essential. The teacher must continually ask how best to select experiences that will be motivating, challenging, and timely. For this reason, instructional assessment to meet shorter-term planning objectives is often concerned with issues of student interest and motivation. That is, once the instructional goals have been chosen, as designated on the IEP, the teacher must plan how to secure the student's enthusiastic cooperation in those activities that will lead to accomplishing these goals. This points up a distinction between (1) planning as goal setting and (2) process planning for goal accomplishment.

Relating

The most fundamental social and emotional developments in children and adults come about through the process of relating to people. Special educators are keenly aware of this reality of instruction. Content is used to teach, but as the saying goes, "We teach children rather than content." Thus, a fundamental objective in instructing mildly handicapped students is teaching them more mature, responsible, and satisfying forms of relating to others.

Opportunities for student learning through relationships can commonly be arranged through teacher–student, student–student, and student–family interactions. While it is agreed that such learning is fundamental, many of the opportunities for it are in fact missed when teachers become so absorbed with the content of learning that they do not focus on the varied interpersonal events that are taking place all around them. (Some assessment procedures discussed in this chapter can provide the teacher with information needed for arranging learning through relationships.)

The Domain for Assessment

Over several years, researchers have had opportunity to thoroughly explore the question: "What areas of affective development can be studied in young children?" (Butler, Gotts, & Quisenberry, 1975; Butler, Gotts, Quisenberry, & Thompson, 1971). During the same years, in the process of designing and teaching a course in affective assessment, the question was stated differently: "What aspects of affective development can be studied in children and adolescents?" (Gotts, 1972–1974). One outcome of these studies is a definition of the domain for assessment, stated in terms of the characteristics to be studied (Table 13-1).

As can be seen from Table 13-1, the affective domain is broadly defined to include: (1) social behavior; (2) environmental forces (which often influence affective reactions); (3) social or emotional perceptions and communications; (4) motivational factors both in the environment and within the individual; and (5) other internal factors including personality traits and intrapsychic organization (e.g., Table 13-1, *E-10* and *E-15*).

Obviously, the teacher cannot assess every area in every category. It is, nevertheless, worthwhile to keep these areas in mind, because together they provide a framework for thinking about affective behavior. Thus, Table 13-1 provides much more than a list of behaviors. Instead, it provides a classification of affective behaviors into five major categories. In general, these categories reflect both be-

Table 13-1
The Domain for Assessment

A. Observable Social Behaviors
   1. Aggression, dominance
   2. Imitative behavior (modeling)
   3. Sex typing, identification (role-taking, role-playing, game preference)
   4. Development of controls (resistance to temptation, guilt reactions; cf. *E-9*)
   5. Attachment, dependency
   6. Maturity (responsibility taking, self-directed behavior, independence, competence; cf. *E-14*)
   7. Prosocial behaviors (cooperation, sharing, empathy, generosity, prosocial approach)
   8. Detachment; movement away from supervision
   9. Other social behaviors

B. Affective Ecology
   1. Social, cultural, or familial constraints on behavior
   2. Physical environmental constraints on behavior
   3. Examiner and procedure constraints on behavior
   4. Reactive or induced states (inhibition, disinhibition)
   5. Behavior carry-over effects after transitions

C. Social Perceptions and Communications
   1. Status awareness (SES, ethnicity, age)
   2. Social abstraction (social desirability, affective meaning)
   3. Person preference (sociometric and group behavior)
   4. Emotional communication; affective awareness
   5. Social roles and institutional arrangements
   6. Social attribution, stereotypes, moral judgment (cf. *E-9*)

D. Motivational Processes
   1. Types of feedback the child can use (threat, failure/success, reward schedules, types of reward, peer effects, teacher effects, higher needs, locus of control, punishment)
   2. Preference (interest, choice behavior, selective attention, attitudes)
   3. Stimulus variation (curiosity, exploratory behavior, responses to novelty or complexity, adaptation level, expectancy level)
   4. Responses to cognitive demands

E. Intrapsychic Factors
   1. Temperament (cf. *E-8*)
   2. Creativity and expressiveness
   3. Self-concept (body image, awareness of group identity, academic self-concept)
   4. Personality—global aspects (traits)
   5. Social and emotional adjustment (cf. *E-12*)
   6. Fantasy process and contents
   7. Typical mood and affective reactions
   8. Vitality and energy output (cf. *E-1*)
   9. Character (delay of gratification, internal controls, socialized self, conformity, values; cf. *A-4* and *C-6*)
   10. Ego organization (defenses, coping mechanisms, styles of processing data, conceptual tempo, field orientation)
   11. Humor
   12. Stigma and reactions (cf. *E-5*)
   13. Acquiescence/negativism
   14. Social skills development (cf. *A-6*)
   15. Psychosocial orientation

havioral contents and corresponding groups of study methods by which the contents are typically studied. The five categories should be continually addressed in assessment efforts. This can be done by asking in each child assessment situation, "Have I considered observable social behaviors, environmental influences, and so forth?" Asking questions about these five categories repeatedly serves as a reminder of the kinds of assessment data that are needed to provide a comprehensive picture of the child's current situation. The list in each category identifies those specific areas that should, perhaps, be considered relative to the issues being faced with a particular child or adolescent. Thus, the full list provides the details of what should be assessed.

What Teachers Need to Know

Teachers do *not* need to know everything about each child's affective development. They do not need to know everything about each child in every area of behavior identified in the lists of Table 13-1. However, they do need to know about those areas of behavior that have a bearing upon the goals of the IEP in terms of the four teacher objectives: understanding, predicting, planning, and relating.

Teachers do not need to think in terms of such categorical distinctions as mentally handicapped, learning disabled, and behavior disordered. Affective assessment and instruction can proceed quite effectively without regard to the child's diagnostic classification. And, to be effective in instruction, the teacher must go beyond classification to identify specific problem areas for the child.

Teachers need to know how to organize information from the affective assessment process into a coherent whole. At a first level, this means comprehending how the various bits of affective data relate to one another. At a second level, it means understanding how the affective data relate to cognitive-linguistic and perceptual-motor development. This large picture is needed if the IEP is to be more than a patchwork of unrelated goals that have been blindly pulled from "objectives sequences" provided by the school district or the state education agency. That is, after objectives have been tentatively selected from such lists, the integrative job of assessment is to inquire "How does the organized perspective of this child suggest the ingredients of the IEP should be blended and sequenced?" (From my observations of the IEP conferencing process, this simply is not happening. The final section of this chapter provides some perspectives on how to integrate affective assessment findings.)

Assessment Strategies: Critical Questions

At this point, the task of performing affective assessment may seem larger and less manageable than might be hoped for. How can it be made manageable? The first answer is: Only by thinking about it. Table 13-1 provides a framework for thinking about affective assessment, but, to be useful, the framework must become an automatic part of the teacher's thinking. Therefore, rehearse and then use the five major categories to analyze the affective situations of a few familiar children. Try to state the categories in the form of questions, as suggested earlier. Jot down answers in brief phrases and then ask what these descriptions suggest together about IEP goals and learning activities for each child.

A second answer is: By systematically recording. Recording is best accomplished with a simple form that meets personal requirements. A form can be prepared to fit onto a single sheet of paper. At the top, place the heading, *Affective Assessment,* and provide space under it for the child's name and the school year. Then divide the remainder of the page into five approximately equal spaces by drawing horizontal lines across the page. Somewhere at the top of each space, place a caption corresponding to each of the five major categories of Table 13-1. The caption may be a complete question or just a phrase. The wording for categories *A–E* as it appears in Table 13-1 may be used or the categories can be named as each teacher chooses, which will help each person remember more exactly the meaning of each category.

This kind of form becomes more useful if the teacher inserts documentation notes next to assessment findings. One way to set documentation apart from findings is by placing documentation information in parentheses. An entry with documentation might appear under *A* as follows: "Mary has been getting along well with Susan but seems jealous and frustrated when Susan selects someone else as a work partner. (Observed jealous reaction with anger directed toward Tawnya on 1/15)." If more space is needed, comments may be continued on the back of the form. The presence of a continued note may be signaled on the front side by *cont.* Another comment might be "(See *Billy's* form dated 10/19)."

The need for an assessment strategy is highlighted by the question: "When should affective findings be recorded?" For observations, they should be recorded while they are fresh in memory. Record keeping is, consequently, a process that is to be completed at the first available opportunity. On the other hand, a particular behavior process may be going on for some time before what is occurring can be understood. Such ongoing observations can be noted on the form at any convenient time, e.g., under *B*: "(Monitoring when Tom seems preoccupied and lapses into fantasy, to determine what events precede his withdrawal—3/6)." This might be followed by a numbered series of observations, each dated, regarding possible "preceding events" that lead up to the observed behaviors.

Anecdotal records tell about the observation of a particular isolated event or incident. Such isolated events are likely to be forgotten if they are not recorded soon after they occur—unless of course they are humorous or otherwise especially memorable. Even if they are not forgotten, some of the details will be lost if they are not recorded until considerably after they occur. If it is not convenient to make a record at the time, jot down a reminder on a pad while it is still fresh in memory, for example: "Record incident with Terry and Allen."

Unlike the recording of critical incidents, the recording of systematic planned observations is done on a special form or sheet. This form is referred, as needed, on the main affective assessment recording form for each child. Conclusions or inferences based on planned observations will also be entered on the main recording forms. Systematic observations can be used for many behaviors from Table 13-1 categories *A, B,* and *D,* and to a lesser extent for some parts of category *E.* (Actual observational and recording procedures are discussed in the sections of this chapter that deal with each specific category.)

A third assessment strategy question asks: "What should be observed and recorded?" As many details as possible. Timely recording of detailed observations is essential, since the ideal is to capture exactly what occurs in terms of (1) frequency; (2) intensity; (3) associated circumstances; (4) duration; (5) sequences (such as who initiates and who responds); and/or (6) response latency (i.e., the time that elapses before a child reacts or responds to a particular question or stimulus). Such details are almost always lost unless immediately recorded.

In the case of information obtained from children by self-report or in their comments to others, it is necessary to make sure that they understand what is being asked. This is not only a problem with questionnaires and paper and pencil tests; interview questions must also be administered with considerable perceptiveness regarding whether a child actually comprehends the meaning intended. When there is some doubt about whether the child understands, it is far better, for classroom affective assessment purposes, to depart, if necessary, from "standardized" administration procedures in order to make sure that the child does understand.

Children's answers to interview questions should be recorded verbatim. The same rule should be followed for recording children's answers to affective assessment procedures that do not involve self-reporting or telling about others. An example of this kind of assessment procedure is the Tasks of Emotional Development Test (TED) (Cohen & Weil, 1975). Children are asked to tell stories about a set of TED pictures. There is no self-report; the child is asked to respond to a stimulus in a particular manner.

Such procedures as the TED are called objective tests (Cattell, 1965), whereas self-report measures of all types are called questionnaires. The reason for recording children's exact answers to questionnaire and objective test items is that, often, as much can be learned from the way that a question was answered as from the actual content of the answer.

Cattell (1965) identified observations of behavior in life situations as another main source of data. The formal observation of this behavior has already been mentioned. What is important to realize is that the teacher may sometimes need to rely on life-situation data from informal sources, such as school cumulative records and other people. Common information sources are (1) other teachers (e.g., those who supervise the lunchroom or playground or who have the child in their class); (2) parents; and (3) the child's peers. Unlike direct observation, life-situation data reports from other people usually are based in part on their evaluations, judgments, and reactions—unless they have used systematic observations and recordings of behavior.

Yet other people's reports of life-situation data can be of much value if the teacher receiving them seeks to isolate the detailed factual basis underlying the reports. This is done pursuing the following general strategy: Use follow-up questions to sample the other person's knowledge of particular instances of behavior on which their opinions are based. The questioning might proceed, for example, like this: "You mentioned that Ann does not stand up for her rights and that she lets others take advantage of her. Try to recall a particular situation when this happened, and then tell me in as much detail as possible what took place." This can be followed up with, "Can you give me any other examples that you remember?" In this way, the teacher generally can decide which reports have some genuine basis in life-situation data and which reports do not.

This emphasis is on using a strategy for determining if other people's reports are based on specific facts. This emphasis should not, however, be interpreted as suggesting that undocumentable reactions are of no value. These reactions also are a kind of data. It is quite important, for instance, to know whether, and which, peers like or wish to associate with a particular child (Table 13-1, *C-3* and *C-6*). Such evaluative reactions help to define the actual environmental influences (Table 13-1, *B-1*) to which the child is reacting. Such data represents the data source that may be called child social-stimulus-value data.

In the process of examining assessment strategy questions, four kinds of data sources have been introduced and illustrated. It will be useful to remember these: questionnaire data (*Q*-data), objective test data (*T*-data), life-situation data (*L*-data), and social-stimulus-value data (*S*-data). Like the five main behavior categories of Table 13-1, these four data sources should become automatic ways of thinking about affective assessment data sources. As Cattell (1965) and others (Campbell & Fiske, 1959) have shown, the goal of reaching valid conclusions about complex behavior patterns or traits can be more surely approached when different kinds of data sources or methods are used simultaneously. It is, therefore, recommended that affective assessment be based on a good mix of *T-*, *L-*, *Q-*, and *S*-data sources.

Limits of Current Knowledge and Techniques[1]

Hoepfner et al. (1972), who are editors at the Center for the Study of Evaluation (CSE), thoroughly examined hundreds of *T-* and *Q*-type measures of higher-order affective and interpersonal skills for use at elementary and secondary levels. Each measure was evaluated on seven criteria: (1) validity; (2) examinee appropriateness; (3) normed excellence; (4) teaching feedback; (5) usability; (6) retest potential; and (7) ethical propriety. The criteria which most pertain to classroom usage, in descending order of importance, are 5, 2, and 4, followed by 1, 7, 6, and 3. The order, naturally, would differ for diagnostic usage.

CSE's evaluations were performed using rating scales. All numeric ratings were then converted to overall grades for each of the first six criteria: *good, fair,* or *poor.* A measure receiving a rating of *poor* would not be recommended relative to the particular criterion. A rating of *fair* indicates a need for caution in the use of a measure; it would only be used if nothing better were available.

A summary appraisal of the state of the art of measurement of higher-order skills appears in Figures 6 and 7 of Hoepfner et al. (1972, pp. xxiv–xxv). Those figures are worth careful examination. The CSE staff's conclusion was that instruments were predominantly rated in the *poor* to *fair* range. Criterion areas that were uniformly judged as *poor* were validity, normed excellence, teaching feedback, and retest potential. Overall ratings for examinee appropriateness and usability were predominantly *fair.*

Thus, for the most important criterion for classroom usage (i.e., teaching feedback), available measures have little to recommend them. Available measures were also rated only *fair* on the two other criteria judged most important for classroom usage. A few individual measures looked somewhat better than these overall ratings, but it was rare to find any affective/interpersonal measure that did not

---

[1]In preparation for writing this chapter, standardized and classroom tests, observations, and questionnaire procedures were reviewed in several sources (Buros, 1974, 1978; Butler et al., 1971, 1975; Hoepfner et al., 1970, 1972, 1974; Johnson, 1976; O'Leary & Johnson, 1979). Individual abstracts were prepared for more widely used measures to determine their potential usefulness for the classroom. This appraisal was not designed to evaluate the usefulness of measures for diagnosis, classification, and other administrative purposes.

receive at least two ratings of *poor*. Moreover, no individual measure seems able to provide teaching feedback in classroom usage.

The other CSE reports (Hoepfner et al., 1970, 1974) present a similar picture, although the latter reports are of more limited value for classroom measurement selection; they considered only four criteria: (1) validity; (2) examinee appropriateness; (3) usability; and (4) normed excellence. The most prominent weaknesses revealed by these two reports for the affective measures were on validity and normed excellence. Careful study of all three reports shows that the measures were evaluated as somewhat more effective in meeting the criteria with increasing grade level (i.e., with older children). This fact, however, does not help much with the mildly handicapped as a group, because their slower rate of development suggests that the measures are less appropriate for them over most of the school years.

The foregoing critique of affective tests and questionnaires would seem to make observational measures all the more appealing. This seems especially so in light of the widely held view that observational measures are inherently valid and error free. But a recent review of empirical studies of observational methods shows, quite to the contrary, that they are subject to several sources of bias and are not necessarily more trustworthy than other types of measures (Baker, 1980; O'Leary & Johnson, 1979).

This tends to strengthen the earlier recommendation that, in order to assure validity, a combination of *T-*, *L-*, *Q-*, and *S*-data sources should be used. There is strength to be found in using a diversity of data sources and in synthesizing the findings across these sources. No single type of measure can by itself guarantee an unbiased assessment; however, when data are synthesized first across the five affective categories (Table 13-1) and then harmonized across the three behavioral domains (i.e., cognitive-linguistic, perceptual-motor, and affective-social), the chances are greater of making correct inferences. It is reassuring in this connection to reflect on the human capacity of teachers to "understand students as individual human beings."

Two final considerations regarding the limits of current techniques are practicality and cost. The kinds of measures available from publishers may not be reproduced by teachers or other school personnel. Many are expensive, despite the limitations pointed up by the CSE staff. Furthermore, individual purchases are subject to various restrictions. Teachers cannot even expect that their schools will have examination copies of the most widely used tests.[2]

---

[2]To look into the test purchasing situation, it is recommended that a local committee be formed and that one person from it request a catalogue for examination from each of the following publishers: American Guidance Service; Association Press; California Test Bureau; Consulting Psychologists Press; Educational and Industrial Testing Service; Harcourt Brace Jovanovich; Institute for Personality and Ability Testing; Psychological Corporation; Scholastic Testing Services; Science Research Associates; and Western Psychological Services (for addresses, see Butler et al. 1971; Hoepfner et al., 1970, 1972, 1974). These catalogues briefly describe a majority of the standard affective domain measures available.

As a result of considering practicality and cost, it seems reasonable in the remaining sections of this chapter to recommend only a few commercially available measures for local purchase. These are recommended only when their value appears to justify their purchase for instructional purposes.

In the text the reader will be provided or referred to certain measures that are in the public domain (i.e., not under copyright). In other instances, the text provides specifications and sample materials, which teachers are encouraged to use in constructing affective assessment procedures for their own classroom use.

OBSERVABLE SOCIAL BEHAVIORS

For a comprehensive look at social behaviors, the model of interpersonal behavior developed by Leary and Coffey (1955) is especially useful.[3] This model resembles a circle or pie that has been cut into equal pieces. Each of these pieces is assigned the name of a social behavior pattern. As with a watch, start at one o'clock, and, going clockwise, the order in which these names occur around the rim of the circle is (1) competitive-exploitative; (2) managerial-autocratic; (3) responsible-overgenerous; (4) cooperative-overconventional; (5) dependent-docile; (6) modest–self-effacing; (7) distrustful-skeptical; and (8) blunt-aggressive.

Since the circle starts with 1 and ends with 8, 8 is immediately next to 1 on one side and 7 on the other; 1 is between 8 and 2; 4 comes after 3 and before 5; and so forth. Thus, the arrangement of social characteristics around the circle is like that shown in Figure 13-1. This type of model or physical arrangement is called a *circumplex*.

After much research, Leary and Coffey (1955) discovered a systematic set of findings that could best be represented by the circular arrangement of the dots shown in Figure 13-1. This circumplex arrangement is intended to express the following relationships:

1. Characteristics that are placed next to each other were found to be similar and highly positively related (e.g., someone described by 1 is also likely to be described by 2 and 8—that is, these characteristics are positively correlated).
2. Characteristics that are two steps removed from each other were found to be unrelated (e.g., if someone can be described by 8, it is not possible to predict whether the person will be described by 6 or by 2—that is, 6 and 2 are uncorrelated with 8).
3. Characteristics that are four steps removed from each other were found to be opposites and, thus, were highly negatively related (e.g., someone who is described by 2 is highly unlikely to be described by 6—that is, 6 and 2 are negatively correlated).
4. Each of the types of social behaviors was found to increase in intensity at points farther out from the center of the circle.
5. The less extreme behaviors falling within the innermost circle were normal or adaptive.
6. Behaviors falling between the innermost circle and the next or middle circle were more exaggerated and tended to cause others to respond in a particular reciprocal style.
7. Behaviors between the center circle and the outermost circle were of extreme or pathological intensity.

It is well to recall that the circumplex model was selected after the research and not before. Thus, the circumplex was used because it accurately fit the actual findings from many studies (Leary & Coffey, 1955) and not simply because the researchers preferred a circumplex. Once the findings had been converted to a

---

[3]To obtain rating scales for observable social behaviors, see Butler et al. (1971, ED 059 783, pp. 230–231, plus the associated references, which appear in the main bibliography, ED 059 781, and the supplemental bibliography, ED 059 784, appendix D). All of the references cited there are available as books or bound journals that can be found in most college libraries.

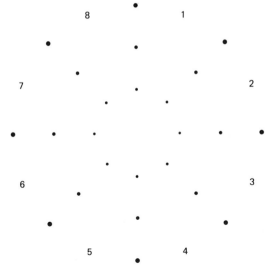

Fig. 13-1. Circumplex arrangement of Leary-Coffey (L-C) social behavior patterns.

clear, spatially represented model, it became possible to make the general statements listed above. This spatial model is, therefore, worth committing to memory, since it includes a large number of validated findings about social behavior.

An activity that will quickly add to recall and understanding of the model calls for these materials: a compass for drawing circles, a ruler or other straight edge, a pencil, and paper. First, use the compass to draw three circles, one inside the other, to resemble the spacing of the circular patterns of dots in Figure 13-1. The point of the compass needs to remain on the same spot for all three circles. Next, use the ruler to draw a horizontal line and a vertical line through the center of the circles to the outermost circle on all sides. The circles will now be divided by the lines into quarter circles. Next, draw two more lines through the center of the circles such that they divide each of the four sets of quarter circles in half. The circles should now be divided into eight equal segments. All that remains is to number the eight segments of the outer circle and to write in the Leary-Coffey (L-C) labels that apply to each.

To obtain more detailed labeling for the inner, center, and outer circles to reflect differing intensities of the various L-C social behavior patterns, consult Leary and Coffey (1955) or McLemore and Benjamin (1979). With this information, it can be decided, relative to each of the social behavior patterns, whether the child's behavior is like that in the innermost, middle, or outermost zone. Another possibility is that the characteristic does not apply to the child at all.

Related work was done to determine how well the L-C circumplex model applies to school-aged children (Gotts, Adams, & Phillips, 1968–1969). That research showed that the eight segments of the circumplex are arranged in the same order around the circle for children as for adults. The measurement procedure used in this work was a checklist for individual students and a "nominations" form for use with entire classrooms (Johnson, 1976, pp. 574–576). The teacher writes down on the specially designed nominations form the names of those children who manifest each of the behaviors or characteristics. Gotts et al. began

their research by using a 72-item nominations form with items that had been collected and assembled by Phillips (1966). Later, the form was expanded to 140
items to do a better job of sampling particular parts of the circumplex (Johnson,
1976). This longer form was tested in both the individual checklist and group nominations formats.

The 140-item form uses a scoring system that has been validated relative to
the L-C circumplex. Thus, it provides a means of assessing a child's social behavior in terms of the model, as do ratings made on the individual dimensions. Experience using both ratings of the L-C dimensions and the checklist/nominations
forms suggests that the ratings are a bit more abstract; it is, accordingly, difficult
to decide just which rating may apply. The checklist/nominations method requires
only that the user identify whether each item does or does not describe the child.
The 140 statements are less abstract than the L-C dimensions, making it easier to
reach decisions.[4]

During development of the nominations method of sampling behaviors to
match the L-C model, an interesting discovery was made. It was found that the
circumplex could be divided into four equal parts (i.e., quadrants) by combining: 1
and 2; 3 and 4; 5 and 6; and 7 and 8 (Gotts et al., 1968–1969). Returning to Fig. 13-1,
imagine dividing the circumplex first with a horizontal line, leaving 7, 8, 1, and 2
above the line and 3, 4, 5, and 6 below it. Careful inspection of the names of the
behavior patterns shows that those above the line indicate an active or forceful
approach and those below the line indicate a passive or compliant approach.

Imagine next dividing the circumplex with a vertical line into a left half (5, 6,
7, and 8) and a right half (1, 2, 3, and 4). Careful study of these two halves suggests
something new about the circumplex. It appears that even mildly exaggerated
behavior patterns in the left half of the L-C model are ones more likely to be
regarded socially as problems, while mildly exaggerated behavior patterns in the
right-hand side are less likely to be defined as problems. Thus, it was suggested
that behavior patterns in the left half of the circumplex more often would be seen
by teachers and peers as troublesome or problematic than right-hand behavior
patterns. Evidence from a variety of measures supplied by teachers, peers, tests,
and children's self-reports consistently supported this view (Gotts et al., 1968–
1969).

When Leary and Coffey (1955) tried to identify psychiatric conditions that
might be equivalent to the more extreme forms of the eight behavior patterns, they
found none to match (1) competitive-exploitative or (2) managerial-autocratic.
Moreover, their descriptions of social maladjustment types for the eight behavior
patterns make those on the left-hand side of the circumplex seem more disturbed
or disturbing than those on the right—i.e., (5) easily influenced and dependent, (6)
passive, submissive, and self punishing, (7) passively resistant, bitter, and dis-
trustful, and (8) aggressive and sadistic versus (1) managing, autocratic, and
power-oriented, (2) self-centered, showy, and exploiting, (3) hypernormal and
overly generous, and (4) naive and overconforming.

---

[4]The original, shorter version of the scale nominations instrument is in the public domain and may
be obtained in the appendices of Phillips' study (1966). The newer, longer version with scoring instructions may be obtained at a nominal cost as described in Johnson (1976) or by writing the author of this
chapter.

The eight behavior patterns of the circumplex appear thus to break into a top and bottom half and a left and right half. Hence, the circumplex divides into quadrants when a horizontal line is used to separate the more active from the more passive behavior patterns and a vertical line is used to separate the more troublesome behavior patterns from the exaggerated, yet more socially accepted behavior patterns. These four quadrants of the circumplex were designated by alphabetic letters and names going counterclockwise around the circumplex as follows: A, aggressive (7 and 8); B, self-effacing and dependent (5 and 6); C, responsible and conforming (3 and 4); and D, manipulative and controlling (1 and 2). Thus, the 140 nominations or checklist items can be used to identify children as being one of the four quadrant types.

Statistical comparisons of children of these four types suggested that those in quadrants A and B were less able to cope with the social and academic environment of school than were those in quadrants C and D (Gotts et al., 1968–1969). This distinction between coping and noncoping, therefore, provides another way of describing how the left and right halves of the circumplex differ from one another. Figure 13-2 summarizes the information on the quadrants in relation to the horizontal and vertical divisions of the circumplex model. Figure 13-2 should be reviewed carefully to assist in the recall of the several perspectives on social behavior it summarizes.

The meaning of the four quadrants is as follows: Children who resemble type A have active behavior disorders; those resembling type B have passive behavior disorders; and those resembling types C and D, even if their behaviors are exaggerated, are usually coping with the school environment. Children of types A and D have active or forceful temperaments or dispositions; those of types B and C have more passive or compliant temperaments or dispositions. Certainly, children of types A and B need help in developing social interactions that they and others will find more rewarding. Children who exhibit exaggerated behaviors of type C or D also need to broaden their repertoire of social behavior, yet their needs are often overlooked, because, from some perspectives, they seem to be doing all right. For this reason, teachers should arrange learning experiences to enhance appropriate interpersonal skills for all children, irrespective of where they fit in the circumplex.

A widely used measure of social problem behavior and personality difficulty is the Behavior Problem Checklist (Quay & Peterson, 1979).[5] There are important parallels between the Behavior Problem Checklist (PBC) and the school behavior checklist (SBC) in terms of (1) item similarity; (2) checklist format; and (3) content composition of various subscales. The PBC's first scale, conduct problem, resembles quadrant A; the second scale, personality problem, resembles quadrant B; and the third scale, inadequacy-immaturity, resembles portions of quadrant B and portions of the SBC intrapsychic scale, "personal disorganization." An advantage of the PBC is that it has been extensively studied, thereby providing the user with a wealth of information on how it relates to family background, national origin, adoption, birth order, race, learning disability, and other factors (Lindholm

---

[5]This instrument and manual may be obtained by writing to Dr. Donald R. Peterson, Busch Campus, Rutgers State University, New Brunswick, N.J. 08903.

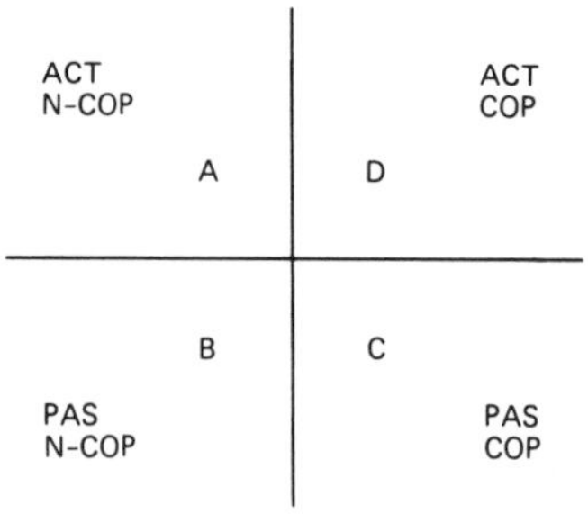

```
ACT                    ACT
N-COP                  COP

          A      D



          B      C

PAS                    PAS
N-COP                  COP
```

Fig. 13-2. Circumplex quadrants related to the coping/noncoping (COP/N-COP) dimension and the active/passive (ACT/PAS) dimension.

& Touliatos, 1976; Quay, 1977; Quay & Peterson, 1979; Touliatos & Lindholm, 1980).

Social Maturity

In addition to using the comprehensive perspective of interpersonal behavior, it is also possible to assess social behavior in terms of maturity. This is usually done by relying on reports of parents, teachers, and/or other people in the position to know how the child behaves. To insure that valid reports are obtained, it is well to be sure that all questions are understood and to obtain supporting specifics whenever possible. Adaptive behavior scales formalize such sampling.

The Vineland Social Maturity Scale is the best known of these scales (Doll, 1965). Over the past 10 years, several other scales of adaptive behavior have been developed and studied (Coulter & Morrow, 1978). In general, however, the Vineland remains as useful as any of the newer instruments for classroom purposes when judged in terms of ease of administration, suitability for the respondent, simplicity of scoring and interpretation, and relevance to instructional planning. The Vineland social quotient [(Sociological Age/Chronological Age) $\times$ 100 = Social Quotient (SQ)] is of less interest; for instructional purposes, teachers will be more interested in identifying each child's accomplishments. It is also important to consider the skills that need to be developed, whether they can most readily be learned at home, school, or elsewhere in the community.[6]

Another area in which social skills mature is play. Children who are socially isolated or who have difficulty fitting into peer group activities inside and outside the classroom often show delayed skill development in this area. Butler, Gotts, and Quisenberry (1978, pp. 27–37) provided observational guidelines for assessing children's play. They gave a specific outline of play stages together with extended examples of typical forms of play manifested at different levels of maturity. They also suggested ways of enhancing play development and of using play as a vehicle for promoting learning and development.

Other Data Sources on Social Behavior

The measures identified above for social behaviors and social maturity are generally based on life-situations (L-type) data. However, the more specific the social behaviors being observed, the more closely they will correspond to L-data.

---

[6]For teachers who wish to pursue social skill development in other areas, Coulter and Morrow (1978) may be helpful.

The more general the behavior categories being considered, the more closely the findings will correspond to social-stimulus-value (S-type) data; i.e., they will be more strongly loaded with judgment and reactions to the child.

Some forms of objective test (T-type) data are available, but they cannot be recommended for classroom use because of (1) limited age range, (2) no norms, and (3) limited populations studied. Nevertheless, teachers who wish to secure T-data on social behaviors can do so by improvising tests in conversational role-playing situations. For example, to measure possible reactions to mild aggression or provocation, the teacher might say, "Imagine, Joe, that you are playing catch and that a boy who's about your size sneaks up behind you and trips you so that you fall. Then he grabs the ball and runs, while laughing at you. Act like I'm that boy. Don't really do it, but show me what you would feel and say and do if I were that boy. Then I'll pretend to react to what you do. Let's keep going that way until I say, 'Okay, Tom, time to stop.' Do you understand?" After answering any questions, the teacher might say, "Let's begin. I just tripped you and I'm running with the ball and laughing." With a little imagination, situations can be improvised to fit any social behavior issues.

Some important points to remember about such simulated situations: (1) provide the child enough visual and action imagery to support the role-play; (2) make the social issue involved very clear and focused; (3) create the exact social details to which the child is to react, both by methods of describing the situation and of playing later reactions; (4) emphasize the imaginary nature of the situation, being certain before commencing that the child understands that this is "not for real"; (5) offer an unmistakable signal for stopping the role-play sequence; and (6) hold a debriefing session with the child.

At first, children may feel a little awkward or silly in the role-play situation. It is necessary to bring them beyond this type of interaction until they are more natural in their role-play. Only then, can possible T-data correspondences be inferred between the child's actions and those that might occur in actual social interactions. The role-playing procedure has the potential, moreover, of being shifted into a direct instructional mode. This can be done during the play action itself by reactions to the child, as, for example, in the foregoing situation, reacting in an apologetic or conciliatory manner. In other play situations, reactions might be calculated to provide insights into others' motives and feelings; to affirm the child's worth; to acknowledge special concerns or sensitivities; and so forth.

In any event, the role-play should be followed up with a debriefing. After stopping the action, ask the child to recount what happened. This step affords insights into the child's ability to hold onto reality during imaginative activity. It also gives the child's self-report (Q-data) version of the action. If the line between pretending and reality seems to be blurred, this is the time to reemphasize that the activity was a form of play and that the purpose was to help the child become more effective in social interactions. Next, the child should be asked about how the people and the situation might be seen and responded to in other—perhaps more effective and constructive—ways. The objective in debriefing is not to moralize or make critiques, but to explore alternate ways of perceiving and behaving in social situations. Additional ideas for carrying out this kind of dialogue with children by means of a "mutual storytelling" technique can be found in a very readable book by Dr. Richard Gardner (1971).

Children who are more mature (i.e., above a social age of around 10 years) can often collaborate with the teacher as observers. In this way, they can help generate *L*-data. Some children can learn to monitor and keep records of their own behavior. They can also help keep records of target behaviors of children with whom they frequently interact. Teachers can creatively draw upon these potential data-collection assistants. It is necessary at the same time to arrange the consequences so that accurate observing and recording are rewarded, and so that the process of helping the teacher neither becomes burdensome nor serves as a possible source of interpersonal strain or conflict among peers. Such conditions can be established where there is a climate of mutual respect and helpfulness.

Additional *Q*-data regarding any aspects of social behavior may be obtained by using a modified semantic differential technique (Osgood, Suci, & Tannenbaum, 1957). This technique uses a series of bipolar adverb or adjective pairs (for example, *good/bad*) for rating or making judgments about the meaning of particular concepts. Examples of social behavior concepts that might be rated in this manner are (1) I am _____ ; (2) my classmates think that I am _____ ; (3) adults think that I am _____ ; and (4) I would like to be _____ . The following modified bipolar pairs, which would be used by the child to rate each of the four preceding concepts, are based on the circumplex model plus the quadrant system (see Fig. 13-3 for actual format to be used in scoring): (1) easy to get along with/ hard to get along with; friendly/unfriendly; kind/not kind; nice/mean (i.e, 4, cooperative-overconventional, versus 8, blunt-aggressive); (2) softhearted/hardhearted; helping others/protecting myself; gentle/tough; willing to share/stingy (i.e., 3, responsible-over-generous versus 7, distrustful-skeptical); (3) weak/ strong; obedient/bossy; follower/leader; shy/powerful (i.e., 6, modest–self-effacing versus 2, managerial-autocratic); (4) helpless/trying to win; courteous/selfish; respectful/disrespectful; dependent/independent (i.e., 5, dependent-docile versus 1, competitive-exploitative); (5) speedy/pokey; lively/quiet; full of energy/tired; starting things/waiting around (i.e., A and D, active versus B and C, passive); and (6) winning/losing; ahead/behind; liked by kids/not liked by kids; good in school work/not good in school work (i.e., C and D, coping versus A and B, noncoping).

To prepare and administer the preceding semantic differential materials, on paper or orally, present only one concept at a time. Begin, for example with "I am _____ ." Then ask the child to complete this concept in terms of each of the 24 rating pairs above. Then present the second concept in this manner, and so forth.

For children under the mental age of 7, try using a three-position scale for each pair. A three-position scale for kind/not kind would be: kind/both/not kind. The one selected by the child should be circled. Use the center position for answers meaning *both, equally,* or *undecided.* For children above mental age 7, use a five-position scale, e.g., kind/X/both/X/not kind. These more mature children can make finer discriminations regarding degrees of intensity. Rather than trying to define exactly these in-between positions, the semantic differential technique presents the scale visually in a spatial format, as above, and asks the child to point to the position that most nearly matches his or her judgment. Then the teacher or examiner circles the position selected. When all of the administration and recording has been completed, the scale can be scored. This is most easily accomplished by using a summary form like that depicted in Fig. 13-3.

To score a child's record, simply count or sum the number of times a particular answer position was selected across all four of the bipolar pairs that were used for each of the six rows of the form (Fig. 13-3). Enter the sum for each answer position in the correct column and row. For example, if the three-position format

	Left-Hand Position	Middle-Left Position	Center Position	Middle-Right Position	Right-Hand Position
4, Cooperative-Overconventional versus 8, Blunt-Aggressive					
3, Responsible-Overgenerous versus 7, Distrustful-Skeptical					
6, Modest–Self-effacing versus 2, Managerial-Autocratic					
5, Dependent-Docile versus 1, Competitive-Exploitative					
A and D, Active versus B and C, Passive					
C and D, Coping versus A and B, Noncoping					

Fig. 13-3. Sample scoring form for semantic differential. Concept: "I am."

was used, and a child had selected easy to get along with, friendly, kind, and nice—then the sum, 4, would be entered in the first column (i.e., left-hand position) of the form's first row (i.e., cooperative-overconventional versus blunt-aggressive). This score would be interpreted as representing a high amount of cooperative-overconventional behavior, as determined from self-report (Q-data). After the form is filled out by summing and entering all of the selections made, it is possible to examine the results by seeing how the top four rows fit together on Fig. 13-1 and how the bottom two rows fit on Fig. 13-2. This provides a crosscheck, because the child's position should be approximately the same on both figures. The final step is to study how social behavior data from all sources fit together to form a unified picture.

AFFECTIVE ECOLOGY

Many environmental circumstances influence and interact with behavior. Thus, these environmental influences help to explain why particular behaviors occur under particular conditions. Motivational processes also help to explain why certain behaviors occur. Behavior does not result simply from what the child is like inside; behavior is the result of interactions among the five kinds of factors represented in Table 13-1. The practical value of considering environmental influences is that the teacher can thereby work to modify those influences in desired directions, using affective ecology, which is the study of the relationship between the environment and children's social and emotional behaviors.

Environmental conditions provide cues for behaviors; impose limitations or constraints on behavior; and sometimes even prompt or push children into particular courses of action. The analysis of the environmental events that precede or accompany affective behaviors suggests these important classes of influences: (1) discriminative stimuli cue, signal, or provide the occasion for behaviors to start, stop, increase, decrease, etc.; (2) evoking stimuli have a more commanding or compelling effect; and (3) maintaining stimuli support the continuation of certain behaviors. Notice that the term "causes behavior" was not used, since that would imply a simple one-to-one correspondence between the environmental stimuli and the behavior. As was said earlier, other factors besides the environment influence behavior.

Social, Cultural, or Familial Constraints on Behavior

Some environmental stimuli are more difficult to observe than others because they are more or less in the eye of the beholder; they are matters of perception and comprehension based on internalized meanings from the child's social, cultural, or family background. If the teacher does not come from a similar background, it is necessary for him or her first to become familiar with that entire meaning system, even to the extent of sensing the familiar feelings that go along with environmental messages.

Courses have been offered and books written to help teachers understand the inner city child, the black experience, the culturally different child, the rural child, the lower-class child, and so forth. These kinds of resources are only able, however, to introduce their respective subject matters. To enter a meaning system calls for authentic contact through experience. Autobiographies or other first-hand accounts by persons from the relevant backgrounds can add further dimensions to understanding. But because social expressions are dynamic and constantly changing, and because children's comprehension of social meanings does not always match that of adults from the same backgrounds, the final source of a teacher's education in social, cultural, and family environmental factors must come from diligent and sensitive listening to what the children say, mean, and understand. Affective data of this type are sensed and felt as much as they are seen.

The relevance of these suggestions for the teacher's self-education can be gauged by the following observations and questions. Children will seemingly tolerate many personal slights and affronts without fighting, but when other types of provocations occur they will begin fighting at once. What is known about the social rules and meanings that regulate children's social aggression? Some environmental stimuli account for cooperative, friendly, and helpful responses by children. Which stimuli occasion positive social behaviors? Once cultural influences have been identified, without rejecting or trying to change those influences, what can be done to rearrange the environment to increase desired patterns of social interaction?

In a bilingual south Texas school system, the superintendent demonstrated that Hispanic children were only willing to display publicly their creative and academic abilities and products if this could be done in a noncompetitive atmosphere. They did not wish to appear immodest; giving the appearance of competitiveness in school was viewed by them as acting immodestly. Their own reaction to seemingly immodest behavior was resentment, so they avoided behaving in ways that would make others feel envious. Thus, culturally defined and perceived cues of competitiveness and immodesty served as discriminative stimuli that inhibited the Hispanic children's participation in recitation and other school activities. Once school officials removed the element of competitiveness, however, by receiving students' work without public comment or evaluation, Hispanic students were comfortable about displaying their academic and creative work. Thus, understanding and accepting cultural influences on social behavior allowed school personnel to devise a way of getting all the children to take pleasure in performing and displaying their work.

Observable Environmental Influences

Unlike cultural background influences, some environmental stimuli are more clearly observable. Understanding their meaning is not really difficult. The difficult work is in carefully observing and documenting the connections or relations between the environmental events and behavior. What must be recorded is the fact that particular stimuli preceded particular behaviors. Therefore, each time the behavior of interest occurs, the circumstances surrounding it should be recorded. The purpose is to discover the connections.

Some of this information will come from direct observation, some from the particular child's story of what happened, and some from questioning other children. If a nonjudgmental attitude of inquiry can be established, the other children will be helpful. A judgmental attitude, in contrast, encourages children to slant their reports, in self-protection, to gain favor, or to influence what happens to another child.

The following are some of the kinds of observable events that should be looked for as discriminative, evoking, and behavior-maintaining stimuli: reactions to transitions or to changes of pace, interruptions, physical contact, verbal interaction, facial expressions and body gestures, suggestive noises made by children, whispering, the presence or absence of certain persons, excessive motion, noisiness, confusion, bright or pulsating lights, someone being socially excluded, someone having too many choices or decisions to make, someone being hurried by others or by deadlines, certain school subjects, excess or insufficient resources for completing assignments, introduction of novel materials or people, and so forth. Any observable stimuli which can be imagined influencing behavior may in fact do so. It is documentable, repeated linkages between behaviors and stimuli that should interest the teacher.

Other Influences

Children may be influenced by drug abuse, prescribed or over-the-counter medications, illness, hunger, thirst, need to go to the bathroom, fatigue, need for physical activity to release muscle tension, moods, pain, discomfort from poor posture, clothing that is too tight, being too hot or cold, and so on. It is important to inquire into these possibilities, because they are not all self-evident. What will be evident in connection with all of them, however, is that the child's energy level will be altered or out of keeping with the general pace of school events. The child will be overactive or lethargic. The child's facial appearance, as well as overall energy level, often reveals that something is amiss.

How the child will react to being out of sorts is an individual matter that should be documented by the teacher. Try using a checklist made up of the items in the preceding paragraph. Each item on the list will suggest a set of simple questions. The most obvious first question is "How are you feeling?" This is followed up with other questions, as needed. The time of day may suggest hunger, fatigue, or need to use the bathroom. Younger children often have difficulty localizing what is bothering them, so it may take some ingenuity to learn the source of the disturbance. Thus, questions about more factual matters may be most productive. For example, "Can you tell me what you ate this morning?" or "When did your mother give you your medicine?" All children can think more clearly and better answer such questions if they are relaxed. Thus, it may be necessary to get a child relaxed first. In addition to trying to understand the immediate situation, look for data on physical states that may repeatedly influence a child affectively.

Another group of influences may be thought of as having carry-over effects; that is, there is a time delay between the event and how the child responds to it. Examples of this: a child is disappointed with the grade assigned on a worksheet, forgets the disappointment, but keeps feeling bad; a child is intimidated on the way to school and remains anxious about what will happen on the way home; and a child is irritated by another child and cannot immediately express the anger but does so later in the day without any apparent reason. The last two examples would more easily be figured out during questioning, whereas the first would be difficult to fathom. Puzzling behaviors that cannot be directly connected to preceding events may be of the type where the child has forgotten the original incident but, nevertheless, continues to be affected by it.

Always consider (1) social, cultural, and family influences; (2) observable environmental factors; (3) the physical state of the child; and (4) carry-over effects. When the first three seem to give no explanation, consider the fourth possibility, i.e., that a behavior may not relate to anything that immediately preceded it but instead to situational factors that are further removed in time. While many data in the environment are observational (L-data), judicious use of questioning (Q-data) is also important.

SOCIAL PERCEPTIONS AND COMMUNICATIONS[7]

Status Awareness

If sampling children's perceptions of racial, ethnic, and other social status issues is required, construct a modified semantic differential.[8] The concepts to be used will be those of interest in your situation. Sample concepts might include

---

[7] A review of literature regarding this third major area of the affective domain revealed that many of the available measures are complicated to administer and score (Butler et al., 1971). Moreover, at least one of the characteristics in list C of Table 13-1 is not likely to be of general interest for classroom use.

[8] Instruments previously used to study $C-1$ (Table 13-1) are intentionally left out.

white girls, black girls, Vietnamese girls, children from the Hilltop housing project, children who speak Spanish, boys who wear motorcycle outfits, my friends, and myself.

A different group of bipolar descriptors may also be used, since the ones given earlier were prepared specifically to fit the L-C circumplex. The following three groups of pairs should work well for many uses: (1) good/bad; happy/sad; clean/dirty; kind/mean; friendly/unfriendly; beautiful/ugly; (2) weak/strong; soft/hard; small/large; quiet/loud; thin/thick; far/near; and (3) fast/slow; sharp/dull; hot/cold; moving/still; excited/calm; active/not active.

These three groups were selected to represent three dimensions discovered by Osgood et al. (1957): (1) the evaluative dimension; (2) the potency dimension; and (3) the activity dimension, respectively. The bipolar pairs are arranged so that the first and the second terms of each pair consistently have the following meanings: (1) positive versus negative evaluation; (2) low versus high potency, power, or strength; and (3) activity versus passivity, respectively. Children under mental age 7 will have difficulty responding to some of the bipolar pairs, so use only those that they comprehend.

Scoring and recording the results calls for constructing a form resembling Figure 13-3, with the three Osgood dimensions set up as the rows of the form. Since there are six bipolar pairs for each dimension, when the child's judgments are totaled up there will be scores ranging from zero to six in the five columns for each row.[9] What will prove most instructive is to score each concept for the three dimensions and then to compare and contrast the scores assigned to each concept with those assigned to the other concepts, especially for "my friends" and "myself."

Social Abstraction

Affective meaning is one of the main variables measured in the category of social abstraction. The capacity of the child to comprehend and make judgments with the semantic differential technique provides an indication of the extent to which the child's affective use of language has been socialized (Gotts, 1967, pp. 113–134). What is being assessed is not *how* the child views particular concepts but *whether* the child is able to use the bipolar pairs to make judgments about concepts. The larger the number of bipolar pairs that the child can apply to concepts, the better the child understands the generalized system of affective meanings. Therefore, one instructional objective for mildly handicapped children would be to have them better understand this important system of connotative meanings.[10]

---

[9]For further information on the interpretation of the three Osgood dimensions, consult Gotts (1967) as well as Osgood et al. (1957).

[10]Social desirability measures are not especially useful for classroom use. If, nevertheless, there is some need for the assessment of children's internalization of the social meanings that account for social desirability, see Gotts (1967, pp. 113–134). The appendices of Phillips's report (1966) contain the social desirability scale of Crandall, Crandall, and Katkovsky (1965) and Phillips's measures of approach and avoidance styles of defensiveness, which provide additional perspectives on the development of socially desirable responses.

Preference for Persons

Of all the assessment measures in the social perceptions and communications area, sociometric techniques have experienced the widest classroom use. Sociometrics are of great value in identifying (1) socially isolated children; (2) children who engender negative reactions and rejection in others; (3) those children with whom a specific child would like to interact; and (4) children who would in turn be willing to interact with that particular child.

Phillip's sociometric items (1966) are in the public domain and can, therefore, be reproduced for classroom use. They are designed for children who can look at a class roster and copy names from it. Thus, lists of names must be visible for inspection. The technique is easily adapted to nonreaders or those who cannot write by orally administering the items to children individually. With children who do not know each others' names well, a set of class pictures is used so that children can point to those who fit the descriptions.

Two parallel forms should be constructed at the elementary level, one for boys and one for girls, following Phillips's practice (1966). Boys choose boys; girls choose girls. At the secondary level, a single form can be used, with the word *student* replacing the word *boy* or *girl*. Phillips's sociometric items are as follows:

1. If you could select a boy/girl in this class to sit by, whom would you pick?
2. Suppose that the teacher picked someone to sit by you. If there is any boy/girl you hope your teacher would not pick to sit by you, write his/her name here.
3. If you could select a boy/girl in this class to play with, whom would you pick?
4. Suppose that the teacher picked someone to play with you. If there is any boy/girl you hope your teacher would not select to play with you, write his/her name here.
5. If you could select a boy/girl in this class to work with you on a school project, whom would you pick?
6. Suppose that the teacher picked someone to work with you on the project. If there is any boy/girl you hope your teacher would not select to work with you, write his/her name here.
7. If you could select a boy/girl in this class to be the leader, whom would you pick?
8. Suppose that the teacher picked someone to be class leader. If there is any boy/girl you hope your teacher would not select to be the class leader, write his/her name here.
9. If you could select a boy/girl in this class to take with you to the movies on your birthday, whom would you pick?
10. Suppose that your mother picked someone for you to take to the movies on your birthday. If there is any boy/girl you hope she would not select to go with you, write his/her name here.

Of course, other items that suit particular classroom needs can also be used.

It will be apparent that the odd-numbered items call for positive choices, and the even-numbered items call for negative choices. This is, therefore, called the choice/rejection method. The instrument should be administered to all children in the classroom. The total number of times that each child's name is mentioned for items 1, 3, 5, 7, and 9 by all same-sex peers indicates the child's popularity (high) or degree of isolation (low). Total mentions for items 2, 4, 6, 8, and 10 indicate rejection (high) or nonrejection (low). Another way of totaling the answers is by counting for each child only the number of different children who make positive mentions (odd-numbered items) and the number who make negative mentions (even-numbered items). Finally, list, for each child, those children who choose that child, plus list the children whom that child chooses. Other help in scoring the sociometric procedure is available in Gordon (1966) and Phillips (1966).

One of the most positive characteristics of sociometric results is that their meaning is immediately obvious. What may not be apparent, however, is that the choice items do not simply measure the opposite of the rejection items (Phillips, 1966); they are negatively related, but the relationship is a very small one. Other research has shown that the information provided by the choice items cannot be statistically derived from the rejection items and vice versa (Gotts, Froehle, & Leventhal, 1970). A low choice score does not mean that a child is rejected. Children who have both low choice and low rejection scores are socially isolated. Only those with high rejection scores are rejected.

The application of sociometric findings in the classroom is also straightforward. Children who are socially isolated are found primarily in quadrant B of Figure 13-2, self-effacing–dependent. Those who are socially rejected are found mainly in quadrant A, aggressive. The former group (B) needs to have a social skill-building curriculum that will make them more socially effective. The latter group (A) needs assistance in reducing their aggressive behaviors, since these seem to alienate them from their peers (Gotts et al., 1970). Also, the lists of positive choices permit the teacher to operate as a peer matchmaker. That is, children who choose one another can be given work assignments together to increase their opportunities to experience peer acceptance.

Emotional Communication: Affective Awareness

Children's ability to engage in emotional communication can be sampled by various tests (T-data), but these are not generally available. Effectiveness of emotional communication can, nevertheless, be sampled in a simulated situation using role-playing. Such role-play can be used to assess both (1) the child's ability to hear and be responsive to what the other person is saying and (2) the child's success in expressing his or her own viewpoint. Direct observations in naturally occurring situations may offer additional findings (L-data). Emotional communication skills are learned, but less by direct instruction than by having opportunity to interact. Learning in this area needs to be provided for, accordingly, in an interactive social situation.

Affective awareness, particularly of facial expressions, is essential to social effectiveness. Children's recognition of facial expressions can be both tested and improved through the use of photographs in a book by Ekman and Friesen (1975). Awareness of the affective meaning of tone of voice is obviously important too. Unfortunately, there are no widely available procedures suited to assessing these skills.

Social Roles

An interesting and usable frame of reference for assessing the perception of social roles, relative to the self, is the fundamental interpersonal relationship orientation (FIRO). The author of this framework, William Schutz (1966), identified three fundamental orientations in the need to establish and maintain a satisfactory relationship with others: (1) interaction and association (inclusion); (2) control and power (control); and (3) love and affection (affection). Each of these need dimensions operates at an expressed and a wanted level. The combination of the three dimensions with the two levels generates the following six interpersonal need cells: need to include others, need to be included by others, need to control others, need to be controlled by others, need to express love toward others, and need to have others express love toward self.

These six needs are measured with a self-report instrument (Q-data) called the FIRO-BC for children or the FIRO-B for adults and older adolescents. Six scores are produced.[11] An understanding of the meaning of results from the FIRO-B or FIRO-BC usually comes automatically after inspecting the self-report statements for each scale. The six needs, however, can be further understood in relationship to one another by studying Schutz (1966) and Ryan (1971). A number of very interesting relationships have been discovered between the two FIRO-BC inclusion scores (i.e., wanted and expressed) and sociometric findings obtained by the choice/rejection method (Froehle, Gotts, & Leventhal, 1971). The FIRO instruments can provide complementary linkages to the L-C circumplex data as well as to sociometric results, so their use is strongly recommended.

Social Attributions, Stereotypes, and Moral Judgment

These assessment procedures do not generally recommend themselves to classroom use because of the unavailability of measures from standard publisher sources, and because some require considerable testing skill to use and score.[12]

MOTIVATIONAL PROCESSES

Earlier the impact of the environment upon affective behavior was presented in terms of influences which precede or which accompany behavior. In thinking about motivation, the focus is upon how those events that follow behavior can influence behavior. Thus, the point in time at which the influence occurs is one of the main differences between environmental influences and motivational processes. That is, if time and events are examined on the basis of whether they occur before, during, or after particular behaviors, then those events that occurred before or during roughly belong with environmental influences, and those that occur

---

[11]The tests and interpretive materials can be ordered from Consulting Psychologists Press, 577 College Avenue, Palo Alto, Ca. 94306.

[12]For those who, nevertheless, wish to know more about social attribution, consult de Charms (1968) and Heider (1958). The study of moral judgment was started by Jean Piaget and refined by Lawrence Kohlberg. The work of both Piaget and Kohlberg in this area has been reviewed and integrated into the broader perspective of ego development by Jane Loevinger (1976).

afterwards are motivational processes. However, there are important exceptions to these assignments.

The first major exception to the time-zone notion is raised by the distinction between extrinsic and intrinsic motivation. By definition, extrinsically motivated behavior is linked to the consequences that follow it. In general, then, the time-zone notion applies to extrinsic motivation. Intrinsically motivated behavior, by definition, is not linked to the external consequences that follow it. Thus, the time-zone notion does not apply to intrinsic motivation.

Extrinsic Motivation

As in the case of environmental influences, the first concern in assessing extrinsic motivational processes is to identify and document connections or relationships between motivational stimuli and behavior. Motivational stimuli are those consequences that follow behavior. Yet there is another limit to the time-zone notion, even in extrinsic motivation; it should be recognized that although extrinsic motivational stimuli follow behavior, the expectation or anticipation of such consequences can precede or accompany behavior. For example, children may both commence (i.e., before) and complete (i.e., during) an assignment (i.e., the behavior) in anticipation of the consequences that will follow. Nevertheless, with extrinsically motivated behavior, it is the end result that explains a child's anticipations and expectations of consequences. Anticipations are, thus, not exceptions to the rule of consequences, although they do change the notion of time zones. Therefore, the consequences that follow extrinsically motivated behavior are what ultimately account for the behavior.

Motivational Stimuli

The motivational stimuli anticipated by children may be as varied as a grade, the teacher's praise, personal satisfaction, peer recognition, parental pleasure, or the avoidance of negative consequences for not performing. Both observational (L-data) and self-report (Q-data) information sources can be usefully combined to assess which consequences motivate children. This information can then be used by the teacher to manage the learning environment.

Some children, however, are not yet mature enough to be motivated by any of the preceding types of motivational stimuli. Such children are not able to stay on task or to accomplish reasonable work objectives called for by their IEPs. Careful study of their off-task behaviors, using observational play-analysis methods (Butler et al., 1978), will often reveal that they are involved in earlier forms of developmental behavior. For example, they may engage in repetitious behavior sequences or may try to engage other children in social play at inappropriate times. While they are not aware of why they act as they do, they behave as if they have a motive to complete developing those preschool skills, which are normally mastered by engaging in these forms of play. A reasonable instructional conclusion is that these children still require experiences of the sort offered in a planned preschool program. An appropriate IEP for them will include some preschool activities. Methods of assessing and planning appropriate individualized programs for these developmentally younger children are discussed in Butler et al. (1975, 1978) and Gotts (1979).

Another group of children can be identified who are tied into another earlier motivational system. They engage in misbehavior as a means of getting attention (goal 1); demonstrating their own power (goal 2); getting even or hurting someone (goal 3); or being left alone by others (goal 4) (Dreikurs, 1968). Dreikurs suggested that observation (*L*-data) may be used to identify these goals. Moreover, if the teacher tries to stop the behavior, the underlying motive will be more clearly expressed (*T*-data). Finally, he suggested that examining personal reactions to such misbehavior (*S*-data) is a powerful assessment tool. A feeling of mild irritation about the behavior or the child's dependency suggests goal 1 or a child who is developmentally stuck. If the teacher feels angry or senses being in a power struggle with the child, this suggests that the child is acting on goal 2. Goal 3 is considered if the teacher feels deeply offended by the child's actions. If the teacher is at a complete loss about what to do and feels like giving up, goal 4 may very well apply.

Children whose goal is to get attention (goal 1) may do so in any of four styles: active-destructive (i.e., butting in, showing off, mischievousness, toughness); passive-destructive (awkwardness, dependency, clinging, laziness); passive-constructive (overgenerous, excessive goodness); and active-constructive (performing to attract attention, working hard to get ahead of others). It is interesting how closely these four styles match the four quadrants of the circumplex (Fig. 13-2). The considerable overlap of Dreikurs's approach and the quadrant version of the L-C circumplex relative to attention getting was confirmed and expanded in research done by Evans (1971). Teachers react to the active-destructive and passive-destructive forms of attention getting as described in the preceding paragraph, whereas they react to the constructive forms of attention getting as if they are socially useful and pleasing. Evans's research (1971) showed that behaviors matching goals 2, 3, and 4 were perceived by teachers as socially useless or noncoping.

Children who do not respond to the usual extrinsic motivational stimuli can be motivated, by other means, to perform regular school work. The least mature will work if given concrete reinforcers such as food or small desirable objects. Some children will stay on task or complete a certain amount of work for the opportunity to participate in an activity they enjoy. Yet other children, who are somewhat more mature, will work for tokens or points that they can later exchange for privileges or desired commodities. What is necessary, in light of these possibilities, is to assess the commodities and activities for which a child would be willing to work. Simply asking children to state or select their preferences (*Q*-data) is an effective way to determine what they want.

The literature on children's responses to motivational stimuli makes it clear that all of the following influence their effectiveness with children: feedback on failure/success, intensity of negative consequences, types of rewards, reward schedules, and stimulus variation (Butler et al., 1971, ED 059 783, pp. 100–118). For further help with the management of learning through use of motivational stimuli, consult Clarizio (1971).

Intrinsic Motivation

Intrinsically motivated behavior is not linked to the external consequences that follow it. In this sense, the four goals of misbehavior are *not* intrinsically motivated. This is so because they are oriented to the observable outcomes they produce, i.e., attention, sense of power, revenge, and being left alone. But a distinction must be made regarding the constructive forms of attention getting. Much evidence suggests these are normal developmental behaviors. Thus, the instructional goal should not be to eliminate all attention getting. Instead, children who engage in destructive forms of attention getting should be taught the skills needed for constructive attention getting.

On the same grounds, it may be reasoned that those less mature children who engage in earlier forms of play are intrinsically motivated to do so. They behave as they do for intrinsic reasons related to developmental processes. Thus, it would appear to be instructionally unsound to use motivational stimuli in school to systematically stop these children from "working" toward the attainment of their developmental potential, while seeking to divert all of their energies into academic types of work for which they are not truly ready. Because most IEP behavioral sequence charts are, however, primarily oriented to academic attainments, the formulation of IEPs that cannot meet the needs of many mildly handicapped children who are below developmental age 7, is encouraged by these charts. The wisdom of early childhood special education needs to be heeded by public school personnel if this IEP imbalance is to be corrected for the developmentally young. The concern is to not destroy these children's intrinsic motivation to develop.

The evidence is overwhelming to support the case for intrinsic motivation (White, 1959). Since White's review, the most important single line of work on intrinsic motivation was introduced by Richard de Charms (1968). Since then, de Charms and his associates have turned this viewpoint into a workable program for schools (de Charms and associates, 1976). De Charms' position somewhat resembles the familiar concept, locus of control, but goes beyond it. The various measures of locus of control estimate how much an individual believes he or she is in control of or can influence events. De Charms acknowledged the value of this but further identified an external locus of control (i.e., belief in low personal influence or control) as making people feel that they are helpless pawns. De Charms' research shows that people prefer instead to be origins of influence in their environments. Much recent evidence is in agreement with White's (1959) and de Charms' (1968) observation that extrinsic motivators can interfere with intrinsic motivation and can even destroy it.

What is recommended, based on the foregoing, is that children's sense of personal causation be assessed using procedures reported by de Charms and associates (1976). Because these are somewhat demanding procedures to learn and use, for a general beginning consider using the expressed control scale of the FIRO series as an indicator of how strongly the child wants to have a sense of control. Look also at the FIRO's wanted control scale as showing how much control the child is willing to let others have. For further help in interpreting control scores, see Ryan (1971) and Schutz (1966). Combine this information with that from the L-C circumplex (Fig. 13-1) as this relates to control; look at both the school behavior checklist and the semantic differential results for circumplex dimensions 1, 2, 5, and 6.

To get at those areas of personal causation that can be developed through classroom experiences, it is particularly important to assess a child's sense of personal causation or locus of control in relation to the school environment. A personal scale can be developed, by writing plainly and colloquially worded statements, using the following sample statements as guides:

1. If I do my schoolwork, I can learn to add numbers.
2. I am too unlucky to learn to add numbers.
3. If I listen carefully to the teacher, I can learn to add numbers.
4. Learning to add numbers is too hard for me.
5. My teacher will give me a good grade if I get the problems right.
6. My teacher will only give me a good grade if he or she likes me.

Notice that the preceding statements attempt to sample the child's belief in locus of control within the school setting. These statements are written for children who still experience addition as an academic challenge. Items should be prepared to reflect the subjects studied by students and the level of difficulty of work typically assigned. For example, items might deal with copying from the board, writing a letter, spelling, division, and so on. All items should take yes/no answers. Half of the items should be stated to reflect an internal locus of control (e.g., 1, 3, and 5) and half an external locus (e.g., 2, 4, and 6). Unlike the sample items, a full scale should be based on the whole variety of subjects being studied. This is because a scale based only on arithmetic may in part assess the child's actual degree of success in that area. By writing items across several subject areas, that source of bias will be reduced.

To score the preceding sample items so that the score reflects how "internal" the child's beliefs are about locus of control, proceed as follows. Each odd-numbered item that is answered *yes* counts one point. Each even-numbered item that is answered *no* counts one point. The scoring key should, of course, be based on the actual content of the items. Add the total points. That is the child's internality score. In general, if a child answers more than one half of the questions in an internal direction, the child's view is more internal. If fewer than half are answered in the keyed direction, the view is more external.

If a child's view is more external, then the child does not feel like an origin of influence in school. This can be remedied by (1) providing feedback that shows that there is a direct relationship between success and the child's efforts; (2) assigning skill-building work that is challenging but at which the child can still succeed; and (3) allowing the child to function as much as possible as an origin by means of giving him or her choices instead of exact instructions. The overall goal is to help children develop a sense of personal causation (de Charms and associates, 1976). A rule of thumb to use in gauging whether work is of a proper difficulty level is to think of the daily assignment as a test. Ask if the child would be able to do 70–80 percent of the work correctly. If the daily work is much more difficult than that, it is very likely discouraging and may contribute to a child's feelings of externality.

Miscellaneous Motivational Measures

When assessing preference for types of motivational stimuli, let children express their choices by using the evaluative dimension bipolar descriptors of the semantic differential. This procedure will more clearly establish the effective extrinsic motivators. A checklist or yes/no format provides a list of possibilities, while the semantic differential enables them to be ranked in order from most to least effective. In this connection, it is important to recognize when using concrete reinforcers that their effectiveness needs to be periodically reevaluated; children's preferences are constantly changing.

Phillips (1966) constructed a scale of school motivation that has worked extremely well in several studies. The scale is in the public domain, so it can be used in the classroom without seeking special permission. The scale requires the sorting of students into groups on the basis of whether they are high or low on a series of motivational characteristics such as: "Tries hard to do well in school." The actual scores are probably less interesting than the insights that the sorting process gives into the variety of components that make up positive school motivation.

Motivational content is available from the series of thirteen stories that children tell about the Tasks of Emotional Development Test (TED) pictures (Cohen & Weil, 1975). As in the case of the preceding instrument, the overall score is less interesting than the insights provided by each child's stories regarding his or her comprehension of motivation and the types of motives he or she attributes to the characters. These insights can serve as a solid basis for planning group discussions of why people feel and behave as they do, which can teach students to analyze and understand this important dimension of human interaction and communication.

INTRAPSYCHIC FACTORS

Intrapsychic assessment is often called personality assessment, although, as Table 13-1 shows, this area of the affective domain consists of many specialized kinds of assessment. Many of these are, in fact, left out of a typical personality assessment. These kinds of assessment have in common that they seek partly to get at the more internal, less observable affective characteristics and they seek to describe some of the more stable or enduring aspects of the person.

Temperament

Temperament refers to the style of behavior in contrast to the content of behavior. Nine dimensions of temperament have been identified, described, and studied across time in the same group of children through an extensive program of research (Thomas & Chess, 1977; Thomas, Chess, & Birch, 1968); scales for measuring the characteristics are available in these same reports. Children have been found to vary along these temperament dimensions: activity level, rhythmicity, approach/withdrawal, adaptability, intensity of reaction, threshold of responsiveness, quality of mood, distractibility, and persistence. While the last two may at first seem like opposites, they are in fact separate characteristics.

Thomas and Chess (1977) and Thomas et al. (1968) did an excellent job of introducing and illustrating the use of scales for measuring temperament. Their research should be studied and their methods used. Temperament is a very stable aspect of human personality. It would, therefore, be a mistake to try to change it. Understanding temperament can help the teacher to avoid this mistake. Understanding a specific child's temperament is also essential for creating a more favorable match between the child's style and the classroom environment.

Self-Concept

Among the various commercially available measures of self-concept, the Piers-Harris children's self-concept scale (Piers, 1969) is perhaps the most usable and well constructed. It is strong in its coverage of school-related content. Children from about mental age 8 can complete the scale.[13]

Teachers can also resort once more to the semantic differential technique. The evaluative dimension bipolar scales will come closest to measuring what the Piers-Harris measures, if the concepts rated include: "My classmates think I am;" "My teacher thinks I am;" "My family thinks I am;" and "I am."

Coopersmith (1967) studied self-concept using self-report (Q-data) plus teacher ratings based on observation (L-data containing some mix of S-data). From this combination of self-report and rating scores, it is possible to study whether a child is defensive about self-concept (i.e., whether the two sets of scores agree or disagree). The rating scale is a valuable source of self-concept information, which teachers should consider using. The scale is brief and easy to use, score, and interpret (Coopersmith, 1967).

Self-concept in relation to particular academic areas has also been studied. Academic self-concept and general self-concept are only modestly related to one another. Information on the availability of one such scale can be found in Johnson (1976, pp. 677–679). The sample items presented there can also be used as models for writing a scale to fit the subject areas and levels of difficulty appropriate to children in every classroom.

Personality—Global Aspects

Self-report measures of the global aspects of personality generally do not lend themselves to use in classroom instruction, nor do they provide teachers with particularly useful insights into their students' personalities. Such tests do have important guidance and administrative uses, however, e.g., to screen for children who may need individual assessment. Unfortunately, none of the most widely used scales come out very well when evaluated by the CSE criteria (Hoepfner et al., 1970, 1972, 1974). From personal preference, therefore, the 16 P-F (personality-factor) series of tests is recommended: early school personality questionnaire, children's personality questionnaire, and junior-senior high school personality questionnaire.[14] Also, an experience that can be of real value to teachers is to study Ferguson's very readable book (1970) on personality development.

Social and Emotional Adjustment

Many questionnaire measures are available for social and emotional adjustment. They have the same problems and limitations noted for personality measures. The Quay and Peterson (1979) Problem Behavior Checklist has much to recommend it for screening purposes. The school behavior checklist (Johnson,

---

[13]This scale can be obtained from the publisher at Box 6184 Acklen Station, Nashville, Tn. 37212.

[14]This preference is based on positive regard for the extensive and systematic research performed by the senior author of the series (Cattell, 1965). This series of measures is available from IPAT, 1602 Coronado Drive, Champaign, Il. 61820.

1976, pp. 574–576) measures, in addition to the social behaviors discussed earlier, personal disorganization, which means such things as difficulty (1) paying attention; (2) concentrating; (3) remembering; and (4) performing in the classroom. It shares some content with the Problem Behavior Checklist's third scale, inadequacy-immaturity.

Typical Mood and Affective Reactions

Very satisfactory observational (L-data) results can be obtained for affective reactions. Once again, a book by Ekman and Friesen (1975) is recommended for sharpening these observational skills. The school behavior checklist (Johnson, 1976, pp. 574–576) contains scales of both anxiety symptoms and symptoms of depression. Ekman and Friesen (1975) emphasized the observation of momentary, passing emotional states. The two checklist scales, in contrast, measure ongoing or frequently present emotions.

School anxiety is of obvious importance to classroom functioning. Phillips (1966, 1978) has done more than any other person to define and study this characteristic; his scale can be used by teachers. Phillips's most recent research (1978) provides suggestions for ways of reducing school anxiety.

Children's attributions of affect are obtained when the TED (Cohen & Weil, 1975) is administered. As was said before, the scores will not be of as much interest to teachers as will the insights afforded by children's discussion of affect in the context of the thirteen tasks of emotional development. What is revealed is the kinds and depths of emotions that are understood and expected of people. Affect responses can further be studied in terms of how congruent they are with the outcomes of the stories in which they appear.

Vitality and Energy Output

This characteristic is assessed observationally together with typical mood and affective reactions. The main purpose of assessing vitality is to determine whether such states as anger, anxiety, and depression are significantly reducing the child's energy level, producing fragile health, and so forth. Reduced vitality and energy level suggest a serious degree of emotional interference and should lead to referral and careful diagnostic appraisal.

Character

The more superficial aspects of character are reflected in the assessment findings for social behavior. As an intrapsychic function, character means internal controls. One important aspect of this is whether the child behaves impulsively. A general impression that the child has impulse control problems (e.g., as reflected in periodic loss of control in social situations, speaking before thinking, etc.) can be checked out by (1) asking the child to see if he or she can remain still for a specified period; (2) asking the child to draw a line as slowly as possible, using first one hand and then the other; (3) observing whether, on special request, the child can avoid interrupting under circumstances that would usually lead to interruptions; (4) having the child alternately start and stop motor activities on verbal command but in the face of sometimes conflicting visual information (i.e., as in Simon Says); and (5) timing by stopwatch the child's solution of the problems of Ravens's test (1963). On each task, the goal is good control. Impulsivity on the Ravens's task shows up when, as the visual problems become increasingly difficult, the child answers incorrectly after spending less time scanning the six answer choices before making a selection; that is, a sudden drop in measured scanning time, coupled with the selection of incorrect answers, suggests cognitive impulsivity when under pressure.

Ego Organization

In recent years, Jane Loevinger (1966, 1976) has been the principal theorist and researcher of ego development. Teachers generally will not wish to assess this group of characteristics. But it will prove to be of great value to study Loevinger's presentation (1976, pp. 24–25) of the ego developmental levels through which children progress. She considers 10 ego stages in terms of the related occurrences in (1) impulse control and character development; (2) interpersonal style; (3) conscious preoccupations; and (4) cognitive style. Specifically, Loevinger's work will help to provide a sense of how to integrate various data sources within the intrapsychic area and between the intrapsychic area and social behavior.

Stigma and Reactions

Children who have experienced major psychological or physical traumas, or who have more obvious handicaps, often have a sense that there is something wrong with them personally—that they are "bad." This sense of stigma is not usually concealed; rather it is an accessible conscious preoccupation of the child. Such feelings will readily manifest themselves on a semantic differential. They can also be seen in the children's sensitivities, personal guardedness against psychological hurt, or excess deference to others. The instructional concern here is similar to that for self-concept. But where feelings of stigma are present, it will not be sufficient merely to work toward having the child feel better about him- or herself in relation to school. Specific plans must also be made for activities that will reduce the sense of stigma.

Psychosocial Orientation

Erik Erikson's theory (1963) of psychosocial development is the primary conceptual framework for this group of characteristics. Most readers have been exposed at some time to his view of development as proceeding through a series of normative stages or crises, which for the years of childhood are: trust versus mistrust; autonomy versus doubt or shame; initiative versus guilt; industry versus inferiority; and identity versus identity confusion. What is needed to make this framework practical for teachers is careful study of Erikson's "Eight Stages of Man" chapter (1963, pp. 247–274). The chapter should be read and reread until the reader thoroughly understands what is at issue in each stage and how different degrees of stage resolution are likely to affect later development. Some modest suggestions have been made elsewhere by the writer (Gotts, 1979) for how some existing rating scales can be applied to Eriksonian assessment. Nevertheless, no satisfactory measures exist for assessing what, for example, a particular child's balance might be between initiative and guilt. The only measure of which the writer is aware that might be adapted to this purpose is TED (Cohen & Weil, 1975).

TED consists of four sets of photographs, to be administered, respectively, to preadolescent boys, preadolescent girls, adolescent boys, and adolescent girls. The sets are essentially parallel in the sense that each deals with the same twelve developmental tasks or issues, and each uses approximately the same style and visual content to depict the tasks. A thirteenth task uses only a single photograph for both adolescent girls and boys; it may, if needed, be administered to preadolescent girls and boys as well.

Children are asked to tell stories about each picture. They are to tell what is happening (i.e., perception); how the story turns out (i.e., outcome); how the characters feel (i.e., affect); and why they act and feel the way they do (i.e., motivation). If a child omits or fails to state understandably any of these four elements of a story, the person administering the test is to ask standard follow-up questions to encourage the child to try commenting on each one of the four. Stories that have been completed in this way can be scored according to a standard scoring system, or the user can instead simply interpret the stories in terms of their clinical meaning.

The thirteen tasks represented by the photographs are (1) peer socialization (belonging to the same-sex group); (2) trust (believing that adults are nurturent); (3) aggression (handling angry feelings and defending oneself against physical aggression); (4) learning (working alone on school tasks); (5) conscience (recognizing and resisting temptation); (6) separation (going outside without parents and without concern over parental restrictions or being abandoned); (7) identification (wanting to be a part of what the same-sex parent is doing; wanting to help); (8) sibling rivalry (sharing parental attention with sibling); (9) acceptance of limits (tolerating adult-imposed limits that frustrate needs or wishes); (10) affection between parents (overcoming feelings of jealousy, rivalry, and abandonment); (11) orderliness, cleanliness (accepting the need to keep things neat and clean); (12) self-concept (developing a positive attitude toward oneself); and (13) heterosexual socialization (forming positive and self-adequate feelings around contacts with the opposite sex).

The writer has taught teachers and school psychologists to administer TED. Test administration normally requires 15–20 minutes. School users have found the pictures to be acceptable, nonoffensive, and well-suited to the purpose of obtaining stories that deal with the thirteen intended tasks of emotional development. By a mental age of 5 years, children can tell meaningful stories. This is in contrast to many of the self-report measures, which may be of little value before mental age 7 or 8.[15]

The TED is a test to which most teachers would not normally be introduced. The test is most typically administered and interpreted by psychologists. Never-

---

[15]This test is supplied by T.E.D. Associates, 42 Lowell Road, Brookline, Ma. 02146.

theless, putting the TED into use among special education teachers would, in this writer's opinion, be a correct move. This is not to suggest that they will wish to use either the standard scoring system or to make clinical inferences. Teachers should, however, study the scoring system sufficiently to understand when a perception is adequate and when it is not; when an outcome is successful or unsuccessful; and so on. With this much preparation, teachers using the TED can learn a great deal that will help them to understand their students and to plan to meet their learning needs in thirteen of life's most fundamental areas. Receiving a psychologist's report, based on the TED, is not an acceptable substitute. What the teacher needs to see is the raw data—the stories told by the children.

Some of the things that a teacher can learn about a child from a child's TED stories include if the world seems friendly; how the child perceives human relations; how interpersonal conflicts are seen as being resolved; whether developmental challenges are seen as being successfully handled; for which tasks the child can see no successful resolution; if the emotions that are inferred as being present sensibly match the outcomes with which they are associated; whether the motives attributed to characters are mature or immature, constructive or destructive; the resourcefulness of the child characters in handling developmental challenges; and the attitudes seen as being exchanged between children and adults. These are insights around which a great deal of thoughtful individualized educational planning could take place.

Other Factors

For measures of creativity and expressiveness, consult Butler et al. (1971, ED 059 783).

Fantasy process and contents are characteristics that lack practical value for classroom applications, so are intentionally omitted from discussion.

Humor is not of great relevance to instructional planning, except in the isolated case of a child who is so overly serious as to feel left out and distressed when others enjoy something humorous.

Assessment of acquiescence/negativism is not of much practical relevance to the classroom, so it is omitted.

Social skills are those properties of behavior that enable a child to be effective in social situations. It is unfortunate that little assessment help is available to teachers for measuring the more complex intrapsychic components of social skills. Therefore, intuition must remain the most dependable tool for such assessment.

INTEGRATING THE DATA

No one could gather all the kinds of assessment data suggested in this chapter on one individual child. But there are times when each of the kinds of data will be needed. Usually what will be assembled will be several separate bits of information that do not fall together automatically. Their assembly requires both analysis and synthesis. The question is how to go about this.

Knowing as Science

To review the high points,[16] the following frameworks and models were commended to the reader as tools which would provide insights: (1) four types of data sources which complement one another—*T, L, Q,* and *S* (Cattell, 1965); (2) the classification of affective behaviors into five major categories (Table 13-1); (3) the Leary-Coffey (1955) circumplex model of social behavior (Fig. 13-1); (4) a division of the L-C model into a four quadrant typology (Gotts et al., 1968–1969) based on two dimensions (Fig. 13-2); (5) the three-dimensional semantic differential model of affective meaning (Osgood et al., 1957); (6) an affective ecology based on discriminative, evoking, and maintaining stimuli—none of which means direct causation; (7) the three-dimensional FIRO model (Schutz, 1966); (8) extrinsic and intrinsic motivation; (9) a time-phased relationship between environmental stimuli and extrinsic motivation; (10) the "goals of misbehavior" model (Dreikurs, 1968); (11) correspondences between the L-C quadrants and Dreikurs's model of attention getting; (12) personal causation theory (de Charms, 1968; de Charms and Associates, 1976); (13) Loevinger's (1966, 1976) model of ego development; (14) the stage theory of psychosocial development (Erikson, 1963); and (15) the 13 fundamental tasks of emotional development (Cohen & Weil, 1975). Together with the suggested measures, these comprise the current basis for a science of affective assessment.

Knowing as Art and Humanity

After the applicable scientific frameworks have been applied and the data gathered, there comes a time of summing up what is known and what it means. The case study method takes over at this point.

The case study is a form of art in the sense that there is no single right way to do it, nor is it likely that the perfect case study has even been or ever will be written. Everyone who does case studies strives to paint with words a picture that reveals an interpretation. The interpretation must have a feel of wholeness and balance. It must be there.

In addition to being art, case studies are also humanity. The person who emerges from the study must be believable and knowable as a person. Otherwise the case study misses its mark. The humanity of the case study depends, of course, on the humanity of the writer. As was noted early in the chapter, our capacity to understand students as individual human beings derives first from our knowledge of ourselves as persons (Polanyi, 1958). If we can see ourselves whole and complete, then we can rely on that capacity to see others.

But to label case studies as art and humanity does not imply that one cannot learn about them. Two small volumes, both now out of print but available in libraries, illustrate some of the basics to be considered in case studies. Rothney

---

[16]Some procedures that would ordinarily be given attention in a chapter on affective diagnosis have not been discussed here. O'Leary and Johnson (1979), Group for the Advancement of Psychiatry (1974), Freedman and Kaplan (1972), and Long, Morse, and Newman (1971, Sec. 2) will be useful references for those whose concern—unlike this chapter's—is diagnosis leading to classification of children and adolescents as being disturbed in social-emotional functions.

(1968) suggested five general criteria for assembling data for the case study: (1) consider individual idiosyncracies; (2) evaluate the data with specific reference to the internal consistency among the various parts, attempting to reconcile all inconsistencies; (3) appraise cultural influences; (4) obtain a longitudinal (i.e., across time) perspective, if possible; and (5) continuously conceptualize the person as new data are added. When writing, try to discover a pattern against which it will be possible to decide whether particular data should be included or excluded. Any case report can deal only with development that has occurred up to a given time. There is a need to think and write in terms of probability rather than certainty. Statistical generalizations, no matter how strongly supported for people in general, cannot dictate how the data should go together for the individual. Rothney (1968) wrapped up his presentations with four case studies, each written with a different objective in view.

Sears and Sherman (1964) produced a very different approach to the case study. They tried, for example, to collect much of the same kinds of data for each of eight children. After getting together a preliminary account of each child, they went on to make various comparisons and contrasts among the findings for different children. Thus, there is the potential for learning more about a specific child from comparisons with other children. In a classroom group, where several children may be studied over a year, this raises the possibility of systematically using the understanding of some children to increase the understanding of others. Between Rothney (1968) and Sears and Sherman (1964), there are twelve individual case studies available for analysis.

Beyond Knowledge

The study of the individual child is not to develop knowledge only. Teachers would not do case studies if knowledge were the only objective. Aside from knowledge, child studies are completed in order to accomplish these other purposes: understanding, predicting, planning, and relating. If the case study does not satisfy these purposes, it is better left undone. The special education case study, moreover, has a product in view: the IEP. The collecting of all data and the assembling of it into a usable form must be carried out so as to satisfy these purposes. Beyond knowledge there is purpose. Purpose must influence assessment as does science, art, and humanity.

REFERENCES

Baker, E. H., & Tyne, T. F. The use of observational procedures in school psychological services. *School Psychology Monographs,* 1980, *4*(1), 25–44.

Buros, O. K. (Ed.). *Tests in print. II*. Highland Park, N.J.: Gryphon Press, 1974.

Buros, O. K. (Ed.). *The eighth mental measurements yearbook*. Highland Park, N.J.: Gryphon Press, 1978.

Butler, A. L., Gotts, E. E., & Quisenberry, N. L. *Early childhood programs: Development objectives and their use*. Columbus, Oh.: Charles E. Merrill, 1975.

Butler, A. L., Gotts, E. E., & Quisenberry, N. L. *Play as development*. Columbus, Oh.: Charles E. Merrill, 1978.

Butler, A. L., Gotts, E. E., Quisenberry, N. L., & Thompson, R. P. *Literature search and development of an evaluation system in early childhood education* (5 Vols.). (ERIC

Document Reproduction Service Nos. ED 059 780–ED 059 784) Bloomington, In.: Indiana University, 1971.

Campbell, D., & Fiske, D. Convergent and discriminant validation by the multitrait-multimethod matrix. *Psychological Bulletin,* 1959, *56*, 81–105.

Cattell, R. B. *The scientific analysis of personality.* Chicago: Aldine, 1965.

Clarizio, H. F. *Toward positive classroom discipline.* New York: Wiley, 1971.

Cohen, H., & Weil, G. R. *Tasks of emotional development test: Kit.* Brookline, Ma.: T.E.D. Associates, 1975.

Coopersmith, S. *The antecedents of self-esteem.* San Francisco: Freeman, 1967.

Coulter, W. A., & Morrow, H. W. (Eds.). *Adaptive behavior: Concepts and measurements.* New York: Grune & Stratton, 1978.

Crandall, V. C., Crandall, V. J., & Katkovsky, W. A children's social desirability questionnaire. *Journal of Consulting Psychology,* 1965, *29*, 27–36.

de Charms, R. *Personal causation. The internal affective determinants of behavior.* New York: Academic Press, 1968.

de Charms, R., & associates. *Enhancing motivation. Change in the classroom.* New York: Irvington Publishers, 1976.

Doll, E. A. *Vineland social maturity scale.* Circle Pines, Mn.: American Guidance Service, 1965.

Dreikurs, R. *Psychology in the classroom: A manual for teachers.* New York: Harper & Row, 1968.

Ekman, P., & Friesen, W. V. *Unmasking the face. A guide to recognizing emotions from facial expressions.* Englewood Cliffs, N.J.: Prentice-Hall, 1975.

Erikson, E. H. *Childhood and society* (2nd ed.). New York: Norton, 1963.

Evans, J. H. *The influence of teacher personality and pupil misbehavior upon teacher impressions of pupils.* Unpublished doctoral dissertation, Indiana University, 1971.

Ferguson, L. R. *Personality development.* Belmont, Ca.: Brooks/Cole, 1970.

Freedman, A. M., & Kaplan, H. I. (Eds.). *The child: His psychological and cultural development* (Vol. 1). *Normal development and psychological assessment.* New York: Atheneum, 1972.

Froehle, T. C., Gotts, E. E., & Leventhal, R. B. *Classroom sociometrics and FIRO-BC interpersonal relationship orientation: Basic research and treatment implications.* Unpublished manuscript, 1971. (Available from AEL, Inc., P. O. Box 1348, Charleston, W. Va. 25325.)

Gardner, R. A. *Therapeutic communication with children. The mutual storytelling technique.* New York: Science House, 1971.

Goffman, E. *Interaction ritual. Essays on face-to-face behavior.* Garden City, N.Y.: Doubleday, 1967.

Gordon, I. J. *Studying the child in school.* New York: Wiley, 1966.

Gotts, E. E. *Affective Assessment of Children.* Unpublished manuscript, 1972–1974.

Gotts, E. E. Delay of verbal response in relation to verbal behavior control (Doctoral dissertation, The University of Texas, 1967). *Dissertation Abstracts,* 1967, *27*, 4126–A. (University Microfilms No. 67–8107).

Gotts, E. E. Early childhood assessment. In D. A. Sabatino & T. L. Miller (Eds.), *Describing learner characteristics of handicapped children and youth.* New York: Grune & Stratton, 1979.

Gotts, E. E., Adams, R. L., & Phillips, B. N. Personality classification of discrete pupil behaviors. *Journal of School Psychology,* 1968–1969, *7* (3), 54–62.

Gotts, E. E., Froehle, T. C., & Leventhal, R. B. *Consistency behavior and validity in classroom sociometrics.* Unpublished manuscript, 1970. (Available from AEL, Inc., P. O. Box 1348, Charleston, W. Va. 25325.)

Group for the Advancement of Psychiatry. *Psychopathological disorders in childhood. Theoretical considerations and a proposed classification.* New York: Jason Aronson, 1974.

Heider, F. *The psychology of interpersonal relations.* New York: Wiley, 1958.

Hoepfner, R., & The staff of the School Evaluation Project (Eds.). *CSE elementary school test evaluations.* Los Angeles: UCLA, Center for the Study of Evaluation, 1974. (ERIC Document Reproduction Service Nos. ED 113382-ED 113384.)

Hoepfner, R., Hemenway, J., DeMuth, J., Tenopy, M. L., Granville, A. C., Petrosko, J. M., et al. (Eds.). *CSE-RBS test evaluations: Tests of higher-order cognitive, affective, and interpersonal skills.* Los Angeles: UCLA, Center for the Study of Evaluation, 1972. (ERIC Document Reproduction Service No. ED 076713.)

Hoepfner, R., Coniff, W. A., Jr., Hufano, L., Bastone, M., Ogilvie, V. N., Hunter, R., et al. (Eds.). *CSE secondary school test evaluations.* (3 Vols.). Los Angeles: UCLA, Center for the Study of Evaluation, 1974. (ERIC Document Reproduction Service Nos. ED 113382–ED 113384.)

Johnson, O. G., (Ed.). *Tests and measurements in child development: Handbook II*. San Francisco: Jossey-Bass, 1976.

Leary, T., & Coffey, H. S. Interpersonal diagnosis: Some problems of methodology and validation. *Journal of Abnormal and Social Psychology*, 1955, *50*, 110–124.

Lindholm, B. W., & Touliatos, J. Comparison of children in regular and special education classes on the behavior problem checklist. *Psychological Reports*, 1976, *38*, 451–458.

Loevinger, J. The meaning and measurement of ego development. *American Psychologist*, 1966, *21*, 195–206.

Loevinger, J. *Ego development*. San Francisco: Jossey-Bass, 1976.

Long, N. J., Morse, W. C., & Newman, R. G. (Eds.). *Conflict in the classroom: The education of children with problems*. (2nd ed.). Belmont, Ca.: Wadsworth, 1971.

McLemore, C. W., & Benjamin, L. S. Whatever happened to interpersonal diagnosis? A psychosocial alternative to DSM-III. *American Psychologist*, 1979, *34*, 17–34.

O'Leary, K. D., & Johnson, S. B. Psychological assessment. In H. C. Quay & J. S. Werry (Eds.), *Psychopathological disorders of childhood* (2nd ed.). New York: Wiley, 1979.

Osgood, C. E., Suci, G. J., & Tannenbaum, P. H. *The measurement of meaning*. Urbana: University of Illinois Press, 1957.

Phillips, B. N. *An analysis of causes of anxiety among children in school*. Austin, Te.: University of Texas, 1966. (ERIC Document Reproduction Service No. ED 010179.)

Phillips, B. N. *School stress and anxiety. Theory, research, and intervention*. New York: Human Sciences Press, 1978.

Piaget, J. *Six psychological studies*. New York: Random House, 1967.

Piers, E. V. *Manual for the Piers-Harris children's self concept scale*. Nashville, Tenn.: Counselor Recordings and Tests, 1969.

Polanyi, M. *Personal knowledge*. Chicago: University of Chicago Press, 1958.

Quay, H. C. Measuring dimensions of deviant behavior: The behavior problem checklist. *Journal of Abnormal Child Psychology*, 1977, *5*, 277–287.

Quay, H. C., & Peterson, D. R. *Manual for the behavior problem checklist*. New Brunswick, N.J.: Donald R. Peterson, 1979.

Ravens, J. C. *Coloured progressive matrices*. New York: Psychological Corporation, 1963.

Rothney, J. W. M. *Methods of studying the individual child: The psychological case study*. Waltham, Ma.: Blaisdell, 1968.

Ryan, L. R. *Clinical interpretation of the FIRO-B*. Palo Alto, Ca.: Consulting Psychologists Press, 1971.

Schutz, W. C. *The interpersonal underworld*. Palo Alto, Ca.: Science & Behavior Books, 1966.

Sears, P. S., & Sherman, V. S. *In pursuit of self-esteem. Case studies of eight elementary school children*. Belmont, Ca.: Wadsworth, 1964.

Thomas, A., & Chess, S. *Temperament and development*. New York: Brunner/Mazel, 1977.

Thomas, A., Chess, S., & Birch, H. G. *Temperament and behavior disorders in children*. New York: New York University Press, 1968.

Touliatos, J., & Lindholm, B. W. Teachers' perceptions of behavior problems in children from intact, single-parent, and step-parent families. *Psychology in the Schools*, 1980, *17*, 264–269.

White, R. W. Motivation reconsidered: The concept of competence. *Psychological Review*, 1959, *66*, 297–333.

PART IV

Educational Programs and Materials

Patricia Gillespie-Silver

14
Meaning-Seeking Strategies and Special Reading Programs

The *types* of questions teachers ask about students' special reading needs will influence the teachers' selection of reading materials. For example, a teacher may ask on what level a child reads and what specific skills the child possesses. Such questions focus on the product, or outcome, of the student's reading process. These product-oriented questions do not address the way the student interacts with words, sentences, and paragraphs; how the student views the reading process per se; or how the student feels about reading in general or specific situations, such as reading aloud.

Product-oriented questions lead to product-oriented strategies and materials. For example, a teacher may determine that a child does not know all of the consonant sounds and, as a result, choose a program that teaches these sounds. This practice is useless if (1) the teacher does not also determine how the student uses these sounds and (2) the program does not give the student the opportunity to try out his knowledge of consonant sounds in sentences and paragraphs. Furthermore, the strategies may never give the student the opportunity to practice these newly acquired skills.

Teachers who are interested in the processes students use in predicting or guessing unknown words, in confirming their predictions, and in attempting to provide meaning will choose materials that encourage students' use of their skills or facilitate the development of new skills through interactions with sentences, paragraphs, and stories. Also, in a process-oriented program the teacher will consider the different developmental stages in the reading process. For example, a child must learn to predict what an unknown word is before she or he can acquire successful reading strategies.

This chapter presents external criteria for judging curricular materials for students with special reading needs. These criteria are based on the processes students use in attempting to comprehend what they read. The criteria also take into account the developmental stages in the reading process itself. The emphasis in this curricular analysis will be on the fact that many different types of approaches and strategies can be used as students progress in their ability to obtain meaning from written language.

MEANING-SEEKING STRATEGIES

Studies that have investigated special needs students' use of meaning-seeking strategies have found that, for the most part, these students use the same strategies as normal readers (Gutkneckt, 1971; Rhodes & Brinson, 1976). These studies have also found that the types of materials used in instruction greatly affect the special student's reading strategies (Rhodes & Brinson, 1976). Here Goodman's paradigm of meaning-seeking strategies will be used to examine curricular materials that facilitate the special needs student's use of effective reading strategies. According to Goodman (1976), the major types of strategies are the *predicting, confirming,* and *comprehending,* and they can be defined as follows:

> In developing the paradigm we have organized all the strategies around three major ones: predicting, confirming, and comprehending. Predicting strategies are those which the reader employs when he samples, selects, and predicts from any one or from an integration of the three language systems [graphophonics, syntax, and semantics]. Confirming strategies are those which the reader uses when he asks himself if what he is reading sounds like language and if it makes sense. In addition, confirming strategies are those which a reader uses as he confirms or disconfirms as he reads. Comprehending strategies include the complex process of integrating the meaning the reader is receiving with the knowledge he brings to the reading task. (p. 95)[1]

Related to these three strategies is the strategy of *self-correction* (Allen, 1976). When constructing a profile of the student's meaning-seeking strategies, it is important to ask whether a student corrects as he or she predicts, confirms, and comprehends. Moreover, teachers can select programs that emphasize self-correction and encourage students to use this important meaning-seeking strategy.

Predicting Strategies

When students attempt to use *predicting* strategies and to figure out an unfamiliar word or to obtain meaning from a passage, they have available to them their own experiential and conceptual backgrounds and the three language systems of *graphophonics, syntax,* and *semantics* (see the next three sections of this chapter). A student may select only one of the three systems or all of them. The teacher must consider how effectively the student uses the systems chosen and whether the student uses one system more effectively than others.

In examining curricular materials, the teacher must determine whether the material emphasizes one language system to the exclusion of the others and how these systems are presented to the student. For example, if the materials present only one system, the student may ignore the other systems completely (Allen, 1976). Furthermore, if only one system is presented, in isolation from the others, the student may define the reading process exclusively in terms of that one system (e.g., the student may conclude that reading is sounding out words).

---

[1]Reprinted with permission from Goodman, Y. Strategies for comprehension. In P. D. Allen & D. J. Watson (Eds.), *Findings of research in miscue analysis: Classroom implications.* Urbana, Ill.: ERIC Clearinghouse on Reading and Communication Skills, 1976, p. 95.

Graphophonic System

The student relying on graphophonic cues uses the visual configuration of the words, the sound–letter relationships, or a combination of the two. Developmental data concerning the graphophonic cueing system indicate that with readers in the first and second grades, all substitution miscues tend to have at least some letter–sound similarity about 90 percent of the time" (Goodman, 1976, p. 118). According to Goodman, readers in the early grades rely more on graphic similarities than on sound–letter relationships, and they rely on initial letters and, to a lesser degree, on final letters as their primary word-attack skills. As they grow older, their miscues have closer phonic and graphic similarity to the text, regardless of their reading proficiency or their reading methodology. And more efficient readers rely less on the graphic display than less efficient readers (Goodman, 1976). Other investigations confirm that efficient readers use a combination of cueing systems rather than rely only on graphophonics systems and that they attend to large units of information rather than to such discrete units as individual letters (Bower, 1970; Smith, 1971).

If a less proficient reader relies on the graphic display but confuses the configurations of similar-appearing words, concentrating on phonics or word-recognition strategies may actually reinforce the incorrect associations, especially if the words are taken out of context. A student who has difficulties with graphic displays may approach a word according to the teaching approach used. For example, the practice of using product-based assessments of graphophonic cueing systems may result in choosing approaches that merely reinforce the student's inefficient strategies rather than correcting them. Teaching approaches that emphasize the use of graphophonic strategies to the exclusion of other systems may result in expected gains, especially on test items measuring graphonic skills; however, comprehension may suffer if the student does not find meaning or purpose for these isolated activities (Pennock, 1979). Furthermore, teachers who choose to concentrate on graphophonic cues should determine students' specific needs, rather than use every lesson in the program (Lamb, 1975).

Syntactic System

When students use the *syntactic* cueing system, they use the grammatical structure of their language to predict unfamiliar material (e.g., they may substitute a noun for a noun). Students may use their own knowledge of the grammatical system to obtain meaning from the text. Also, readers may substitute their own language structures for the authors' without changing the meaning of the text. For example, a child may read "James asks" for "Asks James."

The student's language development will affect his or her use of the syntactic cueing system. Also, miscues (responses that vary from the text), will reflect the student's use of syntax as a predictor. For less efficient readers, words in relatively uncommon grammatical slots (e.g., a noun functioning as an adjective) will be harder to identify than words in more common grammatical positions. "As readers develop proficiency, they are able to handle the less common grammatical units" (Goodman, 1976, p. 121), and to change the order of the sentence and still retain the meaning. Less proficient readers will attempt to remain close to the print rather than transform the sentence or phrase into their own words in order to obtain meaning (Goodman, 1976).

The teacher who elects to use reading materials that emphasize or incorporate the syntactical elements of our language must (1) determine the student's knowledge of syntax, (2) select materials that have predictable syntactical units rather than complex, less predictable ones, and (3) select materials that reflect the student's overall language and conceptual development.

Semantic Strategies

Syntax is closely related to the semantics, or the meaning, of a word, a phrase, a paragraph, and so on. "Things can be syntactically acceptable and not make sense, but they can't be semantically acceptable unless they're syntactically acceptable" (Goodman, 1976, p. 66). The semantic cueing system is closely related to conceptual development and to all aspects of comprehension (Goodman, 1976, p. 123). Also, students' experiential backgrounds will affect their use of the semantic cueing system. The student who substitutes a word that does not appear to have graphic or sound similarities to the text but has a similar meaning (e.g., *car lights* for *headlights*) is using semantic cues. More proficient readers will rely on semantic cues rather than graphophonic or syntactical cues.

The use of semantic cues should be an on-going integral part of the student's reading instruction rather than a separate activity, (e.g., decoding skills should be taught along with skills of comprehension). Students should be encouraged to predict on the basis of the meanings of words, sentences, and passages. And of course the closer reading material is to students' interests, experiences, and conceptual development the more likely it is that they will be able to make such predictions.

Confirming Strategies

Students attempt to confirm or verify their predictions by asking, "Does it sound right?" or, "Does it make sense?" The *self-correction* strategy is closely related to the *confirming* strategies (Goodman, 1976). Students cannot attempt to confirm their predictions, however, if they fail to correct attempts that do not make sense or sound right, and a teacher may need to encourage a student to self-correct. For a reading approach to develop confirmation and correction strategies, it must provide "reading situations outside of the formal reading instructional periods" (Allen, 1976, p. 111), must not introduce strategies in isolation, and must present materials that are within the student's linguistic, experiential, and conceptual levels.

Reading Opportunities

Many reading materials and approaches do not provide opportunities for students to engage in free reading. Allen (1976) describes his observations of many reading lessons in which students spent 40 minutes on such tasks as working in workbooks, responding to isolated sounds on cards, and dividing words into syllables, whereas they spent only five or ten minutes actually reading. Allen (1976) stresses the importance of providing students with the opportunity to read:

It seem ludicrous to make such a statement, but it is possible for a great deal of reading instruction to take place without having the children actually read. Skills taught in isolation, words taught in lists, and other such practices lead to such conditions. Our subjects have shown us again and again that they are capable of teaching themselves a story or article. More importantly, they are dealing with the real rather than the contrived. If they do run into problems, it is then possible to develop strategy lessons that will help in overcoming them, and as it has been pointed out, these strategy lessons always involve the reader in a real reading situation. (p. 111)[2]

Skills in Isolation

One of the major problems in presenting skills in isolation is that, in most cases, materials used for this purpose do not provide enough actual language for students to use all three language systems and their own experiences for confirming their predictions. For example, in many approaches that concentrate on graphophonic strategies, students must confirm their predictions only on the basis of whether they sound right. If a word is not within a student's language experience, she or he will not be able to answer that question. Readers should be encouraged to use more than one language system for confirming their predictions.

Comprehending Strategies

Most readers who are not using effective reading strategies are not fully aware that the main goal in reading is to gain meaning (Goodman, 1976, p. 100). This may often be the case with special students who have been taught isolated word skills. First of all, many of these skills are abstract and may appear arbitrary to the student. (Who *says* a letter must have a specific sound?) If the student is prepared to view written language as a separate symbol system that says something or conveys meaning (Smith, 1977), he or she may attempt to read for meaning. Without the realization that written language conveys meaning, isolated reading exercises confuse the student.

The teacher can facilitate comprehending strategies by presenting materials that are within the student's conceptual level (Goodman, 1976). New ideas or concepts introduced in the student's reading materials should be presented prior to the student's reading of the material. On this topic, Goodman (1976) states:

> Concepts and ideas can be introduced through demonstration, experimentation, concrete illustration. Vocabulary can be developed orally in relationship to these experiences. Then, and only then, is the child ready for the task of reading about the same concepts in the text. He reads then not so much to gain new concepts as to reinforce them. In the process, he learns to handle the unusual language uses of textbooks. If textbooks are well written and handled well in elementary schools, he may, by the time he is in high school, be able to initiate study at times through a textbook with the teacher following up and reteaching the concepts he meets in books. (p. 446)[3]

---

[2]Reprinted with permission from Allen, P. D. Implications for reading instruction. In P. D. Allen & D. J. Watson (Eds.), *Findings of research in miscue analysis: Classroom implications*. Urbana, Ill.: ERIC Clearinghouse on Reading and Communication Skills, 1976, p. 111.

[3]Reprinted with permission from Goodman, K. Beyond the eye: What happens in reading. In H. Singer & R. B. Ruddell (Eds.), *Theoretical models and process of reading* (2nd ed.). Newark, Del.: International Reading Association, 1976, p. 446.

As Goodman notes, textbooks should be well written, to facilitate the student's comprehension. Ambiguous language structures confuse the student. Furthermore, reading materials that stray from our natural language structure—for example, linguistic readers—may deprive the student of the opportunity to use all three language systems in predicting, confirming, and comprehending. Also, reading texts that use such linguistic patterns as "fat cat sat" limit the student's experience with various literary forms. Students may need assistance in dealing with the special demands of various reading styles (e.g., advertisements, poems, and newspaper articles).

The authors of reading materials for special needs students must consider that "the only objective of reading is comprehension" (Goodman, 1976, p. 490). Instructional material must provide students with strategies for obtaining meaning from printed materials. One cannot teach these strategies as separate skills, in the belief that at some point in the student's program, she or he will put all the skills together so as to comprehend relevant reading materials. For the special needs student, isolated skill lessons may be too abstract and the parts may not comprise a meaningful whole.

As students encounter various types of written materials, the teacher can assist them in using such comprehending strategies as signal words (words that indicate transitions or changes in meaning, such as *but* and *in addition to*), main headings, subheadings, and summaries, to obtain the author's meaning.

SPECIAL READING MATERIALS AND MEANING-SEEKING STRATEGIES

Specialized reading approaches have been used with individuals with special reading needs for centuries. For example, the Romans used such multisensory techniques as writing in sand as an aid in teaching the letters. In this country, specialized techniques have been developed to work with students who have varying types of special needs (e.g., the brain-injured, the moderately and mildly retarded, the dyslexic reader). Specialists using these different techniques typically emphasize that a particular approach should be used with a specific type of student.

The research concerning the efficacy of these specialized techniques has yielded few conclusive results (Blanton, Sitko, & Gillespie, 1976). Moreover, most of the early researchers emphasized the differences between special students and normal readers in such skills as phonics, word attacks, and comprehension, and investigated the efficacy of various reading approaches with children designated learning disabled, mentally retarded, and so on. There is little research on the meaning-seeking strategies that special needs students use and on the efficacy of these strategies.

Several studies have found that students identified as *special* (in these cases, the perceptually handicapped and the educably mentally retarded) use the same meaning-seeking strategies as normal readers but may rely more on graphophonic than on other strategies (Gutkneckt, 1971; Rhodes & Brenson, 1976). More research on the meaning-seeking strategies of special students and on the effects of specific reading approaches on special students' reading strategies may assist reading specialists and special educators in the development of individualized reading programs.

This section presents an analysis of special reading materials that focuses on their presentation of meaning-seeking strategies. Reading series that are widely used with special needs students are included. Each program is discussed in terms of (1) its overall structure and components; (2) its types of predicting strategies, including its allowance for guessing; (3) its types of confirming strategies, including the use of self-correction; and (4) its comprehending strategies, as well as its encouragement of student-initiated or constructive strategies. The programs reviewed are the Gillingham–Stillman approach (1970), the Merrill Linguistic Reading Program (Otto, Rudolph, Smith, & Wilson, 1975), the Language Experience approach (Lee & Allen, 1968), the Fernald approach (Fernald, 1943), the Direct Instructional System for Teaching Arithmetic and Reading, or DISTAR (Englemann & Bruner, 1969), and the Sullivan Programmed Readers (Buchannon & Sullivan Associates, 1968).

Gillingham–Stillman Approach

General Description

This program uses a multisensory approach to the teaching of reading that is "based upon the close association of visual, auditory and kinesthetic elements forming what is sometimes called the 'language triangle'" (Gillingham & Stillman, 1970, p. 40). Three *associations* are presented to the student:

1. Association I: association of visual symbol with letter name and association of child's speech organs with sounds he or she produces
2. Association II: association of sound of letter with its name (e.g., /a/ with *a*
3. Association III: association of written symbol (written from memory by the student) with its sound.

Predicting Strategies

Graphophonic language system. The Gillingham–Stillman method emphasizes the student's use of graphophonic cues as the primary reading strategy. The authors of this approach discourage guessing. They state:

> Since the core of the alphabetic approach is to establish the concept of words as built out of phonetic units, the first essential of our technique is to break down the pupil's attitude toward words as ideograms to-be-remembered-as wholes, and to eliminate all guessing. (p. 42)[4]

While students are learning the sound–symbol relationships that will provide the basis for their predictions, they are not to do any reading or spelling outside the remedial reading sessions.

---

[4]Reprinted with permission from Gillingham, A., & Stillman, B. W. *Remedial training for children with specific disability in reading, spelling, and penmanship.* Cambridge: Educators Publishing Service, 1970, p. 42.

Little stories are introduced after the student can read and write phonetic three-letter words perfectly. The little stories are comprised largely of phonetic words but, because "it is very difficult to construct stories with only phonetic words" (Gillingham & Stillman, 1970, p. 59), a few nonphonetic words are included. The teacher tells the student these nonphonetic words in order to discourage guessing. Gillingham and Stillman emphasize that teachers should not encourage students to try unless they can successfully manipulate the known elements. "Confident effort cannot be developed if 'trying' too frequently brings failure for which the child is not responsible" (Gillingham & Stillman, 1970, p. 60).

The emphasis on providing students with phonic strategies for prediction and with materials that will insure that students consistently succeed in their predictions is one of the most salient features of the Gillingham–Stillman approach. This approach was developed for dyslexic children and students with specific learning disabilities. Many such students have severe reading disabilities, and many have inconsistent, unsuccessful reading strategies. This method provides them with strategies for prediction and opportunities for success.

Developmental stages.   Although the Gillingham–Stillman approach discourages the use of the syntactic and semantic language systems as primary prediction strategies, the nature of a student's predictions changes as she or he progresses in the program. After the student is able to predict perfectly phonetic language with success, ambiguities are presented and "both the character and the relative difficulty of the processes change" (p. 73). Instructional procedures change at this stage.

At this point, the teacher explains the history of the English language to the student, emphasizing the way the irregularities in our language appeared. Associations II and III are eliminated at this stage. The teacher emphasizes varying visual representations for one sound (e.g., *eigh, ay,* for $\bar{a}$) and the different sounds one symbol may have (e.g., *cow* and *snow*). The student must attend to how the word looks as well as how it sounds.

During this final instructional phase, the student learns to predict with greater discrimination. Students may test a pronunciation in context to determine how to pronounce it (e.g., they may pronounce the *ow* in *snow* like the *ow* in *cow* and then correct themselves because the word doesn't sound right or make sense). Also, the teacher introduces syllables and dictionary usage as additional prediction strategies. The little stories provide additional practice.

After all the phonics are mastered, the teacher introduces the student to a set of readers that allow the student to establish the "facile application of the alphabetic approach to words" (Gillingham & Stillman, 1970, p. 112). Gillingham and Stillman describe this phase as "comparable to practicing scales on a musical instrument" (p. 112).

In this phase, students "try out" their newly acquired skills on words they have never encountered but that have all the characteristics of the rules they have been taught. As in earlier phases, the teacher tells the student the words that do not have these characteristics. The teacher predicts what words the student may not know and underscores them so that the student will not miscall any word.

In this phase, much valuable information about the student's reading strategies may be ignored. The student may be using effective meaning-seeking strategies other than graphophonic ones, and the teacher may not identify and reinforce them. There is no opportunity to determine the student's use of other strategies because guessing is emphatically discouraged during this phase.

After students master this phase, the teacher introduces them to interesting books and allows them to read silently as well as orally. The teacher asks comprehension questions about the books the student reads. Also, the student selects books and reads independently.

Confirming Strategies

In the Gillingham–Stillman approach, the student confirms predictions primarily on the basis of sound. The student reads to determine whether reading verifies the sound pattern she or he has learned. Because the little stories are carefully matched to the lessons, the student is likely to make successful confirmations. The program does not indicate, however, how the teacher is to respond when the student miscalls a phonetic word. As noted in the preceding section, the teacher provides the responses for nonphonetic words immediately. This practice discourages guessing and perhaps self-correction as well. Unfortunately, the latter is an important skill in the confirmation of predictions.

The Gillingham–Stillman program does not particularly stress the overall process of the student's constructing predictions from which students construct predictions based on their language, experiential, and conceptual backgrounds, try out their guesses, and self-correct. At the stage where ambiguities are presented, the program's authors imply, however, that students will correct miscalls instantly from the sense: for example, *stream*, when read /strem/, will be readily changed to /strēm/. Students must confirm their predictions by asking, "Does it make sense in *this context*?". This meaning becomes part of a confirmation strategy at this stage.

In addition, throughout the lessons, the student is instructed to read the sentences as in speaking; intonation, including reading in phrases, must be emphasized to complete this process. This practice probably enables students to use other language systems in confirming predictions. If students are to read passages as if speaking, they may be more likely to attend to the meaning of what they read.

Comprehending Strategies

In its earlier stages, the Gillingham–Stillman program does not emphasize comprehension. The little stories are similar to stories designed for translations of a foreign language; they lack literary content and are like those found in many linguistic readers. As stated in the preceeding section, students are instructed to read these stories as if they were speaking. To read with meaning, one must comprehend the text. The emphasis in the earlier stages, however, is not on seeking meaning but on practicing the newly acquired graphophonic strategies. In the more advanced stages, the teacher stresses comprehension, and encourages students to select materials on their own interest levels. Also, according to Gillingham and Stillman (1970), students are reading "great works of literature" throughout the program.

In the beginning stages of the program, teachers provide students with an intensive introduction to regular sound–symbol characteristics of our language. These sound–symbol cues are used as production strategies, and the teacher provides phonetically regular *little stories* by means of which students can verify, or confirm, their predictions. The program permits no guessing, and during the program's beginning stages the student is not allowed to read any materials other than the little stories.

The program emphasizes students' success in confirming their predictions. If a student encounters a phonetically irregular word, the teacher supplies the correct response. Although the program does not emphasize meaning cues in its initial stages, students are instructed to read the little stories as if they were speaking; as a result, they read "with meaning."

As teachers introduce phonetically irregular words, they modify the teaching strategies. In the initial phase, the teacher uses a multisensory approach, with the emphasis on the auditory–visual and kinesthetic associations. In more advanced phases, the program introduces various visual representations for the same sound. The student does not spell words during this phase. The authors acknowledge that during this phase, the "character and the relative difficulty of the program" changes (Gillingham & Stillman, 1970, p. 73). Students make predictions on the basis of sound–symbol associations and can correct their predictions if they do not verify them on the initial attempt.

In the program's final stages, the teacher introduces dictionary techniques and checks the student's comprehension. Finally, the teacher allows students to read other materials and encourages them to select their own materials.

Before students begin the Gillingham–Stillman approach, they should realize that written language says something and that the strategies they use are for seeking meaning. Students who do not have these concepts may find the approach too abstract and may engage in meaningless activities.

The Gillingham–Stillman approach may offer students who have inconsistent prediction strategies and who fail to confirm the majority of their predictions the opportunity to succeed. This success may encourage students to make more predictions—to attempt to use meaning-seeking strategies. However, in attempting to control the student's predictions, the program does not encourage the student to use his or her own sense of language (e.g., syntax and vocabulary) or experience in constructing or verifying meanings.

Specialists who use the program claim success with dyslexic readers (Kaluger & Kolson, 1979). A closer examination of interactions between the reader and the program's procedures and materials may reveal the reasons for the program's reported successes. Researchers may be able to determine what types of predicting, confirming, and comprehending strategies the program encourages. For example, does the practice of reading as one speaks, or with meaning, encourage the student to attend to syntax and semantics as well as the sound–symbol characteristic? As a start in evaluating the approach's overall effectiveness, it may be that, rather than analyze the gain scores (e.g., average grade-level gain) of students in this program, investigators should analyze the strategies students use prior to entry into the program and those they develop as they progress.

Merrill Linguistic Reading Approach

General Description

The Merrill Linguistic Reading Program, one of the several linguistic reading programs available commercially, is based on the principles of *structural linguistics,* developed by Charles C. Fries, and the experiences of several reading specialists (Otto, Randolph, Smith, & Wilson, 1975).

The program stresses Fries's observation that "English words and sentence patterns exhibit a high degree of regularity" (Fries quoted in Otto et al., 1975). As with the Gillingham–Stillman approach, the authors of the Merrill Linguistic Reading Program designed the program for students who need more structure. Otto et al. (1975) state:

> Many pupils can learn to read successfully regardless of the instructional approach. Other pupils need more structure, more practice and a slower pace. From the time of their publication in 1966, the *Merrill linguistic readers,* from which this program stems, proved to be effective with both kinds of pupils, but especially successful with the second type. As a result, the Merrill Linguistic Reading Program was specifically designed to meet the needs of the pupil who might have difficulty getting meaning and satisfaction from reading. (p. 5)[5]

The Merrill Linguistic Reading Program includes levels from the first grade to the sixth grade. Materials include the Merrill Linguistic Readiness Program, eleven readers, eleven Skills Books, a Testing Series, Reinforcement Materials, a Literature Appreciation Kit, a Word Practice Kit, and a Linguistic Word Patterns Program.

The readiness program emphasizes (1) pronunciation of whole words rather than individual sounds within words; (2) oral language growth; (3) learning the alphabet by letter names, not sounds, and without depending on pictures; and (4) recognition of words as separate units. The remainder of the series stresses the linguistic spelling pattern approach.

Predicting Strategies

Otto et al. (1975) stress the importance of the "minimum visual and aural contrasts between words" (p. 7); for example, *fat* and *cat, fat* and *fate.* As a result, students learn to use these contrasts as primary prediction strategies. Pictures are not included in the text, in order "to prevent the pupil from using picture clues to guess words and their meanings" (p. 7).

By the third grade, the student has mastered three major spelling patterns and some minor patterns and irregular spellings. After the third grade these spelling skills are used to decode unfamiliar words, and the program introduces other prediction strategies, such as transitional words (e.g., *in addition to*), paragraph organization, figurative language, and key words that indicate cause and effect.

Other prediction strategies introduced early in the program are a "limited number of sight words" that do not conform to regular spelling patterns and skills in syntax, (Otto et al., 1975, p. 20). As in the Gillingham–Stillman program, "guessing has been completely eliminated from the process" (Otto et al., 1975, p. 37). After the third grade, stories are not restricted to sentences with major spelling patterns and the student has the opportunity to use meaning and syntax as prediction strategies.

Confirming Strategies

In the early stages of the program, the stories are designed to ensure that students will confirm their predictions on the basis of whether words sound and look like the patterns they had been taught. The stories are developed so that the

---

[5]Reprinted with permission from Otto, W., Rudolph, N., Smith, A., & Wilson, K. *The Merrill linguistic reading program.* Columbus, Oh.: Charles E. Merrill, 1975, p. 5.

student can easily confirm predictions based on spelling patterns. Guessing is not encouraged in the program, especially with what the authors term *circle words,* or words that do not fit the spelling patterns. Thus self-correction may not be encouraged.

Comprehending Strategies

The authors note that "reading is treated as a means of acquiring meaning—not only the meaning of individual words, but also the cumulative meanings of sentences, paragraphs and entire stories. Comprehension is always stressed as the students' most important goals" (Otto et al., 1975, p. 7). The teacher's guide provides questions that check the student's comprehension of the stories included in the program. For example, after the student reads the sentence "Nat is fat" (I can, Level A, 1975, p. 6), the teacher is to ask, "What can you tell about how he looks?" (Otto et al., p. 7). Although the program provides for checking the comprehension of the short stories, it does not stress comprehending strategies per se (e.g., using titles or the organization of text) in the initial phases. Reading with proper intonation (which implies reading with meaning) is included from the beginning.

As students advance in the program, they are introduced to such comprehending strategies as "transitional words that denote shifts in meaning" (Otto et al., 1975, p. 9). Because the program does not stress comprehending strategies in the initial stages, the student may not construct meanings and verify them (Gregg & Farnham-Diggory, 1979). The student may be merely recoding spelling patterns (e.g., providing sounds for visual symbols). The stories may lack sufficient appeal to interest students sufficiently for them to get involved in the process of integrating the stories with their own experiences.

Although comprehension is supposedly the most important emphasis in the program, the student may not necessarily begin with a construction mode (e.g., construct meanings and verify them) in the initial phases. Furthermore, the stories used to confirm predictions and check comprehension may not interest the student. There are, however, supplementary stories and poems in the Literature Application Kit that "give the pupil a chance to do extra reading for pleasure at his own reading level—and meet with success" (Otto et al., 1975, p. 38).

The student with special reading needs may experience success by using basic spelling patterns as predicting strategies in the initial phases of this program. Students' own language and experiences, however, are not used. Students do not have the opportunity to construct meanings of their own and to experiment with various patterns and structures of our language.

The Language Experience Approach

General Description

The Language Experience approach, first advocated by Lee and Allen (1968), is a method of teaching reading that makes specific use of the student's experiences and language. Although the authors designed their approach for normal readers, special educators and reading specialists have used it with special students, particularly as a corrective approach for older students (Kirk, Kleibhan, & Lerner, 1978). Also, such reading specialists as Kenneth and Yetta Goodman (1979) and Carolyn Burke (Goodman & Burke, 1972) advocate the use of the language experience approach because it uses a whole-language approach. These authors stress that reading is part of the student's language and conceptual development. Goodman and Goodman (1979) write as follows:

> Readers are active participants in communication with unseen writers. They are seekers of meaning, motivated by the need to comprehend, aware of the functions of print, and adaptive to the characteristics of print. The environment for reading development must certainly be rich in print, a literate one. But reading instruction, particularly beginning reading instruction, has a vital role to play in creating and enhancing the conditions that will bring the reader's natural language learning competence into play. Children must be among people who talk in order to learn to speak and listen. But that's not enough. Their need to communicate must also be present for learning to take place. This is also the case in acquiring literacy. (pp. 139–140)[6]

In the Language Experience approach, the beginning reader relates a story or event to the teacher, who writes it on paper. As students learn to write, they write their own stories. The student's own words form the basis for lessons on such matters as phonics and word recognition.

Predicting Strategies

In the Language Experience approach, the student may predict words by a variety of strategies. When students have experienced an event and have used their own language to construct a story, they will seek written symbols that represent their oral language. Gregg and Farnham-Diggory (1979), discussing the semantic cues students use in the Language Experience approach, suggest that "one important characteristic of the language experience method of teaching reading is that it puts children into a constructive mode from the outset of reading instruction. The development of language-experience reading programs always involves connections with semantic information the reader always has" (p. 68).

In longitudinal studies with the Book Experience approach, which is similar to the Language Experience method, Clay (1979) found that beginning readers predicted on the basis of syntax (e.g., by substituting nouns for nouns). Interestingly, she also found that the student's consistent use of visual cues did not emerge quickly, and was "unreliable and unstable" (Clay, 1979, p. 152). Moreover, she found that students attempted to self-correct their errors.

It appears that it may take time for a student to determine the redundant visual and auditory patterns of our language. In the Language Experience approach, the teacher must expose students to a considerable amount of print, but if Clay is correct in her findings, the teacher should assist students in sharpening their skills. To use the analogy of jogging, when a jogger first begins to run, she or he may not attend to many important aspects of the sport, for example, gait, proper shoes, and protecting the knees. Runners may learn by experience (e.g., development of blisters or swollen feet) or coaches or more experienced runners may teach them the important aspects of running. The novice runner may acquire many tips from a more experienced runner but will become a good runner only if she or he runs often. Skills will continually be sharpened and extended (by, e.g. learning to sprint, running uphill, running long distances).

In the Language Experience approach, the teacher may be seen as analogous

---

[6]Reprinted with permission from Goodman, K. S. & Goodman, Y. M. Learning to read is natural. In L. Resnick, & P. Weaver (Eds.), *Theory and practice of early reading* (Vol. 1). Hillsdale, N.J.: Lawrence Erlbaum, 1979, pp. 139–140.

to the coach or more experienced runner who watches the beginner's performance and develops special programs for his or her needs. Not all beginning readers will need the same skill. Some readers will attend to visual cues. Others will use one prediction strategy ineffectively (e.g., sound), and when the strategy continues to fail for them, they may not select other strategies.

The teacher should determine the student's predicting strategies and devise programs to fill in the gaps. Lee and Allen (1968) write that when the teacher presents short stories, he or she should talk about "words, names of letters, beginning sounds, ending sounds, sounds in between." (p. 44). These authors stress that such technical aspects should "emerge as a natural language experience" (p. 47). Thus skills should be taught in conjunction with the student's stories. Lee and Allen (1968) list many of the prediction strategies (e.g., phonics and structural analysis) that are found in many reading programs.

One of the major problems with the Language Experience approach vis à vis predicting strategies is that the method is influenced by the teacher. If the teacher is not observant, and if she or he does not take time with every student—especially those with special needs—the student may have difficulties breaking the code, or determining the predictable redundancies of our written language system (e.g., sound–symbol relationships and syntax).

Confirming Strategies

The student verifies or confirms what he or she knows about the story by asking, "Does the written material sound like what I said?" or, "Does the material convey what I was trying to express?" The student may self-correct several times in order to answer these questions. Clay (1979) found that beginners did self-correct in the Book Experience approach. Because students are given the opportunity to construct meanings and to try several predicting strategies, they may be more likely to self-correct. Again, the teacher determines the strategies. Some teachers may supply the correct response before the student has the opportunity to self-correct.

Comprehending Strategies

In the Language Experience approach, the student is reading for meaning in the initial stages. The supporters of the approach emphasize the meaning aspects of reading. Although the student may have experience with the material in the story, she or he may not necessarily use meaning cues. The teacher may need to encourage the student to attend to the meaning cues of the story to avoid memorization and use of only word-analysis skills. Lee and Allen (1968) stress that the main emphasis should be on what the sentence, paragraph, and story means. Lee and Allen (1968) describe these comprehending strategies as follows:

> Can the children visualize and identify with the situation, the characters, their purpose, and behaviors? Can they see alternative behaviors and evaluate them in relation to the behaviors in the story? Can they project beyond the situation? Predict what might happen next? Can they interpret and identify with the feelings of the characters? Can they draw implications from the material read? Can they get a clear, concise understanding of the meaning of the material? (p. 99)[7]

---

[7]Reprinted with permission from Lee, D. M., & Allen, R. V. *Learning to read through experience* (2nd ed.). New York: Appleton-Century-Crofts, 1968, p. 99.

The Fernald Approach

General Description

Like the Gillingham–Stillman approach, the Fernald approach is multisensory. This visual–auditory–tactual–kinesthetic (VATK) method of teaching reading was developed by Grace Fernald and Helen B. Keller at the clinic school of the University of California. The Fernald method was developed for students in the clinic who had normal intelligence but such extreme disabilities as word blindness (Fernald, 1943, p. 3). Fernald and Keller felt that physically tracing the letters and words would aid these student's memories.

Fernald and Keller discovered that the kinesthetic method of teaching reading originated with Quintilian (A.D. 68), who suggested that letters be cut in boards so that children could trace over the grooves. Fernald and Keller combined the visual, auditory, tactile, and kinesthetic methods into an eclectic approach that uses the student's experience as the basis for stories. Fernald (1943) also emphasized "that for satisfactory reading, it is necessary that the individual apperceive a group of words as a unit. That is, he must see words which taken together have certain meaning, as a signal object and not as a set of unrelated words" (p. 21).

Fernald and Keller developed specific stages in their approach. Before students begin the program, the teacher informs them that they are going to learn a new method of reading and that many bright people with reading problems have learned to read with this new approach. The teacher instructs the students to select words that they want to learn. After students write a few words, the teacher starts them on story writing.

Briefly, the four stages of the Fernald approach are as follows:

Stage 1. After a student selects a word, the teacher writes it for the student, with a crayon, in blackboard-size script or in manuscript. The student traces the word with a finger, saying each letter while tracing it. The student continues this process until he or she can write the word from memory. Then the student writes the word first on scrap paper and then as it occurs in his or her story. Finally, the story is typed for the student.

Stage 2. The student continues the activities of Stage 1 with the exception of tracing. According to Fernald (1943), "After a certain period of tracing, the child develops the ability to learn any new word by simply looking at the word in the script, saying it once to himself as he looks at it, and then writing it without looking at the copy, saying each part of the word as he writes it" (p. 34).

Stage 3. The student is able to say the word without writing it. Also at this stage, the student begins to read from books.

Stage 4. The student is able to learn from printed words and "to generalize and make new words he already knows" (p. 51).

Predicting Strategies

The Fernald approach introduces various predicting strategies at different stages in the program. In the beginning the approach emphasizes the semantic associations (the student associates words in the student's oral vocabulary with written symbols), the sounds of the words (the student says the word slowly, matching sound to symbol), and the visual characteristics of the word. Because students trace words it is likely that they will attend to their visual characteristics. Samuels (1967) posits that multisensory techniques that involve tracing are successful because they force the student to attend to visual characteristics of the word.

Fernald assumes that as students learn more words they will develop generalizations about the structure of our written language. These generalizations can then be used in predicting new words encountered in books. Fernald also assumes that the student will recognize many words by sight and will remember many of the words that are used often in the material the student reads and writes. The student's memory of these sight words is facilitated by tracing the words.

In the Fernald approach, predicting unknown words while reading with the teacher is discouraged. According to Fernald (1943),

> When the child reads stories, we let him read along as he wishes, asking any words he needs to know to get the meaning of what he is reading. He is told what the word is, and it is recorded for later reference if it is common enough to be important. The child is never made to sound the word when he is reading nor is it sounded out for him by his teacher. He points to the word and is told what it is. Any detail that he reads is given him by letting him write the word with the method already described. This writing of the word is merely for the sake of developing word recognition and is done only as necessary to accomplish this end. (pp. 52–53)[8]

The teacher allows students to "sound out" the words if they wish; however, they must sound out the words prior to reading the material "and not in the course of reading it" (p. 53).

Confirming Strategies

Fernald emphasizes that the student's story must by typed and read by the student shortly after it is constructed: "Since the individual is able to recognize words in "sight" or print after he has written them, it is essential that his recognition of words in print be established by having him read the printed form of what he writes" (p. 41).

The student confirms predictions by associating the words in his or her oral vocabulary with the written symbols. The student asks the question, "Does it make sense?" Because the approach emphasizes the visual features of the words (word recognition), the student may attempt to recognize the words as those traced.

This program may, to some extent, discourage the student's use of self-correction because the teacher supplies any word the student does not recognize immediately.

Comprehending Strategies

From the beginning, students are constructing meaning from what they read. They are matching their experiences with the written symbols. Fernald (1943) emphasizes that students should select material to discuss that is of interest to them and not below their intelligence level. She also stresses the need to carry the

---

[8]Reprinted with permission from Fernald, G. *Remedial techniques in basic school subjects.* New York: McGraw-Hill, 1943, pp. 52–53.

program through until students can read on their own and by phrases rather than word by word.

Direct Instructional System for Teaching Arithmetic and Reading (DISTAR)

General Description

Carnine (1977) describes DISTAR Reading as "auditory, phonic, and highly structured" (p. 196). Englemann and Bruner (1969) designed DISTAR to teach beginning reading and math to children who were culturally deprived and/or slow learning. Englemann and Brunner (1969) have stated that if the reading program is designed to give the student all the "subskills demanded by the complex behavior we call reading" (p. 199), a student with a mental age of less than four years can learn to read. These investigators isolated a subset of skills that they considered to be important for reading acquisition.

In an earlier publication the present author has described the DISTAR program (1979) as follows:

> Initially, the program emphasizes left–right progression and the association of sound with a symbol. The children are taught that these sounds occur in fixed orders in words and to spell by orally pronouncing the sounds (e.g., /c/-/at/). The program stresses the skills that are considered to be difficult for slower children to master (e.g., blending, rhyming). Children are taught that words that are said slowly (/c/-/a/-/t/) can be blended by saying them fast. In order to minimize confusion in learning the sounds and the symbols, a basic set of nine phonemes that are not similar in sounds or visual appearance are presented initially with the symbols formed in a manner that reduces visual discrimination confusion; some symbols are joined together (e.g., th). After 20 sounds have been introduced, the children are able to read storybooks that contain one to 25 words. Sounds that have not been introduced are represented in small print in words and diacritical marks are placed over the vowels. (pp. 353–354)[9]

Materials for the program include a teacher's guide, related skills books, take-home blending sheets for the students, workbooks, and a recycling book for the advanced stages.

Predicting Strategies

As noted in the general description, the most important predicting strategy is phonics. Carnine (1977), a supporter of the DISTAR program, provides a rationale for emphasizing sound–symbol relationships as the first predicting strategy the student learns.

> Like other reading programs, [the DISTAR] goal is comprehension and although it includes techniques for teaching comprehension, it does not treat reading initially as a comprehension process. The reason for this ordering of priorities is that a child must be able to say the word before the meaning can be considered. A child may comprehend what is meant by the words 'house' and 'horse,' but if the two words cannot be distinguished in print the ability to comprehend will be poorly utilized. Thus, word identification *must* come before comprehension. DISTAR calls this com-

---

[9]Reprinted with permission from Gillespie-Silver, P. H. *Teaching reading to children with special needs.* Columbus, Oh.: Charles E. Merrill, 1979, pp. 353–354.

prehension skill *code cracking*. Code cracking is a collection of subskills that allow a child to develop squiggles-in-pages into words. (p. 196)[10]

In DISTAR 1, the teacher introduces sounds (not letter names) of letters through daily sound exercises. The program stresses the rhyming and blending of sounds. Although the sounds are taught in isolation, the students are encouraged to say them fast—that is, to blend them into words. "Sounding out is used to decode both isolated words and words in stories" (Carnine, 1977, p. 198).

The visual irregularities of our written language are deemphasized, and the student learns visual representations that are not part of our traditional written language.

In Reading II books, the student encounters the traditional alphabet, learns the letter names, begins to read more irregular words, and does comprehension exercises. Comprehension exercises are also included in Reading I books. Also, in the program's later phases, students can "identify" (predict and confirm) words by other strategies "without first sounding them out" (Carnine, 1977, p. 158).

Confirming Strategies

Students read the stories to confirm the predictions they have based on sound–symbol relationships. The program also includes exercises to confirm the predictions of individual sounds before blending them into words. In the later stages, the student may confirm by asking, "Does this make sense?" Because students begin to read stories after 20 sounds have been introduced, they may be confirming on the basis of syntax and meaning. However, they may choose to exclude syntax and meaning and use only graphophonic similarities because the program stresses these strategies in the initial stages.

Comprehending Strategies

Carnine (1977) notes that DISTAR's primary reading goal is comprehension and that the program does not stress comprehension initially. Engelmann (1969) states that DISTAR can give instruction "in all of the subskills demanded by the complex behavior we call reading" (p. 352). The subskills of sounding out, blending, and rhyming are apparently considered to lead to the student's comprehending the text. But we may question at what point all the subskills combine in the skill of comprehension. That is, when does the student, in this approach, decide to read for meaning?

Buchannon and Sullivan Associates Programmed Reading

General Description

The Sullivan Programmed Readers (Buchannon & Sullivan Associates, 1968) is a programmed linguistic approach for the first through the sixth grades. The program starts by teaching the alphabet in addition to the letter sounds. The teach-

---

[10]Reprinted with permission from Carnine, D. Direct instruction—DISTAR. In N. Haring & B. Bateman (Eds.), *Teaching the learning disabled child*. Englewood Cliffs: Prentice-Hall, 1977, p. 196.

er introduces supplementary exercises, and the student completes linear programmed workbooks (in which one step leads to another).

Predicting Strategies

In this linguistic program, individual letters are learned and combined (e.g., *a*
is taught, then *t*, is taught, and then the two are combined to make *at*). In this
approach, graphophonic strategies are the primary predictors. However, the student may learn other predicting strategies as well. Because the student is reading
to produce a response, she or he may be using syntax and meaning cues. Also,
because the program recommends that the teacher use all his/her "favorite devices for teaching reading" (Buchannon, 1968, p. 8), the student may receive
instruction in other strategies.

Buchannon (1968) writes, "Feel free to stop the class at any time and give
comments or explanations. Each teacher has a number of very effective methods
of presentation which suits her personality. These will prove at least as useful with
programmed reading as they did with traditional readers" (p. 5). Such a practice,
of course, will make it difficult to determine the effectiveness of the overall program itself.

Confirming Strategies

Like several of the other programs described in this chapter, the Sullivan
program attempts to control predictions and the material so that students can
consistently confirm their responses. In this program, students receive an immediate confirmation or disconfirmation of their predictions. In addition, students may
make generalizations about the structure of written language other than those
based on the spelling patterns introduced in the program.

Self-correction is encouraged. "If you find that a student has made errors on
a test, let him try to correct them for you" (Buchannon, 1968, p. 6). Also, the
program does not stress the need for reading aloud fluently (which would imply
that the student can stop and self-correct). Buchannon notes that the student will
eventually develop this skill.

Comprehending Strategies

Students may read for meaning initially because they are expected to respond
and to make a choice. The students may not be able to develop the more complex
comprehension strategies, however, because the stories are too simply constructed. Also, students do not construct their own meanings, as in the Language Experience Approach.

IMPLICATIONS

Our review of six programs according to the foregoing criteria, has led to the
following observations:

1. In order to insure consistent and correct response, most of the programs attempt to control the initial predictions that students make.

2. In the beginning phases of instruction, most of the programs use grapho-phonic strategies as primary predictors.

3. Most of the programs write their own stories so as to ensure that the student can readily verify their graphophonic predictions.

4. Two of the programs (the Language Experience and Fernald methods) em-phasize the use of the student's own experiences on the theory that obtaining comprehension in the initial phases will help ensure success in confirming predictions.

5. Several of the programs discourage guessing and self-correction; that is, if the student fails to supply an immediate prediction or supplies an incorrect one, the teacher supplies the response. Rather than view guessing as a strength, most of the authors of these programs, especially the graphophonic ones, seem to believe that if students guess, they will use incorrect or unreliable predicting strategies. Also, in several of these programs, the student does not have the opportunity to attempt various strategies through the self-correction strategies.

6. Only one of the programs (the Language Experience approach, advocated by Lee and Allen, 1968, and Goodman and Goodman, 1979) stresses observation of students to determine the types of strategies they use consistently and cor-rectly and the types that are unreliable and unstable.

7. All the programs seem to have as their goal initial success for the reader, especially the reader who has experienced failure.

In general, the authors of the programs reviewed believe that reading pro-grams should be highly structured and that graphophonic strategies are the most predictable component of our written language system. Clay (1979) makes similar observations and recommends an alternative.

> What adjustments are normally made for slow-reading groups in school? Remedial programs tend to focus children on exercises that draw attention to the elements of words, word attack and sounding out. It is assumed that this is the means by which people do read, the way children learn to read, and the way failing children need to relearn to read. None of these assumptions is necessarily true. Could we be directing poor readers' attention away from the behaviors that would bring about the most rapid improvement in their reading? Identification of letters and words is important but not significant.
>
> A challenge emerges here. Reading materials that are controlled and purport to offer the child one new difficulty at a time, are based on one kind of learning theory. Perhaps materials that are rich in language cues allow for dissonance and permit the cross-checking and self-correction strategies that construct and support a self-cor-recting system. (pp. 155–156)[11]

Specialists who adopt Clay's suggestion that reading materials should be rich in cues will not necessarily develop unstructured programs. Once specialists or teachers determine, through continued observation and such measures as the Reading Miscues Inventory (RMI) (Goodman & Burke, 1972), the types of mean-ing-seeking strategies students use well and those students use poorly, these pro-

---

[11]Reprinted with permission from Clay, N. Theoretical research and instructional changes: A case study. In L. Resnick & O. A. Weaver (Eds.), *Theory and practice of early reading* (Vol. 2). Hillsdale, N.J.: Lawrence Erlbaum, 1979, pp. 155–256.

fessionals can use structured strategies in encouraging students to use their strengths and in helping students to be more consistent and successful in using other meaning-seeking strategies. Many of the techniques developed by the authors of these programs can be used to assist students to develop the meaning-seeking strategies. For example, strategies used in such programmed texts as the Sullivan Programmed Readers can assist readers to use whole-language strategies (graphophonic, semantic, and syntactic cues) as predictors. Also, the introduction of a certain predicting strategy and the presentation of material to reinforce that strategy, as in the Gillingham–Stillman program, can be used by the teacher to facilitate the student's reading process.

Clay notes that one of the most important considerations in developing a program for a student is to determine early in the program the student's areas of confusion and to assist the student in clearing up these confusions before they become habitual. She adds that the teacher must have an on-going monitoring system to determine the patterns of the student's reading process. She also recommends a whole-language approach. According to Clay (1979), "Children should be able to predict on the basis of context, sentence structure, and letter detail; and as children begin to read, they should be encouraged to confirm or correct their own responses by use of meaning, sentence structure, and letter detail" (p. 167).

These programs' success in meeting the objectives outlined by Clay should be the criteria most often used for judging their effectiveness. We must begin to examine the *processes* these programs facilitate rather than merely their *products* (e.g., grade level scores and knowledge of vowel sound). Only then can a realistic appraisal of program effectiveness be attained.

REFERENCES

Allen, P. D. Implications for reading instruction. In P. D. Allen & D. J. Watson (Eds.), *Findings of research in miscue analysis: Classroom implications*. Urbana, Ill.: Educational Resources Information Center Clearning House on Reading and Communication Skills, 1976.

Blanton, L. P., Sitko, M. C. & Gillespie, P. H. Reading and the mildly retarded: Review of research and implications. In L. Mann & D. Sabatino (Eds.), *Third review of special education*. New York: Grune & Stratton, 1976.

Bower, T. Reading by eye. In H. Levin & J. P. Williams (Eds.), *Basic studies on reading*. New York: Basic Books, 1970.

Buchannon, C. D. & Sullivan Associates. *Sullivan programmed readers*. New York: McGraw-Hill, 1968.

Carnine, D. Direct instruction—DISTAR. In N. Haring & B. Bateman (Eds.), *Teaching the learning disabled child*. Englewood Cliffs: Prentice-Hall, 1977.

Clay, N. Theoretical research and instructional changes: A case study. In L. Resnick & O. A. Weaver (Eds.), *Theory and practice of early reading* (Vol. 2). Hillsdale, N.J.: Lawrence Erlbaum, 1979.

Engleman, S., & Bruner, E. C. *Distar reading: An instructional system*. Chicago: Science Research Associates, 1969.

Fernald, G. *Remedial techniques in basic school subjects*. New York: McGraw-Hill, 1943.

Gillespie-Silver, P. H. *Teaching reading to children with special needs*. Columbus, Oh.: Charles E. Merrill, 1979.

Gillingham, A., & Stillman, B. W. *Remedial training for children with specific disability in reading, spelling and penmanship*. Cambridge: Educators Publishing Service, 1970.

Goodman, K. Beyond the eye: What happens in reading. In H. Singer & R. B. Ruddell (Eds.), *Theoretical models and processes of reading* (2nd ed.). Newark, Del.: International Reading Association, 1976.

Goodman, K. S., & Goodman, Y. M. Learning to read is natural. In L. Resnick & P. Weaver (Eds.), *Theory and practice of early reading* (Vol. 1). Hillsdale, N.J.: Lawrence Erlbaum, 1979.

Goodman, Y. Strategies for comprehension. In P. D. Allen & D. J. Watson (Eds.), *Findings of research in miscue analysis: Classroom implications*. Urbana, Ill.: Educational Resources Information Center Clearing House on Reading and Communication Skills, 1976.

Goodman, Y., & Burke, C. *Reading miscue inventory manual: Procedure for diagnosis and evaluation*. London: Collier-Macmillan, 1972.

Gregg, L. W., & Farnham-Diggory, S. How to study reading: An information processing analysis. In L. Resnick & P. A. Weaver (Eds.), *Theory and practice of early reading* (Vol. 3). Hillsdale, N.J.: Lawrence Erlbaum, 1979.

Gutkneckt, P. A. *A psycholinguistic analysis of oral reading behavior of selected children identified as perceptually handicapped*. Unpublished doctoral dissertation, Wayne State University, 1971.

Kalager, G., & Kolson, C. J. Reading and learning disabilities. Columbus, Oh.: Charles E. Merrill, 1979.

Kirk, S., Kliebhan, J. M., & Lerner, J. *Teaching reading to slow and disabled learners*. Boston: Houghton-Mifflin, 1978.

Lee, D. M., & Allen, R. V. *Learning to read through experience*. (2nd ed.). New York: Appleton-Century-Crofts, 1968.

Otto, W., Rudolph, N., Smith, A., & Wilson, K. *The Merrill linguistic reading program*. Columbus, Oh.: Charles E. Merrill, 1975.

Pennock, C. Introduction. In Pennock, C. (Ed.), *Reading comprehension at four linguistic levels*. Newark, Del.: International Reading Association, 1979.

Rhodes, L., & Brenson, B. *A psycholinguistic analysis of EMR children reading materials of varying predictability*. Unpublished paper presented at Indiana University, 1976.

Samuels, S. J. Attentional processes in reading: The effects of pictures in the acquisition of reading responses. *Journal of Educational Psychology*, 1967, *58*, 337–342.

Smith, F. Making sense of reading and of reading instruction. *Harvard Educational Review*, 1977, *47*, 386–395.

Smith, F. *Understanding reading: A psycholinguistic analysis of reading and learning to read*. New York: Holt, Rinehart, & Winston, 1971.

Les Sternberg
George W. Fair

15

Mathematics Programs and Materials

It is generally accepted that mathematics education for, and amelioration of mathematics deficits in, the handicapped are neglected areas in both research and practice. The reasons for this neglect appear to stem from a number of interrelated situations. First, many teachers and parents of mildly handicapped students prefer instructional emphasis on communication, language, and reading skills as these are judged to be more crucial to future academic success (Otto, McMenemy, & Smith, 1973). Second, institutions of higher learning have decreased emphasis upon mathematics training within their teacher-training programs, thereby furnishing the future teachers with somewhat incomplete background (Sternberg & Mauser, 1975). Third, a plethora of research exists in the area of reading and language-related disabilities due to many professionals' awareness of and interest in the topic, whereas the same does not hold true in the mathematics disability area. This third situation is most probably a result of the continuation of the first two and is reflected in the paucity of available comprehensive programs for the remediation of arithmetic or mathematics deficits of the handicapped.

POSITED MATHEMATICS DEFICITS IN HANDICAPPED STUDENTS

Various problems are encountered by the handicapped in their involvement with mathematics. Errors in computation may develop, or inappropriate application of correct computation procedures may be made (Cawley & Goodman, 1968). Children may experience difficulty with shape and size discriminations, which may adversely affect their performance in areas dealing with sets and numbers (Lerner, 1976; Kaliski, 1967). Often, mathematical concepts (e.g., one-to-one correspondence, equivalent sets) present serious problems to handicapped children, as does the language of mathematics (Peterson, 1973). The list of actual problems can go on indefinitely. However, it is important to realize that these are generalized characteristics that may or may not apply to the individual child.

Reasons for the Presence of Mathematics Deficits

Various hypotheses have been put forth to describe the reasons why handicapped children experience problems in the area of mathematics. Chalfant and Scheffelin (1969) posited that problems in mathematics stem from deficits in the functioning of various psychological processes (e.g., memory, spatial ability, language awareness, and perceptual ability). Therefore, a child who is experiencing difficulty in numeral awareness or discrimination may be experiencing the problem due to an inability to remember or to underlying visual-perceptual problems. Support for the psychological processes explanation of deficits is also voiced by Bryant and Kass (1972) and Kaliski (1967), who stress the spatial foundation of mathematics functioning.

A second hypothesis tendered to account for mathematics deficits in the handicapped posits that difficulties arise from the presence of physiological or neurophysiological dysfunctions (Johnson & Myklebust, 1967; Kosc, 1974). Dyscalculia (the inability to do arithmetic calculations) is one of the disorders that is associated with this hypothesis. The basic premise is that difficulty encountered by a child is a direct function of some underlying brain-related deficit.

A third hypothesis involves the issue of cognitive readiness. The emphasis here is upon whether the child possesses the cognitive competence (i.e., a basic combination of maturation and experience) to deal effectively with mathematics or mathematics-related material. The work of Jean Piaget has heavily influenced proponents of this hypothesis (Cawley & Vitello, 1972; Copeland, 1974; Vitello, 1973), who suggest that a child's acquisition of mathematical concepts depends upon that child's level of functioning and his readiness to be exposed to any new mathematics material.

Other hypotheses have been put forth to account for the myriad problems that handicapped children experience with mathematics, ranging from teacher-centered variables (e.g., poor teaching practices; Sternberg & Mauser, 1975) to material-centered variables (e.g., stress upon computational worksheets or rote memorization of number facts; Scheffelin & Seltzer, 1974). Each variable has its place in attempting to account for individual mathematics deficits. However, unless a hypothesis can somehow lead to ideas for amelioration or remediation, little worth can be found in its existence. Suffice it to say, handicapped children do experience difficulties when they try to deal with mathematics, and the development of a systematic approach or model to help alleviate these problems is of major import.

Meaning-to-Skill versus Skill-to-Meaning

Two major approaches to mathematics education are prevalent. In the skill-to-meaning approach, basic behavioral skills are practiced prior to the introduction of the meaning associated with those skills. For example, to train a student to add two single-digit numbers, the student might be presented with many numerical examples upon which to practice. The intent is to have the student develop a "computational habit" so that errors will not be forthcoming. If, once this habit is established, instruction is geared toward the meaning involved in addition (e.g., verbal problems requiring an understanding of the addition process), then a skill-to-meaning approach is being utilized. If, on the other hand, a meaning-to-skill approach is being employed, computational skill development would not be emphasized until the student displayed an understanding of the process (e.g., demonstrating through the use of manipulatives what is done to solve a verbal problem). In the skill-to-meaning approach, the thought is that once the habit is developed, the understanding of the underlying process will be more easily grasped, while the basic assumption of the meaning-to-skill approach is that if the child grasps the meaning of the process first, she will more easily apply the skill associated with the meaning. Although research has been conducted related to the effect of meaning instruction upon future skill acquisition, most of the studies have dealt with nonarithmetic material (Baumeister & Kellas, 1971; Ellis, 1963; Underwood & Schultz, 1960). However, in a recent research study (Sternberg, Fitzmaurice, & Dembinski, 1979) an attempt was made to determine the efficacy of employing a skill-to-meaning instructional paradigm with arithmetic material. The results indicated that (1) meaning introduced after the skill was acquired aided the subjects in retention of the skill (i.e., rote computation), but had only a limited effect upon the subjects' application of the skill to the new situation (i.e., understanding), and (2) the skill-to-meaning approach appeared to force subjects into determining an answer even when no answer was possible. Sternberg et al. concluded that skill-to-meaning mathematics instruction for the handicapped must not be continued. If, then, the opposing, and apparently more relevant, meaning-to-skill approach is used, various programmatic concerns must be addressed and various instructional components utilized.

PROGRAMMATIC CONCERNS

Through the years, a number of concerns have been voiced by professionals in regard to effective and efficacious mathematical programming for handicapped students. Freidus (1966), Callahan and Robinson (1973), and Herald (1974) all advocated specific instructional procedures to meet the deficit needs of handicapped learners. The first is sequential content. If concepts are specified in a subordinate to supraordinate manner, the concepts the child must understand prior to the introduction of further concepts can be understood. In conjunction with this is the use of task analysis, where individual tasks are broken down into smaller behavioral components. In this theory, acquisition of one step in the analysis is based upon acquisition of all prior steps. Third, concrete materials or manipulatives should be used in mathematics instruction to aid the child in providing meaning for the concept being presented. Although many regard the use of manipulatives as being too elementary, it is too simplistic to assume that there is a one-to-one correspondence between concrete materials and concrete thinking. For instance, sometimes a student can display computation involving numerals but cannot prove the solution using manipulatives. Correct computation in this case involves rote memorization, a lower-level cognitive activity, whereas the proof of the solution using manipulatives requires a higher-level thought process.

Another concern involves the general issues of what to teach and how to monitor and evaluate what has been taught or acquired. It appears as if there is much emphasis placed upon the achievement of content with very little regard to the quality of knowing (i.e., how well does the student understand the material). This emphasis can be seen in mathematics programs that use a fixed frequency basis for material presentation. For example, the first ten pages of the program might deal with addition of two single-digit numerals followed by five pages of addition of three single-digit numerals. The assumption is that when the student finishes the first ten pages, he is ready for the next task automatically. This may or may not be the case. Often, the teacher is concerned with the basic level of performance of the student throughout all types of tasks. The teacher wants to make sure that the child achieves at some consistent rate; if this rate is met, the student moves to the next task. This rate may be a percentage correct level. If movement rate is less than 100 percent correct, and, in the new task, the child encounters a similar problem to one that had been previously solved incorrectly, chances are that she will err again. Unfortunately, the student may never understand that type of problem, not because of lack of exposure, but because of lack of opportunity for mastery learning and overlearning. Cawley and Vitello (1972) advocated a change from the fixed-frequency percentage correct model to the criterion-based approach. Here, the teacher establishes a task criterion that is specific to the student. For example, in order for the student to progress to the next task in sequence, he must solve the problems correctly three consecutive times for five consecutive days. Hence, the student is being asked to master the task (i.e., display correct solution of the problem) and is being given the opportunity to overlearn the task (i.e., duplicating his correct solution over a period of trials). Sternberg and Mauser (1975) felt that many problems that handicapped students experience in mathematics are a function of inappropriate monitoring and evaluation systems.

GENERAL ASPECTS

Sternberg and Sedlak (1978) introduced a number of components that they felt are necessary segments of a mathematics program for handicapped children: (1) flexibility; (2) relevance to the real world; (3) diagnostic/prescriptive format; (4) concept and skill emphasis; (5) social skill development; and (6) management and/or treatment free.

In order to meet the individual needs of mildly handicapped students, a program must be flexible in terms of options for both the student and teacher. For example, if the student has difficulty in reading, reading must be eliminated from the mathematics program so that the student's deficit in one area does not produce a deficit in another area. To make the transition from situation-specific meaning (e.g., verbal problems within a classroom situation) to ecological meaning (i.e., applying the meaning and skill to real-life experiences) requires that the program have relevance to the real world in terms of the child's individual needs. It is better to take a student's elementary grasp of a mathematics concept and apply it to some pertinent environmental situation than to simplify the mathematics level without regard to the child's environment. So that instruction is based upon knowledge of the student's present level of performance, a diagnostic/prescriptive approach should be utilized. Here, assessment determines placement within a sequence of objectives, which are directed toward the attainment of specified goals in mathematics. To avoid the misuse of computational habit or rote computation skills, the program must emphasize concepts and skills. The focus should be on material that will teach the student skills that he can use in a meaningful way both inside and outside the school environment. Although one might assume that mathematics is an individual concern (given the stress upon meeting the individualized needs of the mildly handicapped child), one must never lose sight of the social skill development possibilities within a mathematics program. For example, mathematics instruction can help the student conceptualize the divergent thinking properties of reasoning (e.g., the different ways of making a set of five objects) versus the convergent aspects (e.g., a numerical answer to a computational problem). This helps the student to realize the functions of discrimination and decision making, two extremely important socialization skills. In that behavior and instructional management play a crucial role in the education of mildly handicapped learners, the mathematics program utilized should not interfere with or jeopardize the management plan. The independence from management procedure is necessary so that the student operates within a consistent programmatic environment. If a classroom is following a basic behavioral view toward management, the mathematics program utilized should fit consistently within that procedure.

SIX COMPONENTS OF A MATHEMATICS PROGRAM FOR THE MILDLY HANDICAPPED

Fair (1980) identified six specific components of a mathematics program for mildly handicapped students that are crucial for success: (1) individual focus of program; (2) variety of instructional approaches; (3) explicit transition process; (4) explicit analysis of algorithms; (5) problem solving; and (6) affective aspects of instruction.

Individual Focus of Program

A program that attempts to be effective for students must have an individual focus. There are a number of bases by which instruction can be individualized or differentiated. One approach organizes learning materials so that different students may proceed through them at different rates. Traditionally, this has been the emphasis in special education, and it is an appropriate base on which to individualize instruction so long as it is not generalized from an individual to a group of students. For such an individualized plan, materials must be made available and students must be encouraged to proceed through these materials at the rate and sequence that is appropriate for them based on their individual needs. The instructor must recognize that students are working individually and must develop a system by which the instruction can be appropriately paced for each student.

A second base for individualizing instruction is student interest: the student provides input as to a realm of interest, and instruction is provided in that area. This is particularly apppropriate for secondary-school-aged students, who have been unsuccessful in the past but may have an area in which they are particularly interested. This approach to individualization necessitates cooperation between the student and teacher. Oftentimes, students will not specifically know what interests they have, so interests must be developed with the aid and assistance of the teacher. This type of individualization lends itself to developing a contract between student and teacher. In such a contract situation, the student and teacher agree to the amount and type of work that is to be accomplished.

A third base for individualizing instruction is styles of learning. Traditionally, in special education, the modality approach to learning, where visual learners are differentiated from auditory learners, has been promoted. This often has been a difficult dichotomy to implement because no learner is entirely visual or entirely auditory, and it is difficult to prepare materials that are strictly in one modality. A method that seems more appropriate for mathematics instruction is investigating the approach to learning that is most appropriate for individual students. For example, various approaches in subtraction are the additive concept of subtraction, the comparative concept, and the take-away concept. There are also various approaches for multiplication, division, and other operations. Another example of utilizing different styles of learning is through the adaptation of materials in mathematics. Some students are very proficient in understanding instruction in two-dimensional models as compared to others who would prefer a one-dimensional model such as a number line. Other examples are students who have had a history of learning that is related to a particular material such as Cuisenaire rods or multi-base blocks, and these should be used to explain other concepts to these students. All of these are examples of how style of learning can be considered in the process of differentiating instruction for mildly handicapped students.

A fourth and most important way of individualizing learning is considering the level of intellectual development of the student. Piaget (1952) identified four levels of intellectual development, but for instructional purposes the identification needs to be much more specific. Schminke, Maertens, and Arnold (1973) stated that all mathematics instruction must be directed toward the ability of the child to comprehend the material being presented. Specific activities such as those recommended by Copeland (1979) should be used for specific concepts in mathematics to enable the teacher to determine the level of development of the student. After the level of development has been determined, the instruction should be consistent with that level. This is an approach that takes experience on the part of the teacher. Oftentimes, the chronological age of a student is misleading and is not indicative of the student's level of development in reference to particular mathematical concepts.

Variety of Instructional Approaches

A mathematics program for mildly handicapped students must present a variety of instructional approaches in order to be effective. A number of different ways to conceptualize the basic operations and to perform the basic algorithms that are used in arithmetic should be presented. For example, there are at least three generally accepted ways of introducing the notion of subtraction. Given the mathematical statement of $5 - 2 = 3$, the first approach is the take-away explanation. In a word problem, this would be explained as: "John has five dogs. If he gives two away, how many does he have left?" In this situation, the student could hold up five fingers, then fold two down, and observe that the answer is three. A second approach to conceptualizing subtraction is the comparative situation. In a word problem it would be explained as: "John has five dogs and two cats. How many more dogs than cats does John have?" The third approach is an additive interpretation. That is, how many do you have to add to two to get five? In a word problem it would be explained as: "John has two dogs and would like to have five dogs, how many dogs does he need to add?" For such a problem children often say, "I have two" and then count "three, four, five," holding up three fingers. Then they say, "the answer then is three."

It is difficult to predict which approach will be most appropriate for individual children with learning problems. This is why it is necessary for teachers to have a repertoire of approaches available to them. Students who do not have difficulty in learning mathematics often can have one approach explained to them and are able to generalize to the other two approaches easily. A student with difficulties may not be able to internalize one approach, and, therefore, a second or third approach must be tried. First, the teacher needs to make a judgment about the way the student learns; then, the approach should be used that is consistent with the student's style of learning. Each of the three subtraction approaches have advantages and disadvantages; also, all three depend upon the student's previous knowledge and understanding. There are from three to five interpretations of multiplication that are commonly used. For division, the differences between measurement and partitive division must be well understood by the teacher. For fractions, there are a number of ways of conceptualizing the basic processes and interpretations of fractional numbers. The important concept to remember is that individual students learn differently; using one approach will not always be productive for all students.

Explicit Transition Process

An important component of a mathematics program for mildly handicapped students is a transition process from concrete materials to abstract symbols. In mathematics programs, the assumption is made that for students that have difficulties in learning, a sequence of formats is necessary, beginning with the concrete format, then the semiconcrete format, and finally the abstract format. For teachers who use this type of sequence the question that often arises is, "Once the student can do well with the concrete or manipulative aid, how is the student assisted to perform the same operation with paper and pencil *without* the aid?" The answer is that the teacher must develop an explicit transition program for the student from the concrete objects to the abstract symbols. In this context, concrete objects are thought of as materials that can be handled, picked up, touched, smelled, tasted, or manipulated. Semiconcrete objects are pictures of these concrete objects. The abstract format uses symbols in a strictly paper and pencil mode. An example of using Cuisenaire rods may be helpful. Cuisenaire rods are ten different rods of various colors, from 1 to 10 cm long, which can be used to represent the numbers from 1 to 10. The student who is expected to show the addition problem of 2 + 5 with Cuisenaire rods would find the 2 rod and the 5 rod and put them together, end to end, and then measure them against the other rods. Using this method, the student can determine that the answer for 2 + 5 is 7. At this initial level of operation, the student would be working only with the Cuisenaire rods. At the second level of performance, the student might work with the Cuisenaire rods first and then, using the symbols for 2, 5, and 7, solve the addition problem on paper. At the third level, the student would solve the addition problem on paper with symbols and then check the answer by using the Cuisenaire rods. At the fourth level, the student would solve the problem on paper without the use of the Cuisenaire rods. It is important to note that there is a specific transition program from working with the concrete materials to working in the abstract format of pencil and paper. In such a transition program, the amount of time the student works with concrete materials will vary depending on the student's progress. For example, the student may be expected to spend one half of the lesson time working with concrete materials and the other half in the abstract or semiconcrete format. A schedule should be developed with individual needs taken into consideration. The concept that is important is that an explicit transition program is designed that will help the student make the transition from concrete or semiconcrete materials to the abstract format. Oftentimes, students who do not have difficulty in learning mathematics can be presented an example and then generalize their work and be able to perform in the abstract format. With students who have difficulty in learning, more specific steps for moving from concrete materials to the abstract format are necessary.

Explicit Analysis of Algorithms

An example will help to explain what is meant by explicit analysis of operations and algorithms:

$$
\begin{array}{r}
326 \\
-\ 57 \\
\hline
269
\end{array}
$$

The common algorithm, which is a standardized procedure (rule) for the solution of a particular type of problem, if used to perform the subtraction operation in this problem would involve the use of regrouping rules; most students would proceed by regrouping so that 6 becomes 16 and the students would think, $16 - 7 = 9$. The second step would be to regroup again: $11 - 5 = 6$. In the third step, the student would think, $2 - 0 = 2$. The final answer is 269. Most teachers would present the algorithm that is used in subtraction in this way. The important concept for instructing mildly handicapped students is that this process must be explained to them in a very detailed and explicit manner. The instructor must teach the complete process that was used in the example. What is meant by teaching the process? It means that the teacher should say more than "Because 7 is bigger than 6 you have to borrow so you cross out the 2 and make it a 1, then you bring the 1 over and make that a 16." This is not really an explanation of the process. One of the important concepts that needs to be thoroughly understood is the place value system. The place value system for this problem means that the 326 is $3 \times 100 + 2 \times 10 + 6 \times 1$. If the student has difficulty understanding place value, he will naturally have difficulty with the regrouping process.

Some teachers may believe that the concept of place value is too difficult for mildly handicapped students and, therefore, do not expect them to understand it.

On the contrary, the only way that the student is going to become competent with the subtraction algorithm is to understand the place value system. The teacher needs to make a concerted effort to help the student to understand the system before the student is expected to complete the regrouping process. In order to enable the child to understand this process, it should initially be accomplished in a concrete format. This means not working only with numerals or symbols at a chalkboard or with pencil and paper. The student needs to have an opportunity to manipulate objects that can be grouped together and then ungrouped. Examples are toothpicks and multibase blocks. The importance of explicit analysis of operations and algorithms is that these processes must be understood before they can be practiced. This is true for the basic processes of arithmetic. The explicit analysis of operations and algorithms is an important component of any mathematics program that will be useful for students who have difficulties in learning.

Problem Solving

Many opportunities should be provided for mildly handicapped students to solve written word problems, verbal problems, story problems, logical problems, and puzzles. There has been extensive research conducted on problem solving (Riedesel, 1969). Definitive conclusions from this research have not been forthcoming, but there is one conclusion on which most researchers would agree. Students who have had numerous opportunities to practice problem solving are better problem solvers. There are teachers who believe it is more important for students to have many experiences in computational exercises and that problem solving is a secondary priority. These teachers believe that if the student can solve the algorithm then verbal problems to which the algorithm applies can also be solved. It has been demonstrated that some abilities may not generalize to all relevant problems given in a different manner (Carpenter, Corbitt, Kepner, Lindquist, & Reys, 1980). On a national level, the problem solving performance of all students in mathematics is poor.

How can mathematics programs emphasize problem solving? First, the student should have many opportunities to experience problem solving. As problems are presented, the computational level of difficulty should be within the student's competence. The level of difficulty is important, because if the student has to focus on the computational procedure rather than on the actual interpretation of the problem, the purpose of the problem solving exercise has not been fulfilled. For example, if the student is presently doing computational division exercises with a two-digit divisor and four-digit dividend, the word problems should involve a one-digit divisor and a two-digit dividend. This is important so that the student can spend the time reading, interpreting, and understanding the problem.

Second, emphasis should be on the process of problem solving rather than the product of problem solving. For example, what would one do to solve this problem? "If I had some cans of milk and some cans of juice, how many cans of juice and milk would I have altogether?" Obviously, the student would have to combine the number of cans of milk with the number of cans of juice to find the total number of cans. Another approach to problem solving that emphasizes the process rather than the product is an adaptation of the sequence system of problem solving. Teachers should help students to understand a sequence of problem solving, for example:

1. Identify what is being asked for in the problem.
2. Identify the information needed to answer the question.
3. Identify the operation used to solve the problem.
4. Estimate the answer.
5. Compute and solve the problem.

Rather than implementing each of these five steps with a given problem, the process-oriented focus can be put on accomplishing one step at a time with several problems. This approach to the problem solving sequence enables the teacher to identify and focus on the needs of individual students.

A third strategy for emphasizing problem solving should present the mildly handicapped student an opportunity to decide whether to add, subtract, multiply, or divide—rather than presenting all of the same type of problems on one page. This is important because problem solving is a decision-making process. If only one type of problem is presented on one page, the decision making is removed from the problem solving process. The important concept to remember is that problem solving should be an integral part of a mathematics program for students who have difficulty in learning.

Affective Aspects of Instruction

An effective mathematics program must consider the affective aspects of instruction for children who have difficulty in learning mathematics. Mildly handicapped students often have had a history of failure in mathematics; therefore, an effective program must provide for success experiences. Mathematics needs to be made enjoyable and meaningful to the daily lives of these students. There are many persons who strongly dislike mathematics because of the instruction that they received in their school years. This is also the situation for students who have had difficulty in learning mathematics. The important concept is that the teacher and the program must make an effort to make mathematics meaningful and positive for the student.

The key technique that can be used with students who have had a long history of failure is the provision of success experiences. This can be done by the modification of instruction. Poor attitudes toward mathematics instruction are both an internal and an external problem for the student. The internal problem is low esteem and expectations. The external problem is the teacher's low expectancy for the performance of the student. This is particularly important for secondary-school-aged students. Instruction for these students must be presented in a mature way that will be accepted by them, although they may be doing elementary school mathematics.

Johnson and Risin (1967) best summed up the importance of a positive attitude by stating that

> The mathematics student with positive attitudes studies mathematics because he enjoys it, he gets satisfaction from knowing mathematical ideas, and he finds mathematical competency its own reward. (p. 126)

PROGRAM EVALUATIONS

DISTAR

Program Philosophy

The DISTAR Arithmetic System is a tightly structured teacher-directed program that is comprehensive in design. It purports to teach students everything needed in order to perform all the arithmetic functions. The content of the system does not differ from a traditional arithmetic program; however, the method of instruction is significantly different (Englemann & Carnine, 1970).

The following aspects of the DISTAR system of instruction make it unique: The system assumes that the student has no previously acquired knowledge of mathematics and teaches every skill as though it were the student's first exposure to that skill. Every skill is taught in a teacher-directed method. Simple operations such as learning the names of the numerals and signs are delayed, while some higher level operations such as multiplication are introduced earlier than usual. The system stresses moving through the program at a fast pace. Only the precise skills and information needed to solve a problem are presented. The system teaches one way to perform an operation and then presents a variety of situations in which the operation can be applied rather than teaching a variety of ways to perform the operation. Each skill is taught independently and in very precise small steps. The student must have complete mastery of each step before moving on to the next step. The DISTAR system stresses that the mildly handicapped student will move as quickly as the regular student through the program because every necessary component skill is taught to the student. Therefore, there is no reason for the mildly handicapped student not to perform as well as the regular student in this program.

Programmatic Variables

The DISTAR Arithmetic System is composed of three sequential modules. DISTAR I contains 20 different 30-minute daily lessons; DISTAR II contains 180 different 30-minute daily lessons; and DISTAR III contains 160 different 80-minute daily lessons. Each lesson is designed for small-group instruction. Each module comes in a display box containing student and teacher materials. The teacher materials include presentation books and a teacher's guide for each module. The presentation books, *Preskills* and *Books A, B, C,* and *D* for DISTAR I; *Books E, F, G,* and *H* for DISTAR II: and *Books I* and *J* for DISTAR III contain the specific instructions for the teacher. These instructions tell the teacher exactly what to say, what to point to, what kind of response to expect from the student, and the correct procedure to use if the student replies incorrectly. The teacher's guide contains a scope and sequence chart and explains the use of the presentation books and the student materials. The student materials in DISTAR I and II are two- to four-page take-home booklets. These booklets are to be used as an extension of the daily lesson. Other materials included in the modules are geometric figure cards and form boards in DISTAR I; multiplication charts and workbooks in DISTAR II; and a fact game and workbooks in DISTAR III. Five colors of paper clips are included in each module. These are to be used by the teacher to indicate the next lesson for each group. Placement tests, to be given at the beginning of the year, and mastery tests, to be given periodically, are included in the presentation books.

The DISTAR Arithmetic System is designed to teach children the basic arithmetic concepts by a carefully structured teaching method. For the program to work, these guidelines must be strictly followed. The tasks in the DISTAR system are designed to achieve very specific objectives and do not allow for discussion or extraneous observations. The rationale for this position is based on its proposed advantage for low performers. The more the teacher strays from the task as it is specified, the longer it will take for the students to learn the concepts. Suggestions for teaching this system include the following: (1) separate the thinking operations from the repetition of statements; (2) require 100 percent involvement; (3) reinforce only students who are on task; (4) use group activities to teach concepts and individual activities to check the progress of each student; and (5) determine when assistance is absolutely necessary (Englemann & Carnine, 1970).

Assessment/Monitoring Devices

Instructions for teaching should be followed precisely. The system is begun with a placement test, which is administered before beginning arithmetic instruction. Test results are used for forming homogeneous groups of no more than ten children. The teacher begins by teaching the entire group the first track. (A track is a subject that is included in the daily lesson for a certain number of days.) Some of the DISTAR arithmetic tracks are addition, subtraction, multiplication, and fractions. The DISTAR program also includes periodic mastery tests, which specify the criteria for moving ahead in the program. If more than one student fails a particular test, it means that the whole group should go back and repeat the lesson. There are also provisions for skipping some lessons—these provisions are spelled out in the text of certain lessons. The DISTAR Arithmetic System provides the teacher with a comprehensive math program, but the precise methods demanded must be used for it to succeed.

Contents Emphasis and Range

The system covers 42 content areas:

1. Matching	15. Fact derivation and fact learning
2. Rote counting	
3. Rational counting	16. Counting by
4. Symbol identification	17. Multiplication
5. Lines and numerals	18. Counting money
6. Equality	19. Negative numbers
7. Addition	20. Fractions
8. Algebra addition	21. Problems in columns
9. Facts of addition	22. Consolidation
10. Subtraction	23. Subtraction facts
11. Algebra subtraction	24. Substitution
12. Consolidation	25. Relation between addition and subtraction
13. Revaluing	
14. Analogies	26. Writing numerals

27. Fact game
28. Terms
29. Counting by
30. Algebra
31. Addition in columns
32. Story problems
33. More or less
34. Analogies
35. Subtraction
36. Fractions
37. Factoring
38. Place value
39. Multiplication facts
40. Division using factors
41. Multiplication in columns
42. Adding and subtracting fractions

Rating General Aspects

Flexibility. The materials and presentations are tightly structured, which discourages flexibility.

Relevance. Little or no attempt is made to make the program relative to the child's daily activities.

Diagnostic/prescriptive. Placement tests are used for grouping, and mastery tests are used for monitoring progress.

Concept and skill emphasis. Rote skills are emphasized prior to conceptual learning. Concepts are learned through the practice of computational examples.

Social skill development. Convergent thinking is exclusively promoted with few opportunities for divergent activities.

Management and/or treatment free. This is a highly structured program that permits little modification or adaptations.

Rating Specific Components

Individual focus of program. The focus of the program is on work with homogeneous groups of less than ten students, with little attention to individual students.

Variety of instructional approaches. There is no allowance for variety of instructional approaches. Strict adherence to instructional procedures is required for success.

Explicit transition process. No concrete materials are used. There is no transition process as semiconcrete materials and abstract concept are used simultaneously.

Explicit analysis of algorithms. The solution process for algorithms is subdivided into small steps and is dependent upon the student's rote memory.

Problem solving. Story problems are presented and arriving at the solution is a teacher-directed process.

Affective aspects of instruction.   Students are given tangible and social rewards for on task-behavior and help is provided for incorrect responses.

Essential Math and Language Skills Program

Program Philosophy

The Essential Math and Language Skills Program (EMLS) is based upon two key principles: (1) in order to insure that the handicapped child will comprehend the mathematics concept being presented, one must determine the cognitive readiness of that child to be exposed to that concept; and (2) mathematics instruction must follow a meaning-to-skill approach (Sternberg, Sedlak, Cherkes, & Minick, 1978).

Programmatic Variables

A diagnostic inventory that assesses the child's ability to recognize patterns provides information related to readiness for instruction in various levels of mathematics concepts. Once these levels are determined (through the use of prescriptive charts that juxtapose mathematics concepts with pattern recognition level of performance), curriculum guides are provided that both explain the concept to be taught and outline the procedure to be used in teaching the concept. Each concept is related to both a short-term objective (subordinate objective) and a long-term goal (terminal objective). All concepts are presented in a developmental sequence. Teaching strategies outline the manner in which the teacher should interact with the child during the instruction. Often, these strategies require different behaviors on the part of the teacher. Also specified are student behaviors, which are delineations of what behavior the child must exhibit in order for the teacher to judge that the child has acquired the concept. EMLS does not include specific materials (e.g., manipulatives), but for each objective it does suggest easy ways to obtain materials to be used to teach the concept.

Assessment/Monitoring Devices

As described earlier, a diagnostic inventory is used to establish entry level characteristics. Once target concepts are identified by the teacher, she must determine which concepts within the level should be addressed. The child's performance may be monitored through the use of a tracking chart. The chart is color-coded and identifies concepts within each of the six content areas of the program that are basically of the same cognitive complexity. Therefore, the teacher is reminded that the child can be instructed in a number of different mathematics areas at the same time.

Content Emphasis and Range

Six major areas of mathematics are dealt with in the EMLS program: (1) sets and operations on sets; (2) numbers and operations on numbers; (3) patterns; (4) part-whole relations; (5) spatial relations; and (6) measurements. Within the sets area, concepts begin with understanding general characteristics (e.g., shape, color) and end with performing set union and intersection. In the numbers area, students begin with associating numbers with sets and proceed to all operations on numbers. In patterns, progress is from duplicating patterns of pictures and colors of a model pattern to duplicating a pattern with different pictures and colors than in the model. Within the part-whole area, the child begins with the concept of discrete versus blended parts and proceeds to operations on fractions. For spatial relations, the most elementary concept is open versus closed figures, and the most advanced is the concept of rigidity of geometric figures. In the measurement area, nonstandard measure is the first concept, with metric measurement dealt with as the final concept. The thirty-two concepts covered in this program are

Sets and Operations and Numbers and Operations

1. Left/right
2. Visual differences
3. Visual sameness
4. One-to-one correspondence
5. Set descriptions
6. Set manipulations
7. Operations on sets
8. Number associations
9. Addition operations
10. Place value
11. Additive regrouping
12. Subtraction operation
13. Subtractive regrouping
14. Number families $(+, -)$
15. Multiplication operation
16. Distributive property $(\times)$
17. Division operation
18. Distributive property $(\div)$
19. Number families $(\times, \div)$

Patterns

20. Original learning
21. Reverse shift
22. Intradimensional shift
23. Extradimensional shift

Part-Whole Relations, Spatial Relations, and Measurements

24. Concrete part-whole relations
25. Abstract part-whole relations
26. Topology
27. Shapes
28. Advanced geometry
29. Nonstandard measure
30. Days, weeks, and months
31. Time
32. Metrics

Rating General Aspects

Flexibility. The program allows the teacher a number of behavioral and content options in dealing with each level.

Relevance. Although environmental examples are presented within the teaching strategies, no direct attempt is made to tie the concepts being presented to the students' individual environmental needs.

Diagnostic/prescriptive. Through its diagnostic emphasis, prescription of concepts is based upon the students' readiness to acquire.

Concept and skill emphasis. Concepts are presented in a meaningful way and throughout the program skills are practiced after the meaning is insured.

Social skill development. The social skill enhancement criteria is not met by this system.

Management and/or treatment free. The program can be used in various types of management systems.

Rating Specific Components

Individual focus of program.   EMLS focuses upon the individual student by determining that students' readiness to acquire concepts and by emphasizing individual target concepts.

Variety of instructional approaches.   A variety of instructional approaches are outlined for the teacher, although the sequence of instructional steps is fixed.

Explicit transition process.   In every case, the student is asked to display understanding using manipulatives prior to the demonstration of understanding using symbols.

Explicit analysis of algorithms.   All concepts are defined, and algorithms are explained.

Problem solving.   Although verbal problems are presented throughout the program to help the student understand the concept being demonstrated, there is no direct attempt at emphasizing problem solving as a content area.

Affective aspects of instruction.   The affective component of success-oriented interaction is addressed by the use of small-step instruction, reinforcement of the student's acquisition, and overlearning of concepts through the use of different teacher strategies and learner behaviors.

Developing Mathematical Processes

Program Philosophy

The philosophy of developing mathematical processes (DMP) is that an elementary mathematics program should be pedagogically sound, psychologically sound, and mathematically sound. Pedagogically sound means that both the child and the mathematics content should be considered in developing the program, that a teacher's role is to encourage learning, that physical material should be integrated into a mathematics program, and that each child must be planned for on an individual basis (Romberg & Harvey, 1974). Psychologically sound is interpreted to mean that each child should be actively involved in learning mathematics, that instruction should begin with concrete experiences and move to the abstract, and that the program should be so constructed so that the child is motivated to learn mathematics. Mathematically sound means that there is more to elementary mathematics than arithmetic, that a basic goal should be to learn to solve mathematics problems independently, and that mathematics is more meaningful if approached through measurement.

The philosophy of DMP is operationalized through instruction that involves attributes and processes. There are many attributes that are used throughout the DMP program, but some of them that are used extensively in the primary program are length, numerousness, weight, capacity, shape, color, and direction. The basic processes that are used in the primary portion of DMP are describing, classifying, comparing, ordering, equalizing, joining, separating, grouping, and partitioning. As each of these processes is introduced, children work directly with objects or sets. The development from the concrete to the symbolic is the more general process called representing, and the process of determining whether a proposed solution is the actual solution of a situation is called validating. Representing and validating are used as the means of extending beyond the basic processes with concrete objects to the abstract.

Programmatic Variables

DMP is organized into 90 topics for kindergarten through sixth grade. These 90 topics can be classified into five general areas: addition and subtraction, place value and problem solving, multiplication and division, attributes/measuring, and geometry. For each of the 90 topics there is a description of the topic; one, two, or three regular objectives; preparatory objectives; and review objectives. A regular objective is one that most children are expected to master by the end of the topic. A preparatory objective is one that most children are not expected to master by the end of the topic, although some children may do so. A review objective is one that has been a regular objective in a previous topic and is repeated to provide opportunities for practice. For each of the 90 topics, DMP includes a separate teacher's guide and materials. Physical manipulative materials, printed materials, teacher materials, and student materials are an integral part of each DMP topic.

Assessment/Monitoring Devices

Five different types of assessment procedures are included in DMP: (1) observation schedule; (2) topic inventory; (3) pretest; (4) check-up test; and (5) placement inventory. Specific procedures for when and how each of these is to be used are a part of the resource guide for DMP. DMP suggests three levels of description to rate the progress of the student in a particular topic: mastery, making progress, and needs considerable help.

Content Emphasis and Range

The names of the 90 topics that are included in the DMP program for kindergarten through sixth grade are below:

1. Describing and classifying
2. Comparing and ordering on length
3. Equalizing on length
4. Ordering more than two objects on length
5. Representing length
6. Movement and direction
7. Comparing, ordering, and equalizing on numerousness
8. Three-dimensional shape
9. Representing numerous physically
10. Paths and location
11. Representing numerousness pictorially
12. Tallying
13. Time
14. Representing numerousness symbolically
15. Two-dimensional shape
16. Comparing and ordering on weight
17. Writing numbers
18. Comparing and ordering events on time

19. Assigning measurements
20. Paths
21. Comparison sentences
22. Comparing and ordering on capacity
23. Order sentences
24. The numbers 0–20
25. Representing equalizing situations
26. Movement and direction
27. Representing other equalizing situations
28. Symmetry, fractions, and shape
29. Representing joining and separating situations
30. Grouping
31. Geometric shapes
32. Solving number sentences, 0–10
33. The numbers 0–99
34. Units of capacity
35. Solving number sentences, 0–20
36. Describing, classifying, and locating
37. Partitioning
38. Solving number sentences, 0–99
39. Units of length
40. The addition and subtraction algorithms, 0–99
41. Movement and direction
42. Units of weight
43. Solving open sentences
44. Angles and symmetry
45. The numbers 0–999
46. Comparing and ordering areas
47. Grouping and partitioning
48. Geometric figures
49. The addition and subtraction algorithms, 0–999
50. Measuring length
51. Measuring time
52. Investigating problems
53. Location and angles
54. Grouping and partitioning sentences
55. Representing common fractions
56. Describing three-dimensional objects
57. The numbers 0–999,999
58. Units of areas
59. Ordering fractions with representations
60. Multiplication and division sentences
61. Geometric figures
62. Addition and subtraction of larger numbers
63. Measuring
64. Multiplication with larger numbers
65. Problem solving
66. Measuring angles
67. Equivalence of fractions
68. Movements and changes
69. Multiplication algorithm
70. Patterns
71. Common fractions
72. Division algorithms
73. Three-dimensional objects
74. Decimal fractions
75. Standard cubic units
76. Investigating problems
77. Triangles and other figures
78. Very large and very small numbers
79. Multiplying larger numbers
80. Circles and other curved figures
81. Using common fractions
82. Dividing by larger numbers
83. Units
84. Multiplying and dividing decimal fractions
85. Approximating and estimating
86. Quadrilaterals and other figures
87. Graphing and analyzing
88. Ratios and proportions
89. Problem solving
90. Patterns

Rating General Aspects

Flexibility. There are numerous options available to the student and teacher in terms of materials, sequence of objectives, and format of presentation.

Relevance.   Many manipulative materials are provided that exist in the student's environment and make instructional activities relevant.

Diagnostic/prescriptive.   An extensive effort is made to assess and monitor student progress and provide for commensurate instruction.

Concept and skill emphasis.   Concepts and skills are emphasized through measurement activities, working directly with objects and sets.

Social skill development.   The measurement approach lends itself to many practical applications and problem-solving applications. Convergent and divergent situations are present.

Management and/or treatment free.   The flexible design of the system makes it compatible with different management systems.

Rating Specific Components

Individual focus of program.   The focus of the program is on individual student performance, and each child is encouraged to be actively involved.

Variety of instructional approaches.   Although sequence and format of instruction may vary, the instructional approach is based on measurement concepts.

Explicit transition process.   A specific process, named representing, is the transition from the concrete to the symbolic. Extensive materials are provided to enhance the development of this process.

Explicit analysis of algorithms.   Problem-solving activities are present throughout the program in an innovative and fascinating manner that increases student involvement.

Problem solving.   Manipulative materials are used to increase the understanding of the basic algorithms and operations.

Affective aspects of instruction.   Students are encouraged to take an active part in learning and discovering mathematical concepts.

Project MATH

Program Philosophy

Project MATH is a comprehensive developmental mathematics program for students whose overall developmental growth is slower than average. The philosophy of the system is that a program of mathematics for mildly handicapped students must (1) provide the student with wide ranges of experiences with mathematics; (2) be capable of minimizing the effects of inadequately developed skills and abilities on performance in mathematics; and (3) use the qualities of mathematics, and experiences that can be generated via mathematics, to enhance the affective and cognitive status of the learner. Project MATH presents a balanced emphasis on skills, concepts, and social growth. Specifically, it is designed to (1) enhance the learner's chances for success; (2) integrate the mathematics curriculum with the learner's daily life; (3) provide the teacher with numerous instructional options; (4) maximize the opportunities for individualized instruction; and (5) enhance the development of the total student, socially, emotionally, and academically (Cawley, Fitzmaurice, Goodstein, Lepore, Sedlak, & Althaus, 1976).

A unique aspect of the Project MATH system is the design of the input-output combination, around which the behavioral and instructional objectives are built. Each instructional guide is written specifically to a single pattern of instructor–learner interaction. The four basic types of teacher behavior (construct, present, state, graphically symbolize) interact with the four types of learner-response behavior (construct, identify, state, graphically symbolize). The present mode includes presentation of nonsymbolic displays such as pictures or pictorial activity sheets, and the identify mode requires nonverbal selection by the learner and allows for multiple choices. The construct mode involves direct manipulation of the learner's environment. The state mode relies on verbal presentations, while the graphically symbolize mode uses drawn or written symbolic materials. The different combinations provide optional teaching strategies for any one concept. No one interaction is considered cognitively superior to any other. The strategies allow the teacher to adapt the most appropriate combinations commensurate with the needs of the individual learner.

Programmatic Variables

In the Project MATH system, the curriculum is referred to as the Multiple Option Curriculum. At the teaching level, the Multiple Option Curriculum consists of instructional guides, learner activity books, supplemental activity books for the instructor, class progress records, individual progress records, math concept inventories, and manipulative materials. These materials are packaged in four separate boxes. Included with Project MATH are 192 attribute pieces, 400 small discs, 400 plastic chips, 6 rulers, a metric converter, 6 thermometers, and 3 geoboards.

The instructional guides are large cards which form the basic element of the curriculum. They present directed activities in six major strands of mathematics. Each card also notes the area and concept that the guide covers. Each guide also lists (1) the activities; (2) supplemental activities; (3) materials; and (4) evaluation for the concept. The instructor is to prepare the other suggested materials, with the student's help if possible. These materials are repeatedly used in the program.

Assessment/Monitoring Devices

The Project MATH concept inventory is used to assess the student's status in relation to the major concepts in the program. It can be used as a screening device for placement or as a mastery test to evaluate student progress. Project MATH also includes two sets of forms to record and track the student's progress; recording the student's progress through the program enables the teacher to plan each day's activities.

Content Emphasis and Range

The mathematics content of this system consists of a program from preschool through grade six. It presents activities in six major areas of mathematics: geometry, sets, patterns, numbers, measurement, and fractions.

Various problem-solving experiences are stressed throughout the program at all levels.

Rating General Aspects

Flexibility.   The input-output interaction permits multiple options for both the teacher and the student. Teacher creativity is encouraged.

Relevance.   The focus of the program is to provide the learner with a mathematics curriculum designed to facilitate the use of math in the learner's daily life.

Diagnostic/prescriptive format.   The Project MATH concept inventory is used for placement and evaluating student progress. Two sets of forms are included to record and track student's progress.

Concept and skill emphasis.   The multiple options curriculum minimizes the effects of inadequately developed skills and focuses on providing the student with wide ranges of experiences in mathematics.

Social skill development.   Through the emphasis on problem solving, the student is provided with numerous opportunities for divergent thinking.

Management and/or treatment free.   Flexibility is inherent within the system, making it appropriate for various management techniques.

Rating Specific Components

Individual focus of program.   The multiple option curriculum is designed to maximize the instructor's opportunities for individualizing instruction.

Variety of instructional approaches.   The program stresses the creative input of the teacher, and the success of the program is highly dependent on teacher initiative.

Explicit transition process.   Although no specific transition process exists, concrete materials and manipulatives are used concurrently with abstract symbols depending on the student's needs.

Explicit analysis of algorithms.   The approach taken in this system emphasizes understanding concepts before exposure to basic algorithms.

Problem solving.   Problem solving is an integral part of the system and is stressed at all levels.

Affective aspects of instructions.   The program provides a framework in which the mathematics content enhances the affective and social development of the learner.

REFERENCES

Baumeister, A., & Kellas, G. Process variables in the paired associate learning of retardates. In N. Ellis (Ed.), *International review of research in mental retardation* (Vol. 5). New York: Academic Press, 1971.

Bryant, N., & Kass, C. *Leadership training institute in learning disabilities* (Vol. 1). Washington, D.C.: Bureau of Education for the Handicapped, 1972.

Callahan, L., & Robinson, M. Task analysis procedures in mathematics instruction of achievers and underachievers. *School Science and Mathematics,* 1973, *73,* 578–584.

Carpenter, T. P., Corbitt, M. K., Kepner, H., Lindquist, M. M., & Reys, R. E. Problem solving in mathematics: National assessment results. *Educational Leadership,* 1980, *37,* 562–563.

Cawley, J. F., Fitzmaurice, A. M., Goodstein, H. A., Lepore, A. V., Sedlak, R., & Althaus, V. *Project MATH.* Tulsa: Educational Progress, 1976.

Cawley, J., & Goodman, J. Interrelationships among mental abilities, reading, language arts, and arithmetic with the mentally handicapped. *The Arithmetic Teacher,* 1968, *15,* 631–636.

Cawley, J., & Vitello, S. Model for arithmetical programming for handicapped children. *Exceptional Children,* 1972, *39,* 101–110.

Chalfant, J., & Scheffelin, M. *Central processing dysfunction in children: A review of research* (NINDS Monograph No. 9). Washington, D.C.: U.S. Government Printing Office, 1969.

Copeland, R. *How children learn mathematics.* New York: Macmillan, 1974.

Copeland, R. *Math activities for children.* Columbus, Oh.: Merrill, 1979.

Ellis, N. The stimulus trace and behavioral inadequacy. In N. Ellis (Ed.), *Handbook of mental deficiency.* New York: McGraw-Hill, 1963.

Englemann, S., & Carnine, D. *DISTAR arithmetic.* Chicago: Science Research Associates, 1970.

Fair, G. W. *A developmental approach to mathematics for children with learning problems.* Paper presented at National Council of Teachers of Mathematics Dallas Meeting, Dallas, Texas, 1980.

Freidus, E. The needs of teachers for specialized information on number concepts. In W. Cruickshank (Ed.), *The teacher of brain-injured children: A discussion of the bases for competency.* Syracuse, N.Y.: Syracuse University Press, 1966.

Herald, P. Helping the child who can't do math.

Teacher Magazine, 1974, *91*(17), 46–47.

Johnson, D., & Myklebust, H. *Learning disabilities: Educational principles and practices.* New York: Grune & Stratton, 1967.

Johnson, D. A., & Risin, G. R. *Guidelines for teaching mathematics.* Belmont, Ca.: Wadsworth, 1967.

Kaliski, L. Arithmetic and the brain-injured child. In E. Frierson & W. Barbe (Eds.), *Educating children with learning disabilities.* New York: Appleton-Century-Crofts, 1967.

Kosc, L. Developmental discalculia. *Journal of Learning Disabilities,* 1974, *7*(3), 46–59.

Lerner, J. *Children with learning disabilities.* Boston: Houghton Mifflin, 1976.

Otto, W., McMenemy, R., & Smith, R. *Corrective and remedial teaching.* Boston: Houghton Mifflin, 1973.

Peterson, D. *Functional mathematics for the mentally retarded.* Columbus, Oh.: Charles Merrill, 1973.

Piaget, J. *The child's concept of numbers.* New York: Norton, 1952.

Riedesel, C. A. Problem solving: Some suggestions from research. *The Arithmetic Teacher,* 1969, *17,* 54–58.

Romberg, T. A. & Harvey, J. G. *Resource manual, topics 1–40 developing mathematical processes.* Chicago: Rand McNally, 1974.

Scheffelin, M., & Seltzer, C. Math manipulatives for learning disabilities. *Academic Therapy,* 1974, *9,* 357–362.

Schminke, C., Maertens, N., & Arnold, W. *Teaching the child mathematics.* Hinsdale, Il.: Dryden Press, 1973.

Sternberg, L., Fitzmaurice, A., & Dembinski, R. The efficacy of skill-to-meaning mathematics instruction for the mentally handicapped. *Education,* 1979, *100,* 47–55.

Sternberg, L., & Mauser, A. The LD child and mathematics. *Academic Therapy,* 1975, *10,* 481–488.

Sternberg, L., & Sedlak, R. Mathematical programming for problem adolescents. In D. Sabatino & A. Mauser (Eds.), *Intervention strategies for specialized secondary education.* Boston: Allyn and Bacon, 1978.

Sternberg, L., Sedlak, R., Cherkes, M., & Minick, B. *Essential math and language skills program.* Northbrook, Il.: Hubbard, 1978.

Underwood, B., & Schultz, R. *Meaningfulness and verbal learning.* Chicago: Lippincott, 1960.

Vitello, S. Facilitation of class inclusion among mentally retarded children. *American Journal of Mental Deficiency,* 1973, *78,* 158–162.

Marianne Price
Joyce Ness
Mollie Stitt

16

Beyond the Three R's: Science and Social Studies Instruction for the Mildly Handicapped

Instructional programs for the mildly handicapped, both in elementary and secondary schools, have concentrated almost exclusively on the development of reading, writing, and arithmetic skills. Science and social studies have had very low priority compared with the "basic skill" subjects. A review of the literature on science and social studies instruction for the mildly handicapped shows some research and curriculum development involving educable mentally retarded students but little empirical research on how to teach science and social studies to learning disabled and emotionally disturbed youngsters. Limited attention has been given to science and/or social studies curriculum development for the mildly handicapped as well. A review of the content of 16 textbooks in the field of learning disabilities, all published since 1973 (Rose & Lessen, 1980), reveals that none of the texts address either science or social studies instruction. The paucity of research and apparent neglect of these subjects in current textbooks suggests that science and social studies instruction are incidental to, or possibly ignored altogether, in programs for the mildly handicapped. If this is true, then large numbers of mildly handicapped students are receiving little or no systematic exposure to the concepts, processes, and attitudes that are taught through these programs. Yet the importance of such learning opportunities is as great for the handicapped as the nonhandicapped student.

In 1978, the National Science Teachers Association (NSTA) held a conference on science education for physically handicapped students (Hofman & Ricker, 1979). Although science education for mildly handicapped students was not addressed, the position statement that resulted from the conference is, in many ways, applicable to learning disabled, educable mentally retarded, and emotionally disturbed students; many of the points stressed in the position statement apply to science and social studies education for the mildly handicapped (words inserted in brackets are authors' alterations) (Hofman, 1979).

> Science [and social studies] are not considered an important component of the curriculum for [mildly] handicapped students. [Mildly] handicapped students are not receiving comprehensive or regular exposure to sciences [or social studies] at any lev-

el. Present programs . . . and instructional strategies have not been adapted to meet the needs of the [mildly] handicapped students in both special groups and main-streamed science [and social studies] courses.

Teachers are not always aware of and sensitive to the unique needs of the [mildly] handicapped students. . . . When [mildly] handicapped students are placed in regular science [and social studies] classrooms, the teacher has generally not been adequately prepared for the placement of the students, and has not been provided with the insight, special materials, skills, and or techniques to effectively help the [mildly] handicapped student learn science [and social studies]. (p. 17)[1]

It is not difficult to understand why this situation exists. The emphasis on the development of basic skills has been an all-consuming effort in many programs for the mildly handicapped. Unfortunately, the application of basic skills to content area subjects in the context of remedial education of basic skill deficiencies has not been given sufficient attention. But who would deny that science and social studies are an important part of the handicapped student's education, not only for knowledge, skills, and values, but also for the opportunities that these disciplines provide for students to apply and practice basic skills in a meaningful context? Inclusion of these subjects in the curriculum can greatly enhance the development of basic skills.

For the mildly handicapped student, the goals of science and social studies instruction should not differ substantially from the goals for their nonhandicapped peers. Ochoa and Shuster (1980), in their discussion of setting social studies goals for handicapped students, stressed the importance of examining the goals identified for nonhandicapped learners and determining if they should be modified for children with various kinds of disabilities. They concluded that the four categories of social studies goals identified by the National Council for Social Studies are just as important for handicapped students as they are for nonhandicapped students (Ochoa & Shuster, 1980).

The fact that some learners will not attain these goals fully is not a reason to alter the goals; rather, the challenge to teachers is one of finding ways to increase the likelihood that learners will achieve these goals. . . . Obviously, with certain kinds of handicapped learners, instructional goals for social studies must be tempered by reality. (p. 19)[2]

The potential benefits inherent in science and social studies instruction for the mildly handicapped do not diminish the difficulty of teaching these subjects to a population of students who have poor reading and writing skills, difficulty with oral expression, poor attention and concentration, low levels of motivation, and difficulty understanding abstract concepts. Curricular materials and teaching practices must be modified and adapted to enable mildly handicapped students to successfully reach the goals of science and social studies instruction.

When planning a program of science and social studies instruction for mildly

---

[1]Reprinted with permission from Hofman, H. H. Working conference on science education for handicapped students: Position statement. In H. H. Hofman & K. S. Ricker (Eds.), *Science education and the physically handicapped.* Washington, D.C.: National Science Teachers Association (1742 Connecticut Avenue, NW), 1979, p. 17.

[2]Reprinted with permission from Ochoa, A. S., & Shuster, S. K. *Social studies in the mainstreamed classrooms, K–5.* Boulder, Col.: ERIC Clearinghouse for Social Studies/Social Studies Education Consortium, 1980, p. 19. (ERIC Document Reproduction Service No. ED 184 911).

handicapped students, concerns that must be explored include (1) deciding whether regular education or special education classes will be responsible for providing instruction; (2) choosing a pedagogical approach to instruction; (3) selecting content; (4) making modifications in the use of curricular materials and teaching practices; and (5) evaluating and selecting science and social studies materials. (An extensive list of commercially available science and social studies curricular materials has been provided to aid teachers in their search for appropriate programs.[3])

MODELS OF SERVICE

Should regular education or special education classes assume responsibility for providing science and social studies instruction to mildly handicapped students? This question is easily answered at the elementary school level, where there is often a wide range of special education service delivery models, e.g., self-contained classrooms, itinerant and resource room programs, and part-time classroom programs. Students in self-contained classrooms could be expected to receive science and social studies instruction in the special education classroom until their progress warrants a change to a less restrictive environment and/or mainstreaming into a regular classroom. On the other hand, itinerant and resource room programs at the elementary level are clearly intended to provide remediation in basic skill subjects. Students who participate in these programs are not sufficiently handicapped to warrant spending the major portion of the school day in a special education classroom and should be able to function adequately in a regular classroom with support from special education in their area of disability. Therefore, itinerant and resource room students could be expected to receive science and social studies instruction in the regular classroom with minor modifications made by regular classroom teachers if necessary. Part-time students fall somewhere in between self-contained and resource room students in terms of their needs for special education support. In part-time programs, it is entirely possible that some students will receive science and/or social studies instruction in the special education classroom while others may participate in regular education programs.

At the secondary-school level, where the primary mode of service delivery is likely to be the resource room, the issue of responsibility is more complex because of the range of content subjects offered, the organizational complexity of secondary schools, and the varying competency requirements of different schools. Goodman and Mann (1976) felt that the secondary learning disabilities (LD) program should be limited to the teaching of basic skills, and special education teachers should not be expected to be subject matter specialists. They also argued that the LD program should not be expected to provide tutorial help to assist LD students in studying regular education subjects (Goodman & Mann, 1976).

> From a practical standpoint, if the instructional programs for the learning disabilities secondary class have no curricular limits . . . the demands placed on the LD teacher may become so great that they are unrealizable. . . . Although tutorial services are

---

[3]Because of a general dearth of awareness of the availability of science and social studies materials, this extensive bibliography is included as appendices at the end of the chapter. Readers should have little difficulty in acquiring similar bibliographies for reading and arithmetic from several other sources (see Chapters 14 & 15).

legitimate, particularly during the integration of students in regular programs, we feel that they should not be the primary responsibility of the learning disabilities teacher. (p. 102)[4]

This position was supported by Hartwell, Wiseman, and Van Reusen (1979) who believed that the special education teacher should focus exclusively on the teaching of basic skills. To enable the special education teacher to concentrate on basic skills, they advocated the use of programs such as the Parallel Alternate Curriculum (PAC), a program developed by the Child Service Demonstration Program at Arizona State University in cooperation with the Mesa, Arizona, Public Schools. The objectives of PAC are (1) to provide mildly handicapped students with alternative methods for covering the regular education course content by utilizing methods and materials that permit them to bypass their learning problems, and (2) to provide regular education teachers with a means of individualizing instruction for mildly handicapped students. In this program, the regular classroom content is presented through the use of taped books, videotaped materials, movies, slides, lectures, and various forms of discussion. The entire program is directed by the regular classroom teacher, thus freeing the special education teacher to concentrate exclusively on the teaching of basic skills.

Mosby (1979), on the other hand, advocated a resource room program that provides students with tutorial support, such as the Developmental Bypass Program (DBP), developed by the Franklin County, Missouri, Special Education Cooperative. The program, which was developed for junior high school learning-disabled students, is designed to (1) help students gain the knowledge, concepts, and information necessary to cope with the regular classroom curriculum, and (2) provide special education teachers with a framework within which to support the educational program in the regular classroom. As in the PAC approach, reading materials are taped and a variety of audio-visual materials are used to teach content. In schools where DBP is used, regular education teachers *are not* expected to modify their approach to teaching LD students who are receiving tutorial assistance from the resource room teacher. Mosby (1979) stated that while the program has not resulted in higher grades, students made significant gains in learning as measured by a standardized achievement test.

The lack of agreement about the appropriate mission of the resource room program at the secondary level is likely to persist until there is clear empirical evidence to indicate whether or not it is possible to remediate basic learning problems of students at the secondary level and whether remediation of basic skills enhances overall achievement and promotes functional literacy, especially among senior high school students. The solutions to these dilemmas have important implications for the function of resource room programs. If it is possible to remediate basic learning difficulties with general beneficial effects at this age level, the position that Goodman and Mann (1976) and Hartwell et al. (1979) took is justified. On the other hand, if it is not possible to remediate basic skills at this point in students' lives, the instructional time and resources of the resource room program might be better spent on providing students with tutorial assistance in their mainstream subjects. Based on our collective teaching experience, we suggest that

---

[4]Reprinted with permission from Goodman, L., & Mann, L. *Learning disabilities in the secondary school.* New York: Grune & Stratton, 1976, p. 102.

both positions, and all of the alternatives that fall between them, are valid. For some students, an appropriate alternative may be regular class placement with tutorial support from the resource room, and for others, instruction may be more appropriately provided in a special education classroom. The programmatic choice must address the individual student's needs.

While the concern of special educators is on determining the function of the resource room and the role of the resource room teacher at the secondary level, the concern of regular education teachers is on their lack of training in teaching students with learning and behavior problems. Regular education teachers argue that in view of their training in regular education, it is unrealistic to expect them to effectively modify teaching methods and curricula to meet the needs of special education students. If science and social studies instruction for the mildly handicapped is to be offered through regular education programs, then clearly a support system must be designed to assist the regular education staff in (1) using alternative methods for presenting information; (2) providing additional structure for students with organizational difficulties; (3) providing alternative assignments; and (4) utilizing alternative methods for measuring progress. In order to fully understand each student's unique needs, the regular education teacher should have access to the student's individualized education plan (IEP) and other pertinent educational records. In addition, the regular education teacher must be given frequent opportunities to communicate with special education teachers about students' learning styles and characteristics, behavioral motivational needs, and instructional levels. Finally, the regular education teacher must be given assistance in grading students who are working up to their potential but lagging behind the rest of the class. While the needs of regular education teachers are evident, how to fill these needs is not so clear. A number of critical questions warrant consideration.

THE DISCOVERY APPROACH VERSUS THE TRADITIONAL APPROACH

Until the 1960s, a didactic approach to science and social studies instruction was utilized, with emphasis primarily on the major facts, concepts, and principles of these disciplines. As a result of research in the psychology of learning based on the theories of Bruner, Gagne, and Piaget, the instructional emphasis in science and social studies shifted from content per se to an emphasis on the processes inherent in these disciplines (Williamson, Evans, Fox, & Nice, 1973). A variety of new curricular programs emerged, at both the elementary and secondary levels, which focused primarily on the inquiry process. The goal of these new programs was to provide students with a means for handling expanding fields of knowledge rather than for acquiring a finite body of information or facts. Students began to study content not as an end in itself, but as a means of developing concepts; the emphasis changed from rote memorization of content to the analysis and synthesis of content. Teachers were expected to serve as facilitators of the inquiry process by guiding investigations through skillful questioning and the provision of appropriate materials and information.

While the programs that emerged during the 1960s and 1970s were designed for nonhandicapped children, Boekel and Steele (1972) believed that many aspects of these programs are relevant to the education of handicapped students:

> They focus on process rather than collection of facts. They focus on skills utilized in thinking about and solving problems. They highlight exploration in working with materials and doing things. . . . They do develop sequentially a carefully selected set of concepts. Moreover, they have all been tested in the classroom. . . . Materials such as these do help children learn to think as well as interest and excite them. (p. 5)[5]

Two science programs based on the inquiry approach, Me Now and Me and My Environment, were designed specifically for educable mentally handicapped (EMH) students (EMH and EMR are used interchangeably here). The programs were developed by the Biological Science Curriculum Study (BSCS), which was funded in 1969 by the Bureau of Education for the Handicapped to develop and field test instructional materials in the life services for the 11–19-year-old population of EMH students. Both programs[6] stress a "hands-on" approach in which students plan and carry out scientific investigations. Me Now is designed to help students develop an understanding of the human body and how it functions and grows. Me and My Environment is aimed toward the development of an understanding of environmental conditions and how people influence the environment. The curriculum is designed to foster the "development of a sense of relationship and empathy with other living things that will lead to a positive regard and caring about what effects them" (Boekel & Steele, 1972, (p. 8). These programs have undergone extensive field testing and revision (Gromme, 1975; Meyer & others, 1976; Robinson & Tolman, 1970; Tolman, 1973).

In addition to these curricula, which were designed specifically for EMH students, there have been some attempts to modify process approaches designed for science instruction with normal students for special education students. Wilson and Koran (1978) used Science—A Process Approach (S-APA) with a small group of mildly handicapped children. Five of the children were culturally deprived, three were emotionally disturbed, one was brain injured, and two were undiagnosed. Wilson and Koran (1978) concluded that "S-APA materials were suitable for diagnosing the entering behavior of special education students and, with modification, effective materials for initiating an individually prescribed program in special education classes" (p. 31). S-APA has also been used with elementary educable mentally retarded (EMR) and learning disabled students by three school districts in Mississippi as a result of their participation in a project that addressed group and individually prescribed instruction for handicapped children (Aberdeen, 1974).

Another science program that uses a discovery approach is the American Association for the Advancement of Science Program (AAAS). This program has been used successfully with elementary and middle-school learning disabled students in the Wayne-Carroll Public Schools in Wayne, Nebraska. "The AAAS

---

[5]Reprinted with permission from Boekel, N. & Steele, J. M. Science education for the exceptional child. *Focus on Exceptional Children*, 1972, *4*, 5.

[6]These programs are commercially produced by the Hubbard Scientific Company of Northbrook, Ill.

program nearly eliminates the need for Curriculum Modification for children with learning disabilities'' (Owens, 1974, p. 142).

In the area of social studies education, few educators have attempted to adapt the inquiry approach for mildly handicapped students, with the exception of Curtis (1974), who adapted the method to instruct slow learners in the study of community problems. Under Curtis' model, students became active participants in a learning process that included the following steps (Curtis, 1974).

1. The identification and selection of a particular community problem to be studied.
2. The formulation of appropriate hypotheses that suggest reasons for the existence of the problem and serve as guidelines to the inquiry.
3. The collection of relevant data.
4. The analysis of the data by: (a) evaluating the reliability of the sources, (b) distinguishing between fact and fiction, (c) distinguishing among statements of facts, opinions, and values, and (d) drawing inferences from the facts.
5. The acceptance, rejection, or modification of the hypotheses.
6. The discussion concerning the need to take action on the problem.
7. The identification of legitimate courses of action for protesting the existence of the problem or for suggesting possible programs for the remediation of the problem.
8. The identification of the possible consequences of each course of action.
9. The taking of whatever action is considered by the students to be necessary and appropriate.
10. The evaluation of the action. (pp. 458–459)[7]

Curtis (1974) stressed that in using this approach with slow learners, it is important to select problems for study that are relevant to the lives of the students, and to have students collect data through door-to-door surveys, interviews, etc., to provide for learning experiences that are "concrete."

There have been few studies of the effectiveness of the inquiry approach as compared with other methods of teaching science and social studies to mildly handicapped students; the results of these studies are inconclusive. Bacon (1976) did not find any achievement differences between groups of EMH students exposed to an inquiry method of teaching (inductive approach) and those exposed to a deductive method of instruction. In a study involving 207 educable mentally retarded students, Davies and Ball (1978) found that students who used the inquiry approach contained in the Elementary Science Study Curriculum (ESS) performed significantly better than did a non-ESS group on selected science skills including communicating, observing, and inferring. Esler, Midgett, and Bird (1977) conducted a pilot study involving the use of ESS with a group of 12 students with specific learning disabilities. Following a pretest, which was composed of three Piagetian conservation tasks, students were taught the Sink or Float unit of the ESS curriculum in seven 30-minute sessions over a period of 4 weeks. Post-test results indicating the effect of the treatment on the conservation abilities of individual children were as follows (Esler et al., 1977):

1. Conservation of Liquid Volume: three children advanced from nonconservers to conservers.

---

[7]Reprinted with permission from Curtis, C. K. Social studies for the slow learner. *The Clearing House*, 1974, *48*, 458–459.

2. Conservation of Weight: two children advanced from nonconservers to transitional, two from transitional to conservers, and one from nonconserver to conserver.
3. Conservation of Displacement Volume: one child advanced from nonconserver to transitional, one from transitional to conserver, and two from nonconserver to conserver. (p. 182)[8]

Esler et al. (1977) conducted a second pilot study in which the Beginnings unit of the Science Curriculum Improvement Study (SCIS) was taught to a group of 9 students for 4 months for a half hour each day. The Slosson Intelligence Test, the Metropolitan Readiness Test, and five Piagetian conservation tasks were used as pre- and post-test instruments. Students' gains were not significant as measured by these tests. Students' performance on the five Piagetian conservation tasks did not improve significantly as a result of their participation in the study.

In classrooms today, teachers appear to be shifting from the inquiry method to a more traditional approach to teaching science and social studies. This shift is particularly evident at the elementary school level where teachers have not had sufficient training in science and social studies to be comfortable with inquiry methods and do not universally accept the assumptions on which the methods are based. According to Hall and Jones (1976) science and social studies programs based on the inquiry approach

> were and are considered to be innovative . . . use manipulative materials for learners (a la psychological input), and call for student involvement in not-always-memory topics. Of course, each of these procedures stemmed from another set of *assumptions* about learning and instruction—learning is an active process. . . . The problem with the new programs soon became obvious when these latter assumptions were not found to hold in many classrooms. (p. 35)[9]

Choosing the approach for teaching science and social studies to mildly handicapped students is not easy. In light of a dearth of empirical research and practical experience, special educators have to make their selections based upon their knowledge of the learning characteristics of the students, the training and background of the teachers, and the resources of the local school district. No matter how strong the support for the use of the inquiry process, it is unwise to undertake this approach unless teachers are well trained in its application, and administrators are prepared and able to commit the time and resources necessary to support teachers in this effort.

CONTENT FACTORS

The selection of content to be included in science and social studies programs should be based upon the students' ability to understand abstract concepts, their ability to generalize from one learning situation to another, and their overall level of basic skill development. For some mildly handicapped students, the content of regular education science and social studies programs may be appropriate if modi-

---

[8]From Esler, W. K., Midgett, J., & Bird, R. C. Elementary Science materials and the exceptional child. *Science Education,* 1977, *61,* 182. Reprinted by permission of John Wiley & Sons, Inc.

[9]Reprinted with permission from Hall, G. E., & Jones, H. L. *Competency-based education: A process for the improvement of instruction.* Englewood Cliffs: Prentice-Hall, 1976, p. 35.

fications can be made in presentation to minimize the effect of the handicapping condition upon achievement. Certainly, articulate mildly handicapped students should be exposed to the same content that articulate students in regular education programs study. However, there are many mildly handicapped students whose ability to comprehend abstract ideas is very limited, and for these students, the content decision should be "guided by the criteria of relevancy to adult adjustment and community living skills" (Turnbull & Schulz, 1979, p. 260). Heavy emphasis should be placed on the practical application of theory rather than on the study of theory per se, and knowledge and skills should be taught through direct student involvement in a variety of concrete learning activities.

Turnbull and Schulz (1979) advocated an emphasis on the practical application of concepts for children of all ages, not just secondary level pupils (Turnbull & Schulz, 1979):

> Sometimes the issue of relevant curriculum decisions about adult adjustment and community living is postponed until the senior high years. By that time, some handicapped students have wasted inordinate amounts of time on topics that have no personal value to them. Science and social studies instruction even at the early elementary levels is preparing the student for lifelong adjustment. Students who are handicapped by mental retardation, for example, need the most careful use of instructional time. In almost every case, they are going to learn less than their chronological age peers, and they will probably have lower problem-solving abilities as adults. As a result, there is a high premium on the value of every instructional hour that they spend in school. Relevance to concept development is a central curriculum concern. For every topic the teacher considers including in the science and social studies curriculum, questions should be asked: Will it help the student be more independent in the community, employment setting, and/or at home? What is the jeopardy of the student not knowing this information? Will the student be receiving this information from other sources? (p. 260)[10]

Turnbull and Schulz (1979) suggested that in order to identify what is relevant, committees of science and social studies teachers should systematically analyze their curriculum guides to determine which concepts are essential to adult adjustment and community living skills and what information must be learned in order to have an adequate understanding of the concepts. These essential concepts would then be used to form the basis of the science and social studies curriculum for those mildly handicapped students who are unable to master coursework that is highly theoretical and abstract in nature. This type of curriculum analysis requires a major commitment of time, effort, and resources; however, there are many students in regular education programs who could also benefit from the approach.

Consideration must also be given to the sequence of teaching skills and concepts within the science and social studies curriculum. "If curricular design is not organized in sequential learning steps that lead to concept formation or development, there will be major content gaps that contribute to failure experiences" (Herlihy & Herlihy, 1980, p. 45). Herlihy and Herlihy (1980) also propose the use of the content checklist as an instructional tool that will assist the teacher in sequencing skills:

---

[10]Reprinted with permission from Turnbull, A. P., & Schulz, J. B. *Mainstreaming handicapped students: A guide for the classroom teacher.* Boston: Allyn & Bacon, 1979, p. 260.

The content checklist format . . . is made up of broad subject or skill areas broken down into specific subcomponents and placed into a sequence using a task analysis procedure. . . . It would seem that necessary components of a skill-development hierarchy in the social studies would include: access to skill hierarchies/sequences for the different content areas within the social studies curriculum from basic information and facts, extending through related concepts and generalizations, and ending with specific skills to be attained by this sequence . . . [and] identification of which facts, concepts, generalizations, and skills the individual already possesses. (pp. 45–46)[11]

Contrary to an opinion often expressed among teachers, the inclusion of science and social studies in the curriculum of the mildly handicapped need not detract from instruction in basic skills. Science and social studies instruction provides many opportunities to teach and reinforce basic skills. For example, at the elementary level, basic skills may be taught and reinforced through a great many science and social studies related activities: a study of the post office can begin with a visit to an actual post office. As part of the preparation for the visit, the teacher can read a story about the post office and conduct a directed listening activity. Following the trip, students can write thank you letters to the postmaster, thus providing the teacher with the opportunity to teach students the format for a friendly letter. Students may then decide to construct a post office of their own right in the classroom. Lists of required materials will have to be drawn up and a step-by-step sequence of steps outlined. The teacher can teach students to measure to the inch and/or half inch in preparation for the actual construction. "Wanted" posters can be incorporated into the behavior modification program using captions such as "Wanted—The Hardest Worker" or "Wanted—The Student with the Best Manners." Other possible language arts and mathematics activities related to the unit of study include

1. Constructing mailboxes out of cardboard milk containers. The teacher can exchange written messages with the students through the use of the mailboxes.
2. Buying stamps at the post office. This provides the opportunity for the teacher to teach students to count change and make change.
3. Addressing envelopes.
4. Writing and sharing stories.
5. Learning to spell words related to the unit of study.
6. Discussing how the mail gets from one place to another.
7. And so on . . .

The possibilities for incorporating the teaching of language arts and mathematics into science and social studies instruction are limitless.

At the secondary level, as well, the teaching of basic skills should be an integral part of science and social studies instruction. Botel (1977) believed that students must be taught the specific skills involved in reading science and social studies textbooks. Furthermore, he stated that science and social studies teachers

---

[11]Reprinted with permission from Herlihy, J. G., & Herlihy, M. T. *Mainstreaming in the Social Studies, Bulletin 62*, National Council for the Social Studies, 1980, pp. 45–46. (ERIC Document Reproduction Service No. ED 186 346).

at all levels must take the responsibility for providing this instruction (Botel, 1977).

> At early primary levels and continuing on through college, students should be guided and drilled through these routines of study as the means of grasping the content of the subject matter in social studies and science texts. While students will become increasingly self-directing in using these routines for independent or peer group study, it cannot be assumed at any grade level that students know how to use a unified study procedure independently. For that reason the teaching of this key reading/study strategy, as it pertains to a certain subject, is the responsibility of each content teacher at every grade level. (p. 14)[12]

Instruction in reading content materials is especially important to mildly handicapped students who receive science and social studies instruction in regular education classrooms. In addition, Botel (1977) believed that these students should receive specific help in developing other study skills as well:

1. Organizing a notebook to take notes from listening and reading.
2. Preparing for and taking standardized and curriculum-related tests, whether objective or subjective.
3. Writing reports.
4. Solving word problems (in math).
5. Reading scientific articles and lab reports.
6. Following directions in shop manuals and recipes. (pp. 14–15) (See footnote 12 for source.)

The selection of content of science and social studies programs should be based upon the abilities and skills of the students for whom the programs are intended. For mildly handicapped students, instruction in content subjects should provide opportunities to learn and practice basic skills as well as provide exposure to specialized material.

TEACHING THE MILDLY HANDICAPPED

Since most science and social studies programs are designed for use with nonhandicapped students, the suggested lesson plans and methods of instruction provided in the teacher's guides frequently do not address the learning characteristics of the mildly handicapped. Thus, it becomes the responsibility of teachers, whether special or regular educators, to modify their use of the curricular materials and to adapt their teaching methods to meet the needs of handicapped students. This is beginning to be addressed in college textbooks and journal articles, and from a review of a small but growing literature, it appears that within content area subjects, modifications are most likely to be made in the presentation of content, methods for evaluating progress, and structure of assignments. In addition, the literature stresses the need for teachers to provide a tightly structured learning environment for students who have difficulty organizing their work and structuring their use of time.

---

[12]Reprinted with permission from Botel, M. *A comprehensive reading communication arts plan* (Working ed.). Pennsylvania Department of Education, 1977, pp. 14–15.

Content Presentation

Many mildly handicapped students experience similar learning problems regardless of their classification or label. The problems mentioned most frequently in the literature include reading and written-language disabilities; poor attention and concentration; impaired long- and short-term memory for unrelated facts; lack of motivation; poor understanding of temporal, spatial, and quantitative concepts; and poor comprehension of abstract ideas. Because of these problems, mildly handicapped students have difficulty mastering content that is presented to them in the traditional teaching format—reading the textbook, listening to the teacher's lecture, and participating in the follow-up discussion. They may also find it difficult to understand information that they cannot relate to concrete experiences and impossible to memorize isolated facts such as the capitals of the states or the presidents of the United States. Hartwell et al. (1979) offered a number of suggestions for altering content presentation to ameliorate the problems that mildly handicapped students encounter:

1. Lecture/discussion approach. Develop a brief outline of planned material and present it to the class before the lecture.
2. Audiovisual presentation. Use movies, slides, filmstrips, video, radio, transparencies, records, etc.
3. Guest speakers.
4. Small group discussion.
5. Individual discussion with instructor.
6. Programmed learning. Could be reading or a combination of audiovisual and reading.
7. Reading. Silently, simultaneously with taped version, listening to teacher or other student read aloud, listening to a paraphrased version of the material and following with charts, diagrams, or printed material.
8. Field trips.
9. Projects: Hands-on approach to making a model or other art project that would help establish academic concepts, facts, etc.
10. Peer tutoring. To be used outside of the classroom.
11. Buddy system. To be used in the classroom.
14. Independent study. Established upon agreement between teacher and student.
15. Minicourses. Content units are broken into smaller learning components. . . .
17. Learning centers. Smaller area of classroom where individual concepts are taught through self motivating materials (possible audiovisual).
18. Note taking. Have high achievers take notes with carbon paper to be given to low achievers. . . .
21. Supplementary texts and other written material. High-interest and low-vocabulary reading materials. (p. 31)[13]

Modification of content material for mildly handicapped students has been discussed by other authors as well. Turnbull and Schulz (1979) provided a very thorough discussion of the four basic categories of instructional methods used in typical science and social studies classes (discussion, media, reading, and "doing") and the modifications of these methods that may be necessary for handi-

---

[13]Reprinted with permission from Hartwell, L. K., Wiseman, D. E., & Van Revsen, A. Modifying course content for mildly handicapped students at the secondary level. *Teaching Exceptional Children*, 1979, *12*, 31–32.

capped students. Ochoa and Shuster (1980) discussed the learning characteristics of various types of handicapped students, and, for each exceptionality, they provided examples of how to modify actual lessons taken from regular education social studies texts.

Davis (1977) presented a number of techniques designed to help improve reading through the teaching of science. His suggestions were intended to improve the reading of laboratory assignments and textbook assignments and to help students to improve their vocabulary. Deshler and Graham (1980) presented suggestions for the effective use of taped content materials. Specific topics discussed included (1) deciding what should be taped; (2) teaching text usage and study skills; (3) utilizing a marking system to assist students to follow the text while listening to a tape; and (4) using techniques that will foster comprehension of taped materials.

In a recent publication by the National Council for Social Studies, Herlihy and Herlihy (1980) discussed a variety of instructional strategies that teachers can employ in teaching mainstreamed students. These strategies include (1) grouping students for instruction; (2) developing new courses; (3) rewriting textbooks; (4) using a worksheet approach; and (5) preparing individualized programs for mainstreamed students.

Adams, Coble, and Hounshell (1977); Coble, Hounshell, and Adams (1977); Hallenbeck (1974); and Owens (1974) also provided ideas for organizing and presenting science and social studies content to mildly handicapped students.

Evaluating Progress

Many mildly handicapped students have difficulty taking tests because of poor reading, writing, and spelling skills; difficulty following directions; difficulty in working under time restraints; inability to memorize unrelated facts such as dates and lists of names and places; or varied combinations of these disabilities. Hartwell et al. (1979) suggested the following alternative methods for evaluating student progress:

1. Open tests. Students use textbooks, notes, study guides, etc. Short answer and essay responses are most appropriate with this format.
2. Closed tests. Students must rely on skills, concepts, and facts they have learned or mastered without the use of notes or textbook. Multiple choice, true/false, and matching items are most appropriate with this format.
3. Teacher reads tests. Students respond orally, in writing, or both.
4. Reduced reading level of tests.
5. Taped tests. Students listen to pre-recorded tape of the test and respond on answer sheets.
6. Small group tests.
7. Student made tests.
8. Take-home tests.
9. Alternative projects.
10. Oral tests or oral reports.
11. Student answers questions on tape recorder for teacher to correct later.
12. Students administer tests. A competent peer administers test orally and can either write down student responses or have the students write their own responses. This format is recommended for use with individuals or small groups. (pp. 31–32) (See footnote 13 for source.)

The use of alternative approaches to evaluation provides students with the opportunity to indicate what they have learned about science and social studies content without penalizing them for their reading, writing, and related disabilities. No doubt, many nonlabeled students having problems in the classroom could also benefit from alternative approaches to the traditional pencil and paper test.

Assignments

The types of assignments that are traditionally associated with instruction in science and social studies often prove to be extremely difficult for students who have problems with reading, writing, and/or oral expression. It may be necessary to provide these students with alternative means for addressing certain assignments. For example, an eighth-grade assignment involving a description of the current energy crisis in the United States as it relates to the development and use of nuclear power could be completed through one or more of the following activities:

1. Writing a report.
2. Dictating a report using a tape recorder.
3. Developing an outline based on the reading of several articles that address the topic.
4. Developing diagrams or graphs illustrating the United States's increased energy demands over the past decades and projected energy demands over the next decade.
5. Writing questions and conducting a survey to assess the community's feeling about the expanded use of nuclear power.
6. Watching a TV special on the topic and participating in a class discussion about it.
7. Giving an oral report to the class.
8. Creating a collage illustrating energy problems and making an oral presentation about it.
9. Giving an oral report about an article from a weekly news magazine.
10. Giving an oral book report.
11. Participating in a panel discussion.
12. Inviting a guest speaker to class and having several students interview him or her.
13. Making a scrapbook of current events related to the topic.
14. Writing letters requesting free pamphlets and brochures about the topic.

Teachers often state that parents and students would not respond favorably to the concept of alternative assignments. This problem can be minimized if teachers carefully select alternative assignments to insure that they are equally demanding in terms of the time and effort required to complete them, and require students to perform at a level reflecting their capabilities. In this way, students are not penalized for disabilities over which they have no control, and standards for performance are not compromised.

Providing Structure

The inability of many mildly handicapped students to structure content, assignments, and their use of time is a major factor in their difficulty in mastering science and social studies and other content subjects. Mildly handicapped students often are unable to discern main ideas from supporting details and to arrange events in a logical sequence. In addition, they may also find it extremely difficult to organize an assignment into a series of logical steps. Compounding these difficulties is the inability to structure time. To assist students who present these problems, Price, Kane, Bowman, and Ness (1982) recommended the following techniques:

1. Providing students with study guides.
2. Cutting up worksheets (at the elementary level). Reducing the amount of information on worksheets (at the secondary level).
3. Breaking up large assignments, e.g., reports, into series of steps that are monitored by the teacher and on which time limits are imposed for each step.
4. Grading separate parts of an assignment rather than giving one overall grade.
5. Providing students with very structured directions, both written and oral.
6. Providing folders, notebooks, etc., to help students organize their papers: e.g., folders with pockets, one for in-class assignments and one for homework.
7. Giving the student a schedule of expected assignments, tests, reports, etc., at the *beginning* of a unit of study, to help the student structure his or her time.
8. Providing contracts or rewards for students who are working on specific organizational skills.
9. Providing students with a checklist, so they can check off assignments as they complete their work.
10. Providing students with a homework book, so that all assignments are recorded in one book. This is particularly useful in junior high school and high school when students move among so many different teachers.
11. Using a buddy system; i.e., each student has a friend who checks during the day to be sure that all homework assignments have been copied and who offers assistance with any other classroom details, if necessary.
12. Allowing students to use timers to help them structure their time (elementary level).

Modifications must be made if mildly handicapped students are to successfully complete science and social studies courses. Many of the modifications suggested can easily be incorporated into a teacher's repertoire of skills and require minimum changes in existing science and social studies programs. Certainly there are many students, not just the mildly handicapped, who can benefit from these practices.

SELECTING MATERIALS AND PROGRAMS FOR THE MILDLY HANDICAPPED

The selection of science and social studies materials/programs should be based on an evaluation of how well they meet a set of predetermined criteria. The criteria provide a basis for comparing materials/programs and help to insure that the materials/programs chosen are appropriate for a given student(s) within a particular instructional setting. To provide teachers with a framework for evaluating the organization, format, and content of science and social studies materials/programs, the authors have developed a checklist for Evaluating Science and Social Studies Programs (ESSP). The criteria included in the ESSP (Table 16-1) are a result of the authors' own experiences in selecting curricular programs for use with mildly handicapped students, as well as a review of existing checklists and rating scales (Brown, 1975; Cohen, Alberto, & Troutman, 1979; Eash, 1974; Watsen, 1976).

The ESSP has been divided into four areas: teacher's guide, student text, supplementary materials, and evaluation component. Within each area there are a series of questions that are to be answered *yes* or *no*. Each question addresses a specific criterion that has direct impact on an instructional material/program's utility with mildly handicapped students. If the material/program being evaluated meets the criterion, the question is answered *yes;* if it does not, the question is answered *no*. The number of *yesses* and *noes* within each of the four areas provides a basis for comparison of individual components across various materials/programs, as well as a basis for the comparison of materials/programs as a whole. Teachers should be aware that few materials will satisfy every criterion specified. The percentage of positive to negative answers provides a rating, of sorts, of a particular material/program. But teachers should not base their selection on percentage figures alone; while percentages provide an indication of how well the material/program measures up to the desired criteria, the teacher still has to weigh the importance of each criterion against the intended use of the program, the needs of the students, and any constraints that will ultimately affect the final choice.

Teacher's Guide

The teacher's guide is the most important tool available to the teacher for planning instruction. Unfortunately, the teacher's guide often receives very little attention when instructional materials are being evaluated. A teacher's guide, like a student textbook, is unlikely to be used unless it is attractive in appearance, well-organized, and readable. The intent of the instructional material should be discussed, and specific instructions for the use of the guide should be provided. An overview of the major content areas within a given level, as well as a brief outline of the content of preceding and subsequent levels of the program, should be included. This information is helpful in understanding the prerequisite skills needed for a given unit of instruction and provides a sense of where the unit fits into the overall scope of the program.

Careful attention needs to be given to the suggestions in the guide for individualizing instruction. A guide that contains suggestions for a variety of learning experiences and provides lists of resources, including reading materials on the same topic written at a lower/higher reading level, audiovisual materials, and other sources of information, can be of great assistance to the teacher who is planning lessons for a heterogeneous group of students.

In addition to suggesting ways of individualizing instruction, the guide should provide recommendations for managing the instructional process. General curric-

Table 16-1
Science and Social Studies Programs Checklist

Teacher's Guide

Content

   Is there a scope and sequence chart of topics? _____ YES _____ NO

   Does it provide:

     a listing of major topics and subtopics by
     level? _____ YES _____ NO

     a listing of major topics and subtopics for
     preceding and following levels? _____ YES _____ NO

   Are instructional objectives provided? _____ YES _____ NO

   Are the objectives

     listed by chapter/unit and by lesson? _____ YES _____ NO

     written in behavioral terms? _____ YES _____ NO

Instructional Procedures

   Are instructional lesson plans provided? _____ YES _____ NO

   Do they suggest

     alternative methods for presenting information
     to students of differing ability levels? _____ YES _____ NO

     alternative activities and assignments for
     students of differing ability levels? _____ YES _____ NO

     alternative materials for students of differing
     ability levels? _____ YES _____ NO

     alternative methods for measuring student
     progress? _____ YES _____ NO

   Are lesson plans well-organized? _____ YES _____ NO

   Do they include

     a list of objectives? _____ YES _____ NO

     a list of new vocabulary words? _____ YES _____ NO

     lists of materials needed for experiments and
     demonstrations _____ YES _____ NO

     page numbers of corresponding student texts,
     workbooks, and testing materials? _____ YES _____ NO

Reference Materials

Are reference materials suggested for the
teacher? _____ YES _____ NO

   Do they include

     a glossary of terms? _____ YES _____ NO

     a list of books, pamphlets, and periodicals
     that correspond to each unit of instruction? _____ YES _____ NO

(continued)

Table 16-1 (continued)

Do they include

a list of audiovisual materials, including films, transparencies, and records, that correspond to each unit of instruction? _____ YES _____ NO

Are reference materials suggested for the student? _____ YES _____ NO

Do they include

a glossary of terms? _____ YES _____ NO

a list of books, pamphlets, and periodicals that correspond to each unit of instruction? _____ YES _____ NO

a list of audiovisual materials, including films, transparencies, and records, that correspond to each unit of instruction? _____ YES _____ NO

Student Text

Physical Appearance

Do the pages appear uncluttered? _____ YES _____ NO

Is the size of the print appropriate for the maturity level of the students? _____ YES _____ NO

Are the illustrations appropriate for the maturity level of the students? _____ YES _____ NO

Structure

Does the text provide advance organizers such as

study questions? _____ YES _____ NO

study objectives? _____ YES _____ NO

topical headings? _____ YES _____ NO

new vocabulary words? _____ YES _____ NO

introductory paragraph(s)? _____ YES _____ NO

Does the text highlight key words through the use of italics and boldface print? _____ YES _____ NO

Do illustrations

add meaning to and help clarify the written text? _____ YES _____ NO

appear on the same page as corresponding text? _____ YES _____ NO

Does the text reinforce major concepts through the use of

study questions? _____ YES _____ NO

summary paragraph(s)? _____ YES _____ NO

suggested activities? _____ YES _____ NO

suggested readings?	_____ YES_____ NO

Readability

Is the readability level of the text suitable for the intended audience?	_____ YES_____ NO
Are new concepts and vocabulary introduced at a suitable pace for the intended audience?	_____ YES_____ NO
Is the length of written text suitable for the intended audience?	_____ YES_____ NO

Supplementary Materials

Content

Is the readability level of the written text suitable for the intended audience?	_____ YES_____ NO
Do the activities reinforce concepts presented in the textbooks?	_____ YES_____ NO
Can the students use the supplementary materials independently?	_____ YES_____ NO

Format

Are directions clear?	_____ YES_____ NO
Are the activities of sufficient variety?	_____ YES_____ NO
Are the supplementary materials consumable?	_____ YES_____ NO
Can the text and supplementary materials be ordered separately?	

Evaluation Component

Content

Is the readability level of the evaluation component suitable for the intended audience?	_____ YES_____ NO
Does the format of test questions parallel the format of questions used in the student text and supplementary materials?	_____ YES_____ NO
Do tests lend themselves to alternative methods of presentation by the teacher and alternative modes of response from students?	_____ YES_____ NO

Format

Are test questions cross-referenced to specific instructional objectives?	_____ YES_____ NO
Are answer keys provided?	_____ YES_____ NO
Does evaluation occur frequently enough to provide the teacher and student with ongoing information about students' progress?	_____ YES_____ NO

ular goals assist the teacher in developing annual goals for students. Daily lesson plans that include instructional objectives help the teacher to break down large units of instruction into manageable components. A varied list of teaching activities can provide the teacher with ideas for individualizing instruction. Lists of resources related to the topic save time and energy that would otherwise have to be spent locating appropriate audiovisual materials and reading materials. Sample formats for reporting and summarizing progress should be included, as they will facilitate communication with parents and between teachers.

Student Text

Physical appearance, readability, and structure of content are important factors to be considered when selecting science and social studies textbooks. For secondary students who require reading materials written at a low readability level, it is often very difficult to find science and social studies textbooks that are both mature looking and readable. Secondary students are generally concerned about the size of the print and the sophistication of the illustrations. They are embarrassed to use books that have large print, covers that look like they were designed for elementary school students, covers that designate the elementary grade level for which they were intended, and illustrations that depict much younger students than themselves.

In addition to physical appearance, the readability level of the material must also be given strong consideration. Readability levels are often furnished by the publisher of the material/program. However, if these are not available, there are several readability formulas that can be used for estimating the reading level of a particular set of printed matter, including the Fry (1968), the Lorge (1948), and the Dale-Chall (1948) formulas. Holliday and Braun (1979) discussed two other methods for evaluating the readability of science materials: subjective judgment methods and the Cloze Test. In addition, they listed a number of suggestions that have been useful in reducing the readability load of science materials.

The amount and type of structure superimposed upon the written textual materials must be evaluated along with the physical appearance and readability. Advance organizers such as study questions and topical headings are important because they provide direction to the reader and help to identify key concepts and main ideas. The activities that appear at the end of a chapter in a textbook are equally important because they assist the student in summarizing, evaluating, and synthesizing information. In some textbooks, questions are written in the margin next to the portion of the text that contains the answer. This format has the advantages of (1) providing the student with a specific purpose for reading; (2) helping the student to locate answers to questions more easily; and (3) reducing the reading demands on students who read very slowly and laboriously. Illustrations, diagrams, graphs, and charts can help to develop and clarify concepts. In textbooks used with elementary-school level students, these types of visual aids should appear on the same page as the corresponding text to avoid confusion and to encourage students to utilize visual aids as a tool to assist in word recognition. According to Holliday and Braun (1979), the importance of content structures should not be underestimated:

Recent studies . . . suggest that students reading textual materials must organize major and minor ideas in a logical fashion. Students remember textual information by either choosing the structure employed by the author or imposing a structure of their own. Apparently, storage of science content in memory can most effeciently be achieved by using the writer's structure (e.g., organizational strategies). Therefore, science writers should organize their instructional materials in a clear, unambiguous, and coherent fashion. . . . Theoretically, authors describing independent concepts and their definitions should organize their writing in a "compartmentalized" fashion to permit the readers to learn and remember small portions of the total information. In contrast, authors describing broad principles and emphasizing conceptual interrelationships should use a "connective" style of writing. (p. 63)[14]

Supplementary Materials

Many commercially available science and social studies programs include supplementary materials such as records, student workbooks, tapes, pictures, charts, and maps. These materials can be valuable teaching tools; however, teachers should choose supplementary materials with the same care with which a student textbook is selected. Teachers need to ask if the materials will enhance students' understanding of concepts and/or reinforce skills.

Evaluation Component

The evaluation component of science and social studies programs should be judged in terms of how well it assists the teacher in monitoring students' progress toward the goals and objectives stated on their IEPs. An effective evaluation component (1) measures the skills and knowledge or concepts that are essential to help students cope with the demands of their world (and ultimately with the demands of the adult world); (2) provides teachers with a means of measuring students' progress in mastering specific instructional objectives; (3) suggests techniques for managing the evaluation process; and (4) provides students with performance feedback.

If teachers are teaching the skills and knowledge essential to "adult adjustment and community living skills" as noted in Turnbull and Schulz (1979), it is important that the evaluation of student progress focus on these skills as well. In other words, in a situation in which teachers have decided that knowing the names of all the presidents of the United States is not essential to understanding the concept of *president,* students should not need to memorize the names in order to pass a test.

Pencil and paper tests are the most common means of evaluating student progress on specific instructional objectives. For mildly handicapped students, it is important that tests be judged in terms of how well they lend themselves to alternative methods of presentation by the teacher and alternative modes of re-

---

[14]Reprinted with permission from Holliday, W. G., & Braun, C. Readability of science materials. *Science Education: A Probe for Tomorrow.* Viewpoints in Teaching and Learning, School of Education, Indiana University, 1979, 55 (No. 1), 63.

sponse from students. Some tests can be modified very easily. For example, an easy alternative method for giving an essay test to a student with poor reading and writing skills is to read the questions to the student and permit the student to respond orally.

The evaluation component need not be limited to pencil and paper tests, however. Some texts suggest other means of measuring student progress, especially in science where students' ability to carry out certain tasks can only be judged through a hands-on demonstration of skills. Alternative approaches to evaluation must be sought for those students whose handicapping condition makes a pencil and paper test an invalid measure of their knowledge. Students who understand the concepts being tested should not be penalized because they have a reading disability.

The evaluation component should also provide teachers with suggested formats for keeping records of students' progress. Some curricular programs provide lists of objectives cross-referenced to specific test items. In science courses in which there may be a lot of laboratory work, it would be helpful to have checklists of observable skills and a rating scale to be used when judging students' mastery of these skills.

Regardless of the type of evaluation and the method used to record progress, it is important that evaluation take place often enough to fulfill students' need for frequent and periodic feedback. Some students perform best if they are evaluated on a daily basis; for others, weekly or even monthly evaluation may be sufficient. Many science and social studies texts provide chapter tests; some provide unit tests covering several chapters; and others provide both chapter and unit tests.

PROGRAM EVALUATIONS

Numerous materials are available for teaching science and social studies to mildly handicapped students. Some of these materials have been specifically designed for students who have not fully mastered the basic skills they would be expected to know at their grade level. Other materials can be readily adapted for use with the mildly handicapped. Appendices 16-A–16-D, which list and discuss science and social studies materials, were compiled to aid teachers in their search for appropriate materials and programs.

The listing of curricular materials is catalogued by title and publisher. In addition, the components of each program, including texts, filmstrips, activity cards, cassettes, etc., are listed along with the grade level for which the material is intended, the reading level of the material, and a brief description of the content.

Within each area, materials have been subdivided into core programs and supplementary programs. Goodman, Stitt, Ness, and Eells (1976) felt that this distinction is an important one:

> . . . core materials represent complete and comprehensive curricular programs which embody a structure and sequence of content materials frequently ranging over one or more grade levels within a specific content. . . . Supplemental materials, on the other hand, are not generally as comprehensive but rather stress a limited range or specific area of skill development. While the use of a core curriculum extends over

a lengthy period of time, supplemental materials lend themselves to use on an "as needed basis." (pp. 4–5)[15]

The inclusion of materials in the appendices in no way constitutes an endorsement by the authors. The intention is to provide teachers with access to science and social studies materials; teachers will have to make their own judgments about the value of specific curricular materials for their students.

REFERENCES

Aberdeen Municipal Separate School District, Miss., Amory Municipal Separate School District, Miss., & Munroe County School District, Aberdeen, Miss. *Group and individually prescribed instruction for handicapped children; Instructional program model*, 1974. (ERIC Document Reproduction Service No. ED 108 429)

Adams, A. H., Coble, C. R., & Hounshell, P. B. *Mainstreaming language arts and social studies: Special ideas and activities for the whole class.* Santa Monica, Ca.: Goodyear, 1977.

Bacon, W. E. A comparison of two science teaching methods for educable mentally handicapped children (Doctoral dissertation, Loyola University of Chicago, 1976). *Dissertation Abstracts International*, 1976, *37*, 780-A–781-A.

Boekel, N., & Steele, J. M. Science education for the exceptional child. *Focus on Exceptional Children*, 1972, *4*, 1–14.

Botel, M. *A comprehensive reading communication arts plan* (Working ed.). Harrisburg: Pennsylvania Department of Education, 1977.

Brown, V. A. A basic Q-Sheet for analyzing and comparing curriculum materials and proposals. *Journal of Learning Disabilities*, 1975, *7*, 10–17.

Coble, C. R., Hounshell, P. B., & Adams, A. H. *Mainstreaming science and mathematics: Special ideas and activities for the whole class.* Santa Monica, Ca.: Goodyear, 1977.

Cohen, S. B., Alberto, P. A., & Troutman, A. Selecting and developing educational materials: An inquiry model. *Teaching Exceptional Children*, 1979, *12*, 7–11.

Curtis, C. K. Social studies for the slow learner. *The Clearing House*, 1974, *48*, 456–460.

Dale, E., & Chall, J. S. A formula for predicting readability. *Educational Research Bulletin*, 1948, *27*, 11–20, 37–54.

Davies, J. M., & Ball, D. W. Utilization of the Elementary Science Study with mentally retarded students. *Journal of Research in Science Teaching*, 1978, *15*, 281–286.

Davis, J. B. Improved reading and the teaching of science. *Clearing House*, 1977, *50*, 390–392.

Deshler, D. D., & Graham, S. Tape recording educational materials for secondary handicapped students. *Teaching Exception Children*, 1980, *12*, 52–54.

Eash, M. J. Instructional materials. In H. R. Walberg (Ed.), *Evaluating educational performance: A sourcebook of methods, instruments, and examples.* Berkeley: McCutchan, 1974.

Esler, W. K., Midgett, J., & Bird, R. C. Elementary science materials and the exceptional child. *Science Education*, 1977, *61*, 181–184.

Fry, E. B. A readability formula that saves time. *Journal of Reading*, 1968, *11*, 513–516, 575–578.

Goodman, L., & Mann, L. *Learning disabilities in the secondary school.* New York: Grune & Stratton, 1976.

Goodman, L., Stitt, M., Ness, J., & Eells, J. *Curricular materials for secondary learning disabilities programs.* Bluebell, Pa.: Montgomery County Intermediate Unit, 1976.

---

[15]Reprinted with permission from Goodman, L., Stitt, M., Ness, J., & Eells, J. *Curricular materials for secondary learning disabilities programs.* Bluebell, Pa.: Montgomery County Intermediate Unit, 1976, pp. 4–5.

Gromme, R. O. *Me and my environment formative evaluation report 4: Assessing student abilities and performances: Year 4.* Boulder, Col.: Biological Sciences Curriculum Study, 1975. (ERIC Document Reproduction Service No. ED 112 623)

Hall, G. E., & Jones, H. L. *Competency-based education: A process for the improvement of instruction.* Englewood Cliffs: Prentice-Hall, 1976.

Hallenbeck, P. N. Teaching social studies to special children. *Journal of Learning Disabilities, 1974, 7,* 18–21.

Hartwell, L. K., Wiseman, D. E., & Van Reusen, A. Modifying course content for mildly handicapped students at the secondary level. *Teaching Exceptional Children, 1979, 12,* 28–32.

Herlihy, J. G., & Herlihy, M. T. *Mainstreaming in the social studies. Bulletin 62.* Washington, D.C.: National Council for the Social Studies, 1980. (ERIC Document Reproduction Service No. ED 186 346)

Hofman, H. H. Working conference on science education for handicapped students: Position statement. In H. H. Hofman & K. S. Ricker (Eds.), *Science education and the physically handicapped.* Washington, D. C.: National Science Teachers Associations, 1979.

Hofman, H. H., & Ricker, K. S. *Science education and the physically handicapped.* Washington, D.C.: National Science Teachers Association, 1979.

Holliday, W. G., & Braun, C. Readability of science materials. *Viewpoints in Teaching and Learning, 1979, 55,* 55–66.

Lorge, I. The Lorge and Flesch readability formulae: A correction. *School and Society, 1948, 67,* 141–142.

Meyer, D. E., & others. *Me and my environment: Final formative evaluation report, a synthesis of findings.* Boulder, Col.: Biological Sciences Curriculum Study, 1976. (ERIC Document Reproduction Service No. ED 122 465)

Mosby, R. J. A bypass program of supportive instruction for secondary students with learning disabilities. *Journal of Learning Disabilities, 1979, 12,* 54–57.

Ochoa, A. S., & Shuster, S. K. *Social studies in the mainstreamed classrooms, K–5.* Boulder, Col.: Social Science Education Consortium, 1980. (ERIC Document Reproduction Service No. ED 184 911)

Owens, J. *Project success for the SLD child, curriculum modification.* Wayne, Neb.: Wayne-Carroll Public Schools, 1974. (ERIC Document Reproduction Service No. ED 089 483)

Price, M., Kane, J., Bowman F., & Ness, V. *Guide to mainstreaming planning committees.* Montgomery County, Pa.: Montgomery County Intermediate Unit, 1982.

Robinson, J. T., & Tolman, R. R. *A formative evaluation of me now. Unit 1, digestion and circulation, life sciences for the educable mentally handicapped intermediate grades (11–13 yrs.).* Boulder, Col.: Colorado University, 1970. (ERIC Document Reproduction Service No. ED 043 182)

Rose, T. L., & Lessen, E. I. Completeness and readability of 16 learning disabilities introductory texts. *Journal of Learning Disabilities, 1980, 9,* 25–27.

Tolman, R. R. *A formative evaluation of me now, life sciences for the educable mentally handicapped, intermediate grades (11–13 yrs.).* Boulder, Col.: Biological Sciences Curriculum Study, 1972. (ERIC Document Reproduction Service No. ED 071 263)

Turnbull, A. P., & Schulz, J. B. *Mainstreaming handicapped students: A guide for the classroom teacher.* Boston: Allyn & Bacon, 1979.

Watsen, B. L. Materials analysis. *Journal of Learning Disabilities, 1976, 9,* 13–21.

Williamson, S. E., Evans, T. P., Fox, F. W., & Nice, K. J. Science education. In W. J. Ellena (Ed.), *Curriculum handbook for school executives.* Arlington, Va.: American Association of School Administrators, 1973.

Wilson, J. T., & Koran, J. J. Science curriculum materials for special education students. *Education and Training of the Mentally Retarded, 1973, 8,* 30–32.

APPENDIX 16-A: CORE SCIENCE PROGRAMS

Appendix 16-A
Core Science Programs

Title and Publisher	Intended Audience	Reading Level	Components	Description
Biology and Human Progress Prentice-Hall	High school	*	Text, workbook; teacher's handbook and keys; and tests	Text provides basic biology and laboratory experiences for below-average students. Text relates biological concepts directly to people through discussion of topics such as genetic engineering, sickle cell anemia, and biology-related careers. Illustrations, a glossary, summary and discussion questions, and cognates for students whose first language is not English are included to aid learning.
The Elementary Science Study Program (ESS) Webster Division, McGraw-Hill Book Company	Grades K–9		56 activity units	This basal science program was developed under grants from the National Science Foundation. The ESS program utilizes 56 activity modules to introduce basic concepts of life, earth, and physical science. ESS modules provide a hands-on introduction to concepts, which frees students reading below level from the traditional book-centered approach.
ESS/Special Education Teacher's Guide Webster Division, McGraw-Hill Book Company	Teachers		Teacher's guide	Guide provides instructions for teachers on adapting ESS units for use in special education classrooms and adapting ESS units to the needs of special children "mainstreamed" in their classroom. The guide includes specific teaching and classroom management techniques.

(continued)

Appendix 16-A (continued)

Title and Publisher	Intended Audience	Reading Level	Components	Description
Experiential Science Program *Living Things* *The Physical World* Benefic Press	Grades K–1		*Pupil's Activity Book* and *Teacher's Big Book*	This beginning program introduces the young child to science concepts through "Things to Talk About" questions and "Things to Do" activities. It develops the child's skills in using scientific processes of observing, inferring, predicting, classifying, hypothesizing, using number relationships, and recognizing time-space relationships through easy-to-read text and pictures. Each teacher-directed lesson is followed by questions that require the child to use "accepted processes" to arrive at answers. The *Teacher's Big Book* includes sets of question and activities appropriate for children of basic, average, and advanced ability.
Exploring and Understanding Series *Exploring and Understanding Birds* *Exploring and Understanding the Human Body* *Exploring and Understanding Oceanography*	Grades 4–9		Text	This series of 12 texts develops basic concepts in life, earth, and physical science. Each activity-oriented text explores a different topic. Emphasis is placed on scientific inquiry and discovery and on developing students' skills of observing, inferring, predicting, classifying, and hypothesizing. New words are italicized and defined in the text and in a glossary. Evaluation

Title	Grades	Reading Level	Components	Description
Exploring and Understanding Rocks and Minerals *Exploring and Understanding Weather and Climate* *Exploring and Understanding Beyond the Solar System* *Exploring and Understanding Machines* *Exploring and Understanding Heat* *Exploring and Understanding Magnets and Electromagnets* *Science and the Scientist* *Science Through Experiments* Benefic Press				questions and activities are provided at the end of each chapter. *Guide and Index Volume* cross-references concepts presented in the series.
Finding Out About Living Things *Matter and Energy* *Earth and Universe* Benefic Press	Grades K–6	1.5–3.1	Media kit: student book; experiment filmstrips; cassette; experiment cards; and teacher's guide	This multimedia program utilizes the "inquiry approach" to explore concepts in three major areas: living things, matter and energy, and earth and universe. Topics in each of these major areas (e.g., living things: animals, plants, birds, and fish) are developed in four different multimedia kits. Experiments are presented through use of filmstrips and cassettes.

(continued)

Appendix 16-A (continued)

Title and Publisher	Intended Audience	Reading Level	Components	Description
Gateways to Science Webster Division, McGraw-Hill Book Company	Grades K–6	1.5–4.8	Student text; teacher's edition; and class kit	This text-based basal science program develops life, earth, and physical science concepts. Ongoing evaluation is provided through self-checks and end-of-chapter tests at each level and through evaluation appendices of levels 4, 5, and 6. Annotated teacher's edition includes chapter objectives, teaching strategies, answers to all questions in pupil's editions, reproducible activities, and tests. Class kit provides materials for experiments outlined in the teacher edition.
Ginn Elementary Science Ginn and Company	Grades K–8	*	Multimedia kit; student text; annotated teacher's edition; review spirit duplicating master or review activities book; teacher's edition, review activities book; and test duplicating masters	Each level of this program is designed to cover a year of study and is organized into eight units focusing on life, physical, and earth science. This program utilizes a five-step teaching plan: make ready, inform, experience, review, and evaluate. The text carries the burden of instruction in this series. New words are defined in the margin when they are first introduced, with pronunciation in the text. Pictures, dictionaries or glossaries are also included. Full color photographs, charts, and diagrams are used to supply context clues to explain content. Review activity sheet and review books provide

(continued)

Holt Earth Science Holt, Rinehart and Winston	Grades 4–8	Student text; teacher edition; student resource book; student resource book, teacher's edition; and test duplicating masters	game-like exercises to reinforce and summarize major ideas presented in each unit. Achievement tests are keyed to lessons and objectives for grades 3–6. The teacher's edition offers provisions for teaching science to students with sensory handicaps or learning disabilities. This text-based program investigates earth science concepts. Student objectives, summaries, and follow-up questions are included for each lesson.
Holt Elementary Science Holt, Rinehart and Winston	Grades K–6 *	Student text; teacher's edition; workbook; workbook, teacher's edition; and test duplicating masters	This text-based basal program develops basic concepts in life, earth, and physical science. Each lesson presents a single concept and includes student objectives, main idea summaries, follow-up questions, and optional hands-on activities. The teacher's edition provides teaching plans for each lesson and options for adapting materials to various ability levels. Workbooks provide reinforcement as well as enrichment activities.
Holt General Science Holt, Rinehart and Winston	Grades 4–8	Student text; teacher's edition; resource book; and test duplicating masters	This text-based program develops basic concepts in life, earth, and physical science. Each lesson includes student objectives, a summary, follow-up questions, and reinforcement activities. New vocabulary is defined in the margin.

Appendix 16-A (continued)

Title and Publisher	Intended Audience	Reading Level	Components	Description
Holt Life Science Holt, Rinehart and Winston	Grades 4–8		Student text; teacher's edition; student resource book; student resource book, teacher's edition; and test duplicating masters	This text-based program explores life science concepts. Emphasis is placed on ecology and conservation. Lessons include student objectives, summaries, and follow-up questions.
Holt Physical Science Holt, Rinehart and Winston	Grades 4–8		Student text; teacher's edition; student resource book; student resource book, teacher's edition; and test duplicating masters	This text-based program investigates physical science concepts of matter and energy. Lessons include student objectives, summaries, and follow-up questions.
Ideas and Investigations in Science: *Earth Science, 2/E* Prentice-Hall	Junior high	*	Student text, laboratory data book, teacher's manual	This program, designed for below-average students, utilizes guided laboratory experiences to develop eight major earth science concepts. Drawings and photographs illustrate laboratory steps. New words are marked in boldface italics and are included in a glossary. The teacher's manual suggests enrichment activities for individualization and homework.
Ideas and Investigations in Science: *Physical Science, 2/E*	Junior high	*	Student text, five laboratory data books, and teacher's manual	This program, designed for below-average students, develops five major physical science themes: discovery, matter,

Physical Science Idea 1: Discovery *Physical Science Idea 2: Matter* *Physical Science Idea 3: Energy* *Physical Science Idea 4: Change* *Physical Science Idea 5: Technology* Prentice-Hall			energy, change, and technology. These themes are developed through text and laboratory activities.
Introductory Experimental Chemistry Prentice-Hall	High school	Text and teacher's manual	This text-based program provides a "practical chemistry" for below-average students. Science processes and laboratory skills are developed through text and laboratory activities. Chemistry-related careers and consumer product facts are also emphasized.
Me and My Environment *Exploring My Environment* *Me As An Environment* *Energy Relationships In My Environment* *Transfer and Cycling of Materials In My Environment* *The Air and Water In My Environment* Hubbard Scientific	Junior High	Teachers guide; media package: filmstrips, cassettes, and 35-mm slides; game; posters; booklets; supplies kit; chemical kit; student record of progress sheets; and student worksheets	This is a 3-year junior high curriculum consisting of five sequenced units. It utilizes a multimedia, activities-oriented approach. Concepts are taught through the use of the inquiry principle, which allows exploration of the environment and interrelationships within it.

*

(continued)

Appendix 16-A (continued)

398

Title and Publisher	Intended Audience	Reading Level	Components	Description
Me Now *Digestion and Circulation* *Respiration and Body Waste* *Movement, Support and Sensory Perception* *Growth and Development* Hubbard Scientific	Grades 4–8		Teacher's guide; functioning torso; audio visual: student worksheets, posters, pictures, and slides; filmstrips; evaluation instruments; supplies kit; and chemical kit	This 2-year program utilizes a multimedia approach to develop an understanding of the major human body systems. Concepts are taught through the inquiry approach, emphasizing the development of problem-solving skills. Students investigate each body system.
Pathways in Science (Revised Edition) Globe Book Company	Junior and senior high	5.0–6.0	Student text; laboratory workbook; and teaching guide	The workbook series is designed to introduce below-average students to basic concepts in biology, earth science, chemistry, and physics. The series uses observations, demonstrations, experiments, and illustrations to aid learning. Texts include target questions at the beginning of each chapter, definitions and phonetic pronunciations for new terms, and chapter reviews. End-of-chapter exercises emphasize development of reading and study skills and basic computation skills. Text and workbooks can be combined to teach general science or one science area (e.g., chemistry). The series is in available in an English measurement edition or in a metrics edition.
Process/Concepts Science Series	Grades K–1		Texts	This series of six books introduces the young child to basic science concepts and

Title / Publisher	Format	Grade Level	Reading Level	Description
				processes. Each lesson uses pictures and words to develop concepts.
The Five Senses Things Around Us Place and Space One and More All and Part How Much–How Many Benefic Press				
Science for You You Can See You Can Do You Can Learn You Can Explore You Can Discover You Can Experience Steck-Vaughn	Student text and teacher's edition	Grades K–6	*	This series of six consumable texts is designed to introduce general science concepts to students with learning difficulties. Illustrations and photographs reinforce concepts presented in each lesson. Concepts are also reinforced through experiments that utilize easily obtainable materials and do not require teachers to have specialized knowledge in science. New vocabulary is highlighted in the text and is marked phonetically. The teacher's edition contains a "how-to-hints" manual and provides a scope and sequence chart for the text.
Science Workshop Biology Workshop 1,2,3 Earth Science Workshop 1,2,3 Chemistry Workshop 1,2,3 Physics Workshop 1,2,3 Globe Book Company	Text-workbooks and teaching guide	Grades 4–12	4.0–5.0	This series of 12 text-workbooks introduces students who are reading below grade level to basic concepts in biology, earth science, chemistry, and physics. Instruction is accomplished through short, easy-to-read lessons. AIMS are reinforced by simple exercises, based on photographs, drawings, and diagrams, or by hands-on experiments. Emphasis is placed on development of a basic science vocabulary. AIMS incorporates

(continued)

Appendix 16-A (continued)

Title and Publisher	Intended Audience	Reading Level	Components	Description
				vocabulary aids that include short definitions and phonetic spellings of new words and terms. Lessons conclude with a "reaching out" question that relates science concepts to everyday life. Text-workbooks can be utilized to teach general science by using four different books at each level, or to teach a specific science area (e.g., biology) by using three books in one particular area.
Spaceship Earth Series Earth Science Life Science Physical Science Houghton Mifflin	Grades 7–9	4.0–6.0	Student text; teacher's annotated edition; laboratory record book; and test duplicating masters	This activity-oriented series introduces basic concepts in three topic areas: earth, life, and physical science. Hands-on projects and experiments using easily obtainable materials reinforce concepts. Progress tests on duplicating masters provide a means of measuring "mastery" on a half-chapter, chapter, and/or semester basis.
The Wonders of Science Series The Human Body Water Life The Earth and Beyond Land Animals Matter, Motion and Machines	Grades 7–12	*	Student text and teacher's edition	This series of six consumable texts is designed for low achievers and parallels regular general science courses in subject materials. Large-print texts include exercises followed by a large work-space designed to improve study skills while reinforcing concepts presented in the lesson. Activities and lessons are

Title / Publisher	Grades	Reading Level	Materials	Description
Plant Life Steck-Vaughn				designed for students with short attention spans. A one-page unit test summarizes concepts presented in each book. The teacher's edition contains lesson guidelines, suggestions for faster moving students, and answers to exercises and tests.
You and the Environment: An Investigative Approach Houghton Mifflin	Grades 7–9	5.0–6.0	Student text; teacher's annotated edition; laboratory supplement checkpoints on duplicating masters; and learning games	This text uses the inquiry learning approach to focus on real problems facing the world, such as energy needs and pollution. A variety of teaching strategies (labs, role-playing, data banks, and games) are use to sharpen students' observation skills and to reinforce concepts. Checkpoints on duplicating masters provide chapter tests and answers.

*Publisher indicates that the reading level is "adjusted and limited."

APPENDIX 16-B: SUPPLEMENTARY SCIENCE PROGRAMS

Appendix 16-B
Supplementary Science Programs

Title and Publisher	Intended Audience	Reading Level	Components	Description
Animals, Nature and Our Environment Weston Woods	Kindergarten through intermediate		Book; filmstrip; and cassette	This series of 13 books and the cassette and filmstrip packages are designed to help children gain an appreciation of nature, a knowledge of interrelationships between living things, and an understanding of the four seasons.
Beginning Concepts/Science *The Life Sciences* *The Physical Sciences* Scholastic Book Services	Grades K–3		Filmstrip; soundtrack record or cassettes; and teaching guide	Each unit introduces basic concepts of physical or life sciences through five full-color filmstrips with soundtrack record or cassette. The accompanying teaching guide provides suggestions for introductory and follow-up activities, class projects, and bulletin boards.
Concept Science Books Cypress	Grades 1–6		Text	This series of 16 "easy-to-read" books uses a programmed learning format to explore the topic of plants and animals.
Concept Science Crossword Puzzles Cypress	Grades 1–6		Booklet and teacher answer book	This consumable booklet contains 32 crossword puzzles—two puzzles for each *Concept Science* book. Students must reread each book to work out the answers.
Elementary Science Series Xerox Education Publications	Grades 1–9		Filmstrip; cassette; teaching guide; and duplicating masters	This series of six multimedia modules introduces students to basic concepts in earth, physical, life, and space science. Each module contains four filmstrips that

402

	Grade Level	Reading Level	Format	Description
				use photos, drawings, experiments, and demonstrations to illustrate a concept. Teaching guides and duplicating masters provide follow-up questions and activities.
Exploring Our Environments: Science Tasks Love Publishing Company	Elementary through junior high		Text and task cards	Task cards provide over 100 independent science activities designed to allow student to work in learning centers or small groups. Directions, materials, and illustrations are listed on each task card.
Reading in the Content Areas: Animals, K–3 Scholastic Book Services	Grades K–3	Preprimer –3.0	42 books and filmstrip	This collection of books utilizes children's literature to introduce children to the world of animals.
Reading in the Content Areas: Science, K–3 Scholastic Book Services	Grades K–3	Preprimer –3.0	46 books	This collection of books utilizes children's literature to help children develop an awareness of the scientific principles governing the world around them.
Scholastic Animals Adventures Scholastic Book Services	Grades K–3		Filmstrips with cassette or record and teaching guide	This four-unit series helps students develop an understanding of wild life. Each unit contains four full-color filmstrips developed from TV's award-winning *The World of Survival Series*. The teaching guide contains lesson objectives, strategies for presentation, follow-up questions and activities, and a list of books for group and independent reading.
Science Readers Reader's Digest	Grades 3–9	2.0–6.0	Student reader and duplicating masters	This series of six readers is designed to bridge the gap between reading and content area studies. Each reader contains articles on earth, physical, life, and space science. Readers include

(*continued*)

Appendix 16-B (continued)

Title and Publisher	Intended Audience	Reading Level	Components	Description
				follow-up activities, maps, diagrams and experiments. Each reader is supplemented by a set of 16 duplicating masters which provide post-reading activities, emphasizing vocabulary development, comprehension skills, and study skills.
Science Tutor Books *Learn About Molecules* *Learn About Genetics* *Learn About Electricity* *Learn About Machines* Xerox Education Publications	Grades 5–10	4.0–5.0	Worktext and teaching guide	Each worktext uses comic strips, short articles, photos, diagrams, and charts to introduce a specific science concept. Write-in exercises and experiments are provided for follow-up.
The Sea Library *To Love the Sea* *Sea Patterns, Sea Cycles* Cypress	Grades 3–9	3.1	Books; filmstrips; cassettes; and teacher's guide	This series of 12 single-concept filmstrips with accompanying cassettes and books introduces ocean life and environments. The teacher's guide provides synopses, explanations of concepts, vocabulary, and related follow-up activities for each filmstrip.
Weather Cypress	Grades 3–7	3.8	Books; filmstrip; worksheets duplicating masters; and teacher's resource book	Two multimedia kits introduce the concept of weather to students who are ready for content but need extra help in reading. Filmstrips and books use bright artwork and bouncy music to stimulate student

interest. The teachers resource book provides suggestions for teaching strategies and for follow-up activities.

Wonder World of Animals Classroom Read-Alongs
Troll Associates

Grades 2–4

Book; cassette; and classroom guide

This series of 21 "I Can Read" units introduces reluctant readers to the animal kingdom. Each "I Can Read" title is accompanied by a word-by-word cassette with sound effects. The classroom guide provides suggestions for follow-up classroom activities.

Wordex Science Concept Lab
Benefic Press

Grades 4–8

Lab contains wordex cards, placement test, pupil record sheets, and teacher's guide

This lab includes 96 activity cards that develop concepts in three areas of science: living things, matter and energy, and earth and the universe. Each card presents activities at three difficulty levels and contains an introduction, a list of materials needed for the activity, data regarding the activity, a post-test, and reference sources. A placement test is provided to determine appropriate difficulty level for each student. The teachers' guide recommends strategies for using activity cards with individuals, small groups, and the total class.

APPENDIX 16-C: CORE SOCIAL STUDIES PROGRAMS

Appendix 16-C
Core Social Studies Programs

Title and Publisher	Intended Audience	Reading Level	Components	Description
American Adventures *A Nation Conceived and Dedicated* (prehistory to 1840) *Old Hate, New Hope* (1840–1898) *Coming of Age* (1898–1939) *Yesterday, Today, Tomorrow* (1939 to Carter Administration) Scholastic Book Service	Grades 7–12	*	Student texts; teacher's guide; and duplicating masters	This series of four texts traces the history of the United States from its origins to the Carter Administration. Each text contains a resource section including a glossary, chronology of events, an index, "Our Nation's Leaders," and "Facts About Our Fifty States." Pre/post-tests, chapter reviews, and supplementary activities are provided in spirit master format. This multiple-text program is most appropriately utilized with junior high students.
American History *(Fifth Edition)* Follett	Grades 8–12	5.0–7.0	Student text (hardcover) or set of four softcover student texts, teacher's guide, and unit tests	This text focuses on the political, social, and economic histories of the United States. Contributions of women and minority groups are highlighted. Short selections emphasize development of vocabulary and comprehension skills.
The American Nation: Adventure in Freedom Follett	Grades 7–8	4.0–5.0	Student text; teacher's guide; activities book; and activities book, teacher's edition	This text is designed for use with "educationally deficient" students and utilizes structured skills approach in teaching American history. The activities book provides enrichment and reinforcement activities for each concept.

Title/Publisher	Grade Level	Reading Level	Materials	Description
The Americans: A History of the United States Holt, Rinehart and Winston	Grades 7–8	*	Student text; teacher's guide; classroom support unit; and test duplicating masters	This 1-year course of study traces United States history from pre-Columbian America to the present. The classroom support unit provides enrichment through cassette recordings of speeches, interviews, and songs.
American's Story Steck-Vaughn	Intermediate to junior high	2.0–4.0	Worktexts; teacher's guide; and answer key	These two worktexts provide an overview of the growth of our county from early settlers to current times. Contributions of famous men and women to the development of the United States are highlighted. Emphasis is also placed on development of vocabulary and comprehension skills.
Exploring American Citizenship Globe Book Company	Junior and senior high	5.0–6.0	Student text; teaching guide; workbook; and answer key	This text explores "the rights and powers of the people" through topics such as free enterprise, governmental regulations, labor, and consumerism. Emphasis is also placed on the development of basic reading skills such as finding the main idea, using context clues, and interpreting graphs and charts.
Geography Skills Series Lands at Home Regions of the World The American Continents Contents Overseas Steck-Vaughn	Grades 3–6	*	Worktexts	This series of four worktexts develops map reading and reference skills. Geographical concepts such as land formation, climatic effects, and earth–space relationships are introduced in short lessons followed by summary exercises that test understanding and application of the concepts. Topical worktexts can be used individually or can be combined to provide a sequential program.

(continued)

Title and Publisher	Intended Audience	Reading Level	Components	Description
Holt Databank System *Level K-Inquiry About Myself* *Level 1-Inquiry About People* *Level 2-Inquiry About Communities* *Level 3-Inquiry About Cities* *Level 4-Inquiry About Cultures* *Level 5-Inquiry About American History* *Level 6-Inquiry About Technology* Holt, Rinehart and Winston	Grades K-6	*	Student texts; databanks; datamasters; planning calendars; teacher's guide; 16-mm films, and test duplicating masters	This multimedia program is designed as a total social science curriculum for the elementary grades. The program combines student text with various nonprint materials (filmstrips, cassettes, games, and simulations) from the Databank and datamasters to develop problem-solving and thinking skills. The program utilizes a total systems approach that draws upon a variety of resources to achieve specific learning objectives. The teacher's guide presents strategies for coordinating print and nonprint materials to meet the needs of reluctant readers as well as high achievers. Tests combine matching, fill-in, and write-a-paragraph items for determining students' mastery of specific behavioral learning objectives.
The Human Expression, A History of Peoples and their Cultures J. B. Lippincott	Grades 9-12	*	Student text; teacher's edition; duplicating masters; student workbook; and workbook, teacher's edition	The text and workbook provide a course of study emphasizing various cultures of the world. The following topics are highlighted for each world culture: geographic region, people, history, politics, and economics. Chapters averaging five to six pages require minimal reading and contain numerous illustrations.

Title	Grade	Reading Level	Materials	Description
Man and Urban Living Today Benefic Press	Grades 7–8	*	Student text; teacher's edition; and duplicating masters	The inquiry approach is utilized to explore urban life. Emphasis is placed on sharpening the students observation, investigation, comparison, interpretation, and generalization skills. Supplementary activities are provided in spirit master format. The teacher's edition provides learning objectives and annotated student text.
Man in a World of Change Benefic Press	Grades 1–3	*	Student text; duplicating masters; and teacher's edition	This series of three texts utilizes the inquiry approach to explore families, communities, and cities. Emphasis is placed on developing student's observation, investigation, comparison, interpretation, and generalization skills. The teacher's edition provides learning objectives and annotated student text. Lessons can be extended through use of duplicating masters.
The New Exploring A Changing World Globe Book Company	Junior and senior high	5.0–6.0	Student text; teaching guide; workbook; and answer key	The basics of geography are presented. The text is arranged as a tour of eight regions of the world. The students are presented with vocabulary, geographical terms, and concepts. The main issues focus on contemporary problems and possible solutions. To develop these concepts, parts from books, articles, and stories are used to emphasize the issues being discussed.

(*continued*)

Appendix 16-C (continued)

Title and Publisher	Intended Audience	Reading Level	Components	Description
The New Exploring American History Globe Book Company	Intermediate through senior high	5.0–6.0	Student text; teaching guide; and student workbook	This text provides a chronological overview of United States history. Each of the nine chapters is introduced with a motivational question and is concluded with a chapter review and summary activities. The text emphasizes development of study skills such as map reading, outlining, and use of reference materials, while exploring topics such as foreign policy and the role of minority groups in our nation's development. Student text contains a "mini-atlas" of the United States and the world.
The New Exploring World History Globe Book Company	Junior and senior high	5.0–6.0	Student text and teaching guide	The text provides a chronological overview of the development of various Western and non-Western cultures. Each short chapter utilizes a series of guided study questions to introduce topics such as the cold war, the Korean War, the Vietnam War, and today's emerging African nations.

Our American Minorities Globe Book Company	Intermediate through senior high	3.0–4.0	Student text and teaching guide	The text highlights the role of minority groups in the development of the United States. Short chapters utilize personal narratives, photographs, maps, and charts to illustrate the contributions of American Indians, Black Americans, Mexican Americans, Chinese Americans, Japanese Americans, Jewish Americans, Catholic Americans, Puerto Rican Americans, Italian Americans, the poor, and women.
Our Land and Heritage (Revised) Ginn and Company	Grades 1–7	*	Student text; teacher's edition; workbook; annotated workbook; and duplicating masters	This seven-book series is designed as a basal social studies program for the elementary grades. Texts utilize a narrative approach to describe major events in American history and the major principles of American democracy. Emphasis is also placed on skill development, vocabulary development, map and globe reading, and critical thinking skills. This revised edition includes more illustrations and is more balanced on its representation of women and minority groups. Unit tests and outline maps are provided in duplicating master format.

(*continued*)

Appendix 16-C (continued)

Title and Publisher	Intended Audience	Reading Level	Components	Description
Scholastic Social Studies Scholastic Book Services	Grades 1–6	*	Student text; teacher's edition; activity book; teacher's edition activity book; and test duplicating masters	This basal text program provides content instruction in history, geography, economics, and sociology. Texts and activity books introduce basic principles of citizenship and democracy, focusing on these concepts within the context of family, community, city, state, country, and world. Emphasis is placed on development of map reading skills, reading charts and graphs, and problem-solving skills. Activity books provide additional skills practice and review. Test duplicating masters supplement and expand chapter and unit reviews.
The Search for Identity: Modern American History Harper & Row	Grades 9–12	*	Student text; teacher's edition; and test duplicating masters	This text highlights contributions of various cultural groups to the development of the United States. Chapter tests are provided on duplicating masters.
Skills for Understanding Maps and Globes Follett	Grades 4–12	4.0–5.0	Student worktext and teacher's edition	The student worktext is designed to develop map and globe reading skills. The worktext utilizes the developmental approach to build skills, stressing one new skill per lesson, while building on skills presented in previous lessons.

Title/Publisher	Grade Level	Reading Level	Type	Description
The United States in the Making Vol. 1: *The Road to Independence* Vol. 2: *The Development of a Nation* Vol. 3: *Expansion Through the 20th Century* Globe Book Company	Intermediate through senior high	5.0–6.0	Worktext and teaching guide	This series of three worktexts provides a chronological overview of United States history. Each two-page chapter is concluded with a series of exercises that reinforces concepts presented as well as these reading skills: finding the main idea, recognizing supporting details, use of context clues, and study skills. Chapters include full-color maps and drawings.
World History Texts Vol. 1: *The Rise of the West* Vol. 2: *Empires Beyond Europe: Asia, Africa, and the Americas* Vol. 3: *The Age of Europe* Vol. 4: *The Modern World* Scholastic Book Service	Grades 7–12	*	Student text; teacher's guide; and duplicating masters	These texts provide a chronological overview of world history. Each page's narrative is illustrated with a full-color photograph or drawing. Each unit includes discussion questions and suggested supplementary projects.

*Publisher indicates that the reading level is "adjusted and limited."

APPENDIX 16-D: SUPPLEMENTARY SOCIAL STUDIES PROGRAMS

Appendix 16-D
Supplementary Social Studies Programs

Title and Publisher	Intended Audience	Reading Level	Components	Description
Afro-Americans: Then and Now Benefic Press	Grades 2–4	2.0	Student text	This text contains a series of biographical sketches of black leaders.
American History: Activities Westinghouse Learning Corporation	Grades 7–12	4.0	Activity cards	This project file is designed to supplement any high school American history curriculum. The file contains 101 activity cards that provide more than 250 projects in the following topic areas: art, cookery and crafts, settlement, growth and economics, lifestyles and religion, the revolution and internal affairs, and the new government and the Constitution.
American History for Today Ginn and Company	Grades 7–12	*	Student text and annotated teacher's edition	This text utilizes the traditional approach to explore American history. Each topic is introduced with a motivational question, followed by clear, concise explanation of the specific topic, and concluded with additional study questions. Question-answer format is designed to keep reluctant readers "on task."
American All—A Nation of Immigrants Benefic Press	Grades 4–6	4.0	Student text	This text utilizes the inquiry approach to emphasize the role of various cultural groups in the growth of the United States. Key vocabulary is highlighted in the narrative text.

Title/Publisher	Grade level	Reading level	Format	Description
Backgrounds: An American Reader Series / *Women in American Life* / *The Road to Revolution* / *A Nation in Rebellion* / *American Moves West* / *Juveniles and the Law* / *The Great Depression* / *The Labor Movement* / *Our Indian Heritage* / Xerox Education Publications	Grades 5–9	4.0–6.0	Paperback text and teaching guide	Each 48-page book focuses on a different aspect of American social studies through newspaper articles, playlets, biographies, letters, and short fiction.
Basic Understanding Series / Benefic Press	Primary and intermediate	1.0–3.0	Student text	This series of 14 booklets develops concepts such as ''How We Get Our Mail,'' ''How Hospitals Help Us,'' and ''How We Use Maps and Globes.'' Each booklet combines photographs and drawings to illustrate the text.
Claiming a Right / New Readers Press	Intermediate, junior high and senior high	4.3	Student text	This text contains short biographies of 24 American Indians who have made contributions to American growth from colonial times to the 20th century.
Contributions to American Life Series / *Afro-American Contributions to American Life* / *American Indian Contributions to American Life* / *Hispano-American Contributions to American Life* / Benefic Press	Grades 4–9	2.3–5.5	Student text	These texts explore the contributions of three minority groups to American life. Each text contains more than 20 short biographies. Each biography is presented at three different readings and knowledge levels: meeting—2.3; knowing—3.5; understanding—5.5. Evaluation and study questions conclude each biography.

(continued)

Appendix 16-D (continued)

Title and Publisher	Intended Audience	Reading Level	Components	Description
Economics Westinghouse Learning Corporation	Grades 8–12		Activity cards kit	This series of activity cards emphasizes the basic principles of economics such as inflation, interdependence of goods and services, etc. Flexibility allows the kit to be utilized as a total course of study, as a mini-course, or as supplementary material. The kit is based on guidelines and recommendations of the Joint Council of Economics.
Experiential Development Program Benefic Press	Primary		Teacher's big book; child's activity book; and enrichment books	This program emphasizes students' relationships with family, friends, and others. Skills are developed in several instructional areas: social studies, language arts, health, math, science, music, and art.
Exploring Maps: Map Skills for Today Xerox Education Publications	Grades 2–6		Six filmstrips with cassettes and teaching guide	These filmstrips cover the same basic material covered in the *Map Skills for Today* books. The filmstrips introduce students to members of the Explorer's Club at a mythical elementary school. A visiting world traveler teaches club members the basic map skills and takes them on an around-the-world trip where they use their newly acquired skills.
Follett Student Atlas Follett	Grades 4–12		Student atlas and duplicating masters	This teaching atlas contains political and geographic relief maps of the world, each

416

Title and Publisher	Grade Level	Reading Level	Format	Description
(continued from preceding entry)				continent, the United States, and regions of the United States. Climate, land-use, precipitation, population, growing-season, and other maps are also included. This is a good reference material. Spirit masters provide skill development exercises.
Map and Globe Understanding Transparencies Benefic Press	Grades 4–10		Transparencies; teacher's guide; and storage carton	This set of eight transparencies develop map reading skills. The detailed teacher's guide provides suggestions for use of transparencies with students of a wide ability range.
VEC News Program from New Filmstrip Program VEC, Inc.	Intermediate and junior high		Weekly filmstrip package includes filmstrip and teacher's guide	This weekly filmstrip summarizes current news events. The accompanying teacher's guide provides suggestions for discussion and extension activities. Review quizzes are also provided.
News for You New Readers Press	Junior and senior high	4.0–6.0	Newspaper and instructor's aid	This newspaper utilizes adult tone and format to cover topics of interest to teenagers of limited reading ability. The instructor's aid includes suggested activities.
Our United States New Readers Press	Grades 7–12	5.3	Student text and workbooks	This text provides an overview of the history and geography of the United States and its territories.
People and the Way of Living in the New England Colonies Benefic Press	Grades 4–6	4.0–6.0	Kit includes pupil books; pupil activity books; filmstrip; cassette; and teacher's guide	The components explore the relationships and contributions of the Indians to the early settlers' colonization efforts.
The Progress of the Afro-American Benefic Press	Grades 6–9	5.5	Text	The text stresses an understanding of the experiences of Afro-Americans in the United States.

(continued)

417

Title and Publisher	Intended Audience	Reading Level	Components	Description
Reading in the Content Areas, Social Studies K–3 About Myself Families and Friends School/Community Work Our County's History Our Holidays Scholastic Book Services	Grades K–3	Preprimer –3.0	Each collection of books contains 30–50 different books.	Each collection of books explores social science concepts through children's literature.
Scholastic Search Scholastic Book Service	Grades 8–12	4.0–6.0	Periodical	This biweekly magazine focuses on social science concepts.
Social Studies Readers Reader's Digest	Grades 3–8	2.0–6.0	Student reader and duplicating masters	This series of six readers is designed to bridge the gap between reading and content area studies. Each reader focuses on a different part of the world or period of history. Readers include full-color photographs and illustrations. Each reader is supplemented by a set of 16 duplicating masters, which provide post-reading activities emphasizing vocabulary development, comprehension skills, and study skills.
Turning points Continents and Climates Mountains and Valleys Earthquakes and Volcanoes	Grades 4–9		Student text	Each text in this six-book series develops a different geographical concept. Texts include colorful half-page illustrations, suggestions for simple experiments that

Title/Publisher	Level	Reading Level	Type	Description
Weather *Rivers and Lakes* *Seas and Oceans* Cypress				can be carried out in the classroom, and cross-referenced indexes that link related information within the series.
We Honor Them New Readers Press	Intermediate, junior high, and senior high	3.3–4.4	Text	This two-volume series focuses on Black American history through a series of biographical sketches of outstanding Black Americans. Each biography is illustrated with drawings or photographs. Study exercises are also included in each volume.
Your Rights When You're Young New Readers Press	Junior and senior high	4.7	Text	This text outlines the general rights of those under 18 as minors and as members of families, schools, and communities. Their rights when dealing with the police and courts are also explained. Case histories are used to illustrate the implementation of laws and rights in daily life.

*Publisher indicates that the reading level is "adjusted and limited."

Henry Reinert

17
The Development of Affective Skills

Affective education has had a curious history in schools. Nearly all teachers support the notion that emotions are important. Yet, faced with the reality that some youngsters behave in totally unacceptable ways, they aren't readily prepared to accommodate or change these inappropriate behaviors. In fact, teachers may become so frustrated that they proclaim a child unfit (emotionally) for the classroom. Difference is acceptable in reading, arithmetic, and other academic areas—but affective normalcy is expected and required. While not all students are expected to have academic skills at a high level of sophistication, every student is expected to have "normal" emotional behaviors.

Affective education has had a curious history for several reasons—the most obvious being lack of a common definition. Other reasons include the fear of encroaching on other professionals' areas, a feeling of inadequacy, and the belief that a child's affective education will occur without assistance.

DEFINING AFFECTIVE SKILLS

Affective skills include those behaviors, attitudes, and feelings that demonstrate to those around us that we have emotions, that we know how to cope with these emotions, and that we can control these emotions in a healthy and productive manner. The process of teaching affective skills in school is called "affective education." The development of affective education includes the assumption that all students who are identified as mildly handicapped have a need for affective skills and that the school is a legitimate place to teach these skills.

There are many levels of skill development, some of which are most useful in special classes, resource rooms, or the regular classroom—all places where the mildly handicapped child is likely to be taught. Generally, these techniques are appropriate for behaviorally disordered, retarded, or learning-disabled children, both individually and collectively.

The need for development of affective skills is generally an individual matter; however, members of the group labeled emotionally disturbed are more likely to have affective skill deficits than either retarded or learning disabled children (Morse, Ardizzone, Macdonald & Pasick, 1980).

While numerous researchers have expressed the need for, and advantages of, affective education, none has been more provocative than Benjamin Bloom (Bloom, Engelhart, Furst, Hill, & Krathwohl, 1976). Bloom contended that changes in affective education could have dramatic implications for educational productivity, changing the normal curve of learning to an inverted U with most youngsters achieving mastery level in cognitive areas. This would have the effect of bringing most children up to an acceptable level of learning with few or no failures.

Why isn't a better job being done in affective education? During the past several years, teachers have been writing individual educational plans (IEPs) for students identified as handicapped, and affective needs are a part of each IEP. Yet, it is the author's observation that while teachers often identify affective deficits in students, they rarely plan a structured attack on the problem. A recent example follows.

> Alex, aged 11, was identified by his teacher as having an extreme resistance to school, to teachers, and to learning. During evaluation, it was discovered that he was fully 3 years retarded in all educational areas, was truant from school over half the time, and had relatively few friends. Alex was either unwilling or unable to relate to peers or adults. He had an extremely low self-concept and seldom raised his eyes to look at anyone.

What did Alex's IEP include? Placement in a resource room 50 minutes per day for work on reading and arithmetic skills! Sound familiar? It is apparent that this is not an isolated example. While teachers typically identify emotional/affective problems in evaluation, they often neglect to develop a careful attack on the affective problems identified. Typically, teachers are relying on informal approaches to solve affective problems. Clearly, this has not and will not solve difficult problems. The *Colorado Guidelines Handbook for Education & Related Services for SIBD Students* (Benson & Cessna, 1980) says that "shotgun" (broad, general) approaches to affective education must be avoided. Even though formal *and* informal approaches can be used to teach affective skills, both must be planned (Benson & Cessna, 1980).

AFFECTIVE SKILLS AND BIOPHYSICAL THEORY

Biophysical intervention may seem to be an unusual way to introduce the application of learning affective skills; however, it is unlikely that anyone can identify an area of greater concern than personal health. One of the most common greetings is "How are You?" While this greeting is generally rhetorical, its importance is pervasive. People are interested in each others' well-being and want others to be concerned about them. This interest is in both our psychological and physical welfare. Physical well-being contributes to behavior. It is difficult for someone to have appropriate affective behavior if he or she is ill.

In the school, there are several areas in which biophysical concerns are important (Sinacore, 1978): (1) obtaining a health history; (2) obtaining a physical evaluation; (3) appraising present developmental status; and (4) health screening.

In general, biophysical components of the student are evaluated even before he or she is enrolled in school and at regular intervals throughout the child's school life. The teacher's role in the biophysical intervention is one of knowledgeable observer of behavior. Since teachers have had training in growth and development as well as observational skills, they are in a good position to view and evaluate individual behavior. Teachers see many children in a variety of activities each day. This backdrop of normalcy provides the teacher invaluable comparisons, even in areas where differences otherwise would likely go unnoticed (Reinert, 1980).

Observation thus becomes a major part of the teacher's job when dealing with a child's emotions. The youngster who is suffering considerable anxiety may have a body chemistry imbalance or may be under emotional stress. Careful observation by the teacher and other staff members, combined with careful interaction with the appropriate medical official, can have beneficial effects for the child. School personnel should never go beyond their appropriate roles of observation and interaction with medical personnel and parents.

AFFECTIVE SKILLS AND PSYCHODYNAMIC THEORY

Milieu therapy is a concept described by Lewin (1935) and Redl (1959), meaning treatment by or within the environment (Reinert, 1976). While school staffs are generally concerned with maintaining a healthy environment, their emphasis is generally on normalcy rather than on the child who is handicapped. Milieu therapy was developed to be used in a psychiatric unit of a hospital, but its major components can be applied to schools. Redl (1976) described how the components of milieu therapy could be used with moderately and severely disturbed children. The technique has potential applicability with the mildly handicapped who spend some time in resource rooms and spend much of the school day with students not identified as handicapped.

Milieu therapy may be used with any of the mildly handicapped groups, although adjustments will be needed for individuals.

Environment of the School

Two major factors are important about the environment of a school. The first is the physical structure, which should be flexible enough to allow individual educational and affective needs to be met. For the mildly handicapped, the elementary school environment is often more appropriate for affective growth than the secondary-school environment. Elementary programs are generally organized so that each child has a homeroom where he or she spends most of the school day. This allows for a variety of activities and grouping possibilities and offers youngsters the structure of a central stabilizing figure (the classroom teacher). In contrast, the secondary program generally has five to seven structured periods each day, with a different teacher responsible for each class period; hence, affective changes built upon relationships between the teacher and student are less likely to occur.

The second important component of the environment is the attitudes of those who work in the school. In fact, the attitude of the principal and staff toward the handicapped is probably even more important than the physical environment. As Redl (1976) suggested, the social structure is critical for the milieu to be therapeutic.

Social Structure

The social structure that surrounds programming for mildly handicapped is critical. Highlighting this structure is the need to have sufficient staff to provide for the needs of youngsters. In order to be effective change agents for the mildly handicapped, teachers must have access to a social structure that differs in quality and quantity from that required in the regular classroom.

In addition to the need for a sufficiently large staff, the structure of the staff is also important—including lines of authority, the relationship of staff and students, and the lines of communication for planning and implementing programs.

Everyone needs routine in his or her life. The mildly handicapped who are experiencing emotional difficulties need structure that will promote reasonable self-control while providing a means for acquiring new behaviors. The structure of a school program should allow for group and individual activities that promote a good self-concept and good attitudes toward others.

Life Space Interview

The life space interview is a cathartic technique generally credited to Redl (1959). The technique offers a wide range of discussion and interaction techniques that vary in intensity, length of time required, and commitment level. The technique is designed to be used during times of personal crisis; the therapist uses the crisis of the moment to energize interaction with the person being interviewed. Two techniques were described by Redl (1959)—emotional first aid and clinical exploitation of life events.

Emotional First Aid

For the mildly handicapped, the major technique of life space interview is emotional first aid. This technique is designed to be used when the problem is not considered serious, and an immediate return to productive activity is desirable. Redl (1976) outlined five subcomponents of emotional first aid, all of which would be appropriate for use in the classroom with a mildly handicapped person who is experiencing conflict.

Drain off frustration acidity.   Frustration is a common occurrence for the mildly handicapped child. Retarded children are frustrated when they cannot perform at a satisfactory level; learning disabled children become frustrated because they cannot decode certain words; emotionally disturbed children are frustrated when an enjoyable activity is terminated. Although all of these youngsters experience similar feelings, each needs a slightly different approach to treatment—each feels a frustration acidity that the teacher may "disarm" in different ways. Individualized expectation may be the key to children who cannot succeed with the workload. The teacher may say, "Finish only the first three problems, or problem one, two, and four." The children with learning problems can be "defused" by helpful suggestions in decoding troublesome words, and disturbed children can be warned of the project length before work is started. Thus, the teacher is able to lessen the chance for frustration acidity to set in and may avoid major conflicts.

Support for the management of panic, fury, fear, too much anger, or too much guilt.   All youngsters are vulnerable to their feelings, even when these feelings are expected. Having an understanding adult available when fear, anger, or guilt arise will help the child cope with feelings in a way that can strengthen future episodes of runaway emotions.

Maintain communication.   Teachers do not try to stimulate emotional conflict for those who have low threshholds of conflict; however, this often occurs accidentally during a crisis. The scene is familiar to everyone. A student makes an error and is corrected. Defensive behaviors set in, and frustration soon turns to anger. The child eventually "strikes out" at the teacher, who in turn becomes embroiled in the controversy. Panic reigns! Everyone needs to learn techniques that defuse tense situations. Phrases like "Let's talk about this later," "Come back and see me after you feel better," or "I understand how you feel—how can I help?" should replace inappropriate responses like "Don't let the door hit you in the back as you leave," or "Your parents will hear about this." Teachers are not intentionally insensitive to the needs of others; it is just easy to become defensive when authority is challenged.

Regulate behavioral and social traffic.   Of all the first aid techniques outlined, setting rules seems least therapeutic. However, establishing and maintaining an acceptable atmosphere for growth through reasonable social structure can have very therapeutic effects. As Redl (1959) suggested, "Our respect for the clinical importance of our services as social and behavioral traffic cops has gone up . . . over the last ten years" (p. 12). Rules are difficult for youngsters experiencing conflict. Lectures or small sermons seem only to exacerbate the situation. Small sessions with supportive interaction are critical to the understanding and acceptance of structure, which is critical to change.

Act as umpire.   Everyone can remember the desire to have an adult "umpire" a game or activity when fairness seemed to be paramount. Youngsters often want this service provided when they are unsure of their own controls. This need is not just in external activities, but in internal decisions as well. A concerned and trusted adult can be supportive in the decision-making process and can help the child mature in the ability to be honest and fair in future decisions.

Clinical Exploitation of Life Events

While emotional first aid is often used as a technique to defuse crisis situations, another, more intensive, alternative is clinical exploitation of life events. This approach would seem to have little use for the teacher/therapist with the mildly handicapped and should generally be reserved for situations where a more intensive intervention is desirable. Redl (1976) suggested that no one can predict what situation will demand a specific intervention; however, two general guidelines seem appropriate: (1) the time available at the moment of need; and (2) the receptivity of the situation to successful intervention (Reinert, 1980). Five techniques were described by Redl.

Reality rub in.   Youngsters in conflict are sometimes considered to be perceptually impaired in their ability to interact successfully with others. This perceptual impairment is not the same as the perceptual impairment of learning disabilities, but it is devastating in terms of human interaction. "Reality rub in" is a particularly good technique for use with the mildly retarded since it offers a good way to reinforce appropriate social interaction and teach appropriate behaviors in new situations. Redl (1976) called problems in this area "socially nearsighted" behavior and suggested that some children get caught in a "system of near to delusional misinterpretation of life." Socially nearsighted behavior and delusional misinterpretation of life are two different, but related behaviors. both of which are amenable to change with "rub in" techniques applied immediately and with regularity. During these "rub in" sessions, the teacher tries to implant the idea with the child that there is a reality and this reality can be accepted. The goal is never for the child to admit reality. Sentences such as "Admit you did it," or "Tell me the truth, I know you did it" should not be used. The "rub in" process is slow, with many regressions likely. Even as adults, many people deny reality in order to protect fragile egos.

Symptom estrangement.   In the process of protecting themselves from neurotic fears, people often develop various behaviors that are symptomatic. People avoid telling the painful truth to others and to themselves. People make excuses, blame others for their problems, transfer anger to others, and in general, deny parts of reality. If this denial has gone on long enough, some people develop symptomatic traits that become a part of their personalities. People with these traits are identified as being aloof, aggressive, troubled, cold, and guarded in their approach to others. In many cases, these symptoms serve to protect these people from the painful experiences in their daily lives. Symptom estrangement is the technique for ridding people of these behaviors of defense and replacing them with more appropriate behaviors. In order to help people give up inappropriate behaviors, other behaviors must be taught that can be used to get satisfactory results without the trauma of the former behavior.

Massaging numb value areas.   Life has a way of numbing the senses to painful experiences. The youngster who has experienced hurt because learning is difficult and often confusing, or due to problems of social interaction, often copes by ignoring the pain. Over a period of months and years, this ignoring can turn into numbed values. When cries for help go unnoticed or unheeded in the streets of our cities, it is obvious how numbed people's senses have become. The youngster who experiences regular periods of conflict often has feelings that appear to be asleep. These feelings need to be reawakened if a person is to develop appropriate interactions with others. This can be done through communication in times of stress.

New tool salesmanship.   One of the symptoms of emotional disturbance is an inability to respond to situations in a new and flexible manner. Bower and Lambert (1971) included this characteristic in their definition of disturbance. A child who gets into fights seems to be unable to respond to confrontation in any other way. Teachers should provide youngsters with alternatives to fighting. Children must be taught to say they are angry in another, more acceptable way.

Manipulation of boundaries of self.   Of all the topics of the life space interview, this is perhaps the least obvious. Many youngsters are very vulnerable to the suggestions and modeling behavior of others. Consequently, they are always being "sucked in" by every deviant suggestion. They become the butt of jokes or pranks and end up getting into difficulty with other youngsters and the staff. With the teacher's review of the progression of events that triggered the problem, youngsters can be sensitized to potential difficulties and learn more appropriate coping skills.

In addition to individual life space interviewing, the teacher may want to use the group life space interviewing technique. This technique has been used for many years by those who deal with behavior problems. Generally, the technique has not been called life space interviewing, but various other names like class meetings, class problem-solving groups, and therapy groups. While the emphasis of these groups varies widely, group and individual change is generally one of the desired outcomes. The group life space interview technique is a valid tool with all the mildly handicapped groups, if the goals for its use are clearly articulated and pursued with reasonable persistance and logical direction.

Crisis Intervention

Crisis intervention is therapeutic activity that takes place immediately following a crisis. Ideally, an extra staff member whose major responsibility is interaction with persons in conflict acts as crisis counselor (Reinert, 1980). In practice, however, it appears that crisis intervention is usually done by a staff member who already has responsibility within the school. Likely choices include special teachers trained in interviewing techniques, school counselors, school psychologists, and resource teachers. If no one is available to devote a large amount of time to crisis counseling, a staff member may decide to add to their regular assignments so that someone is freed to deal with crisis situations in an efficient and effective manner.

The concept of crisis intervention as described by Morse (1977) offers an alternative to those interventions that fail to change behaviors. Morse (1977) cited the example of meeting pupil truancy with suspension from school, a reaction that is likely to amplify rather than solve the problem. Morse was very perceptive in his suggestions for change in the process of intervention and equally convincing in his beliefs relative to the use of crisis intervention. Several of his assertions offer valuable insight to the hygienic management of behavior:

1. People tend to want quick answers to comprehensive problems. Rather than seeing change as a process, many people look for someone to "fix" the situation.

2. Many teachers believe in the necessity of a "cooling off" period—the opposite of the immediate intervention proposed by crisis intervention. If left to cool off, many behaviors dissipate to a point where no impact is available for subsequent intervention.

3. Teachers are often unable to extricate themselves from group responsibilities long enough to be effective in crisis situations. This often leaves persons who are far removed from the crisis to initiate intervention. Often the person who inherits the crisis is the principal, the least likely individual to know what occurred. As Morse suggested, the principal is in an awkward position. He or she is expected to act, but how? If the principal does act, it is often with few details of what transpired to create the crisis and with little or no follow-up likely with the classroom teacher other than information sharing.

4. Teachers generally do not value their input during crisis situations. Often the teacher sees his or her role as one of regulator of behaviors rather than that of change agent. The function of change agent is left for those who are "trained" to do therapy. Unfortunately, teachers generally do not have the luxury of trained therapists available to interact with children during crisis situations. Also, it is obvious that teachers are capable of effective interaction during a crisis if they have the time and interest in doing so. In fact, teachers have several advantages over those who are physically and psychologically removed from the situation.

5. This is a very awkward time. Parents expect schools to have controls that have long ago vanished, both from the school and from the home. Many parents still want to think that children are subject to the wishes of adults, even while teaching their own children to think for themselves. While parents two or three generations ago were generally blindly cooperative with school personnel, today they ask serious questions regarding educational practices.

The value of crisis intervention lies in the potential for change that occurs at the time of crisis. If the situation is allowed to cool, much of the potential for gain is also lost. This is particularly true when working with the manipulative youngster, who is most vulnerable during times of stress. If cooling off time is allowed, this child is difficult to reach with traditional interventions. By using life space interview techniques when the child's defenses are lowered, the teacher/therapist will be more likely to succeed. Several common ideal characteristics of crisis intervention were outlined by Reinert (1980):

1. An extra staff member is the ideal person to provide for crisis intervention. This counselor should have training in both educational and psychological interventions, including individual and group counseling techniques, life space interviewing, and strategies for relaxation.

2. A small room should be provided where the crisis teacher can interact with an individual or small group.

3. A communication network should be established to keep the crisis teacher informed of problems on short notice.

4. The teacher/therapist should try to capitalize on the vulnerability caused by the crisis.

Play Therapy

Although formal play therapy would not seem appropriate for use with the mildly handicapped, there are useful concepts within play therapy that can be used in the regular classroom with mildly handicapped persons. While the regular classroom teacher would not, under normal conditions, use play therapy, the principles are valuable assets in the affective arsenal. The goals of play therapy principles offer insights for both the teacher and child (Nelson, 1966). The principles of play therapy, as described by Axline (1947), are summarized below:

1. A cornerstone of play therapy is permissiveness, i.e., allowing the child to express feelings openly and without restriction. This freedom to express feelings is not a license to become destructive but rather an opportunity to express oneself without interference, so long as persons or property are not violated through injury or damage. For the classroom teacher, this may be interpreted as allowing the child to paint a picture, to write, and to be creative in music, drama, and play without undue interference or direction. This self-expression is critical for affective growth. Freedom to create does not, in itself, promote growth, but does allow feelings to surface where they may be supported in productive ways. The mildly handicapped should be made aware of the structure operating in the classroom. This is particularly true for the youngster who is perceptually "nearsighted" and, therefore, prone to misreading the environment. Allowance for permissiveness should never be read as approval of anarchy in the classroom.

2. Establishing a warm, friendly relationship is theoretically easy, but, in reality, it is very difficult to implement. Establishing friendship is often a slow task, especially with the child who has lost trust in adults. It is particularly difficult for those children who have failed for several years. With these individuals, it is often easy to build a superficial relationship, but closer relationships are seen as hazardous by the child, and, therefore, relationships are often destroyed by the child before he or she can experience the pain of rejection. Once a relationship is established, the child must be helped to generalize this relationship to others. Of course, this is the most difficult task of all, since children are being asked to do something that adults often find impossible— relate to those who think, believe, and act differently than themselves.

3. The reflection of feelings is an important feature of play therapy and can be a useful tool for the teacher to use during periods of student stress or crisis. This technique is misunderstood more than any other technique in play therapy, perhaps because it is so difficult to use. To some people, it seems almost cynical to mirror feelings when a child makes a statement. With practice, this technique becomes as natural as other forms of casual interaction. Teachers are often more prepared to question, to explain, or to verify a statement than to reflect its content. Reflection of feelings represents good teaching as well as good therapy. Reflecting allows the youngster the opportunity to evaluate what was just said, internalize the implications, and gain new insights.

4. Complete acceptance of children is difficult when interacting with youngsters who often start trouble. Complete acceptance or unconditional regard are

ways of saying that without equivocation, the child is accepted as a person. This does not mean that all exhibited behaviors are accepted; obligations to reject inappropriate behaviors while accepting the child are still required. Acceptance of the mildly handicapped youngster is often most difficult. It is relatively easy to accept the child who has more noticeable handicaps. But when mildly handicapped children fail to learn or behave in a normal manner, they are often labeled rebellious, lazy, or uninterested in school (Reinert, 1980). In short, all situations in school need to be rethought in order to provide acceptance of each youngster.

5. The rights of all youngsters to solve their own problems must be respected. Of course, monitoring the types of problems that children are given so that the level of decision making is within the realm of the child's functioning. A primary-school-aged youngster should not be allowed to decide whether or not to study reading or arithmetic because the consequences of such a decision are too great for the child to be responsible for. The child could be allowed, however, to decide which period to do arithmetic and which to do reading. In the eagerness to reinforce children, they are unwittingly denied their right and need for self-evaluation. When a teacher asks a question, gets a response, and then waits for a few seconds, a child will often change the original answer. The reason for this uncertainty is that the child is insecure, having become accustomed to quick evaluations. Evaluative responses, such as, "That's good," or "No, that's incorrect," followed immediately by calling on someone else for a response does not allow children to evaluate their own responses, or solve their own problems. It is no wonder that students go to college with so little confidence that they sometimes resort to cheating rather than trust their own judgment.

6. The teacher should allow students to "lead the way" in conversation and action. This principle has been learned in teaching techniques like the discovery method used in arithmetic. When behavior problems are the issue, the teacher often wants to tell, threaten, or manipulate rather than listen to the child.

7. Therapists think in terms of weeks or months when behavioral change is considered. It is important for teachers and therapists to consider the length of time a deviant behavior has been occurring, as well as the intensity level of the behavior, when predicting outcomes. When behaviors are of long duration and high intensity levels, change will take time. Teachers who would never expect quick solutions in cognitive areas are often unrealistic in behavioral change.

One principle of play therapy seems inappropriate for the mildly handicapped in the regular class or resource setting. This is the principle of setting limits in therapy in order to keep children in reality. A corollary of this principle in the classroom would not seem feasible since the classroom teacher wouldn't be involved in formal play techniques.

While the principles of play therapy outlined were not developed for use in the regular classroom, they represent valuable skills that seem well-suited for use with the mildly handicapped. Of course, the use of these techniques will not be as therapeutically dramatic in this setting, but from a practical sense, the techniques can be very useful.

Music Therapy

Music therapy is the therapeutic use of any musical instrument or the voice to modify behavior. Its use is so common that we often don't consider it therapeutic. One of the most common uses of music, in a therapeutic sense, is background music. Music is used in many environments to set a mood. Background music is heard at supermarkets, in church, at football games, in bars, and in homes, to name but a few locations. In these cases, the music is used to set a mood, to cover unwanted sounds, to give a message, or to accomplish numerous other effects. While providing a background mood has been one of the major functions of music in the classroom, it is certainly not its only or most useful function.

McKinney (1978) identified several pertinent uses of music as a therapeutic tool. Music is a consistent, predictable structure in which the child can live, grow, and learn. It can provide success at any age level and at various severity levels of emotional conflict. Music provides the mildly handicapped a response medium that is never wrong, only different. Through successful participation, children can learn more about themselves. This, in turn, can lead to more self-confidence, as well as trust and self-control. As McKinney suggested, music entices the child to attend. This enticement seems to vary with the type music and the association the child makes with the music. The teacher can use this seemingly innate appeal that music has for children to entice them to attend and respond. By carefully selecting the length of musical selections, the teacher can build longer attention periods and even generalize attention to various activities.

Another potential of music for the mildly handicapped is for self-expression. Since these children may have difficulty expressing themselves through normal verbal channels, music can be used in a number of nonthreatening activities. These include singing, playing various instruments, and moving to various musical compositions. Youngsters can find acceptable avenues for expression in these activities.

Within McKinney's collection (1978) of songs are many that use the names of children. This is often very effective in opening and closing a class. McKinney (1978) suggested singing the following song to selected parts of the tune of "Mary Had a Little Lamb": "Hello, _____, how are you? We're glad that you're here today!" When singing songs of greeting, the verse is repeated for each child present. If the children are not too shy, they may be asked to stand while their names are sung. In order to provide some variety, the teacher can play the tune in different keys. Nordoff and Robbins (1968) have many excellent ideas for the inclusion of music as a therapeutic tool. Their "Goodbye, Heather," sung to the tune of "Goodnight Ladies," is an example of one way to close a music session. These examples are for primary-school-aged children, although similar techniques that are age appropriate can be used with older children. The use of our name is very important to all of us. For handicapped children, name use is even more critical for the development of self-image.

In the use of music with the handicapped, it is critical that the music be for therapeutic rather than performance value. The youngster who has a low self-concept, for example, will be unlikely to grow emotionally from an experience that emphasizes performance rather than emotional growth. Of course, music teachers want the best for their students. If a teacher has not had experience with mildly handicapped, many errors can be expected. This does not mean that the music teacher is uninterested or a poor teacher. This is an opportunity for cooperative efforts among interested staff members in order to assist the music teacher.

One of the most useful techniques that teachers with limited musical skills can use is movement therapy. Movement techniques offer tremendous possibilities to develop self-esteem, improve coordination, and increase self-expression. They can also be used to develop concepts of laterality (the concept of left and right), of spatial relationships (above and below, up and down, in front of and behind), and of directionality (the projection of concepts out from the person's body) (McKinney, 1978).

Resources for teachers are listed in the appendices of this chapter. In addition to these published sources, the teacher should not overlook the valuable resources available within nearly every school; the special education teacher and the music teacher. By working together with them to solve a specific educational need, you will probably find many additional musical activities that have affective potential for the mildly handicapped. In addition, this consultation will open new opportunities for professional sharing and growth.

Art Therapy

Art therapy is the use of art techniques for therapeutic values. Several common school art activities that can have therapeutic value are finger painting, drawing, working with clay, and paper construction. Like music therapy, art provides another channel for expression not offered by traditional forms of communication. Art expressions can help the youngsters who cannot express their innermost thoughts through verbal means, for example, to express these thoughts by drawing a picture. This technique is the basis for certain projective tests. While this is a valuable use of art techniques, it is not the appropriate use for teachers of the mildly handicapped since art as a projective technique requires special training not generally in the repertoire of the classroom teacher.

The classroom teacher can use art techniques as a springboard for the expression of feelings that would otherwise not surface. This can provide validation for observations made in the classroom (Reinert, 1980). Art therapy techniques should provide support for other affective interventions rather than being used as panacea in their own right. The person functioning as an art therapist should become an ally of the child's creativity by lending both technical assistance and emotional support (Kramer, 1971). Just as in music therapy, the art activity must be selected for its potential as an emotional-change agent rather than for artistic value. Kramer suggested that the end product is not the goal of art therapy. The emphasis must be for the expression of feelings and values that otherwise would go unobserved.

Therapeutic Play

One of the most promising activities for affective change is therapeutic play, which is the structuring of ordinary play activities so that therapeutic benefits can be achieved (Reinert, 1980). In our society, there seems to be a considerable emphasis toward organized play activities. City recreation departments, schools, scouts, 4-H Clubs, and church organizations all offer structured play. The youngster who is experiencing social developmental deficits has difficulties with the rules and interactions required by such structure. Readiness for these rather sophisticated activities needs to be developed in a structured, yet therapeutic, activity. When a child is ready to play alone, he or she is ready for individual skill development, which is the essence of therapeutic play. Generally, skills are developed in the home or preschool, but occasionally, these processes break down and progress in critical skill areas is terminated or is changed dramatically from a normal course of development. Generally, this breakdown involves the socializing process with family members as well as other children. As the situation deteriorates, the youngster is no longer allowed to have meaningful interactions with other children. It is not unusual for this to spread to other socialization processes until the child is virtually isolated. The child plays alone, is left in the car at the grocery store, stays at home when the family goes for a visit, and, in general, is left out of meaningful social situations.

When events like this occur over a long period of time, the child comes to school with few social skills and often has even fewer physical skills. The youngster is not ready for the games that other children are ready to play. Therapeutic play offers a structure to prepare the child for meaningful interaction. Activities such as wrestling, table or lawn tennis, fishing, skating, running and jumping, bowling, camping, hiking, and handball have therapeutic value. These activities, under close supervision and guidance, can help the youngster develop the individual skill and personal confidence to move to the next step, which is group interaction. The teacher must monitor group activities closely so that they don't deteriorate into disputes over rules, who pushed whom first, and eventual refusal to participate (Reinert, 1980).

In order for free-time activities to be therapeutic, they must be well-planned and integrated into needs for the children. Supervision needs to be more than guarding the playground from intruders and breaking up fights. This is an opportunity for the teacher to interact with children in a new social context. How many of us recall with fondness the teacher who participated in free-time activities? From this point, the integration of the child into appropriate peer activities is at least a possibility.

AFFECTIVE SKILLS AND BEHAVIORAL THEORY

Critics of behavioral theory will undoubtedly suggest that behavioral theory has nothing to do with affective education. Behaviorists will argue that one of the most efficient approaches to affective growth is through behavioral intervention.

The possibilities of debate seem limitless. It appears that behavior modification offers several important strategies that can be used effectively with the mildly handicapped.

Operant Conditioning

Operant behaviors are those behaviors that are emitted "voluntarily" without a visible explanation. The rate of occurrence of these behaviors is controlled by the events that follow (Swanson & Reinert, 1979). These voluntary behaviors may prompt a teacher or counselor to say, "John has a poor self-concept," or "Susan is angry today." While initial studies in operant conditioning were done with maladaptive behaviors (Lovaas, Freitas, Nelson, & Whalen, 1967), more recent studies have pointed to the value of operant conditioning as a tool to increase appropriate behaviors (O'Leary & O'Leary, 1977). For the mildly handicapped, we are generally not making massive behavioral changes, but only "fine tuning" affective responses. Operant conditioning that builds appropriate affect is, therefore, very useful.

While an understanding of personality development is not a prerequisite to the use of operant conditioning, it is useful to have an understanding of principles of self-development. It seems reasonable to expect that a teacher has been trained in personality development, and that reasonable goals will eminate from this understanding.

Operant conditioning offers the teacher a useful tool for observing and modifying behaviors in the regular or special class. The teacher simply observes the child and records the observations in a systematic fashion. With this information, a decision can be made whether or not to modify a behavior. Three basic steps are apparent in operant data collection. The data collected before intervention are called baseline data. The first function of these data is to determine if a need for change really exists. Many texts are available that provide the teacher with information useful in gathering baseline data (Buckley & Walker, 1970; MacMillan, 1973). A second function of baseline data is to provide the teacher with information about maintenance of behaviors. This process requires close observation on the part of the teacher to determine the reinforcing stimulus (stimulus that follows behavior) and the eliciting stimulus (stimulus that precedes behavior). Finally, baseline data provide the teacher with a standard of comparison once intervention has begun.

Once the teacher has decided to change certain behaviors, the arrangement of consequences becomes important. Arranging consequences requires the teacher to decide (1) which type of reinforcers to use; (2) the amount of reinforcement necessary; and (3) the type of reinforcement to use. For the mildly handicapped, it seems that mild reinforcers such as praise and attention are generally sufficient to make needed behavioral changes. Of course, more basic reinforcers like food and money would be effective, but these are generally considered inappropriate for mild problems.

The behaviors that might be considered mild problems include talking without permission, even when asked not to do so; failure to attend to classroom activities; causing distractions; talking back or ignoring staff members; showing aggressive behaviors toward others; fighting; and using inappropriate language. These behaviors may follow a pattern that is indicative of poor self-concept. If so, the teacher may wish to undertake activities designed to help the child build self-confidence. Appropriate reinforcement would be given when the youngster exhibits desired behaviors. Whenever possible, it is appropriate to build or increase existing behaviors that interfere with inappropriate responses rather than using extinction (weakening a behavior by withdrawal of reinforcement). Once a behavior is strengthened, it is desirable to encourage this behavior to occur in similar situations. For example, once a child interacts appropriately with peers in the classroom, this appropriate behavior can be encouraged, through appropriate reinforcement, to generalize to other situations. Generalization is an important concept of behavioral theory, and one that causes the mildly handicapped many problems. In fact, most mildly handicapped youngsters exhibit appropriate behavior at least some of the time—however, they do not generalize this appropriate behavior to other situations.

Another aspect of operant conditioning that is important for the mildly handicapped is the concept of discrimination (the opposite of generalization). Discrimination enables the child to know when to be aggressive and when to be more constrained. Social awareness is to some degree an expression of the ability to discriminate effectively between various social situations.

All of the elements of operant conditioning are fueled by reinforcement. These positive consequences are selected for their effectiveness in motivating changes in behavior. As suggested earlier, reinforcers should be selected that are socially acceptable and part of daily life: praise, a smile, a pat on the back, and other forms of personal attention are appropriate ways to encourage behaviors to occur. Once the reinforcers are selected it is necessary to decide when these will be used and under what conditions. This is commonly called scheduling reinforcers. Two basic schedules of reinforcement are used: ratio and interval.

Ratio Reinforcement

One of the most frequently used schedules of reinforcement is ratio reinforcement, which is varying the format of reinforcement according to behaviors. Ratio reinforcement may be either fixed or variable. When a reinforcer is given for every behavior or every fourth behavior, for example, it is called fixed ratio reinforcement. Variable reinforcement occurs when the number of reinforcers is not constant. For example, a reinforcer is given about once in every 10 correct responses in arithmetic. Sometimes a reinforcer is given after 2 responses, sometimes after 8, and sometimes after 13 correct responses. The relationship of responses to reward varies according to the plan of the person monitoring the reinforcement. Both fixed and variable reinforcement are effective tools in changing behavior as long as the reinforcers do not occur too infrequently (Swanson & Reinert, 1979). Acquiring new behaviors occurs best when a fixed ratio system with frequent reinforcement of responses is used. Generally, new behaviors are taught with fixed ratio reinforcement. The next schedule employed—variable ratio reinforcement schedule—makes the behaviors become engrained in the behavioral repertoire. When the number of reinforcers given is too low, the behavior is not maintained and will decrease. This phenomenon explains one of the problems of teachers who work with the mildly handicapped. Since the mildly handicapped generally appear to be very similar to normal children, it is often assumed that they should receive normal reinforcement. Often this is not the case, and appropriate behavior is slowly replaced with inappropriate behavior, which is reinforced.

Interval reinforcement is similar to ratio reinforcement except that the reinforcement is dependent upon the passing of time rather than the emission of responses. Giving a reinforcer for every 2 minutes of work, is called fixed interval reinforcement. When the amount of time between reinforcers is varied, it is called variable interval reinforcement. Both fixed and variable interval reinforcement are effective tools to change behaviors as long as the number of reinforcers is kept at a high level. One of the unique features of fixed interval reinforcement is that behavior increases rapidly before the end of the reinforcement period and slows dramatically during the first part of the interval immediately after reinforcement. In variable interval, the rate of behavior occurs at a relatively high level throughout the interval, since the person does not know when reinforcement will occur. Behavior that is maintained by variable interval reinforcement is more difficult to extinguish than that maintained through fixed interval reinforcement. Reinforcement based on time is used in schools in a less formal way than ratio reinforcement; however, it is an effective tool when used with precision.

Behavior modification offers the classroom teacher one of the most effective tools for changing behaviors of mildly handicapped. Since the focus is not on the pathology that causes the inappropriate behaviors, the system is potentially very efficient. Also, the technique seems to work equally well with all handicapping conditions as well as with nonhandicapped children. Therefore, it can be used within the regular classroom without concern for negative outcome.

The major limiting question is whether the desired behavior is within a child's present or potential repertoire (Swanson & Reinert, 1979). This generally should not be a serious concern when teaching the mildly handicapped. According to Krasner & Ullmann (1965), three general considerations should be considered in practical application of operant conditioning: the teacher must (1) decide which maladaptive behaviors should be decreased and which adaptive behaviors should be increased; (2) determine the environmental consequences that are maintaining maladaptive behaviors and not allowing adaptive behaviors to flourish; and (3) assess the potential environmental consequences to determine their relative value in changing behaviors.

The rationale of teacher involvement in the affective domain was discussed by Clarizio and Yelon (1967). In making a case for the use of behavior modification techniques, they pointed out that teachers are not trained to know the causes of mental problems, are rarely in a position to influence the cause of deviance, and probably would be ineffective in changing the behaviors if causal factors were available since behavior is rarely maintained for the same reasons as originally caused the behavior. Since, by definition, the mildly handicapped are not seriously emotionally troubled, this argument is weakened, but behavior modification still seems to be a useful tool for the management of affective behaviors.

While behavior modification is effective, there remains considerable concern for the appropriate level of modification. Generally, teachers are reluctant to use highly sophisticated techniques with mild problems, even though positive results are likely. Whether or not behavioral practices follow rigid technical standards is probably not critical so long as the teacher is diligent in observation of behaviors and their consequences.

Observation and Recording Behaviors

The basis of behavior modification is the observation and recording of behaviors in a precise and efficient manner. In order to perform the varied requirements of measurement efficiently, the teacher must understand the various observation and recording techniques available. Blackman and Silberman (1975) outlined five steps of observation and recording.

1. Determine the setting for recording behaviors.
2. Decide on a method to code the behavior.
3. Determine the interval of time in which behaviors will be observed.
4. Observe and record a time during which no intervention takes place.
5. Plot the observations on a graph. (Generally, the frequency of behaviors is plotted on the vertical axis while the successive behaviors over time are charted on the horizontal axis.)

Measurement and Recording Behaviors

Two techniques are commonly used for the measurement of behaviors in the classroom: the measurement of permanent products (tangible results of a person's work) and observational recording when permanent products are not produced. When working with affective behaviors, there are often no permanent products available for measurement. Therefore, observational recording is most often used. Five types of observational recording were listed by Hall (1971): (1) continuous recording; (2) event recording; (3) duration recording; (4) interval recording; and (5) time sampling.

Continuous recording. Continuous recording is the most inefficient recording technique available to the classroom teacher, but it is critical for proper interpretation of some behaviors. Continuous recording allows the teacher to have a complete record of occurrences of behavior—including the behaviors that preceded the recorded behavior as well as those following it. This helps the teacher to pinpoint the problem, to determine the constellation of behaviors that are reinforcing the behavior, and to record these behaviors for future reference (Swanson & Reinert, 1979). Using continuous recording and observation is essential for the teacher to get the "big picture" and avoid fragmentation of efforts.

Event recording. Event recording is the continuous recording of discrete behaviors. The results of event observation may be recorded in terms of rate, percentage, or frequency (Swanson & Reinert, 1979). This technique is one of the most frequently used observational recording techniques. It is valuable for use with behaviors common to the mildly handicapped. Fighting, talking out in class, and abusive language are all examples of behaviors that are of short duration and do not occur frequently.

Durational recording. Durational recording gives information about the length of a particular behavior. For example, if daydreaming is the problem, it is useful to know whether the daydreaming occurs for 2 minutes or 20 minutes. Durational recording, like continuous recording, is very inefficient. The decision to use this technique depends upon the need for the data and the availability of teacher time for the observation.

Interval recording. Interval observation and recording is used when it is important to determine whether a particular behavior occurred or failed to occur over a specified period of time. The technique has several advantages: it (1) allows for the recording of several behaviors at one time; (2) can help the teacher predict when and under what conditions the behavior will occur; and (3) allows for behavior from more than one youngster to be recorded concurrently (Cooper, 1974). This technique is especially useful with mildly handicapped youngsters who are integrated into the regular classroom. The teacher often will want to evaluate several behaviors concurrently or observe one behavior with several youngsters. This is possible with interval recording.

Time sampling. Time sampling is similar to interval recording except that only one observation is made during the observation period, at the end of the time block. The behavior of the student during the remainder of the time period is not recorded or even observed. This technique is used when it is important to know whether or not a behavior occurs while the teacher continues teaching.

Time samples are generally made at the end of each time segment (every 2 or 5 minutes, for example); however, Hall (1971) suggested that time samples can also be taken at irregular intervals and with more than one youngster at one time.

Once the teacher has selected a technique for observation and recording behaviors, it is just a matter of time until baseline data is available and teaching strategies are underway. The teacher must decide whether it is important to increase or decrease behaviors, or leave them unchanged.

Increasing Behaviors

Techniques for increasing behaviors include shaping (using reinforcement and extinction in combination), fading (varying the stimuli until a response is made without prompts), and chaining (combining several discrete behaviors into a series of continuous behaviors). The use of positive reinforcement is the most commonly used of all techniques in changing behaviors; however, there are other behavioral techniques available to the classroom teacher.

Negative Reinforcement

Negative reinforcement is one of the most misunderstood techniques available to the teacher. It is essentially an avoidance technique since the child exhibits a desirable behavior in order to avoid aversive stimuli. Negative reinforcement is often confused with punishment, although the two procedures differ in both definition and in outcomes. Negative reinforcement, which is removed in this process, causes an increase in the target behavior while punishment causes a decrease in the target behavior. Punishment provides a "quick fix" of behaviors, which is a very tempting but often not productive way of coping with affective and behavioral problems, although Hall (1972) has shown effective uses for the technique. Gardner (1977) pointed out that punishment may generalize to other areas of the classroom, require regular association with conditioned aversive events, and provide no possibility for acquiring appropriate behaviors. Since it is only natural for an acquired behavior to be continued, the person who is inhibited by punishment may emit another inappropriate behavior rather than developing appropriate ones. For these reasons, the use of negative reinforcement should be preferred to the use of punishment.

Contingency Management

Contingency management is a behavioral concept that is closely related to operant conditioning. The basic difference is the relative structure of each. Homme, Csanyi, Gonzales, & Rechs (1969) outlined several basic rules for the development of contracting or contingency management: (1) the reinforcement should be immediate; (2) the small segments that make up the total contractual agreement should be rewarded; (3) the contract must be fair to all sides; and (4) contracting should concern positive growth rather than simple adherence to a rule or edict of the teacher. Homme, et al. (1969) developed a self-instructional program for use with contingency contracting. It contains pre- and post-tests for the person studying the material to assess individual progress. One of the strengths of contingency management is its accepted use in the regular classroom; however, its weakness is implied by those who consider it a form of bribery.

Behavior Modeling

Bandura (1969) discussed behavior modeling, which is a theory of critical importance to the mildly handicapped. Three different classes of response are affected by modeling: (1) new behavior; (2) old behavior; and (3) responses that are presently dormant. Modeling is considerably different than operant conditioning. Reinforcement is not essential for the development of new behaviors in behavior modeling, although growth can be enhanced by its use (Swanson & Reinert, 1979). Behaviors that include small steps that occur in rapid sequence are easily learned through imitation or modeling. Hitting a baseball and driving a car are both examples of behaviors that can be partially or totally taught through modeling techniques. The concept of behavioral modeling is very important to the affective growth of youngsters. When a child does not perform at a comparable skill level as peers, his or her confidence may be eroded. When this occurs, the youngster may begin to model any behaviors that are readily observable. It is critical that such children have appropriate models for observation and imitation.

In a study of the capitulation behaviors of emotionally disturbed and normal youngsters, Reinert (1968) found that both groups imitate the behaviors of others when there is pressure toward conformity. It is important, therefore, that appropriate models be available whenever possible. As Banudra (1965) pointed out, children can learn from others once they recognize that other people are a source of learning.

Procedures to Decrease Behaviors

Reinforcing Conflicting Behaviors

Three techniques are commonly used to replace behaviors through the use of competing behaviors (Swanson & Reinert, 1979): (1) reinforcement of behavior that will not allow another behavior to occur (reinforce in-seat behavior to compete with out-of-seat behavior); (2) differential reinforcement of other behaviors (DRO) that occur at the same time as the undesirable response; and (3) reinforcement of the child for not responding to an undesirable behavior.

Extinction

Extinction is the process of removing reinforcing stimuli and so decreasing the strength of a behavior. This process will occur in the case of appropriate and inappropriate responses. The usefulness of this technique is dependent upon the ability to identify and remove the stimuli that is maintaining the behavior. Of course, this is often impossible to do since some behaviors are not under the control of reinforcers within the teacher's control. One of the behaviors that is subject to extinction is talking without permission. Ignoring this behavior will cause it to decrease. It is no longer interesting if all attention is taken away. Often, this is impossible since much reinforcement comes from students rather than the teacher. Not only is ignoring the inappropriate behavior important, but reinforcing the appropriate behavior (being quiet or asking permission to speak) is essential. Teachers often have difficulty ignoring behaviors that appear to be direct affronts to their authority, and sometimes find it impossible to praise behaviors that they believe should be exhibited without praise.

Overcorrection

Overcorrection requires a child to overpractice a behavior. This technique has been used by teachers for many generations. It is an extremely difficult technique to use since the overcorrection can be interpreted as a punitive act used to "get even." When a youngster runs down the stairs, the teacher might say, "State the rule about walking down the stairs." In addition, the teacher might require the child to walk down the stairs so the behavior is imprinted on his or her mind. It is the writer's impression that the youngster interprets this episode as punishment and learns to walk down the stairs only when the teacher is present.

Satiation

Another way to decrease behaviors is through the use of satiation or negative practice. Notable examples include having children chew paper wads or bounce a ball after school—five thousand times, practices the writer remembers very vividly. Chewing paper wads makes one's stomach sick and bouncing a ball increases ball-bouncing skills. Neither did anything for behaviors or attitudes toward the teacher who insisted on the completion of these tasks. The tasks are remembered, but then the memory of getting spanked in school does not dim either. It seems that more appropriate methods of coping with inappropriate responses are possible; this technique should be put aside in favor of more useful and humane treatment.

Changing the Stimulus Environment

The stimulus environment includes the events, activities, persons, places, smells, etc., which have a stimulus effect for certain behaviors. Anyone who has worked with emotionally disturbed youngsters knows the effect of stimulus changes. The behaviorally disordered child will often exhibit a positive personality change following a change of classroom. This is sometimes referred to as a honeymoon period and may last for 1 or 2 days or weeks. In fact, a change of environment may have lasting effects if the child begins to experience success in the new environment.

The concept of changing the stimulus environment is similar to the psychodynamic concept of milieu therapy, discussed earlier. Changing the stimulus environment is one of the easiest tasks for the teacher and school to undertake. Matching the right teacher to the right children in a classroom setting can often bring about dramatic changes in affective development.

Desensitization

Another type of extinction is desensitization—the reduction of fears and anxieties in persons through a systematic behavioral process. Typically, this involves the presentation of a stimulus that produces inappropriate reactions without a consequence (extinction). In addition, other stimuli are presented that act to cue other competing responses,which are reinforced (Swanson & Reinert, 1979). The presentation of a weak stimulus, that ordinarily produces anxiety, at the same time as a stronger stimulus, that ordinarily produces joy, will help the child overcome the anxiety. Another example of desensitization that is appropriate for use with the mildly handicapped is progressive relaxation (Wolpe, 1969). In this technique, the child is put in a relaxed state and then exposed to anxiety-producing events or people. The activities are gradually increased until the anxiety-producing state is very similar to the actual situation in which the fear or anxiety is predominant. Another desensitization technique is the use of emotive imagery (Lazarus & Abramovitz, 1962). This technique involves the identification of the child's favorite television hero. The therapist describes a scene in which the hero is a part. Gradually, the child's fears or anxieties are also brought into the story. If anxiety appears, the child is instructed to raise a finger as a signal. When this occurs, the therapist eases off on the inclusion of the fears until a comfortable level is again reached.

Reducing Emotional Behaviors through Observation of Others

Some children learn many of their emotional responses through the observation of others. Just as appropriate emotional responses to animals, people, and machines can be observed and learned, so can inappropriate responses be learned. Gardner (1977) outlined a five-step process for the reduction of inappropriate emotional behaviors through observation: (1) identify events that produce inappropriate responses in the child; (2) identify a model who is not affected inappropriately by these events; (3) arrange for the model to be in the presence of the event that causes inappropriate behavior; (4) have the child observe the model engaged in appropriate interaction with the event; and (5) repeat this interaction several times so that the child will gradually lose the inappropriate response. This concept is similar to behavior modeling except that it is more structured.

Identification of Reinforcers

One of the troublesome areas for teachers is the identification of appropriate reinforcers. Typically, people identify consequences that work but that are too powerful in terms of what is actually needed to modify behavior. When teachers think of reinforcers, they often consider candy, food, or exotic reinforcers such as going to a movie or on a camping trip. Of course, these are good and effective reinforcers. For the mildly handicapped or normal child these seem to be inappropriate, however. Reinforcers should be identified that will maintain appropriate behaviors at a high level without being too far removed from the reinforcement that a regular classroom teacher or parent would use. Some acceptable examples include positive comments by the teacher or other staff, approving gestures, and positive phone calls home. Generally, the use of food or money should be avoided with the mildly handicapped child since these reinforcers will have to be phased out, which is a difficult task with some children. Also, parents and teachers generally will not support the use of these powerful reinforcers in mild problem areas.

The selection of reinforcers becomes more difficult for older youngsters. Secondary-school students can often acquire certain reinforcers more readily for themselves than they can earn them in school. The personal value of the teacher for this age group should not be overlooked. Even though the student may be able to acquire the reinforcement on their own, the value of the person who gives the reinforcer is also important.

Evaluation of Behavioral Change

Once a behavior has changed, the teacher will want to determine whether the change was related to the program or to other factors. Several techniques are available to provide this information. Suppose the teacher has one youngster who persists in talking whenever he wishes. The teacher sets up a modification design to modify this behavior. Every time the youngster talks without permission the teacher turns her back on the child. Baseline behavior is taken, but no follow-up is made following the intervention. How does the staff know if the behavior is changing? Is it becoming less frequent or increasing? The only way to know the answer for certain is to count the behaviors and compare the results with the baseline count.

Return to Baseline

One of the more elementary ways to evaluate the effectiveness of an intervention process is to return to the baseline procedure with no intervention strategy present. This will show if the behavior being modified has been changed. To return to baseline, the teacher or therapist simply stops the intervention procedure for a period of time. If the appropriate behavior maintains itself without intervention, it means that no further intervention is necessary. This procedure does not show whether the intervention is responsible for the change or whether other factors were responsible. If additional information is desired, the teacher may want to use a complete reversal design (Gardner, 1977). For the mildly handicapped child, there seems to be little reason to use more sophisticated methods than the return to baseline; however, if the staff is interested in more sophisticated designs for evaluation, Gardner (1977) offered two possibilities: the multiple baseline and the changing-criterion design.

One of the major strengths of the behavioral approach is in its use to evaluate affective growth, regardless of whether a behavioral design is used to implement the change. This is particularly important for the evaluation of approaches that are innately weak in evaluation (e.g., psychodynamic interventions). The teacher should not hesitate to use a humanistic intervention along with a behavioral evaluation design.

AFFECTIVE SKILLS AND SOCIAL-ECOLOGICAL THEORY

Social and ecological theories both offer the classroom teacher a wealth of techniques and materials for the development of affective skills. Social theory is focused on the environment of the person being studied. In many respects, people are what their environment has been. If everyone reviews what has made them what they are, a high priority will be placed on where they were born and grew up. The games that were or were not played as a child, a parent's love, those with whom one shares his or her life, and the places visited are all important.

Ecological thought includes social interaction but it is much more; it is the interaction with the environment rather than just the experience. People do not simply experience their world; they also interact with it. This interaction gives rise to the ecological approach, which is a holistic theory that is concerned with all facets of life. Since the ecological and social approaches include so many common elements, no attempt will be made to separate the practical application of the two approaches.

Several authors have written about the concept of socialization and its relationship to emotional difficulties (Hobbs, 1966; Morse, 1977). It is now generally believed that social atmosphere is one of the more critical factors in the mental health of youngsters. In a study of the differences in prevalence and incidence of mental illness among social classes, Hollingshead and Redlich (1958) found considerable differences in several areas related to social issues. In general, the number of instances of emotional difficulties increased in the lower social levels. Treatment also varied, with members of lower social classes receiving longer treatment periods.

Some have argued that the labeling process is the cause of emotional difficulties (Becker, 1973; Schur, 1971). From this viewpoint, the behavior becomes deviant and the person who exhibits it abnormal because someone of social value has labeled the act and person as inappropriate to the situation. While this issue has not come to any conclusive settlement, it is obvious that various social levels will tolerate deviance in different areas, to different degrees, and under different conditions.

Project Re-Ed

Project Re-Ed is one of the most widely publicized social-ecological programs for the treatment of emotionally disturbed children. It was designed to treat seriously disturbed people in a total care residential approach. Re-Ed has not been represented as a singular approach, but rather a basic theoretical approach duplicated with some variation by many practitioners (Hobbs, 1966; Lee, 1971; Lewis,

1967; Weinstein, 1969). Project Re-Ed, as a therapeutic tool, is of limited value so far as the mildly handicapped population is concerned since this group will probably be educated in the regular classroom; however, the philosophy of Re-Ed incorporates many useful ideas for the mildly handicapped. Hobbs (1966) outlined the thirteen processes of Re-Ed:

1. *Life is to be lived now.* Traditionally, children were put into educational programs in order to have something for them to do while the "real reason" for being in school took place: "treatment." In other words, children are treated and then educated. In Re-Ed every hour is important for its own sake.

2. *Time is an ally.* Rather than placing a child in the program for 2 or 3 years, which is not uncommon in other total care programs, the goal is for a 6-month treatment program.

3. *Trust is essential.* This statement certainly applies to the mildly handicapped. Once a child is identified and labeled deviant, trust is often at a very low level. The skill of the teacher-counselor in developing trust is much easier in a re-education setting, but it is no less critical in the regular school environment.

4. *Competence makes the difference.* The confidence children have in themselves is to some degree dependent upon experiences in school. This is even more critical if youngsters are not building competence outside of school. Teachers should try to have all youngsters achieve success in school, whether in academics, personal relationships, athletics, drama, or related activities. The idea of therapeutic play, discussed earlier, is related to the importance of this principle.

5. *Symptoms can and should be controlled.* Project Re-Ed believes in the importance of structure within the lives of children. Children are expected to attend to classroom instruction, work, and do the other things that a student is expected to do. Under traditional therapy, it is not so critical to control symptomatic behaviors since this is the "trail" to causal factors. Re-Ed takes a very behavioral approach in this regard, and is based on the belief that symptoms *are* the problem.

6. *Cognitive control can be taught.* Much of the job of self-monitoring is cognitive in nature. This control can be taught through verbal interaction with students. Opportunities for this interaction are provided continually through group and individual interactions with staff and other students. Through interaction, children are expected to gain insight into their behaviors and self-control.

7. *Feelings should be nurtured.* Re-Ed expects children to have feelings and to nurture the healthy release of these feelings in games, art, music, and other useful activities. All destructive release of emotions is not condoned. Fighting, tantrum behaviors, and hurting others is not approved. Often the feelings of children have been blunted by adults and other children. These must be massaged to life before the full potential of their value can be realized.

8. *The group is important to children.* There is concern that each child have a group of peers that he or she can relate to effectively. This group should be as close to the mainstream as possible. One of the misconceptions of a group atmosphere, however, is that any group will be good so long as it is with normal children. Nothing could be further from logical thinking, since a

group in which the child cannot relate is not a therapeutic group. The key to achieving a useful group is careful selection of students and vigilant observation to maintain relationships.

9. *Ceremony and ritual give order, stability, and confidence.* Everyone needs structure in their lives. Some people demand a high degree of sameness while others require less ritual. Whatever the case, structure is important, especially for those who are experiencing frustration in other segments of their lives. The ceremony and ritual of Re-Ed need not be replicated, but some ritual like preparation for lunch or going home can give special meaning and closeness to individuals and to a group.

10. *The body is the armature of the self.* This idea is related to the concept of therapeutic play, discussed earlier. Our self-image is to some degree developed through our physical abilities. The emphasis on physical health, jogging, physical recreation, and sports in our society underscores the importance of physical skill development.

11. *Communities are important.* This is an important concept for all children to develop. The mildly handicapped child is probably very similar to the normal child in this regard. Field trips to study important community activities, to police and fire departments, and to agencies that offer valuable community services are all worthwhile activities. 4-H Clubs, scouts, and community theater are all excellent possibilities for the involvement of young people.

12. *A child should know joy.* One of the missing ingredients in program operation is often a sense of joy, including the feeling that school can be fun, as well as a growth experience. Re-Ed emphasizes this aspect continually by selecting activities that interest youngsters during school and during evening hours. Each day the students are told what new experiences will happen the following day in order to build a sense of anticipation. One of my impressions of visiting Project Re-Ed schools was the joy that appeared to permeate both children and staff.

13. *Middle class values should be taught.* One of the deleterious effects of labeling includes building certain expectations with people who interact with the "handicapped." Normal youngsters are free to express themselves more freely than those who are handicapped by labels. In order to help dispel preconceived ideas of being emotionally disturbed, retarded, or learning disabled, children must be taught "middle class values" in regard to dress, cleanliness, language, and behavior. The more these values can be incorporated into the youngsters' behavior, the more easily social acceptance can be achieved.

AFFECTIVE SKILLS AND COUNTER THEORY

Counter theorists are those who travel to the beat of a "different drum" in their quest for educational growth. Generally, they follow a humanistic approach to change; they question the time-honored principles of educational practice; they see the teacher as a stimulator of growth rather than a fountain of knowledge; and they challenge the concept of literacy. Some would completely destroy the school as it is presently constituted, while others would be satisfied with drastic revisions. All counter theorists are dissatisfied with public schools as they exist

(Cleaver, 1968; Glasser, 1969; Reimer, 1972; Tracy, 1972). While many approaches have been put forth by counter theorists, only one, reality therapy (Glasser, 1965) is discussed here. Of all counter theories presented to date, none has caught the mood of teachers and support personnel as this theory has. A major reason for the success of this approach lies in its simplicity, logic, and positive nature. It gives hope to the school staff. It offers solutions that are believable.

Glasser (1965) proposed a system of intervention (reality therapy), which is useful with mildly handicapped. This therapy is opposed to labeling and is geared to mainstream education. Glasser (1965) defined it as a therapy that leads all patients toward reality. Glasser believed that deviance occurs when people do not have their essential needs met. The basic needs, to love and be loved and to feel worthwhile, are the essential ingredients for a healthy personality. Glasser believed that a person must maintain a satisfactory level of behavior in order to be healthy. In addition, a person must fulfill his or her needs in a way that does not deprive other people of fulfilling their needs. This is called acting responsibly, and it is a trait of the healthy individual.

Glasser (1965) proposed a three-step process: (1) the therapist must develop some acceptable level of involvement with the person under treatment; (2) the therapist must reject the inappropriate behavior, and get the person to also reject this behavior, as unproductive; and (3) the therapist must help the person develop new skills that are appropriate in meeting his or her needs. It appears that reality therapy includes a unique blend of psychodynamic and behavioral thought in such a way as to capitalize on the strengths of both approaches.

AFFECTIVE TRAINING MATERIALS

A considerable number of materials are now available that emphasize the affective needs of youngsters (Appendices 17-A–17-D). Within their individual components, these materials can provide excellent ideas for the teacher to use in both the regular and special class. A major weakness of these materials does exist, however. The materials are not sequenced in any useable fashion. Unless the teacher provides the structure for the activities, there is none. It would be possible, therefore, to work on assertiveness one day and being patient the next. The teacher must decide what is needed by each youngster. In this way, any program can offer continuity and substance. The materials selected for presentation in the appendices were chosen for their relevance to the mildly handicapped. Many of these materials can also be used by normal children.

The affective materials are grouped into four broad categories: (1) published sources for teachers and other professionals; (2) materials for parents; (3) published materials for use with youngsters; and (4) materials adapted for use with mildly handicapped children.

REFERENCES

Axline, V. *Play therapy*. Boston: Houghton Mifflin, 1947.

Bandura, A. Behavior modification through modeling procedures. In Krasner, L. & Ullman, L. (eds.), *Research in behavior modification*. New York: Holt, 1965.

Bandura, A. *Principles of behavior modification*. New York: Holt, 1969.

Becker, H. *Outsiders: Studies in the sociology of deviance.* New York, Free Press, 1973.

Benson, D., & Cessna, K. *The Colorado guidelines handbook for education & related services for SIBD students.* Denver: Colorado Department of Education, 1980.

Blackham, G., & Silberman, A. *Modification of child and adolescent behavior* (2nd ed.). Belmont, Ca.: Wadsworth, 1975.

Bloom, B., Engelhart, M., Furst, E., Hill, W., & Krathwohl, D. *Human characteristics and school learning.* New York: McGraw-Hill, 1976.

Bower, E., & Lambert, N. In-school screening of children with emotional handicaps. In N. Long, W. Morse, R. Newman (Eds.): *Conflict in the classroom* (2nd ed.). Belmont, Ca.: Wadsworth, 1971.

Buckley, N., & Walker, H. *Modifying classroom behavior.* Champaign, Il.: Research Press, 1970.

Clarizio, H., & Yelon, S. Learning therapy approaches to classroom management: Rationale & intervention techniques. *Journal of Special Education,* 1967, *1,* 267–274.

Cleaver, E. *Soul on ice.* New York: McGraw-Hill, 1968.

Cooper, J. *Measurement and analysis of behavior techniques.* Columbus, Oh.: Charles E. Merrill, 1974.

Gardner, W. *Learning and behavior characteristics of exceptional children and youth.* Boston: Allyn & Bacon, 1977.

Glasser, W. *Reality therapy.* New York: Harper & Row, 1965.

Glasser, W. *Schools without failure.* New York: Harper & Row, 1969.

Hall, V. *Behavior modification: Basic principles.* Lawrence, Kans.: H & H Enterprises, 1971.

Hall, V., Axelrod, S., Foundopoulos, J., Shellman, J., Campbell, R., & Cranston, S. The effective use of punishment to modify behavior in the classroom. In K. O'Leary & S. O'Leary (Eds.), *Classroom management: the successful use of behavior modification* (2nd ed.). New York: Pergammon Press, 1972.

Hobbs, N. Helping disturbed children: Psychological and ecological strategies. *American Psychologist,* 1966, *21,* 1105–1115.

Hollingshead, A., & Redlich F. *Social class and mental illness: A community study.* New York: Wiley, 1958.

Homme, L., Csanyi, A. Gonzales, M., & Rechs, J. *How to use contingency contracting in the classroom.* Champaign, Il.: Research Press, 1969.

Kramer, E. *Art as therapy with children.* New York: Schocken Books, 1971.

Krasner, L., & Ullmann, L. *Research in behavior modification: New developments and implications.* New York: Holt, Rinehart & Winston, 1965.

Lazarus, A., & Abramovitz, A. The use of "emotive imagery" in the treatment of children's phobias. *Journal of Mental Science,* 1962, *108,* 191–195.

Lee, B. Curriculum design: The re-education approach. In N. Long, W. Morse, & R. Newman (Eds.), *Conflict in the classroom.* Belmont, Ca.: Wadsworth, 1971.

Lewin, K. *A dynamic view of personality.* New York: McGraw-Hill, 1935.

Lewis, W. Project re-ed. In E. Cowen, E. Gardner, & M. Zax (Eds.), *Emergent approaches to mental health problems.* New York: Appleton-Century-Crofts, 1967.

Lovaas, O. I., Freitas, L., Nelson, K., & Whalen, C. The establishment of imitation and its use for the establishment of complex behavior in schizophrenic children. *Behavior Research and Therapy,* 1967, *5,* 171–181.

MacMillan, D. *Behavior modification in education.* New York: MacMillan, 1973.

McKinney, C. *Music therapy activities for emotionally disturbed children,* Unpublished thesis, the School of Educational Change & Development, Greeley, Co., 1978.

Morse, W. Serving the needs of individuals with behavioral disorders. *Exceptional Children,* 1977, *44,* 158–164.

Morse, W., Ardizzone, J., Macdonald, C., & Pasick, P. *Affective education for special children and youth.* Reston, Va.: Council for Exceptional Children, 1980.

Morse, W., & Smith, J. *Understanding child variance.* Reston, Va.: Council for Exceptional Children, 1980.

Nelson, R. Elementary school counseling with unstructured play media. *Personnel and Guidance Journal,* 1966, *45,* 24–27.

Nordoff, P., & Robbins, C. *The second book of children's play songs,* Bryn Mawr, Pa.: Theodore Pussor, 1968.

O'Leary, K., & O'Leary, S. *Classroom management: The successful use of behavior modification* (2nd ed.). New York: Pergammon Press, 1977.

Redl, F. The concept of therapeutic milieu. *American Journal of Orthopsychiatry,* 1959, *29,* 1–18.

Redl, F. The concept of therapeutic milieu. In N. Long, W. Morse, & R. Newman (Eds.), *Conflict in the classroom.* Belmont, Ca.: Wadsworth, 1976.

Reimer, E. Unusual ideas in education. In W. Rhodes & M. L. Tracy (Eds.), *A study of child variance*. Ann Arbor, Mich.: University of Michigan Press, 1972.

Reinert, H. Decision making in the educationally handicapped and normal child; a comparative study. Ed.D. dissertation, Colorado State College, Greeley, Co., 1968.

Reinert, H. *Children in conflict: Educational strategies for the emotionally disturbed and behaviorally disordered*. St. Louis: C. V. Mosby, 1976.

Reinert, H. *Children in conflict: Educational strategies for the emotionally disturbed and behaviorally disordered* (2nd ed.). St. Louis: C. V. Mosby, 1980.

Rhodes, W., & Tracy, M. (Eds.). *A study of child variance*. Ann Arbor, Mich.: University of Michigan Press, 1972.

Schur, E. *Labeling deviant behavior: Its socio-logical implications*. New York: Harper & Row, 1971.

Sinacore, J. Priorities in health education. *Journal of School Health*, 1978, *48*, 213–217.

Swanson, L., & Reinert, H *Teaching strategies for children in conflict*. St. Louis: C. V. Mosby, 1979.

Tracy, M. Conceptual models of emotional disturbance: Some other thoughts. In W. Rhodes & M.L. Tracy (Eds.), *A study of child variance*. Ann Arbor, Mich.: University of Michigan Press, 1972.

Weinstein, L. Project re-ed: Schools for emotionally disturbed children—Effectiveness as viewed by referring agencies, parents and teachers. *Exceptional Children*, 1969, *35*, 703–711.

Wolpe, J. *The practice of behavior therapy*. Oxford: Pergamon, 1969.

APPENDIX 17-A: PUBLISHED SOURCES FOR TEACHERS AND OTHER PROFESSIONALS

Canfield J., & Wells, H. *One hundred ways to enhance self-concept in the class-room*. Englewood Cliffs: Prentice-Hall, 1976.

This book contains excellent ideas for the development of self-concept activities. The activities are not sequenced.

Carkhuff, R. *The art of problem solving*. Amherst, Ma.: Human Resource Development Press, 1972.

A simple presentation of phases of problem solving is presented along with guidelines for facilitating goal definition.

Casteel, J. *Learning to think and choose*. Santa Monica, Ca.: Goodyear Publishing, 1978.

This is a highly structured professional guide for affective teaching. The material is aimed at middle school level.

Castello, G. *Left handed teaching*. New York: Holt, Rinehart and Winston, 1978.

Ideas and lessons in teaching the hard-to-reach youngster are presented in this professional handbook of ideas. It is an excellent affective sourcebook.

Cedoline, A. *The effect of affect*. San Rafael, Ca.: Academic Therapy Publishing, 1977.

This book presents activities for the development of self-esteem, self-discipline, decision-making skills, and skill in relationship building. Materials are appropriate for middle grades.

Charles, C. *Teacher's petit Piaget*. Belmont, Ca.: Fearon Publications, 1976.

Short, easy descriptions and explanations of Piaget's theory as it relates to young children.

Chase, L. *The other side of the report card*. Santa Monica, Ca.: Goodyear Publishing, 1975.

This material explores the concept of affective education in sample units such as self-disclosure, test-taking, and goal setting.

Dreikurs, R. *Discipline without tears*. New York: Hawthorne Books, 1972.

This reference book for teachers describes useful management techniques and emphasizes democratic functioning.

Dreyer, S. *The bookfinder*. Circle Pines, Mn.: American Guidance Services, 1977.

This is a professional guide to children's book titles that have specific therapeutic value for affective growth.

Elardo, P., & Cooper, M. *Aware*. Menlo Park, Ca.: Addison Wesley Publishing, 1977.

This book offers professionals many activities, games, and problem-solving situations.

Fagen, S. *Teaching children self-control*. Columbus, Oh.: Charles E. Merrill, 1975.

A guidebook for professionals to assist children in gaining self-control.

Freed, A. *T.A. for tots*. Sacramento, Ca.: Jalmar Press, Inc., 1973.

This book explains and illustrates the basics of transactional analysis. It is also available in kit format.

Good mental health in the classroom. Columbia, S.C.: South Carolina State Department of Education, 1973.

This handbook for teachers is designed to give practical tips for student behavior problems.

Hendricks, G., & Wills, R. *The centering book*. Englewood Cliffs: Prentice-Hall, 1975.

This is a useful professional guide that presents activities for awareness and relaxation. Materials are geared to grades 3–10. A second centering book is also available.

Howe, L., & Howe, M. *Personalizing education*. New York: A & W Publishing, 1975.

This is a guide to personal growth through educational processes for use by teachers or other educational professionals.

Kalb, J., & Viscott, D. *What every kid should know*. New York: Houghton Mifflin, 1974.

This is an excellent resource for teachers and counselors in developing affective education programs.

Kniker, C. *You and values education*. Columbus, Oh.: Charles E. Merrill, 1977.

This book provides an excellent presentation of information for values clarification.

London-Dahm, M., & Dahm, J. *An affective learning system for group facilitators*. Centerville, Oh.: Learning Development Systems, 1975.

This is a professional guide with materials for affective education. Use of this material requires professional group work skill.

Merritt, R., & Walley, D. *The group leader's handbook*. Champaign, Il.: Research Press, 1977.

This is a helpful user's guide for teachers and counselors which outlines techniques for organizing and facilitating group activities.

Raths, L., Harmin, M., & Simon, S. *Values and teaching*. Columbus, Oh.: Charles E. Merrill, 1978.

This is a professional-level book on values clarification in the classroom.

Rubin, R. V. *Using bibliotherapy sourcebook*. Phoenix, Az.: Oryx Press, 1978.

This reviews the use of literature for therapeutic purposes. It also discusses the application of bibliotherapy.

Simon, S., Howe, L., & Kirschenbaum, H. *Values clarification*. New York: A. & W. Visual Library, 1978.

This is a handbook of strategies in values clarification for the classroom teacher.

Simon, S., & O'Rourke, R. *Developing values in exceptional children*. Englewood Cliffs: Prentice-Hall, 1977.

This book offers teachers many activities in the development of values. Each technique is paired with an example developed with emotionally disturbed children.

Stanford, G. *Developing effective classroom groups*. New York: Hart, 1977.

This is a practical guide for professionals in the development of group processes.

APPENDIX 17-B: MATERIALS FOR PARENTS

Baker, B., Brightman, A., Heifetz, L., & Murphy, D. *Behavior problems*. Champaign, Il.: Research Press, 1979.

This is a training manual for use with parents who need help with behavior of children.

Briggs, D. *Your child's self-esteem*. Garden City, N.Y.: Doubleday, 1975.

This parent material is excellent as a tool to help parents work with children in affective development. A book and cassette tape are included.

Dinkmeyer, D., & McKay, G. *Systematic training for effective parenting*. Circle Pines, Mn.: American Guidance Services, 1976.

This material is presented in a format similar to the Developing Understanding of Self and Others (DUSO) kits developed by Dinkmeyer and has excellent applicability for use with parent groups.

James, M. *Transactional analysis for moms and dads*. Reading, Ma.: Addison-Wesley, 1974.

This is a useful handbook for parents, which can be read by parents or discussed in parents' groups.

Zuckerman, L., Cost, R., & Yura, M. *Children: The challenge*. New York: Hawthorne Books, 1978.

This is a workbook that focuses on enhancing the family atmosphere, nurturing children's independence, and goal setting. This material can be used by individuals or groups.

APPENDIX 17-C: PUBLISHED MATERIALS FOR USE WITH YOUNGSTERS

Fassler, J. *Child's series on psychologically relevant themes*. Westport, Conn.: Videorecord Corporation of America, 1971.

This videorecord program is based on bibliotherapy concepts (helping children with problems through the study and identification with literary characters who have encountered and dealt with similar conflicts). This program contains six video cassettes ranging from 6 to 8 minutes in length. Each is narrated by a child and is accompanied with illustrations. A teacher's guide accompanies each series. The story titles include "The Man of the House"; "Don't Worry, Dear"; "A Boy with a Problem"; "All Alone with Daddy"; "One Little Girl"; and "Grandpa Died Today." These materials do an excellent job of introducing preschool and elementary school children to emotionally relevant topics.

Dinkmeyer, D. *DUSO D-1 (Developing understanding of self and others)*. Circle Pines, Mn.: American Guidance Service, 1970.

This has been one of the most popular affective materials during the past 10 years. According to the handbook, DUSO "makes extensive use of listening, inquiry, experiential, and discussion approach to learning." Activities are designed to be used in rather brief settings (listen activities last approximately 5 minutes) to allow good attention by young students. The program emphasizes building a vocabulary for the expression of feelings. It contains eight units with four or five themes in each, which is enough material to last a full school year. The material is designed to be used with primary-school and kindergarten children. The eight unit themes are (1) understanding and accepting self; (2) understanding feelings; (3) understanding others; (4) understanding independence; (5) understanding goals and purposeful behavior; (6) understanding mastery, competence, and resourcefulness; (7) understanding emotional maturity; and (8) understanding choice and consequences.

The DUSO program is packaged in a sturdy metal carrying case. The kit contains a manual, 2 story books, 33 colored posters, role-playing cards, 7 puppets, puppet props, and group discussion cards. The DUSO program is delightful. The presentations invite participation in such a way as to be highly stimulating and useful as an affective tool.

Dinkmeyer, D. *DUSO D-2 (Developing understanding of self and others)*. Circle Pines, Mn.: American Guidance Service, 1973.

The DUSO D-2 is similar in format to the DUSO D-1. It is designed for use with youngsters aged 7–10 years. The eight themes in DUSO D-2 are (1) towards self-identity: developing self-awareness and a positive self-concept; (2) towards friendship: understanding peers; (3) towards responsible independence: understanding growth from self-centeredness to social interest; (4) towards self-reliance: understanding personal responsibility; (5) towards resourcefulness and purposefulness: understanding personal motivation; (6) towards competence: understanding accomplishments; (7) towards emotional stability: understanding stress; and (8) towards responsibile choice making: understanding values.

The DUSO D-2 kit contains a manual, social development activity cards, records or cassettes of dramatizations of stories and songs, colored posters, role-playing activity cards, puppets, career awareness cards, discussion cards, and discussion guide cards. While the directions of the program are very explicit, the teacher must be able to run a discussion and provide motivation for continued participation.

Scholastic Magazine. *(Contact) maturity: Growing up strong*. New York: Scholastic Book Services, 1972.

This program is aimed toward affective development through the development of reading, learning, and thinking. It is aimed at eighth- to tenth-grade youngsters who are reading at the upper elementary grade levels. This material is designed for the activity-oriented classroom, and has special adaptability for withdrawn/passive youngsters. Teaching materials include (1) a teacher's guide; (2) an anthology of short stories, poems, plays, letters, comments, and questions designed to motivate the reader to explore his or her feelings; (3) a logbook of activities; and (4) posters corresponding to various activities. This program fits nicely into the language arts program so that a special affective period need not be provided.

Schwartzrock, S. & Wrenn, G. *The "Coping with" series*. Circle Pines, Mn.: American Guidance Service, 1973.

This series includes 23 books that focus on the frustrations of being an adolescent in today's world: *Facts and Fantasies About Drugs; Facts and Fantasies About Alcohol; Facts and Fantasies About Smoking; The Mind Benders; Some Common Crutches; Food as a Crutch; Alcohol as a Crutch; Living With Differences; You Always Communicate Something; Understanding the Law of Our Land; Easing the Scene; In Front of the Table and Behind It; Can You Talk With Someone Else; To Like and Be Liked; My Life, What Shall I Do With It; Do I Know the Me Others See; Crises Youth Face Today; Changing Roles of Men and Women; Coping with Cliques; I'd Rather Do It Myself If You Don't Mind; Living with Loneliness; Parents Can Be a Problem;* and *Grades, What's So Important About Them Anyway*. The variety of materials presented in this series makes it an effective tool for stimulating thought and discussion in the classroom.

The adventures of the lollipop dragon. Chicago Il.: Society for Visual Education, Inc., 1970.

This is a sound filmstrip program developed for primary-school-aged children. The lollipop dragon, the central character, is a delightful way to introduce various concepts for discussion. The morals of the program are sometimes overemphasized, but this doesn't appear to detract from the presentation. The kit contains (1) a teacher guide; (2) coloring book; (3) filmstrips; and (4) cassettes or records.

Anderson, J. & Miner, P. *Focus on self-development, Stage two*. Chicago, Il.: Science Research Associates, Inc., 1971.

This composite of 19 units, designed to promote intelligent thinking by the child on a variety of topics, is to be used by the classroom teacher in elementary grades.

Topics include (1) self-concept; (2) interests; (3) abilities; (4) limitations; (5) goals; (6) concerns; (7) responsibility; (8) physical environment; (9) cultural differences; (10) social influence; (11) communication; (12) honesty; (13) companionship; (14) acceptance and rejection; (15) respect; (16) trust; (17) loyalty; (18) competition and cooperation; and (19) summary. The program includes a teacher's guide, workbook, filmstrips, story records, and photoboards. *Focus on Self-Development* is designed to be a total counseling program when used by a creative teacher.

APPENDIX 17-D: MATERIALS ADAPTED FOR USE WITH MILDLY HANDICAPPED CHILDREN

Even though materials for the handicapped have become more plentiful in recent years, they continue to be far short of what is needed by teachers. Since the teacher's day does not have enough hours to make materials for all youngsters and all situations, it is imperative that some materials be adapted for use. In order to decide what to adapt, the teacher must look at the needs of the youngsters; decide on materials that are likely to be adaptable, and give your ideas a try. The following are examples of adapted materials appropriate for the psychodynamic approach.

Dartboard

A dartboard can be used as a cathartic activity for youngsters who have feelings that are difficult or impossible to share with others. The activity must be controlled so that risk of injury is eliminated. If feelings are exteme regarding one member of the staff, another child, or a sibling, the youngster may put a picture of the person on the dartboard. This is certainly a more therapeutic activity than hitting the person or transferring anger to someone else. Of course, this does not solve the problem, but it is a step toward eventually resolving the feelings.

Punching Bag

Another cathartic technique is the use of a punching bag (actually, a heavy blocking bag used by football teams). Children can wrestle, punch, and kick the bag with no danger to the child or the bag. It is important to use a heavy bag for this purpose so that some resistance is provided. A bag that swings isn't appropriate because it "hits back" rather than being a passive recipient of abuse.

Soft Bats

Large, soft bats are now available that are excellent for hitting, throwing, or swinging without injury. They provide excellent cathartic release without danger of injury or breakage.

Soft Mats

Many activities require something to fall against or on so that injury can be avoided. Soft mats provide this protection. Sometimes teachers can share mats with gymnastics or wrestling programs, although it is best to have the mats available every day. Since they are heavy and bulky, it is difficult to "share" these expensive items. The mats must be large to provide protection during tumbling and wrestling activities.

Materials for Therapeutic Play

The activities discussed earlier for therapeutic play have their own equipment needs. These include such items as rackets for table and lawn tennis, fishing gear, skates, balls and bats, basketballs, hiking and camping equipment, and equipment for bowling, swimming, and other appropriate activities. Much of this equipment is readily available in the school. Also, children can sometimes bring materials from home for use at school.

PART V

The Mildly Handicapped:
A Future Service Distinction?

James K. McAfee
Lester Mann

18

The Prognosis for Mildly Handicapped Students

The ultimate efficacy of special education should be judged in terms of implications for the adult lives of its recipients. This is particularly true for the mildly handicapped who are expected to participate within the mainstream of adult activity. While follow-up research on such individuals is critical, it is also fraught with many pitfalls and difficulties. These difficulties include locating former students and gaining their cooperation for the purpose of systematic long-term follow-up studies. There are also problems created by the very nature of the subject population since the mildly handicapped are often assimilated into the general population in post-school years. In addition, few follow-up investigations have identified or studied *mildly* emotionally disturbed children as a special education category. Thus, in seeking to shed light on their adult adjustment, it is often necessary to extrapolate from studies of individuals with more severe symptoms.

Other difficulties surface when one attempts to generalize from studies of extremely heterogeneous groups lumped together as ''the mildly handicapped'' to judgment about their later adult adjustment. For example, such renowned individuals as Thomas Edison, Auguste Rodin, George Patton, Woodrow Wilson, and Albert Einstein have been described as learning disabled (Thompson, 1971). Did such men have anything in common with the mildly retarded graduates of a work-study program? Can conclusions derived from one group be applied to the other? Finally, can individuals of wide-ranging ability, who are all called the educably mentally retarded (EMR), really be considered a homogeneous group? The answers to these questions, of course, are negative. Problems here are further exacerbated by the fact that most populations that have been studied have been drawn from among the retarded. Research on learning disabled adults is just now becoming a visible element in the literature (White, Schumaker, Warner, Alley, & Deshler, 1980). Similarly, much of the research on emotionally disturbed adults does not follow up emotionally disturbed children, but rather focuses on individuals whose problems were not clearly manifested until adulthood. Clearly, the status, problems, and needs of these adults are not the same as those of former special education students. Furthermore, research that does concern the adult adjustment of former special-education emotionally disturbed students does not usually address vocational adjustment, or economic self-sufficiency.

In spite of these limitations, there are several reasons for continued review and conduct of follow-up research with this population. Martin (1972) presented one of the major reasons: he estimated that only 21 percent of the handicapped leaving school between 1972 and 1976 would be fully employed, while 40 percent would be unemployed. Clearly there is a need to assess such estimations against available facts and to plan and program on this basis.

On the positive side, another reason for conducting follow-up assessments was provided in a study by Safer (1980). She found that a substantial portion of the mildly handicapped passed the communications and/or math sections of the 1977 Florida minimal competency exam. Forty-nine percent of the learning-disabled high school students passed the communications section. Fifty-six percent of the emotionally disturbed, 49 percent of the socially maladjusted, and 6 percent of the educable mentally retarded also passed this section. The percentages of the same groups passing the mathematics section were considerably lower but still impressive. It thus appears that a large segment of mildly handicapped young adults may be graduating from school with a set of competencies that are considered adequate for students who are not considered handicapped. Do they fare as well in adulthood as their normal peers or are their examination results aberrations? If they possess at least minimal competencies, does the handicap label still have a negative effect on their lives? Only carefully planned and executed follow-up research can answer these important questions.

Two extremely volatile issues provide further support for continued concern about the adult status of the mildly handicapped. These issues, getting married and having children, are wrought with emotional impact, as well as implications for special education programs (Krischef, 1972; Reed & Reed, 1970). Most research does not suggest a very favorable outlook for marriages of mildly handicapped people. Yet some of those marriages are successful (Bass, 1964; Shaw & Wright, 1960; State Board of Public Instruction, 1969). What factors contribute to success or failure?

Thus, while there are serious limitations to currently available follow-up studies, there are also compelling reasons for continuing such research. Individuals conducting or interpreting special education follow-up studies must be aware of several factors, including age at follow-up and the elapsed time since the termination of intervention. The Studies of Baller (1936), Charles (1953), and Baller, Charles, and Miller (1967) suggest that initially difficult adjustments are often followed by later stability.

SOCIAL ADJUSTMENT AND INDEPENDENCE

The social adequacy of mildly handicapped adults has been assessed on the basis of a large number of variables. One factor that has been investigated frequently and that consistently sets the mildly impaired adult apart from others is low participation in social organizations (Birenbaum & Re, 1977; Carter, 1964; Clark, Kivitz, & Rosen, 1968; Dinger, 1961; Redding, 1979). The only community activity in which wide participation is reported is church-going, and information on this point is somewhat dated (Dinger, 1961; Peterson and Smith, 1960; State Board of Public Instruction, 1969). Peterson and Smith (1960) also indicated that very few EMR adults belonged to clubs. Dinger reported that 84 percent of his sample belonged to a church, but 75 percent belonged to no other social or community organization. Forty-five percent of a group of former institution residents were found to be church members in one follow-up study (Clark et al., 1968), while another investigator found only 14 percent of the EMR people studied belonged to a church or a social group (Shanyfelt, 1974).

A New Zealand study (Wilton & Cosson, 1977) revealed that EMR adults were more poorly adapted socially than a similar group of slow learners. EMR adults were not integrated into the community, were dependent upon others for housing, didn't participate in sports, attended church infrequently, and had difficulty managing money.

Mildly handicapped adults also participate in fewer constructive leisure-time activities than their normal peers (Clark et al, 1968; Peterson and Smith, 1960; Redding, 1979). Television and reading magazines and newspapers are the most frequently reported recreational pastimes of mildly handicapped adults. Dinger (1961) reported that 66 percent of the group he studied had newspaper subscriptions, and Peterson and Smith (1960) found that EMR adults read newspapers at the same rate as other, *low-income,* adults.

The Baller (1936), Charles (1953), and Miller (1965) series of studies supported certain findings on the social behavior of mildly handicapped adults:

1. Only 2 of 206 mildly retarded adults were members of the PTA and none belonged to any other service organization.
2. Fifty percent were church members.
3. Only 20 percent belonged to a social club.
4. Forty-six percent had regular hobbies or recreation.
5. Television was the primary leisure activity.
6. Social competence increased with age.

In addition to other factors that limit the social activity of mildly retarded adults, they are further hampered by the fact that they often do not seek or obtain driver's licenses (Peterson & Smith, 1960; Wilton & Cosson, 1977). Match (1969) found that those who did obtain licenses (frequently after failing and repeating the test) were generally safe drivers. It may be that a limitation on driving is imposed by societal expectations (i.e., a widespread belief that the mentally handicapped are not competent to drive) rather than the limitations of the handicapped individual.

The social integration of former institution residents has been extensively explored. Birenbaum and Re (1977) discovered a routine of sleep, work, and at-home passive recreations among mentally retarded persons residing in community residences. Clark et al. (1968) described the social adjustment and the level of independence reached by previous residents of a private facility for the mentally retarded. They found that

1. Nearly all had filed federal income taxes, though 90 percent required help.
2. The major social inadequacy was in contact with the opposite sex.
3. The greatest areas of difficulty were budgeting, saving, and temper control.

4. Few displayed psychiatric symptoms.
5. The most frequent leisure activities were watching television, going to the movies, listening to the radio, and shopping.
6. Very few had hobbies or played sports.

While the lives of former residents do not appear especially fulfilling in the above study, it does appear that they can and do adapt, at least to a minimal degree. Adaptation often takes the form of ''invisibility''—a tendency to avoid participation. It is critical to understand the importance of this factor since inadequate social adjustment has been repeatedly linked to subsequent reinstitutionalization (Eagle, 1967). In most cases, inadequate social adjustment is equated with ''creating a disturbance'' or bringing attention to oneself. Thus, invisibility, in the form of passivity and non-participation, may be overlooked while professionals responsible for follow-up look for ''troublemakers''—those who drink, party, stay out all night, and spend their money foolishly (i.e., high-risk activities). Therefore becoming truly integrated into the community requires a high degree of risk and avoidance of any risk may be reinforced.

The magnitude of the problem is evidenced in the investigations of Edgerton (1967) and Edgerton and Bercovici (1976). They reported that

1. Only 3 of the 48 formerly institutionalized individuals did not depend on others for help. This improved with time.
2. The individuals did not accept the fact that they were retarded.
3. As length of time in the community increased, the subjects rated themselves happier, obtained pets, and developed hobbies. They also became more involved socially.
4. Unlike most reports with other samples, only two people attended church.
5. In the second follow-up, 10 of the 30 subjects were more poorly adjusted than they had been; only 8 were better adjusted.

The results reported about the lack of willingness to accept the fact that they were retarded were refuted by the work of Gan, Tymchuk, and Nisahara (1977). A questionnaire administered to mildly retarded adults 18–40 years old showed that 73.3 percent had accurate knowledge of their retardation, 72.2 percent held positive attitudes towards their retardation, 92.2 percent supported the integration of the mentally retarded, and 76 percent were aware of their legal rights. In addition to the differences in populations (institutional versus noninstitutional), the positive effects of advocacy groups may be discovered here.

Moving to a group that might be considered as representative of learning disabled adults, poor childhood readers have been labeled socially backward as adults (i.e., as nonjoiners, and as having few leisure-time activities; Carter, 1964; Hardy, 1968). Howden's research (1967), however, does not support this conclusion. He found no differences in the level of adult social participation among individuals identified as either good, average, or poor readers in the fifth and sixth grades. His follow-up study, incidentally, was rare in that it was conducted 19 years after the pupils' initial identification. Howden's positive findings are not in concert with other researchers, who declared that learning disabled adults are not generally involved in social activities, fraternal organizations, and recreational activities (Scott, Williams, Stout, & Decker, 1980; White et al, 1980). Scott et al.

(1980) reported that 22 percent of the learning disabled adults studied stated that they rarely went out with friends and 36 percent stated that they rarely socialized at all. Comparisons with a nonlearning disabled group were not made. Thus, it is impossible to determine the extent of deviation from norms.

Blalock's study (1981) of learning disabled (LD) adults provides extensive information of the social deficiencies of that population. The subject group included 38 LD adults. Thirteen were in college at the time of initial evaluation. A majority of the group reported specific handicaps that limited their participation in social activities. These deficiencies included problems getting around in the community, inappropriate use of personal space, and the inability to follow conversations.

Certainly, mildly retarded adults experience continuing difficulties with social adjustment. And the research on the social adequacy and participation of learning disabled adults is indicative (albeit inconclusively) of deficits and reticence. But, what of those individuals whose primary handicaps were viewed as affective, not academic? Do their social difficulties persist in adulthood? Surprisingly, this topic has been researched sparingly: follow-up research on this population appears to concentrate on the continued expression of psychiatric conditions via clinical instruments. The relevant research on this population, however sparse, does seem to indicate that symptoms of social inadequacy persist in adulthood but that they have relatively mild impact.

People with neurotic symptoms as children generally adjust well as adults, but they do continue to be impaired by anxiety (Coolidge, Brodie & Feeney, 1964; Eyesenck, 1952; Garber, 1972; J.F. Masterson, 1958; J.F. Masterson, 1967). Glueck & Glueck (1968) discovered higher rates of dependency, excessive drinking, and lack of social participation for adults who had been classified as delinquent as children. More positive results are reported in a recent study in which young adults (17–24 years old) who were diagnosed as hyperactive as children viewed themselves as socially inferior when asked to rate themselves on a personality inventory (Weiss, Hechtman, & Perlman, 1978). However, those same individuals were not viewed as inadequate by their employers. Anderson & Plymate (1962) suggested that hyperactive children frequently manifest severe social abnormalities as adults. Similar evidence is offered by Menkes, Rowe, and Menkes's 25-year follow-up of hyperactive children (1967). They found a pattern of adult dependence and psychiatric disturbance.

Friendship and Interpersonal Relationships

The making and maintaining of friendships has long been recognized as a valid indices of emotional stability and social adequacy. A number of investigators have analyzed the interpersonal behavior of mildly handicapped adults. Most of this research has been conducted through self-report and family interview, neither of which affords great objectivity. Another concern is the application of essentially middle class standards to assess the adequacy of friendships of the mildly handicapped. It is evident that the mildly impaired adult does not join large social organizations. On a more personal level of encounter, less evidence is available. Birenbaum and Re (1977) indicated that deinstitutionalized mentally retarded adults rarely attempt to establish close friendships with normal individuals in the community. Earlier, Clark et al. (1968) detected a similar pattern. These two sources provide some understanding of the lack of interpersonal integration of the mildly retarded who are often new to the community and hardly have the time to establish friendships. Their residences (often just rented rooms) are located in transient neighborhoods. In spite of that, Clark et al. (1968) reported that 78 percent of their subjects entertain friends at least once a month. In fact, that activity was one of the major forms of recreation. The studies of Edgerton (1967) and Edgerton and Bercovici (1976) lend further credence to the contention that lack of friendships on the part of the mildly retarded may be due to the conditions of isolation imposed on them rather than to the actual characteristics of their disabilities. These researchers found that after 10 years in the community, mildly retarded adults had begun to establish friendships that they indicated were satisfying to them.

For noninstitutionalized mildly handicapped individuals, the establishment of friendships has been only sporadically investigated. Wilton and Cosson (1977) compared EMR special class graduates with slow learners. Utilizing subject, parent, and employer interviews, they concluded that retarded adults had fewer and less intense friendships; however, this study was conducted in New Zealand and its application to the United States is tenuous. In a more pertinent study—one of the very few attempts to investigate the quality of friendships—White et al. (1980) found that learning disabled young adults have the same number of intimate friends as a sex- and age-matched nonhandicapped group. However, they have few social friends (i.e., friends with whom to go places). Scott et al. (1980) reported that a sizable number of dyslexic adults reported that establishing friendships was difficult for them. The difficulties that LD adults encounter in making and maintaining friendships have been traced to several limitations: (1) social imperception; (2) inappropriate comments; (3) inappropriate use of personal space; (4) difficulty understanding rules of games; (5) problems with following conversations; (6) problems learning dance steps; and (7) lack of awareness of limitations (Blalock, 1981).

Surprisingly, the friendship patterns of adults who had been classified as emotionally disturbed as children has not been extensively investigated. Once again, this critical subject is neglected in favor of more clinical variables. Garber (1972) followed 40 neurotic adolescents into young adulthood and concluded that they readily established close friendships. Such was not true for adults with more severe emotional disorders. Hechtman, Weiss, Finkelstein, Werner, and Benn (1976) reported that hyperactive children continued to have socialization difficulties as adults. The conclusions offered with regard to general social adjustment of the mildly handicapped adults are equally applicable to the research on friendship and interpersonal relations. There are definite indications of inadequacy and reluctance. Again, environmental variables (housing, income, etc.) may be as important as the presence of the handicap.

Voting and Civic Participation

Just as the mildly handicapped adult does not participate in social activities, he or she is generally a nonparticipant in community, state and national civic organizations and activities (State Board of Public Instruction, 1969). This phenomenon is especially true for mildly retarded adults, although those adults who were educated in regular school classes vote more regularly and participate in community activities to a greater extent than adults who had been "special class students." Dinger's extensive research (1961) revealed that 34 percent of the EMR adults he surveyed had voted. This was substantially below general national figures, but further evidence suggests that participation may be on a par with the rate for nonhandicapped adults who are comparable on variables of socioeconomic status and educational attainment (Peterson & Smith, 1960).

The extensive follow-up study by Clark et al. (1968) provided a more pessimistic picture of civic participation. Of the 128 mentally retarded individuals they studied, only 6 percent had ever voted. Substantial differences between the population they studied and that of the Dinger study provide some insight into the voting rates. First, the Clark et al. research included many individuals whose IQ was substantially below 55, and, therefore, the study did not truly represent an EMR population. Additionally, Clark et al.'s study dealt with former institutional residents, while Dinger's study considered only former public school students. Long periods of institutionalization (in Clark et al., a mean of 15.4 years) do not appear conducive to the development of participation in the affairs of government.

There have been several other investigations of voting behavior of mildly retarded adults. Kokaska (1972) reviewed some of those studies and discerned no trends in participation over the years 1952–1970. Results ranged from zero participation (Edgerton, 1967; Gozali, 1971) to more positive measures of 43 percent registration and 34 percent voting (Cassidy & Phelps, 1955) and 50 percent participation (Miller, 1965). The most favorable study revealed that 64 percent of the people studied had voted at least once during the 12 years since they had left school (Bobroff, 1956). Gozali's study (1971) devastatingly revealed the lack of citizenship knowledge on the part of the mildly retarded. He found that EMR people had almost no understanding of American history and government operation. In fact, very few even knew why July Fourth is celebrated as a holiday. Lack of voting behavior on the part of EMRs, then, may be attributable to both lack of knowledge and to a paucity of citizenship education for this population. Kennedy's investigation (1962) provided a more positive outlook. Increases in the voting behavior of EMR adults were reported over a 12-year period (from 43.9 percent to 86.4 percent during 1948–1960). We need data for more recent years, however, to reach any conclusions.

Research on voting behavior and civic participation of mildly handicapped populations other than EMRs is extremely rare. White et al. (1980) found a low level of political involvement for very young learning disabled adults. That level, however, was no lower than for a sex- and age-matched comparison "normal" group.

From the contradictory evidence presented above, several conclusions can be reached:

1. When matched with nonhandicapped adults on age, socioeconomic status (SES), and educational level, the mildly handicapped vote at approximately the same low rate.
2. Voting behavior increases substantially as the individuals grow older.
3. The farther from the mainstream the individual is educated, the *less* likely he or she is to vote.

4.   Voting behavior is directly related to educational attainment (Levin, Guthrie, Kleindorfer, & Stout, 1971).

VOCATIONAL ADJUSTMENT

No area has been as extensively investigated in follow-up studies of the mildly handicapped as has been vocational success. Vocational adjustment is also the most widely used measure of adult competence. It has been defined in many ways: initial employment rates, salaries, job tenure, occupational level, quantity and quality of production, and job satisfaction.

There are many barriers to the successful employment of mildly handicapped individuals. The mentally retarded and the mentally ill are rejected more often by potential employers than prison parolees (Colbert, Kalish, & Chang, 1973). They are viewed as unpredictable and physically or mentally incapable. Surprisingly, however, a survey of work-study coordinators revealed that the willingness of employers to hire the mentally retarded was less of a problem than transportation to and from jobs, the development of training programs, and the variety of jobs available (Becker, 1976). New problems have, however, recently arisen. Automation is encroaching on jobs that have been the mainstay of the mildly retarded. Thus, the range of occupations available to them is shrinking (Brolin, Kokaska, & Charles, 1974).

Employment Rates and Job Tenure

Obviously, all measures of vocational adequacy are dependent upon initial success at securing employment. Employment rate statistics for the mildly handicapped have ranged from very pessimistic reports to those indicating no difference between the unemployment rates for the mildly impaired and the general population. The means utilized to obtain data for such reports often determine the results. Data from biased small samples are hardly generalizable. Therefore, estimates of employment rates, etc., must be cautiously interpreted.

Tobias (1970) took a random sample ($N = 1836$) of mentally retarded adults who left the New York Public Schools during the years 1960–1963. A follow-up study was conducted in 1966–1967 (which was a time of low unemployment). The findings: (1) 59 percent of the males and 29 percent of the females were competitively employed at the time of the follow-up; (2) only 35 percent of those employed had been in their jobs for 6 months or more; and (3) 20 percent had never been employed (this includes those who had not sought employment).

The National Association for Retarded Citizens (NARC) has developed an on-the-job training (OJT) project that reimburses employers for a substantial portion of a mentally retarded worker's salary during job training. Mirring (1977) reported that 67.94 percent of the mentally retarded in that program had been successfully placed at the end of 8 weeks of NARC-supported training. Other specific training programs report initial placement success as high as 95 percent (Parker, Taylor, Hartman, Wong, Grigg, & Shay, 1976). One of the programs investigated by Parker et al. included 160 pupils who graduated from the Bergen

County Vocational School in Paramus, N.J. Sixty percent of the graduates were mildly retarded, 20 percent were learning disabled, and 20 percent were emotionally disturbed. Eighty percent of these individuals obtained employment.

Redding (1979) and Chaffin, Spellman, Regan, and Davison (1971) studied mildly retarded graduates of work-study programs. Employment rates shortly after graduation were 70 percent and 83 percent, respectively. In the latter study, the rate rose to 92 percent 2 years later. The employment rate reported by Redding was substantially lower than for a group of nonretarded but low-functioning graduates of the same program. Peterson and Smith (1960) also found that EMRs had a more difficult time finding initial employment, but an extensive study in Iowa revealed that 80 percent of the EMRs who had recently left school were employed. Most had obtained employment on their own (State Board of Public Instruction, 1969).

A follow-up of EMR graduates of a comprehensive vocational program revealed that only 1 of 35 was unemployed 1–3 years after graduation (Titus & Travis, 1973). Olshansky and Beach (1974) reported a much higher rate of unemployment (nearly 50 percent among rehabilitation trainees who had been placed a year earlier.

More pessimistic results, published earlier by McFall (1966) suggest that the data provided by Titus and Travis indicate a general trend toward improvement in initial employment rates. Only 30 percent of the 1951–1961 EMR graduates (total sample, 50) McFall studied in East Orange, N.J., were working at the time of the follow-up interview. Twenty-six percent had never worked. Thirty had odd jobs. Most found their jobs by door-to-door searching; only three used public or private agency help to find employment. The improvement trend mentioned above is further supported by Shanyfelt (1974), who found an employment rate of 82 percent for recently graduated mildly retarded males and 67 percent for females. It should be noted that all of the above data concern *initial placement* rates.

Crain's research (1980) provided employment rates for 130 EMR graduates of the St. Louis Special District, who were randomly selected from the 1962, 1965, 1968, 1971, 1974, and 1977 classes. Sixty-eight percent were in the civilian workforce. Their unemployment rate of 7.9 percent was not markedly different from the 5.5 percent local rate for the general population. Unemployment figures reflected only those who had been laid off and were *actively* seeking employment—thus the low numbers. Unemployment rates, generally, for the mildly retarded have been variously estimated at 8–32 percent (Kokaska & Kalawara, 1969), and even as high as 53 percent (Brolin, Durand, Kromer, & Muller, 1975). Kennedy's 9 percent estimate was among the lower ones (1962).

The success of deinstitutionalized retarded adults at finding employment has been found to be very good by Clark et al. (1968). Of the individuals who had been in the community for 2 years or more, 100 percent were employed. Ninety-one percent of those who lived in the community 12 months or less were employed. Another sample of deinstitutionalized adults fared much more poorly according to Edgerton (1967) and Edgerton and Bercovici (1976). Only 21 of 48 people in the first study were employed full time, while in the second study that figure dropped to 8. A later follow-up on the sample used by Clark et al. found an unemployment rate of 12 percent after a mean community stay of 3.6 years (Rosen, Floor, & Baxter, 1974). While previous institutionalization impacts heavily on social adjustment, it does not appear to be related to employment when other factors such as age and academic attainment are considered (Kolstoe, 1961).

Longevity and continuity of employment have also been investigated. Dinger (1961) reported that 36 percent of the 100 EMR adults he studied were still working at their first or second jobs several years after leaving high school. A similar figure (33 percent still in their first job after 3 years) was discovered in Iowa by the State Board of Public Instruction (1969). Clark et al. (1968) found that although better than 90 percent of the deinstitutionalized retarded adults were employed, only 54.5 percent had worked full time continuously since their discharges, and 50 percent had changed jobs at least once. Brolin et al. (1975) found that 28 percent of their sample had been employed more than 70 percent of the time since they left high school. Thirty-six percent had been employed less than 30 percent of the time. Titus and Travis (1973) found that 57 percent of the recent (1–3 years) graduates of a vocational training program were still in their first job, though males changed jobs more frequently than females. Shanyfelt (1974) encountered a similar figure (62.5 percent).

The success of the Texas Cooperative School Program was evaluated by Doleshal and Jackson (1970). Sixty-six percent of its EMR graduates had been employed 100 percent of the time since case closure. Seventy-five percent had been employed at least 80 percent of the time. At the time of follow-up, only 34 of 199 were unemployed. The students had been out of school for 2–4 years. Homemakers and unpaid workers were included in the employed group.

The Baller (1936), Charles (1953), and Miller (1965) series of studies with the same sample (except for attrition) of mildly retarded adults provide an opportunity to assess trends in the employability of EMR adults. At the time of the third study, 77.9 percent of the subjects were employed. This was a huge increase from 20 percent in 1936 and 47.7 percent in 1951. Eight percent of those employed in the Miller study had been in the same job for 3 or more years as of 1965.

Job procurement success of learning-disabled adults appears to be somewhat better than that of the mildly retarded. Many jobs, however, are not available to nonreading or poor-reading adults, even if reading is not a critical job skill (Silberberg & Silberberg, 1978). Applicants must fill out forms that require reading and writing skills, and trainees must read training materials. In spite of this, Robinson and Smith (1962) reported that only 1 of 44 former students of the University of Chicago Reading Clinic was unemployed at age 24. Slightly fewer learning disabled students were employed than those in a matched control group (67 percent versus 77 percent) in an investigation by White et al. (1980). The difference may be partly accounted for by the higher proportion of females in the LD group. Those learning disabled adults who were unemployed had been so for a mean of 7.15 months, a figure that was not significantly different from that of the control group. Surprisingly, Hardy (1968) found that both the rate and the type of employment were unrelated to the severity of the learning disability. Cordero (1975) reported that 45 percent of adult dyslexics were able to find and retain full-time jobs after completing a remedial reading, writing, and occupational preparation program. The percentage on welfare dropped from 69 to 25 after 3 years. Scott et al. (1980) found that only 6 percent of a sample of LD adults in Pittsburgh ($N = 31$) had been on welfare, 68 percent were employed full time, 16 percent were unemployed, and 94 percent reported no problems obtaining their initial jobs after high school. Blalock (1981) reported that only 50 percent of the group of young LD adults (*N* = 38) studied were self-supporting.

The prognosis for employment of emotionally disturbed children stands in direct relation to the severity of the symptoms. Garber (1972) followed 115 former psychiatric patients and found only 57 employed, but this number represented 75 percent of those who were in the labor market. Others were homemakers, in hospitals, etc. Shore and Massimo (1973) supported vocationally oriented psychotherapy for delinquents on the basis of their research. Eight of 10 people in the treatment group were employed 10 years later, while only 2 of 10 in the control group had adjusted adequately. Hyperactive individuals are reported to obtain employment at the same rate as IQ-, sex-, and SES-matched controls (Hechtman et al., 1976). Again, extensive data relative to the mildly disturbed and their vocational adjustment has not been reported.

Occupational Levels and Types of Job Held

As expected, mildly handicapped adults who are employed primarily work in unskilled jobs. Few receive the training, direction, or encouragement necessary to obtain skilled or professional employment even if they possess the capacity to perform adequately. Crain (1980) noted that all but 5 percent of the mildly retarded workers in his sample were in unskilled or semi-skilled positions.

The mildly retarded also hold fewer skilled jobs than nonretarded but low-functioning adults (Clark et al, 1968; Goldstein, 1964; McFall, 1966; Keeler, 1963; Kennedy, 1962; Baller, 1936; Redding, 1978). The Keeler study indicated that not one of the 115 subjects (recent EMR graduates) in San Francisco held a skilled job. The Kennedy study, however, suggests that unskilled positions may be increasingly obtained by the mildly retarded as they grow older. More than 32 percent of the mildly retarded in that study (aged 30 +) were employed as skilled workers. Another 32 percent were semi-skilled, 11 percent were unskilled, 12.3 percent did service jobs, and 4.3 percent held clerical jobs. Doleshal and Jackson (1970) arrived at more specific conclusions. Their investigation found 5 percent skilled workers, 23.8 percent semi-skilled, 26.7 percent unskilled, 23.8 percent service, 1.3 percent clerical, 18.1 percent family workers, and 1.3 percent agricultural. Low representation of the mildly retarded among skilled workers is also to be found in England (Shaw & Wright, 1960) and Norway (Skaarbrevik, 1971).

Considerable variability exists among the specific jobs held by the educable mentally retarded adult worker. Oswald (1968) reported that 100 different federal jobs were held by 2,747 mentally retarded workers. As long ago as 1930, there were at least 118 occupations viewed as suitable for individuals with a mental age between 5 and 12 (Beckham, 1930). Diverse researchers have reported mentally retarded individuals working in many areas:

1. Tobias (1970)—service, assembly, clerical, stockwork, sales, delivering messages, packing, and handling
2. Mirring (1977)—domestic, custodial, handling, maintenance, ground keeping, child care, construction, autobody repairing, and tractor operation

3. Crain (1980)—dish washing, ground keeping, custodial, aiding nurses or teachers, printing, bookkeeping, and assisting librarians
4. Brolin et al. (1974)—managerial, farming, processing, machining, bench-work, and construction
5. Clark et al. (1968)—food service, building service, laboring, and doing stock and factory work
6. Titus and Travis (1973)—cafeteria, shipping, and custodial
7. Strickland and Arrell (1967)—farming, auto service, laundry, construction, domestic, furniture, hotel, and restaurant work, and medical retail

Similar lists have been produced by Becker (1976) and Rosen et al. (1974).

The occupational status of other groups of mildly handicapped adults has (as expected) been less extensively explored than that of the mildly retarded. But it appears that they tend to be employed in lower skill jobs. Herman (1959) reported that 50 percent of individuals who evinced reading disabilities as children were employed in skilled occupations, but there was also a high representation of disabled readers working as domestics, unskilled laborers, and errand boys in the study. Balow and Blomquist (1965) reported that one half of their sample of disabled readers worked in managerial or skilled positions. Robinson and Smith (1962) provided even more optimistic figures. Of the 44 subjects referred to the University of Chicago Reading Clinic as children, only one was working at unskilled labor 10 years later (it should be mentioned that the median IQ of this group of subjects was 120). In a comparison of young learning disabled adults with nondisabled adults, the former group scored significantly lower on a job status index (White et al., 1980). It may be inferred that their occupations were generally of the less skilled variety. Certainly the $2.93 mean hourly wages reported by Scott et al. (1980) is indicative of employment at low skill levels. It appears, however, that the vocational adjustment of learning disabled adults is less problematic than is their social adjustment.

Adults who exhibited childhood behavior disorders also obtain jobs of lower skill levels, although the type of disorder seems to have little or no effect on occupational status. Weiss et al. (1978) found that employers rated individuals who had been diagnosed as hyperactive as children to be as effective as those in a matched comparison group. The subjects, however, may have selected occupations in which their behaviors did not constitute interferences. The same group of hyperactive people had been studied earlier (Hechtman et al., 1976), at which time they held jobs of a status similar to that of the matched control group. Lack of extensive research with this group precludes further statement in this area.

Vocational Competence and Job Satisfaction

It has been established that the mildly handicapped are generally employed in lower skill positions. Once employed, how do they fare? There is considerable disagreement on this issue. This is due in part to the many ways by which performance can be measured. Brolin et al. (1975) reviewed the reasons for leaving a job offered by mildly retarded adults. They found that 22 percent had been laid off; an additional 9 percent had interpersonal problems. Employers of these individuals reported reliability and punctuality in coming to work as positive qualities demonstrated by EMR workers. But they also reported lack of dependability, slowness, need for extra supervision, moodiness, and lack of confidence as deficiencies. The State Board of Public Instruction (1969) reported that most EMR adults lost their jobs because of their own actions. A Civil Service Commission report (1972) stressed the favorable side of things. Of 7442 mentally retarded adults hired by 40 federal agencies during an 8½-year period, 53 percent were still employed at the end of that period. More importantly, 2105 had received promotions. It is possible, of course, that positive biases were operating to produce these favorable results.

The work performance of the learning disabled and the behaviorally disordered adult appears to be indistinguishable from that of the general population when the handicap is mild. Young males who had been treated in vocational/psychotherapy settings for delinquent behavior were found to have relatively stable job histories (Shore & Massimo, 1973). Weiss et al. (1978) reported that a group of hyperactive individuals were just as effective as a control group according to employer ratings. The variables studied included punctuality, finishing work, peer/supervisor relationships, and independence. On the contrary, a more severely disturbed group, studied by Garber (1972), evinced problems with tardiness, absences, peer and supervisor relationships, poor work performance, and boredom. F. L. Jones (1974) reported that adults who were aggressive and antisocial as children showed high job turn over, absenteeism, and poor job performance as adults. Others in the same study whose behavior problems stemmed from family conflict worked steadily but at low-level jobs. Adequate work performance for learning disabled adults is reported by Hardy (1968) and Rawson (1968), but Blalock (1981) reported that young LD adults felt that their employers viewed them as incapable and not trying.

Are mildly disabled adults satisfied with their jobs? Brolin et al. (1974) reported that 70 percent of mildly retarded adults expressed general job satisfaction. General satisfaction was also reported by Clark et al. (1968). Respondents were dissatisfied only with the lack of opportunity for advancement. Learning disabled adults were found to be less satisfied with their employment than non-LD adults (White et al., 1980). In fact, that factor discriminated between the two groups more accurately than any other single variable. Scott et al. (1980) reported similar figures: only 48 percent of the sample of dyslexic adults stated that they were satisfied with their jobs. Thirty percent expressed dissatisfaction.

Job satisfaction of mildly disturbed adults is a topic rarely encountered in the literature. The two studies that do mention job satisfaction lead to different conclusions, which may be traced to the differences in populations. Only 50 percent of the emotionally disturbed adults followed by Garber (1972) expressed vocational satisfaction. No differences in job satisfaction were found for hyperactives when compared to a matched group in a study by Hechtman et al. (1976).

CRIME

Popular beliefs about the mentally retarded have included the notions that they have a "criminal nature," heightened sexuality, and are nonproductive (Santamour & West, 1979). Crime rates would seem to support those beliefs, but several mitigating factors must be considered before the data can be fully interpreted.

Rates

Almost unanimously, higher rates of criminal behavior are reported for the mildly handicapped than for the population at large. Baller (1936) noted from three to seven times more breaches of the law for a group of mentally retarded adults than for normals. At mid-life, the rate of criminal behavior in the mildly retarded had decreased (Charles, 1953). No major crimes were reported, and 10 of 12 civil offenses were for drunkenness. In fact, a single individual was responsible for a large percentage of both the traffic and civil transgressions. High rates were also reported by Shaw & Wright (1960), who found five males from their sample who were in prison at the time of the study, seven more who had served time in prison, and an additional 30 who had been charged with crimes. Of the women, 11 had been arrested but only 1 had been sentenced; crimes included robbery, larceny, and child neglect. Peterson & Smith (1960) reported a crime rate for mildly retarded adults that was higher than that of the general population. More disturbing, however, they found that EMRs engaged in more serious crimes. A state-wide survey in Iowa revealed similar patterns (State Board of Public Instruction, 1969).

Equally dismaying figures are reported by Skaarbrevik (1971). Criminal records were held by 13.1 percent of the retarded male sample (mean age, 26); only 5 percent of the general population had similar difficulties. Information garnered from correctional facilities is even more alarming. The number of prisoners who are mentally retarded has been estimated at 10–27 percent (Allen, 1969; Brown & Courtless, 1967, 1971; Santamour & West, 1979). Allen's study reported that a larger percentage of mentally retarded persons than normals in prison had been convicted of violent crimes.

A single study (White et al., 1980) provided data relative to criminal behavior among LD adults. In that study, only slightly more young LD adults than non-LD adults were found to have been arrested, but more of the learning disabled group were convicted and 4 percent had served time. None of the control group had been in jail.

A large percentage of former psychiatric patients (10 percent) are involved in serious crimes. Garber (1972) found that such individuals are often chronic offenders in thefts, assaults, rapes, and robberies. A higher estimate was offered by Shore and Massimo (1973), who found that after intensive vocational programming and psychotherapy, 1 of 10 delinquent adolescents still entered prison as an adult—without treatment, 4 in 10 were jailed for serious crimes. Glueck & Glueck (1940) followed 1000 juvenile delinquents over three 5-year periods. All but 20 percent were arrested during those periods. Similar results were encountered in a later study by the same researchers (Glueck & Glueck, 1968). F. L. Jones (1974) found that higher rates of police contact are associated with adults whose childhood disturbances were aggressive and antisocial. Others, whose disorders are characterized as passive-negative or withdrawn, have only minor police involvement as adults. Adults who run away as children have a high adult arrest rate, and commit more serious crimes than those who never ran away from home, according to Robins and O'Neal (1959).

More optimistic estimates also can be found, at least for the mildly retarded.

Wilton & Cosson (1977) found no differences in police contacts between slow learners (IQ approximately 85) and mildly retarded (IQ approximately 67). The group had been matched on age, sex, and social background. None of the females studied had police contact. This study, however, was conducted in New Zealand. In the United States, the investigations of Edgerton (1967) and Edgerton and Berconice (1976) revealed that few deinstitutionalized adults had criminal records. Clark et al. (1968), studying a similar population, found similar results. Perhaps institutionalization and follow-along support provided by institutional staff helps to maintain relatively docile behaviors on the part of the retarded. In addition, the retarded may be protected, when clearly identified, from prosecution by interceding counselors and sympathetic police.

Mitigating Factors

Several individuals and groups have extensively explored the above phenomena and offer evidence that the disproportionate representation of mentally retarded (and, to a lesser extent, emotionally disturbed) individuals in prisons is due, in part, to myopic practices in the criminal justice system. Santamour and West (1979) averred that mentally retarded persons with criminal records are likely to have completed no more than the sixth to eighth grades and to function at the second-grade level. They are most often unemployed prior to arrest, are members of minority groups, and are "more likely to be convicted [and] less likely to receive probation" (p. 25). Giagiari (in Santamour & West, 1979) stated that the retarded more readily react to suggestion and intimidation, are apt to confess, and are more willing to plead guilty.

These statements are further evidenced in the work of Brown & Courtless (1967). They offered the following statistics:

1. In 7.7 percent of the cases studied, the mentally retarded were not represented by an attorney.
2. Sixty-nine percent of the attorneys were court appointed.
3. Fifty-nine percent of the defendants pleaded guilty.
4. Eighty percent were convicted.
5. Forty percent waived the right of jury trial.
6. Two thirds confessed or gave self-incriminating statements.
7. The issue of competence was not raised in 92 percent of the cases.
8. No appeals were made in 82 percent of the cases.
9. Only 22 percent had pretrial psychological examinations.

These data are consistently supported by other researchers. Haskins and Friel (1973) and the Kentucky Legislative Research Commission (1975) painted a dismal portrait of life after conviction. They found that retarded prisoners receive poor prison treatment because of their lack of work skills. They are often exploited, and, not understanding the rules, they are frequently guilty of a large number of in-prison infractions. Such factors lead to longer sentences and denial of parole. The Kentucky study indicated that the average length of sentence for EMR prisoners is 2–3 years more than that of nonretarded individuals convicted for the same offense. The inability of retarded prisoners to present employment and living plans to a parole board further reduces their chances for parole. But some changes may occur as a result of a Federal Appeals Court ruling. In *Bowring v. Godwin* (1977), the court held that failure to provide psychological treatment for a mentally retarded individual illegally affected chances for parole.

The legal fate of mentally ill offenders has also been adversely affected by legal aberrations. Whitmer (1980) traced the effects of changes in the involuntary commitment law in California. He found that a large number of the formerly institutionalized mentally ill have become involved with the criminal justice system since their discharges. Pleas of incompetence in criminal cases rose 100 percent in the year after the law was passed—primarily because those discharged individuals continue to engage in criminal behavior but now come before the courts rather than the mental health systems.

Further insight into legal problems of the mildly handicapped was provided by Schilit (1979), whose subjects were police, lawyers, and judges in and around Buffalo, N.Y. The study's findings revealed (1) police, lawyers, and judges were unable to identify mentally retarded individuals among the accused; (2) 90.8 percent of the subjects had no training whatsoever to deal with the retarded; and (3) 73.1 percent overestimated the prevalence of mental retardation. Furthermore, the subjects had little or no knowledge of the mentally retarded individual's ability to understand his or her crime or to participate in his or her trial. It is safe to assume that ignorance about handicapping conditions is also widespread among other professionals concerned with the law and criminal justice.

STANDARD OF LIVING

It is obvious that the economic status of the mildly handicapped will tend toward the lower end of the spectrum. But, to what extent and for what reasons? Certainly, the high rate of unemployment among this group adversely affects its income. In addition, the nature of employment among the mildly handicapped also results in low earning. But how do mildly handicapped adults compare with the general population in income, housing, and other indices of relative affluence? A large and relatively consistent body of evidence is available in this area.

Income

Hurley's work (1969) provided considerable insight into the inter-relatedness of poverty and mental retardation. Hurley especially emphasized the symbiotic nature of this relationship.

Crain (1980) studied 130 mildly retarded graduates of the St. Louis Special School District. Subjects were randomly selected from the district's 1962, 1965, 1968, 1971, 1974, and 1977 classes. The range in income (in 1979) was $2340–$23000. Sex, race, IQ, and vocational training were unrelated to wage but chronological age (19–37 years) was strongly related. The modal earned income of the group was $7000, which was substantially below average for the general population in 1979.

Brolin et al. (1975) reviewed the earnings of 80 EMR former students of the Minneapolis Public Schools. They found that those who were employed worked an average of 30 hours each week and earned a mean salary of $70/week. This is only slightly above the then minimum wage of $2.00 per hour. In another investigation, former students of a work-study program earned nearly 50 percent more per week ($90.45 versus $62.84) than a matched group of mildly retarded adults who had been in a regular high school program (Chaffin et al., 1971). No relationship between IQ and wages was reported, but part of the difference in earnings may be explained by the fact that those in the work-study program had been employed during their high school years and hence had greater employment longevity.

In a recent study, which may be compared to that of Crain (1980), Redding (1979) calculated an average weekly income of $110.74 for a group of 20 mildly retarded young adults. Although this figure is substantially below Crain's, it should be remembered that some of Crain's subjects had been out of school for more than 15 years and would be expected to earn more. Dinger (1961) encountered a more favorable income picture in which the average annual income of $3367 found for 100 former EMR pupils was very close to the national average for a similar age group of unskilled workers. He also found that 82 percent of his sample were self-supporting, and not one was receiving public assistance. Another investigation of this period revealed substantially lower wages (Peterson & Smith, 1960). Female EMRs had a median weekly wage of $19.25, males $55.00. Wages for a normal comparison group were $54.85 and $89.30, respectively.

Titus and Travis (1973) reported a median wage of $2.08 per hour for very young (19–21) mildly retarded adults, but 6 years earlier Howe related a weekly average wage of $85.40 for a very similar group. The variability of findings is further compounded by McFall (1966), who stated that only 5 of 78 former EMR students in East Orange, N.J. earned more than $40 per week. The contradictions in these data are the results of geographically narrow samples, vastly different age ranges, and changing economic conditions, which impact heavily upon the retarded.

Low income of mildly retarded adults is not restricted to the United States. The results of Skaarbrevik's investigation (1971) in Norway revealed that 25.5 percent of the males and 61.1 percent of the females had no income. For those with income, the average annual gross income of males was $1500, and that of females was $750, compared to a national average of $2500. Surprisingly, individuals who changed jobs frequently earned more than those whose employment was stable.

The earnings of the mildly retarded appear to be considerably less than workmates in comparable occupations. Wilton and Cosson's New Zealand study (1977), in which the status of EMR adults was compared to "slow learners," disclosed that the EMR adults were in lower SES occupations and received lower wages that were also substantially below the national average.

Clark et al. (1968) examined the economic status of deinstitutionalized mentally retarded adults. A median gross annual income of $2989 was reported, at a time that the national average was $3391. Income increased substantially with time in the community. The median income of the group rose to $4000 in 1974 (Rosen et al., 1974). This increase reflects three causes: inflation, increases in the minimum wage, and longevity on the job. On the other hand, Edgerton's study (1967) of deinstitutionalized mentally retarded adults revealed a pattern of debt and poverty. Differences in the incomes of the groups from these two studies may be attributed to greater follow-up assistance provided to Rosen et al.'s group (1974).

A near zero rate of welfare assistance was reported by Dinger (1961) and Clark et al. (1968). Others presented somewhat higher estimates: 5 percent (Mc-Fall, 1966) and 16.19 percent (Miller, 1965). Miller also reported that only 68 percent of the mentally retarded that he studied were self-supporting, compared with 96 percent of a control group. These results are, of course, rather dated. Current figures appear to be variable. They will certainly reflect newer sources of public assistance (e.g., SSI) that may diminish incentive for working.

Lower paying jobs are reported for adults who were learning disabled as students (Carter, 1964; Howden, 1967). Learning disabled pupils are also reported as holding lower vocational aspirations. Rawson's investigation (1968) appears to contradict these general observations. All but 10 of the 56 dylexics she studied were found to be in higher SES groups 23 years after leaving a private residential school for the learning disabled. The group, however, was highly atypical. Its members came from wealthy families and their median IQ was 131. Rawson also reported no occupational or income differences on the basis of the severity of the language problem. White et al. (1980) reported similar income distributions for samples of learning disabled and non-learning disabled young adults matched by sex and year of high school graduation. Seventy-five percent of both groups earned less than $7500 annually. The mean hourly income of $2.93 reported by Scott et al. (1980) is certainly indicative of a lower than average income for learning disabled adults.

The lack of follow-up research on mildly disturbed children as adults is again apparent. Only a single study sheds any light on the financial condition of these individuals, and the information provided by that research is very general. Young adults who were emotionally disturbed as adolescents continued to be financially dependent on their families (Garber, 1972).

Housing

Home ownership is an indicator of wealth and stability, and, consequently, research has revealed a pattern of substandard rented housing for the handicapped adult (Clark et al., 1968; Peterson & Smith, 1960; Rosen et al., 1974; State Board of Public Instruction, 1969). A mean monthly rental fee of $54.00 was reported by Rosen et al. (1974). Slum living was found to be the standard for deinstitutionalized mentally retarded adults (Edgerton, 1967).

These trends were contradicted by Dinger (1961), who reported that most of a sample of mildly retarded adults lived in average or above-average homes—but his sample does not appear representative. Another positive trend was noted by Baller (1936) and Charles (1953). From early unstable adjustment (Baller, 1936), a group of 207 retarded adults demonstrated average rates and quality of home ownership 15 years later (Charles, 1953).

Other Indices of Living Standard

There are many measures of standard of living. Income, bank accounts, and home, auto, and furniture ownership have all been investigated as determinants of the economic status of the mildly handicapped. Dinger (1961) found that 51 percent of his subjects had savings accounts. He did not report the balances, but Clark et al. (1968) found a median savings balance of $436, which decreased over time. Clark's research also revealed several other interesting items concerning the affluence of mildly retarded individuals:

1. Most subjects owned televisions.
2. Few owned furniture but ownership increased over time.
3. Fifty-five percent of the group that had been living in the community for 12–23 months had telephones.
4. Only 20 percent did installment buying.
5. Twenty-seven percent of the group in the community for 12–23 months owned cars.
6. Fifty percent of those in the community less than 1 year had life insurance. This number decreased over time.

FAMILY

A major criterion for adult adjustment is the stability of family life. The mildly handicapped encounter special problems when seeking to develop a "normal family." They face the attitudinal resistance of society, legal restrictions, lack of training in family life and child care, and, if they are the products of residential facilities, they also suffer from a paucity of role models.

Marriage Rates

Mildly handicapped adults who reside in the community marry at, or below, the same rate as other individuals of the same age. As with income, the rates reported in the literature vary considerably. Tobias (1970) found that 20 percent of the mentally retarded women who had left the New York City Public Schools during the years 1960–1963 were married by 1967. Only 16 of 130 EMR subjects (ranging in age from 19 to 37) had been married in another study (Crain, 1980).

Brolin et al. (1975) arrived at essentially the same figure as Tobias. A marriage rate of approximately 50 percent has been reported by other researchers investigating young mildly retarded adults (Dinger, 1961; Redding, 1979). Baller (1936) reported that mentally subnormal girls married younger than girls from a control group, but the mean ages at marriage reported by Shaw and Wright (1960; 22.2 years for males, 25.2 years for females) appear to contradict Baller's conclusion and, in fact, are a reverse of the general trend. In the follow-up to Baller's study, Charles (1953) reported a lower-than-average marriage rate for the retarded. No differences in marriage age or marriage rate between mildly retarded adults and the general population have also been reported (State Board of Public Instruction, 1969). Deinstitutionalized retarded adults appear to marry at a lower rate than those who remain in the community, probably due in part to the difficulty encountered in overcoming the effects of the sexual separation often fostered in institutions (Baller, 1936; Baller, Charles & Miller, 1967; Charles, 1953; Clark et al., 1968; Edgerton, 1967, 1976; Miller, 1965). Marriage rates of female mildly retarded adults are reported to be somewhat higher than those of males (Edgerton,

1976; Howe, 1967; Shanyfelt, 1974; Skaarbrevik, 1971). The greatest difference (8.2 percent versus 46.3 percent) can be found in the Shanyfelt investigation.

Learning disabled young adults do not differ in marriage rates from others of similar age, according to White et al. (1980) and Lehtinen and Tuomisto (1976). Contradictory evidence is reported by Scott et al. (1980). Of that sample, only 18 percent were married (mean age, 30 years). Sixty-nine percent had remained single. The remainder were divorced or widowed. Marriage rates for the mildly disturbed are unreported.

Children

Can the mildly handicapped care for their children? Do they have children at the same rate as the general population? As in the case of marriage rates, only partial answers to these questions may be found. There is considerable variability in estimates of the number of children born to mildly handicapped parents and the ways in which the figures are reported. Some researchers have found that there is no significant difference in birth rate between the married mildly handicapped and the general population (Peterson & Smith, 1960; State Board of Public Instruction, 1969). The manner in which Dinger (1961) reported his birth-rate figures (79 children for 100 mildly retarded adults) makes interpretation difficult since he provided no comparative figures for a similar age nonhandicapped group. For a young adult group, however, it does not appear to be substantially different from that which would be expected.

Andron and Strum (1973) found that only 1 of the 12 retarded couples they investigated had children. Seven of the females had been sterilized. Edgerton (1967) uncovered a similar cause for a low birth rate as 44 of the 48 individuals studied had been sterilized. Of a group of 128 graduates (82 percent male) from Elwyn Institute's transitional program, only 30.8 percent were married in the years immediately following deinstitutionalization. Of that group, less than 50 percent had children (Clark et al., 1968).

A comprehensive study on married mentally retarded individuals was conducted in England by Shaw and Wright (1960). Utilizing a sample of nearly 200, the researchers found a live birth rate 50 percent greater than that of the general population, a live birth rate considerably higher than similar unskilled workers, and an infant death rate essentially equal to that of the general population. Miller's extensive follow-up (1965) to the Baller (1937) and Charles (1951) studies provides information that only partially supports Shaw and Wright. While the mentally retarded had larger families than the control group, only 70 percent of the retarded, as opposed to 81 percent of the controls, had children. Thus, the higher birth rate for the mentally retarded is accounted for by a few very large families.

Several complexities in the Baller-Charles-Miller series of research may be noted. At an early age, the mentally retarded women had more children than the contrast group. That trend reversed in later years. Thus, most children were born in the early years of marriage. Finally, when the mother was retarded, the number of children was greater than when the father was retarded.

Only a single study of learning disabled adults even mentions children (White et al., 1980). Since only three of the subjects in the study were married, and they were recent high school graduates, it should not be surprising that only one child was reported.

The quality of child care provided by mildly retarded adults is frequently discussed in the literature. The lone couple with a child in the Andron and Strum (1973) article reported that the presence of children placed a considerable strain on their marriage. An in-depth analysis of a single marriage demonstrated that the mentally retarded parents were totally unprepared for parenthood. The mother did not provide adequate care to her first-born child and a second pregnancy occurred quickly upon his birth (Bowden, Spitz, & Winters, 1971). Bass (1964) cited a California study that indicated that the relationships of mildly retarded couples are severely strained if they have to care for more than one or two children. Specific evidence of incompetence in child rearing is offered by Shaw and Wright (1960); approximately one third of the families that formed the sample had been involved in cruelty and/or neglect cases with their children. The authors concluded, as did Bass, that the chances of successful social adaptation by EMR adults were much greater when family size was three or less.

Lenkowsky and Saposnek (1978) discussed the family consequences of parental dyslexia and revealed that, while the parent was able to care for his family, the disability had some psychological impact on the children who had to "cover up" the father's inability to read. The scarcity of research in this area should be rectified within the next few years so that professionals can help learning disabled individuals develop adequate parenting skills.

Research on the prevalence of handicapping conditions among the offspring of the mildly handicapped has generally been limited to the mentally retarded. Charles' optimistic belief (1953) that the majority of the offspring are not retarded belied the pervasive nature of the problem when more specific data are analyzed. Forty-six of 377 children born of marriages in which at least one parent was retarded were found to be severely retarded (Shaw & Wright, 1960). Fifty-nine percent of the children had IQs between 80 and 100. The most pessimistic evidence is provided by Reed and Reed (1970), who studied 80,000 white members of 289 kinships. They found that (1) when both parents were mentally retarded, 39.5 percent of the offspring were retarded; (2) in a marriage where only one partner was retarded, 11.2 percent of the offspring were retarded; and (3) when both were of normal intelligence, only 0.9 percent of the offspring were retarded. The California study mentioned by Bass (1969) revealed a 25–50 percent chance of retarded offspring when one or both parents are retarded.

Whether the consequent high rates of retarded offspring are caused by genetics or environment is not an issue here. Suffice it to say that the offspring of mentally retarded adults are frequently retarded. This creates further stress on the marriage and taxes the ability of the parents to care for their children. (The concerns of mildly retarded parents will be further discussed in a subsequent section concerning legal restrictions.)

Are the children of the mildly disturbed and the learning disabled similarly afflicted? There is a small body of knowledge that indicates higher rates of dysfunction among the offspring of such individuals. Hutchings and Mednick (1975) reported higher rates of criminal behavior among both adopted and biological children of criminal fathers. Similarly, hyperactive parents are more likely to have hyperactive children (Cantwell, 1975; Morrison & Stewart, 1973). Much of the research in this area has been in the form of behavioral genetics and has focused on more severe behavioral deviations such as schizophrenia (Defries & Plomin, 1978). In addition, research in this area does not always differentiate between individuals whose symptoms were manifested during childhood and those whose symptoms did not appear until adulthood. This lack of discrimination makes it impossible to effectively interpret some of the literature.

Quality of Marriage and Divorce

Divorce rates uncovered by research show considerable variability. Some writers report very low rates that may be attributed to the young age of the sample and the low marriage rate. Those who have studied mildly handicapped adults in later years report fairly high rates. Crain (1980) reported that only 1 of 130 EMR graduates of the St. Louis Special District had been divorced; however, this number must be interpreted in light of the fact that only 16 had ever married. Dinger (1961) related that 3 percent of a sample of 100 EMR adults were divorced. Samples in both studies were young adults. The marriages of mildly retarded individuals tend to be unstable even when they do not result in divorce (Andron & Strum, 1973; Baller, Charles, & Miller, 1967). An interesting note was provided by Porter and Milazzo (1958), who found that EMR graduates of special classes had better marital adjustment than those who attended regular classes.

The most pessimistic report was provided by Shaw and Wright (1960). Twenty percent of the marriages they studied ended in divorce or permanent separation in spite of the fact that the majority of the marriages were reportedly happy and stable. Miller (1965) provided reinforcement for that statistic with a study divorce rate of 22 percent compared with a 10 percent rate for the normal control group. The group studied by Miller had shown a high divorce rate as young adults. At mid-life, it had slowed down and was close to the national average. In later life, it increased again (Baller, 1936; Charles, 1953).

Robins and O'Neal (1959) found that adults who had run away as children experienced a 50 percent divorce rate and frequent marital difficulties. Garber (1972) reported that adult males who had received psychiatric treatment as emotionally disturbed adolescents had very stable marriages. This was not true for females in similar circumstances. Seventy percent of Garber's subjects expressed satisfaction with their marriages. However, the difficulties they did report included finances, lack of mutual interest, and sexual incompatability. Little information has been published on the quality of marriage of learning disabled adults. Scott et al. (1980) reported a divorce rate of 11 percent—a rate that may not seem very high in light of the age of the sample (30 years), but that becomes more significant when one recalls that only 18 percent of the sample was married. Thus, the divorce rate was almost two thirds of the marriage rate.

Andron and Strum's evaluation (1973) of the married life of retarded couples, although based on a small sample ($N = 12$), provided considerable insight. The length of the marriages was from 8 months to 11 years. Only one couple relied solely on the husband's income for support. Eight relied on public welfare. Few couples had established credit, five reported problems with jobs, and two with family quarrels. The man made all of the decisions in five marriages, the woman in five. One couple shared decision making and another relied on their parents. Half reported no marital problems. While all couples expressed a preference for married life, one husband admitted extramarital sex. The preference for married life among the mentally retarded is further evidenced by a California survey in which mentally retarded respondents expressed 50 percent greater satisfaction with their lives if they were married (Bass, 1964).

The Andron and Strum (1973) and Clark, Kivitz, and Rosen (1968) presentations averred that mentally retarded individuals who marry usually wed partners who are also retarded. A different but not contradictory slant may be found in studies in which it is revealed that mildly retarded individuals (especially females) often marry individuals of slightly higher intelligence (Howe, 1967; Shaw & Wright, 1960). The latter phenomenon may appear to provide security for those retarded individuals who marry individuals with normal intelligence, since when both partners are mentally retarded, marital stability and ability to survive are severely impaired (Shaw & Wright, 1960). However, when the nonretarded spouse dies, the retarded adult is frequently unprepared for the independence forced upon him or her (Edgerton & Berovici, 1976). The death of the spouse may then leave the retarded individual without the survival skills he or she might have obtained if not for the dependence upon the now-deceased partner.

Legal Restrictions on Marriage and Family

Reports such as those written by Goddard (1912) and Dugdale (1877), regarding widespread retardation, mental illness and criminal behavior in specific families (the Kallikaks and the Jukes) resulted in the eugenics movement and numerous legal restrictions on marriage for handicapped individuals. A quick perusal of state statutes and litigation reveals that restrictions continue. As late as 1972, twelve states had laws prohibiting the marriage of even mildly retarded individuals. Twenty-four states also permitted routine sterilization of retarded adults (Krischef, 1972).

The parental rights of the mentally retarded and the emotionally disturbed are still very much in doubt. The Family Court of New York (*In the matter of Judy and Donald G.*, Fam. Ct., N.Y., filed February 1, 1980) held that a state statute permitting termination of parental rights for handicapped individuals was in violation of the due process and equal protection clauses of the United States Constitution. The parents in this litigation were considered to be of dull-normal and mildly retarded intelligence. The involved social agency had charged the parents with abandonment—after the children were removed by the agency, which also thwarted the parents' attempts to see their children. Such cases make the high incidence of neglect reported by Shaw and Wright (1960) somewhat suspect. Other similar cases have been resolved, though not always in the same manner. Termination was upheld despite misconduct on the part of the social agency in one suit (*Coffey v. Baltimore* Department of Social Services, No. 471, Baltimore City Ct. 1977). In two cases similar to the New York case, slightly different issues were addressed. The Utah Supreme Court held that a mother with borderline intelligence could not be charged with abandonment because the Division of Family Services had thwarted her attempts to regain her child (*State v. J.T.* 578 P2d, 831-Utah, 1978). Another case, which has not reached resolution, presents a challenge to an Illinois statute that is similar to the one struck down in New York (*Helvey v. Rednour*, No. 79-145, Illinois App. Ct. 5th District). The statute allows the court to appoint a guardian with the power to allow adoption merely upon determining that the parent is mentally retarded. Retarded persons are *not* afforded the opportunity to prove they are capable parents. Plomondon and Soskin (1978) reviewed the legal status of mentally retarded and emotionally disturbed adults and concluded that in many cases their rights have been summarily abrogated. There appears to have been no similar statutes or litigation concerning learning disabled adults.

EDUCATION

Continuing Education

While it is obvious that academic college attendance is not realistic for a large percentage of the mildly handicapped (especially the mentally retarded), there are many other avenues to continuing education. Dinger (1961) found that 47 percent of former high school EMR students had continued education, while an even higher 79 percent indicated that they intended to continue to try to obtain a high school diploma. Astonishingly, 2 of 19 EMR graduates of a work-study program in Peoria, Ill., attended college in the years immediately following their graduation (Parker et al., 1976). Less optimistic findings come from Clark et al. (1968) and McFall (1966), who discovered that only 26 percent of the former students of classes for EMR had any formal post–high school education. Since college and other forms of post–high school education have not generally been available or viewed as practical for the mildly retarded, most of the follow-up research does not even address this issue. This phenomenon may change during the next few years if Section 504 of the Rehabilitation Act of 1973 is utilized to provide access to college programs for the mentally retarded. In 1976, however, only 1 of 500 colleges surveyed had a program for mentally retarded students (L.A. Jones & Moe, 1980).

Post–high school education for learning disabled individuals is more frequent. Robinson and Smith (1962) reported high frequencies of college attendance for 44 reading-disabled former clients of the University of Chicago Reading Clinic. Eleven former students were in college, three had completed master's degrees, two were in doctoral programs, and one had completed medical school during the 10 years following intervention. It is important to note that the median IQ for the group was 120, which made them a highly atypical group. Poor readers were found to be much less likely to continue their formal education in a study by Howden (1967), but Preston & Yarington (1967) disputed that claim and stated that retarded readers had the same dropout and college attendance rates as the national population. Both studies used samples of approximately 50 people.

Rawson's research (1968) was the most favorable of those reviewed; of 56 former pupils of a residential school for the learning disabled, 48 had college degrees 23 years later. These individuals, many of whom were considered moderately to severely dyslexic, were from upper SES backgrounds and had a median IQ of 131. This, obviously, is not a typical sample of dyslexics. Samples utilized by Frauenheim (1978) and White et al. (1980) provided more realistic appraisals. In the White et al. (1980) study, the learning disabled sample held fewer high school diplomas and baccalaureate degrees than a matched sample of nondisabled individuals. Sixty-seven percent of the learning disabled sample (versus 84 percent of the nondisabled group) had plans for future educational activities. Scott et al. (1980) reported that of a small sample ($N = 31$) of LD adults, 68 percent had some post–high school training and 52 percent had specific post-secondary occupational training. The educational status of learning disabled adults was studied in

Finland by Lehtinen and Tuomisto (1976), who reported that from a sample of 91 individuals, 36 percent had graduated from college and 8 percent were pursuing graduate study.

Since follow-up research with the emotionally disturbed concentrates most heavily on psychiatric aspects, it is difficult to draw any conclusions about their adult educational status. Shore and Massimo (1973) found that adolescent delinquent boys who had been placed in a vocationally oriented psychotherapy program had sought more post-school training than a control group that had been retained in a regular high school program. The former group had not been encouraged to return to high school but rather to employ alternatives (i.e., night and correspondence schools).

Educational Attainment

What are the reading levels of mildly handicapped adults? Do they utilize their academic skills? How do they feel about their school experiences and achievements? Do their IQs change from those measured in school? Since educational achievement has long been viewed as a necessary prerequisite for adequate adult adjustment, the achievement status of mildly disabled adults has been investigated frequently.

Tobias (1970) revealed that two thirds of a sample of 1836 EMR adults in New York City had adult IQs within 10 points of those measured when they were in school. The findings of Tobias were essentially echoed by Rosen et al. (1974). No gains in IQ were reported for adults labeled hyperkinetic as children (Menkes et al., 1967). Dinger (1961), on the other hand, found a mean IQ gain of over 30 points in his sample of 100 former EMR pupils.

There exists a considerable body of research on the adult educational achievement of the mildly handicapped, especially those classified as learning disabled. Ellehammer, Larsen, & Rasch (1954) studied 72 "backward" readers who were in their twenties. Half of the sample demonstrated achievement of less than third grade. Ten were able to read well; 32 read at at least a sixth-grade level, while 39 read slowly, although they could still read newspapers and magazines. Only 3 were very poor readers. Similarly optimistic appraisals of reading were offered by Silver and Hagin (1964), who found that two thirds of disabled child readers were effective readers as adults 10–12 years later. Only those with notable perceptual problems continued to be essentially nonreaders.

Howden's research (1967) provided considerably less optimistic results. A 19 year follow-up of 57 poor childhood readers revealed that they continued to be poor readers. These adults reported reading little for pleasure except for newspapers and magazines. This evidence is contradicted by another study, which revealed that nearly 50 percent of a sample of 44 reading clinic clients read more than the average adult (Robinson & Smith, 1962). The discrepancy may be explained in part by the high IQ for the Robinson & Smith group.

Frauenheim (1978) presented one of the most extensive follow-up studies of educational attainment of dyslexic adults. The sample consisted of 40 males who were 8–15 years old at the time of the original diagnosis and 18–21 at the follow-up. The predominately middle class subjects had a mean WISC IQ of 94 and were 3.5 years retarded in reading at the time of diagnosis. Reading difficulties persisted into adulthood with a mean reading grade of 3.6. Ninety-two percent of the sample were at or below a fifth-grade reading level (compared to an average adult reading level of 10.5). Sixty-three percent were below functional literacy. Phonic skills remained poor. Frauenheim, concurring with Ellehammer et al. (in Herman, 1959), reported a mean grade level of 2.9 on spelling, along with the continuation of dyslexic spelling errors. An arithmetic level of 4.6 was also reported, with special difficulty with the multiplication tables. Like the subjects of the Howden (1967) study, this group reported little voluntary adult reading.

No improvement in academic achievement was reported by Rosen et al. (1974) for mentally retarded adults, while Coolidge et al. (1964) reported that school-phobic children, although higher than average in IQ, continued to perform below grade expectation as adolescents and adults.

There is mixed evidence on the relationship between academic achievement and adult adjustment of mildly handicapped individuals. Rosen et al. (1974) found no relationship between IQ, achievement level, and four measures of community adjustment (income, job stability, coping with daily problems, and social adjustment). In other research, IQ has been found to be unrelated to employability, while high academic achievement was correlated with higher level jobs (Chaffin et al., 1971; Kolstoe, 1961; Levin et al., 1971). Eagle's review (1967) of community adjustment of formerly institutionalized mentally retarded adults showed that IQ and academic achievement are not consistent factors in the prognosis of adequate adjustment. Levin et al. (1971) concluded that higher level jobs are obtained by individuals with more years of schooling rather than by those with higher achievement levels or greater intelligence. Thus, it may be the appearance of competence (in the form of diplomas, etc.) that determines initial success in obtaining employment.

A recent investigation (White et al., 1980) revealed that learning disabled adults expressed considerably less satisfaction with their school experiences than an age- and sex-matched contrast group. In spite of that dissatisfaction, neither group pursued any post–high school remedial assistance. Weiss et al. (1978) essentially agreed with the report of dissatisfaction. The sentiments of other groups toward their educations have been largely uninvestigated.

MISCELLANEOUS FACTORS

Health and Accidents

While at least one writer reported that mildly retarded individuals have a life expectancy similar to that of the general population (Meir, 1973) others averred that the health quality of the mildly handicapped appears to be somewhat deficient. That deficiency may occur as a result of coincidental poverty, poor self-care, or constitutional factors, but the evidence for its existence is substantial. Charles (1953) found that the death rate for a group of 151 mildly retarded individuals was substantially higher than that of a normal control group. Violent deaths were especially prevalent. More convincing evidence is offered by Miller (1965), who reexamined 111 of Charles's subjects. The mortality rate of the mentally retarded people was twice that of the controls. The accidental death rate was 30 percent compared to 6 percent for the control group. In addition, the retarded were more prone to illness. Poor health has also been viewed as a cause of reinstitutionalization (Eagle, 1967).

A follow-up study in Norway (Skaarbrevik, 1971) revealed that the mildly retarded were involved in a disproportionately large rate of disability insurance claims. This finding stands in apparent contradiction to that reported in *VR Review* ("Insurance," 1977). Based upon a United States Labor Department survey, mentally retarded workers were found to have fewer disabling injuries than the average worker exposed to the same job hazards. (Perhaps the difference between the American and the Norwegian studies lies in the definitions of disability insurance.) In another study, 9 percent of EMR individuals who had left their jobs did so because of health reasons. Poor health leading to work disability was reported for nearly 50 percent of a middle-aged sample studied by Edgerton (1976).

The extent of use of alcohol, drugs, and tobacco can be viewed as a peripheral index of health. Alcoholism is reportedly only a minor problem among mentally retarded adults. In a study of the stability of 12 marriages of retarded adults, Andron and Strum (1973) found only one couple with alcohol abuse problems. This proportion is less than national prevalence. The evidence from this small sample is supported by Edgerton (1967, 1976) and Miller (1965), who reported that the major proportion of arrests for drunkenness was accounted for by a single individual in his study. The mentally retarded were also reported to be, generally speaking, nonusers of narcotics (Edgerton, 1967). This is not necessarily true today.

The adult health status of the learning disabled and the mildly disturbed has been largely neglected in the literature. No differences were found in the consumption of alcohol and drug and cigarette use between a learning disabled group and a matched nonlearning disabled group (White et al., 1980). Scott et al. (1980) reported that 26 percent of their sample had chronic medical problems, and 10 percent reported epileptic seizures. Since emotional health is so strongly intertwined with physical health, it is difficult to assess the health status of the emotionally disturbed. In addition, most studies do not separate the mildly disturbed from more serious cases. Garber (1972), however, did find a high rate of illegal drug usage (50 percent) among adults who had been treated in a psychiatric hospital as adolescents; 11 percent used narcotics. The sample included psychotics, neurotics, and character-disordered individuals. No breakdown in drug usage by each subgroup was provided.

Presently, it is impossible to reach any general conclusions about the health of mildly handicapped adults. The evidence appears to indicate that the physical health of the mildly retarded is somewhat deficient. In spite of Feingolds's research (1975) linking learning disabilities to presumed toxic substances, there does not appear to be any diminished longevity or higher illness rate for learning disabled adults. The physical health of adults viewed as mildly disturbed as children is generally unknown. The neglect of this subject may be interpreted in two ways. Either the health problems of the population are not acute, or the health deficiencies that do exist among the mildly handicapped may be more readily linked to poverty, and are therefore captured under studies of that subject.

Military Service

Mentally retarded and emotionally disturbed individuals have always served in the military. To what degree and level of success may be shown by examination of several studies. It should be remembered that one of the original forces for the development of a test of general intelligence was the need for higher level recruits by an increasingly mechanized and technological military (MacMillan, 1977). The most extensive study on the mentally retarded recruit was that of Weaver (1946); of 8000 mentally retarded citizens inducted into the United States Army, 56 percent of the males and 62 percent of the females made a satisfactory adjustment.

Dinger's study (1961) revealed that 65 percent of the EMR males had served in the military. Substantially fewer mildly retarded males had military experience than a comparison group of normally intelligent males (Peterson & Smith, 1960). Shanyfelt (1974) reported that very few (1.7 percent) young mildly retarded males were in the armed forces.

Children with psychiatric problems may also serve in the armed services when they become adults. Of the 155 subjects followed by Garber (1972), 13 had been in military service and 5 of those had been unable to adjust to military demands. Thus, the percentage who served was low and characterized by a high ratio of poor adjustment. Roff (1956) compared individuals who had been seen in one of several guidance clinics with a randomly selected group of young men. For the former group he found (1) higher military rejection rates; (2) fewer deferments for dependency and essential jobs during World War II; (3) more dishonorable discharges; and (4) more honorable discharges for psychopathology. These findings should be tempered with the knowledge that 74 percent of the former clinic patients had normal military careers. Glueck and Glueck (1968) reported a higher rate of conduct problems in the military for a group of former delinquents. No figures are available for the learning disabled. However, a large number of men serving in the United States Armed services are reported as having literacy problems; it may be assumed that the learning disabled are among these men.

EFFICACY OF PROGRAMS

Now that the adult adjustment patterns of the mildly handicapped have been discussed, it is critical to review the impact of special education on that adjustment. Have special programs been effective? Are there long-term improvements in academic, vocational, or social functioning that provide an advantage to adults who have been so educated? While there are few pre-planned (and hence well-controlled) follow-up studies on handicapped adults, there are yet fewer that include the controls and precision necessary to allow conclusions about a specific program's efficacy. In addition, zeal for new programs may lead to unwarranted claims and/or spurious interpretations. Another difficulty arises from the selection of criteria for success. Any of the indices of adult (and childhood) adjustment may have been used as criteria for the success of the program. And what is viewed as the success criterion in one program (e.g., the number of job placements) may not have even been investigated in another.

At this point another issue surfaces: the timeliness of the selection of criteria. For a criterion to be truly sound it must be selected prior to the initiation of a program. This prevents extensive *post hoc* analyses in which the researcher gathers data on a large set of criterion variables and eventually discovers the "significant" changes that were being sought. Such analyses are useful only for providing possible areas for future research.

Vocational Programs

The ultimate success of programs is probably nowhere more evident than in vocational training. Do graduates of special programs obtain jobs more easily, hold onto their jobs longer, get better jobs, and perform better on their jobs than comparable non–special program graduates? The evidence in this area leads to a convincing "yes." Which specific type of work training is most effective is a much more elusive problem. Mirring's report (1977) on the NARC-OJT project would seem to indicate that employers can—and will—provide the necessary training, if given the incentive to do so. Others have evaluated comprehensive and complex programs. Parker et al. (1976) found both work-study and traditional vocational programs to be highly effective in providing initial vocational skills. Brolin et al. (1975) analyzed data on young mildly retarded adults who had been in work-study or traditional programs and found that adults with work-study experience performed better vocationally. An interesting insight was provided by Chaffin et al. (1971); in their study, the initial vocational superiority of a work-study group was nearly eradicated 2 years later. The work-study group showed higher unemployment than it had 2 years earlier, while the regular high school group showed considerably less unemployment after 2 years. A 24 percent difference in unemployment rates had decreased to only 8 percent.

A different criterion was employed by Stickland and Arrell (1967) to assess the value of a cooperative vocational training program. Of the 1405 subjects in the study, 80 percent were employed in jobs for which they had been specifically trained. Utilizing the same criterion, Skaarbrevik (1971) found that only 25 percent of EMR graduates of vocational training programs were employed in the lumbering and farming jobs for which they had been prepared.

Social Adjustment Programs

No other area provides such inconclusive evidence as research on programs designed to improve social adequacy. The complexities of defining "social adjustment" and in developing criteria for its measurement are barriers enough, but when one considers other evidence such as that presented by Eyesenck (1952), the issues become even more murky. Eyesenck's evidence, that two thirds of neurotics will recover spontaneously within about 2 years, made it clear that for a treatment effect to be shown, improvement after or during intervention must be over and above that which could be due to spontaneous remission or maturation. Use of a nontreated control group can accomplish that goal.

One investigation that did attempt to utilize a control group was that of Shore and Massimo (1973). Adolescent delinquent boys who received comprehensive vocationally oriented psychotherapy were much better adjusted 10 years later than a group that did not. A problem in interpretation arises when it is realized that assignment to treatment or control groups was not random. Thus, pre-existing differences may have accounted for the positive evidence for the therapy. Cautious interpretation of the data is therefore a requisite.

Similar difficulty is encountered in interpreting the evidence supplied by Levy (1969). He declared that 85 percent of the teens completing inpatient treatment had successful long-term outcomes, while only 33 percent who had not completed the treatment were adequately adjusted. This seemingly positive evidence may be a tautological phenomenon. The fact of completing treatment could have been due to severity, lack of family support, and organicity—all of which would certainly contribute to poor outcomes. Those with milder problems, and hence better prognoses, completed treatment. The outcome differences reported by Levy, therefore, may have been due to differences in the populations studied, not in the treatments given. Interpretation of the Porter and Milazzo (1958) finding (i.e., that EMR graduates of special classes are socially and recreationally more adept as adults than similar graduates of regular classes) is subject to the same difficulty; were their subjects differentially assigned to the programs?

It is risky to compare two or more investigations even though conditions may appear similar. Certainly, unaccounted differences (qualities of staff, community attitudes, etc.) may have existed that would lead to inevitably different results. However, conjecture about such differences may also provide impetus for future research. The studies of Edgerton (1967, 1976) and Clark et al. (1968) presented contrasts that cannot be ignored. The former presents a rather bleak picture of the postinstitution adjustment of mentally retarded adults, while the latter provides cause for optimism. The sharp differences may be attributable to the quality of the transitional programs. Subjects in the Clark et al. study had been favored by extensive training and follow-up, while those studied by Edgerton were released with little preparation, though with a good prognosis.

McCord's follow-up (1978) to the Cambridge–Somerville Youth Study Project (Powers & Witmer, 1951) is illustrative of well-controlled and -designed follow-up research. Thirty years after termination of the project, McCord re-evaluated the effects of the treatment on 235 subjects, including members of both treatment and control groups. Matched assignment of subjects to treatment and control groups had been carried out in 1939. The treatment consisted of counseling, tutoring, medical and psychiatric help, and recreational programming. Both "difficult" and "average" boys were assigned to each group. Treatment continued for an average of 5 years. McCord conducted her follow-up in 1975 and 1976 and found that

1. As adults, equal numbers from the control and treatment groups had been convicted of crimes. The proportion of serious crimes was similar.
2. More individuals in the treatment group committed more than one crime.
3. Equal numbers had been treated for alcoholism but more individuals in the treatment group reported symptoms of alcoholism.
4. Equal numbers had received treatment in mental health hospitals.
5. Forty-three percent of the control group, compared with 29 percent of the treatment group, were white collar or professional workers.
6. The two groups did not differ in the use of leisure time.
7. Two thirds of the treatment group reported that the program had been helpful to them personally.

McCord (1978) suggested several explanations for the apparent failure of the intervention: "the individual may experience symptoms of dependency. . . . [T]hrough receiving the services of a "welfare project," those in the treatment program may have justified the help they received by perceiving themselves as requiring help'' (p. 289). In any event, it would be impossible to point to any success in the Cambridge-Somerville Project.

A more optimistic presentation was made by Phillips (1978). Unfortunately, Phillips's report contains some very obvious sources of invalidity, which cast serious doubt upon the conclusions reached by the author. A group of adults who had participated in a program for mildly disturbed children was compared with a group that had been invited to participate in the program, but had declined or dropped out. Among the findings were (1) a higher rate of high school graduation for the treatment group; (2) higher rates of employment and post–high school training for the treatment group; and (3) a lower crime rate and greater job satisfaction for the treatment group. Of course, utilizing self-selection as the means for assignment to treatment and control groups negates any real generalization from the data. The nontreatment group may have been more severely handicapped and certainly were less amenable to improvement of their conditions.

The paucity of good, comparative follow-up research precludes the presentation of more extensive positive conclusions. It appears that vocational training has achieved some desired results. However, the social behavior of the mildly handicapped is more affected by maturation, family, and pervasive environmental conditions than by the interventions. It would be easy to fault researchers for the inconclusiveness of their research. However, the conditions under which research is conducted are often unfavorable—in the face of the determined and skilled investigators. Attrition of sample; legal and ethical restrictions on utilizing untreated control groups; and the imposition of external, uncontrollable factors are just some of the problems researchers encounter.

CONCLUSION

While there appears to be considerable impetus to group the learning disabled, the mildly retarded, and the mildly disturbed together under the umbrella of ''mildly handicapped,'' it appears that in adult life the subgroups are highly distinguished. The mildly retarded continue to demonstrate subnormal adaptation. They work at unskilled jobs, their marriages are unstable, and their incomes are far below average. In addition, they are more likely to engage in breaches of the law and less likely to partake of recreational and social resources.

The mildly disturbed and the learning disabled, on the other hand, seem to blend in as adults. Perhaps their handicaps are no longer visible when the pressures of academic achievement and social maturation are removed. Another explanation is also plausible: the handicap affecting the mildly retarded has a much more severe and pervasive impact on vocational success. The learning disabled and the mildly disturbed are able to acquire skills that enhance their positions in the job market. Probably no other factor has as much influence on adult adjustment as occupational success. It may be that vocational behaviors continue to highlight the incapabilities of retarded adults, while at the same time providing the means of integration for the learning disabled and the mildly disturbed.

REFERENCES

Allen, R. C. *The retarded citizen: Victim of mental and legal deficiency.* Washington, D.C.: Institute of Law, Psychiatry and Criminology, George Washington University, 1969.

Anderson, C.M., & Plymate, H. B. Management of the brain damaged adolescent. *American Journal of Orthopsychiatry*, 1962, *32*, 492–500.

Andron, L., & Strum, M. L. Is "I do" in the repertoire of the retarded? A study of the functioning of married retarded couples. *Mental Retardation*, 1973, *11*, 31–34.

Baller, W. R. A study of the present social status of a group of adults who when they were in elementary school were classified as mentally deficient. *Genetic Psychology Monographs*, 1936, *18*, 165–244.

Baller, W. R., Charles, D. C., & Miller, E. L. Mid-life attainment of the mentally retarded: A longitudinal study. *Genetic Psychology Monographs*, 1967, *75*, 235–329.

Balow, B., & Blomquist, M. Young adults ten to fifteen years after severe reading disability. *Elementary School Journal*, 1965, *66*, 44–48.

Bass, M. S. Marriage for the mentally deficient. *Mental Retardation*, 1964, *2*, 198–202.

Becker, R. Job training placement for retarded youth. *Mental Retardation*, 1976, *14*, 7–11.

Beckham, A. S. Minimum intelligence levels for several occupations. *Personnel Journal*, 1930, *9*, 309–313.

Birenbaum, A., & Re, M. A. *Resettling mentally retarded adults in the community —Almost four years later.* Paper presented at the annual meeting of the American Association of Mental Deficiency, New Orleans, May 30, 1977.

Blalock, J. W. Persistent problems and concerns of young adults with learning disabilities. In W. M. Cruickshank & A. A. Silver (Eds.), *Bridges to tomorrow: The best of ACLD*, (Vol. 2). Syracuse N.Y.: Syracuse University Press, 1981.

Bobroff, A. A survey of social and civic participation of adults formerly in classes for the mentally retarded. *American Journal of Mental Deficiency*, 1956, *61*, 127–133.

Bowden, J., Spitz, H., & Winters, J. Follow up of one retarded couple's marriage. *Mental Retardation*, 1971, *9*, 42.

Bowring v. Godwin, Federal Reporter, 1977, *551*, 44.

Brolin, D., Durand, R., Kromer, K., & Muller, P. Post high school adjustment of educable retarded students. *Education and Training of the Mentally Retarded*, 1975, *10*, 144–148.

Brolin, D., Kokaska, C., & Charles, D. Critical issues in job placement of the educable mentally retarded. *Rehabilitation Literature*, 1974, *35*, 174–177.

Brown, B., & Courtless, T. *The mentally retarded offender.* Washington, D.C.: National Institute of Mental Health, Center for Studies of Crime and Delinquency, 1967.

Brown, B., & Courtless, T. *The mentally retarded offender.* Rockville, Md.: National Institute of Mental Health, 1971.

Cantwell, D. P. Genetic studies of hyperactive children: Psychiatric illness in biological and adopting parents. In R. R. Fieve, D. Rosenthal, & H. Brill (Eds.), *Genetic research in psychiatry.* Baltimore: Johns Hopkins University Press, 1975.

Carter, R. P. *A descriptive analysis of the adult adjustment of persons once identified as disabled readers.* Unpublished doctoral dissertation, University of Indiana, Bloomington, 1964.

Cassidy, V. M., & Phelps, H. R. *Postschool adjustment of slow learning children.* Columbus, Oh.: Ohio State University, 1955.

Chaffin, J. D., Spellman, C. R., Regan, C. E., & Davison, R. Two follow-up studies of former educable mentally retarded students from the Kansas Work Study Project. *Exceptional Children*, 1971, *10*, 733–738.

Charles D. C. Ability and accomplishment of persons earlier judged mentally deficient. *Genetic Psychology Monographs*, 1953, *47*, 3–71.

Civil Service Commission. *An 8 1/2 year record: Mentally retarded workers in the federal service.* Washington, D.C.: Bureau of Recruiting and Examining, 1972.

Clark, G. R., Kivitz, M. S., & Rosen, M. *A transitional program for institutionalized retarded adults.* Project No. RD 1275P, Final report, Vocational Rehabilitation Administration, Division of Research and Demonstrations, Department of Research and Demonstrations. Washington, D.C.: Department of Health, Education and Welfare, 1968.

Coffey v. Baltimore. Department of Social Services, No. 471, Baltimore City Court, 1977.

Colbert, J. N., Kalish, R. A., & Chang, P. Two psychological portals of entry for disadvantaged groups. *Rehabilitation Literature,* 1973, *34,* 194–202.

Coolidge, J. C., Brodie, R. D., & Feeney, B. A ten year follow up study of sixty-six school phobic children. *American Journal of Orthopsychiatry,* 1964, *34,* 675–684.

Cordero, I. *Study of reading disorders in relation to poverty and crime.* Santa Barbara, Cal.: Work Training Program, 1975.

Crain, E. J. Socioeconomic status of educable mentally retarded graduates of special education. *Education and training of the mentally retarded,* 1980,*15,* 90–94.

DeFries, J. C., & Plomin, R. Behavioral genetics. *Annual Review of Psychology,* 1978, *29,* 473–517.

Dinger, J. C. Post-school adjustment of former educable retarded pupils. *Exceptional Children,* 1961, *27,* 353–360.

Doleshal, L. L., & Jackson, J. L. Evaluation and follow up of the Texas Cooperative School Program. *Rehabilitation Literature,* 1970, *31,* 268–269.

Dugdale, R. L. *The Jukes.* New York: Putnam, 1877.

Eagle, E. Prognosis and outcome of community placement of institutionalized retardates. *American Journal of Mental Deficiency,* 1967, *72,* 232–243.

Edgerton, R. B. *The cloak of competence: Stigma in the lives of the mentally retarded.* Berkley: University of California Press, 1967.

Edgerton, R. B., & Bercovici, S. M. The Cloak of competence: Years later. *American Journal of Mental Deficiency,* 1976, *80,* 485–497.

Ellehammer, M., Larsen, C.A., & Rasch, G. Redegorelse foren undersøgelse af laeesvage børn i København. In Betaenkning vedrrøende forsorgen for talelidende. København, 1954.

Eyesenck, H. J. The effects of psychotherapy: An evaluation. *Journal of Consulting Psychology,* 1952, *16,* 319–324.

Feingold, B. *Why your child is hyperactive.* New York: Random House, 1975.

Frauenheim, J. G. Academic achievement characteristics of adult males who were diagnosed as dyslexic in childhood. *Journal of Learning Disabilities* 1978, *11,* 476–483.

Gan, J., Tymchuk, A., & Nisahara, A. Mildly retarded adults: Their attitudes toward retardation. *Mental Retardation,* 1977, *15,* 5–10.

Garber, B. *Follow-up study of hospitalized adolescents.* New York: Brunner/Mazel, 1972.

Glueck, S., & Glueck, E. *Juvenile delinquents grown up.* New York: Commonwealth Fund, 1940.

Glueck, S., & Glueck, E. *Delinquents and nondelinquents in perspective.* Cambridge, Ma.: Harvard University Press, 1968.

Goddard, H. H. *The Kallikak family: A study in the heredity of feeblemindedness.* New York: MacMillan, 1912.

Goldstein, H. Social and occupational adjustment. In H. A. Stevens & R. Heber (Eds.), *Mental retardation—A review of research.* Chicago: University of Chicago Press, 1964.

Gozali, J. Citizenship and voting behavior of mildly retarded adults: A pilot study. *American Journal of Mental Deficiency,* 1971, *75,* 640–641.

Hardy, M. I. Disabled readers: What happens to them after elementary school? *Canadian Education and Research Digest,* 1968, *8,* 338–346.

Haskins J., & Friel, C. *Project CAMIO: The mentally retarded in an adult correctional institution. (Vol. 4).* Huntsville, Tex.: Sam Houston State University, 1973.

Hechtman, L., Weiss, G., Finklestein, J., Werner, A., & Benn, R. Hyperactives as young adults: preliminary report. *Canadian Medical Association Journal,* 1976, *115,* 625–627, 630.

Helvey v. Rednour. No. 79-145, Illinois Appeals Court, 5th District, *Amicus,* 1979, *4,* 111–112.

Herman, K. *Reading disability.* Springfield, Il.: Charles C Thomas, 1959.

Howden, M. E. *A nineteen year follow-up study of good, average and poor readers in the fifth and sixth grades.* Unpublished doctoral dissertation, University of Oregon, Eugene, 1967.

Howe, C. E. *A comparison of mentally retarded high school students in work-study versus traditional programs.* Final report, Project No. 6-8148, Grant No. OEG-4-6-'068148-1556. Washington, D.C.: U.S. Department of Health, Education and Welfare, Bureau of Education of the Handicapped, 1967.

Hurley, R. L. *Poverty and mental retardation: A causal relationship.* New York: Random House, 1969.

Hutchings, B., & Mednick, S. A. Registered criminality in the adoptive and biological parents of registered male criminal adoptees. In R. R. Fieve, D. Rosenthal, & H. Brill (Eds.), *Genetic research in psychiatry.* Baltimore: Johns Hopkins University Press, 1975.

Insurance coverage and the mentally retarded worker. *VR Review*, 1977, *1*, 48–49.

In the matter of Judy and Donald G. Family Court, New York, Filed February 1, 1980, *Amicus*, 1979, *4*, 230–231.

Jones, F. L. A four year follow up of vulnerable adolescents: The prediction of outcomes in early adulthood from measures of social competence, coping style, and overall levels of psychopathology. *Journal of Nervous and Mental Disease*, 1974, *159*, 20–39.

Jones, L. A., & Moe, R. College education for mentally retarded adults. *Mental Retardation*, 1980, *18*, 59–62.

Keeler, K. F. *Post-school adjustment of educable mentally retarded youth educated in San Francisco.* Unpublished doctoral dissertation, Colorado State College, Greely, 1963.

Kennedy, R. J. R. *A Connecticut community revisited: A study of the social adjustments of a group of mentally deficient adults in 1948 and 1960.* Report of Project No. 655. Washington, D.C.: Department of Health, Education, and Welfare, Office of Vocational Rehabilitation, 1962.

Kentucky Legislative Research Commission. *Mentally retarded offenders in adult and juvenile correctional institutions.* Research Report #125, Frankfort, Ky.: October, 1975.

Kokaska, C. J. Voter participation of the EMR. *Mental Retardation*, 1972, *10*, 6–8.

Kokaska, C. J., & Kalawara, S. Preparing the retarded for semi-skilled occupations. *Education and Training of the Mentally Retarded*, 1969, *7*, 72–74.

Kolstoe, O. P. An examination of some characteristics which discriminate between employed and not employed mentally retarded males. *American Journal of Mental Deficiency*, 1961, *66*, 472–482.

Krischef, C. State laws on marriage and sterilization. *Mental Retardation*, 1972, *10*, 36–39.

Lehtinen, H., & Tuomisto, J. On the construction and application of an activation variable in the planning of adult education systems. *Adult Education in Finland*, 1976, *13*, 3–30.

Lenkowsky, L. K., & Saposnek, D. T. Family consequences of parental dyslexia. *Journal of Learning Disabilities*, 1978, *11*, 47–53.

Levin, H. M., Guthrie, J. W., Kleindorfer, G. B. & Stout, R. T. School achievement and post-school success: A review. *Review of Educational Research*, 1971, *41*, 1–16.

Levy, E. Long term follow-up of former in-patients at the Children's Hospital of the Men-
ninger Clinic. *American Journal of Psychiatry*, 1969, *125*, 1633–1639.

MacMillan, D. L. *Mental Retardation in school and society.* Boston: Little, Brown, 1977.

Martin, E. W. Individualism and behaviorism as future trends in educating handicapped children. *Exceptional Children*, 1972, *38*, 517–525.

Masterson, J. F. Prognosis in adolescent disorders. *American Journal of Psychiatry, 1958, 114*, 1097–1103.

Masterson, J. F. The symptomatic adolescent five years later: He didn't grow out of it. *American Journal of Psychiatry*, 1967, *123*, 1338–1345.

Match, E. Two driver education programs for the physically and mentally handicapped. *Exceptional Children*, 1969, *35*, 563–564.

McCord, J. A thirty year follow-up of treatment effects. *American Psychologist*, 1978, *33*, 284–291.

McFall, T. M. Post-school Adjustment: A survey of fifty former students of classes for the educable mentally retarded. *Exceptional Children*, 1966, *32*, 633–634.

Menkes, M., Rowe, J., & Menkes, J. A 25 year follow-up study on the hyperkinetic child with MBD. *Pediatrics*, 1967, *39*, 393–399.

Miller, E. L. Ability and social adjustment at midlife of persons earlier judged mentally deficient. *Genetic Psychology Monographs*, 1965, *72*, 139–198.

Mirring, P. On the job training in Georgia. *VR Review*, 1977, *1*, 56–59.

Morrison, J. R., & Stewart, M. A. The psychiatric status of the legal families of adopted hyperactive children. *Archives of General Psychiatry*, 1973, *28*, 888–891.

Olshansky, S., & Beach, D. A five year follow-up of mentally retarded clients. *Rehabilitation Literature*, 1974, *35*, 48–49.

Oswald, H. *A national follow-up study of mental retardates employed by the federal government.* Grant RD-2425-6. Washington, D.C.: Department of Vocational Rehabilitation, 1968.

Parker, S. L., Taylor, G. M., Hartman, W. T., Wong, R. O., Grigg, D. A., & Shay, D. E. *Improving occupational programs for the handicapped.* Washington, D.C.: Report prepared for BEH under contract number OEC-0-72-5226 with Management Analysis Center, 1976.

Peterson, L., & Smith, L. A comparison of post-school adjustment of educable mentally retarded adults with adults of normal intelligence. *Exceptional Children*, 1960, *26*, 404–408.

Phillips, G. The turned-off revisited. *Today's Education*, 1978, *67*, 88–90.

Plomondon, A. L., & Soskin, R. M. Handicapped parents: Can they call their children their own? *Amicus*, 1978, *3*, 24–31.

Porter, R. B., & Milazzo, T. C. A comparison of mentally retarded adults who attended a special class with those who attended regular classes. *Exceptional Children*, 1958, *24*, 410–412.

Powers, E., & Witmer, H. *An experiment in the prevention of delinquency: The Cambridge-Somerville Youth Study*. New York: Columbia University Press, 1951.

Preston, R. C., & Yarington, D. J. Status of fifty retarded readers eight years after reading clinic diagnosis. *Journal of Reading*, 1967, *11*, 122–129.

Rawson, M. B. *Developmental language disability: Adult accomplishments of dyslexic boys*. Baltimore: Johns Hopkins Press, 1968.

Redding, S. F. Life adjustment patterns of retarded and non-retarded low functioning students. *Exceptional Children*, 1979, *45*, 367–368.

Reed, S. C. & Reed, E. W. Who are the parents of the retarded children? *Focus on Exceptional Children*, 1970, *1*, 5–7.

Robins, L. N., & O'Neal, P. The adult prognosis for runaway children. *American Journal of Orthopsychiatry*, 1959, *29*, 752–761.

Robinson, H. M., & Smith, H. K. Reading clinic clients—ten years after. *Elementary School Journal*, 1962, *63*, 22–27.

Roff, M. *Preservice personality problems and subsequent adjustments to military service: Gross outcome in relation to acceptance-rejection at induction and military service*. Randolph AFB, Texas: School of Aviation Medicine, USAF, Report 55-138, 1956.

Rosen, M., Floor, L., & Baxter, D. IQ, academic achievement and community adjustment after discharge from the institution. *Mental Retardation*, 1974, *12*, 51–53.

Safer, N. D. Implications of minimum competency standards and testing for handicapped students. *Exceptional Children*, 1980, *46*, 288–290.

Santamour, M. B., & West, B. The mentally retarded offender in the social context. *Amicus*, 1979, *4*, 23–28.

Schilit, J. The mentally retarded offender and criminal justice personnel. *Exceptional Children*, 1979, *46*, 16–22.

Scott, A. J., Williams, J. M., Stout, J. K., & Decker, T. W. *Field investigation and evaluation of learning disabilities*. Scranton, Pa.: University of Scranton Press, 1980.

Shanyfelt, P. A. Occupational preparation of secondary educable students. *The Pointer*, Winter 1974, 20–24.

Shaw, C. H., & Wright, C. H. The married mental defective: a follow up study. *The Lancet*, 1960, 273–274.

Sheltered workshops and their employment of handicapped individuals. *VR Review*, 1977, *1*, 39–42.

Shore, M. F., & Massimo, J. L. After ten years: A follow up study of comprehensive vocationally oriented psychotherapy. *American Journal of Orthopsychiatry*, 1973, *43*, 128–132.

Silberberg, N. E., & Silberberg, M. C. And the adult who reads poorly? *Journal of Learning Disabilities*, 1978, *11*, 15–16.

Silver, A. A., & Hagin, R. A. Specific reading disability: Follow up studies. *American Journal of Orthopsychiatry*, 1964, *34*, 95–102.

Skaarbrevik, K. J. A follow up study of educable mentally retarded in Norway. *American Journal of Mental Deficiency*, 1971, *75*, 560–565.

State Board of Public Instruction. *Post high school adjustment of the educable mentally retarded*. Des Moines, Iowa, 1969.

State J.T. Pacific Reporter, 1978, *578*, 831.

Strickland, C. G., & Arrell, V. M. Employment of the mentally retarded. *Exceptional Children*, 1967, *34*, 21–24.

Thompson, L. J. Language disabilities in men of eminence. *Journal of Learning Disabilities*, 1971, *4*, 39–50.

Titus, R. W., & Travis, J. T. Follow-up of EMR program graduates. *Mental Retardation*, 1973, *11*, 24–26.

Tobias, J. Vocational adjustment of young retarded adults. *Mental Retardation*, 1970, *8*, 13–16.

Weaver, T. R. The incidence of maladjustments among mental defectives in military environments. *American Journal of Mental Deficiency*, 1946, *51*, 238–246.

Weiss, G., Hechtman, L., & Perlman, T. Hyperactives as young adults: school, employer and self rating scales obtained during ten-year follow up evaluation. *American Journal of Orthopsychiatry*, 1978, *48*, 438–445.

White, W. J., Schumaker, J. B., Warner, M. M., Alley, G. R., & Deshler, D. D. *The current status of young adults identified as learning disabled during their school career*. Lawrence, Kan.: Institute for Research in Learning Disabilities: The University of Kansas, Research Report #21, 1980.

Whitmer, G. E. From hospitals to jails: The fate of California's deinstitutionalized mentally ill. *The American Journal of Orthopsychiatry*, 1980, *50*, 65–75.

Wilton, K. M., & Cosson, L. D. Employment and adjustment of special class graduates in a New Zealand city. *Australian Journal of Mental Retardation*, 1977, *4*, 3–7.

Jerry C. Gross
Jay Gottlieb

19

The Mildly Handicapped: A Service Distinction for the Future?

The commonality among the handicapping conditions, especially among mildly handicapped children, calls into question the necessity of continuing separate educational programs for children identified as either educable mentally retarded, learning disabled, or behaviorally disordered. If children in these handicapping categories exhibit a reasonably high degree of functional similarities in their behavior, it may be asked whether it is not more realistic and more economical to provide educational programs based upon children's functional needs rather than on the particular categories to which they have been assigned.

A BRIEF HISTORY OF CATEGORICAL AND NONCATEGORICAL SPECIAL EDUCATION

Special education in this country evolved out of a desire to provide handicapped children with appropriate education. At the turn of the century, when schools had an unusually high percentage of immigrant children, it was immediately evident to teachers and administrators alike that a number of children simply could not keep up academically with the curricular demands of the regular classroom. It was equally, if not more, obvious to the classroom teacher that many of these children were behaviorally "troublesome." In order to provide slow-learning children with more appropriate class placement, special classes for mentally retarded children were established in this country in 1896 (Esten, 1900). The literature records that classroom teachers were so happy to be rid of the slow-learning and the troublesome children that between approximately 1900 and 1920 almost every major city in the northeastern United States established special classes for mentally retarded children. Of course, educators were helped enormously by the development of the IQ test during this same period, since the IQ test provided an objective numerical score that school administrators could use to justify sending certain children out of the regular classroom and into the special class.

For all practical purposes, the placement of children in special classes mainly on the basis of a low IQ score continued unabated in this country through the early 1960s. But there were problems that were destined to arise. Perhaps the major problem was the uncontested fact that many special classes for mentally retarded children were racially segregated. At a time in history when the courts were striking down racial segregation in regular education, special education administrators simply could not defend the practice of continuing racially imbalanced classes— even though racial segregation was not the intended, or desired, outcome. Interestingly, during the same approximate period in history when the courts were attacking the racial composition of classrooms, the field of learning disabilities was coming into existence. There was enormous dissatisfaction, especially among middle class parents with the lack of suitable educational provision for their children. Although many of these children were failing in school, their parents refused to accept the possibility that their children were mentally retarded; the children's IQ scores were usually above the accepted cutoff for classification as mentally retarded. Such children eventually became known as perceptually handicapped and later as learning disabled. Since the main models of special education at that time were self-contained classes, it should come as no surprise that additional classrooms were established for children who were allegedly perceptually disordered. As the name itself might indicate, the focus of the "curriculum" for perceptually disordered children was to provide intensive remediation to correct, or at least to ameliorate, the perceptual deficit. The argument was advanced that if the perceptual deficit could be reduced or eliminated, the child's learning problem would then disappear.

Dissatisfaction with the self-contained class education of the handicapped was also beginning to appear in the professional literature. In 1962, G. O. Johnson published a paper in which he questioned the paradox of special education. The paradox to which he eluded was that special education classes (1) employed teachers who were specially trained; (2) contained fewer children than regular classrooms; and (3) were more expensive to operate than traditional regular classrooms. Despite these apparent advantages, the research literature indicated that there were few, if any, academic benefits for children who attended self-contained classrooms. Indeed, the research tended to show that retarded children who attended regular classrooms achieved as well, if not better, than retarded children who were educated in special classes (Kirk, 1964). Unfortunately, G. O. Johnson's paper, which appeared in 1962, did not provoke outrage among the special education community. It was not until 1968 when Dunn questioned the continued justifiability of special education classes for mildly retarded children that professional special educators followed suit.

Dunn based his arguments on four points: First, he noted the self-contained classes were racially segregated. Second, he cited evidence that failed to uncover academic advantages to mentally retarded children who attended self-contained classes. Third, he alleged that children were unnecessarily stigmatized by the label that automatically accompanied their special class placement. Finally, Dunn contended that regular education had at its disposal a sufficiently wide range of individualized curricula that would enable it to successfully accommodate slow-learning children. Dunn's paper, which was received very well within the professional special education community, resulted in immediate changes in traditional special education practices.

Dunn's paper was not only well-received by the professional community, but it also affected the public at large by highlighting the inadequacies of education in general and special education in particular. As an example, in the early 1970s, The Children's Defense Fund in Massachusetts published a highly critical document on the Boston school system. This document charged that minority group children, who usually attended special classes, were being excluded unfairly from the schools. Public response to this document was partially responsible for the Massachusetts Legislature passing Chapter 766 of the General Laws of Massachusetts. This law provided for noncategorical special education, in the hope that children would no longer be stigmatized by the label that was assigned to them by their special education placements. After Chapter 766 was passed by the Massachusetts Legislature, the United States Congress began to debate the merits of a far more encompassing piece of legislation that would affect all handicapped children in the country. The legislation was eventually passed and became known as Education for All Handicapped Children Act of 1975 (Public Law 94-142).

When PL 94-142 was being debated in the Senate (as Senate Bill 6, 1973), certain school administrators and university personnel argued in favor of a law organized around the functional deficits of children rather than categories of handicapping conditions. In the end, this point of view did not outweigh the basic political wisdom supporting the maintenance of categories. It was reasoned that categories of handicapping conditions enabled Congress and the public to clearly understand the specific populations who received services. Any attempt to organize or present the law in a noncategorical (functional) format would, it was reasoned, reveal a field hopelessly divided on a central definitional issue, which would divert Congressinal attention, and it was feared that further delay would kill the passage of the Act. Eventually, most professionals and other interested persons bowed to this logic and the traditional categories were sustained as the rallying point for PL 94-142.

There can be little doubt that in the years since the passage of PL 94-142, the trend and the delivery of special education services has been in the direction of cross-categorical programming.

NONCATEGORICAL SPECIAL EDUCATION: THE WAY TO THE FUTURE?

The provision of noncategorical special education services to children is not the result of any single force. Instead it is the result of a number of concerns in the professional community. Many of these concerns overlap each other, and some, perhaps, may not even be rectified by noncategorical practices.

Administrative Concerns

One of the ingredients comprising any effective educational program, special or regular, is that it can be effectively and economically administered. The passage of PL 94-142 and its many provisions has simply made traditional categorical programming difficult to administer. This can be illustrated with an example from the Minneapolis Public Schools.

Consider the example of a school building that houses approximately 500 students. Using a federal special education population expectancy rate of 12 percent (Stanford Research Institute, 1977), approximately 60 of the 500 would qualify for special education.

On the average, the following breakdown might be expected in such a school: 15 learning disabled children, comprising 3 percent of the population; 18 speech-impaired children, being 3.5 percent; 11 mentally retarded children, 2.3 percent; 10 emotionally disturbed children, 2 percent; 3 deaf and/or hearing-impaired children, 0.5 percent; 1 visually impaired child, 0.1 percent; and 2 orthopedically handicapped children, 0.5 percent. Because speech-impaired children are usually accommodated in regular classrooms, it may be concluded from our hypothetical example that 42 special education children would conceivably have been placed in self-contained classes. Let us further assume that of these 42 children, the administration and teachers agree that approximately half did not require full-time placement in self-contained classes, thus leaving approximately 21 children who would be placed in resource room programs. However, since these students represent three or four handicapping conditions, they would require three or four categorically defined resource teachers, all located in a single school building. If we assume a typical case load of 15 students per teacher, each teacher would be responsible for between one and four students per building and, thus, to fill their teaching load, would have to cover anywhere from three to ten school buildings. Under this categorical model, resource teachers would spend most of the day traveling from school to school or visiting each school once or twice weekly. Either option is indefensible on educational and economical grounds.

Largely as a result of the fact that a single school building seldom has a sufficient population of handicapped children in a given category to justify the creation of an additional classroom, school systems have relied on centralized services. That is, one school often contains a number of special education classes with the students being fed from other shcools in the general geographical region. Sufficient numbers of handicapped children are thus assured to justify on financial grounds the opening of a special class. The problem with this approach, however, is that it prevents children from attending their neighborhood school, thereby creating a more restrictive environment than may be necessary.

The logistical problems created by categorical services are even more pronounced in rural areas where sparse populations further reduce the number of children located in one school who fall neatly into a particular category. As schools continue to be increasingly hard-pressed for financial resources, they cannot be expected to employ teachers for few students. When noncategorical resource room programming is applied, however, financial savings may be realized. In the example of the 500-pupil school, for example, one resource room may be established for approximately 20 children, rather than having three resource rooms for the same number of children.

There are other concerns from an administrative vantage point with categorical education, concerns that tend to be more pronounced in large city school systems. Because categorical diagnosis is not very reliable, there is often disagreement among professinals as to the exact classification to which a given child should be assigned. Put another way—there is a considerable amount of error that exists in the diagnostic process, which results in the misclassification of many children. Furthermore, because classification systems are intended to serve as a basis for the appropriate delivery of educational services, diagnosticians attempt to be as precise as possible, usually by creating refined categories of classification that theoretically lead to specific educational interventions.

The immediate result of the increased refinement in diagnostic classifications has been a burgeoning number of terms that are used to describe handicapping conditions. To illustrate, children who have learning difficulties and who are not suspected of being mentally retarded have been labeled at one time or another as having: or as being:

minimal brain dysfunction	learning disabled
congenital auditory imperception	dyslexic
specific reading diability	educationally handicapped
primary reading retardation	perceptually handicapped
minimal cerebral dysfunction	hyperactive
hypokinetic behavior disorder	hyperkenetic
congenital word blindness	neurologically impaired
clumsy child syndrome	brain damaged
developmental language disability	aphasic
extreme learning problems	congenitally aphasic
communicative and intellectual deviation	dysgraphic

The refinement in categories has led to administrative attempts to establish classes tailored to each category, an expensive and probably fruitless enterprise.

Labels and Stigma in Categorical Programming

An irrevocable side effect of categorical special education is the classification and labeling of children with a particular identifier. Children who are placed in classes for educable mentally retarded are thereby labeled as *mentally retarded.* Similarly, children identified as behavior disordered have that label applied to them. Indeed, it is almost an impossibility to develop categorical programming without branding the children with the label associated with that category of education.

However, many special educators are becoming disenchanted with the use of labels. In one early integration effort (Deno & Gross, 1973) labels were eliminated except for state report requirements. Within each school, special education services were not only organized in a functional generic framework (Johnson & Gross, 1973), but children were also described by their functional deficits rather than by handicapping labels. The intent was to encourage regular educators to maintain responsibility for children having learning and behavior problems. It was reasoned that if teachers would be able to improve these children's level of functioning, they would be more willing to accept them into their classrooms; that is, teachers would be more receptive to children having a reading, math, or behavior problem than to children who are labeled mentally retarded or emotionally disturbed.

Although this early effort was based more on practical considerations than on empirical data, subsequent research determined, however tentatively, that labels do in fact bias teachers' judgments of students. Algozzine (1977) found that labeled children were placed in more restrictive settings by teachers, even though the behavioral descriptions for nonlabeled and labeled groups were identical. Such data indicated a need for caution in assigning labels to children, especially when working with regular education personnel in mainstream programs.

Although more recent evidence has shown the labeling process does not result in more restrictive placement decisions by members of child study teams (Pfieffer, 1980), the negative impact of labels on the mainstream educator remains a practical consideration for those responsible for implementing least-restrictive placements. Indeed, the negative side effects of regular classroom teachers' expectations of labeled children have been used as a powerful argument against such a practice (Jones, 1977). Generic models, which identify children by functional need rather than by category, help neutralize the problem of teachers' expectations. It should be mentioned, however, that despite the fact that much has been made of the importance of teachers' expectations in affecting the education offered to handicapped children, there is relatively little consistent empirical data to support the point. Even though labels may have an initial impact on teachers' expectations, other data indicate that stereotyped expectations soon give way to perceptions that are based on accumulated experiences with the child (Yoshida & Meyers, 1975). The entire area of labels and stigma is clearly in need of empirical validation.

Impact of the Courts

During the past 15 years, the courts have done a great deal to shape special education programs. The Education of All Handicapped Children Act of 1975 is, in a large measure, the reflection of court consent decrees, consent agreements, and judgments. It should be indicated that the primary reason for the court's involvement in special education was to protect the civil rights of handicapped children.

To illustrate with an early court case: both the tracking system in special education and the use of group achievement tests to make placement decisions, such as those used in the Washington, D.C. public schools in the early 1960s were struck down as a violation of students' rights under the due process clause of the Fourteenth Amendment (*Hobson v. Hansen*, 1967).

In order to understand how the *Hobson v. Hansen* case related to noncategorical special education, a little background information is required. For years, it had been an uncontested fact that classes for EMR children were racially segregated. It was equally clear that classes for children classified as learning disabled had very few minority group children (Kaufman, Agard, & Semmel, in press). Theoretically, one way to correct the problem of racial imbalance in self-contained special classrooms was to develop new classes that included both learning disabled and mentally retarded children. Since the new classroom structure would involve children from two separate categories, the alternative was either to create a new categorical designation or simply to drop the categorical classifications entirely. The former option would have been extremely difficult to implement because parents of learning disabled children, mostly middle class, would have offered substantial resistance to having their children educated in the same classrooms as "retarded" children, who were primarily black and mostly poor. The path of least resistance was certainly to omit categorical designations.

In his decision, Judge Skelly Wright sent an unmistakable signal to the legislative branch of government that it should begin to address a number of educational concerns with its law-making powers. Chief among Judge Wright's concerns was the constitutionality of making placement decisions based upon group administered achievement tests. He indicated that it would be far better indeed for these social-political problems to be resolved in the political arena by other branches of government. The decision encouraged special educators to carefully review special education students' placements on at least an annual basis in order to determine the possibility of providing them more contact with an expanded peer group.

The revolutionary excursion into our nation's special education programs by Judge Wright spawned legal attacks on (1) placement procedures (*Diane v. California State Board of Education*, 1970); (2) exclusionary practices for certain groups of handicapped children, (*Mills v. Board of Education*, 1971); and (3) children's rights to a free and appropriate public education (*PARC v. Commonwealth of Pennsylvania*, 1971).

Of all the court cases that have appeared to date, perhaps none has the potential of affecting contemporary special education practices more than the recent *Larry P.* case (1979) in California. The *Larry P. v. Riles* case was brought to the court's attention in San Francisco in 1972. A group of plaintiffs claimed that they were misidentified as educable mentally retarded and wrongly placed in classes for retarded children. The court granted a preliminary injunction and enjoined the school district from placing black children in classes for retarded children through the use of intelligence tests when the results were racially imbalanced classes. Since that 1972 decision and subsequent decisions by the court and the State of California, the following occurred (Bersoff, 1980):

1. The broadening of the injunction to prohibit the administration of individual intelligence tests to all black children in the state.
2. The issuance in 1975 of a state memorandum banning the use of the then-approved IQ tests for placement of any child regardless of race in EMR classes in the state.
3. The court determining that IQ tests are differentially valid for black and white children, meaning that more errors will be made for black children than for whites for placements, and this is unacceptable.
4. The court noting that tests would continue to be needed, however, not for the purpose of labeling but for "the development of curricula that respond to specific education needs."
5. A conclusion by the court that EMR classes were an educational anachronism "that focused on stigmatizing labels rather than individual needs, which isolate students and relegate them to inferior education instead of providing remedial training designed to return them to regular classes containing nonhandicapped students."

In 1979, the final decree was handed down in the *Larry P.* case. In that ruling, Judge Pekcham maintained that the use of an individual IQ test as the primary tool to diagnose and place children in classes for EMR students was unconstitutional.

The effect of this ruling will undoubtedly be to strengthen the case for noncategorical special education. This is so because with the absence of an IQ score to identify a child as being retarded, educators will be forced to explore alternative methods of identification that tap children's functional abilities and disabilities. The emphasis on functional abilities must of necessity cut across diagnostic labels and concentrate on children's needs. It is the emphasis on children's educational needs that in many ways forms the nucleus of noncategorical special education.

Despite the guidance of PL 94-142 in the governance of special education programs, the courts continued to involve themselves in these programs. We may take heed of the words handed down by Judge Wright in the *Hobson* v. *Hansen* case, where he stated, "while the government may classify persons and thereby object to disparities in treatment, those included within or excluded from the respective classes should be those for whom the inclusion or exclusion is appropriate; otherwise the classification risks become wholly irrational and thus unconstitutionally discriminatory" (p. 513).

Parental Concerns

The views of the courts and school administrators represent two very important influences that affected educational practice. A third, and perhaps equally important, influence is the views of parents regarding an appropriate education for their children.

Most professionals have had the experience at one time or another of struggling to find the right words when informing parents that they have a handicapped child. The task is neither pleasant nor easy, and the way in which it is accomplished is very important; the event will always be one of the parents' most sustained memories. Informing parents that their child is mentally retarded, for example, is apt to be traumatic. Furthermore, since many of the children who were labeled mentally retarded were in all likelihood misclassified, as educators we were placed in the position of wrongly traumatizing many parents. Indeed, it was precisely because many children were falsely labeled that the criteria for inclusion in the category *mental retardation* was made more stringent; that is, children now have to be substantially below their age range in academic performance and IQ score, and exhibit maladaptive behavior, before the label of mental retardation may be applied to them. As a result of this redefinition, there has been a very substantial reduction in the number of children labeled as educable mentally retarded. To illustrate, since 1975, the EMR population in New York City has declined, while the total handicapped population has risen by approximately 80 percent. Were these children simply reclassified by schools as learning disabled, a categorical label that is far easier for parents to accept than the more permanent and incurable term *mentally retarded?*

One can raise the question of how much easier it would be on parents if they were simply informed that their child has academic problems and is in need of specified remedial instruction, rather than being informed that their child is mentally retarded, behaviorally disordered, or learning disabled. Would we not be performing a service to parents if we adopted a more functional and less categorical nomenclature system to describe the needs of their children?

In recent years, there has been movement among parent groups away from their prior support of categorical systems, toward a more noncategorical approach, particularly among parents of children who were labeled as mentally retarded or emotionally disturbed. The majority of these parents are from poor economic backgrounds and often are members of minority groups. At the present time, however, it is not clear if middle class parents of retarded and/or disturbed children are equally inimical to special education categories.

Probably in response to the movement of minority group parents away from categorical labels, lawmakers appear to be following suit. As an example, in Illinois parents and professionals fought several years over labeling. The prolabeling group had pointed out that state special education aid had always been 100 percent funded by the legislature primarily because the categorically framed special education law was easily understood. In 1979, 1 year after the Illinois legislature prorated (underfunded) state special education aid, however, the state moved toward the adoption of a generic model recommended by the legislature's school problem commission (Gross & Lilly, 1976).

As educators, we must ultimately recognize that parents cannot be expected to shift their emphasis away from the traditional categorical programs overnight. For many years, parent groups have fought hard to obtain funding for their children. Many still view noncategorical education mainly as a way to reduce the state's level of funding for special education. It will probably take several years of sustained funding by various state legislatures before parents fully accept the fact that noncategorical special education will continue to offer their children the same level of support, and the same level of service, that they previously received.

There is another side to this issue, however. Noncategorical programming could conceivably provide parents with a far stronger political base than they previously had. As we are aware, parent groups in the past have coalesced along categorical lines. Parents of mentally retarded children, for example, typically were affiliated with the National Association of Retarded Citizens (NARC). Parents of perceptually handicapped children or learning disabled children typically were associated in one fashion or another with the Association for Children with Learning Disabilities. Parents of deaf and blind children belonged to associations confined to those handicapping conditions. It could be expected that as noncategorical special education evolves and becomes a more recognized force, the parent members of these various organizations might unite into a larger single entity with far more political leverage than they ever enjoyed in the past. If NARC alone, or the American Association for Children with Learning Disabilities alone, was able to influence legislation on behalf of the children, how much more powerful would a joint organization be comprised of parents from both groups?

Questioning the Validity of Old Assumptions

The final impetus for the movement away from categorical programming pertains to the appropriateness of instructional methods. As new data are generated by researchers, the results continually call into question the validity of our assumptions regarding the ways in which handicapped children should be taught. A case in point is the failure of empirical studies to support teaching methods associated with "underlying learning processes" (Arter & Jenkins, 1979).

During the early 1960s, the term *learning disabilities* was offered by Kirk and Bateman (1962) and subsequently gained general acceptance by educators. The term served as an umbrella for a number of conditions associated with learning problems, such as perceptual disabilities (Strauss & Lehtinen, 1948), minimal brain dysfunction (Haring & Miller, 1969), dyslexia, developmental aphasia, visual perception, (Frostig & Horne, 1964), and perceptual motor functions (Kephart, 1963). Training programs were developed to remediate defects in children's learning processes and are still recommended and widely used today (Wepman, Cruickshank, Deutsch, Morency, & Struther, 1975). The remediation of these learning processes, especially those encouraging modality instruction, has not proven effective, however.

Bateman (1967), Sabatino, Ysseldyke, and Woolston (1973), and Arter and Jenkins (1977) have reported that no one has successfully demonstrated that beginning reading instruction can be improved by modality (auditory, visual, tactical) and instructional matching. Arter and Jenkins pointed out that it may be that instruments have not been developed to accurately determine modality strength or because reading requires both auditory and visual skills we cannot devise a modality-pure instructional method. Whatever the case, these findings have severely weakened the bases upon which learning disability programs have been developed. Indeed the "differential diagnosis" and "prescriptive teaching" methods, which involve the assessment and remediation of psychological and perceptual motor abilities as a basis for learning academic skills, have been shown to have serious validity problems to the point that their continued advocacy is not defensible. An excellent review of research in this area was presented by Arter and Jenkins (1979).

Professionals who have witnessed the continued demonstration of the failure of this diagnostic-prescriptive teaching model in learning disabilities have been seeking alternatives in more task-centered instructional systems. These task-centered systems analyze skills required in the standard curriculum and require teachers to teach these skills. Such methods are similar to the task-analysis approach used with retarded and emotionally disturbed children. This movement toward a task-centered system, and an abandonment of the diagnostic-prescriptive/modality-prescriptive/modality-preference methods has contributed significantly to a weakening of the categorical groupings by revealing the similarity of instructional procedures shared by these three groups (Hallahan & Kauffman, 1977). Fox, Egner, Paolucci, Perelman, and McKenzie (1972) in Vermont, Deno and Gross (1973) in Minneapolis, and Taylor and Soloway (1972) in California have developed program models of this type. A major objective in these efforts was to use the regular class curriculum as the basis of the special education instructional interventions. In each circumstance, the administrative support system was organized to function interdependently with regular education. These approaches require the close cooperation of regular educators in an effort to place tight controls on the flow of children into full-time special education programs.

One technique used effectively to govern the movement of students, and to interface regular and special education programs, is the operation of school-based teams. Such teams include the normal complement of special education staff, the principal, and other regular education personnel. These teams are constituted to reflect the joint responsibility of regular and special education, but, perhaps more importantly, to give special education a forum within which the service needs of the mildly handicapped can be defined for regular education staff in the context of the regular class curriculum.

As regular and special educators call for a slowdown on the movement of children into special education, and as the demands grow for behaviorally based decision variables for placing pupils, the use of generic programming will also grow. A major difficulty at this time is that the majority of pre-service teacher training in the universities still seems to be tied to categorical special education. Teacher training programs, on the other hand, that *do* emphasize noncategorical methods, such as applied behavior analysis, are weak in the content-related areas, such as curriculum adaptation. Attempts to define the state of the art and unite teacher training and field-based services as provided by the public schools are clearly some of the more important and immediate needs confronting special education today.

To summarize, parents, courts and professional educators all have a stake in the development of appropriate special education programs. The trend today, in our view, is clearly toward noncategorical programming. We should recognize, however, that old ways do not change easily, nor should they. The application of a categorical system was not entirely bad. We believe, however, that noncategorical education offers children more flexible programming than in the past.

It has been indicated at this point that there have been and probably will continue to be advocates of both categorical and noncategorical approaches. Major points for and against categorical special education were well made in an article by H. Goldstein (1975), who highlighted the following points in defense of categories:

1. Because these systems specify clear inclusion and exclusion limits, they reduce ambiguities and provide clear communication devices for professional exchanges of information.
2. In some cases these systems provide a description of a physical condition that has important educational implications.
3. These systems provide a basis for determining the number of students needing special education services.
4. These systems provide a method for accounting for children being served through special education services.
5. Use of these systems at the local level enables a school district to collect reimbursement from the state for special education services.
6. These systems have provided a rallying point for securing both legislative and general public support for special education programs.

On the other side of the issue are strong arguments against the use of categories in the public schools:

1. These systems invite overgeneralizations concerning individual children.
2. These systems are self-sustaining in that they contribute to "reification" of the labels used.
3. These systems ignore the interactive nature of instruction and assume that the root of instructional problems is in the child.
4. These systems remove the "burden of proof" for children's learning from

school personnel, by providing unalterable child conditions as reasons for repeated failure.

5. These systems provide information to the teacher that is in large part irrelevant for instruction.

6. Placement of children in special education programs on the basis of child-based categorization systems is often a one-way street, with little or no opportunity to escape the label or the treatment.

7. These systems discriminate against minority groups and the poor through the use of culturally biased tests and subsequent "tracking" of children based on these test results.

Perhaps the fairest summary of the categorical/noncategorical approach to special education was made by H. Goldstein (1975) in the summary of his chapter:

> In light of the numerous negative aspects noted, we might well ask whether there are any justifiable uses of categorical labels in the school system. We might then notice that most of the positive aspects of present categorization systems cited above relate to program administration, while most of the negative factors relate to child instruction. In short, it may be highly advantageous for school administrators to maintain child-labeling practices for the purpose of obtaining state and federal support funds; at the same time, such practices seem to be detrimental to children and teachers within the school system. (p. 52) [1]

GENERIC MODELS: FAD OR PERMANENT DIRECTION?

In a categorically based program, a great deal of time and effort is spent determining student eligibility for special education service. Yet the correlation between categorical assignment and instructional delivery is often weak. Generally, in categorical models there is heavy emphasis on norm-referenced testing to determine eligibility and placement. In these norm-referenced assessments, there is a greater potential for low correlations between the diagnostic findings and the subsequent remediation plan, because the testing was not developed out of special education instructional approaches.

The generic models tend to have eligibility requirements linked to the behavior (tasks) required for success in regular classes. Eligibility is determined by the discrepancy that exists between competencies the students have mastered and those that students are expected to have mastered at a particular grade level. This approach moves the special educator away from trying to measure and eradicate assumed deficits in underlying processing variables and toward the measurement and remediation of skills or tasks required for success in the regular class. This approach to referral and placement results in close relationships between reasons for referral and subsequent remediation. Generic programming leads one back to the regular curriculum and encourages the use of a discrepancy model based on tasks from the modal curriculum.

Reprinted with permission from Goldstein, H. Schools. In N. Hobbs (Ed.), *Issues in the classification of children* (Vol. 2). San Francisco: Jossey-Bass, 1975, p. 52.

LONG-RANGE IMPLICATIONS

The local administrator of special education (LEA) is in a favored position to impact on the expansion of generic instructional groupings. The degree to which these models gain widespread use will be highly correlated with the degree to which LEA directors pursue them. It seems clear today that most administrators suffering from "distemper of the budget" and a resultant "shrinkage of the empire" have a number of pressing concerns other than overhauling their categorical programs to develop generic-based services. The development of generic services, even when restricted to the mildly handicapped, is not an easy task. It requires the full attention of the LEA staff, free from the current fiscal survival process that most are confronted by today.

The restructuring effort that took place in Minneapolis occurred over a 4–5-year period with a superintendent and school board providing strong support. It was not accomplished by summarily eliminating the entire array of categorical programs—an act that would be similar to starting a diet by shooting yourself in the stomach. Instead, it was started incrementally by establishing generic resource rooms, then moving toward generic services for the mildly handicapped in special classes.

The difficulties LEA staff will face in such efforts include

1. The potential resistance from and alienation of parent groups to whom the advances of special education are historically owed.
2. The fact that the majority of special education teachers are trained along categorical lines; many training institutions have a strong investment in categorical systems because of their previous research efforts and teaching experience.
3. The fact that most state laws are categorically defined today.
4. The assumption that because PL 94-142 is categorically organized, there is a legal requirement to model that system in the state and LEA (an assumption not based in fact).
5. The resistance from teacher organizations who want to protect their members' "rights" to a teaching position in a particular category, a problem currently being faced in New York City (Gross, 1979).
6. The difficulty of explaining the change from categorical to generic programs in understandable terms to reference groups (teachers, boards, superintendents, parents).
7. The effective development of procedures to "crosswalk" a program from categorical to generic service without excessively disrupting the continuity of service to children.
8. The difficulty of isolating functional descriptions (eligibility criteria) for newly established generic groupings.
9. The retraining and redesign of an evaluation and placement staff who can produce behaviorally based assessments.
10. Getting the regular education system to operationally specify the minimum achievement requirements for each grade level, thereby providing special education with guidelines that can justify referrals to special education.
11. The development of instructional strategies for the mildly handicapped,

which are an improvement over the differential-diagnosis/prescription-teaching model. This model, which Haring and Bateman (1977) called the "majority position within the field . . . over the past 20 to 30 years" (p. 130), traditionally seeks to assess underlying abilities and then prescribes instruction consistent with the ability strength and weaknesses.

Each of these hurdles must be addressed if organizations, state and local, are to sustain a movement to break away from our love affair with categories. Probably the single most important hurdle in this change process is offering teachers, parents, and learners a viable alternative to the current system.

REFERENCES

Algozzine, B., Mercer, C. D., & Countermine, T. The effects of labels and behavior on teacher expectations. *Exceptional Children,* 1977, *44,* 131–132.

Arter, J. A., & Jenkins, J. R. Examining the benefits and prevalence of modality considerations in special education. *The Journal of Special Education,* 1977, *11*(3), 281–298.

Arter, J. A., & Jenkins, J. R. Differential diagnosis-prescriptive teaching: A critical appraisal. *Review of Educational Research,* 1979, *49,*(4), 517–555.

Bateman, B. Three approaches to diagnosis and educational planning for children with learning disabilities. *Academic Therapy Quarterly,* 1967, *3,* 11–16.

Bersoff, D. N. *P. vs. Riles:* Legal perspective. *School Psychology Review,* 1980, *9*(2), 112–122.

Deno, S. & Gross, J. The Seward-University project: A cooperative effort to improve school services and university training. In E. Deno (Ed.), *Instructional alternatives for exceptional children.* Arlington, Va.: Council for Exceptional Children, 1973.

Diana v. State Board of Education. No. C-70-37 RFR, District Court of Northern California, Feb, 1970.

Dunn, L. M. Special education for the mildly retarded—is much of it justifiable? *Exceptional Children,* 1968, *35,* 5–22.

Esten, R. A. Backward children in the public schools. *Journal of Psychoaesthenics,* 1900, *5,* 10–16.

Fox, F., Egner, A. N., Paolucci, P., Perelman, P., & McKenzie, H. An introduction for regular classroom approach to special education. In E. Deno (Ed.), *Instructional alternatives for exceptional children.* Reston, Va.: Council for Exceptional Children, 1972.

Frostig, M., & Horne, D. *The Frostig program*

for the development of visual perception. Chicago: Follett, 1964.

Goldstein, A. P., Sprafkin, R. P., Gerahaw, N. J., & Klein, P. *Skillstreaming the adolescent: A structured learning approach to teaching prosocial skills.* Champaign, Il.: Research Press, 1979.

Goldstein, H. Schools. In N. Hobbs (Ed.), *Issues in the classification of children* (Vol. 2). San Francisco: Jossey-Bass, 1975.

Gross, J. C. *Special education in transition.* Unpublished memo, Board of Education, the City of New York, 1979.

Gross, J. C., & Lilly, M., Special education legislation: Moving away from traditional categories. *Illinois School Problems Commission,* Illinois State Legislation, 1976.

Haring, N. G., & Bateman, B. *Teaching the learning disabled child.* Englewood Cliffs: Prentice-Hall, 1977.

Hallahan, D. P., & Kauffman, J. M. Labels, categories, behaviors: ED, LD, and EMR reconsidered. *Journal of Special Education,* 1977, *11,* 139–147.

Haring, N., & Miller, C. A. (Ed.) Minimal brain dysfunction in children. *Proceedings of national project on learning disabilities in children.* Washington, D.C.: U.S. Public Health Service, 1969.

Johnson, G. O. Special education for the mentally handicapped—A paradox. *Exceptional Children,* 1962, *29,* 62–69.

Johnson, R. A., & Gross, J. C. Restructuring special education leadership resources: The Minneapolis model. In R. A. Johnson, J. C. Gross, & R. F. Weatherman (Eds.), *Leadership series in special education* (Vol. 2). Minneapolis: Audio-Visual Library Service, University of Minnesota, 1973.

Johnson, R. A., Gross, J. C., Nash N., & Reynolds, M. C. Problem solving in Boston: A preliminary report. In M. C. Reynolds (Ed.), *National technical assistance systems in special education*. Minneapolis: Leadership Training Institute/Special Education, University of Minnesota, 1974.

Jones, R. A. *Self-fulfilling prophecies*, Hillsdale, N.J.: Erlbaum, 1977.

Kaufman, M. J., Agard, J. A., & Semmel, M. I. *Mainstreaming: Learners and their environments*. Baltimore, Md.: University Park Press, in press.

Kephart, N. C. *The brain-injured child in the classroom*. Chicago: National Society for Crippled Children and Adults, 1963.

Kirk, S. A. Research in education. In H. A. Stevens & R. Heber (Eds.), *Mental retardation*. Chicago: University of Chicago Press, 1964.

Kirk, S. A., & Bateman, B. Diagnosis and remediation of learning disabilities. *Exceptional Children*, 1962, *29*(2), 73–78.

Mills v. Board of Education of District of Columbia, 348 F. Supp. 866 D.D.C., 1972.

Larry P. v. Riles. 343 F. Supp. 1306 (N.D. Cal. 1972) aff'd 502 F. 2d. 963 (9th Cir. 1974) (preliminary injunction); No. C-71-2270 RFP slip op. (Oct. 16, 1979) (decision on Merits), 1974.

Pennsylvania Ass'n. for Retarded Children (PARC) v. Commonwealth of Pennsylvania. 334 F. Supp. 279, E.D. Pa. 1972.

Pfeiffer, S. I. The influence of diagnostic labeling on special education placement decisions. *Psychology in the Schools*, 1980, *17*, 343–350.

Sabatino, D. A., Ysseldyke, J. D., & Woolston, J. Diagnostic-prescriptive perceptual training with mentally retarded children. *American Journal of Mental Deficiency*, 1973, *78*, 7–14.

Stanford Research Institute. *Validation of state counts of handicapped children*. Menlo Park, Cal.: S.R.I., 1977.

Strauss, A. A. & Lehtinen, L. E. *Psychopathology and education of the brain-injured child* (Vol. 1). New York: Grune & Stratton, 1948.

Taylor, F. D. & Soloway, M. M. The Madison school plan, a functional model for merging the regular and special classrooms. In E. Deno (Ed.), *Instructional alternatives for exceptional children*. Reston, Va.: Council for Exceptional Children, 1972.

Wepman, J. M., Cruickshank, W. M., Deutsch, C. P., Morency, A., & Struther, C. R. Learning disabilities. In N. Hobbs (Ed.), *Issues in the classification of children* (Vol. 1). San Francisco: Jossey-Bass, 1975.

Yoshida, R. K., & Meyer, C. E. Effects of labeling as educable mentally retarded on teacher's expectancies for change in a student's performance. *Journal of Educational Psychology*, 1975, *67*, 521–527.

Index